ESTONIA, LATVIA & LITHUANIA

EYEWITNESS TRAVEL

ESTONIA, LATVIA & LITHUANIA

LONDON, NEW YORK,
MELBOURNE, MUNICH AND DELHI
www.dk.com

Managing Editor Aruna Ghose
Design Managers Sunita Gahir, Priyanka Thakur
Project Editor Alka Thakur
Project Designer Rajnish Kashyap
Editors Jyoti Kumari, Ipshita Nandi
Designers Namrata Adhwaryu, Anchal Kaushal
Senior Cartographic Manager Uma Bhattacharya
Cartographers Mohammad Hassan, Jasneet Kaur
Senior Picture Researcher Taiyaba Khatoon
Picture Researcher Sumita Khatwani
Assistant Picture Researcher Shweta Andrews
Senior Dtp Designer Vinod Harish
Dtp Designer Azeem Siddiqui

Contributors
Howard Jarvis, John Oates, Tim Ochser, Neil Taylor

Photographers
Demetrio Carrasco, Nigel Hicks, Linda Whitwam

Illustrators
Chinglemba Chingtham, Sanjeev Kumar, Surat Kumar Mantoo,
Arun Pottirayil, Suman Saha, Gautam Trivedi, Mark Warner,
Chapel Design & Marketing Ltd

Printed and bound in China

First Published In the UK in 2009
by Dorling Kindersley Limited
80 Strand, London Wc2R 0RL

15 16 17 18 10 9 8 7 6 5 4 3 2 1

Reprinted with revisions 2011, 2013, 2015

Copyright © 2009, 2015 Dorling Kindersley Limited, London
A Penguin Random House Company

ISBN 978-0-24100-664-1

MIX
Paper from
responsible sources
FSC
www.fsc.org FSC™ C018179

Front cover main image: House of Blackheads, Town Hall Square, Riga

◀ Striking onion domes of St Nicholas's Orthodox Cathedral, Latvia

Contents

How to Use this Guide 6

Introducing Estonia, Latvia and Lithuania

Door knocker, Tallinn

St Nicholas's Orthodox Cathedral in Karosta, near Liepāja, Latvia

Picturesque Island Castle at Trakai, Lithuania

Amber jewellery, sold in souvenir shops all
over the Baltic region

Statue of King Gustav Adolphus of Sweden,
Tartu, Estonia

HOW TO USE THIS GUIDE

This guide helps you get the most from your visit to the Baltic States. It provides detailed practical information and expert recommendations. *Introducing Estonia, Latvia and Lithuania* maps the three countries, sets them in their historical and cultural context, and describes events throughout the year. Each country has its own chapter, with a portrait, history and descriptions of important sights using visuals and maps. Information about hotels, restaurants, shops and markets, entertainment and sports is found in *Travellers' Needs*. The *Survival Guide* has tips on everything from making a telephone call to using local transportation.

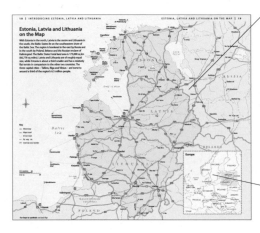

Estonia, Latvia and Lithuania on the Map

The orientation map shows the location of the Baltic States in relation to their neighbouring countries. In this book, each country is divided into three main sightseeing areas that are covered in a full chapter. These areas are highlighted on other maps throughout the book.

A locator map shows the country in relation to other European countries.

Estonia, Latvia and Lithuania Region by Region

Each country has been divided into three regions with a map at the start of the section. The key to the symbols is on the back flap.

1 Introduction
The landscape, history and character of each region are described here, including an account of how they have changed over the centuries and what they have to offer to the visitor today.

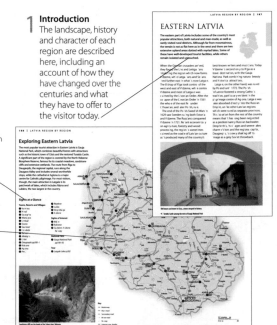

Sights at a Glance lists the chapter's sights by category, such as Churches and Cathedrals, Towns, Resorts and Villages and Islands and National Parks.

2 Regional Map
This map shows the road network and gives an overview of the topography of the entire region. All the sights are numbered and there are also useful tips on getting around by car, bus and train.

3 Street-by-Street Map
This gives a bird's-eye view of interesting and important parts of each sightseeing area. The numbering of the sights ties in with the area map and the fuller description of the entries on the pages that follow.

A suggested route takes in some of the fascinating and attractive streets in the area.

Numbers refer to each sight's position on the area map and its place in the chapter.

Colour tabs refer to the regions. The same tab is used for pages relating to a particular region.

Stars indicate the sights that no visitor should miss.

4 Detailed Information
All the major cities, towns and tourist attractions are described individually. They are listed in an order that follows the numbering on the area map at the start of the section.

The visitors' checklist gives all the practical information needed to plan your visit.

Story boxes provide information about historical or cultural topics relating to the sights.

Practical information provides everything you need to know to visit each sight. Map references pinpoint the sight's location on the road map on the inside back cover. For the three capital cities, map references relate to the *Street Finder* maps.

5 Major Sights
Historic buildings are dissected to reveal their interiors.

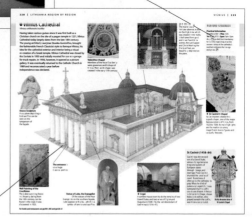

INTRODUCING ESTONIA, LATVIA AND LITHUANIA

DISCOVERING ESTONIA, LATVIA AND LITHUANIA

The following itineraries have been designed to take in as many of the Baltic States' highlights as possible, covering the beautiful and diverse landscapes of each country, while keeping long-distance travel to a minimum. Each of the three itineraries begins with a two-day tour of the country's distinctive and characterful capital city, followed by 12 days exploring the rest of the country. Pick, combine and follow your favourite tours, or simply dip in and out and be inspired.

Kõpu Lighthouse, Estonia
One of the world's oldest functioning lighthouses, this beacon, built in 1531 and reinforced in the 1980s, shines from the western end of ruggedly beautiful Hiiumaa Island.

```
0 kilometres    80
0 miles         80
```

14 Days in Estonia

- Admire the meticulously restored buildings of **Tallinn's Old Town**.

- Visit the historic windmills, thatched barns and inns at the **Estonian Open-Air Museum**.

- Relish the unspoiled nature on sparsely populated **Hiiumaa Island**.

- Marvel at a meteor's impact at the **Kaali Crater on Saaremaa Island**.

- Spend a day boating on **Lake Võrtsjäv**.

- Don a hard hat and head deep under the ground at the **Kohtla Underground Mining Museum**.

Key

—— 14 Days in Estonia
—— 14 Days in Latvia
—— 14 Days in Lithuania

◀ *A View of Tallinn with Hattorpe Tower by Alexander Georg Schlater (1834–79)*

14 Days in Latvia

- Immerse yourself in the warren of narrow streets in **Rīga's Old Town**.

- Appreciate the marvellous Art Nouveau architecture of **Rīga's Quiet Centre**.

- Relax on the windswept beaches of **Latvia's western coast**.

- Look out for bears and elk in **Gauja National Park**.

- Explore the picturesque waters of the **Latgale Lakes region**.

- Visit the stunning 18th-century **Rundāle Palace**, one of the finest in the Baltic States.

Rīga's Art Nouveau Architecture, Latvia
The Quiet Centre in Rīga has the finest collection of Art Nouveau buildings in Europe, including this elaborate edifice designed by Mikhail Eisenstein in 1905.

Lahemaa National Park
Ontika Coast
Palmse
Sillamäe
Narva
Kohtla Underground Mining Museum

STONIA
Mustvee
Raja
Lake Peipsi
Tartu
Rannu
Lake Võrtsjäv
Kiidjärve-Taevaskoja Area

Cēsis
atne

ATVIA
Lake Lubāns
Ludza
Jēkabpils
Rēzekne
Aglona
Lake Ešezers
Daugavpils
Aukštaitija National Park
Ignalina
Vilnius

14 Days in Lithuania

- Lose yourself in the labyrinthine streets of **Vilnius's Old Town**.

- Investigate the quirky cafés and galleries of Vilnius's artists' republic of **Užupis**.

- Step back in time at **Trakai Island Castle** and then drift passed it in a pedalo.

- Enjoy a day of being pampered and pummelled at spa resort **Druskininkal**.

- Discover unspoilt nature at **Aukštaitija National Park**.

- Stand atop the shifting sands of the **Curonian Spit's** giant dunes.

Trakai Island Castle, Lithuania
During the 15th century, this castle was the impenetrable stronghold of the Grand Duchy of Lithuania. Today its picturesque reconstruction is the country's biggest tourist draw.

14 Days in Estonia

- **Airports** Arrive and depart from Tallinn Airport.
- **Transport** This tour can be made using Estonia's bus and rail network, but hiring a car would allow more flexibility.

Day 1 Tallinn

Morning The best starting point for a first visit to Tallinn is the picturesque Old Town where a visit to the **Tallinn City Museum** (p67) provides a fascinating overview of the city's history. Wander down bustling Viru Street, past the colourful façades of historic buildings towards the impressive Gothic **Town Hall** (p64). **Niguliste Church** (p66), another Gothic masterpiece, is nearby.

Afternoon The fortified walls of **Toompea** (pp72–3) enclose a warren of intriguing buildings dating back to the 13th century. Pay a visit to **Toompea Castle** (p74), now home to Estonia's Parliament, and the impressive Russian Orthodox **Alexander Nevsky Cathedral** (p74). Don't miss the splendid views over the Old Town and out to the harbour from **Patkuli Viewing Platform** (p73).

Day 2 Tallinn

Morning Enjoy a stroll through **Kadriorg Park** (pp78–9), Tallinn's most popular green space. The park was originally laid out for Peter the Great with his grand summer residence, **Kadriorg Palace** (p80), at its heart. Pop into **Peter the Great House Museum** (p81), a tiny cottage where the Tsar lived while the palace was being built, and allow time for a visit to the Estonian Art Museum's main collection, housed within the futuristic **Kumu Art Museum** (p80).

Afternoon Choose to either visit the **Estonian Open-Air Museum** (p85) with its remarkable collection of historic rural buildings from all over Estonia, or head to the

Viru Gate, marking the entrance to Tallinn's Old Town

northeast of Tallinn to see the lovely **Botanical Gardens** (p84). Take a lift up to the **TV Tower's** viewing platform (p84) for unbeatable city views.

Day 3 Haapsalu

Dominated by the imposing ruins of its 13th-century castle, **Haapsalu** (p92) is a pleasant seaside resort. Worthwhile attractions include the **Castle Museum** in the ruins' watchtower, the attached **Dome Cathedral** and the **Estonian Railway Museum** where the town's grand 216 m (708 ft) railway platform, built to receive Tsar Nicholas II in 1904, has been preserved.

Day 4 Hiiumaa Island

From the port of Rohuküla, 9 km (6 miles) east of Haapsalu, take the ferry to Estonia's second largest island. Sparsely populated **Hiiumaa** (pp94–5) is a delight for nature lovers with its pine forests and deserted beaches. The small town of **Kärdla** makes a good base from which to explore the island. Be sure to head to **Kõpu**, where you can visit one of the world's oldest functioning lighthouses.

> **To extend your trip...**
> Spend an extra day on **Hiiumaa Island** visiting **Suuremõisa Manor** (p94) and the tiny island of **Kassari** (p95).

Day 5 Saaremaa Island

The picturesque **Saaremaa Island** (pp96–9) can be reached by a short ferry trip from Sõru on the southern tip of Hiiumaa Island. Visit the iconic five wooden windmills of **Angla** (p98) close to the port of Leisi, and stop by the tiny **Karja Church** (p99) to admire its elaborate stone carvings, then travel west along the coast to the unspoiled **Vilsandi National Park** (p99).

Day 6 Kuressaare on Saaremaa Island

Spend a pleasant day in and around **Kuressaare** (p98), Saaremaa's attractive main town. The spectacular **Bishop's Castle**, dating back to the 14th century, is a must-see as is the main street of delightful old buildings. For an afternoon excursion, either travel down the **Sõrve Peninsula** (p96) to

The well-preserved medieval Bishop's Castle in Kuressaare on Saaremaa Island

Saaremaa's magnificent wind-swept southern tip, or visit the intriguing **Kaali Meteor Crater** *(p98)*, 15 km (9 miles) to the northeast of town.

Day 7 Pärnu

Return to the mainland via Muhu Island and head for **Pärnu** *(pp102–103)*, Estonia's summer capital and most popular seaside resort. Attractions include a lovely 7 km (4 mile) sandy beach, historic Old Town buildings and several peaceful parks.

Day 8 Tartu

There's plenty to see in Estonia's vibrant college town, Tartu *(pp118–21)*, home to the venerable **Tartu University** and around 20,000 students. The 14th-century **St John's Church** has a fascinating interior containing terracotta figures and the **Tartu Art Museum** houses a fine collection of Estonian art in a leaning building. The **KGB Cells Museum** sheds a grim light on the activities of the Soviet agency and the suffering of many Estonians under the regime. **Toomemägi** (Cathedral Hill) *(pp120–21)* features pretty historic buildings amidst parkland and a warren of narrow streets.

The renovated medieval cathedral, now a library, in the Toomemägi area, Tartu

Day 9 Kiidjärve-Taevaskoja Recreational Area

In the Põlva region, 50 km (31 miles) south of Tartu and perfect for a day trip, the

Boulders along the coastline of Käsmu peninsula in Lahemaa National Park

picturesque **Kiidjärve-Taevaskoja Recreational Area** is a wonderful spot for picnics and hiking. It's home to **Kiidjärve Watermill** *(p126)* and the stunning **Taevaskoja Sandstone Cliffs** *(p126)*, which tower over the Ahja river.

Day 10 Lake Võrtsjäv

For a day of boating, sun-bathing and swimming, head west to **Lake Võrtsjäv** *(p122)*, Estonia's second-largest lake. Stop at the visitor centre in Rannu to organize boat hire or book a tour of the lake aboard a historic wooden sailing boat *(kalepurjekas)*.

Day 11 North to Narva

From Tartu, travel north to the historic border town of **Narva** *(p116)*, breaking the three-hour journey on the shores of **Lake Peipsi** *(p127)*, which straddles the border with Russia. At over 3,500 sq km (1,350 sq miles), it's Europe's fifth largest lake. Aim for lakeshore villages **Mustvee** and **Raja** *(p127)*, where Old Believers still follow traditional ways of life. Mustvee's small museum offers an illuminating glimpse into the history and daily lives of the community.

Day 12 Narva and Sillamäe

The sheer-sided castle, the museum in the castle's tall white tower and the neighbouring riverside park are the highlights of the border city of **Narva** *(see p116)*, where 96 per cent of the population speaks Russian. Nearby **Sillamäe** *(p115)* was

constructed during the Soviet era along with a uranium mine (closed in 1991), for the Soviet nuclear programme. Today its ornate Stalinist-era buildings are an intriguing sight.

Day 13 Along the north coast

The limestone cliffs of the **Ontika Coast** *(p115)*, just west of Sillamäe, are a magnificent sight and well worth visiting for the views across the Gulf of Finland alone. Spend the afternoon at the **Kohtla Underground Mining Museum** *(p115)* for a fascinating guided tour deep within the oil-shale mine before continuing to **Palmse** within **Lahemaa National Park** *(pp110–14)*.

Day 14 Lahemaa National Park

The grand manor houses at **Palmse** *(p112)* and **Sagadi** *(p113)* both provide an intriguing glimpse of 18th-century aristocratic life. From Palmse consider a trip to the tiny coastal village of **Võsu** *(p112)* or head to pretty **Käsmu** village *(p112)*. If time allows visit the fishing village of **Altja** *(p113)* to see its traditional thatched-roof houses before returning to Tallinn.

> **To extend your trip...**
> Spend a day hiking or hire a bicycle to tour the **Käsmu peninsula** *(p114)*, exploring the striking outcrop of giant boulders and historic **Käsmu** village *(p112)*.

14 Days in Latvia

- **Airports** Arrive and depart from Rīga airport.
- **Transport** This tour can be made using Latvia's bus and rail network, but hiring a car would allow more flexibility

The wonderfully reconstructed buildings of Town Hall Square, Rīga

Day 1 Rīga
Morning Start the day with a visit to the **Old Town**, Rīga's ancient heart. The city lost many of its splendid historic buildings during World War II, but a large number have been meticulously restored in recent years. The area around **Town Hall Square** (see pp150–51) is dominated by the mighty **St Peter's Church** (p153), and many of the area's other magnificent buildings, including **Mentzendorff House** (p152) and the **Town Hall**, have been returned to their former glory. The immense Soviet-era Modernist slab of concrete which normally houses the **Museum of the Occupation of Latvia** (p152), currently closed for renovation, is generally considered an eyesore.

Afternoon After lunching at one of the Old Town's many outdoor restaurants, enter the cool interior of the 13th-century **Dome Cathedral** (p146), the largest place of worship in the Baltics, before continuing to the **Museum of Rīga's History and Navigation** (p146) at the rear of the cathedral. For a more contemporary historical perspective head for the nearby **Museum of the Barricades of 1991** (p146), which documents the Latvian people's overthrow of Communist rule.

Day 2 Rīga
Morning Choose either to explore the UNESCO-listed Art Nouveau architecture of Rīga's **Quiet Centre** (pp156–7) or travel to **Dauderi** (p160), the stately Neo-Gothic mansion once used as the presidential summer residence, and now housing a rather eclectic museum on local history. Neighbouring **Mežaparks** (p160) is a residential district of lovely Modernist and Art Nouveau homes popular with well-to-do Latvians.

Afternoon Don't miss the **Latvian Ethnographic Open-Air Museum** (p163), a vast expanse of woodland on the shores of Lake Jugla dotted with thatched homesteads, churches, windmills and other traditional structures from all over the country – they provide a wonderful insight into Latvia's rural history.

Day 3 Gauja National Park – Around Sigulda
Sigulda (p192) lies 50 km (31 miles) northeast of Rīga and makes a great base for exploring the forested wilderness of **Gauja National Park** (pp190–93). Named after the river that wends its way through the park's sandstone hills, it's a wonderful place to hike and the trails are very well marked. The historic buildings and sculpture park at **Turaida Museum Reserve** (p192) are also worth visiting and are just a few kilometres from Sigulda.

Day 4 Gauja National Park – Līgatne and Cēsis
From Sigulda, travel northeast to Līgatne and the **Līgatne Education and Recreation Centre** (p193). This delightful wooded nature park is home to brown bears, beavers, elk, lynx and European bison and can be explored either on foot or by car. Continue northeast to lovely **Cēsis** (p192), one of Latvia's oldest towns, where the narrow streets are lined with 18th and 19th-century wooden and stone houses.

> **To extend your trip…**
> Rent a canoe and spend a day or two paddling along the Gauja river. You can arrange boat hire and transport through a river-trip specialist (p359 and p361).

Day 5 On to Ventspils
Head back to Rīga before continuing west to the historic coastal town of **Ventspils** (pp180–81), where pleasant cafés, parks and a white sandy beach await.

Day 6 Ventspils
Despite its long heritage as a trading centre and member of the Hanseatic League, Ventspils was little more than a tanker port for much of the Soviet era and has only recently become

Ventspils Castle, a 14th-century Livonian Order stronghold in the resort of Ventspils

For practical information on travelling around Latvia, see pp382–7 the country's most popular seaside destination. The 13th-century **Ventspils Castle** is one of the main attractions, along with the town's attractive Russian and Lutheran churches, and the lovely Blue Flag beach. The **Seaside Open-Air Museum**, with its fishermen's cottages, smokehouses and even a narrow-gauge railway, is also worth a visit.

Day 7 Pavilosta
Reached by a windswept coastal road from Ventspils that affords the occasional glimpse of the sea, **Pavilosta** (p183) is a remarkably laid-back port town with a splendid marina and miles of pristine sandy beaches popular with wind and kite surfers throughout the summer.

> ### To extend your trip...
> Experience life on the waves by joining a fishing trip or taking a sailing lesson at **Pavilosta Marina** (see p183).

Day 8 Liepāja
The coastal road continues through woodland towards **Liepāja** (pp184–5), Latvia's vibrant third city. With both cultural attractions and a fantastic stretch of beach, there's plenty to engage visitors here. The main street, Lielā iela, is dominated by the 18th-century **Holy Trinity Church**, which has superb views from its tower. To the southwest the well-tended **Seaside Park** runs parallel to the town's Blue Flag beach.

Day 9 Jelgava
From Liepāja, take the highway northeast and branch off to **Jelgava** (p170), pausing along the way to admire the turreted **Jaunpils Castle** (p174), an impressive 14th-century affair with a small museum and its own hotel (p301). Despite losing much of its architectural heritage during World War I and World War II, Jelgava still has a number of attractions. Chief among them are the elegant 18th-century **Jelgava Palace** and the **Orthodox Cathedral of St Simeon and St Anna** in the Old Town.

Day 10 Rundāle Palace
Head to stunning **Rundāle Palace** (pp172–3), a Baroque building with Rococo interiors that is one of the finest palaces in the Baltics. It's an easy daytrip from Jelgava, or stop there in the morning before driving on to Daugavpils, four hours away. To get to Daugavpils from Jelgava by public transport, you'll need to travel via Rīga.

Day 11 Daugavpils
Located in Latvia's southeastern corner, **Daugavpils** (pp200–201) is the country's second largest city. It was founded by Ivan the Terrible in the 16th century and, with 90 per cent of the population speaking Russian, it retains a distinctly Russian feel. Among its attractions is the onion-domed **Cathedral of Saints Boris and Glebe**, Latvia's largest Russian Orthodox cathedral. The extensive **Daugavpils**

The ruins of Rēzekne Castle in Rēzekne, the centre of the Latgale region

Fortress is definitely worth exploring, particularly as the **Mark Rothko Art Centre** is now housed in its arsenal.

Day 12 Aglona
Moving on from Daugavpils, head northeast to **Rēzekne** (p199) stopping at **Aglona** (p199) along the way. While Aglona itself is unremarkable, it's home to the towering **Aglona Basilica**; as Latvia's most important Catholic shrine, it attracts worshippers from all across Russia and the Baltic States.

Day 13 Rezekne and the Latgale Lakes
Having been pulverized to rubble during World War II, Rēzekne has few buildings of historic interest, but it makes a good base for exploring the more than 80 bodies of water that make up the picturesque **Latgale Lakes** (p202). **Lake Lubāns**, the largest, is great for bird-watching and fishing. Southeast of Rēzekne, **Lake Ežezers** is considered one of the most beautiful, with many islands to explore by boat. To the east of Rēzekne, the pretty town of **Ludza** (p203), with its many wooden houses, sits between two lakes.

Day 14 Rēzekne to Rīga
Break the four-hour journey back to Rīga at **Jēkabpils** (p198), where a fine Orthodox church and an open-air ethnographic museum are the main sights.

Picturesque Jaunpils Castle, built in the 14th-century and subsequently reconstructed

14 Days in Lithuania

- **Airports** Arrive and depart from Vilnius Airport.
- **Transport** This tour can be made using Lithuania's bus and rail network, but hiring a car would allow you much more flexibility.

Day 1 Vilnius Old Town

Morning The characterful buildings and winding streets of Vilnius's marvellous **Old Town** have changed little in the past several hundred years. Though the city was founded in the 11th century, much of Vilnius's current architectural heritage dates back to the late 18th century, when a series of fires consumed many of its wooden structures and stone houses were built to replace them. A tour of the Old Town should start with its centrepiece – the stunning, temple-like **Vilnius Cathedral** (pp228–9), which stands on the site of an early pagan shrine. Behind is the **Royal Palace**, part of the Lower Castle (p230), home to Lithuania's Grand Dukes for four centuries. The original Renaissance palace was demolished in 1801; the existing building is a reconstruction opened in 2009. Perched on a hill above is the last remaining tower of the **Upper Castle** (p230), with fantastic views of the city. The **Lithuanian National Museum's** (p230) absorbing collection is a short walk from the Upper Castle.

Afternoon Explore the many grand buildings and courtyards that comprise **Vilnius University** (p226) before strolling along **Pilies Street**. Lined with historic churches and houses, the street is the Old Town's main thoroughfare. Look out for **St John's Church** (p226) and the **Church of St Paraskeva** (p227) before reaching the grand **Church of St Casimir** (p236), Vilnius's oldest Baroque church. Exit the Old Town through the **Gates of Dawn** (p239), pausing to view the miracle-working icon, The Madonna of Mercy, within its chapel, which attracts pilgrims from all over Lithuania and Poland.

Day 2 Vilnius

Morning The Old Town boasts a number of excellent museums, including two that cover tragic events in moving detail: the **KGB Museum** (p242) reveals the Soviet reign of terror and includes the basement prison cells of the KGB building; and the **Holocaust Museum** (p242) covers life in the Jewish ghettoes and the horror that befell the community during World War II.

Afternoon Either visit the self-declared artists' republic of **Užupis** (p244), a fascinating quarter of cafés and independent galleries, or head west to the pleasant **Žvėrynas** district (p245), with its wooden villas, lovely park and wonderful views from the nearby **TV Tower** (p245).

The Town Hall in Kaunas, known locally as the White Swan

Day 3 Trakai Island Castle

Lying just 25 km (16 miles) west of Vilnius, **Trakai Island Castle** (pp256–7) is an easy day-trip from Vilnius but can also make an enjoyable overnight stop. Occupying one of Lake Galvė's many islands, the heavily fortified medieval castle is Lithuania's best-known monument and once rivalled Vilnius for power. In summer yachts and peddle boats are available for hire.

Day 4 Kaunas

With its well-preserved Old Town, leafy parks and laid-back pavement cafés, **Kaunas** (pp262–5) makes for an enjoyable stay. Old Town highlights include the pretty 16th-century **Old Town Hall** (p262), the ruins of **Kaunas Castle** (p262) and the Gothic **Cathedral of Sts Peter and Paul** (p263). To learn more about the city's past, visit the **Vytautas the Great War Museum** (p264). The neighbouring **Devil's Museum** (p264) is worth seeing for its quirky collection of sculptures and carvings of devils and witches from all around the world.

Day 5 Around Kaunas

An easy day-trip from Kaunas, the Baroque **Pažaislis Monastery** (p265), founded in the 17th century, can be visited on the way to the **Rumšiškės Open-Air Museum** (p265), a

The remains of Vilnius's Upper Castle, including the symbolic western tower on the right

Tranquil lake fringed by thick forest and marshy shores, Aukštaitija National Park

wonderful collection of traditional buildings from around the country that have been meticulously reassembled in picturesque surroundings.

Day 6 Druskininkai

Travel south to **Druskininkai** *(p259)* and spend the rest of the day relaxing in this tranquil spa resort where numerous spa centres offer massage, mud baths, beauty treatments and mineral water cures.

> **To extend your trip…**
> Spend a day hiking or cycling along well-marked paths in the forests surrounding **Druskininkai**.

Day 7 Aukštaitija National Park

From Druskininkai, take the northeastern road via Vilnius to **Ignalina**, a small rural town that lies just outside Aukštaitija National Park.

Day 8 Aukštaitija National Park

Dotted with glacial lakes, rock formations, and ancient pine, spruce and birch forests, **Aukštaitija National Park** *(see pp270–71)* is a delightful area to explore. Worthwhile sights include **Salos II Cultural Reserve** for its exhibition of traditional thatched houses, and **Ladakalnis Hill** for its panoramic view of the national park.

> **To extend your trip…**
> Hire a rowing boat at Palušė and follow the circular **water trail** around the lakes.

Day 9 Siauliai

Head 240 km (150 miles) west to **Siauliai** *(pp276–7)*, historic site of the Battle of the Sun in 1236, which saw the defeat of the Livonian Order at the hands of the pagan Samogitians. Today it's a thriving modern city with a well-preserved Old Town and numerous museums, but it's probably best-known for the incredible **Hill of Crosses** *(see p277)*, just a little ways north at Jurgaičių. The small hill is covered with thousands upon thousands of crosses and religious sculptures from all over the world, and is almost as much a

The popular 18-km (11-mile) beach at the resort of Palanga

symbol of political will, having been dismantled by the Soviet's numerous times, as it is an outpouring of deep religious faith.

Day 10 Palanga

From Siauliai, head west to the coastal town of **Palanga** *(p286)* and spend a peaceful afternoon on the sandy beach before joining locals and tourists on the pier to watch the sunset.

Day 11 Klaipėda

Lithuania's only seaport, **Klaipėda** *(see pp284–5)* is a popular spot with an atmospheric Old Town and a vibrant nightlife scene. Pay a visit to the **Clock Museum** to marvel at its intriguing collection of time-pieces from all over the world and consider a visit to the **Picture Gallery** and the large sculpture park just behind.

Day 12 Curonian Spit

Accessible by ferry from Klaipėda to Smiltyne, the **Curonian Spit** *(pp288–9)* is one of Lithuania's most remarkable natural sights. No more than 4 km (2 miles) wide at any point and as narrow as 400 m (440 yards) in places, it's a slender sliver of land made up of sand dunes, beaches and woods that stretch from Klaipėda to the Sambian Peninsula in Kaliningrad. Enjoy a peaceful stay at one of the many small guesthouses in and around **Nida** *(p306)*, which can be reached by minibus.

Day 13 Curonian Spit

Spend the day exploring the Curonian Spit on foot or by bicycle. Points of interest include the **Hill of Witches** *(p289)* created by local sculptors just outside Juodkrante, and the 52-m (171-ft) **Parnidis Dune** *(p288)*, which offers marvellous views of the area.

Day 14 Curonian Spit to Vilnius

The journey back to Vilnius by car, bus or train takes around 5 hours.

Estonia, Latvia and Lithuania on the Map

With Estonia in the north, Latvia in the centre and Lithuania in the south, the Baltic States lie on the southeastern shore of the Baltic Sea. The region is bordered in the east by Russia and in the south by Poland, Belarus and the Russian enclave of Kaliningrad. The Baltic States' total land area is 173,000 sq km (66,778 sq miles). Latvia and Lithuania are of roughly equal size, while Estonia is about a third smaller and has a relatively flat terrain in comparison to the other two countries. The three capital cities – Tallinn, Rīga and Vilnius – are home to around a third of the region's 6.3 million people.

Key

═══	Motorway
═══	Major road
⋯⋯	Minor road
───	Railway line
───	International border

0 kilometres   50

0 miles   50

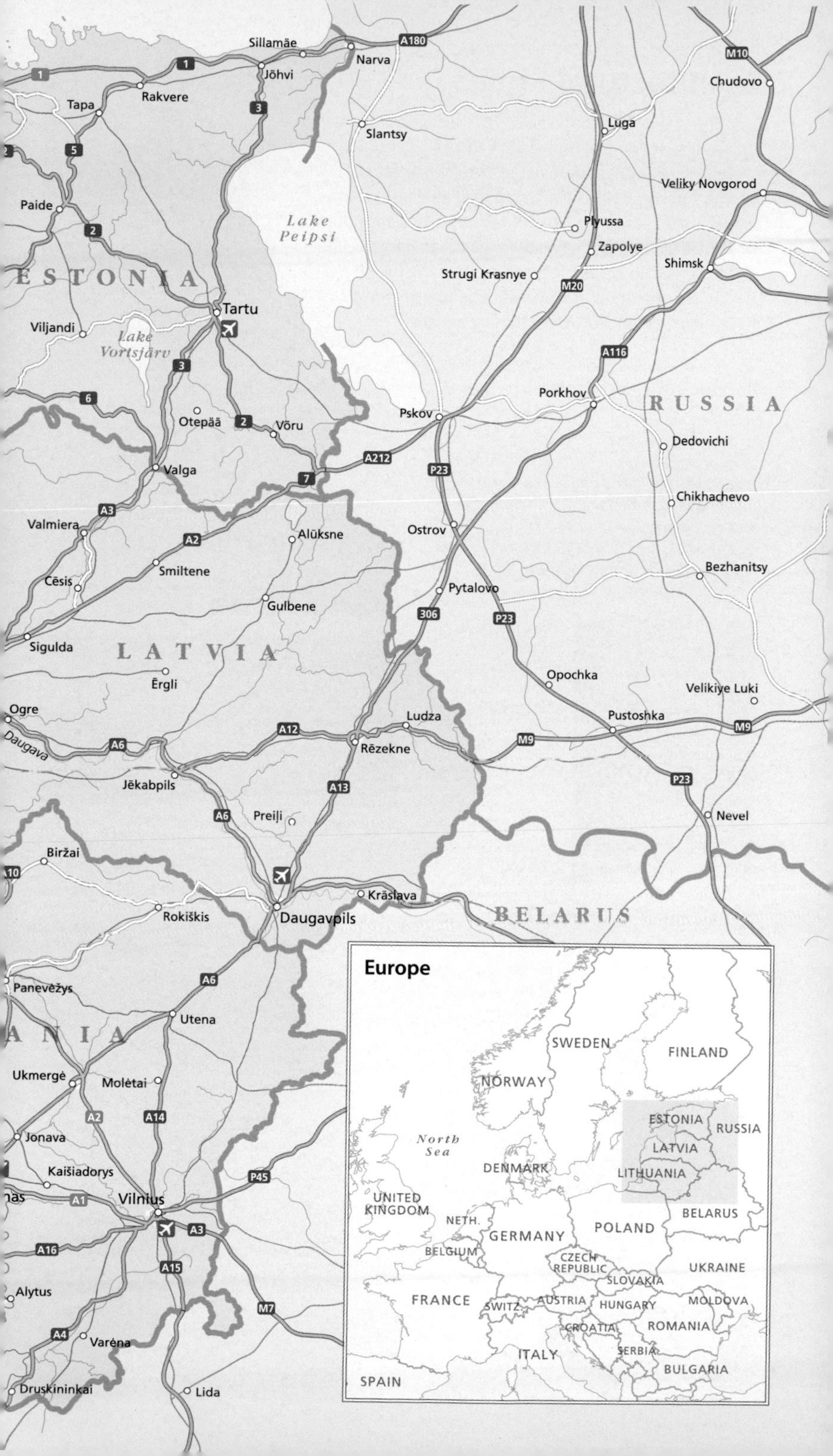

Sillamäe
Narva
1
A180
1
Jõhvi
3
Chudovo
M10
Tapa
Rakvere
Luga
3
5
Slantsy
Veliky Novgorod
Paide
2
Lake
Peipsi
Plyussa
Zapolye
Strugi Krasnye
Shimsk
ESTONIA
M20
Tartu
Viljandi
Lake
Võrtsjärv
3
Porkhov
RUSSIA
Pskov
A116
6
Otepää
Võru
2
Dedovichi
Valga
7
A212
P23
A3
Chikhachevo
Valmiera
A2
Alūksne
Ostrov
Cēsis
Smiltene
Bezhanitsy
Gulbene
Pytalovo
Sigulda
LATVIA
306
P23
Ērgli
Opochka
Velikiye Luki
Ogre
Ludza
Pustoshka
Daugava
A6
A12
Rēzekne
M9
M9
Jēkabpils
A13
A6
Preiļi
P23
Biržai
Nevel
10
Krāslava
Rokiškis
Daugavpils
BELARUS
Panevėžys
A6
Utena
Ukmergė
Molėtai
Jonava
A2
A14
Kaišiadorys
P45
as
A1
Vilnius
A16
A3
Alytus
A15
A4
Varėna
M7
Druskininkai
Lida

Europe

SWEDEN
FINLAND
NORWAY
ESTONIA
RUSSIA
North
Sea
LATVIA
DENMARK
LITHUANIA
UNITED
KINGDOM
NETH.
BELARUS
GERMANY
POLAND
BELGIUM
CZECH
REPUBLIC
UKRAINE
SLOVAKIA
FRANCE
SWITZ.
AUSTRIA
HUNGARY
MOLDOVA
CROATIA
ROMANIA
ITALY
SERBIA
BULGARIA
SPAIN

Architectural Styles

Ever since the wooden fortifications of the Baltic tribes were replaced by stone castles in the 13th and 14th centuries, foreign influences have dominated the architecture of Estonia, Latvia and Lithuania. Today, the Baltic capitals are architectural treasure troves, with Tallinn particularly noted for its medieval buildings, Vilnius for its Italian Baroque and Rīga for its Art Nouveau. The Soviet era saw the building of inexpensive mass housing. Since independence private investment has funded ambitious new projects.

Detail of the extravagant Gothic brickwork of Perkūnas House, Kaunas

Romanesque and Gothic

Brought to Tallinn and Rīga by medieval German invaders, the Romanesque style, with its heavy vaulting, round arches and restrained ornamentation, lasted briefly in the region. The ornate Gothic ribbed vaults, pointed arches and decorative façades were more popular. Tallinn boasts the finest examples, while most of Rīga's were destroyed as part of the 19th-century rebuilding of the city.

The Estonian History Museum was built in Tallinn for the Great Guild, a powerful organization of German-speaking merchants. This early 15th-century building has a stern Gothic façade and vaulted halls.

The Church of St Anne, Vilnius's most celebrated Gothic building, was constructed using 33 types of red brick. So impressed was Napoleon Bonaparte that he is said to have wanted to take it back to Paris.

Kuressaare Castle, on Saaremaa Island, is the only intact Gothic-style medieval castle in the Baltic States. It is built in local dolomite.

Renaissance and Baroque

The 15th- and 16th-century revival of Classical learning, which favoured architectural features such as regularity, symmetry and a central axis, found little expression in Lithuania. In Latvia and Estonia, however, it led to the addition of new façades to existing buildings. The bold 17th- and 18th-century Baroque style, endorsed by the Catholic Church, found favour in the religious climate of Vilnius.

Pažaislis Monastery, in Kaunas, is one of Eastern Europe's most prominent Baroque monuments. Built in the 17th century by Italian architects, the monastery church has a twin-towered façade, behind which soars the 52-m (171-ft) dome. A wealth of marble enriches the interior.

The House of Blackheads, in Tallinn, was used by the Brotherhood of Blackheads. It was formerly a 14th-century building, which was redesigned in a Renaissance style in 1597. The interiors were renovated in Neo-Classical style in 1908.

Neo-Classical and Historicist

The Neo-Classical style arrived in the Baltic States as late as the 1780s. The style had a strong influence on Tartu, as well as some of the finest manor houses throughout Estonia. However, most examples today are found in Tallinn, often as façades on earlier buildings; some Latvian and Lithuanian palaces also exhibit the style. Around 1820, the Historicist movement became popular, drawing inspiration from various styles including Gothic, Renaissance and Neo-Baroque.

Tartu's Town Hall is an elegant Neo-Classical edifice, eye-catchingly painted in lilac and orange. It was designed in the 18th century by J H B Walter for the Pistohlkors family.

Kaunas's Town Hall, locally known as the "White Swan", was renovated in 1870 in Neo-Classical style. It also bears Baroque traces, most obviously in its 53-m (174-ft) tall stepped tower.

The Latvian National Theatre, in Rīga, was designed in a superb Neo-Baroque style. It was completed in 1902 by architect Augusts Reinbergs under the influence of Historicist aesthetics.

Art Nouveau, Modernist and Contemporary

The second half of the 19th century saw Art Nouveau gaining a hold in Rīga. After World War I there was a reaction against earlier flamboyant styles, with Modernists emphasizing function and Soviets favouring severe Functionalism. Since independence, further construction has taken place in the capitals, but it is not always in harmony with older architectural styles.

Alberta iela 13, in Rīga, is a fine example of eclectic Art Nouveau, blending Classical and Symbolist imagery and Neo-Baroque stylistic features.

Europa Tower, in Vilnius, is one of a growing number of skyscrapers in the Baltic capitals, marking the return of the private sector.

The National Library, in Tallinn, is an architectural triumph of the late Soviet period. Raine Karp, the Estonian architect who designed it, used local dolomitic limestone.

Landscape and Wildlife

The three Baltic countries are heavily forested with pine, spruce and birch and enjoy a predominantly flat terrain, although there are hilly areas such as the Vidzeme Upland in Latvia. The highest point in the region is Estonia's Suur Munamägi peak, which rises to about 318 m (1,043 ft) above sea level. The Baltic States are known for their dramatic coastlines, innumerable lakes and rivers as well as extensive wetlands which, along with forests, provide habitats for a wide range of wildlife. The countries are also on major bird migration paths, making them popular with ornithologists all over the world. All three countries are still extensively covered with peat bogs, marshes and lakes.

Erratic boulders, some of them very large, are common on the coastline of Estonia's Käsmu Peninsula (see p114). They were dragged there by glaciers during the last Ice Age.

Forest

Around 40 per cent of the total landscape in Estonia, Latvia and Lithuania is forested. Pine, spruce and birch are the main species, alongside other trees such as oak, ash, elm and maple. Trees were highly valued in the region's pre-Christian religions.

Wetlands

The extensive wetlands of the region are ideal habitats for migrating birds, and for supporting plants such as cranberries and orchids. In Estonia, raised bogs in which thick layers of peat have built up are common. Many are protected by national parks.

Fauna

The Baltic States are home to large mammals such as lynx, elk, deer, wolves and brown bears. With the region lying on major migration routes there are numerous nesting bird species including white stork, crane, barn swallow and grouse. The rivers and lakes teem with fish such as perch, trout and carp.

Bees are highly valued in the region, as apiculture is an important industry and a part of the Baltic States' cultural heritage.

White storks are emblematic of the region and are often found nesting atop chimney pots or telegraph poles. Black storks are a relatively rare sight.

Wolves are found in the region's forests, especially in Lithuania. However, they are a rare sight, as hunting has resulted in dwindling numbers of this predatory animal.

Flora

The Baltic States' extensive forests and wetlands provide an environment in which a diverse range of plants can thrive. Many edible varieties of fungi and berries grow here. There is an orchid trail near Lake Engure, in Latvia, and yellow rattle and sea holly grow in Saaremaa and Curonian Spit.

Arctic lichen is a type of fungus found in Hiiumaa Island's Landscape Reserve. Like other lichen, it usually grows in two layers with a growth of algae in between.

Mushrooms are mostly wood decomposers or parasites. As the virgin forests are depleting, species of the former are becoming rarer.

Orchids grow mostly in the wetlands and woods. Those found here include rare North European species that are facing extinction.

Berries, such as cranberries, are eaten and also turned into wine.

Lakes and Rivers

The region is dotted with lakes, of which Lake Peipsi in Estonia is the largest. There are a number of short rivers in the area. The low salinity of the Baltic Sea limits the number of plants and animal species it can support. Thus many of those present are freshwater species.

Coastline

Estonia has a sprawling coastline. It includes a stretch of the Baltic Klint, which is a long erosional escarpment stretching from Sweden to Russia. Another striking coastal feature is the Curonian Spit, a long sandy strip in Lithuania stretching to Kaliningrad.

The barn swallow, the national bird of Estonia, often builds its nests in man-made structures.

Ringed seals are protected and can be found off the coast of Saaremaa and other Estonian islands.

Brown bears are omnivores and can be spotted in the forests of Estonia and Latvia, although they are usually sighted only with the help of a guide.

Elk is a game species that usually lives in forests and wetlands. It often appears on restaurant menus in the Baltic States.

Religion

Although the Baltic lands were officially Christian by the end of the 14th century, pagan beliefs persisted and mingled with the new religion. Protestantism left its mark in the 16th century, but Lithuania soon returned to the Catholic fold. Today, it is the only Baltic State where the church plays a major public role – in Estonia and Latvia, the surge in religious participation after independence in 1991 proved short-lived. A significant number of ethnic Russians belong to the Russian Orthodox church, while other minority religious groups include Jews and Muslims.

Aerial view of the Orthodox Cathedral in Rīga, Latvia

Priest performing a Romuva ritual based on ancient pagan beliefs

Paganism

Christianity came late to the Baltic region, with the Grand Duchy of Lithuania holding out until 1387, a year after Grand Duke Jogaila was baptized. The details of pagan beliefs are sparse, and scholars rely on surviving traditions and folk songs. Animism, the belief that plants and animals possess spirits, prevailed. Trees had great significance, with prayers offered at sacred groves.

Shamans communicated with the gods, but there was no organized priesthood. For Latvians and Lithuanians major deities included Dievs or Dievas (the Sky God), Saule (the Sun), Pērkons or Perkūnas (Thunder), Velns or Velnias (Trickster), Mēness or Menulis (the Moon) and Laima (Fate). The Estonians and Livs *(see p176)* worshipped Taara (War), Uku (Thunder and Lightning), Vanetooni (the Dead), Maaema (Land), Ahti (Water) and Vanejumi (Fertility). Some scholars argue that these various deities show aspects of one divine being. Pagan overtones are still present in a number of Christian celebrations.

The first period of independence in the 20th century saw attempts to revive old traditions. Some local organizations, such as Dievturība in Latvia, were nationalist in tone. After years of Soviet marginalization, Dievturība has now been revived, though the Lithuanian pagan group Romuva has a stronger following in the country.

Orthodox Christianity

Orthodox missionaries arrived in the region as early as the 10th century but had little success. Orthodox Christianity was largely eclipsed by Catholicism, except among the Setu *(see p124)*. This changed only under Russian rule in the 19th century, with many magnificent Orthodox churches built at that time.

Today, almost all Orthodox worshippers in the region are ethnic Russians. Their churches are known for the abundance of icons – images of Christ, Mary and various saints – often displayed in rows on a screen called an iconostasis. The region also contains small communities of Old Believers *(see p126)*, descendants of worshippers who broke away from the Orthodox Church in protest against reforms introduced by Patriarch Nikon in 1652. Bringing Russian Orthodox rites in line with the Greek, his motives were both religious and political. The Old Believers sought to retain the purity of their faith, and the

Devotees lined up in Alexander Nevsky Church, Tallinn, Estonia

result was the Russian term *raksol* (schism) and their subsequent persecution. Many Old Believers fled from Russia, and today the main communities in the Baltic States are around Lake Peipsi *(see p127)* in Estonia and in the Latgale region of Latvia. Differences in rites include making the sign of the cross with two fingers (the Orthodox church now uses three) and changes to the wording of the Creed. Old Believers regard shaving a man's beard as sinful, and there are restrictions on smoking tobacco. Members often wear long traditional Russian shirts.

Catholic Church of the Holy Spirit, Vilnius, Lithuania

Old Believers' Church, made of wood, near Lake Peipsi

Catholicism

Catholicism was brought to the region by force, with Pope Innocent III authorizing a crusade against the northern pagans in 1198. The areas which are now known as Estonia and Latvia fell first, with Lithuania hanging on until 1387.

The new religion was regarded as alien by the indigenous population, a feeling exacerbated by the use of Latin in services. Catholicism found its strongest roots in Eastern Latvia and Lithuania, both under the influence of Poland. These foundations were strengthened by the Counter-Reformation, the Catholic Church's response to the threat posed by Lutheranism. The newly established Jesuit order built schools and made efforts to use the native language, also emphasizing the importance of the Virgin Mary in an attempt to win back worshippers. Today Lithuania is the only country out of the three Baltic States where religion is central to national identity.

Protestantism

The Reformation was quickly felt in Estonia and Western Latvia with the introduction of the revolutionary ideas of Lutheranism, a major branch of Protestant Christianity. The offshoot emphasized receiving God's grace through faith alone, rather than through good works. It first appeared in Estonian urban centres during the 1520s. Initially, the landowners resisted the change, but soon they recognized it as a useful way to resist the influence of the Pope. Peasants were expected to follow the faith of their landlords. The new beliefs were further bolstered by Swedish rule in the 17th century, when more pastors were trained and there was an increased use of indigenous languages for religious activities. The first Bible in Latvian was published in 1689 by the Lutheran theologian Ernst Glück (1654–1705).

There was a brief revival in religious activity after independence from the oppressive Soviet regime, during which many churches had been converted for other uses. Although Estonia and Latvia are still officially Lutheran, participation has declined in recent years and there are now marginally more Catholics than Lutherans in Latvia.

Virgin Mary's Lutheran Church, Otepää

Famous People

A history of cultural domination by other nations explains why only a handful of figures from the Baltic States are internationally known. It was only with the 19th-century national awakening movements that the notion of distinctive Baltic cultures gained popularity. After the brief confidence of the first independence, the restrictions of the Soviet era meant that most famous people from the region were either of Russian heritage or were living outside their native countries. In the years since independence in 1991, the arts have been hampered by reduced state funding.

A portrait by Michael Sittow, a 15th-century Tallinn-born artist

Visual Arts

Estonia's best-known painter was Eduard Wiiralt (1898–1954), while in the 20th century animators Elbert Tuganov (1920–2007) and Priit Pärn (b.1946) gained international praise. Within Latvia, painter Janis Rozentāls (1866–1916) remains most beloved, although Mark Rothko *(see p200)* is more famed abroad. Lithuania has produced several notable photographers, including Antanas Sutkus (b.1939).

Sergei Eisenstein (1898–1948), one of the most influential film directors and theorists of all time, was born in Rīga. His groundbreaking use of editing is best seen in his early Marxist cinematic works, including *Strike!* (1924) and *Battleship Potemkin* (1925).

Mikalojus Konstantinas Čiurlionis (1875–1911), Lithuania's pre-eminent composer, was also an accomplished artist. His work draws extensively upon Symbolism and the influence of music can be found in his emphasis on mood, interest in harmony and development of themes across a series of paintings. The tempera on canvas shown above is entitled *The Offering (1909)*.

Literature

Key to the 19th-century national awareness was the preservation and creation of stories by authors such as Latvian Andrejs Pumpurs (1841–1902), Estonian Friedrich Kreutzwald (1803–82) and Lithuanian Jonas Mačiulis (1862–1932). Modern literature is equally celebrated and famous contemporary authors include Estonian poets Jaan Kaplinski (b.1941) and Jaan Kross (1920–2007), and Lithuanian novelists Ričardas Gavelis (1950–2002) and Jurga Ivanauskaitė (1961–2007).

Anton Hansen Tammsaare (1878–1940) is regarded as the greatest Estonian writer. His work *Truth and Justice* is a five-volume series of novels covering subjects that include rural Estonia and the Russian Revolution of 1905.

Czesław Miłosz (1911–2004) was born into a Polish aristocratic family and educated in Vilnius. A poet and intellectual, Miłosz won the Nobel Prize for Literature in 1980. He is perhaps best known for *The Captive Mind*, a prose critique of Communist ideology.

Music

Estonia has a strong tradition of classical composition. Veljo Tormis (b.1930) is influenced by Estonian folk music, while Erkki-Sven Tüür (b.1959) mixes avant-garde techniques with early music and progressive rock. The father of Latvian classical music is Jāzeps Vītols (1863–1948), and the country is also known for pop and rock performers such as the band Brainstorm. Lithuania is renowned for jazz musicians, including the Ganelin Trio, while its finest classical composer was M K Čiurlionis.

Arvo Pärt (b.1935), an Estonian composer, made early experiments with Schoenberg's 12-tone technique and the use of chance. He is internationally known for "sacred minimalism", drawing on medieval traditions and Orthodox Christianity. Pärt describes his music as *tintinnabuli* (like bells).

Theatre and Dance

Professional theatre was once the domain of the ruling classes, but from the mid-19th century plays were written by authors such as Estonia's Eduard Vilde (1865–1933) and Latvia's Rūdolfs Blaumanis (1863–1908). Lithuania's lively theatre scene is dominated by director Eimuntas Nekrošius (b.1952). Ballet thrived during the Soviet era, with the Rīga Ballet promoting Alexander Godunov (1949–95).

Mikhail Baryshnikov (b.1948), born in Rīga, is of Russian descent. Baryshnikov began his ballet studies in the Latvian city before progressing to Leningrad (now St Petersburg). He defected while on tour in Canada in 1974. He later became a citizen of the USA and founded a dance centre in New York.

Voldemar Panso (1920–77), the famous theatre director, rejected Soviet ideology in favour of complex characters and the ambiguity of Symbolism. He also founded the Estonian Youth Theatre (later the Tallinn City Theatre).

Sport

The talent of Baltic athletes was, for many decades, obscured by their status as Soviet citizens. Estonia's most famous Olympian was heavyweight wrestler Kristjan Palusalu (1908–87), while Latvian long-distance walker Jānis Daliņš (1904–78) won the Olympic silver in 1932. Lithuania's top Olympic athlete is discus-thrower Virgilijus Alekna (b.1972). The region has also produced exceptional basketball players, including Lithuanian Arvydas Sabonis (b.1964), Latvian Uljana Semjonova (b.1952) and Estonian Tiit Sokk (b.1964).

Erki Nool (b.1970) won a gold medal in the decathlon at the 2000 Sydney Olympics, a controversial result since a judge had disallowed all three of his discus attempts before the competition referee over-ruled him. In 2007, Nool was elected to the Estonian Parliament.

Uljana Semjonova (b.1952), a basketball player of Russian-Latvian origin, won two Olympic gold medals in 1976 and 1980. She dominated the world basketball scene throughout the 1970s and 80s and never lost any official international match.

Folk Songs and Music

The traditional songs of Estonia, Latvia and Lithuania typically deal with everyday events, calendar rituals and rites of passage, though stories of epic heroism and grandeur also exist. These songs are sung by women. Efforts to compile the songs began in earnest in the late 19th century and this was an important facet of the region's growing national awareness. Later, between 1987 and 1990, the struggle for freedom from the Soviet Union came to be known as the Singing Revolution, partly due to the role played by huge open-air concerts.

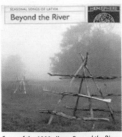

Cover of the 1998 album *Beyond the River: Seasonal Songs of Latvia*

Traditional Lithuanian songs, or *dainos*, deal with daily life. They are sung solo, in unison or polyphonically. One of the best-known forms is the duophonic *sutartinė* from the northeast.

Monophonic Estonian songs, or *runo*, are related to those from Finland, and their roots are much older than those of Latvia and Lithuania. The Setu people of Eastern Estonia have their own distinctive polyphonic singing traditions.

Baltica Festival

This annual international folklore festival was first held in Estonia in 1987 and is hosted cyclically by the Baltic States. The three Baltic flags were hoisted together for the first time during the second festival in 1987. Today, the festival brings together around 3,000 participants and includes concerts, parades and workshops.

Latvian folk songs, or *dainas*, consist of one or two stanzas each with two non-rhyming couplets. This singing tradition is lyrical and usually draws inspiration from pagan mythology or daily life. Traditionally, these songs were accompanied by instruments such as bagpipes and psalteries, with accordions and fiddles added in the 17th century.

Veljo Tormis (b.1930) is a celebrated composer of choral music based on the folk songs of his native Estonia. Many of his more political pieces of the 1970s and 80s were censored by the Soviet government.

Baltic Folk Singers

The Soviet era saw government-approved performers refine folk songs with classical harmonies and accompaniment, but enthusiasts worked to preserve genuine traditions. Today, a number of festivals are held all over the region.

Iļģi, the famous Latvian folk music band, was formed in 1981. Like most folk musicians of the country, they revived forgotten traditions and developed into a band that used folklore as an impulse for creating music of their own.

Veronika Povilionienė (b.1946) has enjoyed success since the late 1960s, initially promoting folk singing as a mode of anti-Soviet protest. In recent years, she has also recorded pop and jazz albums.

The Baltic Psaltery

The most characteristic instrument used by the region's folk singers is the Baltic psaltery. It exists in numerous variations, and is known as *kokle* in Latvia, *kanklės* in Lithuania and *kannel* in Estonia. In the late 19th century, hybrids influenced by German and Austrian zithers were developed.

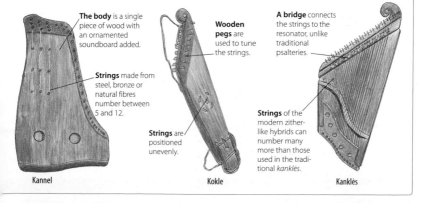

The body is a single piece of wood with an ornamented soundboard added.

Strings made from steel, bronze or natural fibres number between 5 and 12.

Wooden pegs are used to tune the strings.

Strings are positioned unevenly.

A bridge connects the strings to the resonator, unlike traditional psalteries.

Strings of the modern zither-like hybrids can number many more than those used in the traditional *kanklės*.

Kannel

Kokle

Kanklės

Baltic Amber

Amber has been valued for millennia, with amber jewellery found dating back to the early Neolithic period (around 7000 BC). Many medical authorities of the ancient world, including Hippocrates, believed that amber had healing properties. A trade network, now known as the Amber Route, arose at the height of the Roman Empire. In the medieval period, amber was used to make rosaries. Today, it still washes up on Latvian and Lithuanian shores, although 90 per cent of the world's amber is mined in the Curonian Spit of neighbouring Kaliningrad.

One of the many amber stalls found in tourist areas

Identifying Amber

Sellers may pass off copal or plastic as genuine amber. Genuine amber floats in salt water and exudes a pine scent when touched with a red-hot needle, but only laboratory tests are conclusive.

Amber-catchers in the Baltic Sea are shown in this lithograph from the 1850s. In the 13th century, local amber-gathering was forbidden by the Teutonic Knights. Their monopoly was lifted only in the 19th century, reviving amber-working traditions.

Unpolished amber of different colours and shapes

Amber pieces are regularly washed ashore in Pāvilosta (*see p183*), a small port town in Latvia. There are a handful of professional amber-catchers, and tourists can arrange to go out with them.

Formation of Amber

Before it is washed up on the coasts of the Baltic States, which happens especially after raging storms, amber takes millions of years to transform from pine resin into a sought-after substance. Often clear, amber can also contain pine needles or insects which were trapped in the resin before it solidified.

Tree Exuding Resin
Certain trees exude a sticky resin, which has a range of defensive functions. Its antiseptic qualities kill bacteria and fungi, while its stickiness inhibits physical attack from insects.

Insects Trapped in Amber
Any insects stuck in the resin are prevented from decaying, as the substance is antiseptic and lacking in water. Slowly, the volatile components evaporate, leaving behind copal.

Copal Formation
Copal, or hardened resin, becomes incorporated into the ground after the tree dies. The solidification process continues for millions of years, until the inert substance becomes amber.

Uses of Amber

In addition to its decorative value, amber was once considered to have healing powers and even today some Lithuanians consider it to be a cure for goitre. The Aztecs and Maya are known to have burned amber as incense.

Delicately crafted amber jewellery

Knife decorated with amber

Typical inlaid amber box

Exquisite brooch fashioned in amber

The Amber Museum in Palanga
(see p286) features a stunning collection of amber pieces with prehistoric insects trapped inside, as well as amber jewellery. There is also a display presenting the natural history of amber.

An amber-polishing workshop, held by experts, offers participants the opportunity to create their own jewellery. Some amber museums across the Baltic States conduct these worskshops.

The Amber Route

An EU-funded project has devised a modern-day Amber Route that links a series of towns along the Baltic Coast. Starting from Ventspils *(see pp180–81)*, the route takes in Palanga *(see p286)*, Liepāja *(see pp184–5)* and Klaipėda *(see pp284–5)*. While some of these towns have amber museums, Palanga also has an amber-processing workshop. Nida in Lithuania has a museum that exhibits amber. The route also takes in Karklė and Pāvilosta, with professional amber-catchers. Juodkrantė, once the site of major amber-mining activity, boasts a collection of prehistoric amber artifacts. Further south is Kaliningrad, a Russian outpost that is the source of the vast majority of the world's amber.

Key
— Amber Route

Amber in Folklore

A popular Lithuanian folk tale recounts the love between the fisherman Kastytis and the goddess Juratė, who lived in an amber palace at the bottom of the sea. Angry that a mortal had dared to touch a goddess, the god Perkūnas sent lightning to destroy the palace and drown Kastytis. It is believed that pieces of the palace have been washing up on the shore ever since. The well-known story was first recorded in writing by Liudvikas Adomas Jucevičius in 1842, and the tale has even been adapted into a rock opera.

Jūratė kaj Kastytis by Nijolė Ona Gaigalaitė

The Climate of Estonia, Latvia and Lithuania

With the Baltic Sea as a moderating influence, the Baltic region has a temperate climate without the extremes that afflict neighbouring Russia. Winters are gloomy, however, with short days and bitter winds. The first snow usually falls in November, and inland there can be constant snow cover from December to April. The snowy season is shorter on the coast, where temperatures are noticeably lower in summer and higher in winter. At other times the weather is unpredictable, with rain even in the middle of summer, when days are long and warm.

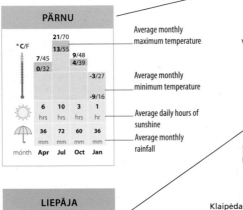

PÄRNU

°C/F			
	21/70		
	13/55		
7/45		9/48	
0/32		4/39	
			-3/27
			-9/16

☀	6 hrs	10 hrs	3 hrs	1 hr
☂	36 mm	72 mm	60 mm	36 mm
mónth	Apr	Jul	Oct	Jan

Average monthly maximum temperature

Average monthly minimum temperature

Average daily hours of sunshine

Average monthly rainfall

LIEPĀJA

°C/F			
	20/68		
	14/57		
8/47		11/52	
2/36		6/43	
			-1/30
			-5/23

☀	6 hrs	9 hrs	3 hrs	1 hr
☂	37 mm	66 mm	77 mm	53 mm
month	Apr	Jul	Oct	Jan

KLAIPĖDA

°C/F			
	20/68		
	14/57	12/54	
9/48		6/43	
2/36			
			0/31
			-5/23

☀	6 hrs	9 hrs	3 hrs	1 hr
☂	36 mm	74 mm	80 mm	50 mm
month	Apr	Jul	Oct	Jan

RĪGA

°C/F			
	22/72		
	12/54		
10/50		10/50	
1/34		4/39	
			-2/28
			-8/18

☀	6 hrs	10 hrs	3 hrs	1 hr
☂	41 mm	85 mm	60 mm	34 mm
month	Apr	Jul	Oct	Jan

KAUNAS

°C/F			
	22/72		
	12/54		
11/52		11/52	
2/36		4/39	
			-3/27
			-9/16

☀	6 hrs	9 hrs	3 hrs	1 hr
☂	42 mm	80 mm	45 mm	39 mm
month	Apr	Jul	Oct	Jan

Kuressaare

WESTERN ESTONI

Pä

Ventspils

WESTERN LATVIA

Rīga

Jelgava

Liepāja

WESTERN LITHUANIA

Šiauliai

Klaipėda

Kaunas

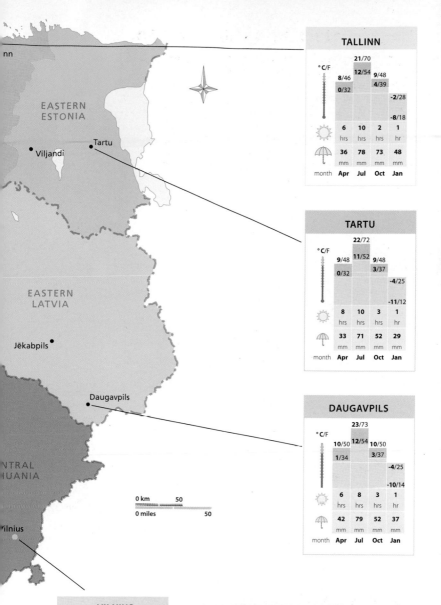

TALLINN

°C/F			
	21/70		
	12/54	9/48	
8/46		4/39	
0/32			
			-2/28
			-8/18

☀	6 hrs	10 hrs	2 hrs	1 hr
☂	36 mm	78 mm	73 mm	48 mm
month	Apr	Jul	Oct	Jan

TARTU

°C/F			
	22/72		
	11/52	9/48	
9/48		3/37	
0/32			
			-4/25
			-11/12

☀	8 hrs	10 hrs	3 hrs	1 hr
☂	33 mm	71 mm	52 mm	29 mm
month	Apr	Jul	Oct	Jan

DAUGAVPILS

°C/F			
	23/73		
10/50	12/54	10/50	
1/34		3/37	
			-4/25
			-10/14

☀	6 hrs	8 hrs	3 hrs	1 hr
☂	42 mm	79 mm	52 mm	37 mm
month	Apr	Jul	Oct	Jan

VILNIUS

°C/F			
	22/72		
11/52	12/54	10/50	
2/36		3/38	
			-4/25
			-9/16

☀	6 hrs	10 hrs	3 hrs	1 hr
☂	46 mm	78 mm	53 mm	41 mm
month	Apr	Jul	Oct	Jan

EASTERN ESTONIA

Viljandi
Tartu

EASTERN LATVIA

Jēkabpils

Daugavpils

NTRAL HUANIA

ilnius

0 km — 50
0 miles — 50

Estonia's winter landscape with snow-capped forest

THE HISTORY OF ESTONIA, LATVIA AND LITHUANIA

The history of the Baltic region begins in 3000 BC with the arrival of the early Baltic tribes, the ancestors of today's Estonians, Latvians and Lithuanians. Despite a shared experience of conquest, foreign occupation and struggles for independence, the three countries have preserved their distinct cultural identities, emerging in 1991 as sovereign states.

Archaeological evidence suggests that the Baltic region was inhabited as early as 10,000 BC, at the end of the Ice Age. The earliest occupied site, at Kernavė in Lithuania, dates back to 9000 BC. These Stone Age people used bows, arrows and spears for hunting and fishing. It was not until 3000 BC, however, that the ancestors of the current inhabitants began to arrive. Surviving by hunting and fishing, the Finno-Ugrians – the future Finns and Estonians – were among the first to drift across Europe from Asia. They were pushed back by the Indo-European groups that arrived in 2000 BC. The Indo-Europeans, who introduced crop cultivation and animal rearing to the traditional modes of subsistence, mingled with the existing groups, eventually forming the races now known collectively as the Balts.

During the first centuries AD, distinctive regional tribes began to form. These were the Samogitians (Lowlanders) and Aukštaitijans (Highlanders) in western and eastern Lithuania, the Curonians along the coast, the Prussians beyond the Nemunas river, the Zemgalians in central Latvia and the Selonians and Latgalians further east. For several centuries, the Balts remained firmly rural, living off the land. Until the early 1200s, there were similar but unrelated settlements all along the coast, from what is now Klaipėda as far as St Petersburg. There are very few records of life at that time as the local communities used wood rather than stone for all their fortifications and housing. Archaeological research has shown that there were extensive trading networks across the sea from this area to Sweden and Germany and inland towards Russia. The little written material from that time talks about the Balts as good boat-builders and dreaded pirates.

At a time when the rest of Europe had embraced Christianity, the Balts staunchly practised paganism. After haphazard attempts by small groups of Western European missionaries to convert the area to Christianity failed, the first Baltic crusade was sanctioned by Pope Innocent III in 1198.

10,000 BC	5000 BC	AD 1	AD 600	AD 1190
10,000 Earliest traces of human life in the Baltic region	**3000** Finno-Ugrians arrive in the region	**98** Roman writer Tacitus describes the "Aestii" people	**700** Vikings use Latvian rivers to trade with Persia and Turkey	**1198** The first Baltic crusade sanctioned by Pope Innocent III
9000 Hunting-fishing groups flourish in Kernavė	**2000** Indo-European groups arrive	**100** Romans begin trading in amber along the Baltic coast		**1009** The name Lithuania appears in written form for the first time

Pope Innocent III (1160–1216)

Early Neolithic bone objects, Narva, Estonia

◀ Detail from Jan Matejko's *Battle of Grünwald* (1878) showing Grand Duke Vytautas defeating the Teutonic Knights

Germans in Estonia and Latvia

After the papal declaration of the crusade, the Teutonic Knights, or the German warrior-monks who had previously called themselves the Brotherhood of the Sword, began to venture along the Baltic Coast. The phrase *"Drang nach Osten"* ("Thrust Eastwards"), which would become notorious in World War II, dates from this time. Religious and commercial zeal drove the crusaders to establish colonies along the Baltic Coast. In 1201, a bishopric was set up in Rīga, which became the basis for the Baltic conquest. Expanding into Estonia from the south, the Knights created Livonia in 1207. Comprising Latvia and Estonia, Livonia was recognized as part of the Holy Roman Empire, with Rīga as the capital. Estonia's largest island,

A 19th-century lithograph showing the Battle of Grünwald (1410)

Saaremaa, was subjugated in 1227. A fortress built in 1260 at its capital, Kuressaare, is the only one in the Baltic region to be preserved largely as the Teutonic Knights built it. Livonia flourished under the Knights, as they built cities throughout the region. After joining the Hanseatic League, a trading confederation of German port-cities and merchants' associations, Tallinn and Rīga began to thrive. The new social order, dominated by the Germans, excluded the local inhabitants not only from mercantile activities, but also agriculture, where they could only be hired as serfs.

Polish Domination in Lithuania

Lithuania has a very different history from that of the area to its north. While Christianity was dominant in much of the Baltic region, Lithuania continued to be resolutely pagan until 1385, when Duke Jogaila married a Polish princess, embraced Christianity and assumed the crowns of Poland and Lithuania. Long before him, in 1251, Mindaugas had briefly adopted Christianity so that he could be crowned by the Pope. In 1410, Jogaila and his cousin Vytautas (r.1410–30), Grand Prince of Lithuania, decisively defeated the Teutonic Knights in the Battle of Žalgiris, or Grünwald. Under Vytautas, the Grand Duchy of Lithuania *(see pp216–17)* emerged as one of the largest states in Europe. Eventually, however, it came increasingly under the control of the Poles, with the relationship culminating in the creation of the Polish-Lithuanian Commonwealth in 1569. With the Polish takeover, the right to

1201 German crusaders set up a bishopric in Rīga

1237 The Brotherhood of the Sword becomes Livonian Order

1260 Building of Kuressaare Castle starts

Kuressaare Castle

1372 German replaces Latin as the official language in Rīga and Tallinn

1410 Lithuanians and Poles defeat the Teutonic Knights at the Battle of Žalgiris (Grünwald)

1200   **1250**   **1300**   **1350**   **1400**   **14**

1230 Mindaugas unites the Grand Duchy of Lithuania

1207 Livonia becomes part of the Holy Roman Empire

1282 Rīga joins the Hanseatic League; Tallinn follows three years later

1385 Lithuania united with Poland under Jogaila

1430 The Gra Duchy reache the Black Sea

Siege of Narva by the Russians in 1558 during the Livonian Wars

own land was lost, the privileges of the peasantry were curbed and serfdom was firmly established in Lithuania.

The Swedes and the Russians

Sweden and Russia fought two major wars to ensure control over the Baltic Sea and the surrounding land. In the Livonian Wars (1558–83), Poland and Lithuania were involved in resisting the armies of Russia's Ivan the Terrible (r.1533–84), in view of the destruction he had wrought in Livonia. The immediate aftermath of the war resulted in most of Estonia coming under Swedish rule, while Latvia endured a Polish occupation and Lithuania's full union with Poland was formalized. Southern and Eastern Latvia, commonly known as Courland and Latgale respectively, became duchies owing allegiance to Poland.

War soon broke out again, this time between the Poles and the Swedes, and in 1621, the Swedes seized Rīga and northern Latvia. The Duchy of Courland stayed in Polish hands, although the dukes almost became rulers in their own right. The most prominent of them, Duke Jakob Kettler (r.1642–82), brought the duchy to the pinnacle of its wealth and power, even establishing short-lived colonies in Africa and the Caribbean. The Swedish occupation, regarded as the gentlest Livonia ever endured, was marked by a benign governance. The Germans, meanwhile, continued to hold sway in Livonia, socially and culturally. When an alternative to Latin was needed in the churches, German was the obvious choice. The universities at Rīga and Tartu taught exclusively in German. German merchants were granted special rights by the Swedish rulers, Charles XI (r.1660–97) and Charles XII (r.1697–1718), to ensure the continuity of commerce.

After the German barons' estates were expropriated by the Swedish crown, they turned to Russia for help. In 1700, Charles XII defeated Peter the Great of Russia at Narva, marking the beginning of the Great Northern War (1700–21). The loss at Narva inspired the Tsar to create a modern army and, in 1709, using a bitter winter to his advantage, he defeated the Swedes at the Battle of Poltava. In 1710, Tallinn and Rīga were occupied and soon Estonia and Latvia were brought under Russian control.

Battle of Poltava, a work by M Lomonosov (1711–65)

1520 Lutheranism established in Estonia, and a year later in Latvia	1572 First reference to a synagogue in Vilnius	1600–29 Polish-Swedish War	1642–82 Courland flourishes under Duke Jakob Kettler	
1500	**1550**	**1600**	**1650**	**1700**
1536 First record of Jewish merchants in Rīga		1558–83 Livonian Wars between Sweden and Russia	1700–21 Great Northern War between Sweden and Russia	

King Charles XII of Sweden (1682–1718)

Tsar Alexander I, with a soldier holding the Imperial Standard

Under Tsarist Rule

Peter the Great treated his new conquests with respect, as the Swedes had done before him. He continued to give the local German community considerable autonomy, both with their trading rights in the towns and with their manor houses in the countryside. After his death in 1725, a unique century of peace followed. There were neither invasions nor local uprisings. The Jews *(see pp40–41)*, who had flourished under the Duchy of Lithuania, gradually spreading into Latvia and parts of Estonia, continued to thrive.

By the 18th century, Vilnius had become the Jewish capital of Eastern Europe, and was referred to as Vilna. Under Catherine the Great (r.1762–96), the Russian Empire expanded to include Lithuania's Grand Duchy, which resulted from the third, and final, partition of Poland in 1795.

Tsar Alexander I (r.1801–25) was forced to forsake his dreams of reconstituting the Grand Duchy, when, in 1812, Napoleon's Grand

An 1864 print in Lithuanian, using the Latin alphabet

Army marched through Vilnius en route to Moscow, and was greeted by the people as liberators. In the same year Napoleon returned there, retreating ignominiously, not because the Russians had fought him successfully, but because they denied him supplies. In a pre-emptive move, the Russians burned down the wooden suburbs of Rīga to give them a clear firing line for defending the town. Eventually, the French army was forced to retreat.

A Century of Uneasy Peace

Under Alexander I, a series of agrarian laws were passed. Serfdom was abolished between 1816 and 1819, and peasants were allowed to buy and sell land. Civil unrest, however, came from the intelligentsia in the towns who were dissatisfied with the religious domination of the Orthodox Church and the increasing use of the Russian language. Between 1830 and 1831, the movement was at its strongest in Lithuania and one of the counter-measures taken by the Russian authorities was to close Vilnius University in 1832, in the hope that this would quell the unrest. In 1864, they resorted to banning the publication of books in Lithuanian using the Latin alphabet; books were now to be transcribed into Cyrillic. This encouraged publishers in Prussia to produce books in the Latin alphabet and to smuggle them across the border. By the 1860s, nationalist movements

---

1721 Sweden surrenders Estonia and Latvia to Russia

Napoleon Bonaparte (1769–1821)

1812 Napoleon's failed attempt to conquer Russia

1725	1750	1775	1800

Catherine the Great (1729–96)

1767 Completion of Latvia's Rundāle Palace under Catherine the Great

1795 Lithuania absorbed into the Russian Empire

were equally active in Latvia and Estonia. In 1869, the first Estonian Song Festival was held, and in the following year, the writer Lydia Koidula produced her first play in Estonian, having previously only written in German. It is significant that both events took place in Tartu and not in Tallinn, where German and Russian influence was still too strong. The Latvian writer Krišjānis Valdemārs also caused a stir in Tartu by printing his name-card in Latvian. It was not until 1900, however, that Estonians, Latvians and Lithuanians could freely proclaim their nationalities in their capital cities.

In the 19th century, as in the 18th, the Russians delegated local administration to the Germans. It was, therefore, the Germans, and not the Russians, who gained from the commercial potential of mass production, railways and steamships. Rīga and Tallinn expanded hugely as ports and manufacturing centres. The prospect of work drew many people from rural areas into the larger towns.

Latvian writer Krišjānis Valdemārs (1825–91)

War Returns

Strikes and demonstrations took place in 1905 in many cities throughout Russia, to pressurize the Tsarist regime to grant civil rights and improve social conditions. Given the size of its industrial workforce at this time, Rīga was an active participant in this unrest. In the countryside, the protests were directed against the German landed gentry and manor houses all over the region were attacked. These were social rather than nationalistic movements, partly as the Balts were now able to use their own languages openly and could also take part in local administration. National aspirations were, however, forcibly dampened at the outbreak of World War I (1914–18). The Russian Revolution of 1917, which resulted in the collapse of Tsarist Russia and brought the Bolsheviks to power, played a significant role in changing the course of the region's history. The Civil War that followed soon after was seen as an opportunity for the Baltic States to take control of their destiny.

A turn-of-the-19th-century postcard impression of Rīga, one of Eastern Europe's most vibrant cities

1854 Crimean War breaks out; British Navy blockades Russian Baltic ports

1870 Tallinn–St Petersburg railway opens

1917 Russian Revolution and Civil War stimulate Baltic independence movements

1825

1850

1875

1900

1832 Russians close Vilnius University to curtail spread of nationalist ideas

1899 First Baltic electric tram line opens in Liepāja

Liepāja tram 1 at Liela iela, Latvia

1905 Urban and rural attacks on German and Russian businesses

1916 Election of first Latvian mayor of Rīga

Jewish History

The history of Jewish settlement in the Baltic region began in the 14th century, when Grand Duke Gediminas invited merchants and craftsmen into the Grand Duchy of Lithuania. Estonia only ever had a small Jewish population, while Jews arrived in Latvia in the 15th century, but were only allowed to settle in Rīga much later. During World War II, almost all Jews who did not flee were killed. Although some returned, the Jewish communities today are dwindling, partly due to emigration to Israel.

Jewish Vilna's itinerant clothes-sellers, photographed in 1915

The Gaon of Vilna *(1720–97)* was Lithuania's most famous Jewish scholar, whose writing and research still guide many in the Jewish community today. In 1997, the celebration of the bicentenary of his birth brought Litvaks, former Lithuanian Jews, back to Vilnius from all over the world.

Jews in the Baltic Region

Banned from buying property and taking up professions until the late 19th century, the Jewish population lived largely as itinerant tradesmen and market stall-holders. After World War I, they were granted full rights as citizens. Until their persecution by the Nazis in 1941, when Jews were killed in large numbers, the Jews were active in the professions, business and politics.

Rīga's Great Choral Synagogue was built in 1869 for the city's Jews, who thrived after the laws restricting Jewish residence were lifted in 1840. The site of a Jewish massacre executed by the Nazis in 1941, the synagogue no longer exists.

Children celebrating Purim were photographed in 1933 in Vilnius. Purim, a joyful festival in the Jewish calendar, is still celebrated by the Jewish community in the Baltic region today.

Kenesa, a 20th-century synagogue in Trakai, is where the Karaim *(see p257)* congregate. An ethnically Turkish community from the northern shores of the Black Sea, they first settled in Trakai in the 14th century.

The Makkabi Sports Association was one of the Jewish organizations that thrived in independent Latvia between 1920 and 1940, when the government worked hard to eliminate anti-Semitism.

The Paneriai Holocaust Memorial *(see p248)*, just outside Vilnius, commemorates the 70,000 Jews who were murdered here during the Nazi occupation (1941–44). In Latvia, 66,000 Jews were massacred, while Estonia, where 4,300 Jews lived prior to World War II, was declared "Jew free".

Rīga's Museum of the Jews in Latvia documents 500 years of Jewish history in the region, and includes this poster used by anti-Semitic groups.

Tallinn's Beit Bella Synagogue was opened on 16 May 2007. The city had been without a synagogue since the destruction of an earlier one during World War II. Today, a 3,000-strong Jewish community lives in Estonia, while in Latvia and Lithuania, the Jews now number over 9,000 and 4,000 respectively.

Estonia's Constituent Assembly in session, 1919

Independence Declared

As Western Europe welcomed peace in November 1918, the Baltic area was one enormous battlefield. Anti-Bolsheviks still hoped to overthrow the new Soviet regime, and the Germans wanted to make up for losses in the West with victories in the East. The Poles were keen to form another commonwealth with Lithuania. As a result, there was little interest in supporting the declarations of independence made by the three Baltic States early that year. Only a large British fleet, stationed off the Estonian coast, was happy to supply arms to Estonia and Latvia and, therefore, help them achieve independence.

By early 1920, Estonia and Latvia were able to fight off all their enemies and get them to agree to borders, which would hold until 1940. Lithuania was forced to give up Vilnius, after the Poles seized it later that year. Subsequently, Kaunas was made the temporary capital. Lithuanians compensated themselves

The USSR and Germany signing the Molotov-Ribbentrop Pact of 1939

to some extent by seizing Memel (Klaipėda) in 1923 from French troops.

For the next 20 years, the three countries operated in a very similar manner. Weak, ever-changing governments in the 1920s gave way in the 1930s to strong statesmen who ran the state on Mussolini's corporatist model. Even though nobody in any Baltic government had held a senior position before independence, it was remarkable what they were able to achieve in such a short period of time. In Estonia and Latvia, the German estates were seized but the many successful urban businesses that had been established in the previous century were allowed to continue as before.

The Soviet Occupation

On 17 June 1940, the Baltic countries fell to the Russians, as had been agreed in the Molotov-Ribbentrop Pact, a non-aggression treaty signed between Germany and the USSR in 1939. All traces of the previous 20 years of independence were removed. Senior members of the three governments were executed. Flags, national anthems and Bibles were banned. The Soviet Union did not want to be reminded of its failure to conquer the Baltic States at the end of World War I. In June 1941, a massive deportation to Siberia was organized of around 10,000 Estonians, 15,000 Latvians and 30,000 Lithuanians, most of whom died. A week later, Germany invaded the Baltic States, violating the Molotov-Ribbentrop Pact. Soviet forces, who called

1918 The three Baltic States declare independence	**1939** Molotov-Ribbentrop Pact signed between the USSR and Germany	**1941** German occupation of the Baltics begins	**1956** Baltic deportees allowed back from Siberia
1922 Russia becomes Soviet Union (USSR)		**1945** Soviet reoccupation	
1925	**1935**	**1945**	**1955**
1920 Russia recognizes independence of the three Baltic States	**1940** The three Baltic countries incorporated into the USSR		**1960** Foreign tourists are once more allowed to visit the Baltic capitals

Soviet tanks in Rīga, 1940

A chain of people joining hands to form the "Baltic Way" across the three Baltic States

themselves "liberators", slowly reconquered most of the Baltic region during the autumn of 1944, as they drove the Germans westwards. In anticipation of their return, many locals fled to Sweden or Germany. Others who stayed joined the partisans based in the countryside. Known as the Forest Brothers, they were a very effective guerrilla force until the mid-1950s, disrupting the Soviet administration throughout the region. All the links with the outside world were broken, including trading routes.

Aware that it had only minimal popular support, the Soviet government knew that the incorporation of the Baltic States could only be achieved and maintained with brute force. In each country, the Russian military occupied large parts to which access was strictly controlled and all the paperwork needed was only in Russian. The Russification policies followed by the Tsars were enforced once again in order to stamp out the national identities of Estonia, Latvia and Lithuania. They imposed such uniformity that it became challenging for an outsider to distinguish one Baltic State from the other. In 1989, a human chain, referred to as the "Baltic

Soviet President Mikhail Gorbachev

Way", was formed across the three Baltic States to draw the world's attention to their shared history of suffering.

Independence Returns

Perestroika (reform) and *glasnost* (openness), the two buzzwords of Mikhail Gorbachev's regime (1985–91), had a dramatic effect in the Baltic region. Independence could be discussed openly and national flags reappeared. By 1990, independence for Estonia, Latvia and Lithuania could be predicted, but only in the long term. However, its sudden arrival on 21 August 1991, when an attempted coup in Moscow against Gorbachev failed, was unexpected. During a 48-hour period of total uncertainty, the three Baltic States took the opportunity to declare independence. Russia under Boris Yeltsin did likewise, dissolving the USSR. Suddenly, what had been provincial backwaters became serious European countries, with their own airlines, currencies and embassies and, above all, recognition on a worldwide basis. In 2004, the three Baltic States joined the EU and NATO (North Atlantic Treaty Organization), and by 2015, all had adopted the EU's common currency, the euro.

1994 Last Russian troops leave the Baltic region

1991 Independence restored to the three Baltic countries

2002 Eurovision Song Contest held in Tallinn; a year later in Rīga

2011 Estonia joins the Eurozone

2015 Lithuania joins the Eurozone

1975   1985   1995   2005   2015

1980 Moscow Olympics sailing events held in Tallinn

1989 Two million people hold hands from Tallinn to Vilnius in a chain known as the "Baltic Way"

2004 Baltic States join EU and NATO

2014 Latvia joins the Eurozone

Coin issued in 1999 to mark the tenth anniversary of the "Baltic Way"

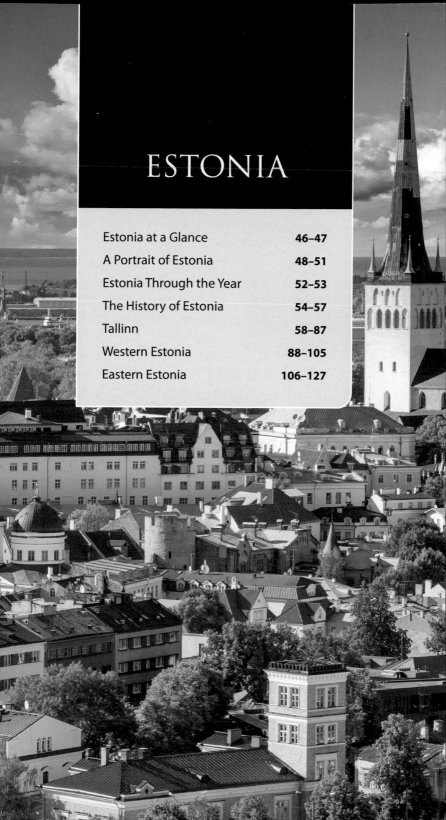

ESTONIA

Estonia at a Glance

The smallest of the Baltic States, Estonia is divided into two geographical regions, Western Estonia and Eastern Estonia. Apart from the hilly region in the southeast, most of the country is low-lying and is punctuated with innumerable lakes and rivers. Estonia's deeply indented coastline and archipelago of many islands offer some dramatic scenery. The country is sparsely populated and made up of forests, wetlands and peatbogs that teem with wildlife.

Tallinn *(see pp58–87)*, the capital of Estonia, is among the best-preserved historic cities in Northern Europe. The city is a compact and harmonious blend of medieval and modern architecture.

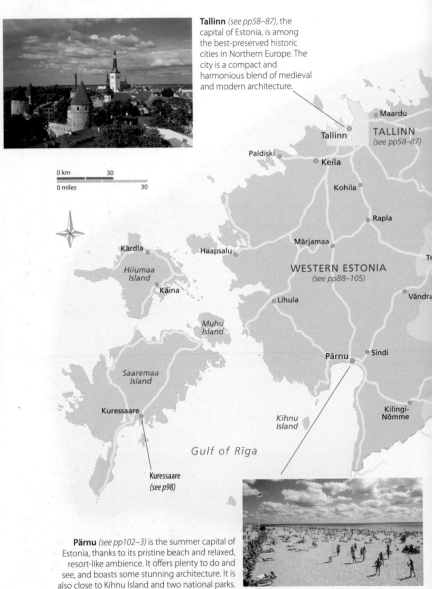

Pärnu *(see pp102–3)* is the summer capital of Estonia, thanks to its pristine beach and relaxed, resort-like ambience. It offers plenty to do and see, and boasts some stunning architecture. It is also close to Kihnu Island and two national parks.

◀ The red roofs of Tallinn's Old Town, with the industrial port beyond

Lahemaa National Park *(see pp110–13)*, the
largest national park in Estonia, has diverse
terrain criss-crossed by hiking trails. It is dotted
with villages such as Palmse, whose manor
house contains the park's information centre.

Narva *(see p116)* has a fortified
medieval castle, which illustrates
that the largely Russian-speaking
city was at the frontline of regional
power struggles for centuries.

Gulf of Finland

Narva

Jõhvi

Rakvere

Tapa

EASTERN ESTONIA
(see pp106–127)

Lake
Peipsi

Jõgeva

Põltsamaa

Tartu

andi

Lake
Võrtsjärv

Elva

Põlva

Karksi-Nuia

Võru

Vastseliina

Valga

Lake Peipsi *(see p127)* is a huge body of
water bordering Russia. A number of
settlements with wooden houses mark the
lakeshore. The Old Believers *(see p126)* live
in numerous little lakeshore villages
towards the north, while the Setu people
(see p124) live in the southern environs.

Tartu *(see pp118–19)*, Estonia's second-largest city,
is famed for its university and has an exciting
cultural and nightlife scene. One of its notable
sculptures is of an imaginary meeting between
English writer Oscar Wilde and Estonian writer
Eduard Vilde. The city rivals Tallinn in charm and
splendour, as well as historic significance.

A PORTRAIT OF ESTONIA

Now presenting a heady mix of medieval heritage and technological advancement, Estonia rebuilt itself in the post-Soviet era, adapting to the demands of the modern world while preserving a distinct cultural identity. With its rich historic architecture, natural landscapes and dynamic culture, the country makes a significant impression on the ever-growing number of visitors that it attracts.

Estonia has had a tumultuous history, a result of its geographical position at a crossroads between Eastern and Western Europe. With Russia dominating its eastern border, Scandinavia surrounding it to the north and west and the other two Baltic States to its south, Estonia was considered a prize strategic asset by the ruling powers in the region over the centuries.

After regaining independence from the Soviet Union in 1991, Estonia was left severely dilapidated. During the long slog towards NATO and EU membership throughout the 1990s, the country was often held up by Eastern Europe as an example of how to rapidly modernize while preserving national heritage and improving overall living conditions.

Estonia is sometimes referred to as e-Estonia due to its reputation for technological innovation, and is home to many IT companies. It pioneered electronic voting and Wi-Fi is available throughout most of the country. Although the rural areas still lag behind the cities in raising living standards, Estonia has grown into a major travel destination. Its forests and marshlands, pristine islands and traditional villages are as alluring as its capital, Tallinn, a pulsating city with a medieval Old Town.

Society and Culture

In general, Estonians are more strongly influenced by Scandinavian culture than by that of their Baltic neighbours. Finns and Estonians also share close linguistic

A typical Estonian rural scene, with the bright colours of autumn

◀ One of the five Angla Windmills on Saaremaa Island

Participants awaiting their turn at the Estonian Song and Dance Festival

life, although hundreds of years of foreign occupation led to many people converting to Christianity, including Lutheranism and Russian Orthodoxy. The most important aspects of Estonian culture are distinctly pagan in origin. The hugely popular midsummer festival Jaanipäev (St John's Day), characterized by drinking, dancing and revelry in the evening on 23 June and through to 24 June, has a pagan origin.

Political Life

Estonia underwent a major political transition in the 1990s, adopting a parliamentary democracy which introduced neo-liberal economic and political policies.

In the early years of independence, there was a lingering cynicism towards politics, as many former Communist Party leaders continued to hold high offices, and corruption was a regular part of the political process. This changed in 2000, as the nation prepared to join the European Union and decisions from Brussels now have just as much effect as local ones. Estonia is governed by a coalition of parties. The major parties are the centre-right Reform Party and the populist Centre Party, while several smaller parties often hold the balance of power.

links through the Finno-Ugric language family. A sizeable Russian-speaking minority remained in Estonia after the Soviet withdrawal, leading to some diplomatic skirmishes with Russia over the years. Today, there are fewer instances of conflict between Russians and Estonians.

Estonians take great pride in their heritage. The country's medieval past is visible not only in some of its architecture, but also in festivals that have their roots in that era. Folk culture is central to national identity, as Estonians were predominantly reduced to serfdom, with no right to own land or property, until the country's first spell of independence in 1918. The Estonian Song and Dance Festival, which was first held in 1869 and has since taken place every five years, remains a significant icon for the nation, rousing affirmation of Estonian identity.

Religion does not play a particularly large part in Estonian

Parliamentary session in progress

Tallinn's new modern city centre, with the Radisson Blu Hotel *(left)* and SEB bank buildings *(right)*

Economy

Until about 2005, Estonia had a large growth in GDP and low unemployment. Its capital, Tallinn, underwent a transition with the economic boom, with office towers shooting up and expensive new shops and restaurants enjoying good trade. The property market boomed, as did the market for new cars, paid for mostly on credit borrowed from Swedish banks.

This changed with the global financial crisis, which wiped out the growth rate and pushed unemployment beyond 10 per cent. The government cut its spending as it attempted to meet the economic criteria necessary to enter the Eurozone, and in July 2010 the EU gave approval for the adoption of the euro in Estonia with effect from January 2011.

Income levels are still below the EU average, although consumer prices are relatively similar to those in the richer western EU countries. The main industries are real estate, manufacturing, retail, transport and communications. There is also a large focus on information technology, a sector that has been breeding start-ups.

Tourism

Tourism has been instrumental in transforming Estonia from a drab post-Soviet state into a thriving nation, and the private sector has been quick to adapt and respond to the business opportunities that have opened up. Tallinn was inevitably the first part of the country to benefit, but tourism has stimulated a social renaissance in parts of the country that had languished in poverty for many years, and towns throughout the country have seen a steady increase in tourism-related investment. Many Estonians fly south for their holidays, although domestic tourism is strong and weekend spa breaks are popular.

Tourists enjoying Tallinn's roof-top panorama from Toompea Hill

ESTONIA THROUGH THE YEAR

Estonians celebrate a host of seasonal festivals through the year. These encompass everything from religion, folk culture and handicrafts to art, music, dance and theatre, making the festival calendar both colourful and remarkable. Much of the festive frenzy occurs in the summer, peaking with the Midsummer's Eve celebrations. Summer is also the time when a series of concerts are held throughout the country, and when the Folklore Baltica Festival *(see p136)*, which showcases the region's distinct traditional culture, takes place. In addition to the annual festivals, a number of commemorative days are observed throughout Estonia.

Spring

As is to be expected in a country so attuned to the seasons, spring is a joyful time marked by a lively range of long-established festivals.

March
Estonian Music Days *(Mar)*. Contemporary Estonian classical music is showcased in Tallinn and other cities.

April
International Choir Festival *(one week, late Apr)*, Tallinn. As well as a choral contest, concerts are staged at churches around Tallinn.
Jazzkaar *(late Apr)*. This big jazz festival held throughout Estonia includes local and international names.
Tartu Student Days *(late Apr–early May)*. During this festival, Tartu's students hold bizarre concerts, shows and parties open to everybody.

Saxophonist playing at a concert during Jazzkaar

Horse-riders in medieval costumes, celebrating Tallinn Old Town Days

May
Spring Farm Days *(mid-May)*, Tallinn. The Estonian Open-Air Museum celebrates the traditional spring farming tasks, such as growing crops and rearing livestock.
Tallinn Literature Festival *(late May)*, Tallinn. Local and international authors gather in the Old Town.
Tallinn Old Town Days *(late May–early Jun)*. Tallinn's medieval past is celebrated with re-enactments of old traditions like jousting. The streets are filled with market stalls and people in costume.

Summer

After months of wintry gloom and darkness, Estonians make the best of their short but resplendent summers with an abundance of festivals.

June
Midsummer's Eve (Jaanipäev) *(23 Jun)*. This summer celebration is marked by a night of joyous drinking, eating and age-old rituals around a bonfire.
Pärnu Hanseatic Days *(late Jun)*. This two-day festival includes a procession, a crafts fair and a knights' tournament.
Juu Jääb Muhu Music Festival *(late Jun)*, Muhu Island. A small and enjoyable open-air festival of local and international music, tending towards jazz and world music.

July
Haapsalu Early Music Festival *(early Jul)*. Set in the pretty surroundings of Haapsalu Castle, this is a celebration of early classical music.
Õllesummer Festival *(early Jul)*, Tallinn. This huge beer festival also features major concerts, from jazz to rock, as well as sideshows.

Audience watching performers on stage, Viljandi Folk Festival

Old Town Medieval Market *(early Jul)*, Tallinn. An exciting series of concerts, workshops and costumed performances, as well as traditional market stalls.

Viljandi Folk Festival *(late Jul)*. Folk music ensembles from all over Estonia perform in the castle grounds.

August

Birgitta Festival *(mid-Aug)*, Tallinn. Operas, concerts and recitals are held in the ruins of Pirita Convent. Food is served on the summer terrace.

August Dance Festival *(late Aug)*, Tallinn. The best in contemporary dance, including guest performances by famous international troupes.

Autumn

The festival season winds down a bit in the autumn, though most cities have a few annual events on offer.

September

Credo International Festival of Orthodox Sacred Music *(early–late Sep)*, Tallinn. Orthodox sacred music concerts held in churches and concert halls.

Matsalu Nature Film Festival *(late Sep)*. An unusual festival screening the works of various natural history film-makers.

October

NYYD *(mid-Oct)*, Tallinn. The best in experimental compositions from Estonia and abroad are featured in this festival of new music.

November

Black Nights Film Festival *(Nov–Dec)*, Tallinn. A celebration of some of the best independent and world cinema films, most of which are screened with English subtitles. Tickets can be purchased from Piletilevi outlets. The festival also runs smaller events in other towns.

Winter

Despite long and bitterly cold spells, winter also holds the promise of a wonderful snow-blanketed landscape and a season of festivity.

December

Christmas Jazz Festival *(early Dec)*. A series of jazz concerts held in Tallinn and several other towns in the run-up to Christmas.

Old Town Christmas Market *(Dec–early Jan)*, Tallinn. Equally popular with tourists

and locals, the market has a variety of goods on sale from the traditional to the novel.

January

Pärnu Contemporary Music Days *(mid–late Jan)*. An outstanding festival of classical music which also features lectures, workshops and theatre performances.

Skiiers participating in the popular Tartu Ski Marathon

February

Baroque Music Festival *(early–mid-Feb)*, Tallinn. A festival favourite offering a series of Baroque music concerts in various venues around the Old Town.

Tartu Ski Marathon *(early Feb)*. This hugely popular ski-fest features events and competitions, but the highlight is the 63-km (39-mile) ski marathon.

Public Holidays

New Year's Day (1 Jan)

Independence Day (24 Feb)

Good Friday (Mar/Apr)

May Day (1 May)

Võidupüha Victory Day (23 Jun)

St John's Day (24 Jun)

Restoration of Independence (20 Aug)

Christmas (24–26 Dec)

A brightly illuminated Christmas tree in the Old Town Christmas Market, Tallinn

THE HISTORY OF ESTONIA

Historical references to Estonia date from the early 13th century, when the German crusading knights arrived, introducing a new social order in which the Germans dominated for several centuries. A brief but benevolent period of Swedish rule in the 17th century was followed by Russian and German oppression, which continued with a short-lived inter-war independence. Estonia became a republic only in 1991.

The German crusading order, the Brotherhood of the Sword, started a bitter struggle for control of Estonia that lasted from 1208, when they established their hold over Otepää, until 1211. The Danes, too, were contending for control. In 1206, they tried in vain to

Fragment of a seal of Danish King Valdemar II

subjugate Saaremaa, the country's largest and most prosperous island. Denmark's King Valdemar II (r.1202–41) occupied Tallinn in 1219, but his attempts to expand Danish territory further were unsuccessful.

German Conquest

In 1227, the whole of Estonia had been conquered. In 1237, the Brotherhood of the Sword was absorbed into another crusading order, the Teutonic Knights, who controlled Tallinn until 1238, when it was returned to the Danes. The Knights took over a stone castle built by the Danes and rebuilt it as the Toompea Castle the same year. The foundations for a new social order were laid, with the Germans serving as the nobility, as well as merchants and craftsmen. The Estonians were forcibly converted to Christianity and

their land given away to the Knights and bishops. The feudal system, in which the Germans owned manor estates and the locals were obliged to work as serfs, survived until the 19th century. Tallinn was acquired again by the Germans in 1346, when large-scale protests against feudal exactions forced the Danes to relinquish their possessions in Estonia. During this time, many guilds and merchants' associations emerged, and towns such as Tallinn, Tartu, Viljandi and Pärnu thrived as members of the Hanseatic League. Tallinn, particularly, prospered as one of Northern Europe's largest towns.

An impression of Tallinn's Toompea Castle in 1227

1208 Germans capture Otepää in southern Estonia

1227 Germans conquer all of Estonia

1219 Danes seize Tallinn

1343 Peasants' uprising (St George's Night) against the Danes

1346 Danes sell Tallinn to the Germans

1372 German replaces Latin as the official written language

Detail, Town Hall Pharmacy door

1422 Tallinn Town Hall Pharmacy opens on site, where it still operates today

1200 **1300** **1400** **1500**

St Olav's Church, Old Town, Tallinn

1574 First Lutheran se preached in Estonia Olav's Church in Ta

Tartu University, Estonia's prestigious seat of learning

The Swedish Rule

The 16th century saw Estonia as the major battleground between Russia and Sweden in the Livonian Wars (see p37). By 1629, the whole country was in Swedish hands. The Swedes achieved much over the next 50 years, including the establishment of Tartu University, the introduction of schools all around the country, printing of books in Estonian and the construction of several buildings, especially in Narva and Tartu. Narva was built as the second Swedish capital. The social system created by the Germans was left undisturbed, however. Later Swedish kings interfered by seizing German-owned estates, incurring the wrath of the Germans who turned to Russia's Peter the Great for help.

Struggle Against the Russians

The Swedish troops were initially able to resist the Russians, but in 1709, the final battle between the Swedish king, Charles XII, and Peter the Great sealed Estonia's fate for the next 200 years, during which time there would be little threat to Tsarist rule. The Russians as well as the Baltic Germans actively kept Estonians out of any positions of responsibility,

as well as curbing use of the Estonian language. The resulting discontent among the intelligentsia found expression in the rebellion led by the students of Tartu University in the late 19th century.

In 1905, as in many other places in Russia, Estonia witnessed widespread unrest. In the towns, factory workers lent support to the nascent Bolshevik movement, while several German manors were burned down in the country-side. During World War I (1914–18), the prospects for Estonian independence seemed bleak. However, the 1917 Revolution that

Estonian Army recruiting poster, 1918

ended the Tsarist regime in Russia and the chaos that followed in Moscow, encouraged Estonia to declare independence in February 1918, in Pärnu. The Treaty of Tartu, signed with Russia in February 1920, formally confirmed Estonian independence.

Declaration of independence in February 1918, Pärnu

1632 Opening of Tartu University by Swedish Lutherans

1710 Treaty of Nystadt brings Estonia into the Tsarist Empire

1872 The first strike organized by the women of Narva

1885 Russification of the Baltics begins

1918 Declaration of Estonian independence signed

00   1700   1800   1900

1629 Estonia passes into Swedish hands

1869 First Estonian Song Festival held in Tartu
1886 First Estonian newspaper, Postimees, launched

1920 Treaty of Tartu confirms Estonia's independence

1905 Uprisings in Tallinn

Diamond order of Peter the Great

President Konstantin Päts *(centre)* in 1939

Freedom and World War II

Although there were 20 coalition governments between 1919 and 1933, they all
agreed to immediately distribute the
Baltic-German landholdings among the local
community. Education and state pension
systems were introduced nationwide. People
who had been active in the national movement before World War I took senior positions
in government. The most prominent of
these politicians was Konstantin Päts, who
staged a coup in February 1934 and dissolved
Parliament, although he began to restore
democratic institutions in 1938. For most
Estonians day-to-day life was hardly
affected by these developments. Industry, agriculture
and international trade
continued as before. Päts
ruled until the Soviet invasion on 16 June 1940, which
brought a sudden and
brutal end to independent
Estonia. The Russians
executed several prominent
Estonians, including Päts
himself, and many others
were deported to Siberia.
The German invasion, which
came a year later, was seen

Soviet tanks thwarting the Germans' landing attempt
in Estonia in September 1941

by many in Estonia as a sort of liberation.
Tallinn-born Alfred Rosenberg, who was
appointed by Nazi Germany to run the Baltic
States, treated the general population less
harshly than his counterparts in other
countries subjected to Nazi occupation. In
September 1944, the advancing Red Army
returned to Estonia, forcing the Nazis to
surrender, and Estonia once again became
part of the Soviet Union.

Soviet Estonia

The 10 years which followed the Soviet
reoccupation were traumatic for Estonia. The
deportation programme, restarted in 1944,
saw its climax in March 1949 with the arrest of
20,000 Estonians. The Soviets wanted to curb
any opposition to the establishment of
collective farms. The deportations were also
meant to sabotage the successful guerrilla
campaign run by the Forest Brothers, a
resistance group active until the early 1950s
throughout Estonia. Stalin's death in 1953 led
to a slightly less oppressive regime in Estonia,
as it did throughout the
USSR. From the 1960s,
Estonia's link with the
non-Soviet world began
to grow. A ferry link
between Tallinn and
Helsinki was started
twice a week. The 1980
Moscow Olympics turned
out to be invaluable for
Estonia because it
staged the yachting
events, which brought
thousands of foreign visitors to Tallinn. As a result,

1921 Flights from Tallinn to Stockholm begin	**1939** Molotov-Ribbentrop Pact puts Estonia under USSR **1934** Bloodless coup staged by Konstantin Päts		*Estonia's Tallink ferry service linking Tallinn and Helsinki* **1941** Nazi Germany occupies Estonia	**1965** A ferry linking Tallinn and Helsinki begins sailing
1925	**1935**		**1945**	**1955**	**1965**
1924 Coup attempted by Estonian Communists	**1937** The navy acquires its first British-built submarine	**1940** Soviet occupation begins	**1944** Return of Soviet forces; Stalinist era begins	**1964** Finnish president visits Estonia **1953** Stalin dies; Soviet oppression slightly relaxed

Olympic torch inaugurating the yachting events held in 1980, Tallinn

Independence

The years 1992 and 1993 turned out to be a challenging time for Estonia. The immediate reintroduction of the kroon as the national currency wiped out savings accumulated in Soviet roubles and inflation was not immediately curtailed. Prime Minister Mart Laar, who served his first term from 1992 to 1994, coined the phrase "the little country that can" and it did, very quickly. Many suffered temporarily, as factories closed and collective farms were abandoned, but few suffered long-term as tourism, Finnish assembly plants and international call centres quickly absorbed any spare labour. Returning to power in 1999, Laar was able to steer the country out of the financial crisis that stemmed from the collapse of Russia's economy in 1998.

foreign newspapers, direct-dial international phone calls and a range of consumer goods not seen in Tallinn since 1940 were introduced. After the Games, all these quickly disappeared, but the memory of them did not; frustration with the USSR turned in the 1980s to total disillusionment as Finnish TV showed the different lifestyle being enjoyed just 50 km (31 miles) from Tallinn.

When Mikhail Gorbachev came to power in 1985 as General Secretary of the Communist Party of the Soviet Union, Estonians took advantage of his liberal policies to revitalize the cultural scene and to restructure factories and small businesses. Plans to reform the economy were made, the key element of which was the introduction of a stable currency. At the time of the collapse of the USSR in 1991, Estonians were better prepared, at least in theory, for a capitalist economy than were any of the other Soviet republics.

Former Estonian prime minister Mart Laar

From 2000 onwards, Estonia enjoyed record growth and increased prosperity. Many public works projects were built with European Union funds and foreign banks gave generous private loans. This ended with the global financial crisis in 2008, and although Estonia was not as badly affected as other Baltic nations, the economy slowed considerably. In July 2010, Estonia was given approval to enter the Eurozone. In January 2011 the euro replaced the kroon as legal tender. Relations with Russia have improved markedly, although diplomatic, cultural and even trade hiccups still occur.

1980 Olympics sailing and yachting events open in Tallinn

1992 Lennart Meri elected as president

President Lennart Meri (1929–2006)

2004 Estonia joins NATO and EU

2011 The euro replaces the kroon as Estonia's currency; Toomas Hendrik Ives re-elected president for a second term

1975   1985   1995   2005   2015

1991 Estonia declares independence

1994 Russian troops withdrawn; MS Estonia sinks, claiming 850 lives

2007 World's first national Internet election held

Pirita Yachting Centre, venue for 1980 Olympics yachting events

TALLINN

In a little over 20 years, the Estonian capital has grown into a dynamic, chic and exciting city. An architectural wonder, Tallinn has some stunning examples of modern architecture that reflect the newfound confidence of its people. In addition to restoring the medieval architecture of its Old Town, the city has experienced a major construction boom.

An overview of Tallinn from Toompea Hill shows how the city has made the best of its extraordinary historic foundations. Tallinn first appeared on the Western European map in 1154. The city came to be known as Tallinn after the Danes conquered it in 1219 and built a stronghold on Toompea Hill. "Tallinn" is an abbreviation of the Estonian name Taani Linnus, meaning "Danish stronghold". However, Tallinn officially bore the Teutonic name of Reval until Estonia's first period of independence in 1918. With the arrival of German merchants in 1230, the city was divided into the Upper Town (Toompea) and the Lower Town.

In 1346, the Danish king sold Tallinn to Germany. The city flourished in the 14th and 15th centuries, when it was one of the leading members of the powerful Hanseatic League. The brilliantly restored Old Town, a UNESCO World Heritage Site since 1991, is a living monument to this golden period of Tallinn's history. Tallinn was relatively stagnant during the Tsarist Russian period, which began in 1710 under the rule of Peter the Great. For most of the 19th century, it was little more than a summer resort for wealthy Russians. However, the introduction of the Tallinn–St Petersburg railway in 1870 restored the city's former glory as a major trading centre. During the Soviet occupation a vast influx of predominantly Russian-speaking workers swelled Tallinn's population.

Since independence in 1991, improved air and sea transport links with Western Europe has made Tallinn easily accessible. The city has forged close ties with neighbouring Finland and the Tallinn–Helsinki ferry line is among the busiest in the world.

Young ballerinas performing in a street in Tallinn during the summer festivities held in June

◄ Alexander Nevsky Cathedral with its striking onion domes

Exploring Tallinn

The vast majority of sights in Tallinn are
concentrated in and around Town Hall Square
and Toompea, in the medieval Old Town.
Relatively easy to explore on foot, the winding
cobbled streets are dotted with elegant back
alleys, courtyards and spired churches, as well
as fascinating museums that present the
city's historic and cultural traditions. There
are also many notable buildings around the
fringes of the Old Town, all within easy walking
distance. On the eastern section of the city wall,
Viru Gate serves as one of the main access
points into the Old Town.

Viru Gate, one of the best-known
landmarks in Tallinn

Sights at a Glance

Churches and Monasteries

3 Holy Spirit Church
6 *Niguliste Church pp68–9*
10 Dominican Monastery
14 Church of the Transfiguration
of Our Lord
15 St Olav's Church
19 Alexander Nevsky Cathedral
20 Cathedral of St Mary the Virgin

Museums

4 Great Guild Hall
5 Museum of Estonian
Photography
7 Museum of Theatre and Music
11 Tallinn City Museum
13 Estonian Museum of Applied
Art and Design
21 Museum of Occupations
24 Adamson-Eric Museum

Historic Buildings and
Sights of Interest

1 Town Hall
2 Town Hall Pharmacy
8 Viru Gate
9 St Catherine's Passageway
12 House of Blackheads
16 Three Sisters
17 Fat Margaret Tower
18 Toompea Castle
22 Knights' House
23 Kiek-in-de-Kök

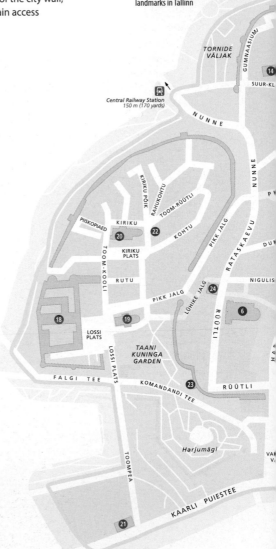

For hotels and restaurants see pp296–7 and pp314–16

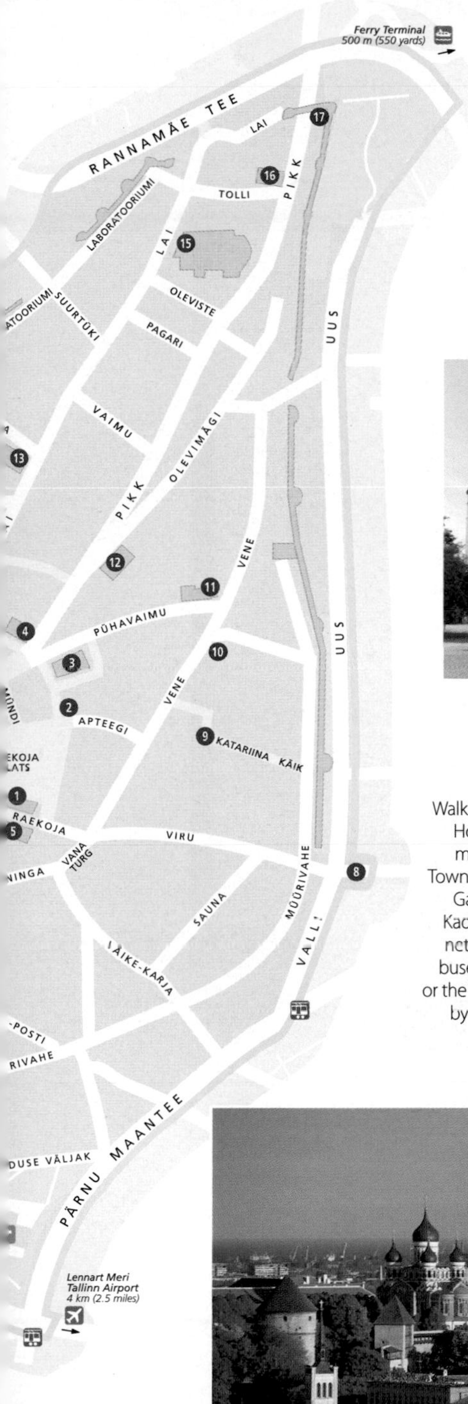

RANNAMÄE TEE

LAI

PIKK

TOLLI

LABORATOORIUMI

LAI

OLEVISTE

ATOORIUMI SUURTÜKI

PAGARI

VAIMU

PIKK

OLEVIMÄGI

VENE

UUS

UUS

PÜHAVAIMU

VENE

MÜNDI

APTEEGI

KATARIINA KÄIK

EKOJA
LATS

RAEKOJA

NINGA

VANA
TURG

VIRU

SAUNA

MÜÜRIVAHE

VALL!

VÄIKE-KARJA

-POSTI

RIVAHE

PÄRNU MAANTEE

DUSE VÄLJAK

Ferry Terminal
500 m (550 yards)

Lennart Meri
Tallinn Airport
4 km (2.5 miles)

| 0 metres | | 200 |
| 0 yards | | 200 |

Key

Place of interest

Pedestrian street

Fat Margaret Tower, a formidable 16th-century fortification,
now housing the Estonian Maritime Museum

Getting Around

Walking is the best way to explore Tallinn's Old Town.
However, public transport is required to see some
major sights, such as Kadriorg Park east of the Old
Town, as well as Pirita, the TV Tower and the Botanical
Gardens, which are all situated to the northeast of
Kadriorg Park. The city's public transport system is a
network of buses, trolleybuses and trams. Nearly all
buses and trolleybuses leave from Vabaduse Square
or the Viru Keskus terminal, while most tram lines pass
by the Old Town. Tallinn has transport links with all
major towns and cities in Estonia.

The city's skyline, as seen from Toompea Hill

For keys to symbols see back flap

Street-by-Street: Around Town Hall Square

In the heart of the Old Town, the magnificent Town Hall Square has, for centuries, served as a marketplace. Gently sloping, the cobblestoned square is surrounded by a ring of elegantly designed medieval buildings. The early 14th-century Town Hall is Northern Europe's only surviving late Gothic town hall. A meeting point for locals and visitors, the square captures the essence of the Old Town. In summer, it is filled with the tables of open-air cafés and restaurants.

Locator Map
See Street Finder Map pp86–7

House of Blackheads

⓫ Tallinn City Museum
Housed in a medieval merchants' house, this museum presents Tallinn's history through a variety of fascinating exhibits and artifacts.

❷ ★ Town Hall Pharmacy
Worth a visit just for the impressive interior, this long-running pharmacy also has a charming little museum displaying old curiosities.

Key

— Suggested route

| 0 metres | 100 |
| 0 yards | 100 |

❸ Holy Spirit Church
Regarded as one of Tallinn's most attractive churches, this splendidly preserved structure houses a treasure trove of medieval and Renaissance features.

⑩ Dominican Monastery
Among Tallinn's oldest buildings, this monastery complex also includes an atmospheric museum which has some beautiful stone carvings.

Viru Street
One of the most famous streets in the Old Town, Viru Street is packed with a variety of restaurants, bars, cafés and shops.

❶ ★ Town Hall
Taking pride of place in Town Hall Square, this imposing Gothic building with an octagonal tower has been the focus of civic life since the Middle Ages.

❺ The Museum of Estonian Photography has an extensive collection housed in two buildings.

❻ Niguliste Church
This remarkable Gothic church is now a Tallinn landmark boasting an excellent museum of religious art. The church holds organ recitals every weekend.

❶ Town Hall
Tallinna raekoda

Raekoja plats 1. **Map** 1 C2. **Tel** 645
7900. 🚌 5, 40. 🚋 1, 2, 3, 4. **Open** Jul–
Aug: 10am–4pm Mon–Sat; Sep–May:
by appointment. Tower: May–Aug:
11am–6pm daily. 🏛 🚻 🖼
W tallinn.ee/raekoda

One of the most revered
symbols of Tallinn, the Town Hall
dates back to 1404. Its high-
pitched roof is supported by
two tall gables and a late-
Renaissance spire crowns the
slender octagonal tower. The
narrow windows and
crenellated parapet complete
the building's impressive
appearance. Facing Town Hall
Square, a vaulted arcade runs
along the north façade, where a
small café puts out tables in the
summer. Inside, it is possible to
see the Citizens' Hall and the
Council Hall, although most
visitors head straight for the
tower and the 115-step ascent
to the top.

❷ Town Hall Pharmacy
Raeapteek

Raekoja plats 11. **Map** 1 C2.
Tel 631 4860. 🚌 5, 40. 🚋 1, 2, 3, 4.
Open 10am–6pm Tue–Sat. 🖼
W raeapteek.ee

The Town Hall Pharmacy is
famed for being one of the
oldest pharmacies in Europe.
The building's exterior dates
back to the 17th century, but
there is evidence that a
pharmacy existed on the site as
long ago as 1422. In one corner
of the shop's interior there is a

modest museum with a small
selection of historical exhibits
including medical instruments
and curative treatments. Ask to
try the spiced wine, which was a
popular purchase in medieval
times. According to a local
legend, marzipan was
accidentally created here and
named Martin's Bread

Graceful Baroque tower of the Holy
Spirit Church

❸ Holy Spirit Church
Pühavaimu kirik

Pühavaimu 2. **Map** 1 C2. **Tel** 646 4430.
🚌 5, 40. 🚋 1, 2, 3, 4. **Open** Oct–Apr:
10am–2pm Mon–Fri; May–Sep: 9am–
5pm Mon–Sat. 🏛 🕐 3pm Sun (in
English). **W** eelk.ee/tallinna.
puhavaimu

The 13th-century Holy Spirit
Church is one of the most
beautiful churches in Tallinn.
The Gothic building served as
the Town Hall chapel before
being converted into a church.

Its whitewashed exterior
includes the oldest public clock
in Tallinn, with carvings dating
from 1684. The stepped gable is
topped by a striking Baroque
tower. The spire was nearly
destroyed by fire in 2002,
but was restored within a year.
Inside, the church is a treasure
trove of religious artifacts and
architecture, from the
magnificently intricate Baroque
pews to the Renaissance-era
pulpit. The sublime altar
triptych, *The Descent of the Holy
Ghost* (1483), by Lübeck artist
Berndt Notke, is the main
highlight. The church holds a
special place in Estonian history,
as the first Estonian-language
sermons were delivered here in
1535 following the Reformation.

❹ Great Guild Hall
Suurgildi hoone

Pikk jalg 17. **Map** 1 C2. **Tel** 696 8690.
🚌 5, 40. 🚋 1, 2, 3, 4. **Open** May–Sep:
10am–6pm daily; Oct–Apr: 10am–
6pm Thu–Tue. 🏛 🖼
W ajaloomuuseum.ee

One of the most important
buildings in medieval Tallinn, the
Great Guild Hall was constructed
in 1417. It was owned by a
powerful union of wealthy
merchants. The building holds a
significant place in the city's
history. It was mainly used as the
gathering place for its members
but at times it was also rented
out for wedding parties and
court sessions. It was the
starting as well as the end point
of most festive processions in
Tallinn. The late Gothic building
has retained its original appearance through the centuries,
although the windows were
remodelled in the 1890s.

The Great Guild Hall's majestic
interior provides a perfect setting
for a branch of the **Estonian
History Museum** *(see also p82)*.
The museum's collection of
historical artifacts covers Estonian
history from the Stone Age to the
mid-19th century in fine detail.
The exhibits, which include
everything from jewellery to
weaponry, are accompanied by
explanatory texts in Estonian,
Russian and English.

Interior of the Town Hall Pharmacy, with well-stocked shelves

Medieval Architecture

Tallinn's Old Town is one of the best-preserved examples of medieval architecture in Northern Europe. With its winding cobblestoned streets and rows of elegantly gabled façades, the Old Town retains the true character of a medieval town centre. The labyrinthine street structure developed in relation to the power seat of Toompea above and the harbour below, with the all-important Town Hall Square and marketplace at the heart of it. Although Tallinn flourished as a centre of trade in medieval times, it was relatively quiet in the 19th century, which is probably why the Old Town was spared from demolition. Tallinn's medieval fortifications are also very well preserved, with some 2 km (1 mile) of the town wall and half of the original 46 towers still intact.

The gabled upper storey was used for storage, with a winch used to hoist up merchandise.

A model of a medieval merchant's house can be seen at the Tallinn City Museum (see p67), a 14th-century building. The upper storey was used to store merchandise, and guests were entertained on the first floor.

Medieval towers are famous symbols of the city's history. Kiek-in-de-Kök (see p75) and Fat Margaret Tower (see p71) are now museums. Visitors can get a view of the area by climbing the adjoining Nunna, Sauna and Kuldjala towers.

Saiakang alley, which is just off Town Hall Square, is one of the narrow medieval streets and passageways that make the Old Town so fascinating.

Lühike jalg, also known as the "Short Leg", is a steep, atmospheric passageway that was built in the 13th century as a link between the stronghold of Toompea, or the Upper Town, and the rest of Tallinn. In the Middle Ages, a number of coppersmiths and locksmiths had their workshops on Lühike jalg.

A dragonhead waterspout can be seen just below the Town Hall's roof. This, and the other waterspouts on the Town Hall's façade, are fine examples of the mischievous details that adorn many of Tallinn's medieval buildings.

An 1898 photograph, Museum of Estonian Photography

❺ Museum of Estonian Photography

Fotomuuseum

Raekoja tänav 4/6. **Map** 1 C3. **Tel** 644 8767. 🚌 5, 40. 🚋 1, 2, 3, 4. **Open** Mar–Oct: 10:30am–6pm Thu–Tue; Nov–Feb: 10am–5:30pm Thu–Tue. 📷 🚫 📷 **W** linnamuuseum.ee

Tucked away behind the Town Hall, the Museum of Estonian Photography consists of two separate buildings, one dating back to the 14th century and the other to the 18th century. They once served as the town prisons and were also used to hold court sessions. The buildings now house an extensive collection of Estonian photography, covering the period from 1840 to 1940.

The display, which includes rare daguerreotypes, ambrotypes and ferrotypes, showcases some of the finest works by well-known early Estonian photographers, including H Tiidermann, B Lais and N Nyländer. Pride of place is given to the tiny Minox camera which was reputedly invented in Estonia in 1936. The gallery also hosts temporary exhibitions of contemporary works.

❻ Niguliste Church

Niguliste kirik

See pp68–9.

❼ Museum of Theatre and Music

Teatri-ja muusikamuuseum

Müürivahe 12. **Map** 1 C3. **Tel** 644 6407. 🚌 5, 40. 🚋 3, 4. **Open** 10am–6pm Tue–Sat. 📷 🚫 call in advance. **W** tmm.ee

This museum focuses on a much-loved part of the country's cultural heritage, and also serves as an academic centre. Founded in 1924, the music museum was combined with a theatre museum in 1941. There is much for music and theatre aficionados to enjoy, from a fine selection of folk instruments to a collection of original theatre production programmes. The papers and instruments of the eminent Estonian composer Peeter Süda (1883–1920) form a small part of the museum's collection. The staff are happy to play the instruments for a small fee. The museum owns the copyright to the work of composer Heino Eller (1887–1970) and since 1998, it has been awarding the prestigious Heino Eller Music Prize to distinguished figures.

❽ Viru Gate

Viru tänav. **Map** 2 D3. 🚌 5, 40. 🚋 1, 2, 3, 4.

On the eastern section of the city wall, the Viru Gate serves as one of the main access points into the Old Town. Its picturesque, slightly skewed stone towers are one of Tallinn's best-known sights. The pair of towers that make up the gate were built in the 14th century and were part of a larger gatesystem. The surrounding stretch of city wall dates back to the 16th century. A moat and water mill, which once existed between the foregates and the main gate, were demolished in 1843. In the early 20th century, Viru Street was regarded as one of the city's most fashionable and is now a major tourist spot.

Stone towers of the Viru Gate, one of the most iconic sights in Tallinn

For hotels and restaurants see pp296–7 and pp314–16

9 St Catherine's Passageway
Katariina käik

Katariina käik. **Map** 2 D2. 📷 5, 40. 🚊 1, 2, 3, 4.

A fascinating medieval alleyway with uneven stone walls and overhead vaulting, St Catherine's Passageway joins Vene and Müürivahe streets. A string of arts and crafts workshops line the passage, where it is possible to watch resident artisans working with jewellery, ceramics and glass or binding books. The passage runs along the surviving wall of St Catherine's Church, which was built in 1246. The church was Tallinn's largest in its day and several gravestones, some dating from the 14th century, still line this narrow passageway.

The medieval St Catherine's Passageway, home to arts and crafts workshops

10 Dominican Monastery
Dominiiklaste klooster

Vene 16/18. **Map** 2 D2. **Tel** 515 5489 or 511 2536. 📷 5, 40. 🚊 1, 2, 3, 4. **Open** No regular opening hours. Call to arrange a visit. 🎧 📷 tour offered to the monastery's inner chambers through the cloister. 📷 W **kloostri.ee** or W **claustrum.eu**

Founded by Dominican monks in 1246, this monastery was a renowned centre of learning. It thrived until the Reformation riots broke out in 1524. The Lutherans destroyed the

A passageway in the medieval Dominican Monastery, Old Town

monastery and forced the monks into exile. In 1531, a fire damaged most of the desecrated St Catherine's Church, which had formed its south wing.

After suffering neglect for four centuries, the ruined monastery was renovated in 1954. Today a serene cloister, its atmospheric passageways and pretty inner garden draw visitors. The star attraction, however, is the fine **Dominican Monastery Museum**, with Estonia's largest collection of medieval and Renaissance stone carvings by local stonemasons. One of the prominent works, a decorative relief of an angel on a triangular slab, is attributed to Hans von Aken, the 16th-century German Mannerist painter.

Dominican Monastery Museum
Open mid-May–mid-Sep: 10am–6pm daily. 🎧

11 Tallinn City Museum
Tallinna linnamuuseum

Vene 17. **Map** 1 C2. **Tel** 615 5195. 📷 5, 40. 🚊 1, 2, 3, 4. **Open** Mar–Oct: 10:30am–6pm Wed–Mon; Nov–Feb: 10:30am–5pm Wed–Mon. 🎧 📷 W **linnamuuseum.ee**

Located in a 14th-century merchant's house, the Tallinn City Museum was opened in 1937 to introduce locals to the city's rich cultural heritage. Today, the vast collection, set over three floors, offers a fascinating overview of Tallinn's history. Highlights include a cutaway model of a 16th-century merchant's house and a fine model recreating a 19th-century domestic interior. There is also a replica model of Old Thomas, the famous weather vane that sits atop the Town Hall steeple. The floors are interspersed with lifelike wax figures, dressed in period costumes. Also on view are collections of silverware, porcelain and pewter and numerous tapestries.

The museum's display of 20th-century exhibits includes photographs of the vast crowds that congregated in the Old Town after Estonia regained its independence from the Soviet Union in 1991. One of the main draws is the intriguing exhibit entitled *The Town That Will Never Be Ready*. It was inspired by a local legend that claims Tallinn will disappear the moment someone proclaims it is finally completed as a city.

Model of Tallinn from the 1820s displayed in the Tallinn City Museum

❻ Niguliste Church

Niguliste kirik

Dedicated to St Nicholas, Niguliste Church was originally built in the 13th century, although nearly all that remains today is from the 15th century. Most of Tallinn's medieval artworks were destroyed in the Reformation riots of 1524. However, according to legend, Niguliste Church escaped being ransacked due to the laudable efforts of the church warden, who sealed the door with melted lead. Today, Tallinn's most impressive collection of medieval religious artworks are housed here. The building has served as a museum ever since it was extensively rebuilt during Soviet times after being damaged by Soviet air raids in World War II. The church regularly holds organ and choral concerts.

Exterior of the Niguliste Church, one of Tallinn's medieval treasures

★ **Altarpiece Depicting St Nicholas**
Painted in 1482 by Hermen Rode of Lübeck, this superbly detailed altarpiece shows a variety of scenes from the life of St Nicholas, as well as the beheading of St George.

Altar Triptych of St Mary and the Brotherhood of Blackheads
The main panel shows St George and St Maurice standing beside the Madonna, while St Francis and St Gertrude stand in the wings.

KEY

① **The Silver Chamber** is located in the far corner of the church.

② **A collection of bells** from churches all over Estonia is displayed inside the church.

③ **The spire**, originally built in 1696, was finally restored in 1984.

④ **Bernt Notke's frieze** *Danse Macabre*, which is kept inside the church, depicts the universality of death.

Stone Figure
This sculpture is one of the wonderfully evocative stone figures that are part of the original design of Niguliste Church.

Entrance

Stone Carving
A stone skull and crossbones can be seen at the entrance to the chapel, near the church's main door. Stone carving, a vital element in Estonian architecture, was largely done in dolomite and sandstone.

★ **Bernt Notke's Danse Macabre**
The 15th-century frieze by Bernt Notke (1440–1509) is widely considered the pièce de résistance of the church. Only a fragment of the 30-m (98-ft) original remains.

Display, the Silver Chamber
This small side chamber contains a fascinating display of ornate silverware that belonged to various guilds and organizations, such as the influential and wealthy Brotherhood of Blackheads.

Dancing with Death

Part of a 15th-century frieze by Bernt Notke, *Danse Macabre* is considered one of Estonia's most prized works of art, as it is the only known surviving example of its genre on canvas. Skeletal figures of death are shown as enticing a king and his nobles to dance along with them. No one knows exactly how the painting came to Tallinn, but it is possible that Notke had reproduced a similar frieze he completed in 1461 in his native Lübeck in Germany.

Detail showing a king

Renaissance-era House of Blackheads, with ornate front door

⑫ House of Blackheads
Mustpeade maja

Pikk 26. **Map** 1 C2. **Tel** 631 3199.
🚌 5, 40. 🚋 1, 2, 3, 4. **Open** only for
chamber music concerts (call for
timings). 🌐 **mustpeademaja.ee**

This 15th-century Renaissance
building was the meeting
place of the Brotherhood of
Blackheads, an association of
unmarried merchants and
shipowners who were then
able to join the more powerful
Great Guild upon marriage.
The unusual name was derived
from the North African St
Maurice, the organization's
patron saint, whose image can
be seen on the ornate front
door of the building.

Unlike their counterparts in
Rīga *(see p152)*, the Tallinn
Blackheads were obliged to
defend the city in times of strife
and proved themselves
especially formidable adversaries
during the Livonian Wars
(1558–83). However, in general,
it seems that the wealthy young
Blackheads lived somewhat
leisurely and hedonistic lives.
The association survived until
the Soviet invasion in 1940, and
today the House of Blackheads

regularly hosts chamber music
concerts in its elegant main hall,
which is noted for its wood-
panelled interior.

⑬ Estonian Museum of Applied Art and Design
Eesti tarbekunsti ja disainimuuseum

Lai 17. **Map** 1 C2. **Tel** 627 4600.
🚌 3. 🚋 1, 2. **Open** 11am–6pm
Wed–Sun. 🌐 **etdm.ee**

Housed in a converted
17th-century granary, the
Estonian Museum of Applied
Art and Design features the best
in Estonian design from the
early 20th century to the
present day. The vast selection
of exhibits, which include
jewellery, ceramics, glass, furniture and textiles, is a splendid
example of the pride that
Estonia takes in applied arts.
Many of the exhibits meld
Scandinavian-style refinement
with subtle Baltic irony to
excellent effect. Some of the
fantastic examples of furniture
are especially eye-catching and
a delight for art enthusiasts.
There are also some fine pieces

of porcelain, dating from the
1930s to the 1960s, by the
legendary Estonian artist
Adamson-Eric *(see p75)*.

Since the museum opened in
1980 it has done a formidable
job of promoting Estonian
design at home and abroad.
Be sure to pick up a copy of the
map, which highlights some
notable examples of public
design around Tallinn.

⑭ Church of the Transfiguration of Our Lord
Issandamuutmise kirik

Suur-Kloostri 14–1. **Map** 1 C2. **Tel** 565
1090. 🚌 3. 🚋 1, 2. **Open** 9am–2pm
Sun. 🎦 🕙 10am Sun.
🌐 **teelistekirikud.ekn.ee**

Located close to a stretch of the
medieval city wall, the secluded
Church of the Transfiguration of
Our Lord has an impressive
Baroque-style spire and a richly
decorated interior. The church
originally belonged to St
Michael's Convent of the
Cistercian Order but was closed
down during the Reformation.
Briefly serving as a church for
the Swedish garrison, it was
handed over to the Orthodox
Church in 1716 during the rule
of Peter the Great, who donated
the extraordinary iconostasis by
Russian architect Ivan Zarudny.
The church also has a bell
dating from 1575, the oldest
in Tallinn.

Baroque spire of the Church of the
Transfiguration of Our Lord

View of Tallinn and the Baltic Sea from St Olav's Church

ⓖ St Olav's Church

Oleviste kirik

Lai 50. **Map** 1 C1. **Tel** 641 2241. 🚌 3. 🚊 1, 2. **Open** Apr–Oct: 10am–6pm daily. 🚗 🚻 🖳 **oleviste.ee**

St Olav's 124-m (407-ft) spire is a major Tallinn landmark and the church holds a proud place in local history. The legend goes that Tallinners wanted to build the tallest spire in the world to attract merchant ships and a complete stranger promised to help them. As payment he wanted the city people to guess his name. When the church was nearing completion, the city fathers sent a spy to his home and found out his name. They called out "Olev" when he was fixing the cross and he lost his balance and fell. In fact, the name of the church was in homage to King Olav II of Norway. The original 159-m (522-ft) spire made the church the tallest building in the world until a lightning strike burned it down in 1625. Amazingly, the church was struck by lightning six times and burned down twice between then and 1820.

Detail of stone carving on rear of St Olav's Church

The original 16th-century structure of the church was renovated extensively in the 19th century. St Olav's interior is not especially striking, although the vaulted ceiling is impressive and the church tower has a viewing platform with breathtaking vistas of the city. The exterior rear wall features an elaborately carved 15th-century tombstone of Johann Ballivi, a victim of the plague.

⓰ Three Sisters

Kolm õde

Pikk 71. **Map** 2 D1. 🚌 3. 🚊 1, 2.

Situated at the northern end of Pikk Street, the Three Sisters are three adjoining medieval merchants' houses that have been tastefully converted into a single luxury hotel *(see p297)*. The houses were built in 1362 and were functional commercial premises, complete with loading hatches and winches to hoist sacks of goods up and down. The houses' original owners, who were mostly guild elders, town councillors and burgomasters, also used their premises to entertain foreign guests whom they met on their business trips abroad. The elegant gabled houses are among the best-preserved buildings from the 14th century and form a valuable addition to the magnificent surroundings of Pikk Street. The Three Sisters Hotel proudly counts the UK's Queen Elizabeth II and the singer Sting among its many famous past guests.

⓱ Fat Margaret Tower

Paks Margareeta

Pikk 70. **Map** 2 D1. **Tel** 641 1408. 🚌 3. 🚊 1, 2. **Open** 10am–6pm Wed–Sun. 🚗 🗲 call in advance. 🖳 **meremuuseum.ee**

The 16th-century tower's evocative name derives from the fact that it was the largest part of the city's fortifications, with walls measuring 4 m (13 ft) thick. It was originally built to defend the harbour as well as to impress visitors arriving by sea. Later, the tower was transformed into a prison and was the scene of an outbreak of violence during the 1917 Revolution, when the prison guards were murdered by a mob of workers, soldiers and sailors.

Fat Margaret Tower now serves the more peaceful function of housing the **Estonian Maritime Museum** (Eesti meremuuseum), with a curious collection of nautical paraphernalia spread out over four storeys. The exhibits include an insight into shipbuilding and historical accounts of Estonia's harbours. There is also a scale model of the *Estonia*, the car and passenger ferry that sank between Tallinn and Stockholm in 1994. There are gorgeous views of the Old Town and Tallinn's harbour and bay from the top of the tower.

🏛 **Estonian Maritime Museum**
Pikk 70. **Tel** 641 1408.
Open 10am–6pm Wed–Sun. 🚗

Metal ship replica on the entrance wall, Estonian Maritime Museum

Street-by-Street: Toompea

Set on Toompea Hill, some 50 m (164 ft) above sea level, Toompea lies southwest of the Old Town. It dates back to the 13th century, when the Danes erected a stone castle on the site. The hill has changed hands many times over the centuries, but still remains enclosed in the impressive limestone fortifications built during the Livonian Wars (1558–83). The eclectic complex of Toompea Castle now houses the Riigikogu, Estonia's Parliament, in Castle Square. The centre of the square is dominated by the imposing Alexander Nevsky Cathedral. Toompea Hill offers a spectacular view of the Old Town and makes an ideal starting point for a tour of Tallinn.

Locator Map
See Street Finder Map pp86–7

⑱ ★ Toompea Castle
This hilltop castle compound comprises several architectural styles, from medieval stone towers to a vibrant pink Baroque façade.

Pikk Hermann Tower

⑲ ★ Alexander Nevsky Cathedral
Tallinn's most grandiose Russian Orthodox cathedral was named after the war hero who victoriously led Russian soldiers into battle at Lake Peipsi in 1242.

㉓ ★ Kiek-in-de-Kök
The superbly preserved medieval cannon tower now houses a large museum on Tallinn's history.

Kiek-in-de-Kök Museum entrance

⓴ Cathedral of St Mary the Virgin
Originally built as a wooden church by the Danes in 1240, St Mary's is the oldest church in mainland Estonia. Most of its austere Gothic exterior, however, dates from the 14th century.

Patkuli Viewing Platform
One of Toompea's secluded hideaways, this picturesque spot has great panoramic views of the Old Town's red roofs as well as of the harbour.

Key

— Suggested route

The Kohtuotsa viewing platform, swarming with postcard sellers and tour groups, looks out over the Old Town.

Pikk Jalg Gate Tower
With a striking red roof, the tower at the end of cobbled Pikk jalg dates from the 14th century.

| 0 metre | 100 |
| 0 yards | 100 |

⓾ Knights' House
The Neo-Renaissance building was built in 1848 to serve as the headquarters of the Knighthood, the then local aristocracy. The well-preserved interior is a blend of various styles.

The Neo-Byzantine Alexander Nevsky Cathedral

⑱ Toompea Castle
Toompea loss

Lossi plats 1a. **Map** 1 B3. **Tel** 631 6345.
🚋 3, 4. **Open** 10am–4pm Mon–Fri.
📅 call in advance. ♿ ✉
🌐 riigikogu.ee

The elegant and unassuming pink Classical façade of this vital seat of power belies its history. The castle is now home to Riigikogu (Estonia's Parliament), but for some 700 years it belonged to various occupying foreign powers. In the 9th century, a wooden fortress stood on the site, which was conquered by the Danes in 1219, who then constructed the stone fortifications around the hill, much of which still survive.

The architecturally diverse castle complex features the 50-m (164-ft) Pikk Hermann Tower, above which flies the Estonian flag. The unique-looking Riigikogu building, which was built in 1920–22, is situated in the castle courtyard. Toompea as a whole enjoyed its own rights and privileges until 1878, when it was officially merged with the rest of the city below.

⑲ Alexander Nevsky Cathedral
Aleksander Nevski katedraal

Lossi plats 10. **Map** 1 B3. **Tel** 644 3484. 🚋 3, 4. **Open** 8am–8pm Sat, 8am–7pm Sun–Fri. ✝ 8:30am Mon–Sat, 10am Sun. ✉ 📷
🌐 teelistekirikud.ekn.ee

The imposing Alexander Nevsky Cathedral was built between 1894 and 1900, under the orders of Tsar Alexander III. As intended, the Neo-Byzantine edifice dominates Castle Square with its towering onion domes and golden crosses.

Legend has it that the cathedral was built on the grave of the Estonian folk hero Kalev. It is named after the sainted Russian duke Alexander Nevsky (1219–63), who defeated the Livonian Knights on the banks of Lake Peipsi in 1242. Disliked by many Estonians as a symbol of the Russification policies carried out by Alexander III, it was due to be demolished in 1924, but the controversial plan was never carried out.

The extravagant altar is made up of a dazzling display of icons, while the sheer scale of the cathedral's interior is equally impressive.

⑳ Cathedral of St Mary the Virgin
Toomkirik

Toomkooli 6. **Map** 1 B2. **Tel** 644 4140.
🚋 3, 4. **Open** Jun–Aug: 9am–5pm daily; Sep–May: 9am–5pm Tue–Sun.
✝ 5pm Wed, noon Sat, 11am Sun.
🌐 eelk.ee/tallinna.toom

Popularly known as Dome Church, St Mary's is believed to be the oldest church in Estonia. It was built in 1240 by the Danes and underwent extensive rebuilding over the years. The somewhat plain Gothic exterior dates from the 14th century, while the beautiful interior boasts an elaborate Baroque pulpit and a widely admired organ built in 1878. Other significant features include 107 aristocratic coats of arms and the fine Renaissance tomb of the French-born mercenary Pontus de la Gardie, who captured Narva for the Swedes from the Russians in 1581, during the Great Northern War (1558–82). In

Intricately designed Baroque pulpit, Cathedral of St Mary the Virgin

1684, the church was badly damaged in a fire that swept Toompea and had to be substantially reconstructed. Today, the church remains at the very heart of Estonian Lutheranism.

㉑ Museum of Occupations
Okupatsioonide muuseum

Toompea 8. **Map** 1 B3. **Tel** 668 0250. 🚋 3, 4. **Open** 11am–6pm Tue–Sun. 🅿 🕐 call in advance. ♿ 💻 📷 🌐 **okupatsioon.ee**

This comprehensive museum provides a look at life in Estonia under both the Nazi and Soviet occupations. The fascinating exhibits include examples of bureaucratic paperwork, gut-wrenching accounts of mass deportation and execution, as well as posterart propaganda, which was an essential weapon for the occupying forces.

The open-space museum remembers the countless victims of the occupations, and its symbolic location at the foot of Toompea adds a certain poignancy. It was partly founded by Kistler-Ritso, an Estonian World War II refugee to the United States. He donated 2 million dollars to the museum, the largest private donation in Estonian history.

㉒ Knights' House
Rüütelkonna hoone

Kiriku plats 1. **Map** 1 B2. 🚋 3, 4.

Built in 1848, the Knights' House originally served as a meeting place for the knighthood, an influential segment of the Toompea gentry. It was home to the Foreign Ministry during the first independent republic, which lasted from 1920 to 1940. During Soviet times, the building housed the Estonian National Library.

It temporarily accommodated the main collection of the Art Museum of Estonia before it moved to its new permanent home in the Kumu Art Museum *(see p80)*. The building,

Exterior of the 19th-century Knights' House, now a venue for concerts

which occasionally hosted concerts, is currently closed to the public.

㉓ Kiek-in-de-Kök

Komandandi 2. **Map** 1 B3. **Tel** 644 6686. 🚋 3, 4. **Open** Mar–Oct: 10:30am–6pm Tue–Sun; Nov–Feb: 10am–5:30pm Tue–Sun. 🅿 🕐 call 644 6686 for a guided group tour of secret tunnels under the bastion. 📷 🌐 **linnamuuseum.ee**

One of the strongest cannon towers in 16th-century Northern Europe, Kiek-in-de-Kök was built in 1475 as Toompea's main bastion. The tower stands 38 m (125 ft) tall and its walls are 4 m (13 ft) thick. The curious Low German name means "to peek into the kitchen", suggesting that soldiers had a good vantage point over the enemy. Some, however, believe that they literally peeked into people's kitchens. The tower fell into disuse in the mid-18th century

Painted porcelain plate, Adamson-Eric Museum

Bitter Death, a cannon replica displayed in Kiek-in-de-Kök

and now houses a five-floor museum devoted to Tallinn's history. The highlights include medieval artillery and a plague doctor's protective uniform.

㉔ Adamson-Eric Museum

Lühike jalg 3. **Map** 1 C3. **Tel** 644 5838. 🚋 3, 4. **Open** 11am–6pm Wed–Sun. 🅿 🕐 group tours of 10–35; call in advance. 📷 allowed only without the flash. 📷 🌐 **adamson-eric.ee**

Located in a medieval house on a narrow stairway connecting the Old Town with Toompea, the Adamson-Eric Museum is a branch of the Art Museum of Estonia. Adamson-Eric (1902–68) is one of the key figures of 20th-century Estonian art. His idiosyncratic and diverse body of work spanned several decades and influenced countless artists after him.

The Tartu-born artist was primarily a painter, but also worked with ceramics, metal forms, jewellery and leather, among other media. Although he held several prominent positions in various Soviet art committees during the latter part of his life, he was thrown out of the Communist Party in 1949 and forced into factory work for four years. After suffering a stroke in 1955 and losing the use of his right hand, he taught himself to paint using his left hand. The collection on display was donated to the Art Museum of Estonia by the artist's widow.

Exploring Beyond the Old Town

There is much more to Tallinn than its tourist-packed Old Town. A little way east is Kadriorg Park, with its splendid palace, the Kumu Art Museum and the nearby Song Festival Grounds. Further east is Maarjamäe Palace, which houses the Estonian History Museum. A little further north of this lies the fascinating Pirita Convent. A short distance west of the Old Town is the Estonian Open-Air Museum with some of Estonia's oldest rural architecture. The well-connected suburb of Nõmme to the south is also worth exploring. Most places are within easy reach of public transport.

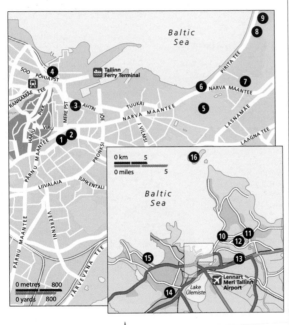

Key

- ▢ Central Talinnn
- ═ Motorway
- ▬ Main road
- ═ Minor road

Sights at a Glance

Theatres, Concert Halls and Museums

- ❶ Estonian Drama Theatre
- ❷ Estonian National Opera
- ❹ Energy Centre
- ❼ Song Festival Grounds

- ❽ Maarjamäe Palace
- ⓯ Estonian Open-Air Museum

Historic Buildings

- ❸ Rotermanni Quarter and Salt Storage Warehouse
- ❻ Russalka Memorial
- ❾ Soviet War Memorial
- ❿ Pirita Convent
- ⓫ TV Tower

Parks and Gardens

- ❺ Kadriorg Park pp78–81
- ⓬ Tallinn Botanical Gardens

Islands and Suburbs

- ⓭ Lasnamäe
- ⓮ Nõmme
- ⓰ Aegna Island

For keys to symbols see back flap

❶ Estonian Drama Theatre

Eesti draamateater

Pärnu mnt 5. **Tel** 680 5555.
🚌 5, 36, 40. 🚋 3, 4. **Open** 10am–5pm Mon–Fri. 🅿 ♿ ✉ 💻 🌐 **draamateater.ee**

This popular theatre occupies one of the most striking buildings on the fringes of the Old Town. Built in 1910 as a German-language theatre, it was purchased by the Estonian Drama Theatre in 1939.

The elegant Art Nouveau exterior includes rustic-style features in a manner unique to the Baltic States. Under Soviet occupation, the theatre's name was changed to the Tallinn Drama Theatre, in an effort to remove nationalist affinities associated with it. However, in 1989 it reverted to its original name.

The theatre is the largest in Estonia, with a 40-member company and an average of 500 performances per season. The productions are usually in Estonian, with rare exceptions during theatre festivals.

Grand entrance of the Estonian Drama Theatre

❷ Estonian National Opera

Rahvusooper Estonia

Estonia pst 4. **Tel** 683 1215. 🚌 5, 36, 40. 🚋 3, 4. **Open** 11am–7pm daily (box office). 🅿 ♿ ✉ 💻 🌐 **opera.ee**

The imperious bulk of the Estonian National Opera dominates the view along the stretch of Estonia Avenue that skirts the eastern edge of the Old Town. The sprawling building

Imposing façade of the Estonian National Opera

houses the Estonian National Opera and its ballet company in one wing and the Estonian National Symphony Orchestra in another, while the Winter Garden is regularly used to host state functions.

The Estonian National Opera was completed in 1913, through public donations, and was intended to serve as an impressive showcase for Estonian culture that would overshadow similar German and Russian institutions in Tallinn. In recent years, the opera company has gained an outstanding international reputation and its cutting-edge productions can be seen for a fraction of the price visitors would pay in most European capitals.

Charles Abraham Rotermann

❸ Rotermanni Quarter and Salt Storage Warehouse
Eesti arhitektuurimuuseum

Ahtri 2. **Tel** 625 7007. ▣ all buses to Viru Bus Terminal. ▣ 1, 2, 3, 4. Museum of Estonian Architecture: **Tel** 625 7007. **Open** 11am–6pm Wed–Sun. ▣ ▣ ▣ ▣ ▣
Ⓦ arhitektuurimuuseum.ee

The Rotermanni Quarter is situated east of Mere Avenue on the fringes of Tallinn's port area and within comfortable walking distance of the Old Town. The district is named after Charles Abraham

Rotermann, a 19th-century industrialist, and was a major industrial hub before most of its factories and warehouses fell into disuse and disrepair during the Soviet era. In 2007 the district underwent a major redevelopment. Several buildings with brave architectural designs were constructed to house boutique shops, offices and restaurants.

The impressive limestone building of the Salt Storage Warehouse, located nearby, is home to the **Museum of Estonian Architecture**. It was once used as the city's salt warehouse, and today, it houses a range of architecture-related exhibits, spread out over its vast three-floor interior.

❹ Energy Centre
Tehnika-ja teaduskeskus

Põhja pst 29. **Tel** 620 9020. ▣ 3. ▣ 1, 2. **Open** 10am–7pm Mon–Fri, 11am–7pm Sat & Sun. ▣ ▣ ▣
Ⓦ energiakeskus.ee

Situated in a former power station, the Energy Centre is an enormous museum that forms part of the Tallinn Science and Technology Centre. It has numerous interactive exhibits which are used to demonstrate the rudiments of science.

The centre is charmingly old-fashioned and relies on the joy of learning through entertainment, rather than the slick presentation and hi-tech gadgetry used by most modern science institutes. There is an especially enjoyable array of hands-on exhibits downstairs. The centre also hosts various other more serious science-related exhibitions and seminars.

Salt Storage Warehouse, home to the Museum of Estonian Architecture

❺ Kadriorg Park

Kadriorg Park is one of Tallinn's most interesting features outside the Old Town. It centres on the magnificent 18th-century Baroque palace built as a summer residence for Peter the Great and boasts a wealth of small museums, historic monuments and art galleries. The park stretches for 1.5 km (1 mile) from its southwest corner to the northeast. It is a popular and picturesque place for a leisurely stroll. The elegant and affluent residential streets near the south entrance are also well worth a look and include museums dedicated to Eduard Vilde and Anton Hansen Tammsaare, two of Estonia's most prominent 20th-century literary figures.

Statue of Friedrich Reinhold Kreutzwald
This grand statue honours the writer of *Kalevipoeg*, considered the founding work of Estonian literature.

Swan Lake
The Swan Lake is one of the park's focal points, although its elegant island pavilion is mostly enjoyed by swans.

Anton Hansen Tammsaare Museum
The museum offers an insight into how the writer Tammsaare (1878–1940) lived and also exhibits his literary works and personal items.

| 0 metres | 200 |
| 0 yards | 200 |

Eduard Vilde Memorial Museum
This attractive summer house serves as a living memorial to one of Estonia's most revered writers. Vilde lived and worked here until his death in 1933.

★ Kadriorg Palace
Peter the Great's Baroque palace now houses the Estonian Art Museum's foreign collection. However, the museum's main exhibits are displayed at the Kumu Art Museum.

Russalka Memorial
This imposing monument *(see p82)* commemorates the sinking of the *Russalka* near Finland in 1893.

President's Palace

Peter the Great House Museum
The great Russian Tsar once used this cottage as a temporary residence.

Mikkel Museum
The small museum is renowned for its porcelain vases and beautiful figurines.

★ Kumu Art Museum
Arguably the most architecturally impressive museum in the Baltic States, the magnificently designed Kumu houses the main exhibits of the Estonian Art Museum.

Exploring Kadriorg Park

With forested paths, statues and ponds, Kadriorg Park is a charming place to explore. The surrounding area has a number of beautiful houses and manicured gardens and is also associated with art because of the museums, such as the Kumu Art Museum and Mikkel Museum, located here. Nearly all the park's main sights are on, or close to, Weizenbergi. Kadriorg Park is not very large and it is quite easy to cover its entire length on foot. Located a short distance from the Old Town, the park and its quiet neighbourhood are, nevertheless, a pleasant 30-minute stroll away. Regular buses and trams connect Kadriorg Park with the Old Town.

The attractive garden of Kadriorg Palace

🏛 Kadriorg Palace

Weizenbergi 37. **Tel** 606 6400.
Open May–Sep: 10am–5pm Tue–Sun; Oct–Apr: 10am–5pm Wed–Sun. 🏛
🖼 🔊 🖥 📷 🆆 ekm.ee

This palace was built in 1718 under the orders of the Russian Tsar Peter the Great, who intended it to serve as a summer residence for the royal family. It was later named in honour of his wife Catherine. Kadriorg Palace was designed in the Northern Baroque style by the famous Italian master architect Nicola Michetti. The Russian emperor intended the three-winged palace to look like an Italian villa, and no expense was spared in creating a magnificently lavish building in the Italian Baroque style of which he was so fond.

Portrait of Thomas Chaloner by Van Dyck

After undergoing extensive renovation, the palace now houses the Estonian Art Museum's foreign collection. Johannes Mikkel (1907–2006), whose collections are exhibited in the Mikkel Museum, donated some 600 works of foreign art to the Estonian Art Museum in 1994. The museum boasts a fine selection of European painting. However, its main attraction is the astonishingly ornate Great Hall, which ranks among the finest examples of Baroque exuberance in Northern Europe. The well-manicured ornamental garden with fountains behind the palace is also open to the public.

🏛 Mikkel Museum

Weizenbergi 28. **Tel** 601 5844.
Open 10am–5pm Wed–Sun. 🏛 🖼
🆆 ekm.ee

Located in the former kitchen of Kadriorg Palace, the Mikkel Museum comprises the private collection of the art collector Johannes Mikkel. He began collecting art during the interwar period and over the years amassed a valuable private collection that is today considered one of the best in Estonia.

The exhibits range from the 16th to the 20th centuries and include an impressive selection of porcelain vases and figurines. There are some fine examples of classical European art, such as *Portrait of Thomas Chaloner* (1620), attributed to the Flemish painter Anthony Van Dyck.

🏛 Kumu Art Museum

Weizenbergi 34. **Tel** 602 6000.
Open May–Sep: 11am–6pm Tue, Thu–Sun, 11am–8pm Wed; Oct–Apr: 11am–8pm Wed,11am–6pm Thu–Sun.
🖼 🔊 🖥 📷 🆆 kumu.ee

The Kumu Art Museum is the Estonian Art Museum's first purpose-built building; it was designed to provide a fitting home for the museum's main collection. The structure is built into a limestone bank on the edge of Kadriorg Park and is a work of art in itself.

The museum's enormous and beautifully designed interior is a labyrinth of artistic discovery, with one exhibition hall leading to another. The exhibits in the rooms are arranged in chronological order. Among the many delights on show, Konrad Mägi's brilliantly coloured canvases stand out as a wonderful example of early 20th-century Estonian art. Eduard von Gebhardt's *Sermon on the Mount* (1904) is another painting to relish for both its epic excellence and subtle irony. The

Row of busts on display in a room at the Kumu Art Museum

fourth floor is devoted to a permanent exhibition entitled "Difficult Choices", exploring the complex relationship between art and the Soviet state, while the fifth floor is given over to the best in contemporary art. However, the most striking exhibition of all is the room filled with hundreds of busts eerily staring into space.

Catherine I's bedroom, Peter the Great House Museum

🏛 Peter the Great House Museum

Mäekalda 2. **Tel** 601 3136. **Open** May–Aug: 10am–6pm Tue–Sun; Sep–Apr: 10am–5pm Wed–Sun. 🖼
W linnamuuseum.ee

This museum is housed in the 17th-century cottage which the Russian emperor used as a summer residence while Kadriorg Palace was being built. The cottage was purchased along with the surrounding land in 1713 and was enlarged with an additional wing so that it contained a hall, a kitchen and four rooms.

After Peter the Great died in 1725, his successors opted to stay in the more lavish Kadriorg Palace and the cottage fell into disrepair until Alexander I ordered it to be restored after a visit to Tallinn in 1804. The house contains few remains of Peter the Great's time, but it still affords an intriguing glimpse into the life of the enigmatic ruler. The bedroom has a four-poster bed and a pair of slippers which supposedly belonged to the Tsar himself. There is an exhibition in the basement about his life and achievements.

Eduard Vilde (1865–1933)

Author of Estonian classics such as *The War in Mahtra* and *The Milkman from Mäeküla*, Eduard Vilde is one of the most revered figures in Estonian literature and is generally credited as being the country's first professional writer.

Vilde spent a great deal of time travelling abroad and he lived for some time in Berlin in the 1890s, where he was influenced by materialism and socialism. His writings were also guided by the naturalism of the French writer Emile Zola (1840–1902). In addition to being a writer, Vilde was also an outspoken critic of Tsarist rule and of the German landowners. With the founding of the first Estonian republic in 1919, Vilde served as a diplomat in Berlin for several years. He spent the last years of his life editing and revising an enormous volume of his collected works.

Eduard Vilde, writer and diplomat

🏛 Anton Hansen Tammsaare Museum

Koidula 12a. **Tel** 601 3232. **Open** 10am–5pm Wed–Mon. 🖼 🖼
W linnamuuseum.ee

Anton Hansen Tammsaare (1878–1940) is Estonia's most important literary figure. His five-volume epic *Truth and Justice* takes a sweeping look at Estonian society from the 1870s to the 1930s.

The museum is situated in the attractive wooden house in Kadriorg where the novelist and his wife lived from 1932 until his death in 1940. The building was converted into a museum in 1978. On the first floor is the couple's five-room flat, while a separate wing serves as a museum dedicated to

Exterior of the modest A H Tammsaare Memorial Museum

Tammsaare's life and work. The collection of almost 6,000 artifacts includes several photographs, letters and manuscripts and even the writer's death mask.

🏛 Eduard Vilde Memorial Museum

Roheline aas 3. **Tel** 601 3181. **Open** 11am–5pm Wed–Sun. 🖼 🖼
W linnamuuseum.ee

The Eduard Vilde Memorial Museum is housed in a Neo-Baroque summer house beside Kadriorg Park which was presented to the writer as a 60th birthday gift by the Estonian government.

Vilde was one of Estonia's most prolific writers, and his works amount to a staggering 33 volumes. The museum showcases the six-room flat where Vilde lived with his wife from 1927 to 1933. The authentic furnishings are accompanied by period art pieces and provide a fascinating look at literary life in Tallinn in the 1920s. It is said that Vilde could often be seen enjoying long talks with his neighbour, the famous writer A H Tammsaare, in the nearby park.

The museum has been in existence since 1946 and is an interesting monument. The balusters of the wooden staircase, dating from the turn of the 19th and 20th century, have survived.

6 Russalka Memorial

Near the junction of Pirita tee & Narva mnt. 🚌 1a, 34, 38. ♿

This imposing memorial was erected in honour of the 177 soldiers who drowned when the Russian ship *Russalka*, or "Mermaid", sank en route to Finland in 1893. Designed by the renowned Estonian sculptor Amandus Adamson (1855–1929), the monument was erected in 1902. It features a bronze angel standing on tiptoe, holding aloft an Orthodox cross. The pedestal on which the angel stands is made of roughly hewn blocks of granite, evoking stormy sea conditions. The monument is one of several locations around Tallinn which young couples visit to be photographed on their wedding day.

Angel with an Orthodox cross, standing atop the Russalka Memorial

7 Song Festival Grounds

Lauluväljak

Narva mnt 95. **Tel** 611 2102. 🚌 1a, 5, 8, 34a, 38 (to Lauluväljak); 19, 29, 35, 44, 51, 60, 63 (to Lasnamägi). **Open** daily. ♿ 🌐 **lauluvaljak.ee**

The centrepiece of the Song Festival Grounds is the **Song Festival Bowl**, the large, shell-like amphitheatre built in the 1960s. During the four-yearly Estonian Song and Dance Festival, the stage holds up to 15,000 choral singers, with room for many more on an extra

Aerial view of the impressive shell-like Song Festival Bowl

platform. It has been a strong symbol for Estonians ever since thousands of people gathered here during the 1988 Song and Dance Festival in a show of unity against Soviet occupation.

In summer, the venue hosts concerts, as well as the Beer Festival. The 42-m (138-ft) high Light Tower beside the Song Festival Bowl offers good views of the Old Town. On weekday evenings, the tower is used as a climbing post.

8 Maarjamäe Palace

Pirita tee 56. **Tel** 622 8600. 🚌 5, 34, 38. **Open** 10am–5pm Wed–Sun. 📷 📹 call in advance. 🌐 **ajaloomuuseum.ee**

An elegant Neo-Gothic summer house, Maarjamäe Palace was built in 1874 by the Russian Count Orlov-Davydov. The building has since served as a consulate, a hotel and restaurant, and a base for trainee pilots as well as the Soviet army. However, today it houses another branch of the **Estonian History Museum** *(see also p64)*.

The museum, inaugurated in 1987, picks up where its counterpart in the Old Town leaves off, in the mid-19th century, to cover the political and social upheavals of the 20th century. The exhibits include historically costumed mannequins and

recreations of domestic interiors. The 1940s and 50s are represented by army uniforms, photographs and weapons. There is an original hut used by the Forest Brothers *(see p122)*, the legendary partisans who fought against the Soviet occupation, and a replica of a desk used by a Communist Party secretary.

Visitors can go to the back of the palace to see some of the gigantic Soviet-era bronze monuments lying there in an unceremonious heap.

🏛 Estonian History Museum
Open 10am–5pm Wed–Sun. Research: 9am–5pm Mon–Fri.

Maarjamäe Palace, housing a branch of the Estonian History Museum

Peter the Great (1672–1725)

Russia had long coveted Estonia as a much-needed outlet to Western Europe, but it was Peter the Great who finally achieved this. When the Treaty of Nystad ended the Great Northern War between Russia and Sweden in 1721, Estonia finally fell under Russian control. The Russian Tsar visited Tallinn 11 times during his reign and left an impressive legacy behind. From the magnificent Kadriorg Palace (see p80), which was built as a royal summer residence, to the reconstruction of the ports in Tallinn and Paldiski, Peter the Great's formidable influence is still visible. The Tsar so loved Estonia that he once remarked, "If Tallinn and Rogewiek [Paldiski] had been mine in 1702, I would not have established my residence and the capital of European Russia on the low-lying river Neva but here."

The epic battle of Narva took place in 1700 between Russia and Sweden during the Great Northern War. It ended in a severe loss for Peter the Great, but by 1721, Russia had defeated the Swedes to become the dominant regional power.

Peter the Great is represented as a great statesman in this portrait by Hippolyte Delaroche, painted in 1838. The Tsar's political intelligence and military prowess turned Russia into a major European power.

The cottage in Kadriorg Park (see p81) was used by Peter the Great and his wife Catherine I as a summer residence while Kadriorg Palace was being built. The cottage is now a museum.

Portrait of Catherine I, painted by Jean-Marc Nattier in 1717

Catherine I (1684–1727)

Originally named Marta Skavronskaya, Catherine I was a Lithuanian peasant's daughter and is thought to have been born in present-day Estonia. A beautiful girl, Marta joined the household of Prince Aleksandr Menschikov, who introduced her to Peter the Great in 1703. They became lovers soon after that. In 1705, she converted to Russian Orthodoxy, whereupon she changed her name to Catherine. The couple lived a modest life in a two-room log cabin during the construction of St Petersburg and were secretly married in 1707. In 1709, Catherine gave birth to Elizabeth, who later ruled Russia from 1741 to 1762. In 1724, Catherine was officially declared co-ruler of the Russian Empire with her husband. Kadriorg (see pp78–81), or Catherine's Valley, was named in her honour.

❾ Soviet War Memorial

Maarjamäe

Pirita tee. 🚌 1a, 8, 5, 34a, 38. ♿

The Soviet War Memorial is a typical example of Soviet war monuments in both its grand scale and rather kitsch appearance. The 35-m (115-ft) obelisk at the centre of the complex was erected in 1960 to commemorate the Russian sailors who died in 1918, during World War I. The surrounding features were built in the 1970s, in memory of the Soviet soldiers killed in 1941 under the Nazi onslaught. In a dilapidated state today, the site includes an eerie concrete amphitheatre and large concrete and iron figures.

A German cemetery filled with stone crosses lies just behind the memorial site, serving as yet another reminder of the fierce struggle for control over the region.

❿ Pirita Convent

Pirita klooster

Merivälja Tee 18. **Tel** 605 5044. 🚌 1a, 5, 8, 34a. **Open** Nov–Mar: noon–4pm daily; Apr–May: 10am–6pm daily; Jun–Aug: 9am–7pm daily; Sep–Oct: 10am–6pm daily. 📷 🌐 piritaklooster.ee

Founded in 1407 by the St Bridget Order, Pirita Convent was consecrated in 1436. It served as the largest convent in then Livonia (present-day Estonia and northern Latvia), until it was badly damaged in a siege by Ivan the Terrible in 1577. Over the following decades, the convent was reduced to a skeletal structure, as locals plundered it for building materials. In the 17th century, a cemetery was established in the compound.

Despite centuries of neglect and oblivion, the impressive ruins retain some splendour. The most striking feature is the perfectly intact 35-m (115-ft) high gable and the walls of the main hall. The site is run by Bridgettine nuns, who live in a state-of-the-art, award-winning building close by. The nuns offer lodgings in their home, continuing a tradition that has existed for hundreds of years.

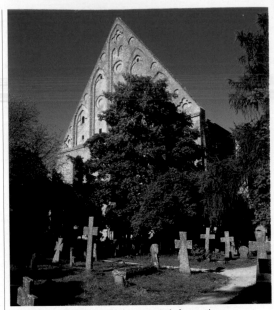

Pirita Convent, screened by trees, with the cemetery in the foreground

⓫ TV Tower

Teletorn

Kloostrimetsa 58a. 🚌 34a, 38. **Open** 10am–7pm daily. ♿ 📷 🏛 🌐 teletorn.ee

Inaugurated in 1980, the 314-m (1,030-ft) tall TV Tower, or Tallinn Tower, was designed as an impressive demonstration of superior Soviet engineering. It was the scene of a tense stand-off between Estonians and Soviet troops in 1991, which was resolved peacefully when the Soviet troops withdrew. The tower is an amazing spectacle, despite its increasingly crumbling condition. There are great views from the observation deck.

⓬ Tallinn Botanical Gardens

Tallinna botaanikaaed

Kloostrimetsa tee 52, 10 km (6 miles) NE of city centre. **Tel** 606 2666. 🚌 34a, 38. **Open** Apr–Sep: 11am–6pm; Oct–Mar: 11am–4pm. 📷 🎫 ♿ 🌐 botaanikaaed.ee

Located in a beautiful stretch of woodland, the Tallinn Botanical Gardens have an exotic palm house as the main attraction. Adjoining the palm house are several greenhouses containing a superb selection of rare orchids and fascinating cacti. The outdoor collections include a rose garden, an arboretum, a limestone rock garden and a permanent display of "useful plants".

The grounds are located in a protected area of the Pirita River Valley and have a designated

The TV Tower, a brilliant example of Russian engineering

4-km (2-mile) nature trail that goes through a lush range of habitats, from dry meadows to pine forests.

⓭ Lasnamäe

5 km (3 miles) NE of Tallinn.

A vast Soviet-era suburb founded on a limestone plateau in 1977, Lasnamäe houses almost a third of the city's population. The industrial part of the district is centred around Peterburi Street. Seemingly endless rows of housing blocks are lined up beside Laagna Street, which is a smaller road that passes through the so-called "Canyon", a road blasted through limestone.

The ambitious plans for the making of Lasnamäe were never finished and several aborted building projects that abruptly came to a halt when Estonia broke away from the Soviet Union, can still be seen. Although there is little of interest, the area as a whole is a strangely impressive sight and offers an intriguing glimpse of a side of the city that most visitors rarely see.

⓮ Nõmme

8 km (5 miles) S of Tallinn. 🚍 from Tallinn. 🚌 14, 18, 33.

The beautiful residential district of Nõmme was developed as a suburb after a railway station opened there in 1872. Soon after, wealthy Tallinners began building elegant summer villas with spacious gardens, and by 1926, the area had grown sufficiently to officially become a town. However, in 1940 the Soviets incorporated it into Tallinn.

Today, Nõmme is one of the most attractive areas of the city, with its own outdoor market, historic centre, cafés and restaurants, and some fine museums. The Kristjan Raud Museum is dedicated to the artist who illustrated the epic poem *Kalevipoeg*, while the **Baron von Glehn Castle**, built by a Baltic-German landlord who largely founded the area, is

Baron von Glehn Castle in lush surroundings, Nõmme

an impressive sight. The castle is only open for special events but the surrounding park, with some particularly eye-catching statues, can be visited any time.

🏰 Baron von Glenn Castle
Vana-Mustimäe tee 48. **Tel** 652 5076. **Open** by appointment only.

⓯ Estonian Open-Air Museum

Eesti vabaõhumuuseum

Vabaõhumuuseumi tee 12. **Tel** 654 9100. 🚌 21, 21b. **Open** May–Sep: 10am–8pm daily; Oct–Apr: 10am–5pm daily. 🎫 📷 call in advance. ♿ 🖥 📷 🌐 evm.ee

One of the few major sights outside the city centre, the Estonian Open-Air Museum is situated in the sprawling grounds of the former Rocco al Mare summer estate, with a stunning backdrop of Kopli Bay. The museum is an enormous village made up of historic rural buildings from all around the country. The exhibits range from the 18th to the 20th centuries and give a fascinating picture of how rural architecture developed in Estonia over the years. There are wooden windmills, thatched barns, a village inn and an 18th-century wooden church alongside numerous farmsteads and outbuildings.

A variety of activities are offered, including nature trails and horse and carriage rides, while regular music and theatre productions are held here too. Annual highlights include the Midsummer's Eve celebrations (*see p52*) and the Autumn Fair.

⓰ Aegna Island

Aegna saar

14 km (9 miles) NE of Tallinn. 🚢 from Pirita Harbour.

The tiny 3-sq-km (1-sq-mile) island of Aegna is situated in the northeastern part of Tallinn Bay. It has pristine sandy beaches and unspoiled nature, which may, however, be the target of future development.

The few traces of human activity that can be found are almost all military. There was a cannon battery here during Tsarist rule, and after being briefly used by the Estonian army during the country's first period of independence, Aegna became a closed Soviet military zone.

The island is now governed by Tallinn City Council and improved ferry links have led to a steady increase in visitors. It is a popular place to pitch a tent in summer.

Old wooden house by the sea, Estonian Open-Air Museum

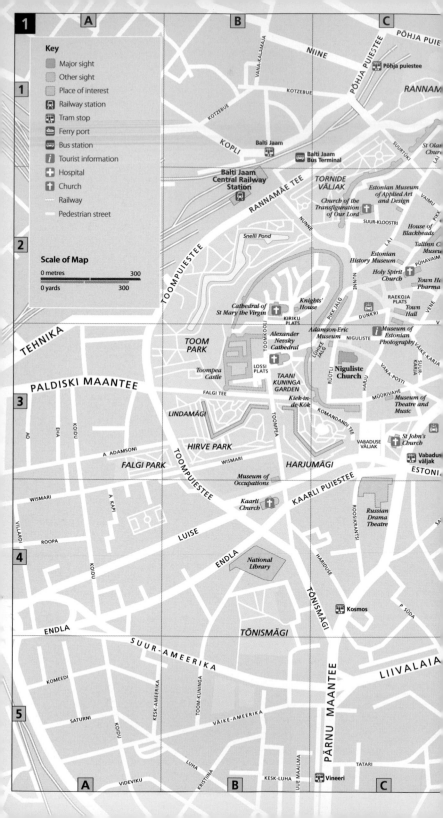

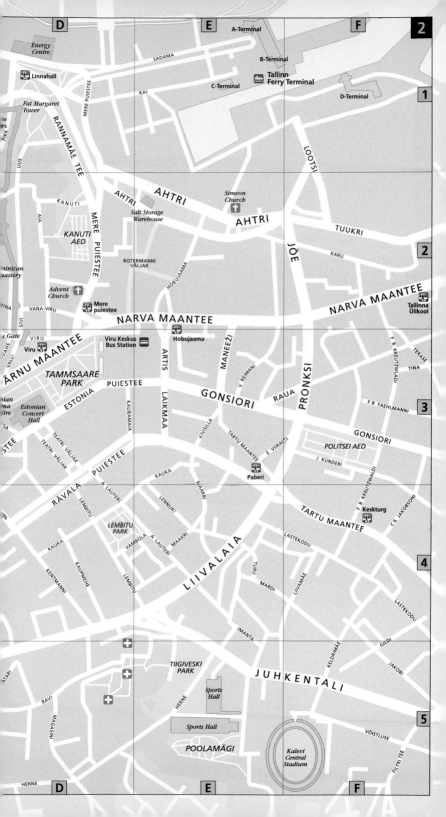

WESTERN ESTONIA

The region enjoys some of the country's most stunning natural landscapes and is also historically entwined with the Estonian national identity in countless ways. The erratic, time-worn coastline is punctuated with numerous places of cultural interest as well as some lively summer resorts, while the archipelago is remarkable for its unspoiled, timeless beauty.

Estonia's history has, to a large extent, been shaped by its west coast. Swedes settled in large numbers on the islands and around Haapsalu, as they were in the path of Nordic trading routes. Peter the Great seized Estonia and, in 1718, built a port and naval base at Paldiski because he wanted a "window into the West". In Soviet times, the coastline served as a heavily guarded border zone.

Western Estonia's main coastal town is Pärnu, in the south, the country's "Summer Capital". Further north, Haapsalu was a stylish resort during the 19th century and has remained every bit as attractive today. Soomaa National Park, which lies just inland, is an enchanting waterworld of bogs and rivers, while Matsalu National Park is one of the biggest nesting grounds for birds in Europe. On the northwest coast, Paldiski offers testimony to the Soviet occupation in the form of countless crumbling buildings that once served the enormous submarine base there, while the beautiful cliffs around the peninsula make it a wonderful place for hiking. The whole coastline is dotted with tiny, picturesque villages, while countless manor houses, medieval churches, iconic lighthouses and other places of interest are strewn throughout this region.

Of the Estonian islands, Saaremaa is both the largest and the most popular. The island of Vilsandi is the remotest of all of Estonia's national parks but, covered with interesting sights, it is one of the most rewarding to visit. The islands of Hiiumaa, Vormsi and Muhu are less developed but their rugged beauty is a strong attraction for visitors seeking the serenity of a pristine and somewhat remote environment.

Traditionally attired dancers forming a circle at a celebration on Hiiumaa Island

◄ The historic Ekesparre Boutique Hotel *(see p298)* in the grounds of the Bishop's Castle in Kuressaare, Saaremaa Island

Exploring Western Estonia

Western Estonia offers an irresistible blend of cultural heritage and wild natural beauty. Pärnu is a good base from which to explore the bogs and wetlands of Soomaa National Park to the east and the flourishing bird sanctuary of Matsalu National Park to the north. The popular spa resort of Haapsalu is within easy driving distance of Tallinn and visitors can explore the ruggedly beautiful coastal area around Paldiski on the way. The islands of Kihnu, Muhu, Saaremaa, Vormsi and Hiiumaa are well connected to the mainland by ferry and can be reached from Pärnu and Haapsalu.

Wooden trail through a bog in Soomaa National Park

Row of old buildings in cobblestoned Rüütli Street, Pärnu

Sights at a Glance

Towns and Cities

1 Paldiski
2 Haapsalu
6 Lihula
9 Pärnu pp102–3

National Parks and Reserves

4 Matsalu National Park
10 Soomaa National Park pp104–5

Islands

3 Vormsi Island
5 Hiiumaa Island
7 Muhu Island
8 Saaremaa Island pp96–9
11 Kihnu Island

Sights of Interest

12 Tori Stud Farm

For hotels and restaurants see pp297–8 and pp316–18

Nõ
Spithami

Riguldi

Sutlep

Lehtma   VORMSI ISLAND 3
Kärdla   Hullo
Lauka   80 Hellamaa   HAAPSALU
82   Rohuküla
Kalana   81   Heltermaa   Ahi
HIIUMAA 5   Kaina
ISLAND
84   Kassari
Leisu
83
Sõru   Emmaste   Nõmmküla
MUHU 7
Metsküla   ISLAND
Angla Leisi   Kuivastu V
Tagaranna   Karja   Põide
Undva   10
Kõruse   Laimjala
Vilsandi Kihelkonna 8 Kõljala
National   79
Park   SAAREMAA ISLAND   Siiksaare
Kipi   Kuressaare
Nasva   Vätta   Gulf
Tiirimetsa   of Rīg
77
Mõntu
Sääre

0 kilometres   20
0 miles   20

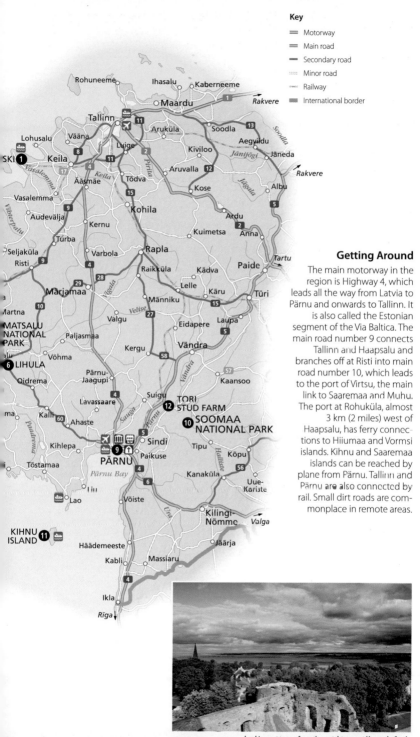

Key

━ Motorway
━ Main road
━ Secondary road
┈ Minor road
⌁ Railway
▬ International border

Getting Around

The main motorway in the region is Highway 4, which leads all the way from Latvia to Pärnu and onwards to Tallinn. It is also called the Estonian segment of the Via Baltica. The main road number 9 connects Tallinn and Haapsalu and branches off at Risti into main road number 10, which leads to the port of Virtsu, the main link to Saaremaa and Muhu. The port at Rohuküla, almost 3 km (2 miles) west of Haapsalu, has ferry connections to Hiiumaa and Vormsi islands. Kihnu and Saaremaa islands can be reached by plane from Pärnu. Tallinn and Pärnu are also connected by rail. Small dirt roads are commonplace in remote areas.

Looking out to sea from the watchtower at Haapsalu Castle

For keys to symbols see back flap

❶ Paldiski

Road Map C1. 🔼 4,000. 🚊
🚌 145 from Tallinn. 🔲 **paldiski.ee**

Deriving its name from the Estonian pronunciation of *baltiyskiy*, which means "Baltic" in Russian, Paldiski was established by Peter the Great in 1718. Paldiski was known to be of strategic importance for the Russian Empire. In 1962, when the Soviet Navy nuclear submarine training centre was set up here, the area already had two nuclear reactors and employed some 16,000 people. The Soviets finally withdrew in 1994 and the town quickly fell into chronic disrepair. The Swedish director Lukas Moodysson shot his extraordinarily bleak film *Lilya-4-Ever* (2002) in Paldiski, though it was described as an unnamed "former republic of the Soviet Union" in the film.

Located 52 km (32 miles) west of Tallinn, Paldiski is a fascinating place to visit and it attracts a steady stream of tourists. The countless derelict military buildings testify to the prominent role Paldiski once played in the Soviet defence system. Today, however, the town is slowly but surely being revitalized. The port area is booming and Paldiski's natural beauty makes it an attractive site for residential development.

Haapsalu's medieval castle, with an adjoining cathedral

Environs

Pakri, a stunning peninsula 3 km (2 miles) west of Paldiski, boasts Estonia's tallest lighthouse. Also here are the ruins of Peter the Great's ambitious but unfinished fortress project.

The red-painted lighthouse at Pakri, near Paldiski

❷ Haapsalu

Road Map C2. 🔼 12,000. 🚌 from Tallinn. 🚢 from Hiiumaa, Vormsi. ℹ️ Karja 15, 473 3248. 🎵 Early Music Festival (4–8 Jul), White Lady Days (Aug). 🔲 **haapsalu.ee**

Situated on a small spit of land jutting out into a narrow bay, the popular resort town of Haapsalu dates back to the 13th century. Its impressive Bishop's Castle ruins still serve as the main focal point for the town, despite the fact that its formidable fortifications were largely dismantled by Peter the Great in the 18th century. The castle watchtower houses the **Castle Museum**, displaying medieval weaponry. The adjoining **Dome Cathedral** is the largest single-nave church in the Baltic region.

Over the course of the 19th century, Haapsalu became a fashionable holiday resort, famed for its curative mud treatments and pretty beaches. Its landmark 216-m (709-ft) long train platform is an enduring monument to the era when Russian royalty and high society flocked to the town every summer. The platform was built in 1904 to receive Tsar Nicholas II and his entourage, and its ornate wooden canopy was designed to protect them from bad weather. The station closed in 1995 and the building now houses the **Estonian Railway Museum** with models of engines used between the late 19th and early 20th centuries.

Paralepa Beach, just to the west of the station, is Haapsalu's most popular bathing spot.

Estonia's Swedish Community

Swedish settlers in Estonia were first mentioned in 1294 in Haapsalu's town records. It is generally thought that Swedes settled along the western coastal areas in the 13th and 14th centuries to secure trade routes. From 1561 to 1700 Estonia was directly under Swedish rule. By the early 20th century, there were some 8,000 Swedish-speaking Estonians, most of whom lived on Vormsi Island and in the Haapsalu region. The Estonian-Swedes were a recognized minority with their own periodical and distinct cultural identity. However, the majority of them fled to Sweden during World War II. It is estimated that some 2,000 Estonian-Swedes remained behind, but life in the Soviet Union soon effaced their way of life and they effectively disappeared as a minority.

Swedish circular crosses in St Olav's Church cemetery, Hullo

On the east coast, the promenade is another fine legacy of the town's imperial glory days. From Africa Beach the promenade winds its way past the spa hall at Kuursaal and leads to the **Museum of Coastal Swedes**, which traces the history of the Swedes.

🏛 **Museum of Coastal Swedes**
Sadama 31/32. **Tel** 473 7165.
Open 11am–4pm Tue–Sat. 🖼
W aiboland.ee

Picturesque houses in one of the villages on Vormsi Island

❸ Vormsi Island

Road Map C1. 🚹 350. 🚌 from Haapsalu. 🚢 from Rohuküla, 10 km (6 miles) W of Haapsalu. **W** vormsi.ee

Estonia's fourth-largest island, Vormsi is only 10 km (6 miles) by 20 km (12 miles) in size. The island is ruggedly beautiful and blissfully unspoiled despite being only 3 km (2 miles) from the mainland. The size of

Tchaikovsky in Haapsalu

Russian composer Pyotr Ilyich Tchaikovsky and his brothers Anatoly and Modest spent the summer of 1867 in Haapsalu. Living in a small house on Suur-Mere Street, the 27-year-old Pyotr worked on *The Voyevoda*, his first opera and one of his major compositions. Tchaikovsky Bench on the promenade commemorates his stay and, at the press of a button, blares out a part of the Sixth Symphony, thought to have been inspired by an Estonian folk song.

Tchaikovsky Bench on the promenade in Haapsalu

the island and its beautiful landscapes make it perfect for hiking and cycling. The island is well known for its lush pine forests and an abundance of juniper bushes, as well as spectacular stretches of rocky coastline.

Some people believe that Vormsi means "Snakes Island", as the name derives from the old Swedish word for snake. Others, however, claim that it was named after a pirate called Orm. Either way, Vormsi Island was home to some 2,000 Swedes prior to World War II, and their influence can be seen all over the island.

The island's main settlement is **Hullo**, 3 km (2 miles) west of the ferry port at Sviby. The 14th-century **St Olav's Church** is especially worth visiting for its Baroque pulpit and a cemetery with a striking collection of circular Swedish crosses looming out of hand-made mounds of grass.

❹ Matsalu National Park
Matsalu rahvuspark

Road Map C2. ℹ Matsalu Nature Centre, Penijõe Manor; 472 4236.
Open 9am–5pm Mon–Fri, 10am–6pm Sat & Sun. 🖼 **W** matsalu.ee

Situated around the narrow Matsalu Bay, Matsalu National Park was founded in 1957 as a sanctuary for nesting and migratory birds. The area is a bird-watcher's paradise, with some 275 species found in its coastal wetlands. Six observation towers dotted along the coast offer the chance to see the fauna and birdlife up close. Viewing platforms overlook some of the islets and coastal meadows. Most of the observation towers are reached by car or bus, although Penijõe tower, on the bank of the Penijõe river, is a short walk from the Matsalu Nature Centre.

The Matsalu Bay islet, part of the idyllic Matsalu National Park

The pristine coastline of Hiiumaa Island

❺ Hiiumaa Island

Road Map C2. ✈ Hiiesaare, 5 km (3 miles) E of Kärdla. 🚌 from Tallinn. 🚢 from Rohuküla, Triigi. 🛈 Hiiu 1, Kärdla, 462 2232. 🎉 St John's Day (Jun). 🖵 **hiiumaa.ee**

Estonia's second-largest island, Hiiumaa is a paradise for nature lovers due to its rugged and diverse landscape. Although it is only 22 km (14 miles) from the mainland, it is far less developed as a tourist destination than neighbouring Saaremaa (see pp96–9). Over half the island is covered in forest that is home to an abundance of wildlife, such as elk, wild boar and lynx. The rest of the territory consists of meadows, peat bogs, heathland and endless miles of unspoiled coastline. Although there are plenty of interesting sights on the island, the majority of visitors come to Hiiumaa to enjoy its amazing natural beauty and revitalizing atmosphere. The shallow waters off the northeast coast are very popular for canoeing and kayaking in the summer, and numerous hiking and cycling routes traverse the island. Public transport is limited and is best not relied on as the main means of getting around.

Kärdla

🏠 4,000. 🛈 Hiiu 1, 462 2232. 🖵 **hiiumaa.ee** Hiiumaa Museum: Vabriku Väljak 8. **Open** 10am–5pm Mon–Fri. 🅿

This small town is of interest primarily as a base for exploring Hiiumaa. However, it is also a picturesque place, full of pretty wooden houses, nearly all of which have well-tended gardens. A branch of the **Hiiumaa Museum** is housed in a one-storey wooden building which was the home of a Swedish manager of a textiles factory in the 19th century. A seaside park lies just north of the museum and is filled with families and sunbathers throughout the summer.

The **Hill of Crosses** (Ristimägi), located 4 km (2 miles) west of Kärdla, is an impressive sight. The hill is packed with crosses made out of local wood. It is believed that the tradition of placing crosses at the site began with the deportation of Swedes in 1781 by the Russians. Today, most of the new crosses at the site are brought by tourists.

🏠 Suuremõisa Manor
Suuremõisa.

Although Estonians customarily refer to Suuremõisa (Big Manor) as a castle, it is actually a manor house. It was built in 1755 for Ebba Margaretha Stenbock, a relative of the powerful de la Gardie family, who owned much of Hiiumaa until the Russians acquired it in 1710. The widowed Stenbock lived in the manor with her children, after winning back the rights to her ancestral land. In 1796, the manor was bought by a shipping magnate who was deported to Siberia in 1803

Key

— Major road

= Minor road

For keys to symbols see back flap

The Sprawling Suuremõisa Manor, fronted by a verdant lawn

for murdering one of his ships' captains in the house. There are 64 rooms in this grand manor, which currently houses two schools. Although the interior is not open to the public, it is possible to take a stroll around the manor's vast grounds.

🏕 Kassari

🗺 90. 🚌 from Kärdla. 🛒 🏔
Hiiumaa Museum: **Open** May–Aug: 10am–5:30pm Mon–Sun. 🎫

A small island connected to Hiiumaa by a causeway, Kassari is known for its natural beauty. The 18th-century Kassari chapel-turned-church is the only functioning church with a reed roof in Estonia. Near the church is the village of Kassari itself, home to the **Hiiumaa Museum**, which gives an overview of Hiiumaa from the Stone Age through to the present. The island culminates in the stunning Sääre Tirp peninsula in the south, a 2-km (1-mile) spit that can be covered on foot or by car.

The Orjaku Nature Trail explores Käina Bay, a major bird sanctuary. The coastal water around Kassari is said to be the warmest in Estonia and the island has plenty of good beaches, especially in the south. With only four villages, Kassari retains its peace even in the height of summer.

🔆 Kõpu Lighthouse

Kõpu village, 35 km (22 miles) W of Kärdla. **Open** May–end Sep: 10am–8pm daily. **Tel** 469 3474. 🎫 🛒

Midway along the rocky Kõpu peninsula, this is the world's third-oldest working lighthouse. Built on the highest hill of Hiiumaa, it was commissioned by the Hanseatic League in 1500 and completed in 1531. At the end of the 1980s, the crumbling edifice was reinforced with four thick sloping buttresses, giving it its highly distinctive appearance.

The equally distinct Ristna Lighthouse (1874) stands only 10 km (6 miles) further west, at the tip of the peninsula.

Kõpu Lighthouse, one of the world's oldest functioning lighthouses

➏ Lihula

Road Map C2. 🗺 1,600. ℹ Tiigi 5, 477 8191. 🔳 lihula.ee

The quiet town of Lihula leads to Matsalu National Park (see p93) and also serves as the last stopping-off point en route to the islands of Muhu and Saaremaa. Lihula was the site of a major castle in the 13th century, which was almost destroyed during the Livonian Wars (1558–83). The impressive ruins stand atop a hill offering spectacular views of the region. Housed in an old manor house, the nearby **Lihula Museum** offers a comprehensive account of the town's history.

🏛 Lihula Museum

Linnuse tee 1. **Tel** 477 8880.
Open irregular hours; call for timings.

➐ Muhu Island

Road Map C2. 🚌 from Tallinn, Pärnu. 🚌 from Virtsu. 🛒 🖥 🎫
🔳 muhu.info

Most people generally pass through Muhu Island on their way to Saaremaa without spending much time here. However, Muhu is an extremely attractive island whose small size makes it easy to explore. The village of Liiva, just 6 km (4 miles) from the ferry terminal, is home to the 13th-century St Catherine's Church, while the nearby coastal village of **Koguva** is a picturesque ensemble of stone farmhouses with thatched roofs.

Muhu Island has preserved its charming tradition of brightly painted farmhouse doors, some of which depict symbols that are said to keep evil spirits away.

The rugged natural beauty of the island also makes it a wonderful place for long walks, especially along the pristine coastline.

Stone farmhouses in the fishing village of Koguva, Muhu Island

8 Saaremaa Island

Saaremaa is Estonia's largest island and the jewel of its archipelago. The capital, Kuressaare, is a strikingly picturesque town whose relatively tranquil atmosphere makes it an ideal base from which to explore the island. The place has a lot to offer in terms of things to see and do, but its extraordinary natural beauty is the real attraction and the reason why so many people feel compelled to return here. The breathtaking landscape of Vilsandi National Park, the abundance of old churches and the fascinating historic relics dotted throughout the island are just some of the main highlights *(see pp98–9)*.

Art Nouveau lion statues outside the information centre, Kuressaare

★ Vilsandi National Park
Known for its awe-inspiring landscapes, unspoiled islets and bird sanctuaries, this park was established in 1993 to preserve the ecology of Estonia's coast.

0 km   5
0 miles   5

Sõrve Peninsula
The scenery along Sõrve Peninsula is some of the most spectacular on the island, culminating in the magnificently wild and windswept tip. The best way to explore the ravishing coastline is to take a bike or car trip.

Key
━━ Major road
═ Minor road
- - Ferry route
-·- Park boundary

For hotels and restaurants see pp297–8 and pp316–18

★ **Angla Windmills**
Standing along the main road from Kuressaare to Leisi, the five wooden windmills at Angla are an iconic symbol of Saaremaa Island and one of Estonia's most photographed sights.

Poppy Fields
Due to its temperate climate and fertile soil, Saaremaa has over 200 local species of flora. Orchids and poppies grow wild in some parts.

KEY

① **Mihkli Farm Museum,** an authentic 19th-century farmstead, offers a fascinating glimpse into rural life on the island in the past.

② **Kihelkonna Church,** a splendid 13th-century place of worship, has a steeple that was added in 1897.

③ **Kiipsaare Lighthouse**

④ **Kaarma Church,** which dates from the 13th century, has a striking 15th-century pulpit.

★ **Bishop's Castle**
The formidable castle is the most important landmark in Kuressaare. It has Teutonic order architecture with a powerful defence tower and a slender watchtower. Today the castle houses an informative museum.

For keys to symbols *see back flap*

Exploring Saaremaa Island

The best way to explore Saaremaa Island is by car. The island's size makes it difficult to visit the major sights by bicycle, while public transport is extremely limited and erratic. Saaremaa has excellent, well-signposted roads on the whole, although bumpy dirt tracks are common in the more remote parts. The majority of visitors stay in Kuressaare but there is an abundance of excellent farmstead-style guesthouses scattered throughout Saaremaa for a more authentic experience of rustic island life. All the major sights are within comfortable driving distance of the capital.

Buildings interspersed with greenery in the attractive town of Kuressaare

Kuressaare

🚂 16,000. ✈ 4 km (2 miles) SW of town centre. 🛈 Tallinna 2. 🎭 St John's Eve (23 Jun). 🖾 **kuressaare.ee**

This small, attractive and serene town epitomizes the spirit of Saaremaa. Kuressaare's main thoroughfare, Lossi, which turns into Tallinna, is lined with a stunning stretch of beautiful buildings, including the green-domed St Nicholas's Church (Nikolai kirik) and the step-gabled Weigh House, which now serves as a pub known as Vaekoja. Most of all, though, the town makes a delightful place for a stroll, especially on a pleasant evening.

🏰 Bishop's Castle

Lossihoov 1, Kuressaare. **Tel** 455 7542. **Open** May–Aug: 10am–6pm daily; Sep–Apr: 11am–6pm Wed–Sun. 🅿 🎟 call in advance. 🖵 🖾 **saaremaamuuseum.ee**

Dating back to the 14th century, the Bishop's Castle (Piiskopilinnus) in Kuressaare is one of the best-preserved medieval castles in the Baltic States. Built out of local dolomite, it is a spectacular sight, as visitors approach it through the surrounding landscaped park. The castle houses the intriguing Saaremaa Regional Museum, whose labyrinthine interior is a joy to explore. The exhibits about Saaremaa are well arranged and offer a vivid account of the island's epic history.

Highlights of the castle include the Bishop's Living Quarters with a dingy, spartan little room where the resident bishop could retire for reflection, and a particularly eye-catching medieval lavatory.

Kaali Meteor Crater

Kaali. 🚌 from Kuressaare to Kõnnu, 15 km (9 miles) NE, then walk for 3 km (2 miles). 🛈 Kaali Visitors' Centre, 459 1184. 🅿 🖾 🖾 **kaali.kylastuskeskus.ee**

The meteor crater at Kaali is arguably one of the most extraordinary geological sights in Estonia. At first glance, it appears to be a small lake, until visitors notice the perfectly rounded banks above the water and the protruding shards of dolomite that were thrown up by the impact.

Scientists estimate that the meteor struck sometime between 4,000 and 7,500 years ago. With a diameter of 110 m (360 ft), the crater is the eighth-largest in the world, and it exudes atmosphere, inspiring visitors to look upwards.

🏰 Angla Windmills

15 km (9 miles) N of Kaali. 🚌 from Kuressaare.

Lined up along the Upa–Leisi road, the five Angla Windmills (Angla tuulikud) are the last remaining group of windmills in Saaremaa. In the mid-19th century, there were 800 working windmills on the island. Four of the Angla Windmills are constructed on the traditional Saaremaa model, while the largest is a wooden version of a Dutch windmill. Together, they form a mesmerizing sight amid the wide open landscape. Although the windmills are not

The Bishop's Living Quarters set in the lush grounds of the Bishop's Castle

For hotels and restaurants see pp297–8 and pp316–18

Two of the five Angla Windmills, standing tall in an open landscape

open to the public, there is a wonderful assortment of traditional play apparatus for children just behind them.

Karja Church

2 km (1 mile) NE of Angla Windmills, Karja village. **Open** mid-May–mid-Sep: 10am–6pm daily.

The medieval Karja Church (Karja kirik) is the smallest church in Saaremaa, but also one of the most beautiful. It is well known for its elaborate stone carvings, which include a relief of the Crucifixion above the side door and some remarkable figures inside depicting saints. There is also a famous bas relief showing Mary and John at Cavalry, along with the two thieves whose souls depart their bodies in the form of children.

Stone carving outside Karja Church

Kaarma Church

15 km (9 miles) NW of Kuressaare, Kaarma village. **Tel** 459 5322. **Open** no regular opening hours.

Dating from the 13th century, Kaarma Church (Kaarma kirik) is one of the oldest churches in Western Estonia. A stone tablet over the front portal attests to repairs made to the church in 1407 and is considered to be the first written example of the Estonian language. The 15th-century pulpit with a polychrome figure of Joseph beneath it is especially impressive. The church may appear incongruously large, standing in the middle of nowhere, but people once flocked here for Sunday services from the surrounding villages.

Mihkli Farm Museum

28 km (17 miles) NW of Kuressaare. Viki. **Tel** 454 6613. **Open** mid-May–Aug: 10am–6pm daily; Sep–mid-Oct: 10am–6pm Wed–Sun. **saaremaamuuseum.ee**

In the sleepy village of Viki, the Mihkli Farm Museum (Mihkli talumuuseum) is a picturesque farmstead consisting of beautiful thatched cottages, a windmill, a brewery and even an old sauna. Most of the buildings date from 1827–56. The museum has authentic displays of rural architecture and traditional living styles. The farm was active until Soviet times, when collectivization broke it up. Today, visitors can learn traditional methods of making bread and butter.

Kihelkonna Church

3 km (2 miles) NW of Kihelkonna. **Tel** 454 6558. **Open** Jun–Aug: 10am–5pm daily.

On the west coast of the island, along the border of Vilsandi National Park, this 13th-century church is a treasure trove of religious architecture and artifacts. The organ, built in 1805, is the oldest in the country, while the beautiful pulpit dates from 1604. The altar triptych, *The Last Supper*, is a superb example of Renaissance church art.

Vilsandi National Park

10 km (6 miles) W of Kihelkonna. from Papisaare. **Tel** 454 6510. Vilsandi National Park Visitors' Centre, Loona Manor. **Open** 9am–5pm Mon–Fri. **vilsandi.ee**

This huge national park comprises Vilsandi Island along with some 150 islets and a narrow strip of coast culminating in the rugged Harilaid Peninsula. The park was established thanks to a lighthouse keeper named Artur Toom, who set up a bird sanctuary here in 1910. The 239-sq-km (92-sq-mile) park in its present form was founded in 1993.

The most significant bird sanctuaries are located on the Vaika Islands, off the western tip of Vilsandi, from where the imposing 40-m (131-ft) Vilsandi Lighthouse can be seen. For some of the most striking scenery, head to the Harilaid Peninsula. From here, it is possible to take an invigorating hike up to the leaning lighthouse. The trail offers evocative scenery.

Display showing the interior of a rural household, Mihkli Farm Museum

The leaning Kiipsaare Lighthouse, Harilaid Peninsula, Saaremaa Island ▶

❾ Pärnu

Often referred to as Estonia's summer capital, Pärnu has historic buildings, pastel-coloured wooden houses and elegant late 19th-century villas set along leafy streets. The town centre is situated on an estuary between the Pärnu river and the Baltic Sea, with all the main sights located within walking distance. The Old Town is centred around the pedestrianized Rüütli Street, with the most popular beach a 10-minute walk away. With an ultra-modern concert hall and high-quality theatre, Pärnu also has an exciting cultural scene.

🏛 Town Hall
Uus 4/Nikolai 3.

The elegant Neo-Classical building that is now the Town Hall was erected in 1797 as a wealthy merchant's residence. In 1819, the structure was slightly altered to serve as the house for the town's governor and, in 1839, it took on its current function as Pärnu's Town Hall. What makes it worth visiting is the magnificent Art Nouveau extension built in 1911. Its brooding dark exterior is in total contrast to the bright yellow façade of the original structure and provides a fascinating juxtaposition of two radically different architectural styles.

⛪ Elizabeth's Church
Nikolai 22. **Tel** 443 1381. **Open** Jun–Aug: 10am–6pm daily, Sep–May: 10am–2pm Mon–Fri. 🛈
🌐 eliisabet.ee

Another excellent example of local Baroque architecture, Elizabeth's Church (Eliisabeti kirik) has an elegant ochre exterior and a maroon spire towering above the surrounding narrow side streets. It was founded specifically as a Lutheran church, in 1747, by the Russian Empress Elizabeth (1709–61). Today, it serves as the largest Protestant place of worship in Pärnu.

The wood-panelled interior is refined and understated, but all the more impressive for it. The church's spire was built by Johann Heinrich Wülbern, who also constructed Rīga's St Peter's Church. Elizabeth's Church is also renowned for its organ, one of the best in Estonia, built in 1929 by H Kolbe.

Green domes and yellow walls of St Catherine's Church

⛪ St Catherine's Church
Vee 16. **Tel** 444 3198. **Open** 9am–5pm daily. 🛈

Built in 1768 for the Pärnu garrison during the reign of Catherine the Great, St Catherine's Church (Ekateriina kirik) is arguably the finest Baroque church in Estonia. With bottle-green domes and lemon-yellow walls, the church boasts an elegant exterior and an equally opulent interior. Intended as an architectural showpiece, St Catherine's had a significant influence on Orthodox churches throughout the Baltic States.

🎭 Pärnu Concert Hall
Aida 4. **Tel** 445 5800. **Open** 10am–6pm Mon–Fri, 10am–4pm Sat (box office). 🅿 ♿ 🏛 🌐 concert.ee

The Pärnu Concert Hall is a source of great pride for local people. The curvaceous glass and steel building is a strong example of modern architecture in the country and compares favourably with similar structures in other European cities. Its seashell-like shape was intended to symbolize Pärnu's status as a coastal town. The multifunctional building mostly hosts theatre performances and concerts, although it also houses an art gallery, music school and music shop.

🏛 Tallinn Gate
Mere pst.

The only trace of the 17th-century ramparts that protected Pärnu at one time, Tallinn Gate still offers a significant glimpse of the once impressive fortifications. Until 1710, when Swedish rule came to an end, it was known as Gustav's Gate, named after King Gustav Adolphus of Sweden (1594–1632).

Today, the Tallinn Gate's only function is to provide an elegant portal between the Old Town and the area leading to the sea. The cobblestoned passageway offers a pleasant walk.

Verdant setting of the Tallinn Gate, formerly known as Gustav's Gate

Detail featuring an Art Nouveau mask, Ammende Villa

🏛 Ammende Villa

Mere pst 7. **Tel** 447 3888. *See Where to Stay p298 and Where to Eat and Drink p317.* 🔲 ammende.ee

Built in 1905 by a wealthy local merchant for the wedding party of his beloved daughter, Ammende Villa is one of the most impressive examples of Art Nouveau architecture in the country. Over the years, it has served as a casino, a health establishment and a library, before two Estonian business-men renovated it and converted it into a luxury hotel, with a beautiful fine-dining restaurant. The villa is located a short walk from the sea and the Old Town.

🏛 Lydia Koidula Museum

J V Jannseni 37. **Tel** 443 3313. **Open** 10am–6pm Tue–Sun. 🔲 🔲 call in advance. 🔲 parnumuuseum.ee

A short walk across the Pärnu river, the Lydia Koidula Museum provides a moving testimony to Estonia's most revered female poet. Established in 1945, it is situated in the building where her father, Johann Valdemar Jannsen, ran a primary school from 1857 to 1863.

A highlight of the museum is a reconstruction of the bedroom where Koidula died of cancer in 1886 in the Russian town of Kronstadt. Although very little of Lydia Koidula's work is available in English, the museum is worth visiting for an interesting insight into Estonian literature of the period.

Lydia Koidula (1843–86)

Lydia Emilia Florentine Jannsen is a highly influential figure in Estonian history. Although she was forced to write under the pseudonym Koidula, meaning "of the dawn", because writing was not considered a suitable career for a woman at that time, her poetry was ecstatically received. Her *My Country is My Love* became the unofficial national anthem during Soviet times. Some critics believe that Koidula's finest writing was her passionate correspondence with the writer Friedrich Reinhold Kreutzwald, although his jealous wife eventually put an end to it. Koidula later married a Lavian doctor. She died of cancer in Kronstadt, in the Gulf of Finland, pining for her country to the last.

Lydia Koidula, a major Estonian writer and poet

Pärnu

① Town Hall
② Elizabeth's Church
③ St Catherine's Church
④ Pärnu Concert Hall
⑤ Tallinn Gate
⑥ Ammende Villa

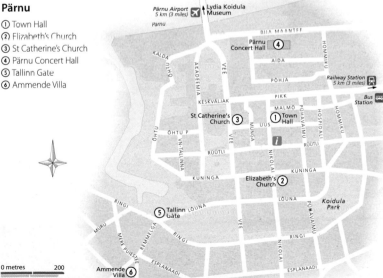

0 metres 200
0 yards 200

⑩ Soomaa National Park

Soomaa National Park, an enchanting self-enclosed world of bogs, rivers, swampland, meadows and virgin forest, was established in 1993. The 390-sq-km (151-sq- mile) park gets flooded in spring, which locals call the "fifth season". However, Soomaa's five bogs are its best natural feature. Approximately 6 m (20 ft) high in places, they can be accessed along a series of hiking trails set on wooden platforms. The park's stunning wildlife includes wolves, roe deer, brown bears, lynx, elk, wild boar and lesser spotted eagles.

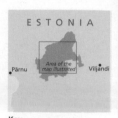

Key
Soomaa National Park

★ Riisa Bog Trail
The 5-km (3-mile) long bog trail, close to the border of the park, culminates in a group of bog pools.

Ingatsi Bog Trail
Half of the 4-km (2-mile) trail is a boardwalk that leads through swamp forest and bog pools.

Karuskose Farm
Close to hiking trails and bog-land, this farm offers guided walks, fishing, canoeing and traditional canoe-building courses.

Key
= Minor road
··· Trail
= = Park boundary

For keys to symbols *see back flap*

★ Tõramaa Wooded Meadow Trail
A 2-km (1-mile) walk leads to this pretty trail, which allows visitors to explore the park and its well-preserved meadow.

Flora
The peat moss of the bogs is ideal for heather, cranberries and Labrador tea. The sundew plant gets additional nutrition by catching insects.

Kihnu Jõnn's grave on Linaküla, the main village on Kihnu Island

⓫ Kihnu Island

Road Map C2. 🄿 600. ✈ from Pärnu. 🚢 from Munalaid, 40 km (25 miles) SW of Pärnu. 🆆 kihnu.ee

The tiny island of Kihnu has a significant place in Estonian culture. It is the only part of the country where women still wear traditional dress and the islanders continue to live largely traditional lifestyles. Fishing remains a major source of income, as do the much-admired handmade clothes and mittens. There are four villages on the island, but as it is only 7 km (4 miles) long and 3.5 km (2 miles) wide, it is easy to get around.

In the main village of **Linaküla** lies the grave of the legendary Kihnu Jõnn (1848–1913), the island's most famous inhabitant. Born on Kinhu, Jõnn was a larger-than-life, hard-drinking sailor who sailed around the globe.

⓬ Tori Stud Farm
Tori hobusekasvandus

Pärnu mnt 13, Tori. **Road Map** D2. 🚐 from Pärnu. **Tel** 503 1892. **Open** 8am–5pm Mon–Fri. 🄿 call one day in advance. 🆆 torihobune.ee

Situated in the beautiful village of Tori, Tori Stud Farm is a good stopping-off point on the way to nearby Soomaa National Park. Estonia's oldest horse farm, it was established in 1856 by the Livonian gentry with the aim of breeding a strong local stock. After several failed attempts at improving the local breed, a crossbred Norfolk-Roadster horse was brought in, which became the basis for the new breed. The stud farm is still used for breeding purposes today, although its horses are far more likely to be used for giving horse-riding lessons than for ploughing the fields.

Tori Stud Farm is also a worthwhile excursion in itself. Visitors to the farm can partake in a range of activities, including a guided tour of the farm which introduces them to some of the 90-odd horses. Those interested in old-fashioned transport can take a tour of the farm and village in a horse-driven carriage for a small fee charged on an hourly basis. It is possible to go sleigh-riding in winter.

The farm also boasts a wonderful little museum situated in a thatched wooden barn. Its collection features a fascinating assortment of exhibits relating to the history of horse-breeding as well as the history of the local village.

Tori Stud Farm, breeder of some of Estonia's finest horses

EASTERN ESTONIA

The landscape of Eastern Estonia, punctuated with rolling hills, lush forests, limestone escarpments and pristine lakes, is more diverse than the country's western part. This truly fascinating region combines idyllic scenery with picturesque old manor houses and the unique cultural heritage of the Setu people and Old Believers, which have survived through the centuries.

Despite its stunning landscape, some parts of Eastern Estonia are less frequented by tourists, especially the far northeast, southeast and around Lake Peipsi. The vast mass of Lake Peipsi dominates the central part of this region. The western shores of the lake are dotted with the sizeable settlements of Russian Old Believers who have been living here for countless generations.

Captured and conquered repeatedly by Russians from 1558 until Estonia's independence in 1991, the historic fortress city of Narva still bears testimony to the enormous role Russia has played in shaping Estonia's history. During World War II, the value of oil-shale mining rose significantly, bringing Kohtla-Järve into sharp focus. Today, this heavily industrial town serves as a vast, sprawling living monument to Soviet-era industry.

East of Tallinn, Lahemaa National Park is arguably the most beautiful of the country's nature reserves for the variety of its landscape and natural features. Further along, the Ontika Coast, with its huge limestone escarpments and cascading waterfalls, is breathtaking.

Sights of political, historic and social history abound in the southeast as a whole. Viljandi is famous for its Folk Music Festival, while Estonia's national flag was sanctified in Otepää, the winter sports capital, where snowboarding and ice skating bring the town to life. Tartu, Estonia's second-largest city and its spiritual and intellectual capital, is home to the nation's oldest university. With attractions such as the grand Sangaste Manor and the captivating Suur Munamägi viewing tower at the country's highest point, the south and southeast are among Estonia's most scenic areas. In the far southeast, the ethnographically distinct Setu people continue to live traditionally.

Migrating flock of gulls flying across Lake Peipsi

◄ Cathedral ruins rebuilt during the 19th-century as the university library, Tartu

Exploring Eastern Estonia

Eastern Estonia has strikingly diverse attractions. Lahemaa National Park boasts some of the country's most beautiful landscapes, with countless villages dotted throughout the area. A stunning coastline stretches to the medieval city of Narva and the pristine beach at Narva-Jõesuu. To the south is Lake Peipsi. The picturesque landscape of the southeast provides a beautiful backdrop to attractive towns such as Viljandi and Otepää, as well as to countless places of historic significance. Tartu makes an ideal base from which to explore the region.

| 0 kilometres | 20 |
| 0 miles | 20 |

Sights at a Glance

Towns, Cities and Resorts

- **4** Sillamäe
- **5** Narva
- **6** Narva-Jõesuu
- **7** Kuremäe
- **8** Rakvere
- **9** Väike-Maarja
- **11** Paide
- **12** Põltsamaa
- **13** *Tartu pp118–21*
- **15** Viljandi
- **16** Otepää
- **19** Rõuge
- **21** Vastseliina
- **22** Võru
- **23** Põlva

Buildings and Sights of Interest

- **2** Kohtla Underground Mining Museum
- **17** Sangaste Manor
- **18** Mõniste Open-Air Museum
- **24** Kiidjärve Watermill

National Parks and Reserves

- **1** *Lahemaa National Park pp110–113*
- **10** Endla Nature Reserve

Areas of Natural Beauty

- **3** Ontika Coast
- **14** Lake Võrtsjärv
- **20** Suur Munamägi
- **25** Taevaskoja Sandstone Cliffs

Tour

- **26** *Lake Peipsi p127*

Medieval Ivangorod Castle, seen from Narva

For hotels and restaurants see pp298–9 and pp318–19

Getting Around

Highway 1 (the E20 under the European system) leads east out of Tallinn and skirts Lahemaa National Park before following the coast to Narva. Highway 2 (E263) connects Tartu and Võru and Highway 3 (E264) links Tartu and Valga, skirting the northern part of Lake Peipsi along the way. The town of Rakvere also has a road leading to Tartu. A railway connects Tallinn with Rakvere, Narva, Tartu and Viljandi. Tartu also has a small airport. In the southeast an intricate network of signposted dirt roads connects most of the villages in the area.

Fishing village in Lahemaa National Park

Key

= Motorway

= Main road

— Secondary road

=== Minor road

— Scenic route

-- Railway

■ International border

△ Peak

For keys to symbols see back flap

❶ Lahemaa National Park

Extending across the north coast of Estonia, Lahemaa National Park, or Lahemaa Rahvuspark, is a nature lover's paradise. It is the largest park in Estonia and also the first area to be designated a national park in the erstwhile Soviet Union. The diverse terrain covers four peninsulas jutting out into the Gulf of Finland and stretches inland over an area of 725 sq km (280 sq miles). The park teems with wildlife and has several marked trails through its forests and bogs and along its meandering coastline. Many impressive manor houses and picturesque villages can be found throughout the area (see pp112–13).

Key
▢ Lahemaa National Park

Viinistu
Once a fishing village, Viinistu has developed into a local cultural centre. It is home to an impressive art gallery.

★ Käsmu Peninsula
The rugged coastline of Käsmu Peninsula, strewn with giant boulders left behind by retreating glaciers after the last Ice Age, has an ethereal beauty.

Flora and Fauna
With forest covering more than 70 per cent of Lahemaa, the area is rich in flora and fauna. The landscape has many raised bogs, including the 7,000-year-old Laukasoo Reserve. The thriving wildlife includes a population of wolves, bear and lynx.

0 km 2
0 miles 2

Key
= Minor road
··· Trail
-- Park boundary

Võsu
A beautiful stretch of beach, a tranquil atmosphere and stunning natural surroundings make this historic village a very popular holiday resort.

The Oandu Forest Nature Trail is a well-signposted 5-km (3-mile) long route. Wildlife can be seen foraging along the largely moss-covered path.

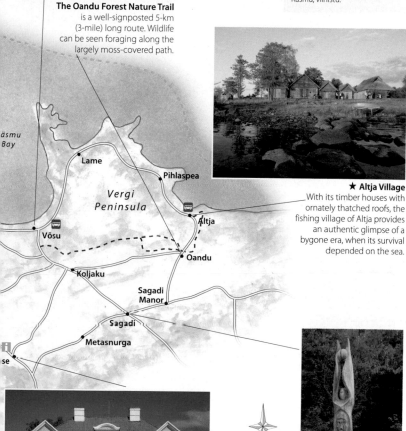

★ **Altja Village**
With its timber houses with ornately thatched roofs, the fishing village of Altja provides an authentic glimpse of a bygone era, when its survival depended on the sea.

Sagadi Manor
The grounds of Sagadi Manor, one of the most attractive of the region's manor houses, are filled with sculptures, while its numerous outhouses include the Forestry Museum.

★ **Palmse Manor House**
The stately Baroque house has now been restored as a museum, while its converted outhouses and extensive grounds offer several other attractions.

For keys to symbols *see back flap*

Exploring Lahemaa National Park

The sheer size of Lahemaa National Park makes getting around it by bike or car the best option. When driving to Lahemaa along the Tallinn-Narva Highway, turn off at the crossroads at Viitna and head north towards Palmse village, where there is a National Park Visitors' Centre. From Palmse, it is a relatively short drive to all the main villages, sites and areas of natural beauty. Käsmu and Võsu make convenient hiking and cycling bases, with plenty of good accommodation, although most places are often booked up well in advance during summer.

Regal interior of the ornately decorated Palmse Manor House

🏛 Palmse Manor House
8 km (5 miles) N of Viitna. **Tel** 324 0070. **Open** May–Sep: 10am–7pm daily, Oct–Apr: 10am–6pm daily. 📷 call in advance. ♿ 🚻 💻 🌐 **palmse.ee**

The attractive village of Palmse is the ideal starting point for a tour of the enchanting Lahemaa National Park. It also has a well-run visitors' centre. The focus of the village is the splendid Palmse Manor House, an elegant Baroque building that originally served as a Cistercian convent. In 1677, it became the family home of the von Pahlens, a leading family of Baltic barons.

Today, the manor house serves as a museum, offering an interesting overview of the estate's history. The old distillery has been converted into a hotel with an excellent restaurant, while a lovely café now occupies the bathhouse.

The manor house runs a wine tour, where visitors can enjoy a glass of sparkling wine or locally produced wine made from berries grown in the nearby Brest Pavilion. The manor grounds are beautifully landscaped. In summer, visitors can take a boat tour of the serene Swan Lake and soak up the surrounding tranquility.

🏖 Võsu
8 km (5 miles) N of Palmse. 🏠 480. 🚌 from Tallinn. 🚻 💻 🌐 **lahemaa.ee**

A charming and quiet little coastal village, Võsu is a popular holiday resort. Its peaceful ambience and stunning natural beauty have made it a favourite summer getaway for families

Tourists enjoying themselves at the pine-fringed beach in Võsu

since the late 19th century. The resort is 2 km (1 mile) long and packed with elegant wooden houses from end to end.

The most distinctive building in the village is the old Fire Tower, which now houses an art gallery. Its beach, with its Blue Flag status, is also one of the most attractive along the north coast. With its soft white sand and pine-fringed dunes, it offers gentle shade during the hot summer days. It is also a convenient base for further explorations of Oandu and Altja.

🏖 Käsmu
16 km (10 miles) N of Palmse.) 🏠 130. 🚻 💻 Käsmu Maritime Museum: **Tel** 323 8136. **Open** May–Sep: 10am–7pm daily; Oct–Apr: 10am–5pm Mon–Fri. 🌐 **kasmu.ee**

Approximately 6 km (4 miles) long and 3 km (2 miles) wide, Käsmu village is situated on the smallest of the four peninsulas in Lahemaa National Park. It is often referred to as the prettiest village in the region due to its proudly kept homesteads.

Käsmu has a history as a shipbuilding centre of repute in the 19th century, while the largely ice-free bay made it a regular place of anchor in winter. A maritime school was set up in the village in 1884 and the building now houses the **Käsmu Maritime Museum**. The museum's emphasis is on the 1920s and 30s through World War II and the Soviet era, and it has an eclectic collection of artifacts honouring the village's seafaring past.

Käsmu is also called the Captain's Village, because of the 62 captains who resided here between World War I and World War II. It was decimated by the Soviets in the 1940s, with many families sent to Siberia and others fleeing across the sea.

Today, the village enjoys a reputation as one of the best holiday resorts in the park. It also boasts a fascinating coastline strewn with giant erratic boulders, a large scattering of which lie in a stone field near the village. This is the highlight of the famous Käsmu Boulder Walk (*see p114*).

🦅 Altja

15 km (9 miles) E of Võsu. Altja Tavern:
Tel 520 9156. **Open** May–Sep: 11am–
9pm daily; Oct–Apr: 11am– 8pm
Sun–Thu, 11am–9pm Fri–Sat.
🏕 Oandu: 10 km (6 miles) S of Võsu.
🏕 free National Park campsite.
🌐 **altja.ee**

Situated to the east of Lahemaa
National Park, Altja is a lovely
tiny fishing village that skirts the
rugged coastline of the park. Its
main landmark is a large
wooden swing that
stands in an open
space at the eastern
end of the village.
Just beyond,
along the beach,
are the abandoned
huts of fishermen. The
village's timber
houses with
thatched roofs make
it seem like an open-air
museum. There is a picturesque
wooden suspension bridge.

**Water barrel,
Viinistu Art Museum**

Beyond Altja, in nearby
Oandu, there are two fantastic
nature trails where visitors can
get a taste of Lahemaa National
Park's varied forest landscape.
The 2-km (1-mile) long Oandu
Beaver Trail passes by several
beaver dams and countless
skilfully gnawed tree stumps.
The 5-km (3-mile) long circular
Oandu Forest Nature Trail
passes through sweet-smelling
and lush pine forest. Visitors are
likely to spot tracks left by
foraging wild boar, elk and
brown bears.

Viinistu

9 km (6 miles) W of Käsmu. 🏠 150.
🚌 🖥 Viinistu Art Museum: **Tel** 676
7888. **Open** 10am–6pm Wed–Sun.
🚗 🌐 **lahemaa.ee**

Lying on the eastern tip of the
Pärispea Peninsula, the village
of Viinistu is an
intriguing little place.
It profited from the
smuggling of
vodka to Finland
during prohibition
in the 1920s, but
during the Soviet
era it was incor-
porated into the
nearby Loksa indus-
trial complex.

Today, it has been reinvented
due to the efforts of Jaan
Manitsky (b.1943), a wealthy
local businessman who opened
a hotel and the **Viinistu Art
Museum** by the harbour. The
museum has an impressive
collection of 20th-century
Estonian art and uses two
converted water-towers for
temporary exhibitions.

The harbour has been
restored and it is possible to
travel northeast from Viinistu to
the barren Mohni Island.

The beautiful 18th-century manor house
at Sagadi Manor

🏛 Sagadi Manor

8 km (5 miles) NE of Palmse. **Tel** 676
7888. **Open** May–Sep: 10am–6pm
daily; Oct–Apr: by prior arrangement.
🚗 📷 call in advance. ♿ 🖥
🌐 **sagadi.ee**

Built in 1749, Sagadi Manor
(Sagadi mõis) consists of several
buildings symmetrically laid out
around a sprawling courtyard in
front, with a manicured park
and pond to the rear. The attractive 18th-century Baroque
manor house is now home to a
museum which offers an
authentic glimpse of the lives of
the Baltic-German aristocratic
family who lived here in the
mid-18th century. The manor
house later served as a primary
school and part of a collective
farm until it finally opened as a
museum in 1987.

The Baroque gatehouse, which
used to be the main entrance to
the manor house, is particularly
grand. There are also some truly
fascinating sculptures scattered
around the grounds.

Today, the outhouses on
one side of the courtyard are
occupied by the Forestry
Museum (Metsamuuseum),
which provides a detailed
overview of the diverse flora
and fauna of Estonia's forests.
Housed in the building nearby
is a hotel called Sagadi Manor
(see p298). A former bailiff's
residence now serves as the
Sagadi hostel. The historic estate
is also home to a Nature School
where ecological research is
carried out.

Wooden swing in the quaint fishing village of Altja

Käsmu Boulder Walk

The smallest of the four peninsulas in Lahemaa, Käsmu boasts the most impressive chain of boulders. These form a formidable outcrop in the shallow waters, creating a dramatic coastline. Old Jüri, the tallest boulder at 5.5 m (18 ft), lies just off the northwest tip. Starting from Käsmu village, a path leads along the coast to the northwest tip of the peninsula before turning back towards the village through dense forest. There are clearly marked hiking trails and a cycling route.

Cosy wooden cottage snuggled in the heart of Käsmu village

③ Scenic Views
One of the most stunning routes in the park, this path follows the whole length of the coast.

② Saartneem
A path leads from Käsmu village to the northwest tip of the peninsula, where a chain of erratic boulders stretches out to the island of Saartneem.

④ Cycle Route
The scenic bicycle route is about 14 km (9 miles) long and is marked with blue ribbons.

① Käsmu Village
Käsmu village is one of the most popular resorts in Lahemaa. With plenty of B&B accommodation, it is an ideal base for exploring the Käsmu Peninsula as a whole, as well as the other regions of Lahemaa.

Key

••• Walk route
▬ Bicycle route
═ Other road

⑤ Erratic Boulders
The Stone Plantation on the trail west of Käsmu village has a bizarre expanse of boulders. These attract a large number of visitors to the area.

Tips for Walkers

Starting point: Käsmu village.
Length: 11 km (7 miles).
Walking trails: An 11-km (7-mile) long path marked with red ribbons leads north of Käsmu village from Old Jüri. A shorter walk is the path west of Käsmu village, which leads through the Stone Plantation.

0 km   1
0 miles   1

❷ Kohtla Underground Mining Museum
Kohtla kaevanduspark-muuseum

Road Map E1. **Tel** 332 4017. 🚌 from Kohtla-Järve. **Open** May–Sep: 11am–7pm Tue–Sat, 11am–5pm Sun & Mon; Oct–Apr: 10am–6pm Tue–Sat. 🅿 🎫 book in advance. ✎ summer only. 🅆 **kaevanduspark.ee**

Undoubtedly one of the most fascinating museums in Estonia, Kohtla Underground Mining Museum is located in the sprawling industrial area of Kohtla-Nõmme. Set in a massive oil-shale mining complex, the museum operates guided tours in which the history, technology and purpose of mining are explained before visitors are taken to explore the dark, damp labyrinth of the mines.

Visitors can see the infernal mining machines at work and can even attempt to drill for oil-shale or ride an underground bike. There is also the added option of sampling a miner's lunch under ground.

The outdoor tour continues on to the very impressive mountains of mined stone and it is possible to see one of the biggest diggers in the world. Wall and mountain climbing are some of the adventure sports offered here. Located nearby is the vast industrial town of Kohtla-Järve. A small town

Exhibit at the intriguing Kohtla Underground Mining Museum

before World War II, it saw speedy development during the Soviet era with the expansion of the oil-shale mines in the area.

❸ Ontika Coast

Road Map E1. 🚌 from Tallinn to Jõhvi, then bus or taxi to Toila, Ontika. 🅆 **ida-virumaa.ee**

The coastal limestone cliff of Ontika forms one of the most striking areas of natural beauty in Estonia. Sprawling over almost 20 km (12 miles) between Saka and Toila, the Ontika cliff is the highest point of the North Estonian limestone escarpment. At Ontika, the cliff reaches a height of 57 m (184 ft) and offers a view across the Gulf of Finland. **Valaste**, which lies 5 km (3 miles) east, has Estonia's highest waterfall. The 26-m (85-ft) stream of cascading

water has carved its way through a bed of 470 to 570 million-year-old rocks to create an amazing sight.

Environs
The beautiful **Oru Park, Toila** is located 14 km (9 miles) east of Ontika Coast and is worth visiting. The park is spread out over an area of 1 sq km (0.4 sq m) along the coast.

❹ Sillamäe

Road Map E1. 🏚 17,000. 🚌 from Tallinn, Narva. 🅆 **sillamae.ee**

Situated midway between Kohtla-Järve and Narva, Sillamäe makes for a fascinating excursion. This Soviet-era town was the site of a uranium mine for the Soviet nuclear programme. However, it was so secret that it was not even marked on official maps.

The town is a living example of the more elegant side of late-Stalinist residential architecture. Many of the ornately decorated apartment blocks set along tree-lined boulevards and manicured parks are very attractive. The mine was closed in 1991 and a number of other industries have since moved in. Sillamäe is slowly but surely reinventing itself as an upcoming coastal and historical tourist destination of interest.

The limestone cliffs set against the azure Baltic Sea, Ontika Coast

❺ Narva

Road Map E1. 🏛 65,000. 🚆 from Tallinn. 🚌 from Tallinn, Tartu. ℹ️ Puškini 13, 356 0184. 🎭 Narva Days (early Jun), Narva History Festival (Aug). 🌐 **narva.ee**

After centuries of being bitterly fought over, Narva now marks the EU border with Russia. Although most of the city's much-admired medieval centre was levelled by the Soviet air force towards the end of World War II, there is still plenty to see and do.

On the west coast of the Narva river stands the impressive Narva Castle, whose main tower, Tall Hermann, houses the predominantly war-themed **Narva Museum**. A splendid riverside park surrounds the castle.

With a population that is 96 per cent Russian-speaking, Narva has a different feel from Tallinn. The city is also close to a number of attractions in the area.

🏛 **Narva Museum**
Tel 359 9230. **Open** 10am–6pm daily.
🌐 **narvamuuseum.ee**

Narva Castle, home to the war-themed Narva Museum

❻ Narva-Jõesuu

Road Map E1. 🏛 2,600. 🚌 from Narva. 🌐 **narva-joesuu.ee**

The attractive summer resort of Narva-Jõesuu is famed for its pristine beach. Lined with pine trees and old wooden houses, the beach stretches for 7 km (4 miles) from Narva-Jõesuu to Meriküla. It was a fashionable spa resort in the 19th century and was popular with St Petersburg's high society.

Exterior of Pühtitsa Convent in Kuremäe, partially hidden by trees

Present-day Narva-Jõesuu enjoys a white sandy beach, a lively nightlife and a booming water-sports industry.

❼ Kuremäe

Road Map E1. 🏛 370. 🚌 from Tallinn, Narva.

The small village of Kuremäe is celebrated for its Russian Orthodox **Pühtitsa Convent**, one of the most notable sights in Estonia. The convent was founded in 1891 and today some 150 nuns live there. There are six churches in the complex, which is dominated by the striking Dormition Cathedral, built in 1910. The convent is surrounded by a thick granite wall and has a majestic entrance gate with seven large bells. The bright façade and pristine appearance of the place gives

it a cheerful air. The convent also has a hostel for guests and pilgrims.

🏛 **Pühtitsa Convent**
Tel 337 0715. **Open** 7am–7pm daily.
🌐 **orthodox.ee**

❽ Rakvere

Road Map D1. 🏛 17,000. 🚌 from Tallinn, Narva. ℹ️ Laada 14, 324 2734. 🌐 **rakvere.ee**

The town of Rakvere, with restored historic buildings and a striking main square, has been transformed into an attractive tourist destination. Its most famous landmark, the 13th-century **Rakvere Castle** on Linnamägi Hill, is now a medieval theme park. The exhibits cover the castle's history from its early existence until it fell to ruins. A grand and slightly Picasso-esque statue of a bull, created by local

Statue of a bull on Vallimägi Hill, Rakvere

artist Tauno Kangro (b.1966), stands on top of Vallimägi Hill and is a new symbol for the town. Rakvere's inhabitants are proud of the fact that the renowned composer Arvo Pärt *(see p27)* went to school and began his music studies here.

Rakvere Castle
Vallimägi. **Tel** 322 5500. **Open** May–Sep: 11am–7pm daily; Oct–Apr: 10am–4pm Wed–Sun. 🎨 🚌 svm.ee

⑨ Väike-Maarja

Road Map D1. 🏔 5,000.
🚌 from Rakvere. ℹ️ Pikk 3, 326 1625.
🌐 v-maarja.ee

A typical parochial Estonian town, Väike-Maarja is steeped in history and has a number of quirky sights of interest. Housing the local tourism information centre, the **Väike-Maarja Museum** offers an eclectic and detailed overview of the town's history, including exhibits showing how the Forest Brothers *(see p122)* used to live. It is also possible to have a "Forest Brothers' picnic" in a reconstructed bunker. Other interesting sights include a Soviet missile base, the Vao Stronghold Tower Museum and the 14th-century town church.

Väike-Maarja Museum
Pikk 3. **Tel** 326 1625. **Open** May–Sep: 10am–5pm Tue–Sat; Oct–Apr: 10am–5pm Mon–Fri.

⑩ Endla Nature Reserve

Endla Looduskaitseala

Road Map D1. 🚌 from Tartu.
ℹ️ Reserve Headquarters, Tooma, 70 km (43 miles) NW of Tartu, 676 7999. 📞 call in advance.
🌐 endlakaitseala.ee

A scenic maze of peat bogs, rivers, swamp forests and lakes, the Endla Nature Reserve is considered to be one of the most important freshwater systems in the country. Although the reserve straddles three counties, its relatively small size makes it much easier

to explore than the larger national parks. One of the six hiking trails, the stunning **Männikjärve Trail,** stretches for 1 km (half a mile) over a long plank platform. To the east of the reserve, **Emumägi Hill** is the area's highest point. Its observation tower offers a superb view of the countryside.

The medieval octagonal tower amid castle ruins, Paide

⑪ Paide

Road Map D1. 🏔 9,000. 🚌 from Tallinn. ℹ️ Pärnu 6, 385 0400.
🌐 paide.ee

Located in the centre of Estonia, Paide makes the ideal base from which to explore the heartland of the country. To emphasize its central location, the town has adopted a heart shape as its official logo. Paide's biggest tourist draw is the beautifully restored 13th-century octagonal castle tower and surrounding ruins. The tower houses a museum focusing on the town's early history, while

the **Järvamaa Museum** offers a much broader look at the nature and history of the area. The Town Hall Square is the focal point of the well-kept town centre and offers a small variety of decent restaurants and cafés.

Järvamaa Museum
Lembitu 5. **Tel** 385 1867.
Open Apr–Oct: 11am–6pm Tue–Sat; Nov–Mar: 10am–5pm Tue–Sat. 🎨
🌐 jarvamaamuuseum.ee

⑫ Põltsamaa

Road Map D2. 🏔 5,000. 🚌 from Tallinn, Tartu. ℹ️ Lossi 1, 775 1390.
🌐 poltsamaa.ee

The idyllic town of Põltsamaa is set amid the ruins of Põltsamaa Castle. Once the centre of power for Duke Magnus, the king of Livonia in the 16th century, the castle stronghold is an amazingly eclectic jigsaw of architectural styles. The exquisite Rococo palace was built in the 18th century on the site of an old convent, while the elegant Lutheran **St Nicholas's Church** dates from 1633 and was re-constructed in 1952. Located in an old storehouse in the castle yard, the **Põltsamaa Museum** boasts some fine exhibits.

St Nicholas's Church
Lossi 3. **Tel** 776 9915. **Open** Jun–Aug: 10am–3pm daily 🕇 11am Sun. 🎨

Põltsamaa Museum
Loss tänav 1. **Tel** 775 1390.
Open May–Sep: 10am–6pm daily; Oct–Apr: 10am–4pm Mon–Sat. 🎨

Well-maintained church inside the castle grounds at Põltsamaa

⓭ Tartu

Best known for being home to the venerable Tartu University, the city is frequently referred to as the intellectual capital of Estonia. The university was founded in 1632 by King Gustav Adolphus of Sweden (1594–1632) and has played a major role in Estonian history ever since. With the second-largest population in the country, Tartu has a thriving cultural scene and exciting nightlife, and makes a convenient base from which to explore the southeast of the country.

Town Hall Square, with the Kissing Students Fountain in the centre

🏛 Town Hall Square

Tartu's historic centre is set around Town Hall Square (Raekoja plats), with the Emajõgi river in the front and Toomemägi (see pp120–21) just behind it. The gently sloping cobblestoned square is distinctly Neo-Classical, with the pink Town Hall overlooking it from the top. The Great Fire of 1775 burned down most of the city and today the square's Neo-Classical look is in sync with the rest of the city centre. The famous **Kissing Students Fountain**, in front of the Town Hall, was erected in 1998.

🏛 Tartu University Main Building

Ülikooli 18. **Tel** 737 5384. **Open** 11am–5pm Mon–Fri. 🚫 📷 ♿ 🅆 ut.ee
Finished in 1809, Tartu University Main Building (Tartu ülikooli peahoone) is one of Estonia's finest Neo-Classical buildings. It contains the impressive Art Museum, from where the imposing Assembly Hall and the far more amusing Lock-Up can be visited. Unruly students were confined to the Lock-Up as punishment, and their doodles and scribbles, which adorn its walls, make for amusing reading.

⛪ St John's Church

Jaani 5. **Tel** 744 2229. **Open** May–Sep: 10am–6pm Mon–Sat, 10am–1pm Sun. 🚫 ⛪ 11am Sun. 🅆 **jaanikirik.ee**
Dating from 1330, St John's Church (Jaani kirik) was severely damaged by bombing during World War II. However, even after extensive renovations and the addition of a new spire in 1999, the church remains one of the best examples of brick Gothic architecture in Northern Europe. Hundreds of elaborate terracotta figures, dating from the Middle Ages, adorn the church's interior. It is believed that there were originally more than 1,000 of them.

Tartu

① Town Hall Square
② Tartu University Main Building
③ St John's Church
④ Tartu Art Museum
⑤ Father and Son Statue

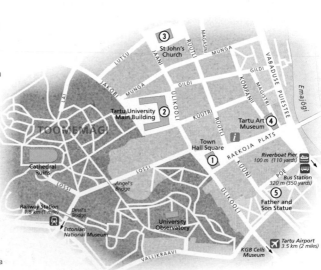

Key

▮ Street-by-Street area
see pp120–21

For keys to symbols *see back flap*

Leaning building in which the Tartu Art Museum is housed

🏛 Tartu Art Museum

Raekoja plats 18. **Tel** 744 1920.
Open 11am–6pm Wed–Sun. 🎫 📷
call in advance. 🖥 🅦 **tartmus.ee**

Housing one of the finest collections in the country, Tartu Art Museum (Tartu kunstimuuseum) features the works of prominent Estonian artists such as Elmar Kits (1913–72), Ülo Sooster (1924–70) and Marko Mäetamm (b.1965). A thorough and captivating overview of Estonian art, which spans the 19th century through to the present, is also provided. The museum's other impressive aspect is the building that houses it. Leaning conspicuously to one side, it belonged to the famous Russian Field Marshal Barclay de Tolly (see p122), who successfully led the Russian army against Napoleon in 1812.

Father and Son Statue

Küüni (close to Poe St).

Originally planned for Tallinn, this delightful little statue by Ülo Õun (1940–88) was conceived in 1977. It was cast in bronze in 1987, purchased by the Tartu Town Government in 2001 and, finally, unveiled on Children's Day (1 June) in 2004. The father figure is modelled after the sculptor, and the child is modelled after his son Kristjan, when he was around 18 months old. Interestingly, both father and son are proportionately equal in this highly unusual and extremely touching monument.

🏛 KGB Cells Museum

Riia 15b. **Tel** 746 1717. **Open** 11am–4pm Tue–Sat. 🎫 📷
🅦 **linnamuuseum.tartu.ee**

In the basement of the regional headquarters of the KGB/NKVD (People's Commissariat for Internal Affairs), the KGB Cells Museum (KGB kongid) offers grim testimony to the nightmare of the Soviet occupation. Some of the former cells have been turned into exhibition spaces, while others have been restored to their original condition to give a picture of what so many Estonians suffered under the Soviet regime. Much attention is paid to the mass deportations that took place between 1940 and 1949, including the official plans for carrying them out. There are gut-wrenching artifacts from the Gulags, the notorious correction camps where thousands of Estonians died.

A desk in the KGB Museum, with Stalin's portrait on the wall

VISITORS' CHECKLIST

Practical Information
Road Map E2. 🅰 100,000.
🛈 Raekoja plats 9, 744 2111. 📷
Tartu City Day (29 Jun), Student Days (around 1 May). 🅦 tartu.ee

Transport
✈ 🚂 A3, Vaksali 6, 1.5 km (1 mile) W of centre. 🚌 C2, Soola 2, E of the centre. 🚌 Narva mnt 2.

🏛 Estonian National Museum

Kuperjanovi 9. **Tel** 735 0445.
Open 11am–6pm Tue–Sun. 🎫 📷
call in advance. ♿ 🖥 📷 🅦 **erm.ee**

Estonia's most important ethnological centre, the Estonian National Museum (Eesti rahva muuseum) boasts over one million artifacts collected since 1909. The museum focuses on Estonia and other Finno-Ugric cultures, and its collection covers every imaginable aspect of life. From chairs made of gnarled birch wood to warped wooden beer tankards, the displayed objects eloquently attest to a way of life that seems quaintly anachronistic today.

In addition, there are vast photographic and documental archives and a fascinating costume collection, which includes a punk jacket (circa 1982–85). The museum is dedicated to the great Estonian folklorist and linguist Jakob Hurt (1839–1907). The museum occasionally holds temporary exhibitions that encompass themes from furniture to photography.

Karl Ernst von Baer (1792–1876)

A Baltic-German biologist, Karl Ernst von Baer was one of the founders of embryology. His pioneering work in this area was recognized by Charles Darwin, although Baer himself was extremely critical of the theory of evolution. Baer studied at Tartu University and later taught at Königsberg and the St Petersburg Academy of Sciences, before living out his last years in Tartu. A statue of Baer, looking pensive, takes pride of place on a plinth on Toomemägi. A rather endearing tradition takes place every year, on the eve of St Philip's Day (1 May), when Tartu University students wash Baer's bronze hair.

Statue of Karl Ernst von Baer on Toomemägi

Street-by-Street: Toomemägi

With its labyrinthine layout of narrow, winding streets and elegant historic buildings, Toomemägi (Cathedral Hill) is full of delightful surprises. In medieval times a fortress and cathedral stood on the hill but both were abandoned during the Livonian Wars (1558–83). Today, Toomemägi is home to a variety of prominent public buildings. Many of them belong to Tartu University, which was re-established here in 1802. There are several impressive monuments to some of the university's most esteemed graduates in the landscaped parks dotted around the hillside. The hill also commands some wonderful rooftop views of the city of Tartu spread out below.

Statue of two Wildes outside Vilde's Health Café (see p319)

Devil's Bridge
The bridge was built in 1913 to honour three centuries of rule by the Russian Romanov dynasty. The bridge was dedicated to Tsar Alexander I.

Key

— Suggested route

0 metres   100
0 yards   100

★ University Observatory
When it was built in 1820, the observatory had the most powerful achromatic telescope in the world. It was separated from the university in 1946 and now serves as a science centre.

★ Angel Bridge
It is a local tradition to hold one's breath and make a wish while crossing this 19th-century yellow-and-black bridge.

Cathedral Ruins
The massive ruins bear testimony to the original grandeur of the cathedral. Damaged during the Livonian Wars, it was rebuilt as a library after the reopening of the university in 1802. Visitors can climb the renovated towers.

The sacrificial stone was the site of worship for pagan Estonians.

★ Statue of Karl Ernst von Baer
This impressive monument befits Tartu University's most eminent graduate and founder of modern embryology.

L O S S I

Tartu University
When the first students registered here in 1632, it was only the second university in the province of Swedish Livonia. Since its establishment, the university has played a crucial role in Estonia's history.

Town Hall
Dating back to 1786, the current Town Hall is the third of its kind to occupy this position at the heart of Tartu. Its elegant early Classicist architecture was considered very fashionable in the 18th century.

⓮ Lake Võrtsjärv

Road Map D2. 🚌 from Viljandi, Otepää. ℹ️ Visitor Centre, Rannu, 527 5630. **Open** May–Sep: 10am–6pm daily; Oct: 11am–5pm daily; Nov–Apr: by arrangement. 📷
Ⓦ vortsjarv.ee

Straddling the counties of Viljandi, Tartu and Valga, Lake Võrtsjärv is the second-largest lake in Estonia after Lake Peipsi *(see p127)*. The northern part of the lake has some beautiful sandy beaches, while the southern part is swampier.

The Visitor Centre is a great place to gather information before your visit, and you can also rent a canoe or boat from here. There are several attractions scattered around the lake. The mausoleum of Barclay de Tolly (1757–1818), the Russian general credited with helping to defeat Napoleon, is in **Jõgeveste**, south of the lake. The bagpipe farm in Riidaja, at the southwest corner of the lake, is one of the area's more unusual sights. A popular summer activity is to take a tour of the lake aboard a *kalepurjekas*, a traditional sailboat.

A section of the medieval castle on Castle Hill, Viljandi

⓯ Viljandi

Road Map D2. 🏛️ 20,000. 🚆 from Tallinn. 🚌 from Tartu. ℹ️ Vabaduse 6, 433 0442. 🎭 Viljandi Folk Festival (late Jul). Ⓦ viljandi.ee

The pleasant town of Viljandi is centred on the medieval castle ruins sitting atop Castle Hill, which afford spectacular views of the nearby lake and

surrounding landscape. A crucial staging post on the Hanseatic trade route *(see p36)*, Viljandi emerged as one of Estonia's leading strongholds in the 16th century. By the end of the 19th century, the local area had become one of the wealthiest in Estonia.

Viljandi is notable for its well-preserved historic buildings, with an abundance of pretty timber cottages and early 20th-century brick houses.

In the small plaza, at the junction of Lossi and Tartu, is a statue that pays homage to Carl Robert Jakobson (1841–82). This zealous 19th-century Estonian nationalist helped get the National Awakening underway by founding the Estonian-language newspaper *Sakala* in Viljandi in 1878. The statue is the main focal point for the town.

Viljandi is also a major centre for folk art and music, with a large music academy and a popular yearly festival.

Magnificent view of Otepää, set amid lush landscape

⓰ Otepää

Road: **Map** E2. 🏛️ 2,300. 🚌 from Tartu, Võru, Tallinn. ℹ️ Tartu mnt 1, 766 1200. 🎿 Tartu Marathon (Feb). Ⓦ otepaa.ee

Situated amid the beautiful rolling hills of southeast Estonia, Otepää is equally popular as a summer and winter holiday retreat. The town also holds a special place in Estonian history. In 1884 the national flag was consecrated in the parish church, which now houses the **Flag Museum**. The totemic Energy Column at Mäe Street is an intriguing reminder of how strongly pagan beliefs prevail in Estonia.

Lake Pühajärv, 3 km (2 miles) south of Otepää, has some splendid beaches and dining spots from which to enjoy the magnificent scenery.

🏛️ **Flag Museum**
Tel 765 5075. **Open** 11am-4pm Tue-Sat.

The Forest Brothers

After the Soviet Union reoccupied Estonia in 1944, thousands of men fled to the woods to take up arms. They became known as the Forest Brothers and fought a guerrilla-style campaign against the Soviet system, most prominently in Viljandi and Tartu, with strong support from locals. However, the NKVD units ruthlessly targeted the partisans' families and by 1949 their support network had largely been broken. By 1953, only a few of the Forest Brothers were left. The last active member died in 1980.

An underground bunker used by Forest Brothers

Skiing and Snowboarding

Skiing is a popular winter pastime in Estonia. When Estonia won three gold medals for skiing events at the 2006 Winter Olympics, the medallists were hailed as national heroes and "ski fever" gripped the country. Although Estonia has a flat terrain, there are numerous ski hills, such as the 318-m (1,043-ft) high Suur Munamägi, that offer snowboarding and downhill skiing. There are many ski resorts around Otepää. However, since Estonia is blanketed in snow throughout winter, the ski resorts are crowded until spring. The annual Tartu Ski Marathon *(see p53)* is held at Kuutsemäe Ski Resort and has seen as many as 10,000 participants. Snowboarding is also fast gaining popularity in the region and Baltic snowboarders compete with the best in Europe in "trick park" acrobatics.

The Tartu Ski Marathon is one of the highlights of the winter sports calendar in Estonia. This 63-km (39-mile) WorldLoppet series event attracts competitors from all over the world. The festive proceedings also provide plenty of other skiing activities for non-professionals as well as children.

Winter time in Otepää draws hordes of ski-lovers, as this idyllic "Winter Capital" has several resorts, such as the one on Väike Munamägi (Small Egg Hill), 2 km (1 mile) from Otepaa. Snowboarding, ice skating and snowtubing are popular in this attractive southern town.

Kuutsemäe Ski Resort is a seven-slope skiing facility about 14 km (9 miles) outside Otepää. Its cross-country skiing tracks are well marked out.

Kristina Šmigun-Vähi (b.1977)

A cross-country skier, Tartu-born Kristina Šmigun has achieved remarkable success in her field, which has made her a national hero among sports enthusiasts in Estonia. Her parents, Anatoli Šmigun and Rutt Rehemaa, were also successful skiers. Kristina has won six medals at the FIS Nordic World Championships, including a gold medal in 2003. Her greatest success to date, however, was to become the first Estonian woman to win two gold medals at the 2006 Turin Winter Olympic Games. She won the 2 x 7.5 km (4.5 miles) double pursuit and the 10 km (6 miles) classical.

Kristina Šmigun at the Turin Winter Olympic Games

Andrus Veerpalu (b. 1971), winner of two Olympic gold medals and one silver medal, is Estonia's most successful Olympic athlete. The cross-country skier has also won gold and silver in the World Championships.

The English Gothic Revival exterior of Sangaste Manor

⓱ Sangaste Manor
Sangaste loss

Road Map D2. **Tel** 767 9300. 🚌 from Tartu, Otepää. **Open** 10am–4pm daily. 🎨 📷 call in advance. ♿ 🚻 📷
W sangasteloss.ee

One of the most attractive buildings of its kind in Estonia, Sangaste Manor was built in the English Gothic Revival style between 1879 and 1883. It was commissioned by Count Friedrich von Berg to prove to an English aristocrat, whose daughter he was wooing, that he was not the "savage from Russia" that the prejudiced nobleman deemed him to be. Sangaste's striking redbrick façade, crenellated gables and elegant towers lend it the appearance of a whimsical castle rather than a parochial manor house. The arched vestibule Dome Hall on the ground floor used to hold grand balls and still retains an air of grandeur, while the spacious dining room, which is criss-crossed with Tudor-style rafters, is particularly impressive. Sangaste is surrounded by a 0.8-sq-km (0.3-sq-mile) forest park, making it a favourite place for wedding receptions.

⓲ Mõniste Open-Air Museum
Mõniste muuseum

Road Map E2. Kuutsi, Mõniste village. **Tel** 789 0622. 🚌 from Tartu. **Open** May–Sep: 10am–5pm daily, Oct–Apr: 10am–4pm Mon–Fri. 🎨 📷
W monistemuuseum.ee

Established in 1948, Mõniste Open-Air Museum is the oldest museum of its kind in the country. It is located in 19th- and early 20th-century farm buildings, which are surrounded by the tranquil and beautiful forests of the Võru countryside. The museum offers plenty of activities for visitors and special events are regularly held throughout the summer, which focus on the essential aspects of traditional rural life such as milking cows, working with wood and flax and baking bread. Apart from trying their hands at authentic farm work, visitors can also spin yarn, roll linen and make rope. One of the most interesting activities is learning how Estonian farmers used local plants and trees to treat ailments.

St Mary's Church, set in lush rolling fields, Rõuge

⓳ Rõuge

Road Map E2. 🗺 440. 🚌 from Võru. 🛈 Haanja mnt, 785 9245. **Open** May– Sep: 10am–6pm daily. **W** rouge.kovtp.ee

The small village of Rõuge perfectly embodies the languid charm of southeast Estonia and is considered by many Estonians to be the most beautiful village in the country. Situated on the shores of Lake Rõuge Suurjärv, the deepest in the country at 38 m (125 ft), and with the magnificent Valley of the Nightingales looming behind it, the village is an exceptionally tranquil place. There are a series of nature trails through the valley which start behind **St Mary's Church**. The church dates back to 1730 and

The Setu People

A Setu woman wearing a traditional headdress and full-skirted dress

Living in the southeast of Estonia, the Setu people form a distinct ethnographic group. Unlike the majority of Estonians, the Setu are Orthodox, having lived in a region that was Christianized by the Russian Orthodox Church. They also have their own unique language, known as Võru-Setu, which differs considerably from standard Estonian. Traditional Setu folk music is among the most beautiful in Estonia, although its plaintive polyphonic form is strikingly Slavic-sounding. The Setu people are also famous for their traditional costumes and handicrafts. The best starting point to explore Setu culture is Obinitsa. Located at the centre of Setumaa, or "the Land of the Setu", the little village celebrates several Setu festivals.

was the site of an Estonian stronghold until the 12th century. Adjacent to the church is an old wooden school dating from 1888 which has some beautiful wooden carvings and sculptures on its exterior. Opposite the church is a monument honouring the Estonians who lost their lives in the war of independence (1918–20).

⑳ Suur Munamägi

Road Map E2. **Tel** 786 7514. 🚌 from Võru. **Open** Apr–Aug: 10am–8pm daily; Sep–Oct: 10am–5pm daily; Nov–Mar: noon–3pm Sat & Sun. 🖥 💻 🌐 **suurmunamagi.ee**

Situated just south of the village of Haanja, Suur Munamägi (Great Egg Hill) is the highest point in the Baltic States. At a mere 318 m (1,043 ft) above sea level, it gives an idea of how flat the Baltic region is. However, the surrounding landscape of farmsteads, forests and hills is breathtaking enough to merit a trip to the top of the hill. On clear days, it is possible to see all the way to Russia and Latvia.

At the peak, there is an elegant observation tower which was built in 1939 and renovated to include the glass-fronted Suur Munamägi Tower Café *(see p319)* and a lift. Delightfully quirky wooden carvings, which peer down from the trees, can be seen while walking up the steep path to the top of the forested hill.

F R Kreutzwald (1803–82)

One of Estonia's best-loved writers, Friedrich Reinhold Kreutzwald is revered as one of the most pivotal figures in the National Awakening of the 19th century. The enormous body of literature created by him in the Estonian language still instils a strong sense of identity and confidence among patriotic Estonians. Despite being impoverished, he studied medicine at Tartu University, where he developed a passionate interest in national folklore. He wrote many epics based on Estonian folklore, the most celebrated of which is *Kalevipoeg* (Son of Kalev). Published between 1857 and 1859, it was part fiction, part influenced by existing folk stories.

Kreutzwald Memorial Monument in Võru

㉑ Vastseliina

Road Map E2. 🚌 from Võru. 🚐 620. 🌐 **vastseliina.ee**

The small town of Vastseliina is visited mainly for the 14th-century castle located 4 km (2 miles) east of it. The castle was originally a border stronghold built by the Germans as a defence against the Russians. It became the site of a miracle in 1353, when a cross was seen suspended in the middle of the castle's chapel altar. The incident was reported by the Bishop of Rīga to Pope Innocent VI and the castle subsequently became a place of pilgrimage. In 1702, the castle was completely destroyed during the Northern War (1700–21), but the ruins are a vivid reminder of this once fiercely contested area.

In Vana-Vastseliina, at the foot of the castle hill, **Piiri Tavern** – first mentioned in 1695 – still serves food.

Well-preserved wooden house on Jüri Street in Võru

㉒ Võru

Road Map E2. 🚐 14,000. 🚌 🛈 Tartu 31, 782 1881. 🎭 Võru Folklore Festival (mid-Jul). 🌐 **voru.ee**

Situated in the centre of the southeast corner of Estonia, Võru is a good base for exploring the surrounding region. The town is best known for its impressive 18th-century wooden architecture.

Võru's main sight is the **Kreutzwald Memorial Museum**, the former house of writer F R Kreutzwald, who had a medical practice in the town. The sandy shores of Lake Tamula almost reach the town centre and are perfect for walks.

Environs
Obinitsa, 30 km (19 miles) east of Võru, is the largest village of the Setu community.

🏛 **Kreutzwald Memorial Museum**
Open Apr–Sep: 10am–6pm Wed–Sun; Oct–Mar: 11am–5pm Wed–Sun. 🖼

View from the observation tower, Suur Munamägi

Sweeping view of Lake Põlva with the spire of St Mary's Church in the background

㉓ Põlva

Road Map E2. 👥 6,500. 🚌 from Tartu. ℹ️ Kesk 42, 799 5001.
🎭 Town Days (first weekend in June).
🌐 polva.ee

The town is set around the artificial Lake Põlva, whose sandy shores are crowded with sunbathers in summer. Legend has it that a girl was immured in a kneeling position in **St Mary's Church** to keep the devil away. This is reputedly how Põlva, meaning "knee" in Estonian, got its name.

The town was developed around St Mary's Church, which lay in ruins for a long period until it was rebuilt after the Northern War *(see p37)*. Nearby, the Cultural Centre, an award-winning building, houses an art gallery, concert hall and café, and offers panoramic views of the town from its terraced roof. Põlva is also famous for the Intsikurmu Song Festival Grounds. Set in a small forested area on the west side of the town, it regularly hosts concerts.

㉔ Kiidjärve Watermill

Road Map E2. 🚌 from Põlva.
ℹ️ Kiidjärve village, 799 2122.
📷 🌐 polvamaa.ee

Built in 1914, the Kiidjärve Watermill is situated in the Kiidjärve-Taevaskoja Recreational Area, a 32-sq-km (12-sq-mile) pocket of stunning natural beauty that also

includes sandcliffs. The watermill is the largest redbrick structure of its kind in the Baltic region. There are many hiking trails that start at Kiidjärve village. Horse-riding, cycling and canoeing are also popular ways to see the area. The famous Akste Anthills, some of which stand 2 m (7 ft) high, are among the area's most fascinating sights.

㉕ Taevaskoja Sandstone Cliffs

Road Map E2. 🚌 from Põlva.
🚉 from Tartu. 🏢 Taevaskoja Tourism & Holiday Centre, 5373 6406.
🌐 taevaskoja.ee

Taevaskoja, meaning "Heaven's Hall", is famous for its sandstone cliffs and natural beauty. The Big and Small Taevaskoja cliffs are among the main attractions in the Põlva area. They run along the striking Ahja river, which is regarded as one of Estonia's

most beautiful. Close to the Small Taevaskoja is the Maiden's Cave, which was carved by the spring water flowing out of the Devonian sandstone and is also a source of numerous legends and myths. Nearby is the Big Taevaskoja, a striking sandstone wall, widely regarded as a national symbol.

Sandstone cliffs at Taevaskoja, along the Ahja river

The Russian Old Believers

Opposing the sweeping reforms brought about by Patriarch Nikon (1605–81), the Old Believers split from the Russian Orthodox Church in the 17th century. Due to persecution, many moved to southeast Estonia, especially near Lake Peipsi where they have adhered to their traditional way of life ever since. Today, there are 11 congregations of Old Believers in Estonia, comprising about 15,000 members. They are known for their love of onions, which they grow in abundance. It is a local belief that onions ward off various ills if eaten in large amounts.

Congregation of Old Believers

⑳ Lake Peipsi

The fifth-largest lake in Europe, Lake Peipsi stretches across a large part of the eastern border with Russia. It is a tranquil place, steeped in history and tradition, with the immense lake dominating every aspect of life. The region is famous for being home to the Old Believers as well as the Setu people *(see p124)*. The lakeshore has beautiful stretches of sandy beach dotted with small fishing villages.

Fishing, a common activity on the coast of Lake Peipsi

① Mustvee
A small museum dedicated to the Old Believers and three churches are the main sights here.

② Raja
Famed for its Old Believers' Church, the 4.5-km (3-mile) long Raja is considered to be the longest village in Estonia.

③ Kolkja
The Museum of Old Believers is the highlight of Kolkja. The village also has a good restaurant that offers a taste of local cuisine.

0 km 15
0 miles 15

④ Kasepää
Kasepää is part of a 7-km (4-mile) stretch of villages that adhere to the Old Believers' way of life.

⑤ Piirissaar
This island, on which fishermen and onion-growers live, can be reached by boat from Tartu and Värska.

Tips for Drivers

Starting point: Mustvee.
Length: The road stretching from Mustvee to Varnja is 46 km (28 miles) and Meerapalu to Värska is 56 km (35 miles).
Driving conditions: It is not possible to drive the entire length. There are plenty of places to stay just north of Kallaste.

⑥ Värska
Sandy beaches and wildlife make this village a pleasant getaway. The Setu Village Museum is a big draw.

Key
━━ Tour route
══ Other road
‒ ‒ Ferry route
▪ ▪ International border

For keys to symbols *see back flap*

LATVIA

Latvia at a Glance

Latvia is traditionally divided into four regions, roughly corresponding to the territories of the old Baltic tribes. Its long, sandy coastline includes two of the country's largest ports, while the western region of Kurzeme is heavily forested in the north. To the south, the flat and fertile plains of Zemgale border Lithuania. In the north, Vidzeme has the most varied landscape, with a long coastline as well as forests, wetlands and hills. Bordering Russia and Belarus, the culturally distinct easternmost Latgale region remains largely rural and undeveloped.

Rīga *(see pp142–65)* is the largest city in the Baltic region, boasting a UNESCO-listed historic centre and one of the world's greatest collections of Art Nouveau architecture.

Ainaži

Salacgrīva

Limbaž

Ventspils

Valdemārpils

Mērsrags

Saulkrasti

Talsi

Lake Usmas

Lake Engure

Sig

Engure

Kuldīga

Tukums

Jūrmala

Pāvilosta

WESTERN LATVIA
(see pp166–185)

Rīga

RĪGA
(see pp142–165)

Ogre

Aizpute

Olaine

Lielv

Durbe

Skrunda

Saldus

Dobele

Jelgava

Liepāja

Iecava

Lake Liepāja

Priekule

Auce

Bauska

Rundāle Palace *(see pp172–3)*, Latvia's most impressive surviving stately home, was designed by Rastrelli (1700–71), the Italian architect of St Petersburg's Winter Palace. Most of the rooms at the palace are decorated in the fanciful Rococo style of the second half of the 18th century.

◀ Serene shores of the Latgale Lakes

Gauja National Park *(see pp190–93)* is one of the most attractive parts of the country and a popular destination for both local and foreign tourists. In addition to providing a compelling mix of natural attractions and historic sites, it also offers some of Latvia's best opportunities for outdoor activities, from canoeing to bobsleighing.

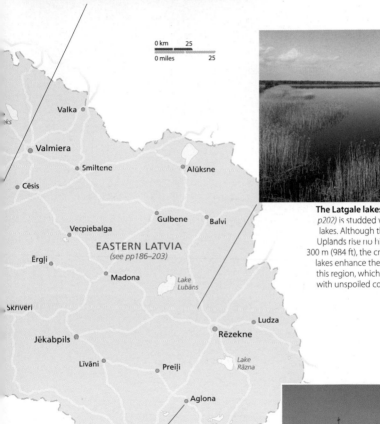

0 km 25
0 miles 25

Valka
Valmiera
Smiltene
Alūksne
Cēsis
Gulbene Balvi
Vecpiebalga
EASTERN LATVIA *(see pp186–203)*
Ērgļi
Madona Lake Lubāns
Skrīveri
Ludza
Jēkabpils Rēzekne
Līvāni Preiļi Lake Rāzna
Aglona
Daugavpils Krāslava

The Latgale lakes area *(see p202)* is studded with many lakes. Although the Latgale Uplands rise no higher than 300 m (984 ft), the crystal-clear lakes enhance the beauty of this region, which is blessed with unspoiled countryside.

Aglona *(see p199)*, the most important site of Catholic pilgrimage in the region, is famed for a 17th-century icon of the Virgin Mary which is only displayed on special occasions. The busiest day of the year is the feast of the Assumption, on 15 August, when thousands of visitors flock to the Baroque church.

A PORTRAIT OF LATVIA

Lying between the other two Baltic States, Latvia is characterized by delightful forests and lakes, fascinating historic towns and dynamic cities, which are, by and large, unexplored. Nonetheless, the country's exciting capital, Rīga, draws hordes of Western Europeans throughout the year. The largest city in the Baltic region, Rīga boasts a well-preserved Old Town packed with cultural treasures and revels in its status as a hedonistic nightlife destination.

Long before the arrival of the German crusaders in 1201, local Latvian tribes had established trading links with merchants as far afield as Byzantium, while Orthodox Christianity had made inroads from the East. Yet, it was the crusaders who were responsible for ushering in eight centuries of foreign domination. A short period of self-determination in the early 20th century ended with occupation first by Nazi Germany and then by Soviet Russia. The Soviet era brought rapid industrialization, while the restoration of independence in 1991 further hastened the pace of the country's modernization. Nonetheless, a distinctively Latvian culture developed and survived, assimilating foreign influences and substantial regional differences. A connection with nature, reflecting centuries of rural toil, has remained intact at the same time. While

still trying to come to terms with the social, economic and political legacies of the 20th century, the country entered the 21st century with confidence. The historic cores of Rīga and other major cities have been restored, while the rural areas are being developed for ecotourism.

People

The most obvious ethnic divide is between the country's Latvian and Russian communities, who make up 60 and 30 per cent respectively of the country's population of 2 million. Although Russians form the majority in Latvia's major cities, a significant proportion of them are not citizens, as they have not taken the mandatory language and citizenship tests. They cannot vote in national elections, nor are they allowed to travel and work freely in the EU.

A splendid view of the countryside in Sigulda, Gauja National Park

◀ One of the many cobbled lanes in Rīga's Old Town

Traditional Latvian folk dancers performing at the Latvian Ethnographic Open-Air Museum, near Rīga

Minority groups include Lithuanians, Poles, Belarusians and Ukranians. Most of Latvia's Jews were executed or fled during World War II, although some of the survivors returned and small communities exist today.

Society and Culture

Latvians are, by and large, socially conservative, and although employment levels are equal for women and men, the latter are usually better paid. Women play a prominent role in public life, including making a mark on Latvian politics, but the female domain is still often considered to be the home.

The strict social hierarchy imposed by the Baltic Germans ensured the survival and adaptation of many folk traditions. Echoes of Latvia's pagan past remain to this day, most obviously in the passionate celebration of Midsummer, and even city-dwellers profess a connection with nature. This is also reflected in the popularity of flowers as gifts, although it is important to give bunches with an odd number of stems, as even numbers are associated with funerals.

Latvians have never taken strongly to organized religion and today only around a third of the population identify themselves as Christians, mostly Evangelical Lutheran.

Politics and Economy

Since the restoration of independence, Latvia has seen the birth of dozens of political parties that have formed a succession of short-lived centre-right coalition governments. The end of Communist rule has not meant the end of widespread corruption, with a small number of powerful oligarchs using political influence to promote vested financial interests. All this has bred a

Spectators at the anniversary of the proclamation of the Republic of Latvia in Rīga

general sense of scepticism towards the political system.

The Soviet authorities took a primarily agricultural economy and transformed it to one based largely around heavy industry, with an associated influx of Russian workers into the cities. The collapse of the Soviet planned economy between 1989 and 1992 meant a sudden loss of markets for Latvia's goods, and the country was plunged into further crisis when four newly privatized banks

Ships docked at Liepāja harbour, a former Soviet naval base

crashed in 1995. From then until the economic crisis of 2008, privatization, economic reform and low wages fostered rapid growth. Most raw materials are imported, with the exception of timber, but industry has succeeded in attracting foreign investment. Exports include pharmaceuticals, timber, textiles, electrical and electronic goods, ships, dairy products, beef and grains. Latvia has capitalized on its status as an East–West trade hub, with oil transit from the former USSR to Western Europe particularly lucrative.

Although money has been flooding into the country, for the average person, living conditions have not improved very much. A lack of employment opportunities has precipitated migration from rural areas, either to Latvian cities or to other EU countries.

Tourism

One very evident change in recent years has been the rapid growth in tourism. While much of the country remains under-explored by foreign visitors, Rīga has firmly established itself on the

tourist map. The area around the Old Town is transforming to accommodate the growing number of visitors. The city is striving to recover its prized epithet of "Paris of the North", which it once shared with several other European cities.

However, the most fertile area for growth probably lies outside of the urban areas, where the forests, rivers and lakes seem serenely untouched. Even though the infrastructure is still developing, tourism offers genuine opportunities for reviving rural economies, with some farmsteads already embracing the possibilities of ecotourism.

A group of rafters in the forested Kurzeme region

LATVIA THROUGH THE YEAR

With the pagan past never entirely erased by the German crusaders, the Latvian calendar is punctuated by celebrations which mark the rhythm of passing seasons. Many folk traditions are incorporated into Christian festivals, and they provide a chance to experience traditional activities. International cultural events are concentrated in Rīga, although other cities, particularly Liepāja, have their share, and many smaller towns celebrate folk festivals. The best time to visit is from May to mid-September. Rīga, however, gets plenty of tourists throughout the year due to its vibrant cultural life and it can look very attractive on a clear winter's day.

Spring

The rain and mud of early spring can dampen the spirits. However, by April the countryside comes alive with dance and music.

March

Piano Stars *(early Mar)*, Liepāja. This festival was established in 1993 and attracts pianists from around the world.

April

International Baltic Ballet Festival *(Apr–May)*. The festival, which features styles of dance ranging from classical to avant-garde, is held in Rīga as well as other towns.

May

Livonian Festival *(late May)*, Cēsis. Highlights include medieval music, food, crafts workshops and battle re-enactments held in the town's Livonian Order castle.

Art Days and Museum Nights. At this lively festival, artists display their work in streets and squares across the country. Concerts and theatre performances are held, and many museums stay open into the night.

Summer

The summer months are the best time to visit, not only because the weather is at its most enjoyable, but because it is festival season.

June

Rīga Opera Festival *(mid-Jun)*, Rīga. An international festival marking the end of the Latvian National Opera season, with an overview of the previous year.
Artisans' Festival and Fair *(first weekend)*, Rīga. This event has been in existence since 1971, with music, theatre, dance and traditional crafts demonstrations at the Ethnographic Open-Air Museum *(see p163)*.

Knights fighting in the Baltic Medieval Festival

Midsummer *(23–24 Jun)*. On Herb Day (Līgo), houses and barns are decorated with branches, flowers and leaves. In the evening, songs are sung around fires which remain lit until the dawn of St John's Day (Jāņi).

July

Sea Festival *(second weekend)*. Fishermen are honoured along with the God of the Sea in this festival.
Latvian Song and Dance Festival, Rīga. This amateur choral festival is the largest of its kind in the world. It is held every five years and is next scheduled for 2018.
Folklore Baltica Festival, Rīga. The three Baltic capitals host the event in turns.
Rīgas Ritmi *(first week)*, Rīga. Jazz and world music artists perform at this music festival.
Summer Sound, Liepāja. This festival confirms the city's claim to be the home of Latvian rock music.

Performers at the Rīga Opera Festival

Dancers in a street performance during Rīga City Festival

Positivus, Mazsalaca. Latvia's biggest pop and rock festival is held next to the Baltic Sea and attracts international artists.

August

Assumption of the Blessed Virgin Mary *(15 Aug)*, Aglona. Thousands of pilgrims visit Latvia's most important Catholic place of worship.

Rīga City Festival *(mid-Aug)*. First held in 2001 for the 800th anniversary of Rīga's founding, the festival includes concerts, street theatre and dance.

Autumn

Autumnal colours can make this season a pleasant time to see the countryside, but temperatures fall rapidly from mid-September.

September

Railway Festival *(first Sat)*, Gulbene–Alūksne Narrow-Gauge Railway *(see p203)*. Events are held at various stops along this 33-km (21-mile) railway line, with a restored steam engine as the star attraction.

October

New Music Festival Arēna *(Oct–Nov)*, Rīga. A month-long showcase for contemporary compositions.

November

Mārtiņdiena *(10 Nov)*. This marks the beginning of winter. Events take place at Rīga's Ethnographic Open-Air Museum *(see p163)*.

Lāčplēsis Day *(11 Nov)*. A number of events are held on this day in honour of Latvian freedom fighters.

Winter

Short days and poor weather can make travelling in winter a challenging proposition, but on a clear day Latvia's snow-bound landscape can be beautiful.

December

Christmas *(25–26 Dec)*. Yule logs are dragged from house to house, collecting the misfortunes of the previous year before being ceremonially burned.

Old Town Christmas Market

(Dec–early Jan), Rīga. Popular with tourists and local people, this festive market has a number of stalls selling handicrafts and warming winter treats, such as mulled wine.

January

Silver Bells International Sacred Music Festival *(mid-Jan)*, Daugavpils. A competition with performances from a range of choirs, ensembles and soloists.

Exhibit at the International Ice Sculpture Festival, Jelgava

February

International Ice Sculpture Festival *(early Feb)*, Jelgava. One of the largest festivals of its kind in the world. After the event, the sculptures remain on display until they melt in the sun.

Public Holidays

New Year's Day (1 Jan)

Good Friday (March/April)

Easter Sunday and Monday (March/April)

Labour Day (1 May)

Restoration of the Independence of the Republic of Latvia (4 May)

Mother's Day (second Sunday in May)

Midsummer (23–24 June)

Proclamation of the Republic of Latvia (18 Nov)

Christmas (24–26 Dec)

Visitors enjoying the beautiful city of Rīga in autumn

THE HISTORY OF LATVIA

Latvia's history is traditionally considered to have begun with the advent of the Teutonic Knights in 1201, which started German dominance of the area for three centuries. From the mid-16th to the early 18th century, Latvia was divided between Poland and Sweden. By 1795, all of Latvia had been absorbed into Russia. Final independence from foreign domination was only achieved in 1991.

Latvia's strategic geographical position, which prompted its more powerful neighbours to gain control over the region, largely decided the course of its history. By the late 12th century, Latvia's trade route up the Daugava river was increasingly visited by merchants from Western Europe. The Teutonic Knights, German warrior-monks who first arrived in 1200, were looking for conquests as well as new converts in a pagan land. In 1201, they founded Rīga, which grew into an important centre for trade between the Baltic region and Western Europe.

King Gustav Adolphus landing near the Baltic coast in 1630

The Germans and the Swedes

Teutonic Knight in battle gear

The power of the Germans quickly extended across all of Latvia. Castles were built in Cēsis (1209), Kuldīga (1242) and Valmiera (1283) to prevent any local resistance. Meanwhile, Rīga, Cēsis and Ventspils began to thrive as members of the Hanseatic League (see p36). The beneficiaries of this growth were the Germans, who also owned large manors in the countryside. The Latvians, on the other hand, were dispossessed and forced to become serfs.

The early 16th century saw the population lending zealous support to the Reformation movement, and soon after, Protestantism was declared as the state religion. In 1561, during the Livonian Wars (see p37), Poland conquered Latvia and Catholicism was firmly established. The separate Duchy of Courland, owing allegiance to Poland, was created in the south and west.

The clash between the Protestant Swedes and Catholic Poles in the late 16th century resulted in Swedish rule in northern Latvia for much of the 17th century. The Swedes were responsible for

---

1201 Rīga founded by Bishop Albert of Bremen

1282 Rīga joins the Hanseatic League

Stone coat of arms of the Hanseatic League

1561 Latvia occupied by Poland

1558 Livonian Wars begin

1200 **1300** **1400** **1500**

1211 Building of Rīga Cathedral begins

Rīga Cathedral

1372 German replaces Latin as official language

1520 First Lutheran service held

1536 F record Jewish mercha in Rīga

spreading education in the Latvian language throughout the country. Under Gustav Adolphus (r.1611–32), Sweden consolidated its hold over Livonia, which was then under Polish rule. Around the same period, the Duchy of Courland flourished under Jakob Kettler (r.1642–81), who built a powerful navy at Ventspils and also founded Latvia's only colonies, on the Caribbean island of Tobago and on the Gambia river in West Africa.

Jakob Kettler, Duke of Courland

The Russian Empire

In 1710, during the Great Northern War (*see p37*), the Swedes surrendered Rīga to Peter the Great of Russia. The Russians introduced 200 years of stability. Serfdom was abolished in 1819, which enabled farmhands to migrate to the towns as industrialization and the railways created a wide range of new employment. Power and money would, however, stay firmly in German and Russian hands. German merchants still enjoyed the privileges that they had secured from the Swedish rulers.

Towards the end of the 19th century, the Russians attempted to replace German with Russian as the national language. This infuriated the Latvian intelligentsia, who saw it as a sign of oppression. They began organizing political movements hostile to the Tsarist regime and continuing German control of many businesses and farms. The 1905 uprisings in Russia found a sympathetic echo in Rīga and across the Latvian countryside, where over 100 manor houses were burned down.

The Fight for Freedom

When World War I broke out in 1914, Latvia became the main battleground between Germany and Russia, neither ever seizing its entire territory. Latvia's national aspirations took a blow as many Latvians were forced to join the Russian army. The Latvians, who were permitted to form their own army in 1915, put up a spirited fight against the Germans at the Battle of Christmas, which began on 23 December 1916. However, the Latvians were ultimately defeated and the Germans captured Rīga. The Allied victory in 1918 forced the German troops to withdraw. Within a few days, on 18 November, Latvian independence was declared.

A 19th-century oil painting of ships at a Latvian port

The First Independence

Latvia's newly formed government was forced to flee to Liepāja in January 1919, returning to Rīga in July, when the city had been freed of Bolshevik troops. Throughout that year, many forces were ranged against Latvian independence and against each other, including the Germans, Poles and Russians. Latvia was only assured of its independence when it signed a peace treaty with Russia on 11 August 1920.

Despite the constantly changing governments that ruled until 1934, much was achieved during this period of independence. Trade was re-directed westwards and away from Russia, the Latvian language had a resurgence and Rīga came to be regarded as the Baltic region's capital. The leading political figure throughout this period was Kārlis Ulmanis (1877–1942), who staged a coup in 1934 and abolished parliament. He proclaimed himself president, taking Mussolini as his role model.

Progress came to a grinding halt with the Soviet invasion on 17 June 1940, making

President Kārlis Ulmanis
(1877–1942)

Latvia a part of the USSR. Anyone who had played a significant role in "bourgeois" Latvia was either executed or deported to Siberia. The German invasion followed a year later, in June 1941, and most of Latvia was occupied within 10 days. The Nazi regime was as brutal, but with different targets. Most of its victims were from the Jewish community, which had grown considerably after the laws which restricted Jewish residence were lifted in 1840.

The Return of the Russians

The Soviets returned to Eastern Latvia and Rīga as "liberators" in autumn 1944, though the Germans held out until May 1945 in the country's west. This enabled nearly 100,000 Latvians to escape to Germany and Sweden, from where many continued on to Britain, Canada and Australia. In March 1949, the Russians carried out more deportations; this time their victims were mostly farmers unwilling to join the new collectives. As Latvians were forcibly removed from their own country, Russians were happy to take their place, and their numbers grew throughout the Soviet era. By 1990, half the population of the country was Russian-speaking and there was a serious threat that Latvian would disappear as the national language. The first public protest took place in 1987, when a crowd gathered around the Freedom Monument in Rīga, to commemorate the 1941 deportations to Siberia. New political groups began to emerge a year later. The most forceful of them, the Popular Front of

Soldiers marching through Rīga in 1940

PLF supporters campaigning during the 1990 elections

Latvia (PLF), demanded full independence and won the elections in 1990.

Independence at Last

The violence that broke out in January 1991 showed the determination of the Latvians for independence. Eight people were killed in clashes with Soviet forces in Rīga. In August, Moscow's conservative Communists staged a coup against President Mikhail

Gorbachev, but it collapsed within two days and Latvia suddenly found itself free.

Latvia was led during the first eight years of independence by Guntis Ulmanis (b.1939). Governments came and went as they had done in the 1920s, but they largely agreed on a slower policy of privatization than the Estonians were practising. The poor salaries being paid in the public sector continued the low-level corruption prevalent in the Soviet era and introduced it at higher levels too.

The beginning of the 21st century saw the effective integration of Latvia into Western Europe, particularly with its joining the European Union in 2004, and subsequent adoption of its shared currency, the euro. Nonetheless, Latvia has still managed to maintain its trading links with Russia. The status of Latvia's population who speak Russian as their first language is a problem likely to trouble its post-independence governments. However, sensitive handling of this issue can ensure the country's long-term security.

Jews in Latvia

In the early 19th century, Jews in the Russian Empire were barred from the academic world, government and the army officer corps. Anti-Semitism worsened under Tsar Alexander III (1881–94). Between the two world wars, President Ulmanis firmly suppressed the activities of fringe groups that wanted to promote anti-Semitism. As part of its Latvian invasion in June 1941, Nazi Germany put its extermination policies into practice at once. The genocide was carried out in two phases that year. By 1945, only about 1,000 Jews, from a pre-war population of 95,000, had survived. Jewish institutions were re-established in 1988, at the end of the Soviet era. A proper evaluation of Jewish history in all eras could only be carried out after independence in 1991.

Pro-German Latvian militia standing guard over captured Jews in Liepāja in 1941

RĪGA

With its long history as a mercantile centre, Rīga is the largest and most cosmopolitan city in the Baltic States. This is reflected in the buildings that line its streets and squares. The Old Town boasts an engaging array of medieval warehouses and Dutch Renaissance apartments. Remarkable Art Nouveau buildings, which secured the city UNESCO World Heritage Site status, can also be found.

When German crusader Bishop Albert von Buxhoevden chose Rīga as a strategic location for his fortress in 1201, the area was already inhabited by tribes who traded with Russian and Scandinavian merchants. The German settlement became the headquarters for the subjugation of the region and prospered as a member of the Hanseatic League of trading cities. Ruled by Sweden from 1621 to 1710, Rīga experienced a 19th-century heyday under the Russians. New suburbs were built for incoming workers, the harbour was expanded, a ring of boulevards was created in place of the old fortifications, and in the 20th century, industries such as auto-mobile construction were developed.

The capital of an independent Latvia between the world wars, Rīga suffered heavily during both conflicts and many of its oldest buildings were devastated. Several, including the striking House of Blackheads, have been rebuilt or restored. The "liberation" of Rīga by the Red Army in 1944 ushered in almost five decades of Communist rule, and there are still more ethnic Russians than Latvians in Rīga; relations between the two communities are cordial but rarely warm.

Since Latvia regained independence in 1991, Rīga has flourished, becoming a vibrant tourist destination with an impressive range of museums and a spirited nightlife. Change has been rapid and not always smooth, with the arrival of low-cost airlines in particular bringing its own challenges. Fashionable new bars and restaurants cater to growing crowds of visitors, and new glass and steel buildings have sprung up alongside the cobbled streets and church spires of the medieval Old Town. This is not a picture-perfect city stuck in time, but a lively metropolis intent on shedding the trappings of Soviet rule.

Outdoor café on Cathedral Square (Doma laukums)

◀ Figure at the top of the Freedom Monument, affectionately referred to as "Milda"

Exploring Rīga

For many centuries Rīga was largely contained within the city walls on the right bank of the Daugava river. Now known as the Old Town, this area contains most of the city's sites of interest. The main route through the tangle of picturesque streets and squares is Kaļķu Street, leading from the Stone Bridge *(Akmens tilts)* to Brīvības Street and the Freedom Monument. When the city walls were removed in the mid-19th century, the space was developed into a ring of boulevards and parks. The main train and bus stations lie on the southeastern edge of this ring. To the north is the late 19th- and early 20th-century extension of the city known as the Quiet Centre, which includes some of Riga's most impressive Art Nouveau architecture.

Sights at a Glance

Churches and Cathedrals

1. Dome Cathedral
4. St Saviour's Church
8. St Jacob's Cathedral
21. St Peter's Church
24. St John's Church
29. Orthodox Cathedral

17. House of Blackheads
19. Latvian Riflemen Monument
20. Mentzendorff House
26. Bastejkalns
27. Freedom Monument

Museums and Galleries

2. Museum of the Barricades of 1991
3. Museum of Rīga's History and Navigation
7. Art Museum Rīga Bourse
10. Arsenal Museum of Art
13. Powder Tower/Latvian War Museum
18. Museum of the Occupation of Latvia
22. Museum of Decorative Arts and Design
23. Porcelain Museum
25. Photography Museum
28. Krišjānis Barons Memorial Museum
30. Latvian National Museum of Art
31. Museum of Jews in Latvia
32. Pauls Stradiņš Museum of the History of Medicine
33. Art Nouveau Museum

Buildings and Monuments

5. Rīga Castle
6. Three Brothers
9. Parliament
11. Swedish Gate
12. St Jacob's Barracks
14. Cats' House
15. Great Guild
16. Small Guild

| 0 metres | 200 |
| 0 yards | 200 |

For hotels and restaurants see pp300–301 and pp320–22

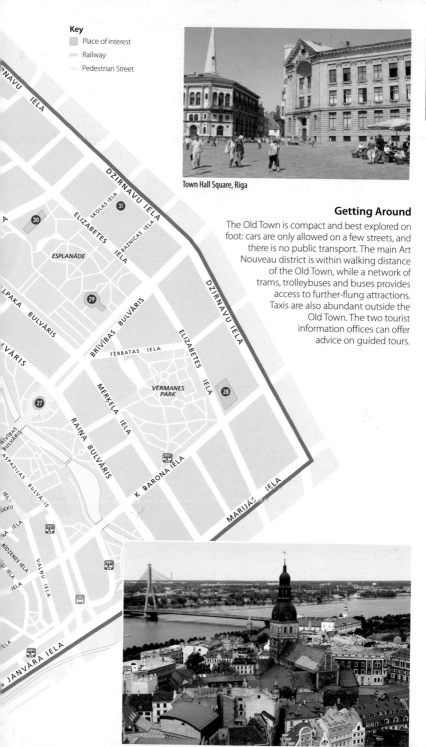

Key

▨ Place of interest

═ Railway

― Pedestrian Street

Town Hall Square, Rīga

Getting Around

The Old Town is compact and best explored on foot: cars are only allowed on a few streets, and there is no public transport. The main Art Nouveau district is within walking distance of the Old Town, while a network of trams, trolleybuses and buses provides access to further-flung attractions. Taxis are also abundant outside the Old Town. The two tourist information offices can offer advice on guided tours.

Rīga's Old Town next to the Daugava river

For keys to symbols *see back flap*

Impressive Cross-Vaulted Gallery of the Dome, Dome Cathedral

❶ Dome Cathedral

Doma baznīca

Doma laukums 1. **Map** 1 C3. **Tel** 6722 7573. **Open** May–Sep: 9am–6pm daily (to 5pm Wed & Fri); Oct–Apr: 10am–5pm daily. **Closed** for special events. 🅿 🛈 8am Mon–Sat; noon Sun. 🆆 doms.lv

Founded as St Mary's in 1211 by Bishop Albert von Buxhoevden, the cathedral became one of the city's three seats of power alongside the Town Hall and the castle. It gained its current name from the German word *Dom*, meaning "cathedral", during the Reformation. The cathedral looks as if it has sunk, but in fact the land around it has been raised to keep out floodwater from the Daugava river.

The largest place of worship in the Baltic region, the cathedral has been altered over the years and its bulky structure exhibits a variety of styles. The altar alcove and the east wing crossing are Romanesque, with a cross-vaulted ceiling and rows of semi-circular windows. Simpler Neo-Gothic additions are characterized by pointed arches, large windows and lierne vaulting, while the eastern pediment and the steeple are in an 18th-century Baroque style. The portal was added in the 19th century, followed by an Art Nouveau vestibule in the 20th century.

Most of the interior decor was destroyed during the Reformation, and it is now very plain except for the tombs of merchants and the 19th-century stained glass. The woodwork of the 17th-century pulpit is ornate, however, as is the organ case, which is Mannerist with Baroque and Rococo additions. It is possible to visit the **Cross-Vaulted Gallery of the Dome**, a Romanesque cloister and courtyard, all year round.

❷ Museum of the Barricades of 1991

1991 Gada barikāžu muzejs

Krāmu iela 3. **Map** 1 C4. **Tel** 6721 3525. **Open** 10am–5pm Mon–Fri. 🅿 donations. 🛈 🆆 barikades.lv

This museum recalls the pivotal days of January 1991 when the people of Rīga took to the streets, following the threat of direct presidential rule from Moscow and the stationing of Soviet tanks outside the Supreme Council in Vilnius. The most fascinating of the exhibits is video footage shot around the barricades, showing people installing huge blocks of concrete to defend strategic points, including the Interior Ministry and TV Tower. Scenes shot at night are punctuated by gunfire and shouting. A final room is dedicated to the people who were killed in Bastejkalns (*see p154*).

❸ Museum of Rīga's History and Navigation

Rīgas vēstures un kuģniecības muzejs

Palasta iela 4. **Map** 1 C4. **Tel** 6721 1358. **Open** Jun–Sep: 11am–5pm daily; Oct–May: 11am–5pm Wed–Sun. 🅿 🛈 🆆 rigamuz.lv

Founded in 1773, this museum is the oldest in Rīga. Housed in an impressive building with tiled stoves and stained-glass windows, it is also one of the city's most interesting and varied museums. The exhibition on navigation stresses the strong maritime history of the city up until World War I, and includes several large model ships and material on Krišjānis Valdemārs (*see p195*). Other rooms cover everything from prehistory to independence. Highlights from the Middle Ages include the *Madonna on a Crescent Moon*, a sculpture of the patroness of the Great Guild dating from the late 15th century, which was taken to Germany during World War II, and *Big Kristaps*, a large 16th-century statue of St Christopher.

Interior of the Museum of the Barricades of 1991

❹ St Saviour's Church

Anglikāņu baznīca

Anglikāņu iela 2a. **Map** 1 C3. **Tel** 6722 2259. 🕐 11am first Sun of the month. Free lunchtime concerts are held at 1pm every Wed. 🌐 **anglicanriga.lv**

Funded by British merchants, this small Neo-Gothic church, built in 1857, is the only Anglican place of worship in the city. The English bricks were brought as ballast on trading ships, and the church was even built on a layer of British soil. During the Soviet era it was used by students as a disco and recording studio, but since the second independence in 1991 it has been reopened for worship, and the congregation includes English-speaking expatriates.

❺ Rīga Castle

Rīgas pils

Pils laukums 3. **Map** 1 C3. History Museum of Latvia: **Tel** 6722 1357. **Closed** until 2016. 🌐 **history-museum.lv**

The city's original Livonian Order castle was destroyed by Rīga's citizens during a war against the Order lasting from 1297 to 1330. After losing, the townspeople were forced to build a new castle on the present site just outside the city. Continuing quarrels led the Master of the Order to leave the capital, but Rīga Castle was destroyed by the citizens once more in 1484. Again they were defeated and the next castle the townspeople were compelled to build forms the core of the current structure and was the headquarters of the Livonian Order until 1561.

As well as being the official residence of Latvia's president, the building houses the **History Museum of Latvia** (Latvijas vēstures muzejs), which is currently closed. The castle was damaged during a fire in the summer of 2013; reconstruction work is scheduled to be completed in 2016.

❻ Three Brothers

Trīs brāļi

17–21 Mazā pils iela. **Map** 1 C3. Museum of Architecture: **Tel** 6722 0779. **Open** 9am–6pm Mon, 9am–5pm Tue–Thu, 9am–4pm Fri. 🌐 donations. 🌐 **archmuseum.lv**

This row of buildings on Mazā pils Street known as the Three Brothers covers three distinct architectural styles. Number 17, with a stepped gable and Gothic niches, dates from the 15th century and is Rīga's oldest residential building made out of stone. The ears of wheat on the stones beside the door indicate that it was owned by a baker. The wooden interior of the 17th-century building at number 19 now houses the small **Museum of Architecture**. The green building at number 21 was built in the 18th century.

❼ Art Museum Rīga Bourse

Mākslas muzejs Rīgas Birža

Doma laukums 6. **Map** 1 C3. **Tel** 6722 3434. **Open** 10am–6pm Tue–Sun (to 8pm Fri). 🌐 **rigasbirza.lv**

This impressive building, built in the ornate Venetian Renaissance style in 1856, was once one of the city's most elegant edifices. However, years of neglect and a fire in 1979 destroyed much of its beauty. After three years of renovation, it opened its doors in 2011 as the home of the new Art Museum Rīga Bourse, which has taken over the collection of the Foreign Art Museum once housed in Rīga Castle. The museum has an extensive

collection of 16th–20th-century European paintings and 19th-century paintings from China and Japan. There is also a collection of porcelain and glass, which features pieces from the Danish Royal Porcelain Factory.

Entrance of St Jacob's Cathedral, the seat of Rīga's Catholic archbishop

❽ St Jacob's Cathedral

Sv Jēkaba katedrāle

Klostera iela 1. **Map** 1 C3. **Tel** 6732 6419. **Open** May–Sep: 9am–7pm; Oct–Apr: 9am–6pm. 🕐 8am.

Sited outside the old city walls, St Jacob's was built in 1225 to serve the surrounding villages. The church was renowned for having its bell not in the Gothic steeple but hanging from a cupola, which is still visible on the southern side although the bell has gone. It was rung to signal that an execution was taking place in the city, although another story insists that it was heard when unfaithful women passed by the church. Today, the cathedral is the seat of Rīga's Catholic archbishop.

Changing of the guard outside Rīga Castle

9 Parliament

Saeima

Jēkaba 11. **Map** 1 C3. **W saeima.lv**

This rather anonymous building, constructed from 1863 to 1867 with Florentine Renaissance features, and renovated several times since, was originally used for meetings of the local landed gentry. From 1919 to 1934, as today, it served as the seat of Latvia's Parliament, while during World War II it was the headquarters of Friedrich Jeckeln – the SS officer who oversaw the killing of Latvia's Jews, Roma and other "undesirables". Later it was used by the Supreme Soviet of Latvia. Nearby stands a monument that was built to commemorate those who died in the Barricades of 1991 *(see p146)*.

Imposing façade of Latvia's Parliament

10 Arsenal Museum of Art

Mākslas muzejs Arsenāls

Torņa 1. **Map** 1 C3. **Tel** 6735 7527. **Open** noon–6pm Tue, Wed & Fri; noon–8pm Thu; noon–5pm Sat & Sun. **W lnmm.lv**

This is Rīga's premier venue for shows of cutting-edge art. There is no permanent collection, but the temporary exhibitions are generally of high quality. The emphasis is on art from the middle of the 20th century onwards, either produced in Latvia or by Latvians living abroad. The imposing one-storey building on Jēkaba Square was built as a customs house between 1828 and 1832 in the style of Russian Classicism. The name "Arsenal" comes from a previous building on the same spot, built by the Swedes. The downstairs exhibition space particularly benefits from airy rooms and high ceilings.

Paintings and sculpture exhibited at the Arsenal Museum of Art

11 Swedish Gate

Zviedru vārti

Between Torņa iela & Aldaru iela. **Map** 1 C3.

The sole remnant of eight city gates, the Swedish Gate was built in 1698 during a period of Swedish rule in Rīga. It runs through the ground floor of the house at Torņa 11, and legend has it that the gate was created illegally by a wealthy merchant to give him more direct access to his warehouse. More likely, it was built for the use of the soldiers stationed at St Jacob's Barracks. Today the gate provides access between the popular strip of shops and bars on Torņa Street and the quieter, but pleasant, Aldaru Street. Newly married couples include the gate on their tour of the city, as passing through it is said to bring good luck.

Swedish Gate, built through the ground floor of an old house

12 St Jacob's Barracks

Jēkaba kazarmas

Torņa iela. **Map** 2 D3.

Built in the 17th century to house Swedish soldiers, this yellow block is now home to shops and restaurants. The barracks also played a brief role in the nation's cultural development, as the site of an artists' commune opened in 1917, although the building retained its military purpose. Many of the members went on to join the influential Rīga Artists' Group of the 1920s and 30s. Opposite is the oldest remaining stretch of the city wall, dating from the 13th to 16th centuries but restored during the Soviet era.

For hotels and restaurants see pp300–301 and pp320–22

⑬ Powder Tower/ Latvian War Museum

Pulvertornis/Latvijas kara muzejs

Smilšu 20. **Map** 2 D3. **Tel** 6722 8147. **Open** May–Sep: 10am–6pm daily; Oct–Apr: 10am–5pm daily. 🎟 donations. 📷 🌐 **karamuzejs.lv**

The cylindrical Powder Tower is all that remains from a total of 18 towers that were once part of the city's defences. Its 14th-century foundations are among the oldest in the city, but the rest of the structure dates from 1650, being rebuilt after it was destroyed by the Swedish army in 1621. The 2.5-m (8-ft) thick walls were intended to protect the gunpowder stored inside, after which the tower was named. Nine Russian cannonballs remain embedded in the walls as proof of the tower's strength.

The tower was bought by a German student fraternity at the end of the 19th century and in 1919 it housed a military museum reflecting on the then-recent fight for independence as well as on World War I. The annexe building was constructed from 1937 to 1940, but the Soviet occupation meant that it did not fulfil its function until several decades later. From 1957 the tower housed the Museum of the Revolution in the Soviet Republic of Latvia.

The current museum, the Latvian War Museum, occupies both the tower and the annexe. While the oldest exhibit – part of a cannon discovered during the 1930s – dates from the 15th century, the museum largely concentrates on 20th-century warfare. World War I is covered with interesting displays of weapons, uniforms and propaganda posters, as well as items made by the Latvian Riflemen *(see p152)*. Other rooms examine the role of Latvians in the Russian Revolution, the Latvian War of Independence, World War II and the Soviet occupation.

Old issue of *Lāčplēsis* magazine at the Latvian War Museum

⑭ Cats' House

Kaķu māja

Meistaru iela 10. **Map** 2 D3.

This yellow Art Nouveau building on the corner of Meistaru and Amatu streets is a popular image of Rīga for its two feline statues on its rooftop. The story goes that before World War I a merchant who owned the building was refused entry to the Great Guild because he was Latvian and membership was reserved for Germans only. In retaliation, he put two statues of black cats – with arched backs and tails up – onto the roof, positioning them so that their backsides faced the guildhall. After a lengthy court battle the merchant eventually gained entry into the guild and turned the cats around.

Statue on the roof of Cats' House

⑮ Great Guild

Lielā Ģilde

Amatu 6. **Map** 2 D3. **Tel** 6721 3798.

Established in the 13th century, the Great Guild had a monopoly on trade in Rīga for centuries. The building that served as the guild's headquarters was built from 1853 to 1860. An old guild chamber displays symbols of Hanseatic cities and the bridal chamber was once used by guild members' children on their wedding nights. Today, the building holds concerts by the Philharmonic Orchestra.

⑯ Small Guild

Mazā Ģilde

Amatu iela 5. **Map** 2 D3. **Tel** 6722 3772. **Open** for concerts and conferences only. 🌐 **gilde.lv/maza**

While the Great Guild counted the city's merchants as its members, the less powerful Small Guild existed to promote the interests of Rīga's German artisans. This guild may have been less prestigious than its neighbour, but with its turret and spire it is a more attractive building. The Italian mosaic floor in the entrance hall is particularly noteworthy. The current structure was started between 1864 and 1866, and then completed after an interval of 20 years.

Splendid exterior of the Small Guild

Street-by-Street: Around Town Hall Square

Until a local government reform in 1877, the Town Hall Square was Rīga's administrative centre. Built in 1334, the Town Hall was one of three focuses of power alongside Dome Cathedral and Rīga Castle, representing the interests of the city's residents. The square has functioned as a marketplace and a site where festivals were held and executions carried out. The impressive step-gabled House of Blackheads has been completely rebuilt, while the Town Hall is a modern building behind a Neo-Classical façade. Out of place at the square's edge is a Soviet-era building housing the Museum of the Occupation of Latvia.

Locator Map
See Street Finder Map pp164–5

Town Hall Square
Many of the square's elaborate buildings, destroyed by German bombs during World War II, have benefited from a restoration project tied to the city's 800th anniversary in 2001.

Town Hall

Statue of Roland
A legendary medieval figure and one of Charlemagne's knights, Roland became a symbol of the independence of cities from the local nobility.

GRĒCINIEKU IEL

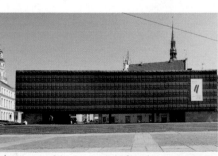

⓲ ★ Museum of the Occupation of Latvia
Covering the Soviet and Nazi occupations of the 20th century, the exhibitions of this museum are housed in the US Embassy while the building undergoes reconstruction.

Key
— Suggested route

㉑ ★ St Peter's Church
This striking building has been destroyed and rebuilt several times over since its original 13th-century incarnation.

Konventa Sēta
The winding Convent Courtyard has been renovated and is now home to shops, galleries and the Porcelain Museum (see p153).

0 metres ─────── 100
0 yards ─────── 100

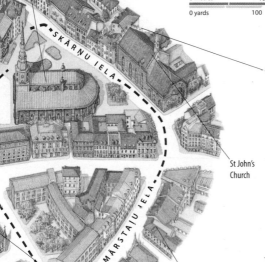

SKĀRNU IELA

MĀRSTAĻU IELA

St John's Church

Jāņa Sēta
The courtyard of St John's Church is lined with tables and chairs in summer.

Photography Museum

Mentzendorff House

Dannenstern House
was the largest dwelling in 17th-century Rīga.

㉒ Mentzendorff House
This restored late 17th-century building is home to a museum of the merchant class.

House of Blackheads, set behind Schwab House

⑰ House of Blackheads

Melngalvju nams

Rātslaukums 7. **Map** 1 C4.
Tel 6704 4300. 🛈 Schwab House.
Closed until 2016.

Together with the adjoining Schwab House, the House of Blackheads is one of Rīga's most impressive reconstruction projects. It was originally built in 1334 for the city's guilds, after the Livonian Order seized the existing guild buildings. Over time, the Blackheads, a guild of unmarried foreign merchants, became the sole occupants. Their name derives from their patron, St Maurice (who was often depicted as a Moor), and they were known for their riotous parties.

The building's ground floor housed shops, while the guild-hall was on the first floor. The step-gabled Dutch Renaissance façade was added in the late 1500s, the astronomical clock in 1622, and the Hanseatic emblems and the four figures (Neptune, Mercury, Unity and Peace) in 1896. Schwab House was built to complement its neighbour in 1891.

The Blackheads disbanded when the Baltic Germans were asked by Hitler to return home at the beginning of World War II. Both buildings were devastated by bombing in 1941 and the Soviet authorities demolished the remnants seven years later; the current structures date from 1999. The building will serve as a temporary presidential residence until 2016, while renovation work is carried out at Rīga Castle (see p147). The city's main tourist information office can be found in Schwab House.

⑱ Museum of the Occupation of Latvia

Latvijas okupācijas muzejs

Strēlnieku laukums 1. **Map** 1 C4.
Tel 6721 2715. **Closed** for renovations; temporarily housed in US Embassy building, Raina bulvaris 7.
🖾 donations. 🎦 🏠
🆆 **occupationmuseum.lv**

This Soviet-era concrete structure was built to house a museum honouring the Latvian Riflemen, but since 1993 it has provided a sobering account of Latvians' suffering at the hands of Nazi Germany in World War II and the later Soviet occupation. The collection includes photographs and eyewitness accounts of deportations and political repression. The replica of a Gulag barracks room offers an insight into the hardship experienced by deportees. The renovated building will include a memorial to the victims of Communist occupation.

⑲ Latvian Riflemen Monument

Strēlnieku piemineklis

Strēlnieku laukums. **Map** 1 C4. ♿

Depicting three brooding Latvian Riflemen, this controversial granite sculpture has stood in the square bearing its name since 1970. The Riflemen were a unit of the Russian army, formed to defend their homeland against Germany in 1915. Radicalized by the heavy losses they suffered during fierce fighting, they went on to support Lenin during the 1917 Revolution. Some of the Riflemen later returned to Latvia, while others became Lenin's most trusted troops. Some local people see the Riflemen as Latvian military heroes, while for others they recall the repressive Soviet period.

⑳ Mentzendorff House

Mencendorfa nams

Grēcinieku 18. **Map** 2 D4. **Tel** 6721 2951. **Open** May–Sep: 10am–5pm daily; Oct–Apr: 11am–5pm Wed–Sun.
🖾 🎦 🆆 **mencendorfanams.com**

Constructed in 1695 as the premises for a glass-cutter, this tall building got its current name from a delicatessen based on the ground floor in the early

Beautifully restored wall paintings in a room of Mentzendorff House

20th century. Extensively restored in the 1980s and 90s, the building is now a museum devoted to the life of Rīga's merchant class in the 17th and 18th centuries. Each room is decorated in period style. One highlight is the wall paintings, influenced by the work of French artist Antoine Watteau, depicting the wealthy relaxing.

㉑ St Peter's Church

Pēterbaznīca

Skārņu 19. **Map** 2 D4. **Tel** 6718 1430. **Open** 10am–6pm Tue–Sun. ♿ except tower. 🎫 for tower W **peterbaznica.riga.lv**

First mentioned in 1209, St Peter's Church was, unlike other churches, largely built by the Livs *(see p176)* and not by foreigners. None of the original wooden church remains, but parts of the walls date from the 1200s. The semi-circular apse and its five chapels were built in the 15th century, while the three Baroque dolomite entrance portals were added in the late 17th century. The church, which had become Lutheran in 1523, was damaged by fire in 1721, when Peter the Great is said to have headed the failed efforts to rescue it.

The church's steeple has been rebuilt several times over. The current one was built in 1973. Reaching a height of 123 m (403 ft), it provides excellent views across the city.

㉒ Museum of Decorative Arts and Design

Dekoratīvās mākslas un dizaina muzejs

Skārņu iela 10/20. **Map** 2 D4. **Tel** 6722 2235. **Open** 11am–5pm Tue & Thu–Sun; 11am–7pm Wed. 🎫 🎫 🎫 W **lnmm.lv**

This museum is housed in the former St George's Church, Rīga's oldest surviving stone building. It was constructed as the chapel

Vera Viduka's 1977 textile at the Museum of Decorative Arts and Design

for Rīga's original Livonian Order castle in 1208, and became a separate church after the castle was destroyed in 1297. After the Reformation it was used as a warehouse, and traces of sacred and profane uses have been retained in the building.

The museum gives an overview of decorative arts from the 1890s to the present day. Temporary exhibitions are shown on the ground floor, while the first floor, covering the 1890s to the 1960s, is the most interesting part of the main collection. Highlights include painted ceramics from the Baltars studio and carpet designs by Jūlijs Madernieks.

Lenin plate, Porcelain Museum

㉓ Porcelain Museum

Rīgas porcelāna muzejs

Kalēju 9/11. **Map** 2 D4. **Tel** 6701 2944. **Open** 11am–6pm Tue–Sun. 🎫 W **porcelanamuzejs.riga.lv**

Situated in the Convent Courtyard, this museum reflects the history of porcelain manu-facturing in Latvia, which dates back to the late 19th century. The 6,000 exhibits include a wide range of dinner services, as well as a huge red-and-gold vase made to celebrate the city's 700th anniversary in 1901. Of historic importance is a display of vases and statues portraying Soviet leaders.

㉔ St John's Church

Jāņa baznīca

Jāņa 7. **Map** 2 D4. **Tel** 6722 4028. **Open** 10am–5pm Tue–Sat. ✝ 6:30pm Wed, 10am Sun.

Built as the cloister chapel for a Dominican Order monastery in 1234, St John's was devastated by 15th-century fighting between the Livonian Order and the city. Only the main door and porch remain, with the rest rebuilt in Gothic style, including a web-vaulted red-brick nave with an apse, choir and tower. In 1582, the Polish king Stefan Bathory gave the church to the Lutherans, and it was further expanded in the Mannerist style. The interior includes a Baroque altar dating from 1769 and a painting, *Krusta sistais* (*The Crucified*, 1912), by Janis Rozentāls in the sacristy.

Impressive ceiling and nave of St John's Church

Boating on the city canal in Bastejkalns park

㉕ Photography Museum

Latvijas fotogrāfijas muzejs

Mārstaļu iela 8. **Map** 2 D4. **Tel** 6722 2713. **Open** May–Sep: 10am–5pm Wed & Fri–Sun, noon–7pm Thu; Oct–Apr: 11am–5pm Wed & Fri–Sun, noon–7pm Thu. 🎫 📷 **w** fotomuzejs.lv

This museum traces the development of photography in Latvia from 1839 to 1941 through displays of photographs and camera equipment. The images also serve to illustrate life in Latvia, depicting events such as the 1905 Revolution *(see p139)* and scenes of daily life during the first period of independence. In one room, an early 20th-century photographic studio has been re-created and in another there is a display dedicated to the Minox, or "spy" camera, invented by Rīga-born Walter Zapp (1905–2003). More unusual items include stereoscopic images and viewers and there is also a gallery that holds temporary exhibitions.

Large plate camera, exhibited at the Photography Museum

㉖ Bastejkalns

Basteja bulvāris. **Map** 2 D3.

Situated next to the Freedom Monument, this leafy park was set out in the mid-19th century on the mound of a 17th-century bastion. It is a pleasant place to relax, but it also contains a reminder that the path to Latvia's independence was not without bloodshed. On the night of 20 January 1991, OMON troops – also known as the Black Berets – tried to storm barricaded government buildings. Two filmmakers (Gvido Zvaigzne and Andris Slapiņš), two militiamen (Sergejs Kononenko and Vladimirs Gomanovics) and a schoolboy (Edijs Riekstiņš) were killed in the ensuing gunfire in Bastejkalns. Local people regularly renew the flowers on the memorial stones which bear their names, located close to a small bridge.

㉗ Freedom Monument

Brīvības piemineklis

Brīvības bulvāris. **Map** 2 D3. ♿

Built in 1935 on a site previously occupied by a statue of Peter the Great, the 42-m (138-ft) tall Freedom Monument is a potent symbol of Latvian independence. It was designed by the sculptor Kārlis Zāle, also responsible for the ensemble at the Brothers' Cemetery *(see p161)*. The granite base is decorated with reliefs and statues representing four virtues – work, spiritual life, family and protection of the fatherland – as well as Latvian heroes including Lāčplēsis. It also bears the motto *"Tēvzemei un brīvībai"* (For Fatherland and Freedom). The slender granite column is topped by a female figure, commonly known as Milda, holding aloft three golden stars, which represent the three cultural regions of Latvia – Kurzeme, Vidzeme and Latgale. During the Soviet era the authorities banned people from laying flowers at the base of the monument and placed a statue of Lenin a short distance away.

The imposing Freedom Monument, designed by Kārlis Zāle

㉘ Krišjānis Barons Memorial Museum

Krišjāņa Barona memoriālais muzejs

Kr Barona iela 3. **Map** 2 E3. **Tel** 6728 4265. **Open** 11am–6pm Wed–Sun. 🎫 📷 📷 **w** baronamuzejs.lv

Located in an apartment where the famous folklorist spent the last years of his life, this museum displays photographs and documents relating to Barons's life and work. The most important exhibit is the *Dainu skapis* (Cabinet of Latvian Folk Songs), a specially designed chest of drawers in which Barons organized the texts of over

Krišjānis Barons

In a nation where singing is one of the most important forms of cultural expression, Krišjānis Barons (1835–1923) is perceived as a hero. Influenced by Krišjānis Valdemārs *(see p195)* and part of the group of nationalist intellectuals known as the Young Latvians, Barons is known for systematizing Latvia's four-line folk songs *(dainas)*. He did not collect them in person, but by selecting certain songs as central and then listening to the differences between them, he was able to include 217,996 songs in the six-volume work he published between 1894 and 1915.

Krišjānis Barons

350,000 four-line folk songs sent by thousands of singers and informants. Each was written according to Barons's instructions on a slip of paper the same size as cigarette-paper boxes, which he used for storage before the cabinet was built. Contrary to popular belief, not all the slips were rewritten by Barons.

㉙ Orthodox Cathedral

Pareizticīgo katedrāle

Brīvības iela 23. **Map** 2 D3. **Tel** 6721 2901. 🕆 8am, 6pm Mon–Sat; 6:30am, 8:30am, 6pm Sun.

Situated on the edge of Esplanade Park (Esplanāde), this Neo-Byzantine Russian cathedral is officially called the Cathedral of Christ's Nativity (Kristus dzimšanas katedrāle). An attractive structure topped by five domes, it was built from 1876 to 1884 for the city's growing Russian community and was part of a deliberate process of Russification. It became a Lutheran church during the brief German occupation of Rīga in World War I, and once again an Orthodox church in 1921.

As with many places of worship, the Soviet authorities found alternative uses for the building during their occupation. In the 1960s they turned it into a lecture hall and planetarium. The interior decorations were nearly destroyed, and are still being replaced.

㉚ Latvian National Museum of Art

Latvijas Nacionālais mākslas muzejs

Kr Valdemāra 10a. **Map** 2 D2. **Tel** 6732 4461. **Closed** for renovation until 2016. 🕆 🗖 🌐 **lnmm.lv**

The interior of this early 20th-century Neo-Baroque building still has its original gilt and marble embellishments. While the collection was originally eclectic, in the 1920s and 30s the director Vilhelms Purvītis (1872–1945), himself one of the country's most famous artists, decided to focus on Latvian works. The first floor, therefore, traces the development of Latvian art from the mid-19th century to 1945, while the ground floor displays 18th- and 19th-century Balto-Germanic and Russian art. The latter collection also includes many icons from the 16th to 20th centuries.

There are, unsurprisingly, many paintings by Latvia's best-known artist Janis Rozentāls *(see p26)* and his works on display include *Leaving the Cemetery* (1895), and *Portrait of Malvīne Vīgnere-Grinberga* (1916). Other Latvian artists represented include Jēkabs Kazaks (1895–1920) and Romāns Suta (1896–1943), who were both members of the Rīga Artists' Group.

㉛ Museum of Jews in Latvia

Muzejs Ebreji Latvijā

Skolas iela 6. **Map** 2 D2. **Tel** 6728 3484. **Open** 11am–5pm Mon–Thu, Sun. 🕆 donations. 🌐 **jewishmuseum.lv**

Housed inside a Jewish community centre, this museum is based around the collections of Holocaust survivors Zalman Elelson and Marģers Vestermanis. It tells the story of the Jewish community in Latvia, which begins in the 16th century with the first records of Jews in the country and progresses to photographs of early 20th-century family life. Inevitably, though, the focus is on the horrific years of the Nazi occupation. The museum does not shy away from distressing images of the Holocaust, and it even includes footage of the massacre of Jews on Liepāja beach.

The elaborate domed roof of the Orthodox Cathedral

㉜ Pauls Stradiņš Museum of the History of Medicine
Paula Stradiņa medicīnas vēstures muzejs

Antonijas iela 1. **Map** 2 D2. **Tel** 6722 2665. 🚌 2, 24. Trolleybus 1, 19. **Open** 11am–5pm Tue–Sat (to 7pm Thu). **Closed** last Fri of the month. 🌐 ♿ 🅦 **mvm.lv**

Opened in 1961, this museum is based around the collection of cancer specialist Dr Pauls Stradiņš and is one of the world's three biggest medical museums. Its aim is to explore the history of medicine in relation to scientific development. Ancient uses of medicinal herbs, trepanning (the oldest known surgery, which involves making a hole in the patient's skull) and Soviet developments in space biology and medicine are covered. The oddest exhibit is a stuffed two-headed dog, which was the result of experimental grafting.

㉝ Art Nouveau Museum
Jūgendstila muzejs

Albert iela 12. **Map** 2 D2. **Tel** 6718 1464. **Open** 10am–6pm Tue–Sun. 🌐 ♿ 🎥 🅦 **jugendstils.riga.lv**

This museum celebrates the Art Nouveau movement for which Rīga is most famous. It is located in the former apartment of the building's architect, Konstantīns Pēkšēns (1859–1928), who lived here around 1900.

Before you enter the apartment, note the elaborately decorated balconies and corner tower. Once indoors, it is worth climbing the staircase to the fifth floor in order to view the paintings that adorn the ceilings. The interior is furnished throughout as it would have been during the time when Pēkšēns lived here, although few of the items are original.

Visitors are guided by staff in period costume, and there is a short film about Art Nouveau buildings in Rīga.

Art Nouveau Architecture

Rīga's collection of Art Nouveau buildings has been recognized by UNESCO as unparalleled anywhere in the world, with most found in the Quiet Centre (Klusais Centrs). Many of the early examples – dating from the turn of the 20th century – are categorized as eclectic Art Nouveau, making use of asymmetry, symbolic ornamentation and details drawn from nature. Two other Art Nouveau styles found here are perpendicular, which placed emphasis on vertical composition, and National Romanticism, which incorporated folk motifs and the use of natural materials.

⑫ **Elizabetes iela 13**
Less ornately decorated than others in the area, and judicious in its use of space, the façade of this building illustrates the principle of *amor vacui* (love of space).

⑨ **Strēlnieku iela 4a**
Symbols of victory adorn this eclectic Art Nouveau edifice, including maidens clutching wreaths and bald eagles. The building, designed by Mikhail Eisenstein, now houses a private school.

⑪ **Strēlnieku iela 2**
An example of perpendicular Art Nouveau, the architectural design of this building is relatively restrained, with ornamental details integrated into the structure, including carvings of grain at the top.

⑩ Elizabetes iela 23
This building has anthropomorphic carvings and a pediment with the words *"Labor vinvit omnia"* (Work conquers all), which commemorates architect Mārtiņš Nukša.

⑧ Alberta iela 13
The numerous female figures on this building display a range of emotions.

④ Alberta iela 4
Lions are uncommon in Art Nouveau, but in this eclectic building their wings indicate their traditional connection with the sun.

0 metres   100
0 yards   100

② Elizabetes iela 33
This early experiment with Art Nouveau by Mikhail Eisenstein, one of the foremost proponents of the eclectic style, draws upon Historicist architecture.

Key List of Sites

① Elizabetes iela 10b
② Elizabetes iela 33
③ Alberta iela 2a
④ Alberta iela 4
⑤ Alberta iela 8
⑥ Alberta iela 11
⑦ Alberta iela 12
⑧ Alberta iela 13
⑨ Strēlnieku iela 4a
⑩ Elizabetes iela 23
⑪ Strēlnieku iela 2
⑫ Elizabetes iela 13
⑬ Vilandes iela 2

⑥ Alberta iela 11
A fine example of National Romanticism, this building, constructed in natural stone, has bay windows resembling turrets.

Elsewhere in the City

Although the Quiet Centre includes some of Rīga's finest examples of Art Nouveau, there are many other buildings worth visiting elsewhere in the city. Examples in the Old Town include Kalēju iela 23, with its tree-shaped portal, and the city's oldest Art Nouveau building at Audēju iela 7. There are excellent examples of National Romanticism at Tērbatas iela 15/17 and A Čaka iela 26, and many impressive buildings on Brīvības iela and Hamburgas iela. *Art Nouveau in Rīga* (Silvija Grosa, published by Jumava) has good walks of the city.

Brightly coloured façade, Kalēju iela 23

Further Afield

Although primarily residential, Rīga's suburbs include numerous places of interest for visitors. The Moscow Suburb, southeast of the Old Town, has long been home to immigrant communities, including many Jews before World War II. In contrast, the exclusive Mežaparks to the north was built for wealthy Baltic Germans. Across the Daugava river is the Left Bank, where old wooden buildings and a variety of museums can be found.

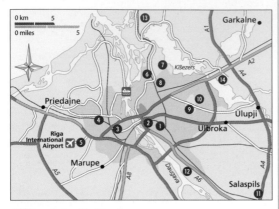

Sights at a Glance

1. Moscow Suburb
2. Central Market
3. Left Bank
4. Botanical Gardens
5. Aviation Museum
6. Dauderi
7. Mežaparks
8. Rīga's Cemeteries
9. Biķernieki Forest
10. Motor Museum
11. Salaspils
12. Rumbula Forest
13. Vecāķi
14. Latvian Ethnographic Open-Air Museum

Key

▨ Central Rīga
═ Motorway
▬ Main road
═ Minor road
— Railway

---

❶ Moscow Suburb

Maskavas forštate

🚌 A18, T15. 🚊 3, 7, 9.

The area to the east of the Central Market has long been known as the Moscow Suburb, for the road to Moscow ran through it and many of its inhabitants were impoverished Russians. They were joined by Jews – who had previously been banned from settling in the city – in the second half of the 19th century. When the German army arrived in 1941, they established a Jewish ghetto in the suburb, bounded by Kalna, Lauvas, Ebreju, Jersikas and Daugavpils streets.

Still home to many non-Latvians today, it is a quiet area with cobbled side-streets and numerous wooden and religious buildings. The nearby **Rīga Ghetto Museum** attempts to depict life inside the Jewish ghetto, with barbed-wire fences, original cobblestones and other artifacts. A memorial was unveiled at the **Choral Synagogue Ruins** on 4 July 2007, exactly 66 years after German soldiers had filled the

building with Jewish families and burned it to the ground. The memorial includes the names of the 270 Latvians known to have rescued Jews during the war and the image of Žanis Lipke, who, with his wife Johanna, saved more than 50 lives.

Other religious buildings in the area include the small and atmospheric **Russian Orthodox Church of the Annunciation** (Tserkva blagoveshtenya) and the domed Grebenshchikov Church (Grebenščikova baznīca) where Old Believers *(see p126)* worship. The distinctive octagonal Lutheran **Jesus Church** (Jēzus baznīca), the largest wooden church in the city, is also worth visiting.

The **Academy of Sciences** (Latvijas zinātņu akadēmija) is a more controversial landmark. Rīga's first skyscraper, it was built between 1953 and 1957 in a pseudo-Baroque style which earned it the nickname "Stalin's Birthday Cake". The ornamentation includes both Latvian folk imagery and hammer-and-sickle motifs, and while parts of it are in need of repair it remains an impressive structure. The

balcony on the 17th floor is open to the public.

🏛 **Rīga Ghetto Museum**
Maskavas 14a. **Tel** 6727 0827.
Open 10am–6pm Sun–Fri.

🏛 **Choral Synagogue Ruins**
Corner of Gogoļa & Dzirnavu iela.

🏛 **Russian Orthodox Church of the Annunciation**
Gogoļa iela 9. **Tel** 6722 0566.

🏛 **Jesus Church**
Elijas iela 18. **Tel** 6722 4123.
🏛 6pm Thu, 10am Sun.

🏛 **Academy of Sciences**
Akadēmijas laukums 1. **Tel** 6722 9350.
Balcony **Open** May–Sep: 9am–6pm daily. 📷

Academy of Sciences, nicknamed "Stalin's Birthday Cake"

Well-maintained locomotives on show at the Railway Museum, Left Bank

Gunnar Birkerts, houses the National Library of Latvia. Its unusual, sloping shape symbolizes a mythic castle said to have sunk into an ancient lake only to re-emerge once Latvians were masters of their own land. Opened in 2014, the library hosts exhibitions and cultural events.

🏛 Railway Museum

2–4 Uzvaras bulvāris. **Tel** 6723 2849. **Open** 10am–5pm Tue–Sun (to 6pm Thu). 🏛 **W** **railwaymuseum.lv**

🏛 Castle of Light

Mūkusalas iela 3. **Tel** 6780 6135. **Open** noon–8pm Tue & Thu, 11am–7pm Wed & Fri, 10am–5pm Sat.

❷ Central Market

Centrāltirgus

Centrāltirgus 1. **Open** 8am–5pm daily. ✉ **W** **centraltirgus.lv**

Housed in five Zeppelin hangars, Rīga's Central Market is one of the most distinctive in Europe. The hangars, which the German Kaiser's army had abandoned in Kurzeme during World War I, were moved to their current site during the 1920s. The market building sells mostly fresh food, while the area around it is crammed with stalls selling other goods.

❸ Left Bank

Pārdaugava

🚌 A8, T9. 🚋 2, 4, 5, 10.

Although most sites of interest lie on the right bank of the Daugava river, the Left Bank includes specialist museums

and some of the country's best wooden architecture, found in Āgenskalns district.

Just across the Stone Bridge (Akmens tilts) is the city's **Railway Museum** (Latvijas dzelzceļa muzejs), the highlight of which is the collection of rolling stock in the yard outside. Exhibits housed inside a renovated engine warehouse include photographs of Latvian stations, old tickets and posters, railway staff uniforms and signalling equipment.

Close by is **Victory Park** (Uzvaras parks), named for the Red Army's victory over the Nazis, which was depicted by the Soviet regime as a "liberation" of the city. The war memorial depicting soldiers being greeted by a welcoming figure of Victory is controversial and Latvian nationalists have twice tried to blow it up.

The massive **Castle of Light** (Gaismas pils), designed by Latvian-American architect

❹ Botanical Gardens

Botāniskais dārzs

Kandavas iela 2. **Tel** 6745 0852. 🚋 5 to Konsula iela. **Open** May–Sep: 9am–7pm; Oct–Apr: 9am–4:30pm. 🏛 📷 in English, Russian or German by arrangement. ♿ **W** **botanika.lu.lv**

Founded in 1922 as part of the University of Latvia, the Botanical Gardens have been in their current location since 1926. The site includes 5,400 species of plants, with approximately 400 of them native to Latvia; many of them are rare or endangered. In the centre of the garden is a complex of five greenhouses, including a palm house, a large collection of ferns, and a greenhouse devoted to cacti and other succulents. The gardens are particularly attractive from spring through to summer.

Greenhouse set amid the lush grounds of Rīga's Botanical Gardens

❺ Aviation Museum

Aviācijas muzejs

Rīga Airport. **Tel** 2686 2707.
Open 9am–6pm Mon–Fri, Sat & Sun
by arrangement. 🚗 📷 💻 📱
🌐 **aviamuseum.org**

Located just beside Rīga's
airport, this private open-air
museum claims to have the
largest collection of Soviet aircraft outside the Commonwealth
of Independent States.
The impressive array of aero-
planes and helicopters is the
legacy of the Young Pilot's
Club, an organization founded
in 1956 which was granted
used military aircraft for
training purposes. After the
break-up of the Soviet Union,
funding dried up, but in 1998
the equipment was moved
onto airport territory. In
addition to the aircraft, both
military and civilian, there
is a small exhibition of
uniforms and other equip-
ment. Opening hours can
be erratic so visitors should
call ahead.

M16 airplane, on show at the
Aviation Museum

❻ Dauderi

Sarkandaugavas iela 30. **Tel** 6739
1780, 6739 2229. 🚌 5 or 9 to Aldaris.
Open 11am–5pm Wed–Sun. 🚗
🌐 **history-museum.lv**

This late 19th-century Neo-
Gothic mansion, 6 km (4 miles)
from Rīga's city centre, was the
summer residence of Latvian
president Kārlis Ulmanis from
1937 to 1940, although he only
ever stayed here for short

Neo-Gothic façade of Dauderi mansion dating from the 19th century

periods of time. The Soviet army
later occupied the building, and
in turn the Germans placed
anti-aircraft guns in the
grounds. The mansion has also
been used as a kindergarten
and as tasting rooms for the
Ministry of Food.

Now converted into a
museum, the rooms are
decorated and furnished in
the style of the 1920s
and 30s. There are
displays dedicated
to the life of
Ulmanis, the
nation's first period
of independence
and the cultural
activities of Latvian
exiles during World
War II and the
subsequent Soviet
occupation. The collection is
eclectic and includes
photographs, medals, puppets
and folk costumes. The mansion
is surrounded by a park
containing sculptures and
artificial ruins.

Cherubs decorating the ceiling
of Dauderi mansion

❼ Mežaparks

🚇 11.

Previously called Kaiserwald
(German for "Emperor's Forest")
in reference to its use as a base
by the invading Swedish king
Gustav Adolphus in the 17th
century, this part of northeast
Rīga became Europe's first
garden city in the early 20th
century. Renamed Mežaparks,
meaning "Forest Park", it was
designed as a suburb for
wealthy Baltic Germans, most of

whom later returned to Germany
at the beginning of World War II.
During the war a concentration
camp was set up in the area by
the Nazis, housing Jews brought
from liquidated ghettos across
Eastern Europe. The camp was
closed when the Red Army
invaded in 1944 and nothing
remains of it today. During the
Soviet period many of the
suburb's buildings fell
into disrepair. Since
independence,
however, property
prices in Mežaparks
have risen, and the
area is now predo-
minantly Latvian
with a significant
number of foreign
owners including
several embassies.
Some of the new residents are
building homes which are
grand, if not always tasteful,
while others are restoring older
buildings. The area is fascinating
to walk around for its mix of
contemporary, Modernist and
Art Nouveau buildings, with
Hamburgas Street a particular
highlight of the area.

Another reason to visit the
area is **Rīga Zoo** (Rīgas
zooloģiskais dārzs), a well-
maintained site which is popular
with families. It is known for its
bears and has an excellent
tropical house, although the
zoo's star attraction is a pair of
rare Amur tigers. Rides in a
horse-drawn carriage are
available during the summer,
and special events take place
throughout the year, including
the weighing of the zoo's

tortoises in June, and Wolves' Day in September.

Close to the zoo is the **Song Stadium** (Mežaparka estrāde), which was built to host the National Song Festival, held every five years. With the finale including more than 10,000 singers on stage at one time, the stadium is built on a very large scale.

🎪 Riga Zoo
Meža prospekts 1. **Tel** 6751 8409. **Open** May–Sep: 10am–6pm daily; Oct–Apr: 10am–4pm daily. 🅿 🅲 **W** rigazoo.lv

🕗 Rīga's Cemeteries

Aizsaules iela. 🚌 A9. 🚋 11. **Open** daily.

Rīga's three most interesting cemeteries are located just south of Mežaparks along Aizsaules Street. The grandest is the **Brothers' Cemetery** (Brāļu kapi), built for Latvians who died defending their country during World War I and the War of Independence. The best-known sculptures are three patriotic works by Kārlis Zāle: *Two Brothers*, *The Wounded Horseman* and *Mother Latvia*. The memorial features the 19 coats of arms of the Latvian administrative

districts as well as soil from every *pagasts* (parish).

The **Rainis Cemetery** (Raiņa kapi) existed before the writer and atheist Janis Pliekšāns, known as Rainis, was buried there in 1929, but it was renamed in his honour. His memorial allegorically depicts a youthful Latvia awakening from its slumber. Rainis's wife Elza Rozenberga, who wrote under the name Aspazija, lies beside him, and many other Latvian artists and musicians have also been buried here.

The **Woodlands Cemetery** (Meža kapi) opened in 1913 and is the burial place for many political figures from Latvia's first period of independence. It was intended that the main alley would lead straight to the memorial to Latvia's first president, Janis Čakste (1859–1927), but during the Soviet era smaller gravestones were put in the way. Janis Rozentāls *(see p26)* was also laid to rest at the site, while the most famous sculpture is the *Grieving Mother*, which marks the suspicious death of the nation's foreign minister in 1925.

Mother Latvia statue, Brothers' Cemetery

🕘 Biķernieki Forest

Biķernieku mežs

🚌 A16, T14.

This site was chosen by the Nazis for the execution and burial of around 40,000 Jews and other "undesirables" brought from Germany and several occupied European countries between 1941 and 1944. The memorial is the most moving of those in the Rīga area. A path leads from Biķernieku Street under a white concrete arch, revealing a field of jagged stones huddled together into sections, each representing a city from which Jews were deported. The centre-piece is a concrete canopy under which a black stone stands, with an inscription reading *"O earth, cover not thou my blood, and let my cry have no place"* (Job 16:18). Further smaller memorials nearby mark mass graves. The site can be reached on foot from the Motor Museum *(see p162)* although the route is not signposted; the trolleybus stop is about 1 km (half a mile) from the memorial.

Evocative jagged stones of the Holocaust Memorial, Biķernieki Forest

Auto Union V16 racing car on display at the Motor Museum

⑩ Motor Museum

Rīgas motormuzejs

S Eizenšteina 6. **Tel** 6702 5888. 🚌 5, 15; minibus 207, 263. **Open** 10am–6pm daily. ♿ 📷 in English or Russian. 🛍 📷
🌐 **motormuzejs.lv**

Row after row of gleaming cars, motorcycles and bicycles are housed in this modern, hangar-like building. There are over 240 vehicles in total – both Latvian-made and foreign. The highlight is a series taken from the Kremlin's collection. The former Soviet president Leonid Brezhnev, in particular, was a motor enthusiast and one of the exhibits is a 1966 Rolls Royce Silver Shadow which he crashed in Moscow – a startled-looking waxwork sits behind the wheel. There is also a heavy armoured ZIS 115S limousine used by Stalin. Small panels give background information on the vehicles and tell the story of the automotive industry in Latvia. The museum shop sells model cars.

⑪ Salaspils

15 km (9 miles) SE of central Rīga. 🚉 Dārziņi. 🌐 **salaspils.lv**

Although its history stretches back to the 12th century, Salaspils is notorious as the location of a World War II German concentration camp. Its original inmates were prisoners of war, but they were joined by Jews brought from several occupied countries after Rīga's main ghetto was closed. The number of people who died in the camp is disputed as the Soviet regime subsequently exaggerated the figures as a propaganda tool, but it is thought that hundreds were either killed directly or died as a result of the camp's harsh conditions.

The entrance to the camp is marked by a long, sloping concrete block placed at an angle to the ground, intended to symbolize the boundary between life and death. The text on the block reads *"Behind this gate the earth groans"* – a line from a poem by Eižens Vēveris, who was a prisoner at camp. Inside the block is a small exhibition which, like the rest of the site, has a rather neglected air. Beyond this, the shape of the camp has been indicated, and a metronome ticks inside a block of stone – its slow beat seemingly coming from deep inside the earth. Dominating the site is a series of huge sculptures erected in 1967, with titles such as *The Humiliated* and *The Unbroken*.

Sculpture at Salaspils

⑫ Rumbula Forest

Rumbulas mežs

11 km (7 miles) from central Rīga, along Maskavas iela. 🚉

At least 25,000 Jews were murdered in Rumbula Forest on 30 November and 8 December 1941. The victims, mostly women, children and the elderly from the Rīga ghetto, were shot and their bodies dumped in five mass graves. Just three people are known to have survived. The location of the killings came to light after the war, when two local people tried to sell jewellery found in the area.

Until the late 1980s, the memorials identified the dead as Soviet citizens, although members of the Jewish community illegally tended the site and were eventually allowed to add a modest stone bearing Hebrew text. The focal point of the memorial, constructed in 2002, is a large menorah (seven-branched candlestick), surrounded by broken stones, each of which is inscribed with the names of a murdered family.

⑬ Vecāķi

15 km (9 miles) NE of central Rīga. 🚉 🚌 A24.

This stretch of coast is a popular escape from the city during summer, although its beach is rarely crowded. At the eastern end there is an area reserved for naturists. It is worth walking west along the coast, towards the mouth of the Daugava river, to see the remains of fortifications built to protect what was one of Europe's biggest ports. Many of the bunkers date from the time of the Napoleonic Wars, but were last used during World War I. The fortifications have not been well maintained, so exercise caution.

Vast sandy coastline of Vecāķi, northeast of central Rīga

⓮ Latvian Ethnographic Open-Air Museum

Latvijas Etnogrāfiskais brīvdabas muzejs

Occupying 86 ha (213 acres) of woodland on the shores of Lake Jugla, this site includes over 118 homesteads, churches, windmills and other structures from across Latvia. Founded in 1924, the museum is organized according to Latvia's ethnographic regions – Vidzeme, Kurzeme, Zemgale and Latgale – drawing attention to variations in building design and living arrangements in different parts of the country. With craftspeople working on-site during the summer, and many buildings containing everyday artifacts, the museum offers an insight into 19th-century rural life and takes at least 2 hours to explore.

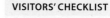

VISITORS' CHECKLIST

Practical Information
Brīvības gatve 440. **Tel** 6799 4510.
Open 10am–5pm daily.
🕙 10am Sun.
w brivdabasmuzejs.lv

Transport
🚌 1.

Dutch Windmill
The windmill (1890) is from Latgale and can operate two grindstones simultaneously.

Vidzeme Spinning Wheel-Maker's Homestead

★ Kurzeme Peasants' Homestead
This wooden building with a reed-thatched roof is typical of 19th-century rural architecture in southwest Kurzeme.

Zemgale Peasants' Homestead
includes a dwelling-house, a bath-house, granaries and a threshing barn.

Handicrafts
Handicraft displays include traditional wickerwork.

Kurzeme Fishermen's Village

Entrance

★ Usma Church
Most wooden churches were replaced by stone buildings in the 19th century, making this a rare survivor.

Old Believers' House
Located in a Latgale village, the house exhibits a loom for weaving thread and a samovar used to boil water for tea.

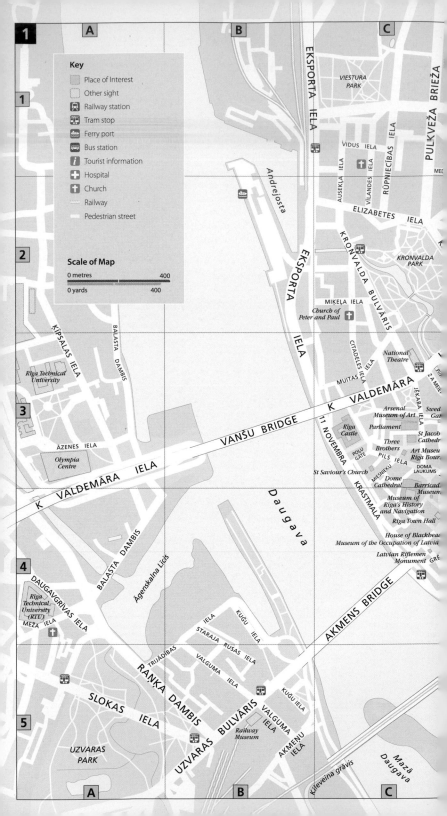

WESTERN LATVIA

Known for its dense forests and fertile plains, lively cities and sleepy rural towns, Western Latvia enchants visitors with its contrasts. The Kurzeme region is quiet and sparsely populated, with the major exceptions of the busy ports of Ventspils and Liepāja. Running along the Lithuanian border, the largely agricultural Zemgale region is dotted with castles and manor houses recalling past glories.

Prior to the arrival of the German crusaders, the heavily forested western region now called Kurzeme was dominated by the Kurši tribe, while the Livs inhabited its northern coast. The fertile and well-drained terrain running along the Lielupe river in the south was home to the Zemgaļi; together with an eastern region formerly called Selonia, this area is now known as Zemgale. The Kurzeme tribes were defeated in 1267 and just over two decades later the same fate befell the Zemgaļi – the last of the Latvian tribes to surrender.

When the Livonian Order collapsed in the 16th century its last master, Gotthard Kettler, retained control of the entire region as a largely independent fiefdom of Poland. With Jelgava as its capital, the Duchy of Courland and Semigallia reached its zenith under Duke Jakob Kettler

(r.1642–81). The Duchy was incorporated into the Russian Empire in 1795, and its fate was thereafter tied up with that of the rest of what is now Latvia.

Today, most of Kurzeme retains its rural character, although the cities of Liepāja and Ventspils are among the largest and most vibrant in the country. The few remaining speakers of the Liv language continue their fishing traditions on the northern coast. The area has several pictur-esque small towns, including Kuldiga and Talsi. The Zemgale countryside consists mainly of flat farmland, with exceptions such as forest parks in the hills around Tērvete. Jelgava's Old Town was devastated during World War II, although the duke's palace is still standing. The most popular tourist attraction, however, is Rundāle Palace with its Baroque exterior and restored Rococo interior.

Bright yellow rape fields in full bloom, Kurzeme

◄ Tree-lined approach to the splendid Rundāle Palace

Exploring Western Latvia

Kurzeme's long, unspoiled coastline has some tranquil villages as well as the cities of Ventspils and Liepāja. Ventspils is one of Latvia's busiest ports, while Liepāja has been transformed from a derelict port to a vibrant cultural centre. Further inland, Kuldīga is among the country's most attractive small towns and makes a good base for exploration, while Pedvāle is popular for its outdoor sculptures. In Zemgale, Rundāle Palace, Bauska Castle and a Neo-Classical palace at Mežotne are highlights. Jelgava, a major transport hub, is a good base from which to explore the region.

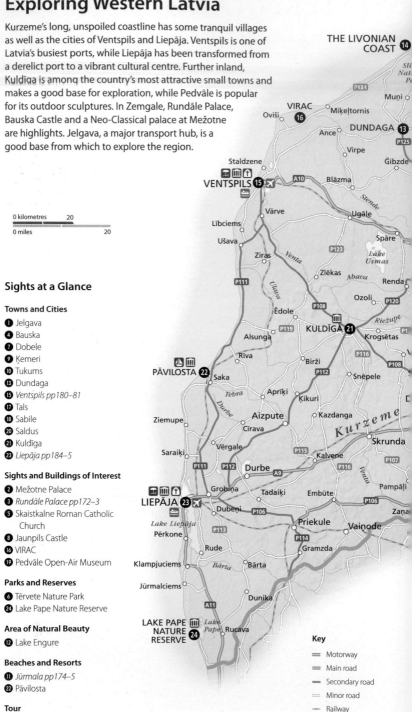

Sights at a Glance

Towns and Cities

1 Jelgava
4 Bauska
7 Dobele
9 Ķemeri
10 Tukums
13 Dundaga
15 *Ventspils pp180–81*
17 Tals
18 Sabile
20 Saldus
21 Kuldīga
23 *Liepāja pp184–5*

Sights and Buildings of Interest

2 Mežotne Palace
3 *Rundāle Palace pp172–3*
5 Skaistkalne Roman Catholic Church
8 Jaunpils Castle
16 VIRAC
19 Pedvāle Open-Air Museum

Parks and Reserves

6 Tērvete Nature Park
24 Lake Pape Nature Reserve

Area of Natural Beauty

12 Lake Engure

Beaches and Resorts

11 *Jūrmala pp174–5*
22 Pāvilosta

Tour

14 *The Livonian Coast p177*

Key

═══ Motorway
─── Main road
─── Secondary road
┄┄┄ Minor road
-··- Railway
▬▬▬ International border

For hotels and restaurants see pp301–302 and pp322–4

Ruins of the 15th-century Bauska Castle atop a grass mound

Getting Around

To explore Western Latvia's remote towns and villages, it is generally best to travel by car. By contrast, it is also possible to visit the region's many other attractions by using public transport. While buses are a good option for reaching Bauska and most of Kurzeme's sights, taking a train is preferable for trips to Jelgava and Tukums. However, as there are no direct routes between Rīga and Rundāle, visitors will need to travel to Bauska and take an onward bus from there. The port towns of Ventspils and Liepāja have good ferry connections with Rīga as well as with other European cities. There are also airports at Liepāja and Ventspils.

For keys to symbols *see back flap*

Jelgava Palace, built on an island in the Lielupe river, Jelgava

❶ Jelgava

Road Map C4. 🅐 66,000.
🚉 from Rīga. 🚌 from Rīga.
ℹ️ Akadēmijas iela 1, 6300 5445.
🎭 International Ice Sculpture Festival
(Feb). 🖥️ **visit.jelgava.lv**

Between 1578 and 1795,
Jelgava was the capital of the
Duchy of Courland. Much of the
town was damaged during the
two world wars. The most
prominent remnant of the
duchy period is the **Jelgava
Palace** (Jelgavas pils), the winter
residence of Ernst Johann Biron
(see p173). Built in the 18th
century by Francesco B Rastrelli,
the building today houses the
Latvian University of Agriculture.
None of the original interiors
remain intact, but a small
museum houses archive
photographs of the palace's pre-
war state. Museum staff also
provide access to the burial
vault of the dukes of Courland.
   The Old Town offers a handful
of interesting sights. The
impressively restored **Orthodox
Cathedral of St Simeon and St
Anna** (Sv Sīmaņa un Annas
pareizticīgo katedrāle) was
designed by Rastrelli for Biron's
patron, Anna Ivanovna. A Baroque
building houses the **History
and Art Museum** (Vēstures un
mākslas muzejs), which documents local history, while the
quirky little **Latvian Railway
Museum** (Latvijas dzelzceļu
muzejs) attracts rail enthusiasts.

Environs
The small **Nikolai Cemetery**,
4 km (2 miles) southeast of
Jelgava, contains the graves of
36 British soldiers and sailors
who died in 1917 in Latvia as
German prisoners of war during
World War I.

🏰 Jelgava Palace
Lielā iela 2. **Tel** 6300 5617. **Open** mid-
May–Aug: 9am–6pm Mon–Sat; Sep–
mid-May: 9am–6pm Mon–Fri. 🔲 🎦

**⛪ Orthodox Cathedral of
St Simeon and St Anna**
Raiņa iela 5. **Tel** 6302 0207.
Open 9am–5pm daily. ✝️ 5pm.

🏛️ History and Art Museum
Akadēmijas iela 10. **Tel** 6302 3383.
Open 10am–5pm Wed–Sun. 🔲

🏛️ Latvian Railway Museum
Stacijas iela 3. **Tel** 6309 6494.
Open 11am–3pm Wed, Fri, Sat;
1–6pm Thu. 🔲 🎦

❷ Mežotne Palace

Road Map D4. **Tel** 6396 0711.
Open 9am–8pm daily. 🔲 🚫
🖥️ **mezotnespils.lv**

This restored Neo-Classical
structure was built in 1802 for
Charlotte von Lieven, governess

Pastel-coloured exterior of the
Neo-Classical Mežotne Palace

to the grandchildren of the
Russian Tsarina Catherine II.
The original design by Italian
architect Giacomo Quarenghi
was developed by local architect J G Berlitz. The Lieven
family lost the manor in 1920
during the agrarian reforms,
and it was partly destroyed
during World War II. Today, the
palace is used for functions and
as a hotel, but it is also open to
visitors. The highlight is the
Dome Hall, with artificial marble
pillars and walls, and a dome
painted to give the illusion of
three-dimensional decoration.
The grounds are in the style of
an English park, and in summer
boats take visitors across the
Lielupe river. On the other side
of the river is a castle mound,
site of one of the largest
Semigallian castles and scene
of their final battle against the
German crusaders (1290).

❸ Rundāle Palace

See pp 172–3.

❹ Bauska

Road Map D4. 🅐 11,000. 🚌 from
Rīga. ℹ️ Rātslaukums 1, 6392 3797.
🎭 Early Music Festival (Jul),
International Country Music Festival
(Jul). 🖥️ **tourism.bauska.lv**

A small country town, Bauska is
known mainly for its 15th-
century **Bauska Castle** (Bauskas
pils), which was built at the
confluence of the Mēmele and
Mūsa rivers to help control the
trade route between Rīga and
Lithuania. Later, it became the

property of the Duchy of Courland and Semigallia and a fortified residence was added for the duke. Restoration work has reversed inauthentic Soviet alterations, including the renewal of the original sgraffito decoration on the towers. It is possible to climb one of the towers for a small fee, and tours of the castle are illuminating.

Besides a number of fine wooden buildings, the town also boasts a 16th-century Lutheran church and the riverside **Bauskas Alus** brewery.

Bauska Castle
Tel 6392 2280. **Open** May–Sep: 9am–7pm daily; Oct: 9am–6pm daily; Nov–Apr: 11am–5pm Tue–Sun.
W bauskaspils.lv

Bauskas Alus
Tel 2945 1942.
Open by appointment.
W bauskasalus.lv

Embellished altarpiece, Skaistkalne Roman Catholic Church

❺ Skaistkalne Roman Catholic Church
Skaistkalnes Romas katoļu baznīca

Road Map D4. Slimnīcas iela 2, Skaistkalne. **Tel** 6393 3154.

Built for the Jesuits in 1692 and now maintained and administered by monks of the Paulian Order, Skaistkalne Church is Latvia's most popular place of pilgrimage after Aglona (*see p199*). Raised on a mound, the white building has a red roof and a rounded apse. The Baroque interior features

artificial marble palisades and an ornate altarpiece. Plump, pastel-coloured cherubs decorate the pulpit and organ, and two sets of paintings represent the Stations of the Cross. Call ahead, as the church is often locked.

❻ Tērvete Nature Park
Tērvetes dabas parks

Road Map C4. **i** Tērvetes Sils, 6372 6212. **Open** 9am–7pm daily (Nov–Feb: to 5pm). partial.
W tervetesparks.lv

This popular nature park was developed in the forest around Tērvete, which was famous as the home of Sprīdītis, a Tom Thumb-like character in the beloved fairytale by Anna Brigadere (1861–1933). Her summer house has been preserved as the **Anna Brigadere Museum**.

Wooden figure, Tērvete Nature Park

The theme of the fairytale is evident throughout the park, with its Dwarf Forest and Fairytale Forest dotted with carved wooden creatures. Summertime attractions include the park's own witch, and there are quieter paths through the Old Pine Forest. Nearby are a Livonian Order castle mound with an imposing replica fort and the **Tērvete History Museum**, which displays a collection of farm utensils and textiles.

Anna Brigadere Museum
Sprīdīši. **Tel** 2653 2691. **Open** May–Oct: 10am–5pm Wed–Sun.

Tērvete History Museum
Lielķēniņi. **Tel** 2695 0975. **Open** May–Nov: 10am–5pm Wed–Sun.

❼ Dobele

Road Map C4. 11,100. **i** Baznīcas iela 6, 6372 3074.
W dobele.lv

Situated on the banks of the Bērze river, Dobele is visited mainly for its ruined Livonian Order castle, built in 1335. Destroyed several times during the Polish-Swedish Wars (1600–29), the castle began to be restored only in 2002. The small **Dobele History Museum** recounts the town's history and mounts temporary exhibitions. On the edge of town, the **Dobele Horticultural Plant Breeding Experimental Station** houses a museum dedicated to noted horticulturalist Pēteris Upītis (1896–1976). One of the largest lilac collections in the world can also be found here. Classical music concerts are held in the gardens every spring, while the flowers are in bloom.

Environs
A drive of 13 km (8 miles) down a gravel road west of town, the **Pokaiņi Forest** is an area of spiritual significance due to its numerous unusual rock formations.

Ruins of the 14th-century Livonian Order castle in Dobele

❸ Rundāle Palace

Designed by Francesco Bartolomeo Rastrelli (1700–71), Rundāle is one of the finest palaces in the Baltic region. Work began in 1736 on a Baroque summer residence for Ernst Johann Biron, but was left unfinished when he was exiled. Following Biron's return, the interiors were renovated in the Rococo style. Biron's son removed most of the furnishings when he left in 1795, after Courland was annexed by Russia. The structure suffered damage during the 20th century, and the rooms have served as an elementary school and a granary. Restoration began in 1972 and is still in progress.

Detail, Rose Room
Rococo touches, such as fake marble, silver detailing and floral motifs, adorn the room.

★ Duke's Bedroom
This room was the focal point of Biron's private apartments, which occupied the central block of the palace.

The Corner Room
The Russian Neo-Classical style reflects the taste of Count Zubov, who inhabited the palace after Courland was absorbed into the Russian Empire.

★ Gold Hall
The initials of the palace's owner, "EJ", can be seen amid the ornate gilt scrolls.

Ernst Johann Biron

The son of a minor landlord, Ernst Johann Biron was asked to leave the academy in Königsberg (present-day Kaliningrad) for bad behaviour. Failing to establish himself in the Russian court, he returned to Jelgava and became close to the widowed Duchess of Courland, Anna Ivanovna. In 1730, Anna became empress of Russia, and three years later Biron was appointed Duke of Courland. After his patron died in 1740, the unpopular Biron was sent into exile,

Duke of Courland, Ernst Johann Biron
(1690–1772)

returning only in 1763. A year later, Catherine II made him duke once more, but he abdicated in 1769 in favour of his son Peter.

VISITORS' CHECKLIST

Practical Information
Road Map D4. **Tel** 6396 2274.
Open May–Oct: 10am–6pm daily; Nov–Apr: 10am–5pm daily.
🅿 ♿ 🚫 📷 Ⓦ **rundale.net**
Park: **Open** May–Oct: 10am–7pm daily (Jun–Aug: to 9pm Fri–Sun); Nov–Apr: 10am–5pm daily.

Transport
🚌 from Bauska.

Duchess's Boudoir
The duchess could rest and receive visitors during the day in the splendidly decorated boudoir, which has now been restored. The duchess and other family members lived in the western wing.

KEY

① **The Grand Gallery** was where guests would dine before dancing in the White Hall. Wall paintings were uncovered during restoration.

② **Rose Room**

③ **Duke's Reception Room**

④ **The Marble Hall** was used as a school gym in the 20th century.

⑤ **An exhibition** on the palace's construction is on display in the building's basement.

⑥ **A display of period clothes** fills three rooms with fashions from the 17th and 18th centuries.

⑦ **The courtyard** has gateposts topped by the duke's emblem – a heraldic lion.

⑧ **The Oval Porcelain Cabinet**, made by Johann Michael Graff, was designed to display the household's collection of fine china.

★ **White Hall**
This ballroom boasts lavish stucco work by German sculptor Johann Michael Graff. The restrained colour scheme gives the room its name.

❽ Jaunpils Castle
Jaunpils pils

Road Map C4. **Tel** 6310 7082.
Open 10am–6pm daily. 🚗 🖥
🆆 **jaunpilspils.lv**

Built by the Livonian Order in
1301, with its distinctive round
tower added in the 15th century,
Jaunpils Castle was owned by
the German von der Recke
family from 1561 to 1922. On 24
December 1905, the castle was
burned down by revolutionaries
(*see p139*), and the current
structure is almost entirely the
result of subsequent
reconstruction. The small
museum inside includes replicas
of weapons and armour, as well
as some interesting photographs
of the castle before 1905. Across
the courtyard from the museum
is a pub, and the castle also has
eight atmospheric hotel rooms
(*see p301*). Guided tours also take
in Jaunpils town's Evangelical
Lutheran Church and the early
19th-century watermill.

One of a dozen bridges across the Vēršupīte river, Ķemeri Park

❾ Ķemeri

Road Map C3. 🚆 from Rīga.
ℹ Meža Māja, 6773 0078. 🛶 canoe
trips & wildlife tours arranged at
visitors' centre. 🆆 **daba.gov.lv**

A popular resort in the early 20th
century, Ķemeri is considered
part of Jūrmala, although it has
not seen the same scale of
rejuvenation experienced further
east. The town's main attraction,

Ķemeri Park, encompasses an
Orthodox church, pavilions and
bridges across the Vēršupīte river.
    Ķemeri is also the entry
point to **Ķemeri National Park**,
which has rivers, lakes, meadows, inland dunes, sulphur
springs and forests. A 3-km
(2-mile) wooden pathway
traverses the park's 6,000-ha
(14,830-acre) bog, which
attracts bird-watchers.

❿ Jūrmala

Literally meaning "seaside" in Latvian, Jūrmala is an attractive
stretch of beaches, pine forests and small towns alongside the
Gulf of Rīga. During the 19th century, the area became
famous for its medicinal mud and sulphur-rich spring water.
Jūrmala soon grew into a popular resort and it became
fashionable to own a summerhouse here. The wooden houses
as well as older sanitaria still dot the area, standing alongside
modern guesthouses and upmarket spas.

Jomas Street in Majori is a
pedestrianized strip that forms the
heart of Jūrmala. It is lined with a
large number of outdoor cafés,
restaurants and hotels, as well as a
variety of shops.

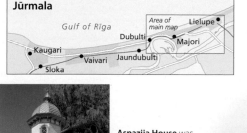

Jūrmala

Gulf of Rīga

Area of main map

Lielupe
Dubulti
Majori
Kaugari
Vaivari   Jaundubulti
Sloka

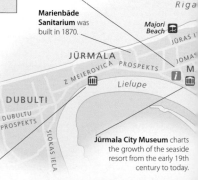

Marienbāde Sanitarium was built in 1870.

Aspazija House was
the last home of one of
Latvia's most famous
poets, Elza Rozenberga
(1865–1943),
nicknamed
"Aspazija". The
house is now a
branch of the
Jūrmala Town Museum.

Gulf of Rīga

Majori Beach

JŪRAS I

JŪRMALA

Z MEIEROVICA PROSPEKTS   JOMAS

Lielupe   M

ℹ

DUBULTI

DUBULTU PROSPEKTS

SLOKAS IELA

Jūrmala City Museum charts
the growth of the seaside
resort from the early 19th
century to today.

For hotels and restaurants see pp301–302 and pp322–4

⑩ Tukums

Road Map C3. 🏔 19,000. 🚆 from Rīga. 🚌 ℹ️ Talsu 5, 6312 4451. ⛴ Tue, Thu, Sat. 🎵 Festival of Female Choirs and Men's Choruses (Jun).
🌐 **visittukums.lv**

Meaning the "Land of the End" in Livonian, Tukums stands at the point where the Zemgale plains meet the Kurzeme uplands. Little remains of the town's history as an ancient Liv settlement, while the only remnant of the Livonian Order castle is the Palace Tower (Pils tornis). Restored in 1767 to serve as a granary and jail, it now houses the **Local History Museum**, which displays dioramas and temporary exhibitions.

The oldest buildings in the old town date from the late 19th and early 20th centuries. The main highlight, **Tukums Art Museum**, houses Latvian art

Monument to freedom fighters, Tukums

from the 1920s and 30s. It is considered to be Latvia's foremost gallery outside Rīga.

Environs
Durbes Pils, a manor house on the eastern edge of Tukums, is an 1820s Neo-Classical building with a 17th-century core. The restored rooms include displays on local history, but the foremost exhibition is the ethnological collection in the former servants' quarters. About 5 km (3 miles) east of Tukums is the 15th-century Šlokenbeka Manor, home to the **Latvian Road Museum**. Many exhibits are of specialist interest but the collections of horse-drawn carriages and road building machines have a more general appeal.

Jaunmoku Pils *(see p323)*, 5 km (3 miles) west of Tukums,

is a distinctive red-brick manor house with step gables and chimneys. Many of the rooms of this former hunting lodge are decorated in an ornate style. A highlight is a large tiled stove bearing images of Rīga and Jūrmala. The forest museum upstairs includes oddities such as a collection of silver cigarette holders. It is possible to climb the tower for stunning views of the surrounding countryside.

🏛 **Local History Museum**
Brīvības laukums 19a. **Tel** 6312 4348.
Open 10am–5pm Tue–Sat, 10am–4pm Sun. 🐾

🏛 **Tukums Art Museum**
Harmonijas 7. **Tel** 6318 2392.
Open 11am–5pm Tue–Fri, 11am–4pm Sat & Sun. 🐾

🏰 **Durbes pils**
Mazā parka 7. **Tel** 6312 2633. **Open** 10am–5pm Tue–Sat, 11am–4pm Sun. 🐾 🎥 📷

🏛 **Latvian Road Museum**
Milzkalne. **Tel** 2990 4147.
Open 9am–4pm Mon–Fri. 🐾

Dzintari Beach, is a popular stretch of sand that draws hordes of tourists in summer. It is dotted with beer tents and volleyball nets during this time.

```
0 km                    1
0 miles                 1
```

Dzintari Concert Hall hosts open-air summer concerts.

Bulduri Beach 🚉

Dzintari Beach 🚉

LIELUPE

BULDURU PROSPEKTS

MEŽA PROSPEKTS

DZINTARI 🏛

EDINBURGAS PROSPEKTS

BULDURI

ZINTARU PROSPEKTS

RĪGAS IELA

Morbergs' Summer Cottage, built in 1883 in Neo-Gothic style, sits amid beautiful gardens.

VISITORS' CHECKLIST

Practical Information
Road Map C3. ℹ️ Lienes iela 5, Majori, 6714 7900.
Aspazija House: Meierovica prosp 20, Dubulti. **Tel** 6776 9445.
Jūrmala City Museum: Tirgoņu iela 29, Majori. **Tel** 6776 4746.
Dzintari Concert Hall: Turaidas iela 1. **Tel** 6776 2086. Morbergs' Summer Cottage: Dzintaru Prospekts 52/54. **Tel** 6722 7175.

Transport
🚉 from Rīga.

The coastal towns which make up Jūrmala are situated among picturesque pine forests. Strict building regulations preserve the 19th-century wooden summerhouses and restrict construction in the area.

Reed-filled part of Lake Engure, with boats moored along the shore

⓬ Lake Engure
Engures ezers

Road Map C3. 🚤 for boating: Abragciems Kempings, 4 km (2 miles) N of Engure, 6316 1668; for fishing permits: Ornithological Centre, Bērzciems, 6947 4420 (open by appointment only). 🖥 eedp.lv

Latvia's third-largest lake, Engure is a significant bird habitat. Around 160 species have been spotted in the wetlands, including cranes and grey herons. A road leads around the western edge of the lake, between the towns Mērsrags and Engure, while the **Ornithological Centre** on the eastern side of the lake can be reached by turning inland just north of Bērzciems. One bird-watching tower is situated close to the centre, while another is directly opposite it across the lake. A 3.5-km (2-mile) orchid trail starts close to the

Ornithological Centre, running through dry pine forest and a chalky grass swamp in which 22 species of orchid can be found.

Many parts of the lake are choked with reeds as a result of pollution by chemical fertilizers, and a number of fish species have disappeared, although fishing permits can still be obtained at the centre.

Environs
The small fishing port of **Roja**, 26 km (16 miles) northwest of Mērsrags, offers more accommodation options than most places on the coastal route from Rīga to Ventspils. Exhibits in the town's **Sea-Fishing Museum** (Rojas jūras zvejniecības muzejs) look at the naval schools of Krišjānis Valdemārs *(see p195)*, sailing

ships in the late 19th and early 20th centuries, fish canning and the local Banga fishermen's collective.

🏛 **Sea-Fishing Museum**
Selgas iela 33. **Tel** 6326 9594. **Open** Jun–Sep: 10am–6pm Tue–Sun, Oct–May: 10am–5pm Tue–Sat. 🏷 🗎

⓭ Dundaga
Road Map C3. 🚹 4,000. 🚌
🛈 Pils iela 14, 6323 2293.
🖥 visit.dundaga.lv

First recorded in 1245, Dundaga has a restored 13th-century Livonian Order castle that today houses the tourist office. The coats of arms of the last owners decorate the tower over the entrance to the northwestern section. The Lutheran church nearby has an altarpiece by Janis Rozentāls (1866–1916). The church's 19th-century wooden organ case is unusual, as it is the work of Latvian craftsmen who generally produced functional items while foreign masters made decorative pieces.

Coat of arms at the castle, Dundaga

Dundaga features a large, bizarre sculpture of a crocodile at the corner of Talsu and Dinsberga streets, honouring local crocodile hunter Arvīds Blūmentāls (1925–2006). He emigrated to Australia during World War II and is said to have been the inspiration for the film *Crocodile Dundee* (1986).

Large concrete crocodile sculpture on a bed of stones in Dundaga

The Coast-Dwelling Livs

A Finnic people related to the Estonians, the Livs settled along the Gulf of Rīga around 5,000 years ago, long before the arrival of the Latvian tribes. They referred to themselves as *raandalist* (coast-dwellers) and *kalāmīed* (fishermen), and the sea has always been central to their way of life. German crusaders devastated Livonian culture in the 13th century and the Livs were gradually assimilated into the other Baltic tribes. During the 19th and 20th centuries, children were educated in German and later Russian rather than in Livonian. Many of the remaining Livs were forced to leave the region when the Soviets declared the coast a military zone. Since 1991 there have been concerted efforts to preserve and strengthen Liv culture. Today, not more than 200 people are officially registered as Livs.

Monument to Livonian Culture in Mazirbe

⑭ The Livonian Coast

A narrow strip of land running along the edge of the Gulf of Rīga and the Baltic Sea and dominated by sand dunes and pine forests, the Livonian Coast is separated from the rest of Kurzeme by the Zilie kalni (Blue Hills). It is home to one of Europe's smallest ethnic groups, the Livs. The coastal route also provides access to some of Latvia's most beautiful scenery. It is only a short walk between fishing villages and attractively secluded beaches.

Tips for Drivers

Tour length: 60 km (37 miles).
Stopping-off points: There are small guesthouses and campsites in several of the coastal villages. Booking ahead is advisable.
Road conditions: Conditions can be difficult once off the main roads, particularly in poor weather.

② **Cape Kolka**
The point at which the Baltic Sea meets the Gulf of Rīga is a popular place for Latvian holidaymakers.

③ **Vaide**
The Museum of Horns is the main highlight of Vaide. It showcases the personal collection of a forest warden, formed over decades.

① **Pūrciems White Dune**
A walkway leads across the dune, while signboards indicate a Neolithic settlement.

④ **Košrags**
The typical coastal village of Košrags is dotted with 18th-century wooden buildings, including a small B&B.

⑤ **Mazirbe**
Located in Mazirbe village, the Folk House of the Livs is a museum with a collection of old photographs showing rope-making, leather-softening and other daily activities of the Livs.

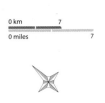

⑥ **Slītere Lighthouse**
Indicating the start of the Slītere nature trail, the lighthouse can be climbed for a view of Slītere National Park's forests. Inside, there is a display focusing on the lighthouses along Latvia's coastline.

Key

━━ Tour route
══ Other road

⓯ Ventspils

Founded in 1290, Ventspils has long been a trading centre and was a member of the Hanseatic League. In the 18th century, war and plague ravaged the city, but it later thrived as part of the Russian Empire.

A hub for Russian oil tankers till recently, Ventspils has gained an air of affluence since independence. In order to limit its reliance on Russia, the city has been spruced up to boost tourism. Enlivened by parks, flower beds and fountains, Ventspils has a bustling modern centre and a well-restored Old Town. The historic core is best explored on foot and a walk along Ostas Street offers a chance to see bovine sculptures left after the 2012 Cow Parade.

Exterior of the 13th-century Livonian Order castle, Ventspils Castle

🏛 Ventspils Castle

Jāņa iela 17. **Tel** 6362 2031. **Open** 10am–6pm Tue–Sun. 🅿 📷 ♿ 🚻
w muzejs.ventspils.lv

On the bank of the Venta river, this Livonian Order castle is one of the finest in Latvia. Although it began life as a late 13th-century stone tower, its current form largely dates from the 14th century. Devastated by the Swedish army in 1659, the castle has been restored many times since. Parts of the redbrick gallery in the inner courtyard were built as recently as the 1870s.

The museum inside the castle recounts its history through engaging displays and touch screens. As a Livonian Order stronghold, it was a self-contained world complete with a dormitory, refectory, chapel and meeting hall. Later, the chapel was used as a Lutheran church, while the building served as a prison at various times from 1824 to 1959. It became the barracks for the German army during World War I and for Soviet border guards from 1962 to 1983. The rooms in which the exhibits are laid out bear fragments of wall paintings from the 15th to the 17th centuries, and there are also displays of traditional costumes and jewellery.

The pleasant restaurant on the premises, Melnais Sivēns Pils Krogs (see p324), is one of the best places to eat in the city. During summer, it is possible to try archery and, by arrangement, fire a small cannon in front of the castle.

🏛 Russian Orthodox Church of St Nicholas

Plosta iela 10. **Tel** 6362 1616.
The onion-domed Russian Orthodox Church of St Nicholas (Sv Nikolaja pareizticīgo baznīca) was consecrated in the early 20th century. Although the Neo-Byzantine exterior needs to be restored, the interior has an excellent collection of icons.

Lutheran Church of St Nicholas

Tirgus 2. **Tel** 6362 2750. **Open** 9am–4pm daily.

With a portico at the front and a tower with an observation platform, this attractive yellow-and-white church (Sv Nikolaja Luterāļu baznīca) stands on the old market square. Dating from 1835, it was built in accordance with the wishes of Tsar Nicholas I.

Seaside Open-Air Museum

Riņķa 2. **Tel** 6362 4467. **Open** May–Oct: 10am–6pm Wed–Sun. **ventspilsmuzejs.lv** Narrow-Gauge Railway: May–Oct: Sat & Sun.

The Seaside Open-Air Museum (Piejūras brīvdabas muzejs) was opened in 1954 to preserve the heritage of Latvia's fishing villages, which began to disappear as the Soviet authorities regarded the shores as areas of military importance. Buildings were moved from their original location and reassembled here and the site now includes homesteads, smokehouses, curing cabins, net sheds and even a large windmill.

Traditional crafts are displayed around the site in summer. There are also large collections of fishing boats and anchors, and a **Narrow-Gauge Railway**. Until the 1960s, the steam engine linked seaside villages, but now it takes a 1.4-km (0.8-mile) trip through Seaside Park.

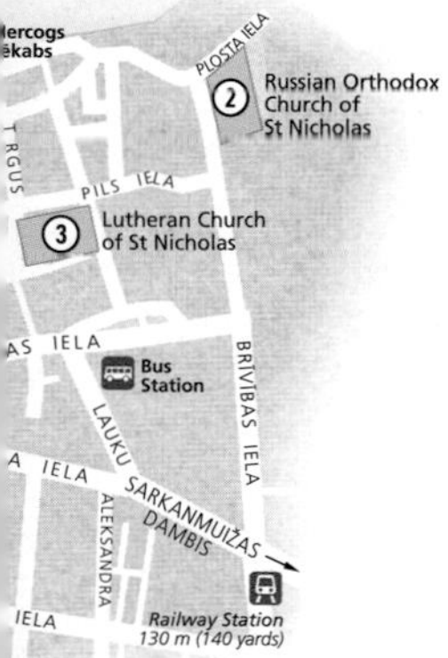

Ventspils

① Ventspils Castle
② Russian Orthodox Church of St Nicholas
③ Lutheran Church of St Nicholas
④ Seaside Open-Air Museum
⑤ Aqua Park
⑥ Ventspils Beach

VISITORS' CHECKLIST

Practical Information
Road Map C3. 44,000.
Dārza iela 6, 6362 2263.
visitventspils.com

Transport
Dzeaizceļnieku iela. Kuldīga iela 5. Plosta iela 7.

Water slides and swimming pools at the Aqua Park

Aqua Park

Medņu iela 19. **Tel** 2642 9684. **Open** May–Sep: 10am–9pm daily.

With three pools, several slides, Jacuzzis and saunas as well as a variety of water playgrounds, the Aqua Park (Akvaparks) is popular with families. Swimming gear can be rented on site.

Ventspils Beach

2 km (1 mile) S of town.

The residents of Ventspils are proud of their beach, particularly the 1.2-km (0.7-mile) stretch that received an EU Blue Flag in 1999 for meeting international standards. This was a remarkable achievement, since the coast had been contaminated by industrial pollution during the Soviet era. Parts of the beach have been set aside for windsurfers, nudists and smokers, and there are playgrounds for children. At the northern end of the beach is a breakwater, with a promenade leading to a lighthouse at the end.

⑯ VIRAC (Ventspils International Radio Astronomy Centre)

Ventspils Starptautiskais Radioastronomijas Centrs

Road Map B3. **Tel** 2923 0818. **Open** Mar–Nov: 6am–6pm daily. call in advance. **virac.venta.lv**

Situated in a former Russian army town, the 1970s military installation is believed to have spied on communications between Europe and the USA for at least a decade. When they left in 1994, the Russians took the smallest dish, leaving the two heavier ones, which are 16 m (52 ft) and 32 m (105 ft) in diameter. The bigger one is the largest radio telescope in Northern Europe and the world's eighth largest.

A combination of size and precision engineering makes the larger dish especially valuable to scientists. Guided tours of it begin with the ground-floor laboratory. Visitors can climb up to a viewing platform and then step into one of the suspended laboratory pods. The structure was built by a naval factory in the Ukraine, and the interiors are reminiscent of a ship.

The unmarked road to VIRAC, leading past eerily empty residential buildings, is just east of an electrical substation on the P124. Book in advance for a guided tour.

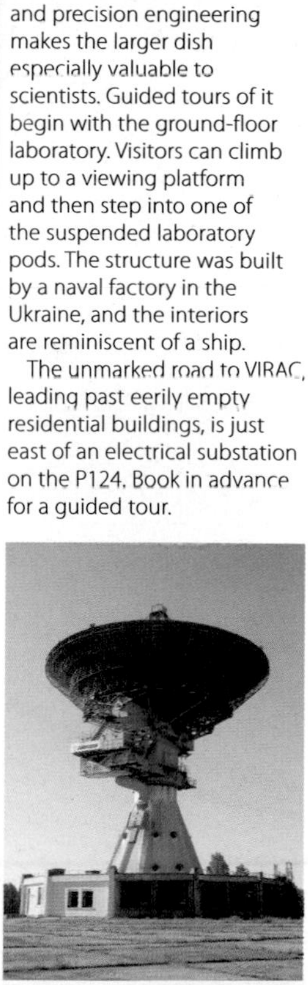

Radio telescope at VIRAC, the largest of its kind in Northern Europe

⑰ Talsi

Road Map C3. 🏔 12,500. 🚌
ℹ Liela iela 19–21, 6322 4165.
🎪 Mara's Craft Market Fair (Aug).
🌐 **talsitourism.lv**

The administrative centre of northern Kurzeme and a transport hub for the region, Talsi is an attractive town spread out around two lakes and across nine hills. It was originally a Liv settlement, captured by the Kurši during the 10th century, and then by the Livonian Order in 1263. A mound remains where the Order's castle stood on Watermill Hill (Dzirnavkalns).

Talsi's oldest surviving building is the 18th-century Lutheran church, atop Church Hill (Baznīckalns). The most noted pastor of the church was Karl Amenda (1771–1836), a close friend of composers Beethoven and Mozart. Nearby, the cobblestoned Kalēju and Ūdens streets are notable for water troughs.

The **Talsi Regional Museum** (Talsu novada muzejs), housed in a late 19th-century Neo-Classical residence, features an interesting exhibition on the Livs. The building's original painted ceiling can be seen in one of the rooms.

Environs

Laumas Nature Park, 20 km (12 miles) north, has several walking and cycle paths. Guided tours are available, including one focusing on bees. It also has a campsite.

🏛 **Talsi Regional Museum**
K Milenbaha 19. **Tel** 2910 2628.
Open 10am–5pm Tue–Sun. 🐾 🖥
🌐 **talsumuzejs.lv**

Latvian grape variety Zilga growing at Vīna Kalns, Sabile's renowned vineyard

⑱ Sabile

Road Map C3. 🏔 3,500. 🚌 ℹ
Pilskalna iela 6, 6325 2344.
🎪 Wine Festival (Jul). 🌐 **sabile.lv**

A small town on the banks of the Abava river, Sabile was first mentioned in 1253, by which time it had long been inhabited by the Kurši tribe. Only a mound remains of the tribe's castle, although the stones were used to repair the town's 17th-century Lutheran church, which houses Latvia's oldest bell, made in 1450.

Just 1 km (half a mile) from Sabile centre is the farmstead **Drubazas**, where you can follow a 2-km (1-mile) guided walk through forests and marshes, and vist the farmhouse for wine tastings.

Sabile Wine Hill, **Sabiles Vīna Kalns**, is said to be the northern-most vineyard in the world. The strong and sour wine it produces was popular in the court of the

Sculpture, Pedvāle Open-Air Museum

Kurzeme Duchy (1561–1795), but viniculture may have begun long before. In the 1930s, the vineyard was used to experiment with grape varieties, but this ceased during the Soviet period. Work began again in 1989, and there are now 650 vines of 15 varieties. Wine-tasting is possible at the annual wine festival.

Environs

Mara's Caves (Māras kambari), named after an ancient Latvian goddess, are 12 km (7 miles) southwest of Sabile. In the Middle Ages, these sandstone caves were used as a hiding place by bandits.

🌿 **Drubazas Botany Trail**
"Drubazas" Abavas pagasts. **Tel** 2837 0702. **Open** call in advance. 🐾

⑲ Pedvāle Open-Air Museum

Pedvāles brīvdabas mākslas muzejs

Road Map C4. Strauta 4. **Tel** 6325 2249. 🚌 **Open** May–Sep: 10am–6pm daily; Oct–Apr: 10am–4pm daily. 🐾
📷 🖥 🌐 **pedvale.lv**

The near-derelict buildings and grounds of Pedvāle Manor, a short walk uphill from Sabile, were bought by sculptor Ojars Feldbergs in 1991. A year later, they were opened as the Pedvāle Open-Air Museum, one of Latvia's most interesting museums. Scattered around the 100-ha (247-acre) site are over 150 works by Latvian and international artists. Many of the artworks are designed specifically for the museum during conferences and workshops. The on-site ticket office provides a map to help visitors in their exploration. Some of Feldbergs's own work can be found exhibited in the attractively decaying estate buildings at the far end of the site, while other buildings have been renovated to accommodate visiting artists. The former manor house is now a guest house open to the public.

Picturesque view of Talsi with a canopy of trees rising behind

For hotels and restaurants see pp301–302 and pp322–4

Rows of crosses marking the graves of German soldiers, near Saldus

⑳ Saldus

Road Map C4. 🚇 11,000. 🚌
ℹ️ Striķu iela 3, 6380 7443.

Set amid scenic countryside, close to Lake Ciecere, Saldus is best known for the **Janis Rozentāls Museum of History and Art** (Jaņa Rozentāla Saldus Vēstures un Mākslas Muzejs). Rozentāls *(see p155)*, who was born near Saldus, reconstructed the building in 1900. The artist's home till 1901, it is now a museum that showcases his works. Temporary art exhibitions are housed in an adjacent building.

**Statue of Janis
Rozentāls, Saldus**

Environs

Vācu Karavīru Kapi, 7 km (4 miles) south of town, is a war cemetery where German soldiers who died in Latvia were re-buried in a single place.

🏛️ **Janis Rozentāls Museum of History and Art**
Striķu iela 22. **Tel** 6388 1547.
Open 9am–5pm Tue–Fri, 10am–4pm Sat & Sun. 🖼️

㉑ Kuldīga

Road Map B3. 🚇 14,000. 🚌 ℹ️
Baznīcas iela 5, 6332 2259. 🎭 Town Festival (mid-Jul). 🌐 **visit.kuldiga.lv**

With a well-preserved Old Town and an attractive location alongside the Venta river, Kuldīga is one of Latvia's most alluring provincial towns. It was founded in 1242 by the Livonian Order, who chose the site to capitalize on the river and a land route linking Prussia with the lower Daugava Valley.

In the 16th century, Kuldīga's castle was one of the residences of Duke Gothard Kettler and the town traded with Rīga and Jelgava. The streets near the attractive old Town hall Square, running alongside the Alekšupīte river, feature 17th- and 18th-century timber buildings. Also here are a couple of attractive churches, St Catherine's (Sv Katrīnas baznīca) and the Holy Trinity (Sv Trīsvienības Katoļu baznīca). A short walk away is the Venta Waterfall (Ventas rumba), the widest in Europe. Close by is a 164-m (538-ft) brick bridge, one of Europe's longest. Overlooking the river is **Kuldīga District Museum** (Kuldīgas novada muzejs), best known for its collection of playing cards.

Environs

The **Riežupe Sand Caves** (Riežupes smilšu alas), 4 km (2 miles) north of Kuldīga, form the longest cave system in Latvia. A quarter of the 2-km (1-mile) site is open to visitors.

🏛️ **Kuldīga District Museum**
Pils iela 5. **Tel** 6332 2364.
Open 11am–5pm Tue–Sun. 🖼️

㉒ Pāvilosta

Road Map B4. 🚇 3,000. ℹ️ Dzintaru iela 2, 6349 8229. 🎭 Sea Festival (Jul).

Founded in 1879, the small port town of Pāvilosta was named after Paul Lilienfeld, Governor of Kurzeme from 1868 to 1885. Tourist activities in Pāvilosta revolve around the sea, including yacht and canoe hire and trips out in a fishing boat. The surrounding area is also a popular spot for windsurfing and is home to the country's first world-class yacht marina, **Pāvilosta Marina**.

The **Regional Studies Museum** (Pāvilostas novadpētniecības muzejs), located in the town's oldest building, exhibits everyday items from the region and displays about local history (in Latvian only).

⚓ **Pāvilosta Marina**
Ostmalas iela 4. **Tel** 6349 8581.
🌐 **pavilostamarina.lv**

🏛️ **Regional Studies Museum**
Dzintaru iela 1. **Tel** 6349 8276. **Open** mid-May–mid-Sep: 11am–5pm Wed–Fri, noon–4pm Sat & Sun; mid-Sep–mid-May: 9am–5pm Mon–Fri. 🖼️

Ferries anchored at the harbour in the port town of Pāvilosta

㉓ Liepāja

Although Liepāja was officially declared a town in 1625, it expanded only in the early 19th century. The deepening of the ice-free port and the building of a railway link were followed, in 1890, by the foundation of a Tsarist naval port at Karosta. Today, Liepāja is Latvia's third largest city and it has a vibrant cultural life. It is dotted with many interesting sights, most of which are located in its historic core. Many of the city's older buildings have been extensively restored.

Beautifully carved Baroque altar of St Anne's Basilica

🏛 Holy Trinity Church

Lielā iela 9. **Tel** 6342 2208.
Open 10am–6pm daily. 🚫
donations. Organ recital: Jul: Sat (call for timings).

The modest exterior of the mid-18th-century Holy Trinity (Svētās Trīsvienības baznīca) belies one of the finest church interiors in the Baltic region,

Details on the exterior of Holy Trinity Church

adorned with gilt detailing and woodcarvings. The centrepiece is an organ built in 1773 by H A Contius, a favourite organ builder of composer J S Bach. Expanded in 1885, it was the world's largest organ until 1912. Wooden steps lead up the clock tower for views.

House of Craftsmen

Dārza iela 4–8. **Tel** 2654 1424.
Open 9am–5pm Mon–Sat. 📷
With a wide variety of fine handicrafts on sale, the House of Craftsmen (Amatnieku namiņš) is a place where one can watch skilled artisans as they weave traditional textiles. The world's longest amber necklace, 123 m (404 ft) long and weighing 60 kg (132 lb), is also on display, along with photographs documenting its creation.

🏛 St Anne's Basilica

Veidenbauma iela 1. **Tel** 2922 7566.
First documented in 1508, the current Neo-Gothic St Anne's Basilica (Sv Annas baznīca) dates only from the end of the 19th century. The plain interior is dominated by the huge Baroque altar, carved for Duke Jakob Kettler (see p139) in 1697 by Nicolas Sefrens. The altar painting depicts the Passion of Christ in three panels, with the Crucifixion at the bottom, the wrapping of his body in the centre and the Ascension at the top.

🏛 Occupation Museum

K Ukstiņa iela 7/9. **Tel** 6342 0274.
Open 10am–6pm Wed–Sun. 📷
The interesting Occupation Museum (Okupāciju režīmos) offers an absorbing account of the city's treatment at the hands of Nazi Germany and the Soviet

Liepāja

① Holy Trinity Church
② House of Craftsmen
③ St Anne's Basilica
④ Occupation Museum
⑤ St Joseph's Cathedral
⑥ Liepāja Museum

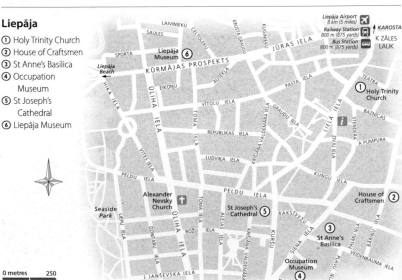

0 metres 250
0 yards 250

Union, with copious notes available in English. Exhibits include everyday objects left behind by repatriated Baltic Germans at the start of World War II, photographs of people deported en masse by the Soviets in June 1941 and an account of the killing of the city's Jews and other "undesirables".

The exhibition ends with a display about the events leading up to independence. The offices of the Popular Front, which was based in the building, have been left intact. Rooms upstairs house an exhibition of antique photographic equipment.

🏛 St Joseph's Cathedral

Rakstvežu iela 13. **Tel** 6342 9775. Decorated inside with scenes from the Bible, the yellow St Joseph's Cathedral (Sv Jāzepa katedrāle) attained its current towering form in the 19th century. The congregation needed a larger church, but had no land on which to build one, which is why they simply expanded the existing building upwards.

🏛 Liepāja Museum

Kūrmājas prospekts 16/18. **Tel** 6342 2327. **Open** 10am–6pm Wed–Sun. 🗝 **w** liepajasmuzejs.lv

Set amid a small sculpture garden, the Liepāja Museum (Liepājas muzejs) is housed in an ornate early 20th-century building with an impressive galleried hall. The displays trace local history, with exhibits including the heads of stone cherubs from St Anne's Basilica, a series of pewter drinking vessels topped by human figures and traditional southern Kurzeme costumes. Also here is a reconstruction of the workshop of the famous sculptor Mikelis Pankoks (1894–1983), who vanished in 1944 and was presumed dead. He had fled the country incognito, and ended his days in a Swiss mental hospital.

🏖 Liepāja Beach

Although the coast here was once an environmental disaster area, it has now been thoroughly cleaned up and proudly flies its

EU Blue Flag. The long, sandy Liepāja Beach (Liepājas pludmale) is separated from the Old Town by the wooded **Seaside Park** (Jūrmalas parks). The nearby streets are lined with elegant Art Nouveau buildings that used to be summerhouses.

Façade of St Nicholas's Orthodox Cathedral, Karosta

Karosta

4 km (2 miles) N of town. 🚌 3, 4, 7. **w** karosta.lv St Nicholas's Orthodox Church: Katedrāles 7. Military Prison: Invalīdu 4. 🗝

A military harbour built by the Russians during the late 19th century, Karosta was off-limits to civilians. In its heyday, it housed 40,000 personnel. Today, it has a ghost-town feel, with streets of huge, unoccupied buildings.

One reason for visiting Karosta is to see the striking onion-domed **St Nicholas's Orthodox Cathedral** (Sv Nikolaja pareizti-cīgo catedrāle), used as a cinema and gym by the Soviets. The old **Military Prison** (Karostas cietums) is now the Kurzeme region's major tourist attraction, offering a chance to be locked up and yelled at by "guards" for a couple of hours or overnight.

24 Lake Pape Nature Reserve

Papes dabas parks

Road Map B4. **Tel** 2922 4331.
ℹ️ Buši, Rucava village, 2913 4903; Bārtas iela 6, Nica, 6348 9501. 🗝 🗝
w pdf-pape.lv

Just 10 km (6 miles) from the Lithuanian border, the wetlands, pine forests, dunes, grasslands and coastline of the Lake Pape area make an excellent trip from Liepāja. Sponsored by the World Wide Fund for Nature, the reserve covers around 52,000 ha (128,495 acres), and is best known for its *savvaļas zirgi* (semi-wild horses) and *sumbru ganības* (European bison). Guided tours, taking around 90 minutes, are available from the ticket office at the entrance to the signposted grazing area.

The reserve is popular with bird-watchers, due to its location on a migration path. Some 271 species have been sighted here, 15 of which are on the European Red List of endangered species. The area is sparsely populated, although there are three villages within the reserve. One of them is the dune-enclosed settlement of Pape, home to **Vītolnieki**, a branch of the Latvian Ethnographic Open-Air Museum *(see p163)*.

🏛 Vītolnieki

Pape village. **Tel** 2926 2283. **Open** May–Sep: 10am–6pm Fri–Wed. 🗝 by appointment.

Bird-watching tower at the Lake Pape Nature Reserve

EASTERN LATVIA

The eastern part of Latvia includes some of the country's most popular attractions, both natural and man-made, as well as rarely visited rural districts. Although far from mountainous, the terrain is not as flat here as in the west and there are two extensive upland areas dotted with myriad lakes. Some of these have well-developed tourist facilities, while others remain isolated and untouched.

When the German crusaders arrived, they found the Livs and Lettgallians inhabiting the region which now forms Vidzeme, while Latgallians and Selians lived further east in what is now Latgale. The Bishop of Rīga took control of the west and east of Vidzeme, while central Vidzeme and most of Latgale was claimed by the Livonian Order. After the collapse of the Livonian Order in 1561 the whole of the east fell under Lithuanian, and later Polish, rule.

The end of the Polish-Swedish Wars in 1629 saw Sweden ruling both Estonia and Vidzeme. The Russians conquered Vidzeme in 1721. Reliant economically on agriculture, forestry and wood processing, the region is sometimes claimed as the cradle of Latvian culture as it produced many of the country's

best-known writers and musicians. Today Vidzeme is second only to Rīga as a travel destination, with the Gauja National Park combining natural beauty and historical attractions.

Latgale, on the other hand, was ruled by Poland until 1772. The Polish influence fostered a strong Catholic tradition, particularly evident in the pilgrimage centre of Aglona. Latgale was later absorbed directly into the Russian Empire, unlike other Latvian regions which were ruled as separate provinces. This isolation from the rest of the country means that it has long been neglected as a predominantly Russian backwater. Despite this, its villages and serene lakes charm visitors and the regional capital, Daugavpils, is slowly shaking off its image as a grey Soviet throwback.

Old houses and tower in Cēsis, a town steeped in history

◀ Turaida Castle among the trees of Gauja National Park

Exploring Eastern Latvia

The most popular tourist attraction in Eastern Latvia is Gauja National Park, which combines beautiful forests with attractions such as the historic town of Cēsis and the restored Turaida Castle. A significant part of the region is covered by the North Vidzeme Biosphere Reserve, famous for its coastal meadows, sandstone cliffs and extensive wetlands. The route from Rīga to Daugavpils, the regional capital, runs along the Daugava Valley and includes several worthwhile stops, while the cathedral at Aglona is a major centre for Catholic pilgrimage. For most visitors, though, the main attraction in Latgale is its patchwork of lakes, which includes Rāzna and Lubāns, the two largest in the country.

Sights at a Glance

Towns, Resorts and Villages

2 Valmiera
3 Ainaži
4 Salacgrīva
5 Mazsalaca
6 Limbaži
7 Dunte
8 Saulkrasti
10 Lielvārde
11 Skrīveri
13 Jēkabpils
14 Līvāni
15 *Daugavpils pp200–1*
16 Krāslava
17 Aglona
18 Preiļi

19 Rēzekne
21 Ludza
22 Vecpiebalga
23 Alūksne

Sights of Interest

9 Ikšķile
12 Koknese
24 Gulbene–Alūksne
    Railway

National Park

1 *Gauja National Park
  pp190–93*

Tour

20 *Latgale Lakes p202*

Sandstone cliffs on the banks of the Salaca river, Vidzeme

Key

— Motorway
— Main road
— Secondary road
⋯ Minor road
⁓ Railway
— International border

For hotels and restaurants see pp302–303 and pp324–5

Getting Around

The highlights of Gauja National Park are easily reached by bus or train from Rīga, while even small towns in Vidzeme usually have at least one bus a day. Rīga and Daugavpils are well connected by buses and trains that run several times a day. The public transport network elsewhere in Latgale is not well developed and it is easier to use a private vehicle, particularly when exploring the lakes. Bus services link all the towns, but services are not very frequent.

Tartu
Valka
Pedele
Sedã
Gauja

Pskov

Zabolova

A3 P24 Vijciems
Gaujiena P39 Lāzbergi P42
Alsviķi 23 ALŪKSNE
Liepna
P18 Smiltene Palsa Vireši P34 P43 Kuprava
P27 Mālumuiža Gauja Jaunanna P41 Viļaka
GULBENE– Kubuli Balvi P35
Ūdrupe ALŪKSNE 24 P45
P29 RAILWAY P47 Čilipine
Gulbene Pededze Medņi P46
Gauja P38 Baltupe Baltinava
P37 Tirza Ostrov
P3 Lake 22 VECPIEBALGA P83 Lubāna P36 Bērzpils Grebņeva
Inests Kuja Iča A13
Ērgļi Lautere Žogotas Goliševa
P30 Madona P82 Lake Rēzekne Drīcāni Aizpūre
P81 Bērzaune P84 Lūbāns Malta Lake 21
Irši Lazdona Zalmežnieki Cirma LUDZA Istalsna
Lake P62 Grozas Viļāni Malta 19 RĒZEKNE Nukši Brigi
Odzes Aiviekste Atašiene 20
12 KOKNESE A12 Troškas P58 A13 Čornaja P49 Rudzīši
P76 Kūkas Nagļi Riebiņi Lake P55 Čerņavski
JĒKABPILS 13 Daugava 18 PREIĻI Puša Rāzna P52
Lake Birži 14 P63 Malta PS7 Lake Bērziņi
steres P75 LĪVĀNI A6 Ežezers P60 Dagda
Viesīte P72 Jersika Aglonas Rušons Kapiņi Asūne
P74 Slate Stacija 17 AGLONA P62
Nereta Aknīste P64 Kalupe Spoģi KRĀSLAVA
Dviete A13 Lociķi 16 A6
P73 Subate P72 A6 Daugava Piedruja
P70 Svente 15 DAUGAVPILS
A13 Silene
Demene
Utena

0 kilometres   20
0 miles   20

For keys to symbols *see back flap*

❶ Gauja National Park

Latvia's first and most popular national park was established in 1973 and stretches for about 100 km (62 miles) along the Gauja River Valley. But the area has been attracting tourists to its so-called "Alpine trails" since the 19th century. Almost half of the 92,000-ha (227,337-acre) park is forested, and it is home to about 900 plant, 149 bird and 48 mammal species. Around 4 per cent of the park forms a closed nature reserve, but the rest is accessible by road. Canoeing and boating are great ways to see the caves, cliffs and ravines carved out by the river since the glaciers receded 12,000 years ago. In addition to its natural attactions, the area also has some of Latvia's most fascinating historic sites *(see pp192–3)*.

Key

▨ Gauja National Park

★ Turaida Museum Reserve
The extensively restored Turaida Castle houses historical exhibitions, while the grounds include outbuildings and a sculpture park.

New Castle in Sigulda
This fanciful manor house was built in 1867 near the ruins of a Livonian Order castle, where there is now an open-air stage.

```
0 km           5
0 miles              5
```

Key

▬▬ Major road

═══ Minor road

─── Other road

─── Railway line

‒‒ Park boundary

Bobsleigh Run
Sigulda offers a rare chance to experience the thrill of a world-class bobsleigh run at a reasonable price. In summer, a slower, wheeled vehicle is used.

★ Līgatne Education and Recreation Centre
Inside the park, footpaths and tracks for vehicles wind past spacious enclosures housing animals, Including elk, brown bears and European bison.

★ Cēsis
Once the seat of the German crusaders, Cēsis is a romantic town with a lakeside park.

Lake Āraiši
Archaeologists found the remains of a fortress on the lake bed here. This reconstruction of it offers a glimpse into Latgallian life in the 9th and 10th centuries.

Zvārte Rock, a 35-m (115-ft) high sandstone outcrop, boasts excellent views. It is locally believed to be a haunt of witches and demons.

The Rose of Turaida

According to a popular legend, in 1601 a young orphan girl found in the aftermath of a battle between the Swedish and Polish armies was named Maija and raised in Turaida Castle. She fell in love with Viktor, a gardener from Sigulda Castle. One day a deserter from the Polish army lured Maija into the nearby Gūtmaṇa Cave under false pretences, but she tricked him into killing her rather than surrendering her chastity. The so-called grave of the Turaida Rose in the Turaida Museum Reserve is considered a romantic spot for newlyweds.

Gravestone of the Turaida Rose, the beautiful Maija

Exploring Gauja National Park

The park follows the Gauja River Valley as it flows southwest from Valmiera. Road access to the park is good, with the A2 and A3 running alongside. The most convenient access points from Rīga are Sigulda, where the park information office is located, and Cēsis. In addition to hotels and guesthouses along the major routes and close to the tourist sites, the park includes a network of 22 campsites. They are arranged along the Gauja, Amata and Brasla rivers, making canoeing an appealing way to see the area. The stretch between Sigulda and Cēsis is particularly attractive.

Sigulda

🚆 from Rīga. 🚌 from Rīga.
ℹ️ Train station, Ausekla iela, 6797 1335. 🌐 **sigulda.lv**

A spacious town set in scenic woodland, Sigulda is a centre for outdoor activities and is also a good base for visiting Krimulda and Turaida. After the Brotherhood of the Sword subdued the Liv population in 1207, they gave the valley's right bank to the Bishop of Rīga and built their own castle on the left bank. The Brotherhood, renamed the Livonian Order, lost the town to the Poles in 1562, and it passed between the Poles and Swedes for 150 years until it was taken by Russia in the Great Northern War (1700–21).

The castle ruins are tucked away behind the 19th-century New Castle (Jaunā pils) and its fine gardens. Close by is a Lutheran church and the impressive viewpoint called Artists' Hill (Gleznotāju kalns). Paths run through the woodland to Satzele Castle Mound, once a Liv fortress, and Peter's Cave on the bank of the Vējupīte river.

Krimulda

🚌 from Sigulda. 🚠 from Sigulda 9am–5pm Mon–Fri. ℹ️ 6797 2232.
🎫 📷 🌐 **krimuldaspils.lv**

The Bishop of Rīga had a castle built in Krimulda after taking control of the right bank of the Gauja Valley in 1207. Krimulda Castle (Krimuldas pils) was destroyed by the Swedish army in 1601, and little remains of the ruins. It is easier to spot the nearby 19th-century Neo-Classical manor house (Krimuldas muižas pils). It is

Cable car carrying visitors from Sigulda to Krimulda

now a rehabilitation centre for children, with a café and basic accommodation.

🏛️ Turaida Museum Reserve

6 km (4 miles) N of Sigulda. 🚌 from Sigulda. **Tel** 6797 2376. **Open** May–Oct: 9am–8pm daily; Nov–Apr: 10am–5pm daily. 🎫 📷 🕐 11am Sun. 🍴 📷 🌐 **turaida-muzejs.lv**

The Turaida Museum Reserve mainly consists of a castle and a group of outbuildings. Turaida Castle was built by the Brotherhood of the Sword in 1214. It was left in ruins after a fire in 1776 and has since been extensively restored. Plaques help visitors to understand the site, while exhibitions inside deal with the history of the castle and illustrate the restoration process. Near the museum entrance are the remains of the Turaida estate, as well as a working smithy and exhibitions on farming and woodcraft.

Close to the castle is the Turaida Church. Built in 1750, it is one of the oldest wooden churches in Latvia. Outside is a memorial to the Turaida Rose (see p191) and tucked away behind the church is the Folk Song Park (Dainu kalns), where 25 sculptures celebrate the work of Krišjānis Barons (see p155). Nature trails lead down slopes from the park.

Cēsis

35 km (22 miles) NE of Sigulda.
🚆 from Rīga. 🚌 from Rīga.
ℹ️ Pils laukums 9, 6412 1815.
🌐 **tourism.cesis.lv**
Museum of Art and History: Pils laukums 9. **Open** May–Sep: 10am–6pm daily; Oct–Apr: 10am–5pm Tue–Sun. 🎫 inc New Castle. 🎫 📷

One of the oldest towns in Latvia, Cēsis has winding streets lined with attractive wooden and stone buildings. It was once an important trading centre, becoming a member of the Hanseatic League in 1383. The town served as the headquarters of the Brothers of the Sword, and later the Livonian Order, for much of the period between 1237 and 1561.

In 1577, Ivan the Terrible took Cēsis. Further damage was inflicted during the Great Northern War and the town also

Row of wooden and stone houses in the Old Town, Cēsis

Picturesque view of the wooden dwellings of Āraiši Lake Fortress

witnessed extremely fierce fighting during the War of Independence (1918–20).

The Cēsis Castle complex is the town's major attraction. Visitors are given builders' helmets and lanterns for the tour of the 15th- to 16th-century towers of the 13th-century Old Castle. The pink New Castle, built in 1777, is home to the **Museum of Art and History** (Cēsu vēstures un mākslas muzejs). The highlight is the well-presented "Treasures of Cēsis" exhibition. Cēsis Exhibition House (Cēsu izstāžu nams), a renovated 18th-century coach house, stands on the square in front of the New Castle. To the north, the Castle Park is a popular place to relax in the summer, while the Old Town is to the southeast of the castle.

Other attractions include the 19th-century Cēsis Brewery, although the beer is now brewed outside the town.

🏠 Āraiši Lake Fortress

10 km (6 miles) S of Cēsis. **Tel** 6410 7080. **Open** Apr–Oct: 9am–7pm daily; Nov–Mar: 9am–4pm daily. 🎫 🖼

Tales of sunken castles are common in Latvian folklore, appearing to stem from the 9th- to 10th-century Latgallian practice of building settlements on islets. In 1965, archaeologists found one such settlement in

Lake Āraiši, now reconstructed as a tourist sight. A wooden platform holds 16 single-room dwellings with log walls and bark roofs. Each of them could accommodate three to eight people. A clay stove was used for heating and cooking, while a small structure to the right of each doorway was used for storage or to keep cattle.

Sign, Līgatne Education and Recreation Centre

Today, guides in costume re-create the atmosphere of the settlement, and a dugout boat can be hired. Back on shore is a ruined Livonian Order castle and several reconstructed Stone, Bronze and Iron Age dwellings.

🏕 Līgatne Education and Recreation Centre

15 km (9 miles) NE of Sigulda. 🚌 from Cēsis. **Tel** 6415 3313. **Open** May–Sep: 9am–6pm Mon–Fri, 9am–7pm Sat & Sun; Oct–Apr: 10am–5pm daily. 🎫 🌐 gnp.lv

A wooded nature park, Līgatne Education and Recreation Park (Līgatnes mācību un atpūtas parks) is home to the likes of brown bears, lynx, beavers, elk and European bison. Large enclosures are connected by 5.5 km (3.4 miles) of walking trails and a 5-km (3-mile) route for vehicles. The site includes a 22-m (72-ft) viewing tower, horse-riding facilities, spots for campfires and several car parks. Dogs are not allowed on the trails.

The Latvian Flag

According to tradition, the Latvian national flag was born in Cēsis around 1280. The story goes that warriors from one of the Latvian tribes wrapped their dying chieftain in a white flag, which they had captured from their Estonian enemies. After giving a stirring speech, the chieftain died and the warriors removed the flag from his body to find that his blood had left two red stripes on it; the white stripe in the middle was where he had lain. The warriors took the new flag into battle and defeated their enemies. The present-day version of the flag was designed by artist Ansis Cīrulis in May 1917. The Museum of Art and History in Cēsis has an exhibition dedicated to the Latvian flag.

Latvian flag hoisted on the New Castle, Sigulda

Forlorn remains of the Livonian Order castle in Valmiera

❷ Valmiera

Road Map D3. 🏙 30,000.
🚂 from Rīga. 🚌 from Cēsis.
🛈 Rīgas iela 10, 6420 7177.
🎭 Winter Music Festival (Jan), City Festivities (Jul), Craftsmen's Festival (Aug), St Simeon's Fair of the Middle Ages (Oct). 🖥 visit.valmiera.lv

Once a Hanseatic League member, Valmiera was founded in 1283 and has a distinguished history of trade due to its position on the Gauja river. Today, it is the second-largest city in Vidzeme after Rīga, but its Old Town was devastated in World War II. Most sights of interest are clustered together beside the river, just east of the city's main roundabout.

The 13th-century **St Simon's Church** (Sv Sīmaņa baznīca) has been destroyed several times and its current appearance dates from 1739. The altarpiece shows a depiction of the Temptation of Christ by Christiana Vogels-Vogelstein. Visitors can climb the church

tower for a view of the city. Just beyond the church lie the ruins of the Livonian Order castle and the **Museum of Local Studies** (Valmieras novadpētniecības muzejs). The museum covers local history and hosts exhibitions. Close by is the city's oldest wooden building, a former pharmacy built in 1735.

🏛 **St Simon's Church**
Bruņinieku iela 2. **Tel** 6420 0333.
Open 11am–5pm Tue–Sun.

🏛 **Museum of Local Studies**
Bruņinieku iela 3. **Tel** 6422 3620.
Open 10am–5pm Tue–Sat. 🎦

❸ Ainaži

Road Map D2. 🏙 1,800.
🚌 from Cēsis. 🛈 Valdemara iela 50a, 6404 3241.

Close to the Estonian border, Ainaži occupies a crucial place in Latvia's maritime history. For centuries, the coastline was sparsely inhabited, justifying the town's name, which is derived from the Livonian word *ainagi* meaning "solitary". However, by the 19th century, it had become an important fishing centre, and in 1864, was chosen by Krišjānis Valdemārs as the location for his naval school, which closed only in 1919 during the civil war. The original school building is now the **Naval College Museum** (Ainažu jūrskolas muzejs), which displays photographs, documents, model ships and a collection of anchors. Ainaži also boasts the

Fire-fighters' Museum (Ainažu ugunsdzēsības muzejs). Exhibits in the main building include hand-operated water pumps, uniforms and insignia, while the garage displays fire trucks. The museum staff are former fire-fighters.

🏛 **Naval College Museum**
Valdemāra iela 47. **Tel** 6404 3349.
Open May–Sep: 10am–5pm Wed–Sun; Oct–Apr: 11am–5pm Tue–Sat. 🎦

🏛 **Fire-fighters' Museum**
Valdemāra iela 69. **Tel** 6404 3280.
Open May–Sep: 10am–4pm Tue–Sat, 10am–2pm Sun; Oct–Apr: 10am–4pm Tue–Fri, 10am–2pm Sat.

Striking snowcapped Liv Sacrificial Caves near Salacgrīva

❹ Salacgrīva

Road Map D3. 🏙 6,000. 🚌 from Rīga. 🛈 Rīgas iela 10a, 6404 1254.
🎭 Positivus (Jul). 🖥 tourism.salcgriva.lv

Positioned at the mouth of the Salaca river, the fishing port of Salacgrīva officially became a town in 1928. There is evidence that German traders may have visited the Salaca before reaching the Daugava river. Salacgrīva is a good jumping-off point for exploring the area nearby.

Environs
On the banks of the Svētupe river, 10 km (6 miles) east of town, are the **Liv Sacrificial Caves** (Lībiešu upurala). Coins and artifacts dating from the 14th to the 19th centuries have been found here, and there are runes carved into the walls. The **Randu Meadows** (Randu pļavas), about 8 km (5 miles) north of Salacgrīva, are rich in birdlife and rare plants.

Nautical objects displayed in the garden of the Naval College Museum, Ainaži

❺ Mazsalaca

Road Map D2. 🏛 1,200. 🚌 from Rīga. ℹ️ Rīgas iela 1, 2837 4774.
🌐 **mazsalaca.lv**

This sleepy town has little to detain visitors, except for the **Mazsalaca Regional Museum**, with its unusual collection of woodcarvings on a Satanic theme by Valters Hirte. It is an ideal base, though, for exploring nearby attractions, such as the spookily named Werewolf Pine and Devil's Caves, 2 km (1 mile) from town, where the spring water is said to have healing powers.

Skaņaiskalns (Sound Hill), a sandstone cliff southwest of Mazsalaca, is noted for its echoes. It can be reached via a park full of wooden sculptures, which can be viewed on the drive through, but are better seen on foot. The 2-km (1-mile) path begins at the Valtenburg manor house (now a school) on Parka Street.

🏛 **Mazsalaca Regional Museum**
Rīgas iela 1. **Tel** 6425 1781.
Open May–Oct: 11am–4pm Wed–Sun; Nov–Apr: 11am–4pm Tue–Thu.

Carved wooden soldiers in the park leading to Skaņaiskalns, Mazsalaca

❻ Limbaži

Road Map D3. 🏛 9,200.
🚌 from Rīga. ℹ️ Torņa iela 3, 6407 0608. 🌐 **visitlimbazi.lv**

Although it is one of Latvia's oldest towns, Limbaži has retained little of its prosperous past. The area, which was known during the 13th century as Metsepole (Indriķis in Latvian), was one of three Liv territories mentioned in the early 13th-century chronicle written by Henry of Livonia.

The Orthodox Church in Limbaži, dating back to the early 20th century

Limbaži's stone castle, built by the Brotherhood of the Sword in 1223, served as the Archbishop of Rīga's residence. A town grew up around the castle and formed part of the Hanseatic League. The castle, now in ruins, was destroyed in the 1602 Polish-Swedish War.

Offering tours of the castle ruins is the **Museum of Regional Studies** (Limbažu muzejs), with its fascinating display of artifacts that recount the region's history. Close by is the 1903 **Orthodox Church**, which still retains some of its original splendour. A statue of Kārlis Baumanis, composer of the national anthem, stands in Jūras Street.

🏛 **Museum of Regional Studies**
Burtnieku iela 7. **Tel** 6407 0632.
Open May–Oct: 10am–6pm Tue–Sat; Nov–Apr: 10am–5pm Tue–Sat.
📷 for castle. 📷

Krišjānis Valdemārs

One of the key figures of the Latvian National Awakening, Krišjānis Valdemārs (1825–91) was a writer, educationist, political thinker and ideologist. During Valdemārs's time the majority of Latvian literary works were written by Baltic Germans, and he sought to change this. From 1862 until its suppression in 1865, Valdemārs edited a Latvian-language publication, *Pēterburgas Avīzes*, alongside Krišjānis Barons and poet Juris Alunāns, which criticized the Baltic German sense of cultural superiority. He encouraged Barons and Fricis Brīvzemnieks to start a Latvian folk songs collection (see pp28–9), and was instrumental in establishing the Ainaži Naval College, where tuition was free and not dependent on social status.

Valdemārs's bust, Naval Museum

House set amid idyllic scenery reflected in one of the many clear-water lakes near Dunte

7 Dunte

Road Map D3. 🏔 2,890. 🚌 from Valmiera.

Otherwise unremarkable, Dunte is known for the **Münchausen Museum** dedicated to Karl Friedrich Hieronymus von Münchhausen (1720–97). An officer in the Russian cavalry, Baron Münchhausen married a local woman and visited Dunte on his honeymoon. He became unwittingly famous when a collection of fantastical stories featuring him was published anonymously in 1781, and his association with exaggeration continues to this day. Museum staff dress in period costumes, and one room is a fanciful reconstruction of his wife's boudoir. A screen shows a 1943 German film adaptation of his tales. Upstairs are waxworks of famous Latvians.

🏛 Münchausen Museum
Duntes Manor. **Tel** 6406 5633. **Open** May–Oct: 10am–5pm daily (to 6pm Sat & Sun); Nov–Apr: 10am– 5pm Sat & Sun, by appt Wed–Fri. 🐾 🎫 📷

8 Saulkrasti

Road Map D3. 🏔 5,550. 🚆 from Rīga. 🚌 from Rīga. ℹ Ainažu iela 13b, 6795 2641. 🎭 Town Festival (Jul), International Jazz Festival (Jul), Organ Music Festival (Sep). 🌐 **saulkrasti.lv**

A seaside resort since the 19th century, Saulkrasti is little more than a string of homes and guesthouses along the main road. Nonetheless, it remains a popular getaway for Rīga residents. The main activity is walking along the coastline, and a trail stretching for 4 km (2 miles) has several viewing points, including a platform on the White Dune (Baltā kāpa). The privately owned **Bicycle Museum** (Saulkrastu velosipēdu muzejs) is housed in a large shed in the owners' garden. The superb collection, a work of many years, features oddities such as a wooden bicycle made by an aeroplane engineer. There are also mock-ups of a repairs workshop and a shop of bicycle parts.

Cycle badges at Bicycle Museum, Saulkrasti

🏛 Bicycle Museum
Rīgas iela 44a. **Tel** 2888 3160. **Open** call in advance. 🐾

9 Ikšķile

Road Map D3. 🏔 6,250. 🚆 from Rīga. 🚌 from Rīga.

In the mid-12th century, the Augustinian monk Father Meinhard, the first Bishop of Ikšķile, accompanied German merchants along the Daugava river. He built **St Mary's Church** here, the first church in the territories of Latvia's tribes. The local Livs resisted being converted to Christianity and Meinhard made little headway. The church was the first stone building in the Baltics, and its ruins have been covered with a metal roof to protect them from the elements. Following the construction of a hydroelectric dam on the river, the ruins stand on an island, although there is nothing much to see.

Ruins of St Mary's Church in Ikšķile, one of Latvia's earliest churches

⑩ Lielvārde

Road Map D4. 🏔 7,350. 🚌 from Rīga. ℹ️ Edgara Kauliņa aleja 20, 6505 3759. 🎭 Regional Festival (Jul), Birthday of Andrejs Pumpurs (Sep). 🌐 **lielvarde.lv**

The town of Lielvārde is best known as the site of the climactic battle between the heroic Lāčplēsis and the Black Knight. The conflict ended when the two warriors disappeared into the Daugava river close to an early 13th-century castle, the ruins of which stand on a hillock. Tall wooden sculptures nearby illustrate Lāčplēsis's story, while a pair of large stones are said to be the bed and blanket of the hero, who reputedly returns to the bank each night to sleep.

Also close to the river is the **Andrejs Pumpurs Museum** (Andreja Pumpura muzejs), dedicated to the eminent writer. A small display is devoted to *Lielvārdes josta*. These belts, used in traditional weddings, are for sale at the museum.

At the western end of town is **Uldevena Castle** (Uldevena pils), a reconstruction of a wooden Liv fortification. It was built in 1997 to the design of a local artist and takes elements from other structures, thus representing an "ideal" rather than a single castle.

Wooden sculpture of Lāčplēsis

🏛 Andrejs Pumpurs Museum
E Kauliņa aleja 20. **Tel** 6505 3759. **Open** 10am–5pm Tue–Sun (Nov–Apr: 11am–3pm Sun). 🖼 📷

🏰 Uldevena Castle
Parka iela 3. **Tel** 2946 5792. **Open** Apr–Nov: 10am–6pm Thu–Sun. 🖼 📷

⑪ Skrīveri

Road Map D4. 🏔 4,000. 🚐 from Rīga. ℹ️ Daugavas iela 58, 2863 3643. 🌐 **skriveri.lv**

Although the town has a long history, Skrīveri was devastated during World War I. Its main attraction is the **Andrejs Upīts Memorial Museum** (Andreja Upīša memoriālmajā), which draws visitors interested in Latvian literature. The exhibition about the noted author, critic and Communist polemicist is displayed in his former home. The **Tree Park** (Dendroloģiskais parks) close to Skrīveri is a pleasant, peaceful place to wander, its paths running through forests made up of almost 400 species of tree from around the world. Each one has been tagged with both its Latvian and Latin names.

🏛 Andrejs Upīts Memorial Museum
Daugavas iela 58. **Tel** 6519 7221. **Open** mid-May–Oct: 10am–5pm Tue–Sun. 🖼 🌐 **upisamuzejs.lv**

Andrejs Pumpurs and Lāčplēsis

Mural of Lāčplēsis and Laimdota at the Andrejs Pumpurs Museum

Born in Birzgale, close to Lielvārde, Andrejs Pumpurs (1841–1902) was an unlikely literary figure. Working on the land before volunteering to fight in Serbia against the Ottoman Empire in 1876, he became a loyal officer in the Russian army but was also a staunch promoter of Latvian culture. Convinced of the need for a national epic, he chose the folk story of Lāčplēsis the Bear Slayer, whose mixed animal-human parentage is evident in his bear-like ears. Pumpurs also drew from Latvian folklore to create a strongly allegorical plot filled with demons and witches. Lāčplēsis defeats the Estonian giant Kalapuisis and convinces him of the need to work together against their foreign foes. Towards the end of the epic, Lāčplēsis unites the Latvian people and repels the invaders, but the wicked turncoat Kangars reveals the hero's secret – his strength is in his ears. The Black Knight, a Germanic giant, cuts off Lāčplēsis's ears, plunging Latvia into 700 long years of misery. The story goes that Lāčplēsis will rise again after he defeats his rival.

⑫ Koknese

Road Map D4. 🏔 3,000. 🚉 from Rīga. 🚌 ℹ️ Melioratoru iela 1, 6516 1296. 🎭 International Folk Music Festival (Jul). 🌐 **koknese.lv**

Once the main settlement of the Selonian tribe, which was subjugated by the Livonian Order in 1208, Koknese also appears in the tale of Lāčplēsis as the home of Laimdota – the beautiful and virtuous young woman with whom the hero falls in love. Today, the picturesque ruins of the Livonian Order castle, built in 1209 but destroyed during the Great Northern War (1700–21), makes Koknese popular with visitors. The site was even more attractive before a hydro-electric power station was built on the Daugava river in 1965.

Livonian Order castle with the Daugava river in the distance, Koknese

Neo-Byzantine St Nicholas's Orthodox Church in Jēkabpils

⓭ Jēkabpils

Road Map D4. 28,000.
from Rīga. from Rīga,
Daugavpils. Brīvības iela 140/142,
6523 3822. jekabpils.lv

Founded as a settlement for
Old Believers (see p126),
Jēkabpils received town rights
from Jakob Kettler, Duke of
Courland (see p139), in 1670.

In the town centre, the
Neo-Byzantine **St Nicholas's
Orthodox Church** (Sv Nikolaja
pareizticīgo baznīca) was built
in 1910. Close by, the large
private **Mans's Gallery** was one
of the first to open in post-
Soviet Latvia. East of the centre,
the **Selian Farmstead** (Sēļu
sēta) is an open-air museum
with 19th-century buildings,
including a farmhouse, a smithy
and a windmill.

On the opposite side of the
Daugava river lies the 13th-
century **Krustpils Castle**
(Krustpils pils). Destroyed during the Livonian Wars (1558–
83), it was reconstructed in
1585 and modified in 1849.
Though the castle is largely
dilapidated, several of its rooms

have been restored, and one
of them displays Russian
military memorabilia.

🏛 **St Nicholas's Orthodox Church**
Brīvības iela 202. **Tel** 6522 3886.

🏛 **Mans's Gallery**
Brīvības iela 154. **Tel** 6523 1953.
Open 9am–6pm Mon–Sat.
🌐 manss.lv

🏛 **Selian Farmstead**
Filozofu iela 6. **Tel** 6522 1042.
Open May–Oct: 9am–6pm Mon–Fri,
10am–5pm Sat & Sun. 🏛

🏛 **Krustpils Castle**
Rīgas iela 216b. **Tel** 6522 1042.
Open May–Oct: daily; Nov–Apr:
Mon–Sat. 🌐 jekabpilsmuzejs.lv

⓮ Līvāni

Road Map E4. 11,000.
Domes iela 1b, 6538 1856.
🎭 Town Festival (Jul), International
Folk Festival (Sep). 🌐 livani.lv

With a long history as an industrial centre, Līvāni takes pride in
its glass factory, which opened
in 1887. The on-site **Glass
Museum** (Stikla muzejs) offers
glass-blowing demonstrations.

During the post-war era, the
Soviet regime built large bio-
chemical and construction facilities, many of which became
obsolete after independence.
Recent efforts to improve the
town's fortunes include the
establishment of the **Latgale
Art and Craft Centre**, which
hosts exhibitions, besides con-
ducting ceramics and weaving
workshops for visitors.

🏛 **Glass Museum**
Domes 1b. **Tel** 6538 1855. **Open** Jun–
Aug: Tue–Sun; Sep–May: Tue–Sat. 🏛
🏛 🌐 latgalesamatnieki.lv

🏛 **Latgale Art and Craft Centre**
Domes 1. **Tel** 6538 1855.
Open Tue–Sat. 🏛 🏛 🏛

⓯ Daugavpils

See pp200–201.

⓰ Krāslava

Road Map E4. 11,500. from
Daugavpils. Pils iela 2, 6562 2201.
🌐 visitkraslava.com

Attractively set alongside the
Daugava river, the town of
Krāslava is largely composed of
two-storey wooden buildings.
Although there are few specific
sights to draw visitors, it is a
pleasant place to visit.

Standing on an artificial hill, the
1750 Baroque Krāslava Castle
(Krāslavas pils) houses the
Krāslava Museum, dedicated to
local arts and history. The
Catholic Church (Katoļu baznīca)
stands on the town's other hill. It
is the finest of the Baroque buildings in Latgale. Its imposing
fresco, depicting St Ludovik leaving for the Crusades, was painted

Krāslava town, with rows of pretty houses along the Daugava river

by the Italian artist Philippo Kastaldi in the 18th century.

🏛 Krāslava Museum
Pils iela 8. **Tel** 6562 3586. **Open** 10am–5pm Mon–Fri, 10am–4pm Sat, 10am–2pm Sun. 📷

Dazzling exterior of the majestic Aglona Basilica

⓱ Aglona

Road Map E4. 🚌 from Rīga.
ℹ️ Somersetas 34, 6532 2100.
📅 Feast of the Assumption (15 Aug).

Catholic pilgrims from across the Baltic region and Russia flock to this otherwise unremarkable town to visit **Aglona Basilica** and attend the Feast of the Assumption. Lithuanian members of the Dominican Order were invited by a local landowner to build a monastery and school in 1697. The basilica, then a church, was built in the 18th century. Pope John Paul II declared it a basilica in 1980, marking the 200th anniversary of its completion, and visited it in 1993. The basilica is famous for its early 17th-century icon of the Virgin Mary, brought by the Dominicans and said to have healing powers. It is hidden behind a lesser icon, which slides down only during special services.

⓲ Preiļi

Road Map E4. 🚶 10,000. 🚌 from Rīga. ℹ️ Kārsavas iela 4, 6532 2041.
🌐 **preili.lv**

From about 1475 until 1866, the market town of Preiļi was under the control of the Borgh family, who were originally from southern Italy. The most recent

of the family's three manor houses still stands but is in poor condition. In the gatekeeper's house, the **History and Applied Arts Museum** (Preiļu vēstures un lietišķ mākslas muzejs) has exhibits including old photographs of Preili and samples of the pottery for which it is renowned. More local ceramics can be found – and bought – at the **P Čerņavskis Pottery Workshop-Museum** (P Čerņavska keramikas darbnīca-muzejs). The late 19th-century **Roman Catholic Church** (Romas katoļu bazīca) contains an 18th-century crucifix, and two sculptures stand outside; one is dedicated to Mother Latvia and the other is a monument to the politically repressed during the Soviet regime.

Jug, Latgale Culture and History Museum

🏛 History and Applied Arts Museum
Raiņa 28. **Tel** 6532 2731.
Open 11am–6pm Tue–Fri, 10am–4pm Sat. 📷

🏛 P Čerņavskis Pottery Workshop Museum
Talsu iela 21. **Tel** 2942 9630.
Open by appointment.

⛪ Roman Catholic Church
Tirgus laukums 11. **Tel** 6532 2041.
Open by appointment.

⓳ Rēzekne

Road Map E4. 🚶 37,000. 🚉 from Rīga. 🚌 from Daugavpils. ℹ️ Krasta Iela 31, 6460 5005. 🌐 **rezekne.lv**

Although most of its old buildings were destroyed during World War II, Rēzekne is one of the cultural centres of

the Latgale region and also serves as a good base for visiting the area's lakes.

The best-known sight is *Latgales Māra*, a statue created by Leons Tomašickis, which stands in the centre of a large roundabout on Atbrīvošanas Avenue. The religious iconography of the statue depicting the pagan goddess Māra holding aloft a Christian cross may be ambiguous but the politics are not: the plinth simply reads "*Vienoti Latvija*" ("United for Latvia"). Unveiled in 1939, it commemorates the 1917 meeting in Rēzekne which decided that Latgale would no longer remain a part of Russia's Vitebsk province. Removed by the Russian authorities in 1940, the statue was reinstated by the occupying German army. Destroyed in 1950, the statue was rebuilt by Iomašickis's son after Latvia gained its independence in 1991. The inauguration of the replica took place in 1992.

Just north of the statue is the **Latgale Culture and History Museum** (Latgales kultūrvēstures muzejs), which focuses on the ceramics of the region, including traditional branched candelabra. South of the statue, on a small mound with excellent views of a Catholic church, are the ruins of the city's castle.

🏛 Latgale Culture and History Museum
Atbrīvošanas aleja 102. **Tel** 6462 2464.
Open May–Sep: Wed–Sun; Oct–Apr: Tue–Sat. 📷

Exhibits displayed inside the History and Applied Arts Museum, Preiļi

⓯ Daugavpils

The second-most populous city in Latvia, Daugavpils is often regarded as a "Russian city" as the majority of its residents are Russian. Its history can be traced to 1275 and a Livonian Order castle called Dinaburga. In the 16th century, a settlement grew on the banks of the Daugava river, and was occupied by Poles, Russians and Swedes at various times. When the town was developed into a Tsarist fortress in the early 19th century, civilians were relocated southeast to the land that today forms the city centre. An industrial hub for the erstwhile Soviet Union, Daugavpils has suffered from economic neglect since independence, though the city's image is improving.

Stately exterior of the Museum of Regional Studies and Arts

🏛 Museum of Regional Studies and Arts
Rīgas iela 8. **Tel** 6542 4155. **Open** 10am–6pm Tue–Sat. 🚫 📷 📷
w dnmm.lv

Housed in an attractive building dating from 1883, this museum is dedicated to local history from the 9th century BC to the present day, but focusing on the period between the second half of the 18th century and 1918. Paintings by the city's second-most famous artist, Leonīds Bauļins, occupy one room, while other rooms document regional flora and fauna.

Mark Rothko (1903–70)
The artist Mark Rothko was born Marcus Rothkowitz into a Jewish family in Daugavpils at a time when the Russian Empire was scarred by pogroms. His family emigrated to Portland, Oregon, USA, in 1913. He received a scholarship to study at Yale University, but left after two years and trained in art in New York. Rothko changed his name in 1940, and by 1950 he had developed a unique style, in which soft-edged rectangular forms are aligned in front of coloured backgrounds. They are described as Abstract Expressionist, although Rothko himself insisted that he was interested in pure form. Following an aneurysm and the breakdown of his marriage, Rothko committed suicide in 1970.

Mark Rothko, Abstract Expressionist

✡ Synagogue
Cietokšņa 42. **Tel** 6542 0092.
Open by appointment.

Prior to World War I, over half of the town's population was Jewish. There were at one time 48 synagogues, of which only one remains in use. It was renovated in 2006 with the help of Mark Rothko's children, who had visited it in 2003, the centenary of their father's birth.

⛪ Cathedral of Sts Boris and Glebe
Tautas iela 2. **Tel** 6545 3544.

This blue-and-white building, resplendent with its ten golden cupolas, is the largest Russian Orthodox cathedral in the country. Built in 1905, it is named after the two saints on whose feast day the Russian army entered Daugavpils in 1656. The Russian name for the town, Borisoglebsk, was also taken from the saints' names. The icons and frescoes inside were copied from those in Sophia Cathedral in Kiev, Russia.

⛪ St Mary's Church
Puškina 16a. **Open** services only. ✉
A solid pink structure with diminutive blue domes, this Old Believers' *(see p126)* church is rarely open to the public. Visitors may, however, be able to look inside during services, when candles are lit in front of the dozens of icons that line the walls. The solemn chanting of the congregation adds to the atmosphere.

Beautiful interior of the Cathedral of Sts Boris and Glebe

Rose-coloured façade of St Mary's Church

VISITORS' CHECKLIST

Practical Information
Road Map E4. ⬛ 110,000.
ℹ️ Rīgas 22a, 6542 2818.
🌐 **visitdaugavpils.lv**

Transport
🚉 Rīgas iela. 🚌 Viestura iela 10.

🏛 Daugavpils Fortress
Cietokšņa iela. **Tel** 6542 4043.
Open 8am–6pm. 🏛 Mark Rothko Art
Centre: Mihaila iela 3. **Tel** 6543 0279.
Open 11am–5pm Tue & Sun, 11am–
7pm Wed–Sat. 🌐 **rothkocenter.com**

The construction of this walled
Russian fortress began in 1810
but was interrupted when
Napoleon's army attacked in July
1812. The moat encircling it once
contained tunnels that connected it to the Daugava river,
but they have since been
blocked. The fortress served as a
German concentration camp
and was later occupied by the
Soviet Army until 1993. The **Mark
Rothko Art Centre**, located in
the former arsenal building,
provides space for exhibitions
and displays original works by
the world-famous artist,
donated by his children. Guided
tours and maps are available
from the renovated water tower
that now houses the fortress's
culture and information centre.

🏛 Martin Luther Church
18 Novembra iela 66. **Tel** 2957 4349.
Open Sun or by appointment.
This redbrick, Neo-Gothic
church dates from 1893 but has
been completely renovated.
During the Soviet regime, it was
used as a boxing gym.

🏛 Virgin Mary Catholic Church
A Pumpura 11a. **Open** evening mass.
According to local legend
the daughters of a rich
merchant drowned in a lake
on the spot where the church
now stands.

Daugavpils

① Museum of Regional Studies and Arts
② Synagogue
③ Cathedral of Sts Boris and Glebe
④ St Mary's Church
⑤ Martin Luther Church
⑥ Virgin Mary Catholic Church

| 0 metres | 500 |
| 0 yards | 500 |

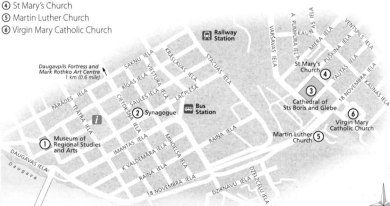

⑳ Latgale Lakes

Latvia's relatively hilly southeastern corner, known as the Latgale Uplands (Latgales augstiene), is covered with a patchwork of many lakes. On a sunny day it is easy to see why this part is called the Land of Blue Lakes. Unfortunately, public transport is limited here, although if time permits the area can be explored by bus. The route also passes through Rēzekne, where the tourist office can provide advice on activities such as angling and bird-watching in the area, and a trip to Ludza en route is also possible.

Lake Lubāns, one of Latvia's favourite spots for bird-watchers

⑧ Lake Lubāns
One of the best places for bird-watching and fishing in the country, this is Latvia's largest lake by surface area.

⑥ Musical Instruments Workshop, Gaiglava
Visitors can watch artisans at work and learn to play traditional instruments.

⑦ Teirumnīki
A boardwalk circles the lake and runs through a swamp where cranberries grow.

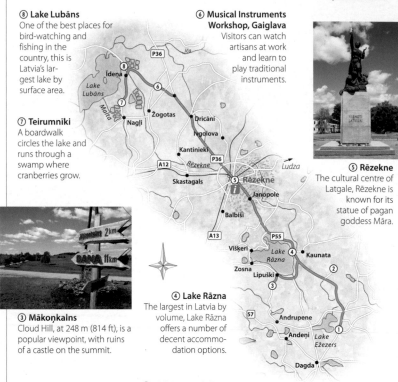

⑤ Rēzekne
The cultural centre of Latgale, Rēzekne is known for its statue of pagan goddess Māra.

③ Mākoņkalns
Cloud Hill, at 248 m (814 ft), is a popular viewpoint, with ruins of a castle on the summit.

④ Lake Rāzna
The largest in Latvia by volume, Lake Rāzna offers a number of decent accommodation options.

Key

▬ Tour route

═ Other road

② Lielais Liepukalns
At 289 m (948 ft), this hill is the highest point in the region and the third-highest in the country.

0 km | 10
0 miles | 10

Tips for Drivers

Starting point: Lielais liepukalns.
Length: 114 km (71 miles).
Stopping-off points: Rēzekne is an ideal stop. It is possible to stay at Ežezers, Rāzna and Lubāns.
Driving conditions: Avoid driving around the western edge of Lake Rāzna in bad weather.

① Lake Ežezers
Translated as "Hedgehog Lake", Lake Ežezers is considered one of the most beautiful lakes in Latgale. Its 36 islands can be explored by boat.

㉑ Ludza

Road Map E3. 🗺 10,500. 🚉 🚌 ℹ️ Baznicas 42, 2946 7925. 🚢

Perhaps the oldest town in Latvia, Ludza traces its foundation back to about 1177. The central square is home to the tourist information office and the Orthodox Cathedral.

The **Handicrafts Centre** (Ludzas amatnieku centrs), close to the central square, has a potter's kiln and space for artisans. Visitors can participate in workshops by prior arrangement. Handicraft objects are on sale here as well. There is also a monthly food and crafts market.

The town's **Museum of Local Studies** (Ludzas novadpētniecības muzejs) occupies the former villa of Jakov Kulnev (1764–1812), a Russian war hero who lived in Ludza. The grounds contain late 19th- and early 20th-century wooden buildings from various parts of Latgale.

🏛 **Handicrafts Centre**
Tālavijas iela 27a. **Tel** 2946 7925. **Open** Mon–Sat. 🌐 ludzasamatnieki.lv

🏛 **Museum of Local Studies**
Kulneva iela 2. **Tel** 6572 3931. **Open** Mon–Sat. 🖼

㉒ Vecpiebalga

Road Map D3. 🗺 1,000. 🚌 ℹ️ 2611 0724. 🌐 vecpiebalga.lv

With a history dating back to the early 14th century, this small town is famed as the home of prominent cultural figures. Notable among them were the brothers, Reinis (1839–1920) and Matīss Kaudzīte (1848–1926), who wrote *Mērnieku laiki* (The Times of the Land Surveyors). Among the best-loved Latvian novels, it is based on the sale of a landlord's estates to peasant farmers. The authors' home is now the **Kaudzīte Brothers Memorial Museum**.

Environs
There are other interesting sites close to Vecpiebalga. The Kārlis Skalbe Museum is about 4 km (2 miles) from the town.

Statue of Liena, heroine of *Mērnieku laiki*, in Vecpiebalga

It occupies the summerhouse of revolutionary writer Kārlis Skalbe (1878–1945). Further along the road is the Janskola Museum, housed in the former home of composer Emīls Dārziņš (1875–1910). The displays include works by Latvian poet Janis Sudrabkalns (1894–1975).

🏛 **Kaudzīte Brothers Memorial Museum**
Kalna kaibēni. **Tel** 2618 5382. **Open** mid-May–mid-Oct Wed–Sun. 🖼

㉓ Alūksne

Road Map E3. 🗺 9,500. 🚉 from Gulbene. 🚌 from Cēsis. ℹ️ Pils 25a, 6432 2804. 🌐 aluksne.lv

In 1342, the Knights of the Sword built a castle on an island in Lake Alūksne, after destroying the existing fortress. The Swedish army demolished the castle in 1702 rather than let it fall into Russian hands. Alūksne is best known for its association

with Ernst Glück (1654–1705), a German Lutheran clergyman who was the first to translate the Bible into Latvian. His home has been turned into the **Ernst Glück Museum of the Bible**.

The Museum of Local Studies and Art is housed in a manor house built in 1861 for Baron Vietinghoff. There are displays on local history, arts and crafts, and the museum can also arrange excursions.

🏛 **Ernst Glück Museum of the Bible**
Pils 25a. **Tel** 6432 3164. **Open** May–Oct: Tue–Sat; Nov–Apr: by appointment. 🖼

㉔ Gulbene–Alūksne Narrow-Gauge Railway

Road Map E3. **Tel** 6447 3037. 🎫 Railway Festival (first Sat in Sep). 🌐 banitis.lv

This 33-km (21-mile) stretch of railway track constitutes the only functioning narrow-gauge railway within Latvia. The 90-minute journey has stops en route, including Stāmeriena, which has a manor house, and Umernieki.

The **Ates Mill Museum** is the primary incentive for visiting Umernieki. Around the mill is an ethnographic museum, consisting of 13 buildings which have been brought from around Vidzeme.

🏛 **Ates Mill Museum**
Ate, Kalncempji village. **Tel** 2940 0393. **Open** Tue–Sun (Nov–Apr: closed Sun). 🖼 ♿ 🎫 Harvest Festival (Sep).

Soviet-era steam engine locomotive at Gulbene railway station

LITHUANIA

Lithuania at a Glance

An unblemished natural landscape of rolling hills, Lithuania is blessed with thousands of lakes that create a complex network of streams and rivers. In this low-lying, post-glacial countryside, almost all the land lies at less than 200 m (656 ft) above sea level. The eastern half of the country is known as the "highlands" and the western half the "lowlands". The main features of the Lithuanian coast are its fascinating sandy dunes and beaches. Despite Lithuania's tumultuous history, many of the country's fine historic buildings have survived.

Hill of Crosses
(see p277)

Mažeikiai
Skuodas
Naujoji Akmenė
Joniškis
Kuršėnai
Palanga
Telšiai
Plungė
Šiauli
WESTERN LITHUANIA
(see pp272–89)
Radviliškis
Klaipėda
Rietavas
Priekulė
Kelmė
Šilalė
Šilutė
Raseiniai
Tauragė
Jurbarkas
Šakiai
Marijampolė
Kalvarija

0 km   25
0 miles   25

Palanga (see p286) is a popular beach resort that draws hundreds of visitors each summer. Once a quiet little fishing hamlet, today it is a vibrant place filled with innumerable bars and cafés.

Parnidis Dune towers over the fishing village of Nida, on the Curonian Spit (see pp288–9). Views from the summit take in both the Baltic Sea and the Curonian Lagoon and stretch southwards to Kaliningrad.

◀ Farm on the shore of the Nevis river at the archaeological site of Kernavė

Kernavė *(see p258)* is a UNESCO World Heritage Site, set in the Neris River Valley. Once the capital of the Grand Duchy of Lithuania, it is now one of the largest archaeological sites in the Baltic region. The state museum, established here in 1989, was converted into a cultural reserve in 2004.

Vilnius Cathedral *(see pp228–9)*, a Neo-Classical structure, houses the lavish Baroque Chapel of St Casimir and a crypt that provides an insight into Lithuania's complex history.

CENTRAL LITHUANIA
(see pp252–271)

VILNIUS
(see pp220–251)

Pažaislis Monastery
(see p265)

Trakai Island Castle *(see pp256–7)*, in the picturesque village of Trakai, is a fairytale fortress that makes a beautiful day-trip from the capital during any season of the year. An optional trip by yacht or rowing boat rounds off the experience.

A PORTRAIT OF LITHUANIA

The largest of the three Baltic States and one of the hidden jewels of Europe, Lithuania takes pride in its relatively secluded landscape of clean lakes, ancient forests and coastal dunes. The capital, Vilnius, which has a UNESCO-protected Old Town, combines the romance of its breathtaking Baroque architecture with the modern trappings of 21st-century Europe.

Lithuania successfully repelled Germanic invaders as early as 1410 at the Battle of Grünwald. In the subsequent centuries, however, the country experienced a tumultuous series of invasions. Most recently, the two world wars and the massacre of one of Europe's largest Jewish communities were followed by the neglect of the Soviet era.

Since its independence in 1991, Lithuania has strived to restore its national identity. Vilnius possesses one of Europe's finest Old Towns, with several Baroque masterpieces. Across the country, areas of serene natural beauty have become protected reserves teeming with wildlife. Excellent roads wind through attractive villages and towns that are remarkably tranquil. A resurgence in the popularity of folk culture is colouring every corner of the country, with wooden crosses, altars and shrines being crafted and folk song and dance traditions being explored. An explosion of printed and electronic materials in Lithuanian, a language related to Sanskrit, has taken place since the Singing Revolution (1987–90). At the same time, Lithuania is forging a positive political and cultural role for itself in the expanded European Union.

A sweeping view of Parnidis Dune, or the Great Dune, in the Curonian Spit National Park

◀ Façade of Rokiškis Manor House, embellished with Neo-Baroque details

Catholics worshipping the Virgin Mary in Vilnius

Ethnic and Religious Identity

Lithuania is the most ethnically homogeneous of the Baltic countries. By staying largely agrarian it managed to stem the incoming tide of large numbers of Russians and other nationalities whom the Soviet authorities wanted to man the new factories being built across the Baltic region. Of its population of 3 million, 84 per cent are Lithuanian, while only 5.8 per cent are Russian and 6.6 per cent Polish. Other minorities include Belarusians and Ukrainians, as well as a small group of Tatars and Karaim. In Vilnius, the most ethnically diverse city, Russian and Polish can commonly be heard.

Despite its pagan past, Lithuania has a strong Catholic identity that sets it apart from Estonia and Latvia, where the Germans introduced Lutheranism. The efforts of the Soviet authorities to stamp out religious worship by converting churches into warehouses, cinemas, art galleries and museums, destroying their interiors and deporting large numbers of priests to Siberia, failed. As a result, only 10 per cent of the people do not identify with any religious group today. Religious groups other than Catholics include Russian Orthodox (5 per cent) and small communities of Old Believers and Lutherans.

Politics

Since regaining independence in 1991, Lithuania has vacillated between left- and right-wing governments, while struggling to find its feet on the international stage. Achieving the goals of NATO and EU membership in 2004 was of huge significance for the Baltic region, wrenching it away from Russia's influence. The impeachment of President Rolandas Paksas for violating the constitution, also in 2004, was the climax of a wave of public scepticism in politics. High-profile corruption cases

A Lithuanian folk dance group dressed in national costume

Former Lithuanian president, Valdas Adamkus

revealing how politicians have lobbied on behalf of business interests in exchange for money have created the feeling that moral leadership in Lithuania is waning. Some politicians, however, including two-time president Valdas Adamkus, remained untainted by scandal.

Economy

The Lithuanian economy is one of the fastest-growing in Europe. A dynamic private sector feeds strongly on niche industries including laser optics and biotechnology, as well as core industries such as construction and energy. Lithuanian laser and biotech companies are among the strongest in Europe. Lithuania's largest company by turnover is the Mažeikių Nafta oil refinery near Mažeikiai. The Soviet-era Ignalina Nuclear Power Plant has been decommissioned, but a new nuclear power plant is likely to be constructed to reduce reliance on Russian energy.

Agriculture was rapidly privatized following independence, and then heavily subsidized once Lithuania joined the European Union. Although this has made much of the land more productive, negative results include large swathes of abandoned land and widespread rural poverty. However, ways are being found to invest in sustainable industries such as tourism. Many small farms have been turned into attractive countryside farmsteads providing tourist activities and accommodation.

Modern Life

The countless art galleries in the cities and towns reveal the importance of art and culture to Lithuania. The walls of most households are adorned with real paintings and graphics rather than framed reproductions.

Cultural figures, such as M K Čiurlionis and adored novelist and painter Jurga Ivanauskaitė, have apportioned their skills to more than one medium. Symphonies, chamber concerts, classical ballet and opera are performed regularly throughout the country. On the stage, the dark, post-industrial version of *Hamlet*, by acclaimed theatre director Eimuntas Nekrošius, is one of the most popular theatrical pieces.

In sport, Lithuania has produced achievers such as the discus-thrower Virgilijus Alekna and ice-dancer Margarita Drobiazko, but basketball remains its national obsession. While the Kaunas-based Žalgiris team and Vilnius-based Lietuvos Rytas team dominate the domestic scene, the Lithuanian Olympic basketball team has put the country on the world sporting map.

High-energy Euroleague basketball match

LITHUANIA THROUGH THE YEAR

Lithuanians celebrate a host of festivals where traditional events and folk culture blend with ancient pagan and Catholic rituals. Most of the year's events take place in summer, when after months of wintry gloom the country comes alive with music, dance, cinema, folk culture, handicraft and food festivals. Music is at the centre of most of the country's events, and it ranges from classical, jazz and blues to electronic and contemporary. Christmas is usually white but the thick snows fail to thwart the merrymaking, which culminates in New Year's Eve celebrations. A number of commemorative days are observed in addition to the traditional annual events.

Kaziuko Crafts Fair, held every year to mark St Casimir's Day

Spring

Lithuanians welcome spring with joyful celebrations. The warmer weather wakes the country up to a new season of fairs and festivals.

March
Kaziuko Crafts Fair *(4 Mar)*, Vilnius. A feast of traditional arts and crafts marking St Casimir's Day, with stalls selling all manner of curios.
Cinema Spring *(late Mar– early Apr)*, Vilnius. One of the largest international film festivals in the Baltic region, it showcases the best foreign-language films of the year, most with English subtitles.

April
Garso Galerija, Vilnius. A festival of new electronic music, often featuring radical international songwriters.
Kaunas Jazz *(late Apr)*. One of the best international jazz festivals in the country.

May
New Baltic Dance *(early May)*, Vilnius and Klaipėda. This eclectic event celebrates modern dance and theatre.
Poetry Spring, Vilnius. An international poetry festival and the most outstanding annual literary event in Lithuania.
Kaunas City Day *(20 May)*. A folk art fair with concerts, funfairs and fireworks.

Local folk dressed in traditional costume, Kaunas City Day festival

Summer

The sultry Lithuanian summer initiates great festivities. Classical music takes precedence in the warm evenings, along with jazz and blues.

June
Cow-Swimming Festival, Aukštaitija National Park. A quirky custom where locals dress in folk costumes and watch as cows wearing wreaths are led into a lake to swim to the other side.
Medieval Festival, Trakai. Knights' fights with swords and battleaxes are the festival's highlight.
Joninės *(24 Jun)*. The summer solstice is celebrated all over Lithuania on St John's Day. It is also known as Rasos, meaning "of the dew", for dew's healing properties.
Pažaislis Music Festival *(Jun– Aug)*, Kaunas. Hosted at the Baroque Pažaislis Monastery, it stages music performances.

July
Christopher Summer Festival *(Jul–Aug)*, Vilnius. A hugely enjoyable musical fiesta with performances at different venues all over the city.
Statehood Day *(6 Jul)*. Pomp and ceremony are the hallmarks of this national holiday dedicated to the coronation of King Mindaugas.
Lake Lukštas Blues Nights features blues and jazz performers with the isolated Lake Lukštas as the backdrop.
Sea Festival *(late Jul)*, Klaipėda. The freedom of the seas expressed in a carnival.

Guards at the Presidential Palace in Vilnius, on Statehood Day

August
Christopher's Guitars, Vilnius. A festival featuring classical guitar and flamenco concerts as its highlight.
Mėnuo Juodaragis *(late Aug)*. Translated as "Black Horned Moon", this annual musical event of folk, metal and electronica is held in a different location every 3 years.
Capital Days *(late Aug–Sep)*, Vilnius. A multi-art event during which Gedimino Avenue is flooded with crafts and food stalls, while the squares of central Vilnius become rock and pop music venues.

Autumn
Autumn, which is from mid-September to December, is a visual treat. However, there are fewer annual events

September
Sirenos Theatre Festival *(Sep–Oct)*, Vilnius. Works by international and local artists are showcased.
Mushroom Festival *(late Sep)*, Varėna. A traditional festival dedicated to mushrooms that includes the Lithuanian Mushroom-Picking Championship.
Fire Sculptures Festival *(21–23 Sep)*. Straw figures are set alight at night in this festival that honours Grand Duke Gediminas and also celebrates the autumn equinox.

October
International Festival of Modern Dance *(early Oct)*, Kaunas. A festival of free-style contemporary dance, it attracts the best dancers from all over the world.

Vilnius Jazz *(mid-Oct)*. Jazz, blues and swing are performed by talented contemporary Lithuanian musicians and singers at this festival.

Winter
Lithuania looks stunning in winter as it is often covered in a blanket of snow. However, the chill does not curb the festive spirit.

November
Scanorama *(mid-Nov)*, Vilnius. Scandinavian films take over the capital's multiplexes for this annual 10-day film festival.

December
Christmas *(24–26 Dec)*. The festivities culminate in most homes with a 12-course meat-free meal on Christmas Eve. Christmas Day is celebrated with mass in church, and concerts.
New Year's Eve *(31 Dec)*. Celebrations and parties take place throughout the country, and at the stroke of midnight fireworks light up the sky.

January
Epiphany *(6 Jan)*, Vilnius. Shortly after New Year, a colourful procession of the Three Kings graces the streets of the Old Town.

February
Užgavėnės *(mid-Feb)*. People throughout Lithuania don masks of witches, devils, goats and other creatures and feast on heartwarmingly rich food in this farewell to winter.

Public Holidays
New Year's Day (1 Jan)
Independence Day (16 Feb)
Restoration of Independence (11 Mar)
Easter (Mar/April)
Labour Day (1 May)
Midsummer's Day (23 Jun)
Joninės (24 Jun)
Statehood Day (6 Jul)
Assumption Day (15 Aug)
All Saints' Day (1 Nov)
Christmas (24–26 Dec)

Musicians jamming at the Vilnius Jazz festival

THE HISTORY OF LITHUANIA

Europe's last pagan stronghold, Lithuania rose as a powerful state by the late 14th century, surviving until the 16th century. It was thereafter subjugated first by the Poles and then the Russians. The long periods of occupation endured by the country stirred a reawakening of national identity in its people. An independent republic, briefly created during the inter-war era, was finally established in 1991.

At the start of the 13th century, Lithuanian tribes, such as the Samogitians in the west and Aukštaitiai in the east, began to unite in the face of regular incursions by Germanic crusaders. The brutal attacks grew with increasing intensity before the resolutely pagan Samogitians vanquished the Knights of the Sword at the Battle of the Sun in 1236.

13th-century seal of the Germanic crusaders

of Lithuania *(see pp216–17)*, led by a dynasty established by Gediminas (r.1316–41). The crusaders occupied the Grand Duchy for 100 years, until they were finally and decisively defeated at the Battle of Grünwald (Žalgiris) in 1410 by the powerful allied armies of Lithuania and Poland.

The Lithuanian Grand Duchy

Duke Mindaugas (r.1235–63), who was rapidly adding territory to his base in Aukštaitija, united the tribes in 1240, crowning himself king in 1253. His acceptance of Christianity to appease the crusaders enraged the Samogitians, who murdered him, took over his land and reverted to paganism. By the beginning of the 14th century, large numbers of crusaders returned from the Middle East and joined the fight against the pagan Grand Duchy

Polish-Lithuanian Commonwealth

Grand Duke Jogaila (r.1362–1434) married Jadwiga of Poland in 1386 and accepted Christianity, which led to mass baptisms throughout Lithuania in the ensuing years.

Impression of the Union of Lublin by 19th-century artist Jan Matejko

1236 Samogitian victory at the Battle of the Sun	**1253** Duke Mindaugas crowned	*King Mindaugas (c.1203–63)*	**1386** Lithuania and Poland unite	**1392** Grand Duchy of Lithuania reaches the Black Sea

1200		**1300**		**1400**
1240 Duke Mindaugas unites Lithuania	**1316** Accession of Gediminas	**1382** Crusaders seize Samogitia		**1410** Battle of Grünwald (Žalgiris) destroys the Teutonic Knights

The marriage formed a Polish-Lithuanian alliance that endured for centuries. This proved particularly effective as a bulwark against enemies in the West and in the East. Under Grand Duke Vytautas (r.1401–30), Lithuania was able to extend its reach between the Baltic and the Black seas. Throughout the first half of the 16th century, however, a militant Russia compelled a stronger union between Lithuania and Poland, cemented at the Union of Lublin in 1569. The Commonwealth that resulted lasted for over 200 years.

Portrait of Grand Duke Vytautas on a tile

Decline of the Commonwealth

When King Sigismund Augustus (r.1548–72) died without an heir, the combined position of Grand Duke of Lithuania and King of Poland became an elected one, chosen by the all-powerful nobility. Warsaw, midway between the old capitals of Vilnius and Kraków, became the base. Stefan Bathory (1533–86) was one of the most successful of these elected heads of state. Apart from founding Vilnius University, he also introduced sweeping military and judicial reforms. During the Livonian Wars (see p37), he successfully led a decisive campaign against the Russians, regaining control over Livonia in 1582.

Under the Commonwealth, Poland established its hegemony, with the Poles dominating the Lithuanian nobility. The bourgeoisie, on the other hand, were deprived of all political rights as well as the right to own land, while the peasants were forced to become serfs, subject to severe punishment if they attempted to flee.

The 17th century was a disastrous period for Lithuania, with misrule in Warsaw, plague and fires in Vilnius and a calamitous invasion by the Russians in 1655. Governed by a string of ineffective rulers and noblemen who were either deliberately divisive or simply uninterested in state affairs, the steadily weakening Commonwealth became, throughout the 18th century, little more than a puppet state to Tsarist Russia. In a series of partitions in 1772, 1793 and 1795, the vast lands of the Commonwealth were divided between Russia, Prussia and Austria, despite brave armed resistance by Lithuanian patriots. One such failed uprising was led by Jokūbas Jasinskis (1761–94). By 1795, with the final partition of the Commonwealth, Poland and Lithuania had ceased to exist.

Russians paying tribute to Stefan Bathory in a painting by Jan Matejko

1569 Union of Lublin creates Polish-Lithuanian Commonwealth

1579 Vilnius's academy assumes the status of a university

Bronze doors of the Vilnius University library

1772 First partition of the Commonwealth

1795 Final partition of the Commonwealth

1600

1700

1800

1568 Jesuits found an academy in Vilnius

1655 Russian army sacks Vilnius

1793 Second Partition of the Commonwealth

Coat of arms, Polish-Lithuanian Commonwealth

The Grand Duchy of Lithuania

Founded in the 13th century by King Mindaugas and strengthened further by Grand Duke Gediminas in the 14th century, the Grand Duchy of Lithuania reached its greatest territorial extent under Vytautas the Great. Originally a defensive military union, the Duchy quickly started expanding eastwards and southwards, eventually stretching across much of present-day Belarus and Ukraine. The Duchy was dominated in Vilnius by a military class that later became a privileged nobility. Vilnius flourished as the capital of culture and architecture.

Key

Grand Duchy under Vytautas

The Battle of Grünwald

Nothing quite symbolizes the Grand Duchy at the height of its achievements like Jan Matejko's masterpiece, painted in 1878. Vytautas the Great is shown at the centre, victorious in the Battle of Grünwald (Žalgiris) against the Teutonic Knights in 1410. The Knights were decisively defeated by the combined armies of the Grand Duchy and Poland, led by Vytautas and King Jogaila, respectively.

Grand Duke Gediminas (1275–1341) extended the Duchy's borders, moved the capital to Vilnius and built a powerful chain of defensive fortresses.

Albert II Radvila (1595–1656), who was descended from a long line of influential nobles, effectively ruled the Grand Duchy as Grand Chancellor of Lithuania within the Polish-Lithuanian Commonwealth.

Grand Duke Vytautas (1350–1430), shown here in a 17th-century portrait, is today revered as a national hero. Under his reign, the Grand Duchy grew to its greatest geographical extent, covering swathes of land between the Baltic and Black seas.

Surviving the Centuries

Artifacts found during excavations of the remains of the Royal Palace in Vilnius include decorative tiles, coins and exquisitely crafted jewellery. While the tiles and coins date from the 16th century, some of the jewellery dates back to the 14th century. The collection is likely to go on display once the newly reconstructed palace is completed.

Tile, 16th century   Coin, 16th century

Vilnius University, which the Jesuits had founded as an academy in 1568, was upgraded to a university 11 years later by Stefan Bathory (1533–86), the Grand Duke of Lithuania and King of Poland.

The icon of the Virgin Mary at the Gates of Dawn in Vilnius is a fine example of religious painting from the period. It was originally painted on oak panels in the 1620s.

Grand Duke Vytautas

The first book printed in the Lithuanian language was *Catechism* (1547) by Martynas Mažvydas. Appearing in the Duchy at a time when Polish was the preferred language of the aristocracy, the book had a great appeal for the pagan rural masses.

The Christianization of Lithuania took place in 1387, following the union of Lithuania and Poland. However, unlike the dramatic mass conversion depicted in this 19th-century painting by Jan Matejko, many parts of Lithuania remained pagan into the 16th century.

Napoleon's Grand Army crossing the Nemunas river in 1812

Tsarist Russian Rule

More than 120 years of occupation followed the break-up of the Commonwealth, with most of the land once governed by the Grand Duchy of Lithuania now absorbed into the Russian Empire. Resistance constantly simmered under the surface, however, and hopes of independence were revived when Napoleon marched through Kaunas and Vilnius in June 1812. These hopes were crushed six months later when the demoralized, half-frozen remnants of the French Grand Army retreated from Moscow through Vilnius.

When a rebellion led mainly by the rural nobility failed in 1831, repressive measures were launched such as the closure of Vilnius University and the enforced use of Russian in Lithuanian schools. Even harsher oppression followed another rebellion in 1863, with over 100 of the resistance leaders hunted down and hanged, while others were deported with their families to Siberia. The Russification of the whole country followed, which involved a conscious eradication of all traces of traditional Lithuania. Catholic churches were converted to Orthodox ones and Lithuanian-language books in the Latin alphabet were banned. However, language and identity were kept alive by smuggling books in from East Prussia as well as the printing and circulation of the first Lithuanian-language newspapers, *Aušra* (Dawn) and *Varpas* (Bell).

Nationhood Regained, and Lost

As the chaos of World War I and the 1917 Revolution weakened Russia, an elected council in Vilnius declared Lithuanian independence on 16 February 1918. International recognition was slow in coming. In October 1920, Józef Piłsudski (1867–1935), the nationalist head of state of Poland, which had also regained its independence in 1918, sent an army to occupy Vilnius. The Lithuanian government was, therefore, forced to re-establish itself in Kaunas. Vilnius was indisputably Lithuania's historical capital, but by now, almost half of the city's population was Jewish, and the other half consisted of Polish-speakers. Kaunas was declared Lithuania's temporary capital and remained so until 1939. An element of pride was restored when Lithuania snatched control of Memel from a caretaker French garrison in early 1923 and renamed it Klaipėda.

President Antanas Smetona (r.1926–40)

Dr Jonas Basanavičius, one of the signatories of the Lithuanian Independence Act

1812 Napoleon's advance and disastrous retreat

1832 Russians close down Vilnius University

1918 Lithua decla independe

1815

1855

1895

1831 Rebellion against Tsarist rule

1863 Lithuanian rebels persecuted by Russia

1866 Ban on Lithuanian-language books in the Latin alphabet; 40 years of book-smuggling from East Prussia begins

Adolf Hitler entering Klaipėda in 1939

The Republic of Lithuania

In 1988, encouraged by the greater openness of Soviet premier Mikhail Gorbachev's reforms, a group of intellectuals founded the Sąjūdis movement to rally popular support for the demonstrations that had begun the previous year. The response was immediate. Peaceful protests increased and, on 11 March 1990, Lithuania declared its independence, the first of any of the Soviet republics to do so. In January 1991, Soviet tanks and troops stormed the Vilnius TV Tower, killing 14 unarmed civilians and injuring 700.

In August 1991, the failure of the hardliners' putsch in Moscow finally gave Lithuania freedom. The first presidential elections brought Algirdas Brazauskas to power. Several years of economic hardship followed, marked by rising unemployment. Lithuania's EU and NATO membership in 2004 has brought the country far greater security and prosperity.

Independent Lithuania was led, between 1926 and 1940, by the authoritarian Antanas Smetona. For Lithuanians, this was a time of growing prosperity as agricultural exports boomed. However, they were also uneasy years, as the resurgent powers of Germany and Russia loomed on either side. Klaipėda was retaken by the Nazis in 1939 and the Red Army occupied the rest of Lithuania following an ultimatum from Moscow in 1940. The Red Army carried out mass deportations and horrific massacres. The reign of terror continued under the Nazis, who, in June 1941, launched Operation Barbarossa, the code name for Germany's invasion of the Soviet Union. An estimated 200,000 people, most of them Jews, were taken outside virtually every town and city to be executed. In 1944, as part of its Baltic Offensive, the Red Army pushed back through Lithuania. Over the next 10 years, between 120,000 and 300,000 people were deported to the Siberian Gulags. A brave, but futile, partisan war was fought from the Lithuanian forests until the early 1950s.

A Lithuanian independence rally in 1989, Kaunas

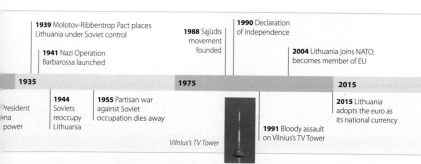

1939 Molotov-Ribbentrop Pact places Lithuania under Soviet control

1941 Nazi Operation Barbarossa launched

1988 Sąjūdis movement founded

1990 Declaration of independence

2004 Lithuania joins NATO; becomes member of EU

1935

1975

2015

President
na
power

1944 Soviets reoccupy Lithuania

1955 Partisan war against Soviet occupation dies away

Vilnius's TV Tower

1991 Bloody assault on Vilnius's TV Tower

2015 Lithuania adopts the euro as its national currency

VILNIUS

Whether viewed from one of the hills that overlook the Old Town or from one of the many pavement cafés with tall spires rising all around them, Vilnius is unmistakably a city of great beauty. The Old Town, on the UNESCO World Heritage list since 1994, blends Gothic and Neo-Classical styles with a breathtaking late flourish of Baroque. Vilnius is in itself an architectural monument.

The character of Vilnius, the Lithuanian capital, has been retained partly because of its isolated location. Yet, the ebb and flow of history has given it a more multicultural feel than the country's other cities.

The earliest written reference to Vilnius exists in a letter from Grand Duke Gediminas in 1323, inviting citizens from towns in Germany to settle here, pledging freedom from taxes and granting other rights. Pagan Vilnius sustained many attacks during the Northern Crusades, yet by the 14th century it had become the capital of an empire that stretched from the Baltic Sea to the Black Sea. Vilnius was reduced to the status of a provincial city in the Polish-Lithuanian Commonwealth, but following a period of devastating wars, invasions and fires between the early 17th and mid-18th centuries, efforts to rebuild the city resulted in the rich offshoot of the Baroque style that is typical of its architecture today.

Vilnius regained its status as the capital of Lithuania in 1918, but only for a year. Occupied by Poland, with Lithuania's government forced to relocate to Kaunas, it declined in economic importance until the Soviets invaded it in 1939. World War II devastated Vilnius and annihilated most of its Jewish population, but under the ensuing Soviet occupation the city expanded.

Vilnius has been transformed from a sleepy backwater to a lively, modern European capital that provides a wonderful setting for shopping, dining and nightlife. However, with Vilnius University, Town Hall Square and several carefully restored churches, the city has retained its charm.

Colourful mural by Antanas Kmieliauskas decorating the ceiling of Vilnius University's bookshop, Littera

◀ Bronze doors of Vilnius University Library

Exploring Vilnius

Although its Old Town is one of the largest in Europe, Vilnius is a surprisingly compact city that can easily be explored on foot. Two of the best places to begin a tour of the Old Town and its Baroque treasures are Vilnius Cathedral in the north and the Gates of Dawn in the south. Gedimino Avenue, the main shopping street where the KGB Museum is located, stretches west from Cathedral Square, while the Church of St Anne lies immediately to the east of the Old Town. Vilnius is also a good base for exploring much of Central Lithuania.

Outdoor cafés along cobblestoned Pilies Street, Old Town

Sights at a Glance

Churches

2 St John's Church
5 Church of St Paraskeva
8 *Vilnius Cathedral pp228–9*
15 Holy Mother of God Church
16 Bernardine Church
17 Church of St Anne
18 Church of St Michael
20 Orthodox Church of St Nicholas
24 Church of St Casimir
26 Church of the Holy Spirit
27 Church of St Theresa
31 Church of St Nicholas
32 Franciscan Church
33 Dominican Church
34 Church of St Catherine

Museums and Galleries

4 Vilnius Picture Gallery
7 Šlapelis House Museum

12 Lithuanian National Museum
13 Applied Arts Museum
19 Mickiewicz Museum
21 Čiurlionis House
23 Contemporary Art Centre
29 Kazys Varnelis Museum
35 Theatre, Music and Film Museum
37 State Jewish Museum
38 Holocaust Museum
40 KGB Museum

Sights of Interest

1 Vilnius University
3 Presidential Palace
6 House of Signatories
9 Cathedral Square
10 Lower Castle
11 Upper Castle
14 Hill of Three Crosses

22 Town Hall Square
25 Basilian Gate
28 Gates of Dawn
30 Artillery Bastion
36 Radvila Palace
39 Frank Zappa Statue

For hotels and restaurants see pp304–305 and pp326–8

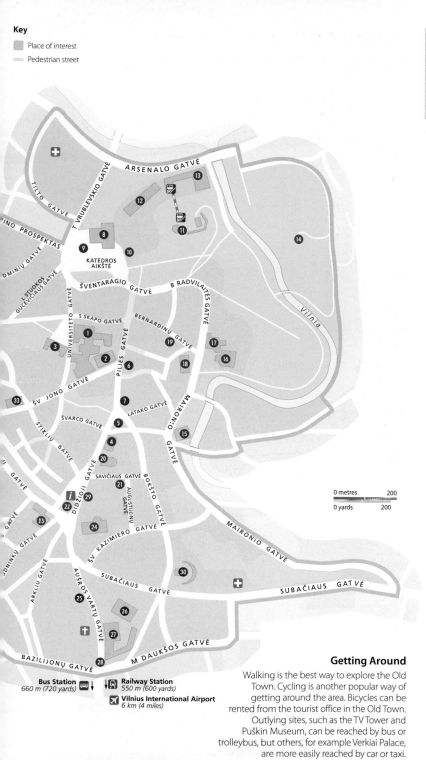

Key

Place of interest

Pedestrian street

ARSENALO GATVĖ

TILTO GATVĖ

T. VRUBLEVSKIO GATVĖ

...INO PROSPEKTAS

DMINIŲ GATVĖ

L. STUOKOS GUCEVIČIAUS GATVĖ

UNIVERSITETO GATVĖ

KATEDROS AIKŠTĖ

ŠVENTARAGIO GATVĖ

B. RADVILAITĖS GATVĖ

S. SKAPO GATVĖ

BERNARDINŲ GATVĖ

PILIES GATVĖ

ŠV. JONO GATVĖ

ŠVARCO GATVĖ

LATAKO GATVĖ

MAIRONIO GATVĖ

STIKLIŲ GATVĖ

...I GATVĖ

SAVIČIAUS GATVĖ

DIDŽIOJI GATVĖ

AUGUSTIJONŲ GATVĖ

BOKŠTO GATVĖ

ŠV. KAZIMIERO GATVĖ

MAIRONIO GATVĖ

...GATVĖ

...JONINKŲ GATVĖ

ARKLIŲ GATVĖ

SUBAČIAUS GATVĖ

SUBAČIAUS GATVĖ

AUŠROS VARTŲ GATVĖ

M. DAUKŠOS GATVĖ

BAZILIJONŲ GATVĖ

Vilnia

0 metres 200

0 yards 200

Bus Station
660 m (720 yards)

Railway Station
550 m (600 yards)

Vilnius International Airport
6 km (4 miles)

Getting Around

Walking is the best way to explore the Old Town. Cycling is another popular way of getting around the area. Bicycles can be rented from the tourist office in the Old Town. Outlying sites, such as the TV Tower and Puškin Museum, can be reached by bus or trolleybus, but others, for example Verkiai Palace, are more easily reached by car or taxi.

For keys to symbols *see back flap*

Street-by-Street: Pilies Street and Vilnius University

Narrow lanes, hidden courtyards and some of the Old Town's finest architecture make Pilies Street and nearby Vilnius University a delight to stroll around and explore. The university, which is over 400 years old, is one of the oldest in Eastern Europe. Traffic is restricted, and in summer restaurants and cafés spill out onto the streets. Souvenir stalls and shops on Pilies sell amber and interesting gifts, while the surrounding buildings are testimony to the city's long and eventful history.

Applied Arts Museum lies inside the Old Arsenal.

⑪ Upper Castle
The best visual introduction to Vilnius is from the viewing platform on the castle's last surviving tower. The Lithuanian flag was raised here in 1919 and in 1988.

⑩ Royal Palace
Also known as the Lower Castle, it was the main residence of the Grand Dukes and was the political and cultural heart of Lithuania.

⑨ Vilnius Cathedral
The austere Neo-Classical exterior of Lithuania's main basilica belies its hidden jewels, which include the Baroque Chapel of St Casimir and the winding passages of the crypt.

UNIVER

⑧ Presidential Palace
A 14th-century nobleman's residence, this building has hosted many historical figures. It became the Presidency in 1997.

Key

— Suggested route

For hotels and restaurants see pp304–305 and pp326–8

★ Pilies Street
With a view of the Upper Castle ever present, Pilies is one of the city's oldest streets. It was once Vilnius's commercial centre but today the street is popular with visitors hunting for amberware and other local products.

Locator Map
See Street Finder Map pp250–51

```
0 metres          100
0 yards           100
```

BERNARDINŲ GATVĖ

PILIES GATVĖ

ŠV. MYKOLO GATVĖ

St John's Church has a sweeping Baroque façade.

⑰ Church of St Anne
The flamboyant Gothic redbrick church fell victim to Napoleon's soldiers, who used it as a barracks on their way to Moscow in 1812. Fortunately, the beautiful façade has survived the turbulent centuries.

Littera Bookshop
This charmingly decorated bookshop at the eastern edge of the university's Sarbievijaus Courtyard also sells university souvenirs.

❶ ★ Vilnius University
Lithuania's largest university, it occupies a sizeable part of the Old Town. The university has over 13 courtyards and multiple buildings.

❶ Vilnius University
Vilniaus universitetas

Universiteto 3. **Map** 2 D3. **Tel** 268 7001. **Open** 10am–5:30pm Mon–Sat. for prior booking call 268 7103. vu.lt

The oldest university in Eastern Europe was founded as a Jesuit College in 1568, before becoming a school of higher education in 1579. The current campus, constructed between the 16th and 18th centuries, is a combination of different architectural styles.

The most impressive of the university's 13 courtyards, the Great Courtyard has open galleries dating from the 17th century, which were later lined with dedications to professors. Accessed via a passage from the western side of the Great Courtyard, the Observatory Courtyard by contrast is a serene enclosed garden from which the observatory and its zodiac symbols can be seen.

North of the Great Courtyard is the Sarbievijaus Courtyard, the oldest part of the university. At its far end, a bookshop, **Littera**, can be found. The frescoes caricaturing professors and students that decorate the interior of the bookshop were painted in 1978 by Antanas Kmieliauskas (b.1932).

Façade of St John's Church and the adjacent belfry

❷ St John's Church
Šv Jono bažnyčia

Šv Jono 12. **Map** 2 D3. **Tel** 261 1795. **Open** 10am–5pm Mon–Sat. 6pm Tue–Thu, 11am & 1pm Sun.

At the southern edge of the university campus, the impressive façade and separate bell tower of the Church of St John the Baptist and St John the Evangelist dominate the Great Courtyard. The original Gothic church, built here in 1426, was reconstructed in 1749 in flamboyant Baroque style by Jan Krzysztof Glaubitz *(see p237)*. The 10 magnificent altars in faux marble with Corinthian columns illuminate the otherwise austere interior. Initially there were 22 columns, most of which were

removed during further rebuilding in the 19th century. At 68 m (223 ft), the bell tower, which was given two extra tiers by Glaubitz, is the tallest structure in the Old Town. A lift runs to the top, from where there are fine views.

❸ Presidential Palace
Lietuvos respublikos prezidentūra

Daukanto aikštė 3. **Map** 2 D3. **Tel** 266 4154. **Open** 9am–5pm Sat (call in advance). for group tour call 266 4073. president.lt

Formerly a residence for high-ranking bishops, this ornate building has existed since Lithuania's conversion to Christianity at the end of the 14th century. The palace was rebuilt in the late 1820s in the Neo-Classical style by Vasily Stasov (1769–1848), an architect from St Petersburg. It has hosted a number of important personalities, including Napoleon Bonaparte and Tsar Alexander I. The former used the palace during his doomed advance on Moscow.

The palace was later used for a variety of ceremonial purposes before becoming the Presidential Palace in 1997. When the president is in Vilnius, a flag flies showing his coat of arms.

Colourful interior of Littera, with its collection of books for leisure and study material, Vilnius University

Elegantly displayed paintings in one of the exhibition rooms, Vilnius Picture Gallery

❹ Vilnius Picture Gallery

Vilniaus paveikslų galerija

Didžioji 4. **Map** 2 D4. **Tel** 212 4258.
Open 11am–6pm Tue–Sat, noon–5pm Sun. 🎨 🎫 📷 📶 ldm.lt

The imposing, enclosed Neo-Classical courtyard of this gallery offers a reflection of 19th-century Vilnius, when these premises were used by Vilnius University and the Medical Academy. Inside, the paintings on display show how the main art movements of the 19th and early 20th centuries influenced the development of Lithuanian art. *Lithuanian Girl with Verbos* by Kanutas Ruseckas (1800–60) is an icon of the Romantic aesthetic in Lithuanian art. Similarly, the later movements of Realism and Impressionism are reflected, respectively, in intimate portraits, such as Alfredas Romeris's *Study of a Girl's Hands*, and open landscapes, such as Juozas Balzukevičius's *Across a Ryefield*.

❺ Church of St Paraskeva

Šv Paraskevos cerkvė

Didžioji 2. **Map** 2 D4. **Tel** 215 3747.

Also known as Pyatnitskaya Church, this attractive little Orthodox church stands on a site that has been used for rituals and prayer for many centuries. In the mid-14th century, Grand Duke Algirdas built a church here for his Orthodox wife, before which it had been a pagan sanctuary. Here, at the beginning of the 18th century,

Peter the Great baptized a nine-year-old African slave by the name of Hannibal, later Major-General Abram Petrovich Hannibal (1696–1781), great-grandfather of the Russian poet Alexander Pushkin. The current building, designed by Nikolai Chagin, dates from 1865. Closed during the Soviet period, it has been returned to the Russian Orthodox faith.

The small Russian Orthodox Church of St Paraskeva

❻ House of Signatories

Signatarų namai

Pilies 26. **Map** 2 D3. **Tel** 231 4437.
Open 10am–5pm Tue–Sat. 🎫 🖥

The House of Signatories, with an extravagant façade, has played a crucial role in Lithuania's modern history. It was here that, on 16 February 1918, the newly created Council

of Lithuania signed the deed that restored Lithuania's independence. The Štralis Coffee House on the ground floor, created during renovation in the 1890s, was a popular meeting place for leading figures in the Lithuanian national revival.

The second-floor room, where the independence act was signed, has been re-created. Unfortunately, the displays on this historic event are a little sparse.

❼ Šlapelis House Museum

Šlapelių namas-muziejus

Pilies 40. **Map** 2 D4. **Tel** 261 0771.
Open 11am–5pm Wed–Sun (call in advance). 🎫

Presenting a journey back in time to Vilnius during the troubled first half of the 20th century, this modest, yet evocative, museum is dedicated to Marija and Jurgis Šlapelis. Although a native Polish-speaker, Marija secretly ran a Lithuanian-language bookshop on nearby Domininkonų Street while the city was under Russian, Polish, Nazi and Soviet occupations between 1906 and 1949.

On display are furnishings, newspapers, books, music sheets and postcards from this time. In addition, photographs showing a number of family reunions following the end of Soviet occupation can be found beneath 17th-century beams in what used to be the kitchen.

❽ Vilnius Cathedral

Vilniaus arkikatedra bazilika

Having taken various guises since it was first built as a
Christian church on the site of a pagan temple in 1251, Vilnius
Cathedral today largely dates from the late 18th century.
The young architect, Laurynas Stuoka-Gucevičius, brought
the fashionable French Classicist style to Baroque Vilnius, his
idea for the cathedral exterior and interior being a visual
re-creation of a Greek temple. Vilnius Cathedral was closed by
the Soviets in 1950 and initially mooted for use as a garage
for truck repairs. In 1956, however, it opened as a picture
gallery. It was eventually returned to the Catholic Church in
1989 and reconsecrated a year before
independence was declared.

Valavičius Chapel
Members of the Valavičius family
were governors and bishops of
Vilnius. Their lavish chapel was
created in the early 17th century.

Stucco Sculpture
A sculpture depicting a
bird sacrifice can be
seen on the
tympanum of
the façade.

**Wall Painting of the
Crucifixion**
The oldest surviving fresco
in Lithuania, dating from
the 14th century, can be
found in the crypt. It was
discovered in 1925.

The entrance is
via a huge
Classical portico.

Statue of Luke, the Evangelist
Of the statues of the Four
Evangelists on the southern façade,
Luke appears with a bull, which is a
symbol of service and sacrifice.

High Altar
The marvellously intricate tabernacle door on the High Altar, which was created in the 1620s, is fashioned from gold and silver. Two biblical scenes, the Last Supper and Christ Washing the Disciples' Feet, are beautifully depicted on the panel.

VISITORS' CHECKLIST

Practical Information
Katedros aikšė 1. **Map** 2 D3.
Tel 85261 0731. **Open** 7am–7pm daily. 🎧 guided tour mandatory to visit the crypt. Enquire at the souvenir shop at the cathedral's northern entrance for timings and prices. 📷

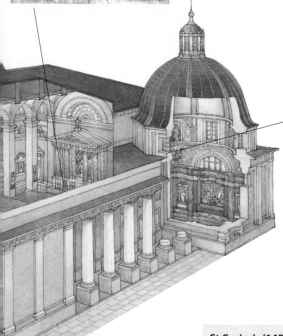

★ St Casimir's Chapel
Italian masters created this superb chapel, one of the major Baroque jewels of Vilnius, from 1623 to 1636. Its main highlights are the marble columns, magnificent stucco figures and colourful frescoes.

St Casimir (1458–84)

Casimir was the second son of a Grand Duke, whose siblings became kings and queens of European states through lineage and marriage. Pious Casimir shunned the luxuries of court life and would often go to the cathedral to pray. When he died of tuberculosis aged 25, it was rumoured that his coffin could cure disease. A fresco in St Casimir's Chapel shows how a sick orphan, who prayed beneath the coffin, was miraculously cured.

Richly decorated altar of St Casimir's Chapel

★ Crypt
A sombre mausoleum holds the remains of two Grand Dukes and two wives of Sigismund Augustus (r.1548–72), the last descendant of Gediminas (r.1316–41).

Vilnius Cathedral Belfry, Cathedral Square

9 Cathedral Square
Katedros aikštė

Map 2 D3. 10, 11, 33.

The paving stones around the square show the outline of the wall around the Lower Castle, a defence that made Vilnius a 14th-century bastion against the crusades.

At the square's western end is the **Vilnius Cathedral Belfry**. It was originally part of the fortifications. There was also a western gate where Vilnius Cathedral stands today. The square's eastern end is dominated by a statue of Grand Duke Gediminas. Unveiled in 1996, it conveys the city founder's predilection for diplomacy over force. In the square's centre is a tile marked *stebuklas* (miracle), reputed to be the point where the Baltic Way *(see p43)*, the human chain linking Vilnius, Rīga and Tallinn in 1989, started from. Locals believe that turning around on it three times makes a wish come true.

10 Lower Castle
Žemutinė pilis

Katedros 4. **Map** 2 D3. **Tel** 212 7476.
10, 11, 33. **Open** 8am–5pm Mon–Fri (to 3:45pm Fri).
W valdovurumai.lt

A group of buildings, including Vilnius Cathedral, the Old Arsenal and the Royal Palace –

the residence of the Grand Dukes that stood at the foot of Castle Hill and survived the sieges of the 14th century – form the Lower Castle. In the 1520s, the Royal Palace was renovated in Renaissance style by Italian architects invited by Sigismund the Old (r.1506–48) and his wife. The palace became the hub of a vibrant cultural life. Excavations carried out here in 1987 to 2001 unearthed decorative tiles, tapestries, jewellery and armour from this period and earlier. These objects are thought to have lain buried since the palace was destroyed by Tsarist authorities in 1802 as they did not want a symbol of Lithuanian power dominating the city.

11 Upper Castle
Aukštutinė pilis

Arsenalo 5. **Map** 2 D3. **Tel** 261 7453.
10, 11, 33. **Open** 10am–5pm Tue–Sun.

The western tower, the only remaining part of the Upper Castle complex, which once included defensive structures, is today the symbol of independent Lithuania. The viewing platform at the top provides a panorama of the spires and rooftops of the Old Town to the south, as well as a glimpse of the new skyscrapers rising to the west. A funicular offers a ride to the Upper Castle.

The original stone buildings of the Upper Castle were built in 1419, with restoration work taking place in the 1950s. According to legend, while on a hunting trip, Grand Duke Gediminas dreamed of an iron wolf howling from the hills in the park. This, his pagan priest said, was a sign that a powerful fortress should be built there. Wooden upper and lower castles and another on the adjacent hill were the result.

12 Lithuanian National Museum
Lietuvos nacionalinis muziejus

Arsenalo 1. **Map** 2 D3. **Tel** 262 9426.
10, 33. **Open** May–Sep: 10am–5pm Tue–Sat, 10am–3pm Sun; Oct–Apr: 10am–5pm Wed–Sun.
W lnm.lt

An early 19th-century building, known as the New Arsenal, houses the Lithuanian National Museum. In front of it stands a statue of King Mindaugas, which was unveiled together with the nearby bridge in July 2003. The museum presents a glimpse of everyday life in

Western tower, the Upper Castle's lone surviving structure

Lithuanian traditional costumes on display, Lithuanian National Museum

Lithuania before World War II. Ordinary lives are evocatively documented in the exhibits, which include plates and spoons, decorative boxes and perfume bottles, and even an old stone with a hollow used for pagan rituals.

The museum's main highlight is the first-floor room, which gives a pictorial history of the Lithuanian Grand Duchy from the Battle of the Sun to the 18th-century partitions (see p215).

The museum as a whole gives a concise overview of Lithuanian history from the 13th century to the present. Fascinating exhibits show-cased in the museum include an executioner's sword, tellingly broken into two pieces, a wonderfully ostentatious 18th-century sleigh and a handprint in iron of Peter the Great. There is also a display of folk costumes and a superb life-size re-creation of a typical Lithuanian peasant family farmstead.

⓭ Applied Arts Museum

Taikomosios dailės muziejus

Arsenalo gatvė 3a. **Map** 2 E3. **Tel** 262 8080. **Open** 11am–6pm Tue–Sat, 11am–4pm Sun.

The 16th-century Old Arsenal houses the Applied Arts Museum, which hosts major state-sponsored exhibitions on topics mainly relating to the history of Lithuania, the Grand Duchy and sacred art.

One of the permanent exhibitions in the museum displays Lithuanian folk art from the 17th to the 19th centuries, illustrating the heavy impact that Christian themes had on traditional mediums such as sculpture. The collection includes wayside wooden crosses, shrines, saints and *rūpintojėlis* (Lithuanian folk-art representations of a weary Christ holding his head in his right hand). Particularly illuminating is the work of Vincas Svirskis (1835–1916), a prolific craftsman who carved hundreds of shrines for rural farmsteads and villages in the Kėdainiai and Kaunas regions (see pp262–5).

⓮ Hill of Three Crosses

Trijų kryžių kalnas

Kalnų parkas. **Map** 2 E3.

A recognizable landmark and symbol of Vilnius, the three crosses on the hill adjacent to the Upper Castle are replicas of a monument destroyed by the Soviet authorities in the 1950s. Three wooden crosses were first placed here in the 16th century to commemorate, according to legend, Franciscan friars tortured and murdered by a pagan rabble. The incident took place during the rule of Grand Duke Algirdas, when Lithuania was stubbornly resisting Roman Catholic conversions. Seven of the friars were hacked to death, while the others were tied to crosses and cast into the Vilnia river.

The view of the Old Town from the crosses is unrivalled. A footbridge and a path along the Vilnia leads to steps up the hillside. An easier alternative route is via a side road leading up through the park from where T Kosciuškos Street crosses the Vilnia.

Hill of Three Crosses, a distinctive symbol of Vilnius

Elegant façade of the Russian Orthodox Holy Mother of God Church

ⓑ Holy Mother of God Church

Skaisčiausios Dievo Motinos cerkvė

Maironio 14. **Map** 2 E4. **Tel** 215 3747. 🚌 10, 11, 33. 🕆 10am, 4pm Sat, 9am Sun.

The current structure of this Russian Orthodox church, designed by Russian architect Nikolai Chagin, dates from the 19th century. One of the icons, *The Mother of God*, was brought by Tsar Alexander II, who also gave funds for the reconstruction work. For over 60 years before its renovation the church had been used as dissection rooms for the Medical Academy and as a military barracks. Just like the Church of St Paraskeva *(see p227)*, it stands where pagan Grand Duke Algirdas built a place of worship for his wife, in the 14th century.

ⓖ Bernardine Church

Bernardinų bažnyčia

Maironio 8. **Map** 2 E3. **Tel** 260 9292. 🚌 10, 11, 33. 🕆 7:30am Mon–Thu; 6pm Sat; 9am (in English), 10:30am, 1pm, 5pm Sun.

In 1469, the austere Franciscan Observant friars, known as the Bernardines after their founder St Bernardino of Siena, arrived in Vilnius. The Bernardine Church, which they built in around 1525, still retains the late Gothic crystal vaulting above the aisles. In the 1770s, a series of Baroque wooden altars and confessionals

were added to the interior. However, of these only the main altar, carved by Italian craftsman Daniele Giotto, remains today. The intriguing façade combines Gothic windows and Baroque scrolls.

Both church and friary were closed after the 1863 uprising *(see p218)*, becoming barracks for Russian troops, but were

eventually given back to the friars. The church's original 16th-century frescoes are being restored and include depictions of the sobriety and solemnity observed by friars, as well as St Christopher, and scenes from the Passion of Christ.

Just outside the church grounds is a statue of Adam Mickiewicz, created in 1904. In August 1987, the statue was the meeting point for the first public rally under Soviet occupation that called for Lithuania's national rights.

ⓗ Church of St Anne

Šv Onos bažnyčia

Maironio 8/1. **Map** 2 E3. **Tel** 6981 7731. 🚌 10, 11, 33. 🕆 6pm Mon–Sat, 9–11am Sun.

According to local folklore, this church charmed Napoleon into exclaiming how he wished he could take it back to Paris

Church of St Anne, a Gothic gem said to have dazzled Napoleon

Adam Mickiewicz (1798–1855)

Statue of Adam Mickiewicz, outside the Bernardine Church

"Oh Lithuania, my country, thou art like good health; I never knew till now how precious, till I lost thee." So begins *Pan Tadeusz*, the lyrical masterpiece of the great Polish Romantic poet Adam Mickiewicz. He was born into a family of Polish nobles near Nowogrodek, in present-day Belarus, three years after the partition of the Polish-Lithuanian Commonwealth. His nomadic life was dominated by a strong yearning for an idyllic lost home-land. His epic poems are full of ancient forests, groves and open landscapes. *Grażyna* (1822), written in his youth, is about the female chief of a pagan Lithuanian tribe who outwits the cross-and-sword-wielding Teutonic Knights. The Byronesque *Konrad Wallenrod* (1828) describes these battles with even greater mastery.

on the palm of his hand. St Anne's is a Gothic beauty; its ornate façade of flowing ogee arches and slender windows is a unique monument to the style in a city of Baroque. The finials and the spires are covered evenly with decorative crockets – bricks made to resemble flowers or curled leaves and so favoured by Gothic architects. One set of historians found 33 different shapes of brick used in the façade. Inside, the three Baroque altars were designed by Jan Krzysztof Glaubitz *(see p237)*. The free-standing bell tower was built much later, in the 1870s.

⑱ Church of St Michael

Šv Mykolo bažnyčia

Šv Mykolo 9. **Map** 2 E3. **Tel** 269 7803. **Open** 11am–6pm Tue–Sat.

The Renaissance-style Church of St Michael was built during the early 17th century, as a convent for Bernardine nuns and a mausoleum for the Sapiega family. Its interior features several of the nobles' funerary monuments. These include one to Leonas Sapiega, whose initials mark some of the crests, motifs and rosettes

that decorate the ceiling. Since 2009, the building has housed the Church Heritage Museum, which displays treasures from Vilnius Cathedral and other sacred art.

⑲ Mickiewicz Museum

Adomo Mickevičiaus memoralinis butas-muziejus

Bernardinų 11. **Map** 2 E3. **Tel** 279 1879. **Open** 10am–5pm Tue–Fri, 10am–2pm Sat–Sun.

The legendary poet Adam Mickiewicz, who romanticized his Polish-Lithuanian homeland, stayed at this apartment, which belonged to a university professor, for a brief period in 1822. Set inside a lovely enclosed courtyard, the museum attempts to re-create the atmosphere of the era in which the poet lived.

Period furniture, which Mickiewicz himself is said to have used while writing his first folk-inspired ballads, includes a table and chair from Kaunas and a chair from Paris. Portraits of the poet are set alongside volumes of his works

in various languages. The museum also houses the first editions of a number of his great poems. The museum often hosts literary meetings and poetry evenings.

⑳ Orthodox Church of St Nicholas

Šv Mikalojaus cerkvė

Didžioji 12. **Map** 2 D4. **Tel** 261 8559. **Open** 1–6:30pm Mon–Fri, 7:30am–3pm Sun. 🔔 5pm Tue–Sat, 9am Sun.

The serene, candlelit interior of the Orthodox Church of St Nicholas contrasts sharply with the bustle on Didžioji, the Old Town's main street. Originally a Gothic church dating from 1514, it passed into the hands of the Uniates, or Greek Catholics, in 1609 before getting a Baroque overhaul, including the bell tower. The church was returned to the Russian Orthodox Church in 1827. The overtly Russian Byzantine façade of the church, together with most of the interior, is an example of the change that took place in the city's religious landscape following the doomed January 1863 uprising.

The domed chapel on the left is dedicated to Count Mikhail Muravyov (1796–1866), the governor-general who dealt harshly with the uprising's participants.

Façade, Orthodox Church of St Nicholas

Street-by-Street: Town Hall Square to the Gates of Dawn

Lithuania's distinctive Baroque architecture, known as Vilnius Baroque, can be admired in the outstanding monuments clustered around the Gates of Dawn and the Church of St Casimir. The enchanting collection of towers and sculptures was created during the 17th and 18th centuries by Italian and Polish architects and their Polish-Lithuanian noble patrons. The buildings are elegantly designed with symmetrical façades, reflecting an unmistakable Italian influence. Nonetheless, the mystical atmosphere, so unique to Vilnius, distinguishes the area from any other European city.

㉔ ★ Church of St Casimir
This church was the city's museum of atheism from 1963 to 1991. The crown symbolizes St Casimir's royal lineage.

㉒ Town Hall
With a bold Classical portico, the Town Hall was designed by the renowned Lithuanian architect Laurynas Stuoka-Gucevičius.

DIDŽIOJI GATVĖ

VOKIEČIŲ GATVĖ

RŪDNINKŲ GATVĖ

Key

— Suggested route

Vokiečių Street
One of the city's oldest, Vokiečių Street resembles a park during the summer months, with its outdoor cafés and a pleasant central tree-lined walkway.

㉓ Contemporary Art Centre
is a Soviet-era venue for groundbreaking modern art.

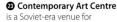
| 0 metres | 100 |
| 0 yards | 100 |

Šv Kazimiero Street
A narrow cobblestone street named after St Casimir snakes around the back of the church towards Užupis, with its jumble of roofs.

Locator Map
See Street Finder Map pp250–51

Church of the Holy Spirit

㉗ ★ Church of St Theresa
Scenes from the life of St Theresa, revered for her mystical writings, adorn the vaulted nave of the church. The frescoes were painted in the late 18th century following a fire.

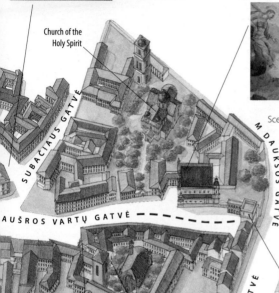

SUBAČIAUS GATVĖ

AUŠROS VARTŲ GATVĖ

M DAUKŠOS GATVĖ

BAZ¹LIJONŲ GATVĖ

Basilian Gate

㉘ ★ Gates of Dawn
A site of pilgrimage, this gateway to the Old Town protects a silver-covered painting of the Virgin Mary, said to have miraculous powers.

Basilian Monastery
The now dilapidated monastery complex was used as a prison to hold anti-Russian activists, including the poet Adam Mickiewicz, in the 1820s.

Panoramic view of Town Hall Square, with flagpoles and church spires

㉑ Čiurlionis House

Čiurlionio namai

Savičiaus 11. **Map** 2 D4. **Tel** 262 2451. **Open** 10am–4pm Mon–Fri. Entrance from side door.

The former house of Mikalojus Konstantinas Čiurlionis *(see p265)* was turned into a museum in 1995, to mark the 120th anniversary of the birth of Lithuania's beloved artist and composer. Čiurlionis lived here in relative poverty with his wife Sofija, from October 1907 until June 1908, when they left Vilnius in search of success in St Petersburg.

Quite modest in scale, this museum does not attempt to rival the more extensive one dedicated to Čiurlionis in Kaunas *(see p264)*. Instead, it mainly serves as an information resource and a venue to hear his chamber music concerts. Reproductions of the artist's paintings adorn the walls, as do photographs of him. Even today, Čiurlionis's grand piano stands here.

㉒ Town Hall Square

Rotušės aikštė

Didžioji 31. **Map** 2 D4. Kaziuko Crafts Fair (Mar). **vilniausrotuse.lt** Town Hall: **Tel** 261 8007. Didžioji 31, 262 6470. **Open** 11am–6pm Mon–Thu, 11am–5pm Fri.

Fully repaved in 2006, Town Hall Square was for centuries a market place and the centre of public life. It still bustles with activity, mainly during the annual Kaziuko Crafts Fair *(see p212)*, when craft stalls line the square. The square's main building, the **Town Hall**, was earlier the site of

a court, and prisoners were marched from its cells to the square to be beheaded. The hall was constructed at the end of the 18th century and designed by the Classical architect Laurynas Stuoka-Gucevičius *(see p228)*. Today, the hall hosts about 200 cultural and social events around the year.

"Extreme Crafts", art exhibits at the Contemporary Art Centre

㉓ Contemporary Art Centre

Šiuolaikinio meno centras

Vokiečių 2. **Map** 2 D4. **Tel** 212 1945. **Open** noon–7:30pm Tue–Sun. **cac.lt**

The main gallery space for modern art exhibitions in Vilnius, the Contemporary Art Centre features works by both Lithuanian and international artists. The star attraction is the Fluxus Room, with a permanent exhibition dedicated to Fluxus, the radical art movement that emerged in New York in the 1960s. The room pays special tribute to the movement's creator, Kaunas-born George Maciunas (1931–78). Memorabilia evoking the populist spirit of Fluxus festivals and photographs of Maciunas fill the room.

㉔ Church of St Casimir

Šv Kazimiero bažnyčia

Didžioji 34. **Map** 2 D4. **Tel** 212 1715. 5:30pm Mon–Fri, 10:30am & noon Sun.

The city's first Baroque church, St Casimir was destroyed by fire three times after being built by the Jesuits between 1604 and 1635, prompting heavy reconstruction in the 1750s. Much of the interior was destroyed in 1812, when Napoleon's army used the church as a granary. It became a Russian Orthodox church during the 19th century and onion domes were added to it.

During World War I, it served as a Lutheran church for the German army and was then returned to the Jesuits and restored in the 1920s. The dome was rebuilt in 1942 and the crown was added. The Soviets used the church as a museum of atheism from 1963. It was reconsecrated in 1991.

Altarpiece at the Church of St Casimir, depicting the saint's resurrection

Baroque Vilnius

The sensual waves, rich colours and theatrical stucco figures of Baroque architecture reached Lithuania during the first half of the 17th century, replacing Gothic and Renaissance. Italian masters, invited by Lithuania's rulers, built Baroque gems such as St Casimir's Chapel *(see p229)* and the Church of St Theresa. In the mid-17th century came a second resurgence of the style, when architects living in Vilnius began to develop a distinct branch of Baroque. Led by Jan Krzysztof Glaubitz, they began to transform the Old Town's panorama by designing opulent façades, matched by voluptuous interiors and multiple altars. By the end of the 18th century Baroque had been replaced by the far more restrained values of Neo-Classicism.

St Casimir's Chapel, in Vilnius Cathedral, is an early Baroque gem, beautified intricately with marble from Galicia and the Carpathians, lavish stucco and 17th-century frescoes.

St John's Church *(see p226)*, one of Glaubitz's first works in Vilnius, boasts an overwhelming four-tier façade made up of clusters of columns. Inside there are 10 interconnected altars.

The Basilian Gate *(see p238)* of the Basilian monastery was built by Glaubitz in 1761. The 18-m (59-ft) structure carries a depiction of the Holy Trinity, to which the church in the complex is dedicated.

Church of St Theresa *(see p238)* boasts radiant frescoes, glittering altars and an image of the Madonna that is believed to be miraculous.

Jan Krzysztof Glaubitz (1700–67)

The most influential of Vilnius's late Baroque architects, Jan Krzysztof Glaubitz developed a distinct school of Lithuanian Baroque known as Vilnius Baroque. Born in Silesia, Glaubitz was a Lutheran of German origin who moved to Vilnius at the age of 37 and designed structures for all faiths in this multi-religious city. Among his most celebrated works are the magnificent façades of the Basilian Gate, St John's Church, Church of St Catherine *(see p241)*, the Church of the Holy Spirit *(see p238)* and the now destroyed Great Synagogue *(see p243)*.

Exterior of the Church of St Catherine, Old Town

Ornate Baroque entranceway of the Basilian Gate

㉕ Basilian Gate

Bazilijonų vartai

Aušros vartų 7b. **Map** 2 D5.

The awe-inspiring Basilian Gate was designed in 1761 in flamboyant late Baroque style by J K Glaubitz *(see p237)*. An all-seeing eye peers out from the central niche. The white bas-relief at the top portrays the Holy Trinity, a hint of what lies beyond the gate. The **Church of the Holy Trinity**, placed in the hands of the Uniates in 1598, stands at the centre of an enclosed courtyard. This was once a secluded monastery, but in 1823 the Tsarist authorities turned it into a prison for anti-Russian revolutionaries and held Adam Mickiewicz *(see p233)* there the same year. The Uniates who live here now are sometimes willing to show visitors round.

🔼 **Church of the Holy Trinity**
Tel 212 2578. 🔼 5:30pm Mon–Sat, 10am Sun.

㉖ Church of the Holy Spirit

Šv Dvasios cerkvė

Aušros vartų 10. **Map** 2 D5. **Tel** 212 7765. ✉ 🔼 8am, 5pm Mon–Fri; 7am, 10am, 5pm Sun.

This Baroque church is the religious centre of the city's Russian Orthodox faithful. Though completed in 1634, it remains remarkably intact, the only alterations to the exterior being a raised façade and a new dome added in the late 19th century. The painting over the doorway depicts Sts Anthony, Ivan and Eustachius, whose remains lie within, miraculously preserved. In the 14th century, the three were Christians in the court of pagan Grand Duke Algirdas. When the pagan priests demanded that they renounce their faith, they refused and were hanged from an oak tree. They were canonized in 1547 and the nearby Church of the Holy Trinity was built in place of the oak.

Painting, Church of St Theresa

㉗ Church of St Theresa

Šv Teresės bažnyčia

Aušros vartų 14. **Map** 2 D5. **Tel** 212 3513. 🔼 7:30am (Latin), 6:30pm Mon–Fri; 11am, 6:30pm Sun.

Another early feature of the Baroque landscape, built from 1630 to 1655, is the Church of St Theresa, which stands in front of the Gates of Dawn. Materials like black marble in the portal and sandstone from Sweden, used to beautify its façade, were also used in St Casimir's Chapel inside Vilnius Cathedral *(see p229)* around the same time. This has led some researchers to believe that Italian craftsmen who designed the chapel also contributed to the Church of St Theresa. The main attraction of the church is its interior, with its frescoes and altars dating back to the second half of the 18th century. The painting on the high altar is *The Exaltation of St Theresa* by Szymon Czechowicz (1689–1775). St Theresa of Ávila in Spain inspired the formation in 1593 of the Discalced (Barefoot) Carmelites, a Roman Catholic order whose emphasis was on discipline and prayer. A convent was located next door, but today it is a hotel, the Domus Maria *(see p304)*.

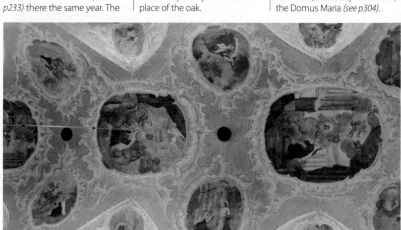

Frescoes on the ceiling of the Church of St Theresa

Image of the Virgin Mary, seen through the window of the Gates of Dawn

㉘ Gates of Dawn

Aušros vartai

Aušros vartų 12. **Map** 2 D5. **Tel** 212 3513. 🕐 7:30am, 9am, 10am, 5:30pm, 6:30pm Mon–Sat; 9am, 9:30am, 11am, 6:30pm Sun. 🔲 ausrosvartai.lt

The Classical chapel of Gates of Dawn follows the centuries-old custom of having a chapel or a religious image in every gateway to safeguard the city from outside enemies and to protect departing travellers. The focus of this chapel is *The Madonna of Mercy*, an image reputed to have miracle-working powers. It was painted on oak in the 1620s and encased in silver 150 years later. The miracles attributed to it were faithfully recorded by nuns at the neighbouring Carmelite convent. The walls surrounding the painting are covered with silver votive offerings .

The Classical chapel that houses the image dates from 1829, when it was rebuilt from an earlier Baroque version. A flight of steps leads up to the chapel from a door in the street. A site of pilgrimage, it was one of the first stops for Pope John Paul II when he visited Lithuania in 1993.

This is the only gateway from the early 16th-century city walls to have survived. It becomes more evident when viewed from the outside, where round holes that were used for cannons are still visible.

㉙ Kazys Varnelis Museum

Kazio Varnelio namai-muziejus

Didžioji 26. **Map** 2 D4. **Tel** 279 1644. **Open** 10am–4pm Tue–Sat (by appointment only). 🖼 📷

An extraordinary collection of modern art, maps, graphics, paintings, sculptures, vintage furniture, books and ceramics, as well as art from around the world, fill the home of the famous Lithuanian-American artist Kazys Varnelis (b.1917).

Some of the rooms look truly avant-garde, mixing Italian Renaissance furniture and French Baroque with 20th-century American modern art. Other rooms have over 150 maps, including some of Lithuania dating from 1507. The book section has around 7,000 volumes of unique publications. The collection includes a number of books by famous illustrators.

Varnelis, renowned for creating optical illusions based on geometric patterns in his paintings, rarely meets visitors now.

㉚ Artillery Bastion

Bastėja

Bokšto 20/18. **Map** 2 E4. **Tel** 261 2149. **Open** 10am–6pm Tue–Sat. 🖼

Constructed as part of the city defences in the first half of the 17th century, the bastion had fallen into ruin by the end of the 18th century. It was used as an orphanage and the city's pre-eminent rubbish heap, and was finally cleaned up by the Germans during World War I to store ammunition. Its cool interior made it an ideal space for storing vegetables during the early Soviet period.

In 1987 it was opened as a museum, and in 2014 it opened again following renovation. Although there is not a great deal to see, the museum holds a certain fascination for history enthusiasts. Outside, there are pleasant views of the Old Town and the hilly Užupis district.

The redbrick Artillery Bastion, dating from the 17th century

㉛ Church of St Nicholas

Šv Mikalojaus bažnyčia

Šv Mikalojaus 4. **Map** 2 D4. **Tel** 262 3069. 🕇 8am, 6pm Mon–Fri; 9am Sat; 8am, 10am, 2pm Sun.

One of the oldest churches in Lithuania, the Church of St Nicholas was built when the country was still pagan. Most of its simple Gothic façade and interior dates from the 16th century. The interior is defined by the decorative brick veins of the vaulting. Some colourful paintings discovered here include a striking image of the sun.

The church has patriotic connotations for Lithuanians, as from 1901 to 1939, when Vilnius was occupied by Russia and then Poland, it was one of the few churches allowed to hold Lithuanian-language services.

In the churchyard, the statue of St Christopher carrying the Infant Christ, created in 1959, also helped to keep the spirits of the people alive. The sculptor, Antanas Kmieliauskas (b.1932), was expelled from the Association of Artists because of it. He later frescoed Littera bookshop in Vilnius University *(see p226)*.

Surviving fragment of a fresco on the ceiling of the Franciscan Church

㉜ Franciscan Church

Pranciškonų bažnyčia

Trakų 9/1. **Map** 1 C4. **Tel** 261 4242. 🕇 5:30pm Mon–Sat; 10am, 11:30am Sun.

The cracked and cavernous, yet highly evocative, Franciscan Church is also known as the Church of Our Lady of the Assumption. It stands on a spot where, in the 14th century, Franciscan friars established a base on the road to Trakai *(see pp256–7)*. The Conventual Franciscans chose to settle in the poorest of urban areas,

reaching out to the destitute, often outside the safety of the city walls. The Gothic main doorway dates from this earlier period, but the rest of the structure was built in the 1770s. After the 1863 uprising *(see p218)*, the church and friary were closed and used as a granary and an archive. The altars and the now unidentifiable frescoes above the nave were virtually destroyed, as was a tall Gothic bell tower that stood on Pranciškonų Street.

㉝ Dominican Church

Šv Dvasios bažnyčia

Domininkonų 8. **Map** 2 D4. **Tel** 262 9595. 🕇 3pm, 6pm Mon–Fri; 8am–6pm Sun.

Also known as the Church of the Holy Spirit, the current building of the Dominican Church dates from the years of repair that followed the destructive war of 1655–61 during the Russian occupation. A church has stood on this spot since the 14th century.

The unassuming doorway, which can be easily missed, belies the sumptuous interior. Figures in stucco stand out on

Lavishly decorated interior of the Dominican Church, featuring Rococo altars

15 lavishly decorated Rococo altars. The altars, which are embellished with colourful paintings, also feature gilded frames and faux marble Corinthian columns – all hallmarks of the late Baroque style. The fresco lined vestibule, which forms a passage into the nave from the street, gives the church a cavern-like quality, emphasized by the dark, candlelit interior.

During Napoleon's chaotic retreat in 1812, the friary next to the church was converted into a hospital and the crypt was used as a morgue. Today, the crypt is still full of stacks of mummified corpses from this period, which have been preserved by the dry air. The crypt is, however, off-limits to visitors.

Movie cameras on display at the Theatre, Music and Film Museum

Façade of the Church of St Catherine, with strawberry-and-cream towers

㉞ Church of St Catherine

Šv Kotrynos bažnyčia

Vilniaus gatvė 30. **Map** 2 D3.

Originally a small wooden structure, the Church of St Catherine formed part of a Benedictine monastery in the early 17th century. The church was rebuilt in stone in 1703, almost 50 years after the Russians burned it down. The structure, as it appears today, was built and considerably expanded between 1741 and 1773. Its sophisticated design, highlighted by the delightful strawberry-and-cream twin towers, is attributed to

Lithuania's much-celebrated Baroque architect, Jan Krzysztof Glaubitz *(see p237)*.

The church suffered some damage during World War II and was reopened in 2006 after lengthy renovation. It is now regularly used as a popular venue for classical music concerts and performances. In the garden facing the church, there is a bust monument of the well-known Polish composer Stanislaw Moniuszko (1819–72), who wrote his first operas while working as an organist in Vilnius. The area to the east of the church is where a large convent for Benedictine nuns stood from 1622 until the Soviet period. The church's interior is highly decorated but not fully repaired, giving it an air of authenticity.

㉟ Theatre, Music and Film Museum

Lietuvos teatro, muzikos, kino muziejus

Vilniaus 41. **Map** 1 C4. **Tel** 231 2724. **Open** 11am–6pm Tue–Fri, 11am–4pm Sat. 📷 **ltmkm.lt**

Housed inside a 17th-century mansion once owned by the powerful Radvila family, who ruled Lithuania in the 16th century, this absorbing museum was founded by the

Phonograph, Theatre, Music and Film Museum

Ministry of Culture. The museum's expansive collection is a tribute to the Lithuanians' love of theatre and classical music. The exhibits include theatre memorabilia ranging from old costumes and puppets to stage-set pieces, mostly from the 19th and early 20th centuries. The superb collection of folk instruments features a number of *kanklės* (decorated Lithuanian stringed instruments related to the zither).

The space given to cinema is limited and not as informative, although there are some displays on cinematography.

㊱ Radvila Palace

Radvilų rūmai

Vilniaus 24. **Map** 1 C3. **Tel** 262 0981. **Open** 11am–6pm Tue–Sat, noon–5pm Sun. 📷 **ldm.lt**

The early 17th-century palace, once grand in size, was reduced to just one wing by the end of the Northern War (1700–21). Now an art gallery, it hosts a permanent display, including 165 portraits of members of the Radvila family. Temporary exhibitions feature little-known, but often surprisingly impressive, paintings by Lithuanian artists from the 19th and early 20th centuries.

Holocaust Museum in the Green House, annexe of the State Jewish Museum

㊲ State Jewish Museum

Valstybinis Vilniaus gaono žydų Muziejus

Pylimo 4. **Map** 1 C3. **Tel** 212 7912. **Open** 9am–1pm Mon–Fri. excursions of the museum & Vilnius Old Town offered. **jmuseum.lt**

The hub of the city's now tiny Jewish community, this small museum displays copies of ghetto diaries and handwritten notes on the backs of cigarette packets about life in the ghetto, plus items that remained from the museum that existed before World War II. Several objects that miraculously survived from the Great Synagogue include a bas-relief of the Ten Commandments.

The museum building also hosts a Union of Former Ghetto and Concentration Camp Prisoners, a Union of Jewish War Veterans, a youth club and a newspaper in Yiddish, English, Lithuanian and Russian called *Jerusalem of Lithuania*.

㊳ Holocaust Museum

Holokausto ekspozicija

Pamėnkalnio 12. **Map** 1 C3. **Tel** 262 4590. **Open** 9am–5pm Mon–Thu, 9am–4pm Fri, 10am–4pm Sun. **jmuseum.lt**

Located in the Green House, this annexe of the State Jewish Museum reveals some of the horrors that befell the Jews of Lithuania during World War II. A display on Jewish life before the Holocaust unfolded is followed by maps and photographs showing how and where the Nazi genocide was executed. Descriptions of the harsh conditions inside the ghettoes are followed by eyewitness accounts of the mass killings in the forests of Paneriai *(see p248)*.

㊴ Frank Zappa Statue

Kalinausko 1. **Map** 1 C3.

The world's first statue of the prolific Californian rock legend Frank Zappa was created in Vilnius shortly after his death from cancer in 1993. A group of local artists wanted to test the limits of newly independent Lithuania's proclamations of democracy and freedom and were pleasantly surprised when their idea for the statue was approved. The bust was created by the then 70-year-old Konstantinas Bogdanas, known for his statues of Lenin and other notable Communists.

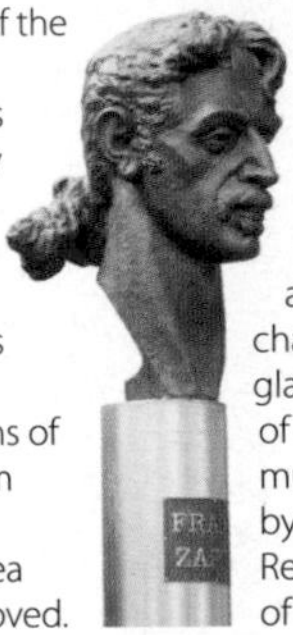

Bust of Frank Zappa

㊵ KGB Museum

Genocido aukų muziejus

Aukų 2a. **Map** 1 C2. **Tel** 249 8156. **Open** 10am–6pm Wed–Sat, 10am–5pm Sun. **genocid.lt**

Also known as the Museum of Genocide Victims, the KGB Museum was opened in 1992 on the ground floor of the former KGB building. In this effectively designed display area, personal stories are used to reveal the regime of terror under Stalin until 1940 and then until 1991 under the former Soviet Union.

The exhibits chronicle the Soviet occupation of Lithuania, the cattle-car deportations to Siberia and the futile efforts of the Forest Brothers *(see p122)* who fought the Soviets. Below ground, the cells were in use right up until the late 1980s and are even more overwhelming. They include tiny cells used in winter with no glass in the window and a floor filled with water, and an execution chamber displaying, under glass, the dug-up remains of victims. In 1997, the museum was taken over by the Genocide and Resistance Research Centre of Lithuania, a state institution dedicated to investigating atrocities that occurred in the country during the Nazi and Soviet occupations.

Exhibits in the corridor outside the former execution chamber, KGB Museum

Jewish Vilnius

Until it was eliminated during the Holocaust, Jewish Vilna, or Vilnius, was home to a large, influential Jewish community. About 250,000 Jews lived in Lithuania at the turn of the 19th century, compared to just 4,000 today, and 40 per cent of Vilnius's population was Jewish. By the early 19th century, Vilnius had emerged as a major centre of Jewish learning and bustled with life. The religious customs of the Litvaks, as Lithuanian Jews are known in Yiddish, were marked by a rigid analysis of the Talmud, the Jewish laws and traditions. As a result, other Jewish communities in Eastern Europe saw the Vilna Jews as being old-fashioned and staunch intellectuals. Decimated by World War II and ravaged further by the Soviets, Jewish Vilna is a ghostly reminder of a vanished world.

Jewish Vilna before World War II had its cobbled lanes crowded with artisans' workshops and cafés. A maze of courtyards and passages that lay around Vokiečių and Žydų streets, concealed synagogues and prayer houses.

The Great Synagogue, built in 1572, was restored with an Italian Renaissance interior by Glaubitz. The Soviets destroyed the remains of the Jewish quarter after World War II, broadening Vokiečių Street and bulldozing this awe-inspiring building.

Vilnius Choral Synagogue was the only synagogue in the country to survive World War II. Located on Pylimo Street 39, it started functioning in 1903. Although it was smaller in scale and simpler in design than Vilnius's other synagogues, the Choral Synagogue has an enchanting interior.

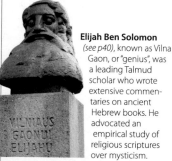

Elijah Ben Solomon (see p40), known as Vilna Gaon, or "genius", was a leading Talmud scholar who wrote extensive commentaries on ancient Hebrew books. He advocated an empirical study of religious scriptures over mysticism.

A map of Vilna Ghetto is shown on the wall at Rūdininkų 18. The ghetto is where the Jews of Vilnius were imprisoned during World War II, and the wall marks the place where its only gate once stood.

Further Afield

As most of Vilnius's main sites are concentrated in the Old Town, visitors often ignore the suburbs. It can be rewarding, however, to escape the bustling city centre and to discover Vilnius as a living city as well as a picturesque time capsule. A trip to the TV Tower affords excellent views on a clear day, while Vingis Park and Verkiai Palace are ideal for walking and a breath of fresh air. Paneriai and Antakalnis Cemetery, meanwhile, recount Lithuania's often tragic history.

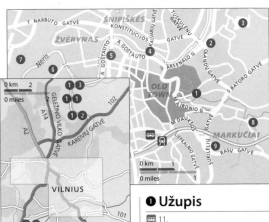

Sights at a Glance

❶ Užupis
❷ Church of Sts Peter and Paul pp246–7
❸ Antakalnis Cemetery
❹ Green Bridge
❺ Parliament
❻ Vingis Park and Žvėrynas
❼ TV Tower
❽ Pushkin Museum
❾ Rasos Cemetery
❿ Paneriai Holocaust Memorial
⓫ Calvary Church of the Holy Cross
⓬ Trinapolis Church
⓭ Verkiai Palace

Key

▨ City centre
— Motorway
— Main road
═ Minor road

For keys to symbols *see back flap*

❶ Užupis

 11.

Tucked inside a bend in the Vilnia river, Užupis translates as "Behind the River". This picturesque part of central Vilnius has narrow streets filled with cafés, art galleries and mysterious hidden courtyards. The artists who live here declared independence in 1997, with their own flag, president and independence day (1 April). Their constitution, which features articles such as "Everyone has the right to understand nothing", is nailed to a wall on Paupio Street. The statue of an angel, the symbol of Užupis, stands on nearby Užupio Street. The bizarre **Alternative Art Centre**, where the door is always open, stands by the river between Užupio and Malūnų. A stroll further east leads to the serene Bernardinų Cemetery.

The terrace of the Tores café on Krivių has one of the city's best views. Another viewpoint can be found on an unmarked footpath behind the school on Krivių Street. The footpath then plunges down the Vilnia Valley into Kalnų Park.

❷ Church of Sts Peter and Paul

See pp246–7.

❸ Antakalnis Cemetery
Antakalnio kapinės

Karių kapų 11. **Tel** 234 0587.

The largest public cemetery in Vilnius brings together much of the city's modern history. Statues and memorial stones cover the verdant landscape, the crosses and tombs inscribed in Lithuanian, Russian and Polish. The main path leads past a wave of identical stone crosses dedicated to Polish soldiers who died during World War I. At the heart of the cemetery is a sweeping semicircular memorial cut into the hillside for the 14 civilians who were killed while defending the TV Tower and the

Imaginatively painted façade of the Alternative Art Centre, Užupis

Graves of civilians killed by Russian tanks in 1991, Antakalnis Cemetery

Parliament in 1991. A path to the right of the cemetery entrance leads to Soviet-era war memorials.

❹ Green Bridge
Žaliasis tiltas

The first bridge crossing the river at this point was built in the 16th century, but the current one dates from 1952, the year before Stalin's death. At its four corners stand Socialist Realist statues and reasons abound for not pulling them down. One is that they are a reminder of the ugliness of Soviet monoculture; another is that locals have come to regard them as genuine works of art. Whatever the reason, the statues of confident workers, peasants and soldiers, once built to instill optimism among the masses in a brave new Communist future, are here to stay, however odd they may seem amid Vilnius's skyscrapers.

Soviet-era statues that adorn Green Bridge

❺ Parliament
Lietuvos respublikos seimas

Gedimino 53. **Tel** 239 6060. 24. lrs.lt

The far end of Gedimino Avenue is marked by the Seimas, Lithuania's Parliament. Built in 1982, the building is typical of the late Soviet era.

The similarly monumental National Library, constructed 20 years earlier, stands beside it on the other side of Independence Square.

It was in the Seimas, on 11 March 1990, that the act declaring independence from the Soviet Union was signed. During the subsequent siege, in 1991, concrete barricades and Catholic shrines were put up around the building to protect it against Soviet tanks. These were finally removed in 1993, and the remnants emblazoned with graffiti demanding freedom and democracy can still be seen on the western side of the Seimas.

❻ Vingis Park and Žvėrynas

11, 24.

The leafy Žvėrynas district was created from the Radvila family's forest-covered hunting grounds, which were sold off from 1893 as plots of land for development. The streets are lined with old wooden villas and contemporary mansions. The silver-domed Orthodox Church of the Apparition of the Holy Mother of God (1903) looms over the Neris river. The tiny Kenesa (1922), where the Karaim (see p257) used to

congregate, stands on Liubarto Street. Vingis Park, reached via a suspension footbridge on the western side of Žvėrynas, is filled with towering pine trees and footpaths. At the centre of the park is an open-air auditorium used for concerts and, every five years, the climax to the World Lithuanian Song Festival. To the east, where the pleasant M K Čiurlionio Street meets the park, a cemetery for German soldiers killed during the two world wars has been restored.

❼ TV Tower
Vilniaus televizijos bokštas

Sausio 13–Osios 10. **Tel** 252 5333. 49. **Open** 10am–9pm daily. tvbokstas.lt

The grand 326-m (1,070-ft) TV Tower is set against a striking backdrop of tall pines. On the ground floor, there is a small display paying tribute to those who were shot or crushed beneath Soviet tanks while trying to defend the tower on 13 January 1991. Granite markers outside show where they fell.

The tower's observation deck houses a state-run café, Paukščių Takas, at a height of 165 m (541 ft). The rotating deck makes a full circle in about 50 minutes and offers spectacular views of the area. On a clear day, visibility is 70 km (43 miles) in every direction, with views stretching into Belarus, about 40 km (25 miles) away.

Elegant TV Tower, soaring high above its surroundings

❷ Church of Sts Peter and Paul

Šv Petro ir Povilo bažnyčia

With its breathtaking interior of over 2,000 white stucco figures featuring angels and demons, biblical scenes and some gruesome historical images, the Church of Sts Peter and Paul is essentially a glorified Baroque mausoleum to its wealthy patron, Michal Kazimierz Pac (1624–82). He was a Lithuanian military leader and the provincial governor of Vilnius. Pac's portrait hangs by the altar, his crest is positioned over the door and his body lies under the front steps. Built over the remains of two earlier wooden churches, the second of which was badly damaged during a brutal war with Moscow from 1655 to 1661, the church was intended to stand as a lasting monument to peace.

Twin-towered façade of the Church of Sts Peter and Paul

Boat-Shaped Chandelier
A late addition to the interior and a reference to St Peter's profession as a fisherman, the glass-bead chandelier was made by Latvian craftsmen in 1905.

Altar
The original high altar was replaced by *The Parting of St Peter and St Paul* (1801), created by the Polish historical painter Pranciškus Smuglevičius (1745–1807).

KEY

① **The interior** is a fine ensemble of exquisite stucco and richly decorated chapels.

② **The inscription above the balcony** reads *"Regina pacis funda nos in pace"* ("Queen of Peace protect us in peace"), probably a play on the patron's name.

★ **Chapel of the Holy Queens**
The chapel to the north of the nave is rich in stucco. The female figure perched over the arch giving a coin to a beggar denotes compassion.

★ Vaulted Nave and Cupola
The exuberance of the decoration attains a dizzying scale as the nave reaches the cupola – the rectangular reliefs, flowers and cartouches giving way to a spiral of animated angels and the face of God at the apex.

VISITORS' CHECKLIST

Practical Information
Antakalnio gatvė 1. **Tel** 234 0229.
🕆 7am, 7:30am, 6pm Mon–Sat;
8:30am, 1pm Sat; 7:30am, 10am,
11:30am, 6pm Sun. Services in
Lithuanian & Polish only.

The Italian Connection

The first flowering of Lithuanian Baroque in the early 17th century took place when Lithuania's rulers invited Italian architects and sculptors to redesign the city. Matteo Castello (1560–1632) designed St Casimir's Chapel (see p229). His nephew, Constante Tencalla (1590–1646), completed it, then created the façade of the Church of St Theresa (see p238). Half a century later, artists Perti, Galli and Palloni arrived in Vilnius to adorn the Church of Sts Peter and Paul.

Smiling Madonna in the Chapel of St Casimir in Vilnius Cathedral

★ Chapel of St Ursula
Ursula was an English princess seized by the Huns with 10 virgin companions and shot with arrows. Images of their fate are balanced by four sculptures of female saints including Mary Magdalene.

Ornate Stucco Portico
The rippling central shield above the doorway, flanked by figures of young boys, displays a fleur-de-lis, a symbol from Pac's coat of arms. The glorious stucco work adorning the entire church is attributed to the Italian masters Pietro Perti and Giovanni Maria Galli.

Delightful wooden building of the Pushkin Museum

❽ Pushkin Museum
Puškino memorialinis muziejus

Subačiaus 124. **Tel** 260 0080.
🚌 10,13. **Open** 10am–5pm Wed–Sun. 🚫 🅿

This museum is located in a bright yellow wooden house, which stands out on a pleasant grassy hill. It was not the great Russian poet, but his son Grigorij (1835–1905) who lived here with his wife Varvara (1855–1935). Founded in 1940 and opened in 1948, the museum is now home to many volumes of Alexander Pushkin's works and the ground floor is furnished in the late 19th-century style. At the back of the house, behind a statue of Pushkin, are acres of tranquil grounds and a small onion-domed family mausoleum. Steps lead down to a lake, and the paths that reach out into the surrounding countryside are a delight to explore.

❾ Rasos Cemetery
Rasų kapinės

Rasų gatvė. **Tel** 265 6563. 🚌 31.

Revered national figures and ordinary Vilnius folk lie side by side in this cemetery, founded in 1769. Some of the distinguished tombstones include those of Jonas Basanavičius (1851–1927), founder of the first Lithuanian-language newspaper, *Aušra* (Dawn), composer and painter M K Čiurlionis *(see p265)* and Marija and Jurgis Šlapelis *(see p227)*. A more controversial monument is the tomb of the man responsible for Poland's annexation of Vilnius in 1920, Józef Pilsudski (1867–1935). His body lies among those of the kings and queens of Kraków, but by his wishes his heart was cut out and placed here under a granite slab. The cemetery is spiritually significant for Lithuanians. In 1956, a crowd gathered here to protest the suppression of the Hungarian uprising against Soviet occupation.

❿ Paneriai Holocaust Memorial
Panerių memorialinis muziejus

Agrastų 17, 8 km (5 miles) SW of Vilnius. **Tel** 6808 1278. 🚆 from Vilnius. **Open** 9am–5pm Mon–Thu, Sun.

Centuries of Jewish culture and tradition in Vilnius ended at this major Holocaust site. About 70,000 Jewish men, women and children were slaughtered in

Imposing tombstones of Marija and Jurgis Šlapelis at the Rasos Cemetery

the forests of Paneriai between July 1941 and August 1944. Around 29,000 Poles, Russians and people of other nationalities were killed, as were many Roma and about 500 Catholic priests. The executions were carried out by Nazi units with the help of a squad of Lithuanians. The sites, including a large pit where, in 1944, the retreating Nazis attempted to destroy the last of the bodies with acid, are now an open-air memorial. The first memorial was raised here in 1948. The tiny visitor centre is closed in winter, but the rest of the site is accessible.

Fresco in a Station of the Cross, Calvary Church of the Holy Cross

⓫ Calvary Church of the Holy Cross

Kalvarijos bažnyčia

Kalvarijų 327. 5 km (3 miles) N of Vilnius Old Town. **Tel** 269 7469. 🚌 35, 36, 50. ✝ 6pm, 7pm Mon–Fri; 9am, 10:30am, noon, 1:30pm, 4pm Sun.

This twin-spire Baroque church towering over the Neris Valley was built by the Dominicans in the 1750s. The prime feature of its interior is a series of ceiling frescoes depicting the life of Christ. The main highlights are the nearby Stations of the Cross. Some 35 chapels, set along a 7-km (4-mile) hillside route, many in the Baroque style, were a popular attraction for 19th-century pilgrims. In 1962, they were destroyed by the Soviets. Several of the chapels have been re-created.

Twin-towered façade of the 18th-century Trinapolis Church

⓬ Trinapolis Church

Šv Trejybės bažnyčia

Verkių 70. 🚌 35, 36, 50.

The original wooden church lasted only 6 years before it burned down in 1710. The solid Baroque structure that replaced it in 1722 was designed by Pietro Puttini, a Veronese architect. Following the 1831 uprising, the church was closed by the Russians and the interior destroyed. In 1849, it was converted into an Orthodox church and the Metropolitan, the city's highest-ranking Russian Orthodox personage, used the neighbouring monastery as his summer residence. In 1917, the church was returned to the Catholics and the Archbishop set up residence here. The church was closed during the Soviet era and is still not open to the public.

⓭ Verkiai Palace

Verkių rūmai

Žaliųjų ežerių 49. **Tel** 210 2333. 🚌 35, 36, 76. **Open** by appointment. 📷 🎦 🎦

This once-immense Classical mansion was designed by Laurynas Stuoka-Gucevičius (1753–98) and Marcin Knackfus (1740–1821). The two distinguished architects were commissioned in 1781 to create a summer retreat for the Bishop of Vilnius. They built the palace on a site that, some 400 years previously, had been granted by Grand Duke Jogaila (see pp214–15) on his conversion to Christianity, to the new diocese of Vilnius.

The Classical gem was unfortunately short-lived. It was ravaged so much by the French army in 1812 that the subsequent owners had the central part pulled down. Only two wings of the palace survive and some decoration is still visible on the ceilings and the woodwork.

Verkiai Palace is also a popular place to visit because of its magnificent location on a hilltop above the Neris river. The views from here of the surrounding forests are stunning. A centuries-old legend tells how a sacred fire here was once tended by a pagan priest and beautiful virgins. A winding path leads from the mansion gates down to **Vandens Malūnas**, a former watermill that is now a restaurant (see p326).

Vandens Malūnas, a former watermill near Verkiai Palace

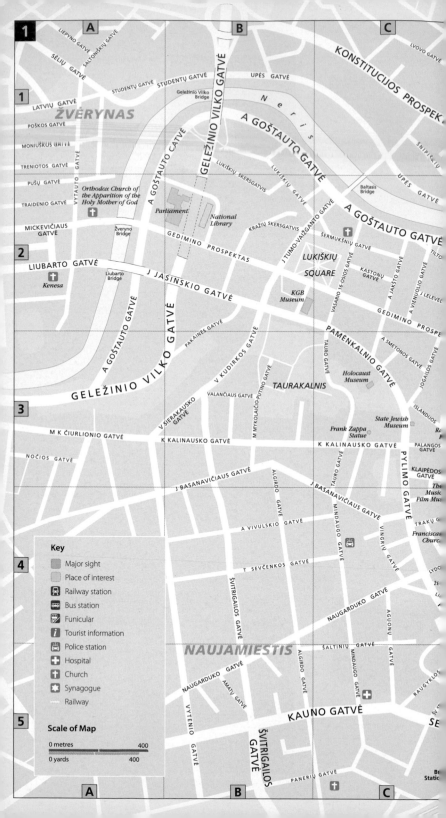

1

LIEPYNO GATVĖ
SALTONIŠKIŲ GATVĖ
SĖLIŲ GATVĖ
A
B
UPĖS GATVĖ
LVOVO GATVĖ
C
KONSTITUCIJOS PROSPEK.

STUDENTŲ GATVĖ
STUDENTŲ GATVĖ
Geležinio Vilko Bridge
N e r i s
ŠNIPIŠKIŲ
UPĖS GATVĖ

1
LATVIŲ GATVĖ
ŽVĖRYNAS
A GOŠTAUTO GATVĖ

POŠKOS GATVĖ
MONIUŠKUS GATVĖ
VYTAUTO GATVĖ
LUKIŠKIŲ SKERSGATVIS
LUKIŠKIŲ GATVĖ
Baltasis Bridge

TRENIOTOS GATVĖ
PUŠŲ GATVĖ
A GOŠTAUTO GATVĖ
Orthodox Church of the Apparition of the Holy Mother of God ✝
A GOŠTAUTO GATVĖ

TRAIDENIO GATVĖ
Parliament
National Library
KRAŽIŲ SKERSGATVIS
ŠERMUKŠNIŲ GATVĖ ✝
TILTO

MICKEVIČIAUS GATVĖ
Žveryno Bridge
J TUMO-VAIŽGANTO GATVĖ
LUKIŠKIŲ
VASARIO 16-OSIOS GATVĖ
KASTONŲ GATVĖ
A JAKŠTO GATVĖ
A VIENUOLIO GATVĖ
J LELEVE

2
LIUBARTO GATVĖ
GEDIMINO PROSPEKTAS
SQUARE
GEDIMINO PROSPE

✝ *Kenesa*
Liubarto Bridge
J JASINSKIO GATVĖ
KGB Museum

A GOŠTAUTO GATVĖ
PAKAINĖS GATVĖ
PAMĖNKALNIO GATVĖ
A SMETONOS GATVĖ

V KUDIRKOS GATVĖ
TAURO GATVĖ
Holocaust Museum
JOGAILOS GATVĖ

GELEŽINIO VILKO GATVĖ
VALANČIAUS GATVĖ
TAURAKALNIS
ISLANDIJOS

3
M K ČIURLIONIO GATVĖ
V SIERAKAUSKO GATVĖ
M MYKOLAIČIO-PUTINO GATVĖ
Frank Zappa Statue
State Jewish Museum
Re
PALANGOS

K KALINAUSKO GATVĖ
K KALINAUSKO GATVĖ
KLAIPĖDOS GATVĖ

NOČIOS GATVĖ
PYLIMO GATVĖ
The Music Film Mus

J BASANAVIČIAUS GATVĖ
ALGIRDO GATVĖ
J BASANAVIČIAUS GATVĖ
TRAKŲ G

A VIVULSKIO GATVĖ
MINDAUGO GATVĖ
VINGRIŲ GATVĖ
Franciscar Churc
LYDO

Key
T ŠEVČENKOS GATVĖ
🏛 *Police station*
ŽE
Li

🟧 Major sight
🟨 Place of interest
🚉 Railway station
🚌 Bus station
🚋 Funicular
ℹ️ Tourist information
🚓 Police station
✚ Hospital
✝ Church
✡ Synagogue
 Railway

ŠVITRIGAILOS GATVĖ
NAUGARDUKO GATVĖ
AGUONŲ GATVĖ

4
NAUJAMIESTIS
ŠALTINIŲ GATVĖ
MINDAUGO GATVĖ

NAUGARDUKO GATVĖ
ALGIRDO GATVĖ
✚
RAUGYKLOS

AMATŲ GATVĖ
VYTENIO GATVĖ
KAUNO GATVĖ
SE

Scale of Map

5
0 metres	400
0 yards	400

ŠVITRIGAILOS GATVĖ
PANERIŲ GATVĖ
✝
Be
Static

A
B
C

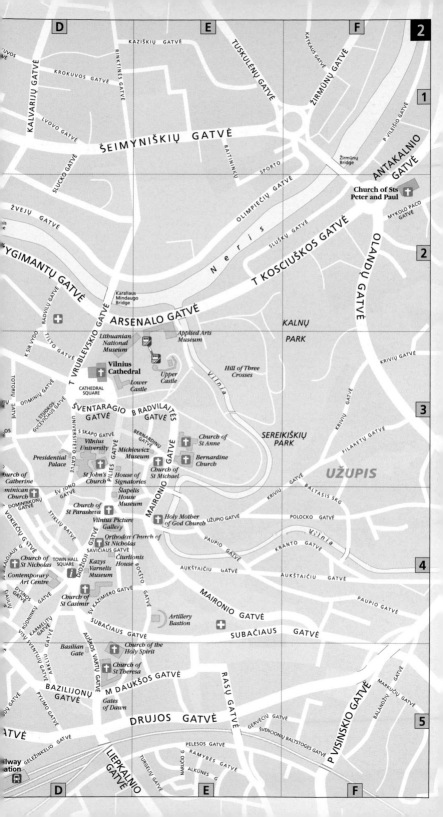

CENTRAL LITHUANIA

Rolling hills, swathes of untouched ancient forest and thousands of clear lakes characterize Central Lithuania. Much of the land is protected, allowing birds, animals and plants to thrive. While Vilnius and Kaunas are the region's most vibrant cities, the less-visited towns and villages of the region, with their beautiful churches and farmsteads, also attract a number of visitors.

Lithuania's heartland is symbolized by the mysterious mounds and fort-hills of Kernavė, where Mindaugas, the first king of Lithuania, is said to have united the Baltic tribes in an effort to hold back the crusading armies of the Teutonic Knights. Similarly, Trakai, with its fairytale Island Castle that once stood as the kernel of one of Europe's biggest empires, stirs romantic nationalism in Lithuanians. Kaunas, which served as the capital of independent Lithuania between the two world wars, is often seen as the original seat of its nationhood, rather than Vilnius, the present-day capital.

Three of the country's four ethnographic regions, each with its own dialect and traditions, are located in this area. Much of Dzūkija, in the south, is thickly forested. In summer and autumn, villagers selling mushrooms or berries line the roads, particularly along the route from Vilnius to the spa town of Druskininkai. Some parts of Dzūkija, which stretches from Alytus in the west to Vilnius in the east, have large Polish-speaking communities. Aukštaitija, which literally means "the highlands", consists of relatively high ground that is dotted with lakes. Although some forest has survived the centuries, much of Aukštaitija was used for agriculture during the 20th century. With the exception of the Russian-speaking town of Visaginas, Aukštaitija is almost exclusively Lithuanian-speaking and is the country's archaic hinterland. Centred around Marijampolė, Suvalkija, or Sūduva, is the smallest ethnographic region, with its dress and customs once influenced by Prussia as well as Poland.

Permanent display entitled "Space of Unknown Growth" at the open-air art museum, Europe Park

◄ The onion-domed Russian Orthodox Church in Druskininkai

Exploring Central Lithuania

The well-kept roads winding through the region offer great opportunities for exploring the forests around the spa town of Druskininkai in the south, as well as the lakes and villages of Aukštaitija National Park in the northeast. The best way to experience this pristine landscape is to venture off the main roads, onto the scenic minor routes connecting Trakai–Birštonas, Varėna–Marcinkonys–Merkinė and Molėtai–Ignalina. However, Central Lithuania is more than just lakes and forests. The towns are scenic and there is a good choice of old-fashioned farmsteads to visit.

Flower beds in the pedestrianized centre of Panevėžys

Sights at a Glance

Towns and Resorts

3 Kernavė
4 Varėna
5 Druskininkai
8 Alytus
9 Kalvarija
10 Marijampolė
11 Birštonas
12 *Kaunas pp262–5*
13 Kėdainiai
14 Panevėžys
15 Biržai
16 Rokiškis
17 Anykščiai
18 Molėtai Lakelands
19 Visaginas

National Parks

1 *Trakai Island Castle pp256–7*
7 Dzūkija National Park
20 *Aukštaitija National Park pp270–71*

Sights of Interest

2 Europe Park
6 Grūtas Park

Getting Around

The A1 motorway between Vilnius and Kaunas and onwards to the coast, and the A2 motorway from Vilnius to Panevėžys are the region's major arteries. Good bases for exploring are Kaunas, Druskininkai, Anykščiai and Palūšė, each of which is reachable by bus. Buses traverse Aukštaitija and Dzūkija national parks, but the best way to enjoy the surroundings is to reach the pretty villages of Zervynos and Salos II on foot. Trains go to Kaunas and Ignalina from the capital, but road transport should be taken to all other areas. There are airports at Vilnius and Kaunas.

Key

- ═══ Motorway
- ── Main road
- ── Secondary road
- ┅┅ Minor road
- ── Scenic route
- ┅┅ Railway
- ▬▬ International border

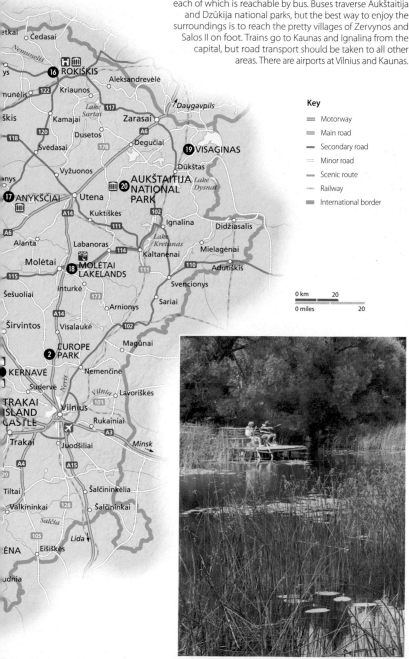

Fishing at Lake Srovinaitis, Aukštaitija National Park

For keys to symbols *see back flap*

❶ Trakai Island Castle

A formidable stronghold for any invader to overcome, the Island Castle in Trakai was built as a seat of power during the reign of Vytautas the Great and completed just before the Grand Duchy's crushing victory over the Teutonic Knights at the Battle of Grünwald *(see p216)*. As Vilnius grew in importance, Trakai lost its significance and was destroyed by the Cossacks during the 1655 Russian invasion. In the late 19th century, the elegiac island ruins captured the imaginations of poets and painters during the national revival. Oddly, it was the Soviet authorities who, in the 1950s, sanctioned the reconstruction of this monument to Lithuania's glorious past. It was completed in 1987.

Dry moat, separating the main castle from the outer courtyard

★ **Lakeside Walk**
One way to appreciate Trakai's idyllic lake-filled landscape and the scale of the castle's construction, is to take the pretty walk that follows the shore of the island.

KEY

① **A wooden footbridge** links the shore to the Island Castle.

② **The circular defence towers** have 4-m (13-ft) thick bases.

③ **The Ducal Palace's keep**, which is 30 m (100 ft) high, served as the residence of the Grand Duke.

④ **Yachts** from the nearby Žalgiris Yacht Club are moored next to the Island Castle between May and October. They can be hired by the hour; charges vary.

Lake Galvė
Serving as a moat around the castle, the lake has 21 tiny islands. Rowing and paddle boats can be hired along the quayside for a spectacular view of the castle.

VISITORS' CHECKLIST

Practical Information
Road Map D5. ℹ️ Vytauto gatvė 69. **Tel** (528) 51 934. Žalgiris Yacht Club: Žemaitės gatvė 3. **Tel** (528) 52 824. History Museum: **Tel** (528) 53 946. **Open** Mar & Apr: 10am–6pm Tue–Sun; May–Oct: 10am–7pm daily; Nov–Feb: 10am–5pm Tue–Sun. 🅿️ 🔤 **trakaimuziejus.lt**

Transport
🚌 from Vilnius. 🚆 from Vilnius.

★ **History Museum**
The museum showcases a wide array of weaponry as well as items found during excavations, including 16th-century tankards, tiles and coins.

The Karaim of Trakai

The Karaim, a community of Turkic settlers practising a particular kind of Judaism, lend a distinctly exotic flavour to Trakai. Their ancestors were taken prisoner by Vytautas the Great during his military venture to the Crimea in 1397, and subsequently served as royal guards. The Karaim have maintained their customs and traditions. Their characteristic wooden houses, each typically with gable ends and three windows facing the street, the Karaim synagogue or Kenesa and the Karaim Museum, are all on Karaimų Street. The Karaim cemetery is by Lake Totoriškiai.

Graves in the Karaim Cemetery, partially hidden by long grass

❷ Europe Park

Europos parkas

Road Map D5. **Tel** (370) 237 7077.
🚌 from Vilnius. **Open** 10am–sunset daily (last adm in summer: 7pm). 🚻
📷 📁 📶 🌐 **europosparkas.lt**

The 55-ha (136 acre) park contains contemporary sculptures. The aim of its founder, Gintaras Karosas (b.1968), was to give an artistic response to the French National Geographic Institute's statement in 1989 that a point about 17 km (11 miles) north is Europe's precise geographical centre.

Around 100 works of art are set in a landscape of forests, hills and lakes. The American artist Dennis Oppenheim (b.1938) created two monumental pieces – *Chair/Pool* (1996) and *Drinking Structure with Exposed Kidney Pool* (1998). *Double Negative Pyramid* (1999) by Sol Le Wit (1928–2007), is a reflection in concrete of ripples on a lake. Karosas's own work, *LNK Infotree* (2000) is a maze of 3,000 old TV sets.

❸ Kernavė

Road Map D5. 🏛 500. 🚌 from Vilnius. 🛈 Kerniaus 4, (382) 47 385. 📅 Days of Live Archaeology (Jul). 🌐 **kernave.org**

The small, sleepy village of Kernavė overlooks the idyllic Neris Valley, where steep-sided fort-hills hint at the passing of a long-lost civilization. Archaeological finds show

Wooden steps crossing fort-hills, Kernavė's archaeological reserve

that the site was inhabited as far back as 9000 BC. In the 13th century, Kernavė was the first capital of the united Lithuanian tribes and a busy trading centre. The Northern Crusaders ransacked the prosperous pagan town in 1365. In 1390, another attack was launched by a mighty army consisting of knights, soldiers and mercenaries from Germany, France, Italy and England. Henry IV (1367–1413), the future king of England, also participated in the assault, from which the town never recovered.

Today, Kernavė is Lithuania's foremost archaeological reserve. In 2004, it was declared a UNESCO World Heritage Site. The protected area comprises five large mounds, which contained medieval ramparts and fortifications. Wooden

steps lead to the summits of the hills, where there are breathtakingly beautiful views of the surrounding terrain.

Environs

The scenic road from Vilnius to Kernavė passes several villages. **Sudervė**, 20 km (12 miles) south of Kernavė, has an unusual white circular church designed by Lithuania's legendary early 19th-century Neo-Classicist, Laurynas Stuoka-Gucevičius.

❹ Varėna

Road Map D6. 🏛 11,000. 🚉 from Vilnius. 🚌 from Vilnius. 📅 Mushroom Festival (Sep). 🌐 **varena.lt**

Surrounded on all sides by thick forest, Varėna is situated on the eastern edge of Dzūkija National Park *(see p260)*. The town is regarded as the mushroom capital of Lithuania. Although a rich variety of mushrooms grows all over the country, here they proliferate like a carpet on the forest floor. One day a year, usually the last Saturday in September, the sleepy town springs to life to celebrate the Mushroom Festival *(see p213)*.

Environs

The road from Varėna to Marcinkonys, 22 km (14 miles) southwest, winds pleasantly through Dzūkija National Park. Immediately on the left

Farmstead with wooden barns, on the edge of the forest in Zervynos, near Varėna

Russian Orthodox Church with striking domes, Druskininkai

inside the park, a road leads to **Zervynos**, a village with unpaved streets and the scenic Ūla river bubbling underneath the foliage and wooden bridges.

❺ Druskininkai

Road Map D6. 🗺 17,000. 🚌 from Vilnius. ℹ Gardino 3, (313) 608 00. 🌐 **druskininkai.lt**

Lithuania's foremost spa resort, Druskininkai is a haven of peace and tranquility. Main roads bypass the town, tucked inside a bend on the thickly forested Nemunas river, and noise restrictions allow peace to prevail. After thriving on 200 years of popularity, Druskininkai suffered an economic shock in the 1990s, when it found itself deprived of Polish, Belarusian and Russian tourists, who once stayed in its sanitaria.

Wellness tourism has, however, been revived since the 1990s. The sanitaria offer water and mineral mud treatments, massages, beauty programmes and fitness trails through the forest. Bike rides and long walks are possible along the Sun Path, which leads through the picturesque Ratnyčia Valley.

The boulevard-lined town centre preserves wooden villas from the 19th and early 20th centuries, mainly found on Laisvės Square. The delightful **Russian Orthodox Church** also stands in the same square. On Vilniaus Street, some

futuristic-style buildings still survive, including the now-closed Soviet-era physiotherapy treatment centre with decorative waves of solid concrete hanging in mid-air.

The serene town inspired painter and composer M K Čiurlionis *(see p265)*, who lived here from 1890 to 1911. The **Čiurlionis Memorial Museum**, located in his family's wooden house, displays period furniture, his notebooks and copies of his artwork. Another museum in the town, the **Jacques Lipchitz Museum**, is dedicated to the Cubist sculptor who was born here in 1891.

🏛 **Čiurlionis Memorial Museum**
M K Čiurlionio 35. **Tel** (370) 313 51131
Open 11am–5pm Tue–Sun.
Closed last Tue of the month. 🖼 📷

🏛 **Jacques Lipchitz Museum**
Šv Jokubo 17. **Tel** (313) 56 077.
Open call ahead for opening hours. 🖼

❻ Grūtas Park
Grūto parkas

Road Map D6. Parko 47, Grūtas village, Druskininkai. **Tel** (370) 3135 5511. **Open** Jun–Aug: 9am–10pm daily; Sep–May: 9am–5pm daily.. 🖼 📷 ♿ 🖥 🌐 **grutoparkas.lt**

Around 90 statues and busts of figures once glorified by the Soviet regime stand in alcoves on a forest trail in Grūtas village. Most of them once graced squares and gardens, before being torn down by cheering Lithuanians in 1991. The park's owner, Viliumas Malinauskas, was awarded the Ig Nobel Peace Prize in 2001, the year the park opened.

Information in English is given on each of these ideological relics. A massive metal statue of Lenin that once stood in front of the KGB building in Vilnius lost a thumb while being wrenched by a crane from its pedestal. Another statue shows Lenin with the Lithuanian Communist Party's First Secretary, Vincas Mickevičius-Kapsukas. Both statues were decapitated in 1991, but their heads have been joined back. There is an image of Stalin, which once stood outside Vilnius train station until it was dismantled in 1960. *Rusų Karys* (Russian Soldier) is a statue made by Nazi prisoners of war from metal taken from the wrecks of German planes shot down by the Soviets. There are also statues of Red Army liberators, poets and other heroes.

Busts of Marx, Engels, Lenin and Stalin in Grūtas Park

View of the Nemunas river and surrounding area from the fort-hill at Merkinė, near Dzūkija National Park

❼ Dzūkija National Park

Dzūkijos nacionalinis parkas

Road Map D6. 🚂 from Vilnius to Zervynos, Marcinkonys. 🚌 from Vilnius to Merkinė. 🛈 Vilniaus 3, Merkinė, (310) 57 245. Headquarters: Miškininkų 61, Šilagėlių 11, Marcinkonys, (310) 44 466. 🎫 English-speaking guides arranged in Merkinė, Marcinkonys.
🌐 dzukijosparkas.lt

This densely forested park covers 550 sq km (212 sq miles) of countryside. Besides an enormous area of ancient pine forest in the sandy Dainava plain, the park also covers sweeping bends in the broad Nemunas Valley. More than 200 species of flora and fauna are protected in the park, including many rare species of stork. The few villages that are located in the park offer a glimpse of Eastern European life that has remained the same for a century or more. The ethnographic reserve of **Zervynos** is on the park's eastern edge.

The ancient settlement of **Merkinė** lies at the confluence of the Nemunas and Merkys rivers. A fort-hill, the site of a 14th-century castle, offers extensive vistas of the park.

Another fort-hill overlooking the Nemunas river is in the scenic hamlet of **Liškiava**, at the southwestern edge of the park. The 14th-century castle that stood here defended the Grand Duchy against the mighty Teutonic Knights. Another striking landmark is the domed 18th-century Holy Trinity Church, with a rich interior featuring seven late Baroque altars. A series of frescoes depicting images from the history of Christianity were covered in plaster in 1823 and were only restored in 1997.

In **Marcinkonys**, a village 8 km (5 miles) southwest of Zervynos, a track leads southwards to **Čepkeliai Reserve**. This area protects the country's most extensive marsh, which stretches into Belarus, and the migratory birds that stop here. Paths and raised wooden walkways reach observation platforms offering great views.

White stork, Dzūkija National Park

❽ Alytus

Road Map D6. 🏘 62,000. 🚂 from Kaunas. 🚌 from Vilnius, Kaunas. 🛈 Rotušės aikštė 14a, (315) 52 010. 🌐 alytus.lt

Lithuania's sixth-largest city began as a hilltop fortress where the tiny Alytupis river trickles into the Nemunas. The hill still offers views of both the city and the Dzūkija forests to the south. In the centre, the **Museum of Local Lore** has a collection of 65,000 antiques. The bridge across the Nemunas has a bas-relief depicting a battle that occured here between Lithuanians and Bolsheviks in 1919. It claimed the life of Antanas Juozapavičius, the first Lithuanian officer to die in the independence struggle. His tomb lies by the **Guardian Angels' Church**.

Much of the city centre was destroyed in 1941. Soon after, all the city's 60,000 Jews were killed in Vidzgiris Forest, a site marked in 1993 by a monument of a broken Star of David. Gravestones in the city cemetery remember the Jews.

Mass of crosses in the churchyard of Guardian Angels' Church, Alytus

Environs

From Alytus, the Nemunas river sweeps towards Kaunas *(see pp262–5)* around several huge, forest-covered bends. One of these bends can be viewed from an evocative fort-hill at the far end of the quiet village of **Punia**, located 15 km (9 miles) north of Alytus.

Museum of Local Lore
Savanorių 6. **Tel** (315) 51 990.
Open 9am–6pm Tue–Fri, 9am–5pm Sat. **alytausmuziejus.lt**

Church of the Blessed Virgin Mary in Kalvarija

❾ Kalvarija

Road Map C6. 12,000. from Kaunas. Bažnyčios 4, (345) 60 759.

Another Lithuanian town deeply haunted by the Holocaust, Kalvarija emerged in the 17th century as a trading town on the Warsaw–St Petersburg road. Jews made up a significant part of the population, some of them wealthy merchants who exported grain to Germany, but the majority were poor workers who manned several factories making brushes and medicinal alcohol. Wooden synagogues were built and, in 1803, a stone synagogue complex was constructed, including a rabbi's house and *beit midrash* (a place of study and prayer).

In 1941, the Nazis and the Soviet army exterminated the entire Jewish population in town. Lithuanian and Jewish Communists were tortured,

then shot on the banks of Lake Orija. The synagogue has been partially restored as a national monument.

The **Church of the Blessed Virgin Mary**, with its statues of angels and kings on the pediments above the portico and gate, was built in 1840.

❿ Marijampolė

Road Map C6. 61,000. from Kaunas. from Kaunas. J Basanavičiaus 8, (343) 91 538. **marijampole.lt**

This town takes its name from an 18th-century monastery built for the Marian Fathers, a religious order founded in 1673. The Church of St Michael became a part of the complex in 1824, but the monastery's activities were restricted after the 1831 uprising. The church was revived by Bishop Jurgis Matulaitis (1871–1927), whose remains are marked by a tombstone and sarcophagus. During the Soviet occupation in 1944, over 6,000 residents were deported to Siberia. Anti-Soviet partisans mounted a struggle, a story told at the **Tauras District Partisans and Deportation Museum**. A cemetery on Varpio Street and a chapel on Tylioji Street remember the victims of the Soviet regime.

Tauras District Partisans and Deportation Museum
Vytauto 29. **Tel** (370) 3435 0754.
Open 9am–5pm Tue–Sat.

⓫ Birštonas

Road Map D6. 4,600. from Vilnius, Kaunas. B Sruogos 4, (319) 65 740. Birštonas Festival (Jun), Birštonas Jazz (Mar, alternate years). **visitbirstonas.lt**

The secluded spa town of Birštonas is quite different from the bustling wellness centre of Druskininkai *(see p259)*. Though open to paying guests as well as patients, Birštonas's clinical sanitaria have remained trapped in a bygone era. Nonetheless, the well-ordered landscape planning and a pleasant pedestrian boulevard alongside the Nemunas river makes it a delightful town to explore. On the town's eastern edge stands Vytautas Castle Hill, the site of a hunting lodge of Grand Duke Vytautas. A large carved stone statue of Vytautas on horseback stands near the fort-hill. Birštonas is dotted with wooden houses, which date from the mid-19th century, when the reputation of the town's mineral waters and muds began to grow. A tiny yellow building in the town centre contains a tap with free access to the rich well of water below. The town

Vytautas's statue, Birštonas

attracts a lot of visitors during Birštonas Jazz, Lithuania's oldest jazz festival. Held once every two years, the three-day marathon features a range of styles. Birštono Seklytėlė *(see p328)*, a valley-top restaurant, has a grand view of the pine-covered Nemunas.

The Nemunas river, seen from the promenade at Birštonas

⑫ Kaunas

Lithuania's second-largest city, Kaunas stands at the confluence of the Nemunas and Neris, the country's biggest rivers. A series of disasters hindered the city's development, including invasions by the Russians (1655), Swedes (1701) and Napoleon's Grand Army (1812). Rapid growth in the 19th century culminated in Kaunas becoming the temporary capital of newly independent Lithuania in 1919. Later, the city suffered under Nazi and Soviet occupations. Today, Kaunas is a modern city with a boulevard and a host of museums. The main historic sights are located in its well-preserved Old Town.

Bridge over the Nemunas river leading to the Old Town

🏛 Old Town Hall

Rotušės aikštė.

Known locally as the "White Swan" and resembling a church with its single-tiered tower, the Old Town Hall has been a marriage registry office since the 1970s. It continues to be the photogenic backdrop for newlyweds. Built in the mid-16th century, it housed merchants, magistrates and the mayor, as well as a subterranean prison. It has been used as an ammunition store, clubhouse,

Elegant Old Town Hall, locally called the "White Swan"

fire station and theatre. Town Hall Square, where it stands, was once a busy marketplace and the focal point of the Old Town.

🏰 Church of the Holy Trinity

Rotušės aikštė 22. **Tel** (37) 323 734. 🕑 10am Sun.

Built for a Bernardine convent in the late 1620s, this church has remained in good condition. Its blend of Renaissance and Gothic styles and pastel colours brighten up the northwestern corner of Town Hall Square. A redesign of the interior was completed just before the outbreak of World War II.

🏰 Church of St George

Papilio 7/9. **Tel** (37) 224 659. 🕑 6pm Mon–Fri, 10am Sat, 10:30am Sun.

Constructed for Bernardine friars in the 15th century, this Gothic church was destroyed twice by fire before its interior was restored in the Baroque style. The church was further damaged by the Russians in the 17th century and in 1812 by Napoleon's soldiers, who used it as a warehouse. It was finally returned to the Franciscans in 1993.

🏰 Kaunas Castle

Pilies 17. **Tel** (37) 300 672. **Open** 10am–6pm Tue–Fri, 10am–5pm Sat.

The ruins of Kaunas Castle are a reminder of the strategic importance of its location, between the two rivers, Neris and Nemunas. Little is known about what stood here before the first stone structure was erected in the 13th century. Crusaders damaged the castle in 1362. Soon after reconstruction, the Teutonic Knights were dealt their decisive blow at the Battle of Grünwald *(see p216)* and the castle consequently fell into ruins. The structure was used as a prison in the 18th century, but was restored in the 1920s.

🏛 Pharmacy Museum

Rotušės 28. **Tel** (37) 201 569. **Open** 10am–5pm Tue–Sat. 🚫

A powder for epilepsy made from the heads of corpses, a tincture of "Venus hair" to improve one's allure and a 19th-century herbal remedy

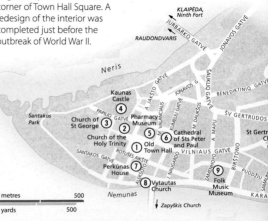

0 metres 500
0 yards 500

for male vitality called Erektosan are among the exhibits at this unique museum. Chilling medicinal apparatus and the occasional waxwork, such as a shaman curing a baby, add to the atmosphere. The museum also runs a homoeopathic pharmacy.

⛪ Cathedral of Sts Peter and Paul

Vilniaus 1. **Tel** (37) 324 093. ⏰ 7am, 8am, 9am, 6pm daily.

Several reconstructions have culminated in the Gothic and Renaissance exterior of this 15th-century cathedral. The broadly late Baroque interior, however, has remained largely unchanged since 1800. A tomb-stone on the exterior of the south wall is that of Maironis (1862–1932), a priest-poet whose verse romanticized Lithuanian legends and land-marks. Inside, the sculptures surrounding the high altar are overpowering. The oldest of the cathedral's

Painting, Cathedral of Sts Peter and Paul

paintings, the 17th-century *Suffering Mother of God*, reputedly has miraculous powers.

🏛 Perkūnas House

Aleksoto 6. **Tel** (37) 6414 4614. **Open** 2–5pm Thu & Fri; other times by appointment. 📷

The ogee arches and pinnacles of this redbrick Gothic building, resemble those of the Church of St Anne *(see p232)*, Vilnius. It was named after Perkūnas, the pagan god of thunder, when renovation in the 19th century revealed that it may once have been the site of a pagan temple. Dating from the early 1500s, it was originally a meeting house for merchants in the Hanseatic League. Bought by the Jesuits, the house was converted into a chapel before becoming, in the 19th century, a theatre and then a school. Later, during the Soviet period, it was used as a warehouse. It is now back with the Jesuits.

Kaunas

① Old Town Hall
② Church of the Holy Trinity
③ Church of St George
④ Kaunas Castle
⑤ Pharmacy Museum
⑥ Cathedral of Sts Peter and Paul
⑦ Perkūnas House
⑧ Vytautas Church

⑨ Folk Music Museum
⑩ Laisvės Avenue
⑪ Mykolas Žilinskas Art Gallery
⑫ Church of the Resurrection
⑬ M K Čiurlionis Art Museum
⑭ Vytautas the Great War Museum
⑮ Devil's Museum

Airport
10 km (6 miles) ✈ / VILNIUS, RUMŠIŠKES

Church of the Resurrection ⑫

Devil's Museum ⑮
M K Čiurlionis Art Museum ⑬
⑭ Vytautas the Great War Museum

Philharmonic Hall

Laisvės Avenue ⑩

NEPRIKLAUSOMYBĖS AIKŠTĖ
⑪ Mykolas Žilinskas Art Gallery

City Garden

KĘSTUČIO GATVĖ

JGO PROSPEKTAS

Bus Station
450 m (500 yards) 🚌
Railway Station
800 m (885 yards) 🚆 ↓ Pažaislis Monastery

VISITORS' CHECKLIST

Practical Information
Road Map D5. 🚉 320,000.
ℹ️ Laisvės alėja 36, 323 436.
🎷 International Jazz Festival (Apr). 🌐 **kaunastic.lt**

Transport
✈ 10 km (6 miles) N of town.
🚌 🚊

⛪ Vytautas Church

Aleksoto 3. **Tel** (37) 203 854. ⏰ 6pm Tue–Thu, 10am & 6pm Sat–Sun.

Standing on the bank of the Nemunas river, this church was built on the orders of Vytautas the Great after the Holy Roman Emperor decided in 1413, much to the ire of the Teutonic Knights, that the land on the river's right bank belonged to the Grand Duchy of Lithuania. Already an army storehouse, the church was converted to serve a Russian Orthodox congregation. A full reconstruction took place after Lithuania's first independence in 1918, post World War I. In 1930, a medallion was placed in the church wall to commemorate the 500th anniversary of Vytautas's death.

Redbrick Gothic structure of Vytautas Church

🏛 Folk Music Museum

Zamenhofo 12. **Tel** (37) 422 295. **Open** 9am–5pm Mon–Fri, 9am–6pm Sat. 📷 📷

This museum boasts a collection of 7,000 wind, brass and stringed instruments, including pipes and whistles. Only 500 of them are on display due to the museum's small size. The staff can give demonstrations of many of these. Stranger pieces, such as the table bass, a pine table with four strings and a pig's bladder, are also displayed.

For keys to symbols *see back flap*

Exploring Modern Kaunas

Stretching eastwards from the Old Town is Kaunas's modernized New Town. The process of its expansion began in the 19th century, and today it is the hub of commercial and cultural life in the city. The museums and other sites are found around the heart of modern Kaunas in Laisvės (Freedom) Avenue. This broad, leafy, pedestrianized boulevard is lined with shops, pavement cafés, restaurants and bars, and is the place local people come to stroll and mingle.

Laisvės Avenue leading to the Church of St Michael

⊞ Laisvės Avenue

At the eastern end of this boulevard are the blue-silver onion domes of the Church of St Michael. Originally Russian Orthodox when it was built in the early 1890s, it was later converted to serve the Lithuanian army. A monument by the park outside the Music Theatre at Laisvės 4 marks the spot where Romas Kalanta, a Lithuanian student, set fire to himself on 14 May 1972 in protest against Soviet rule. His suicide sparked student protests, which were ruthlessly suppressed.

▥ Mykolas Žilinskas Art Gallery

Nepriklausomybės 12. **Tel** (37) 222 853.
Open 11am–5pm Tue–Sun. 🚳 📷

An exile who had fled from Kaunas to West Berlin in advance of the Soviets in 1940, Mykolas Žilinskas (1904–92) later built a valuable art collection, which he donated to Kaunas in the 1970s. Besides canvases and porcelain from the 16th to the 20th centuries, including *The Crucifixion* by Rubens and some early Soviet avant-garde art, there are also pre-war paintings and sculptures by Baltic artists.

⬆ Church of the Resurrection

Žemaičių 31. **Tel** (37) 229 222. 🔼 6pm Mon–Fri; 9:30am, 11am, 12:30pm Sun.

With a 70-m (230-ft) steeple, this church was built in 1918 to mark Lithuanian independence. After World War II, the Soviets turned it into a radio factory. With independence regained, the factory was evicted. After reconstruction the church was consecrated on Christmas Day 2004.

▥ M K Čiurlionis Art Museum

V Putvinskio 55. **Tel** (37) 229 475.
Open Apr–Sep: 11am–5pm Tue–Sun; Oct–Mar: 11am–5pm Tue–Sat. 🚳 📷

Housing virtually all of Čiurlionis's paintings, this museum also covers the development of art in Lithuania. With 335,000 exhibits, it holds Lithuania's biggest art collection, but there is only room to display a fraction of the pieces. Artifacts from other cultures include some oddly juxtaposed pieces from Ancient Egypt.

▥ Vytautas the Great War Museum

Donelaičio 64. **Tel** (37) 320 939.
Open 11am–5pm Tue–Sun. 🚳 📷

Lithuania's national war museum exhibits weapons that the country has used to defend itself.

However, the main focus of the museum is the re-creation of the story of the doomed transatlantic flight of the *Lituanica* in July 1933. The pilots, Steponas Darius and Stasys Girėnas, died in the crash, but the distance covered (6,411 km/ 3,984 miles) was the second-longest flight ever recorded. The plane's wreckage is on display.

▥ Devil's Museum

V Putvinskio 64. **Tel** (37) 221 587.
Open 10am–5pm Tue–Sun. 🚳 📷 🖼 📷

This museum's fine collection of representations of devils, demons and witches from Lithuania and around the world, was brought together by avid collector Antanas Žmuidzinavičius (1876–1966). A sculpture of the horned figures of Hitler and Stalin fighting over Lithuania in a pit of bones is grim, but most of the devils are shown as playful, musical and frequently drunk.

▥ Ninth Fort

Žemaičių 73. **Tel** (37) 377 750.
Open Apr–Oct: 10am–6pm Wed–Mon; Nov–Mar: 10am–6pm Wed–Sun. 📷 🌐 **9fortomuziejus.lt**

The ninth in a series of fortifications constructed by Tsarist Russia to protect its western borders was built in the early 20th century, only to become a prison in 1924. During World War II, it was used for incarceration and extermination by the Nazis. The fort also housed Soviet political prisoners. Part of a farm after the war, it opened as a "museum to the victims of Fascism" in 1958. The dungeon and defence walls have displays on the Nazi and Soviet occupations.

Artillery on show at the Vytautas the Great War Museum

For hotels and restaurants see pp305–306 and pp328–30

🏛 Raudondvaris

5 km (3 miles) W of Kaunas. 🚌 from Kaunas. 🌐 raudondvariodvaras.lt

Built by the crusaders in the 14th century, Raudondvaris (Red Manor) became a part of Lithuania after the Battle of Grünwald (1410). The legend says that it was presented as a gift in 1549, by Sigismund August to Barbora Radvilaitė, a year before their marriage. After her death in 1551, the castle fell into ruin and was rebuilt as a manor house in the 17th century by the Tyszkiewicz family. Its library and collection of paintings were lost during World War I. A chapel close by contains the Tyszkiewicz tombs that survived the 20th century.

A red manor with manicured lawns at Raudondvaris

🏛 Pažaislis Monastery

7 km (4 miles) E of town. **Open** 10am–5pm Tue–Fri, 10am–4pm Sat.
🌐 pazaislis.org

One of Eastern Europe's great Baroque monuments, Pažaislis Monastery and its central, cupola-domed Church of the Visitation of the Blessed Virgin Mary were constructed by Italian architects in the 17th century. There is finely detailed stucco work inside the church and in the corridors of the monastery, much of it framing intricate frescoes painted by the Italian artist Michelangelo Palloni.

🏛 Rumšiškės Open-Air Museum

L Lekavičiaus 2, 15 km (9 miles) E of town. **Tel** (346) 47 392. **Open** May–Sep: 10am–6pm daily; Oct–Apr: 10am–4pm (park only). 🌐 llbm.lt

At Rumšiškės Open-Air Museum, traditional thatched farmsteads and other elements of village life have been carefully

Merchants' houses lining the square of the Old Town, Kėdainiai

reassembled. The rolling country-side overlooking Lake Kaunas creates a perfect backdrop.

🏛 Zapyškis Church

15 km (9 miles) W of town.

One of Lithuania's loveliest buildings, the triangular red-brick Gothic Zapyškis Church is set in a field by the Nemunas river. Built in the 16th century, it has remained miraculously intact despite invasions and occupations.

⑱ Kėdainiai

Road Map D5. 🏙 54,000. 🚆 from Kaunas, Vilnius. 🚌 from Kaunas, Vilnius. 🛈 Didžiosios rinkos 6, (347) 56 900. 🎪 Cucumber Festival (Jul), Broma Jazz Festival (Aug), Ice Cream Festival (Aug). 🌐 kedainiutvic.lt

With a history as a trading town on the route between Kaunas and Rīga, Kėdainiai was first mentioned in written sources in 1372. Its colourful Old Town has a series of elaborately gabled merchants' houses in the main square. Close by, the Renaissance-style Town Hall dates from 1654 and holds Kėdainiai's admin-istrative offices. In another square, two synagogues dating from 1837 stand side by side. They were once used by the town's thriving Jewish commu-nity. Another synagogue, now the **Multicultural Centre**, holds a museum on Kėdainiai's cultural history.

Environs

Paberžė, 30 km (19 miles) north of Kėdainiai, with its delightful wooden church, was the residence of Father Stanislovas (1918–2005), a revered Tolstoyan hermit and Capuchin friar.

🏛 Multicultural Centre

Senoji rinka 12. **Tel** (347) 51 778.
Open 10am–5pm Tue–Sat. 🎨

M K Čiurlionis (1875–1911)

A tortured soul and artistic genius, Mikalojus Konstantinas Čiurlionis is Lithuania's most famous painter and composer. He started out as a prodigious composer of atmospheric symphonic and organ works, but at the age of 27 he began to study drawing. The next nine years were filled with feverish creativity. Before his early death from pneumonia, he had created around 300 works of music, painting and poetry. Many of his mystical paintings mirrored his musical compositions and some were named as pieces of music, such as *Spring Sonata* (1907) and *Funeral Symphony* (1903). Despite their melancholy, Čiurlionis's painted and musical works can be surprisingly uplifting.

Painting by Čiurlionis, displayed at the M K Čiurlionis Art Museum

Interior of the Neo-Baroque Cathedral of Christ the King, Panevėžys

⑭ Panevėžys

Road Map D5. 🏙 105,000.
🚆 from Klaipėda. 🚌 from Vilnius.
ℹ️ Laisvės aikštė 11, (45) 508 081.
🌐 **panevezysinfo.lt**

One of Lithuania's largest cities, with a modern commercial centre, Panevėžys is a crucial transport hub in the region.

South of its centre lies the **Cathedral of Christ the King**, a Neo-Baroque structure built in 1904. A sweeping painting above the altar depicts a victorious medieval Lithuanian army. A few streets north, the **Civic Art Gallery** often holds eccentric exhibitions of local modern art. East of the centre is **Glasremis**, a working gallery creating glass items.

Environs
In **Pakruojis**, 50 km (31 miles) northwest of Panevėžys, the country's largest 18th-century manor lies in a 6-ha (15-acre) park, with a five-arch stone bridge and 40 other structures.

🏛 **Civic Art Gallery**
Respublikos 3. **Tel** (45) 584 802.
Open 11am–6pm Wed–Sun. 🗝

🏛 **Glasremis**
J Biliūno 12. **Tel** (45) 430 403.
Open 10am–5pm Mon–Fri. 🗝

⑮ Biržai

Road Map D4. 🏙 28,000.
🚌 from Panevėžys. ℹ️ J Janonio 2, (450) 33 496. 🌐 **birzai.lt**

The small town of Biržai is best known for its traditional breweries. The local brew can be sampled in the cellar of the **Sėla Museum**, housed in the 17th-century Biržai Castle. Visitors can enjoy the live folk music performed here, but should book ahead.

In 1701, Peter the Great of Russia and King Augustus II of Poland signed the pact against Sweden in this castle on the eve of the Great Northern War *(see p37)*.

In the grounds are the ruins of an older castle, whose defences in the mid-1500s involved damming two rivers to create Lithuania's oldest man-made lake, Širvėna. A 525-m (572-yard) wooden bridge leads across the lake to Astravas Manor Park, with its sprawling 19th-century manor house, watermill and old dam.

🏛 **Sėla Museum**
J Radvilos 3. **Tel** (450) 31 883.
Open May–Sep: 10am–5:30pm
Tue–Sun; Oct–Apr: 10am–5:30pm
Wed–Sat. 🗝 🗝

⑯ Rokiškis

Road Map D4. 🏙 35,000. 🚆 from Panevėžys. 🚌 from Panevėžys, Vilnius. ℹ️ Nepriklausomybės 8, (458) 52 261 or (458) 51 044. 🐎 Lake Sartai Horse Race (first Sat in Feb). 🌐 **rokiskis.lt**

Set amid glorious countryside, Rokiškis is blessed with fort-hills, forests and picnic sites. However, it is best known for its cheese company, Rokiškio Sūris. Having started as a small local dairy, it now sells cheeses all over the Baltic region.

Rokiškis Manor House, the town's main sight, was built in 1801 by the Tyzenhaus family. The Polish architects who redesigned it in 1905 created an English-style interior, but its exterior has Baroque elements. It houses the **Rokiškis Museum**, which offers tours of the lavish Great Hall and a separate building that exhibits fine wooden folk sculptures by Lionginas Šepka (1907–85).

Environs
Kriaunos, 15 km (9 miles) southeast of Rokiškis, has a local **Historical Museum** filled with an eclectic collection of flax tools, linen fabrics, tubs and troughs. Hidden upstairs, the "loft of witches" is a coven of 400 witches, mermaids, fairies and goblins.

The island in Lake Dviragis in the village of **Salos**, 20 km (12 miles) southwest of Rokiškis, was a sanctuary for its inhabitants

Wooden bridge across the castle moat into the older castle, Biržai

Restored Classical façade of Salos Manor House near Rokiškis

in the early 15th century. Now connected by a bridge to the rest of the village, the island forms a calm backdrop to a Classical 19th-century manor and a Neo-Gothic wooden church.

Rokiškis Museum
Tyzenhauzų 5. **Tel** (458) 52 261. **Open** 10am–6pm Tue–Sun.

Historical Museum
Kriaunų village. **Tel** (458) 41 718. **Open** 10am–4pm Tue–Sat.

⓱ Anykščiai

Road Map D5. 29,000. from Panevėžys, from Panevėžys, Kaunas. Gegužės 1, (381) 59 177. **antour.lt** Lithuanian Narrow-Gauge Railway: **siaurukas.eu**

Nestled in a landscape of rolling pastures, Anykščiai creates a picturesque setting for the 160-km (100-mile) **Lithuanian Narrow-Gauge Railway**. Only 68 km (42 miles) of Europe's longest functional narrow-gauge railway is in regular use today. Its locomotives pull carriages across open countryside, along the Šventoji river to the scenic shores of Lake Rubikiai with its 16 islands. Tickets are sold at the tourist information centre. The old station boasts the **Anykščiai Northern Railway Museum**, providing further insights into train travel.

Environs
In **Niūronys**, 6 km (4 miles) north of Anykščiai, the **Horse Museum** hosts exhibitions on various horse-related products. Rides on real horses, around the paddock or in a horse-drawn carriage, can be had for a small fee. There is also a mini-playground for children.

Anykščiai Northern Railway Museum
Vilties 2. **Tel** (370) 38 15 4597. **Open** May–Oct: 10am–5pm daily, Nov–Apr: by appointment.
siaurukas.eu

Horse Museum
Niūronių village. **Tel** (381) 51 722. **Open** May–Aug: 9am–6pm daily, Sep–Apr: 8am–5pm daily.
arkliomuziejus.lt

⓲ Molėtai Lakelands

Road Map D5. 21,000. from Vilnius, Daugavpils. from Vilnius, Daugavpils. Inturkės 4, (383) 53 091.

The lakes that extend east from the town of Molėtai are some of the Baltic region's cleanest, making them perfect for camping and swimming.

Lake Želva's Ethnocosmology Centre, Molėtai Lakelands

Forest-lined lakes with inlets, such as Baltieji and Juodieji Lakajai, and, further south, Asveja, are protected as part of the 55,000-ha (136,000-acre) Labanoras Regional Park. Molėtai is one of the oldest settlements in the country, although it has preserved very few historical monuments. The Molėtai Astronomical Observatory offers sweeping views of area. Inside, the **Ethno-cosmology Centre** displays an intriguing exhibition on the links between cosmology and the pagan rituals of the ancient Lithuanians.

Exterior of the Ignalina Nuclear Power Plant, near Visaginas

⓳ Visaginas

Road Map E5. 22,000. from Vilnius, Daugavpils. from Vilnius, Daugavpils. Jenalina Ateities 23, (386) 52 597. Visagino Country Music Festival (mid-Aug).

With only 15 per cent of its population ethnically Lithuanian, Visaginas has a unique atmosphere in a country that is 85 per cent Lithuanian. It was created in 1974 to house the nuclear scientists who built and then worked at the nearby **Ignalina Nuclear Power Plant**, until recently the Baltic region's only nuclear power station.

Hidden in forests down a single road, Visaginas has no discernable centre. High-rise housing blocks cover the town from east to west. The power station was closed in December 2009, but a new plant may open at the same site in the future.

⑳ Aukštaitija National Park

The oldest and most beloved of Lithuania's national parks, Aukštaitija National Park was established in 1974 to protect local biodiversity. About 60 per cent of the country's plant species can be found here, in addition to ancient pine forests, fort-hills, burial mounds and old thatched cottages in villages such as Salos II. Palušė makes an ideal base for exploring the 400-sq km (154-sq mile) park. The park's central point, Ladakalnis Hill, is its highest, from which five lakes are visible. Rowing boats can be hired from Palušė, enabling visitors to make a circular trip or drift at a leisurely pace along the water trail.

Key

■ Aukštaitija National Park

Taurapilis, one of several ancient fortifications found in the park, is situated above Lake Tauragnas, affording extensive views in all directions.

★ Beekeeping Museum
Sculptures of characters from Lithuanian folklore stand together on a grassy hillside with wooden hives, in the village of Stripeikiai.

★ Ladakalnis Hill
The best panoramic view of the park can be experienced from the hill above Lake Linkmenas. The area is noted for its mesmerizing greenery and clear lakes.

★ Salos II Cultural Reserve
The ethnographic village is arranged like a live, open-air museum, with several well-preserved timber houses.

0 km 2
0 miles 2

Beekeeping

Unusually shaped beehives at the Beekeeping Museum

Lithuanians have a long and enduring history of apiculture. Forest beekeeping, in which bees lived in tree hollows and their keepers mounted elaborate climbing apparatus to collect the honey, was widely practised in the Middle Ages when beeswax and honey were vital to the economy. In the 15th century, a law was passed to prosecute people who harmed the bees, or the trees.

Trainiškis
In the village of Trainiškis stands a mighty tree believed to be more than 800 years old and said to have once been a site of pagan sacrifices.

Valčių Pervežimas Water Trail
Visitors can rent a boat for a circular trip around the park from lake to lake, going via Valčių Pervežimas, the water trail that links Lake Baluošas and Lake Dringis.

Gaveikėnai Watermill
One of several original watermills in the park, Gaveikėnai Watermill was built around 1800. Today, it houses a café.

Key
═ Main road
═ Other road
— Railway
••• Trail
--- Water trail
■■■ Park boundary
△ Peak

For keys to symbols see back flap

WESTERN LITHUANIA

Isolated for centuries, the little towns and villages of Žemaitija, the local name for the low-lying land of Western Lithuania, have a mystical atmosphere. Rustic wooden farmsteads and settlements are nestled between knolls and marshes. Klaipėda and Šiauliai are charming cities with distinct surroundings characterized by tiny, hidden lanes with a surfeit of cafés and museums.

Žemaitija is the ancient heartland of Samogitia, a medieval pagan duchy that managed to repel the innumerable incursions of its hostile, mostly Christian neighbours. With stubborn determination the Samogitians fought off the crusaders for more than 250 years, before finally being absorbed into the Grand Duchy of Lithuania in 1422. It was the last corner of Europe to be converted to Christianity and age-old rituals dedicated to pagan deities continued in more isolated parts until the 20th century.

Klaipėda, the country's only seaport city, is an ideal base for embarking on day-trips into Western Lithuania. Although the port area was secretively closed off during the Soviet era, it has since reopened to cruise ship and ferry passengers. Originally known as Memel, Klaipėda was part of Prussia and Germany for over 500 years.

Some of the surviving Germanic-style half-timbered houses, once used by merchants, characterize the streets of the Old Town today.

A short ferry ride from Klaipėda lies the Curonian Spit, with its towering dunes and scenic villages like Nida. Inland, quaint little towns, such as Šilutė and Kretinga, are easily reachable and a delight to stroll around. The quiet village of Rusnė and the surrounding Nemunas Delta region attract many rare birds, which breed in their lush marshes. Žemaitija National Park, close to Lake Plateliai, conceals a former Soviet missile base. Cycle paths stretch all along the Lithuanian coast from Nida up to the Latvian border and pass the coastal resorts of Palanga and Šventoji, both offering beaches, spas and all-night bars and clubs.

Pretty wooden houses along a street in Nida, a village in the Curonian Spit National Park

◀ Boldly coloured weather vanes, Klaipėda

Exploring Western Lithuania

The northwest corner of Lithuania offers the twin attractions of Žemaitija National Park, with its Soviet-era missile base, and the memorable Orvidas Garden. The UNESCO-protected Curonian Spit, a long and narrow strip of land between the Baltic Sea and the Curonian Lagoon, is worth visiting for its towering dunes, charming fishing villages, cycle paths and beaches. Western Lithuania also gives an insight into the country's unique Catholic and pagan mysticism, which is keenly felt in small towns such as Tytuvėnai and Šiluva.

Sights at a Glance

Towns and Resorts

1 Šiauliai pp276–7
3 Šeduva
4 Tytuvėnai
5 Šiluva
6 Raseiniai
7 Raudonė
8 Panemunė
9 Jurbarkas
10 Telšiai
11 Mažeikiai
12 Plateliai
14 Plungė
16 Klaipėda pp284–5
17 Kretinga
18 Palanga
19 Smiltynė
21 Šilutė

Sights of Interest

2 Hill of Crosses
13 Orvidas Garden

National Parks

15 Žemaitija National Park pp282–3
20 Curonian Spit National Park pp288–9

Area of Natural Beauty

22 Nemunas Delta

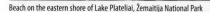

Beach on the eastern shore of Lake Plateliai, Žemaitija National Park

For hotels and restaurants see pp306–307 and pp330–31

Getting Around

The A1 motorway between Kaunas and Klaipėda is the fastest east–west route across the region. Buses serve the region well, and good bases from which to explore it are Palanga, Kaunas, Šiauliai and Klaipėda. Trains offer a less flexible means of transport, and even the Kaunas–Klaipėda line makes a detour via Šiauliai. The regional airport, at Palanga, provides international connections, most notably with the transit hubs of Copenhagen and Rīga.

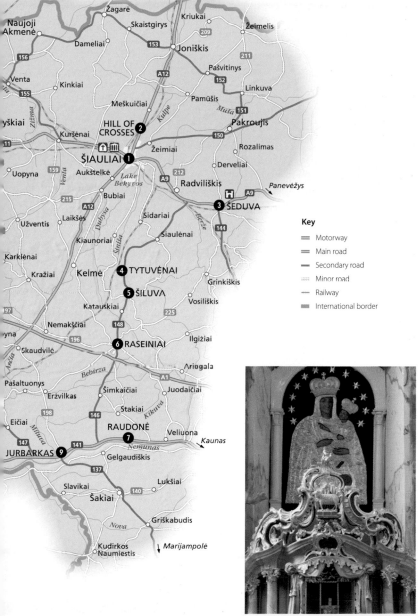

Key

- ▬ Motorway
- ▬ Main road
- ▬ Secondary road
- ┅ Minor road
- ─ Railway
- ▬ International border

Painting of the Madonna and Child, Tytuvėnai

For keys to symbols *see back flap*

❶ Šiauliai

Lithuania's fourth-biggest city, Šiauliai first appeared in historical sources in 1236, the date of the Battle of the Sun *(see p214)*. A major industrial centre since the 18th century, it saw its population rise from 6,200 in 1866 to 23,600 at the outbreak of World War I. The war destroyed more than 60 per cent of the city. Today, Šiauliai is enjoying a wave of development. New shopping centres are being built, pedestrianized streets laid and monuments renovated. The city's most attractive part, with traditional houses and museums, is the Old Town.

Old bicycle outside the Bicycle Museum, a part of the Aušra Museum

🏛 Aušra Museum

Aušra Avenue Palace: Aušros 47. **Tel** (41) 524 391. **Open** 9am–5pm Mon–Fri. Bicycle Museum: Vilniaus 139. **Tel** (41) 524 395. **Open** 10am–6pm Tue–Fri, Sat 11am–5pm. Chaim Frenkel Villa: Vilniaus 74. **Tel** (41) 524 389. **Open** 10am–6pm Tue–Fri, 11am–5pm Sat & Sun. Photography Museum: Vilniaus 140.

Tel (41) 524 395. **Open** 10am–6pm Wed–Fri, 11am–5pm Sat & Sun. 🗓 🎫 times vary. 🌐 **ausrosmuziejus.lt**

The Aušra Museum, founded in 1923, is the oldest museum in the city. It was named in honour of the first Lithuanian newspaper. The museum is a treasure trove of art and culture with a vast collection of historical, architectural and archaeological artifacts, spread over 11 locations. The history of the daily life of the townspeople of Šiauliai is the focus of **Aušra Avenue Palace**. A special section is dedicated to the repression of the Soviet post-war period.

The **Bicycle Museum** reveals the story of cycling in Lithuania, with almost 100 bicycles on display, including a child's tricycle from 1905. Replicas of historic bikes are also exhibited.

One of Lithuania's very few Art Nouveau buildings from the early 20th century, the **Chaim Frenkel Villa**, depicts Jewish daily life in centuries past.

The **Photography Museum**, housed in a reconstructed Art Deco-style building, covers the development of art and photography in the city, and holds contemporary exhibitions.

🏛 Cathedral of Sts Peter and Paul

Aušros Takas 3. **Tel** (41) 528 077. 🕐 7am, 7:30am, 5pm, 6pm Mon–Sat; 8am, 9:30am, 11am, 12:30pm, 6pm Sun.

A church has stood on this spot since 1445 and the precise location of the earlier wooden place of worship is marked by a metal cross. The old church was

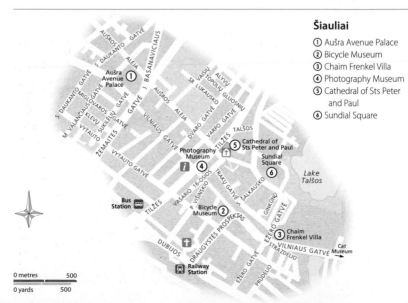

Šiauliai

① Aušra Avenue Palace
② Bicycle Museum
③ Chaim Frenkel Villa
④ Photography Museum
⑤ Cathedral of Sts Peter and Paul
⑥ Sundial Square

0 metres 500
0 yards 500

For keys to symbols *see back flap*

Prominent tower of the Cathedral of Sts Peter and Paul

burned down and in 1625, the existing one was built in stone to give it more permanence. Seen from afar, the cathedral's gleaming white 70-m (230-ft) tower makes the building look more modern than it actually is.

The cathedral is built in Renaissance style with some features typical of medieval architecture. Its thick walls are accompanied by details that appear to have been defensive but in fact were not. On the southern side of the cathedral is Lithuania's oldest sundial. Sts Peter and Paul Church was elevated to cathedral status in 1997.

Sundial Square
Ežero gatvė.

A sundial was erected in the square in 1986 to mark the 750th anniversary of the Battle of the Sun. The slender sundial, surmounted by a sculpture of a golden archer, towers over Lake Talšos.

Sundial Square is laid out like an amphitheatre and brings together three significant symbols of the city – the archer Šaulys, after whom, according to legend, the city was named; the sun, images of which can be found all over Šiauliai; and time, represented on the square by the numbers of the clock, 12, 3, and 6, which when brought together form the date of the battle.

Cat Museum
Žuvininkų 18. **Tel** 6836 9844.
Open 10am–5pm Tue–Sat.
With almost 10,000 exhibits, not just from Lithuania but

VISITORS' CHECKLIST

Practical Information
Road Map C4. 115,000.
Vilniaus gatvė 213, (41) 523 110. Saulės Žiedas Folk Festival (Jul), Šiauliai City Days (Sep). **tic.siauliai.lt**

Transport
Višinkio gatvė 44, S of Draugystės prospektas.
Tilžės gatvė 109.

across the world, from Austria to Zambia, this museum is a haven for catlovers. Established in May 1990, the museum has exhibits of cats in every conceivable pose cramming the display area. They have been crafted from porcelain, amber, marble, crystal, glass and other materials. There are cats in stained-glass windows, cats in artistic photographs, cats on postage stamps, in books and on cards. Interesting odes to cats have been collected in over 4,000 poems written in various languages. There are lamps with cats as ornamentation as well as furniture and a set of banisters with delightful feline designs.

Colourful wooden cats, Cat Museum

❷ Hill of Crosses
Kryžių kalnas

Jurgaičių village. Road: **Map** C4. from Šiauliai. **Tel** (41) 370 860.
kryziukalnas.lt

One of Lithuania's most awe-inspiring sights, this saddle-shaped knoll in a field filled with thousands of crosses, crucifixes and rosaries is an insight into the significance of Catholicism to Lithuania.

Crosses started appearing on the hill after the ruthless suppression of the 1831 uprising against Tsarist Russian rule. By the end of the 19th century, 150 large crosses stood here, 200 by 1914, and many more by the time the Soviets came to occupy Lithuania in 1940.

Seen by the atheist regime as an unnecessary religious symbol, the Hill of Crosses was hacked down in 1961, but the crosses reappeared soon after. It was bulldozed in 1973 and again in 1975, but the crosses kept appearing. Finally, the hill was left in peace. By the time Pope John Paul II visited it, in 1993, it had crosses and religious sculptures from all over the country and around the world.

Collection of crosses in all shapes and sizes at the Hill of Crosses

❸ Šeduva

Road Map C5. 🅰 3,000. 🚉 from Šiauliai, Panevėžys. 🚌 from Šiauliai, Panevėžys.

The little town of Šeduva is a composite of wooden houses preserved as a historic monument. One of its main sights is the twin-towered Church of the Holy Cross. Built in 1649, the church elegantly blends Renaissance and Baroque elements.

Šeduva's most delightful spot is the mid-19th-century estate of Prussian Baron Otto von Ropp, located 2 km (1 mile) east of town. Aside from the original redbrick buildings, which have given the estate the local name **Raudondvaris** (Red Manor), there is a school and a hotel, and the lakeside grounds are a pleasure to stroll through.

Environs

The grounds of **Burbiškis Manor**, 12 km (7 miles) east of Šeduva, are decorated with sculptures of lions, fauns and historical figures created in 1912 by sculptor Kazimieras Ulianskas. A dazzling display of tulips adorns the manor grounds in spring, when the Tulip Festival is celebrated.

🏠 **Burbiškis Manor**
Burbiškis village. **Tel** (422) 42 001. **Open** Apr–Oct: 9am–6pm Tue–Sun; Nov–Mar: 8am–5pm Tue–Sat. 🅿 🅰 Burbiškis Tulip Festival (mid-May).

Crucifix above the altar, Friary of the Blessed Virgin Mary, Tytuvėnai

❹ Tytuvėnai

Road Map C5. 🅰 3,000. 🚉 from Šiauliai. 🚌 from Šiauliai. 🌐 trp.lt

Once the site of a 13th-century hilltop fortress, Tytuvėnai became the secluded setting for a magnificent monastery and the church of the **Friary of the Blessed Virgin Mary** in the 1630s. The buildings were created for the Franciscans and set amid rolling hills and tranquil lakes. The courtyard of the monastery is decorated with faded frescoes, while a beautiful painting on the wooden sacristy door depicts the Resurrection.

The highlight of the church's colourful interior is an elaborate altar encircled by four Baroque figures of Franciscan saints. In the grounds, the Chapel of the Holy Stairs was modelled on the Scala Sancta (Holy Stairs) in Rome. Each of the steps, which pilgrims mounted on their knees, contains a sacred relic brought here from Jerusalem in the 1730s.

❺ Šiluva

Road Map C5. 🅰 800. 🚌 from Šiauliai. 🅰 Šilinės Pilgrimage (Sep).

Šiluva is one of Lithuania's great pilgrimage places. Legend has it that 400 years ago, the town was the site of a miraculous apparition of a weeping Virgin Mary holding the infant Jesus in her arms. In the late 16th century, as Šiluva became Calvinist, its last priest buried a bundle of Catholic documents and a miracle-working painting of the Virgin Mary in an iron box in the grounds of the ruined church.

In 1610, the Virgin Mary appeared, standing on a rock before children tending their herds. The box was later discovered by the rock and, as fame about the apparition grew, a wooden chapel was built close by. It was replaced in 1785 by the Church of the Nativity of the Blessed Virgin Mary. The painting of Mary, now embellished by a golden frame, was hung on the altar. The painting is concealed, except on feast days, by a 1920 painting

Bright evening view of the lakeside buildings at Raudondvaris, near Šeduva

Façade of the Neo-Gothic castle at the Raudonė estate, seen from across its lush grounds

of the Annunciation. On his visit in 1993, Pope John Paul II prayed at the church.

The obelisk-style structure of the Church of the Apparition of the Blessed Virgin Mary, which was completed in 1924, can be seen from afar.

Raseiniai's attractive main square, featuring the *Independence Statue*

❻ Raseiniai

Road Map C5. 🏠 37,000. 🚌 from Kaunas.

An important Samogitian town, Raseiniai played a crucial role in the region's history. In 1941, the town witnessed a fierce four-day battle between hundreds of German and Soviet tanks. By the end of World War II, 90 per cent of Raseiniai had been destroyed. Miraculously, the

hilltop Church of the Ascension, built in 1729, survived the war, as did the *Independence Statue* in the town's main square. Created by Vincas Grybas (1890–1941) in 1934, the statue shows a man in a flowing cloak and bast shoes, together with a bear he has tamed. The bear is a symbol of Samogitia, the independent duchy that fought the Teutonic Order in the 13th century, but it was later ceded to the Grand Duchy of Lithuania.

❼ Raudonė

Road Map C5. **Tel** (447) 45 445. **Open** Jun–Aug: 10am–4pm daily. 🏛

Originally a 16th-century family estate owned by Prussian timber merchants, the castle at Raudonė was acquired in 1810 by Platon Zubov, once a favourite consort of Catherine the Great. Catherine had played an important role in obtaining much of the Polish-Lithuanian Commonwealth during the partitions *(see p215)*. After her death, the count lived in seclusion at Rundāle Palace *(see pp172–3)* in Courland.

The count's daughter gave the family castle in Raudonė its current Neo-Gothic appearance and its tall and slender fairytale tower. Destroyed by the retreating Germans at the end of World War II, the tower was rebuilt in 1968 and today offers a panoramic view of the Nemunas Valley.

Environs
Veliuona, a village 10 km (6 miles) east of Raudonė, is known for its secluded fort-hill where Gediminas *(see p216)* was reputedly slain.

❾ Panemunė

Road Map C5. 🚌 from Kaunas.

Situated on the banks of the Nemunas river, Panemunė boasts a castle with two tall circular towers and red-tiled rooftops. Most of the building was erected by a family of Hungarian nobles during the reign of Stefan Bathory, the Transylvanian prince who ruled the Polish-Lithuanian Commonwealth between 1575 and 1586. Two centuries later, the castle was bought by the Polish-Lithuanian Gelgaudas family. The Tsarist authorities seized it after Antanas Gelgaudas led the 1831 uprising *(see p218)*. Today, the castle belongs to the Vilnius Academy of Art.

One of the castle's tall circular towers in Panemunė

9 Jurbarkas

Road Map C5. 🏔 29,000. 🚌 from Kaunas. ℹ️ Vydūno 19, (447) 51 485. 🌐 jurbarkotic.lt

The ancient **Karšuva Forest**, about 3 km (2 miles) west of the tiny industrial town of Jurbarkas, was the site of one of the earliest fortresses built by the crusaders on the Nemunas river, in 1259. The pagan Lithuanians erected their own castle above the Imsrė river, a tributary of the Nemunas, and both sides fought bitter battles for the next 150 years. Although nothing remains of the castles, the forest can be explored. One of Lithuania's largest and most secluded forests, the 427-sq-km (165-sq-mile) stretch has enchanting trails leading through its towering pines.

Environs
In **Gelgaudiškis**, 10 km (6 miles) east of Jurbarkas, lie the ruins of the 19th-century manor of the Gelgaudas family, the Polish-Lithuanian ancestors of actor Sir John Gielgud. The manor boasted a lavish interior with paintings, silver, crystal, bronze and porcelain works until it was ransacked during World War II. Today, the manor hosts village festivals and music evenings in its grounds.

   Mount Rambynas, 60 km (37 miles) west of Jurbarkas, is a 46-m (50-yard) escarpment, and a mystical location for Lithuanians. A pagan altar that once stood here was used for rituals up until the 19th century. Today, the hill offers views over Kaliningrad.

Embellished interior of the Cathedral of St Anthony of Padua, Telšiai

10 Telšiai

Road Map C4. 🏔 47,000. 🚊 from Vilnius, Šiauliai, Klaipėda. 🚌 from Vilnius, Šiauliai, Klaipėda. ℹ️ Turgaus 21, (444) 53 010. 🌐 telsiaitic.lt

According to legend, Telšiai was founded by a knight named Džiugas on a hill above Lake Mastis. In 1765, the Franciscans built a church here, which became the **Cathedral of St Anthony of Padua**, after Telšiai was made a diocese in 1926. The second-floor gallery has its own altar and paintings framed by Corinthian columns. These include an altar painting of St Anthony and Infant Jesus, embellished with faux gold and held aloft by angels garbed in pink and green.

Environs
One of the worst massacres by the Soviets took place in the forests near **Rainiai**, 4 km (2 miles) southeast of Telšiai.

The terrible event took place on the nights of 24 and 25 June 1941, shortly after Nazi Germany invaded the then Soviet Union. Today, a granite cross marks the spot and the **Rainiai Chapel of Suffering**, consecrated in 1991, stands nearby. Just 30 km (19 miles) southeast of Telšiai, **Šatrija Hill** offers splendid views of the Žemaitija landscape. **Lake Lūkstas**, 40 km (25 miles) south of Telšiai, has beaches that liven up in July during the Blues Night festival.

11 Mažeikiai

Road Map C4. 🏔 57,000. 🚊 from Šiauliai. 🚌 from Šiauliai. ℹ️ Ventos 8a, (443) 67 177. 🌐 mazeikiutvic.lt

A minor village in the mid-19th century, Mažeikiai rapidly grew into Lithuania's eighth-largest city by the end of the 20th century. The Vilnius–Liepāja railway, which reached Mažeikiai in 1869, was responsible for its initial growth; it is also home to the Baltics' only oil refinery.

   The **Mažeikiai Museum** has displays on the town's development and regional folklore, and paintings by Alfonsas Dargis (1909–96), a Lithuanian artist who joined the New York Modernist movement.

Environs
The 4,000-ha (9,884-acre) **Kamanos State Reserve**, 20 km (12 miles) east of Mažeikiai, protects one of the region's most valuable clayfields. Richly diverse in flora and fauna, the reserve has an area of marshland as well as lakes and tiny islands.

   In **Viekšniai**, a small town 15 km (9 miles) southeast of Mažeikiai, the **Pharmacy Museum** is considered miraculous, having survived two fires that devastated the town.

🏛 **Mažeikiai Museum**
V Kudirkos 6. **Tel** (443) 26 037. **Open** 8am–5pm Mon–Thu (until 3:45 Fri). 🐾

🍃 **Kamanos State Reserve**
Tel (425) 59 285. 🐾 📷

🏛 **Pharmacy Museum**
Tilto 3. **Tel** (443) 37 420. **Open** 9am–4pm Tue–Sat. 🐾

Rainiai Chapel of Suffering, commemorating the massacre in 1941

Boats on the eastern shore of Lake Plateliai, bordering Plateliai village

⓬ Plateliai

Road Map B4. 🏔 1,000. 🚌 from Plungė. ℹ️ Didžioji 8, (448) 49 231. 🎭 Shrove Tuesday Carnival (Feb/Mar).

The administrative centre of Žemaitija National Park *(see pp282–3)*, Plateliai is a sleepy lakeside village. It has the wooden Church of Sts Peter and Paul (1744) and a park that was the grounds of a manor. The Witch's Ash, Lithuania's biggest ash tree, which stands in the park, has many legends attached to it. One involves a baker who threw a loaf of bread at a witch sitting on its branches. The loaf is still visible – the knobbly bit where the branches divide.

Across the road on Didžioji Street, elaborate Shrovetide masks are displayed in the manor barn. These are worn during the Shrove Tuesday Carnival. The most popular sight is **Castle Island**, which takes its name from a fortress that stood on the nearest island of Pilies.

⓭ Orvidas Garden

Orvidų sodyba-muziejus

Road Map B4. **Tel** (613) 28 624. **Open** June: 10am–7pm Tue–Sun, July–May: 10am–7pm Wed–Sun. 🅿️

The creative work of local mystic and genius Vilius Orvidas (1952–92), this garden is one of Eastern Europe's most bizarre sights. Eclectic and enormous, it is a complex network of crosses and tombstones, boulders and treetrunks, sculptures of odd

creatures, carvings and rock paintings of pagan and religious imagery, painted missile shells and a disused Soviet tank. Hidden gardens appear out of nowhere and there is no set path, adding to the maze-like feel. The dark caverns conceal further oddities, and a pondside hut hidden among trees is reputedly the home of pixies and gnomes.

⓮ Plungė

Road Map C5. 🏔 39,000. 🚆 from Šiauliai, Klaipėda. 🚌 from Šiauliai, Klaipėda. ℹ️ Dariaus ir Gireno 27, (448) 55 108. 🌐 **plunge.lt**

The town of Plungė is the main gateway to Žemaitija National Park *(see pp282–3)*. One of Lithuania's most opulent manors, the well-preserved **Plungė Manor** was built by Mykolas Oginskis, a descendant of a family of Lithuanian nobles. It includes 16 sculptures of

Samogitian figures and a park featuring the Thunder Oak tree, now a natural monument. The manor also houses the **Samogitian Art Museum**, which displays works by Western Lithuanian artists.

Environs
About 2,236 of Plungė's jews died in the Holocaust. Much of the killing took place in **Kaušėnai**, a village 4 km (2 miles) west of town. Here, a series of moving wooden sculptures have been carved by Jacob Bunka (b.1922), chairman of Plungė's 13-member Jewish community.

Gandinga Hill, 5 km (3 miles) southwest of Plungė, offers a panoramic view of the Žemaitija forests. A fortress, Gandinga, once stood here, built as a defence against the Teutonic Knights. Pagan burial grounds dating from the 9th century have been discovered nearby.

Another remarkable outdoor museum is the **Museum of Unique Rocks** in Mosėdis, 40 km (25 miles) northwest of Plungė. Exhibits range from a display of fossils and rock fragments inside a restored watermill to a park full of mossy boulders and crude stone sculptures. The museum was founded in 1979 by Dr Vaclovas Intas.

🏛 **Samogitian Art Museum**
Parko 1. **Tel** (448) 52 492.
Open 10am–5pm Tue–Sat. 🅿️ 📷

🏛 **Museum of Unique Rocks**
Salantų 2. **Tel** (440) 76 291. **Open** 8am–6pm (10am–6pm Sat & Sun). **Closed** Nov–Apr: Sat & Sun. 🅿️ 📷

Plungė Manor, seen across a lake, with a sculpture in the foreground

⓯ Žemaitija National Park

Shrouded in folklore and legend, the Žemaitija region was the last stretch of Europe to accept Christianity. Pagan gods were worshipped here till the 19th century, and carvings and crosses in the villages still blend Catholic and pagan imagery. Established in 1991, the Žemaitija National Park spreads across 220 sq km (85 sq miles), with its headquarters and information centre in the town of Plateliai. There are several hiking trails that meander around Lake Plateliai through isolated stretches of forest. Campsites and rural farmsteads cater to tourists.

Key

══ Minor road

••• Hiking trail

••• Park boundary

★ Mikytai Hill and Devil's Footprint Stone

The forest-covered "sacred hill" of Mikytai is believed by local people to be haunted. On the hill's northern slope, the Devil's Footprint Stone was once used for pagan sacrifices.

Church of St Stanislav in Beržoras

This church (1746) is made of spruce logs. Its Chapels of the Cross were destroyed by the Soviets but restored in 2001.

KEY

① **Godeliai** has a rare collection of obscure paintings and crucifixes in its Museum of Folk Art.

② **Plateliai** serves as the park's main service and information centre.

Mill-Gallery

A stone watermill, converted into a folk art gallery, stands in the riverside village of Babrungėnai, once famed for its beaver hunters.

★ Žemaičių Kalvarija
Churches and white Chapels of the Cross give this town a spiritual atmosphere. The Church Festival, held in July each year, is its main attraction.

VISITORS' CHECKLIST

Practical Information
Road Map C4. ℹ Didžioji 8, Plateliai, (448) 49 231; to book, 86778 6576. 🅰
🅦 **zemaitijosnp.lt**
Mill-Gallery: **Open** 9am–6pm daily. Plokštinė Former Soviet Missile Base: 📷 book at the park's information centre.

Transport
🚌 from Plungė to Žemaičių Kalvarija.

Mound of Šarnelė
Excavations on this hill, in Šarnelė village, have revealed that it was a small fortified town in the third century BC.

★ Plokštinė Former Soviet Missile Base
Between 1962 and 1978, this secret Soviet rocket site, with its now rusty and overgrown silos, aimed missiles at cities in Western Europe.

Yacht moored along the shore of Lake Plateliai

Folk Legends of Lake Plateliai

Lake Plateliai had tremendous significance to the pagans of the historical regions of Samogitia and Žemaitija. Drownings occasionally occur here and according to one of the many legends associated with the lake, a great white horse lives in the water and takes the life of at least one swimmer every year. The water level has risen in recent times and archaeologists diving in the lake have excavated standing stones with pagan symbols under the surface. To this day, Plateliai, on the lake's western shore, celebrates many colourful traditional Samogitian festivals.

For keys to symbols *see back flap*

⑯ Klaipėda

First mentioned in 1252, when the Christian Livonian Order built a fortress named Memelburg at the mouth of the Danė river, Klaipėda for many centuries was an important Prussian port city called Memel. Today, as Lithuania's only sea port, Klaipėda is thriving, despite serious damage during World War II and its status as a military-industrial centre during the Soviet years. For those who enjoy walking, central Klaipėda and its Old Town, with narrow, criss-crossing streets, is a delightful place to explore. Half-timbered buildings and cobbled lanes conceal gift shops, galleries and café-bars.

Visitors and local people relaxing in cafés in Klaipėda

Ännchen of Tharau

Teatro aikštė.

The heart of Klaipėda's Old Town is **Theatre Square**. A statue called *Ännchen of Tharau*, which stands in front of the theatre, is the focal point of the fountain dedicated to Simon Dach (1605–59), one of the city's distinguished personalities. Born in Klaipėda, then known as Memel, Dach became a leading Prussian poet from the late 1630s until his death. He is well known throughout Germany for his songs, hymns and dialect poems, such as *Ännchen of Tharau*, written in 1637.

The original statue was created in 1912, but it mysteriously vanished on the eve of World War II. Adolf Hitler made a speech from the theatre balcony behind its original location, on 23 March 1939. In 1989, a replica of

Statue of Ännchen of Tharau in Theatre Square

the original *Ännchen of Tharau* statue, made by local artists, was placed in the middle of the fountain.

🏛 Castle Museum

Pilies 4. **Tel** (46) 410 527. **Open** 10am–5pm Tue–Sat (to 4pm Fri). 🐾

Not much remains of the 17th-century castle that houses the Castle Museum. The castle was built on the foundations of the 1252 fortress when Memel was part of the Duchy of Prussia. In 2002, an exhibition opened inside one of the ramparts, illustrating the development of the fortress and the city. The exhibits on display include authentic furniture and re-created models. The highlight is a Renaissance-era gold ring encrusted with diamonds. Today, this castle has become one of the most recognized symbols associated with modern Klaipėda.

🏛 Lithuania Minor History Museum

Didžioji vandens 6. **Tel** (46) 410 524. **Open** 10am–5pm Tue–Sat (to 4pm Fri). 🐾

Lithuania Minor is what the local people call East Prussia, which today is the territory of Kaliningrad as well as Klaipėda. The Lithuania Minor History Museum, inside one of the Old Town's loveliest buildings, tells the region's history. Coins, clothes, maps, postcards, old photographs and models give a glimpse of the lives and the differences between the local German- and Lithuanian-speaking communities before World War II. Situated opposite the museum is the town's old post office.

🏛 Blacksmiths' Museum

Šaltkalvių 2a. **Tel** (46) 410 526. **Open** 10am–5pm Tue–Sat (to 4pm Fri). 🐾 📷

Black metal crosses, fences and cemetery gates in a garden beside an old working smithy are among this museum's exhibits. Some of the crosses were rescued from destruction when the Sculpture Park replaced the city's main cemetery in the 1970s. Lithuania's cross-crafting tradition, in metal and in wood, was recognized by UNESCO in 2001.

Old wooden clock inside the exceptional Clock Museum

🏛 Clock Museum

Liepų 12. **Tel** (46) 410 414; 410 413 (excursions). **Open** noon–6pm Tue–Sat, noon–5pm Sun. 🐾 📷

A fascinating insight into the development of man's attempts to measure time, from sundials to atomic clocks, is the focus of this unique museum. The Clock Museum was opened in 1984 inside a villa built in 1820 by John Simpson, an English merchant. Reconstructions of ancient calendars, sun, fire, water and sand clocks, and timepieces showing the changes in the faces and mechanisms of clocks from Renaissance times form the bulk of the exhibits.

The pleasant courtyard, featuring a large sundial, is a popular venue for music, dance and poetry evenings. The house next door was built by another English merchant and industrialist, Mae Lean. In 1905, it was reconstructed in the Art Nouveau style. The Neo-Gothic post office close by is another striking building in the neighbourhood.

▥ Picture Gallery and Sculpture Park
Liepų 33. **Tel** (46) 410 412.
Open noon–6pm Tue–Sat, noon–5pm Sun. ♿

The city's main state-run art gallery is named after Pranas Domšaitis (1880–1965), a Lithuanian artist who was born near Königsberg and settled in South Africa in 1949. Heavily influenced by the Norwegian Symbolist painter Edvard Munch (1863–1944), Domšaitis won recognition for his art in inter-war Germany and later in South Africa. The gallery exhibits 20th-century Lithuanian art as well as a permanent exhibition of works by Domšaitis.

Dedicated to the author of the first Lithuanian book, Martynas Mažvydas (1510–63), the Sculpture Park is situated behind the gallery. Until the 1970s it was the site reserved for the city's cemetery. It covers almost 10 ha (25 acres) and is scattered mainly with abstract

and intriguing sculptures by various artists. New works are added to the park each year.

Unique creations laid out in the Sculpture Park

Klaipėda

① Ännchen of Tharau
② Castle Museum
③ Lithuania Minor History Museum
④ Blacksmiths' Museum
⑤ Clock Museum
⑥ Picture Gallery and Sculpture Park

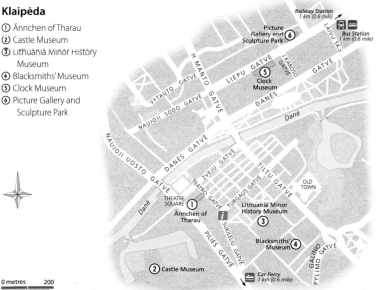

Railway Station 1 km (0.6 mile)
Picture Gallery and Sculpture Park ⑥
Bus Station 1 km (0.6 mile)

H MANTO GATVĖ
VYTAUTO GATVĖ
LIEPU GATVĖ
J KAROSO GATVĖ
GATVĖ
⑤ Clock Museum
DANĖS
NAUJOJI SODO GATVĖ
Danė

NAUJOJI UOSTO GATVĖ
DANĖS GATVĖ
ŽVEJU GATVĖ
TILTU GATVĖ
OLD TOWN
Danė
TEATRO GATVĖ
TURGAUS GATVĖ
THEATRE SQUARE
① Ännchen of Tharau
ℹ️
Lithuania Minor History Museum ③
SUKILĖLIU GATVĖ
Blacksmiths' Museum ④
PILIES GATVĖ
GALINIO PYLIMO GATVĖ
② Castle Museum
Car Ferry 1 km (0.6 mile)

0 metres 200
0 yards 200

⑰ Kretinga

Road Map B5. 🔢 41,000.
🚆 from Klaipėda. 🚌 from Klaipėda.

This pretty town is based around a 17th-century Franciscan monastery, a manor house, now the **Kretinga Museum**, and gardens that stretch alongside a stream and open up into a park. The Franciscans played a major role in developing the town, particularly in independent inter-war Lithuania when they opened a college specializing in agriculture and beekeeping. They also arranged a Lourdes-style grotto in the park with an image of the Virgin Mary.

One of the highlights of the Kretinga Museum is the Winter Garden, originally built when Count Josef Tyszkiewicz reconstructed the manor in 1875. Destroyed during World War II, these gardens were re-created in 1987 and today house around 600 plants. Other museum exhibits include furniture and paintings rescued from the Tyszkiewicz mansions in Kretinga and Palanga, iron crosses that are a blend of Catholic and pagan imagery and Curonian clothing and jewellery. The Church of the Annunciation has a towering steeple and an ornate interior with 17th-century paintings.

🏛 Kretinga Museum
Vilniaus 20. **Tel** (445) 77 323.
Open 10am–6pm Wed–Sun. 🐾 🎫
📱 📷 🌐 **kretingosmuziejus.lt**

Locals and visitors enjoying the sandy beach in Palanga

⑱ Palanga

Road Map B5. 🔢 16,000. ✈ 5 km (3 miles) N of town. 🚆 from Klaipėda. 🚌 from Klaipėda. 🛈 Kretingos 1, (460) 48 811. 🎉 Summer Feast (Jun). 🌐 **palangatic.lt**

The coastal town of Palanga, first mentioned in a 13th-century land partition pact between the Teutonic Order and the Livonians, became a permanent part of Lithuania in 1435. Today, it is a popular beach resort, with its dune-and-pine-bordered sands stretching 18 km (11 miles). It also has boulevards crammed with restaurants, clubs and bars, giving it a carnival-like atmosphere. The pier, first built in 1882, is a popular spot to watch the sunset.

A Neo-Renaissance palace was built in the 1890s by the Tyszkiewicz family, with grounds created by the French landscape architect Edouard André (1840–1911). Since 1963, the palace has housed the **Amber Museum**, which exhibits 4,500 pieces, including some unusual ones such as amber with trapped prehistoric insects and plants. At the far end of the palace's grounds is **Birutės Hill**, said to be where the future wife of Grand Duke Kęstutis tended a pagan sacred fire before he wed her. Close by is one of Lithuania's best-known sculptures, *Eglė, Queen of the Grassy Snakes* (1960), inspired by a fairytale.

Environs
The quiet fishing village of **Šventoji**, 15 km (9 miles) north of Palanga, is blessed with windswept dunes. It was a thriving port in the 16th and 17th centuries. An attraction here is *Fisherman's Daughters* (1982), a statue of three girls dancing on the dunes.

🏛 Amber Museum
Vytauto 17. **Tel** (460) 51 319.
Open Jun–Aug: 10am–8pm Tue–Sat, 11am–7pm Sun; Sep–May: 11am–5pm Tue–Sat, 11am–4pm Sun. 🐾 🎫
🌐 **pgm.lt**

⑲ Smiltynė

Road Map B5. 🔢 100.
🚢 from Klaipėda.

Officially part of Klaipėda city (*see pp284–5*), Smiltynė is the northernmost settlement on the Curonian Spit, directly facing Klaipėda's busy port. In earlier times, the spit was the main land route used by dispatch riders, postmen and the military, between the Prussian cities of Königsberg and Memel, modern Kaliningrad and Klaipėda respectively. However, the final ferry trip was disrupted by storms or trapped ice. In 1525, an inn was established in Sandkrug (Sand Inn), as Smiltynė became known.

A string of elegant villas line the water's edge. The town's star attraction, however, is the **Sea Museum**. It is located in Kopgalis Fortress, a sea bastion built by Prussia in 1865.

Tropical conservatory in Kretinga Museum's Winter Garden, Kretinga

Dolphins performing with trainers before an enthralled audience at the Sea Museum in Smiltynė

The main highlights are the regular dolphin and sea lion shows. Permits must be purchased for photography.

🏛 Sea Museum
Smiltynės 3. **Tel** (46) 492 250.
Open Oct–Apr: 10:30am–5pm Tue–Sun; May–Sep: 10:30am–6pm Tue–Sun (Jun–Aug: to 6:30pm). 🔲 🔲 🔲
🔲 **W** muziejus.lt

⑳ Curonian Spit National Park

See pp288–9.

㉑ Šilutė

Road Map B5. 🔝 21,500.
🚆 from Klaipėda. 🚌 from Klaipėda.
ℹ Lietuvininkų 4, Parko 2, (441) 77 785. **W** siluteinfo.lt

Originally the site of an inn for travellers riding between Klaipėda and Kaliningrad, Šilutė became a part of the German Empire in 1871. It was seized by Lithuania in 1923, but annexed by Nazi Germany 15 years later.
German influence is still visible in the low, red-tiled roofs of the public buildings. On tree-lined Lietuvininkų Street, the tiny **Šilutė Museum** displays 18th-century furniture and folk-themed exhibits. The Evangelical Lutheran Church, built in 1926, is decorated with startlingly colourful murals of biblical scenes.

Environs
Just 3 km (2 miles) northeast of Šilutė, **Macikai** was used as a German prisoner-of-war camp from 1939, then a Soviet camp for German troops after 1944, and was an official unit of the Gulag from 1948 to 1955. Today, it comprises the **Macikai Concentration Camp Museum** and a grave site.

🏛 Šilutė Museum
Lietuvininkų 36. **Tel** (441) 62 207.
Open 10am–5pm Tue–Sat. 🔲 🔲

🏛 Macikai Concentration Camp Museum
Macikai. **Tel** (441) 62 207.
Open mid-May–Oct: 11am–3pm Tue–Sat. 🔲

㉒ Nemunas Delta

Road Map B5. 🔝 1,700.
🚌 from Šilutė. **W** nemundodelta.lt

The low-lying delta of the Nemunas, Lithuania's largest river as it streams into the Curonian Lagoon, has great potential for outdoor activities. The wetlands, protected as a regional park, are a popular spot for angling and bird-watching. Every spring, when the snow and ice melt, 20 per cent of the delta gets flooded, attracting 200 species of birds to breed, while hundreds of other species migrate through the area every year. A bird ringing station at **Ventė** is one of the oldest in Europe, dating from 1929.
The floods annually threaten to cut off **Rusnė**, located 11 km (7 miles) southeast of Ventė. A Lutheran church, built from 1809 to 1827, is a sign of Rusnė's East Prussian background. It was changed into a sports hall in the Soviet period, but reverted to receiving congregations in 1994. An ethnographic farmstead gives a snapshot of past life in the delta region.
Almost 8 km (5 miles) northwest from Rusnė is the village of **Minija**, situated where the Minija river meets the Nemunas Delta. The river serves as the main thoroughfare in the village. Protected as architectural monuments, 19th-century wooden houses stand on both riverbanks.

The Nemunas Delta countryside, near Šilutė

⑳ Curonian Spit National Park

A narrow 98-km (61-mile) strip of land on the Baltic Coast, the Curonian Spit (Kuršių nerija) was formed 5,000 years ago. Its landscape consists largely of pine forests, dunes and sandy beaches. The park's forests are rich in wildlife such as roe deer, elk, foxes and wild boars. The dunes that tower over the village of Nida fall like cliffs into the Curonian Lagoon and villages have been buried beneath the shifting sands. The Curonian Spit National Park was created in 1991 to preserve the dunes, lagoons and surrounding area. The national park, which covers most of the spit, has been a UNESCO World Heritage Site since 2000.

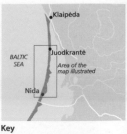

Key

▢ Curonian Spit National Park

★ **Nida**

The highly characteristic red-and-blue fishermen's cottages in Nida have remained unchanged for centuries. Some ancient weatherbeaten fishing boats lie in the gardens outside the cottages.

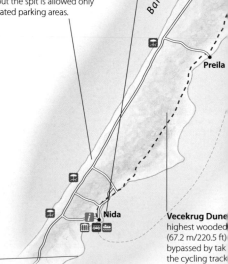

Baltic Beach

The entire length of the spit on the side of the Baltic Sea is one long sandy beach. Areas adjacent to the villages are popular in summer, but other parts are little visited. Parking throughout the spit is allowed only at designated parking areas.

Preila

★ **Parnidis Dune**

Looming 52 m (171 ft) above Nida, Parnidis (Great) Dune offers stunning views and is one of the highest points on the spit. A sundial was erected here in 1995.

Nida

Vecekrug Dune
highest wooded
(67.2 m/220.5 ft)
bypassed by tak
the cycling track

★ **Hill of Witches**
Comically demonic wooden statues, such as this ghoulish figure, lurk alongside a path through the pine forest behind Juodkrantė. The statues were set up by a group of local sculptors in the 1980s.

Juodkrante

Dead Dunes
These once-shifting dunes are now held in place with vegetation and offer a sanctuary to birds, animals and plants. Paths stretch from Avikalnio Dune in the north to Agilo Dune in the south.

alka

Forest Trails
It is possible to walk or cycle the entire length of the spit. The path, indicated by the dotted red line on the map, takes visitors past isolated stretches of sandy beach.

0 km   2
0 miles   2

VISITORS' CHECKLIST

Practical Information
Road Map B5. ℹ Taikos 4, Nida, (469) 52 345. Bike rentals can be arranged at the centre. 🚲 ⓦ **visitneringa.com** or ⓦ **nerija.lt**

Transport
🚌 Naglių 18e, Nida, (469) 52 859. ⚓ Naglių 14, Nida, (469) 51 101. Several operators offer cruises in vessels, including a replica kurėnas. Local trips, as well as excursions across the lagoon or along the shoreline to the Dead Dunes, are available.

Shifting Dunes

In the 17th century, when the forests on the Curonian Spit were cut down to fuel industry and supply constant military campaigns, the mountainous dunes were released. In the Baltic winds, the sand started to shift up to 20 m (66 ft) a year in places, burying entire villages. It was not until the 19th century, when a vast number of trees were planted to reforest the area, that the moving dunes were stopped.

Parnidis Dune, seen from the harbour at Nida

Key

═══ Main road

••• Trail

–– Ferry route

TRAVELLERS' NEEDS

WHERE TO STAY

The Baltic States offer every form of accommodation, from luxury hotels and city-centre hostels to rural guesthouses and lakeside spa complexes. Although there is an abundance of good-quality mid-range and budget stay options in the three capital cities of Tallinn, Rīga and Vilnius, it is still advisable to book in advance during late spring, summer and early autumn. In smaller towns and the countryside, it is very easy to find a place to stay for the night. Booking is straightforward as even the smallest guesthouses have their own website and are advertised through several other sources as well. The recommended options on pages 296–307 will help you get your hotel search started.

The thatched guesthouse at Toomalõuka Tourist Farm, Saaremaa Island, Estonia *(see p298)*

Booking

Reservations can be made by telephone, email, through hotel websites, and via online reservation sites such as booking.com. For more out-of-the-way locations, there are specialist tour operators as well as websites run by local tourist authorities and associations of hotel business owners. Local tourist information offices can also book rooms, and can be helpful if upon arrival you find most hotels are booked up.

Prices and Payment

It is advisable to confirm acceptable modes of payment prior to arriving, especially for rural areas, although all major hotels accept the principal credit cards for payment. Visitors should be aware of what is included in the advertised rate. Many hotels include breakfast and the use of amenities such as a fitness centre, while other facilities, including saunas, can cost extra.

Pricing structures vary considerably from country to country and from hotel to hotel, but across many types of hotel there are significant discounts during the off-season months. It is also worth keeping an eye out for special offers and discounts, or package deals.

Tipping

Generally, it is not customary to tip taxi drivers, bar staff and porters in the Baltic States. As a rule of thumb though, tip those who provide you with especially good service.

Luxury Hotels

Tallinn, Rīga and Vilnius have a large range of luxury hotels, some of which attract heads of state and other VIPs. Often these hotels are in historic buildings that have been converted to provide state-of-the-art facilities while retaining their original features. There are also several superb hotels that are run by the big international hotel groups, such as the Radisson Blu Astorija Hotel in Vilnius *(see p305)* and Europa Royale Rīga *(see p300)*.

Even in the swankiest hotels in the Baltic States, swimming pools remain something of a rarity, although fitness centres, spas and saunas are common, as is high-quality cuisine and Wi-Fi access (although an extra charge is sometimes levied).

Modern Hotels

Affordable, good-quality accommodation is readily available throughout Estonia, Latvia and Lithuania. There is a wide choice of modern hotel accommodation in the mid-price range in all areas within the three Baltic States.

Most of the larger towns and cities provide a variety of modern hotels, although only a handful are located in the Old Town areas of Tallinn, Rīga and Vilnius. Most of the hotels can be found either downtown or in slightly more peripheral locations. The quality of modern hotels can vary considerably so it is always sensible to do some research prior to booking, such as checking the website and some independent guest reviews.

Corner entrance of the Kolonna Hotel, Rēzekne, Latvia *(see p303)*

Pädaste Manor, housed in a 16th-century farmhouse on Muhu Island, Estonia *(see p297)*

Apartments and Private Homes

Apartment rental is an excellent accommodation option that is comparatively under-used in the Baltic States. Several agencies in the capital cities offer this service – **Erel Apartments & Residences** and **Goodson & Red Apartments** in Tallinn, **Lilija Plus Real Estate Agency** in Rīga and **Eldorado Apartments** and **Eugenijus Apartments** in Vilnius. Also available in some other major cities, apartments can be opulent or spartan, but in general most are of a high standard. Most agency-managed apartments are in central locations. Rates are usually very competitive and the apartments often provide better facilities than those offered at a hotel in the same price range. Numerous properties are also listed on vacation rental sites such as **Airbnb**.

Guesthouses

In major cities, guesthouses are small, moderately priced hotels, sometimes family-run, of eight to twenty rooms. They can be convenient places to stay, with many right in the old centres, and often in older buildings with a little character.

In rural areas, guesthouses can be the best form of lodging, offering cosy, clean accommodation at very reasonable rates. Most rural guesthouses tend to be built close to a family home, so a personal touch is assured. Aesthetically, they are loosely

modelled on rustic-style timber buildings and have become an integral part of the Baltic countryside. They invariably offer a range of activities for guests, such as swimming, sports and saunas, and the owners can sometimes arrange guided tours of local sights. Meals are usually optional, but a hearty, home-made breakfast or dinner costs less than similar fare in a local restaurant.

The choice of rural guesthouses is enormous throughout the Baltic States and their availability extends to the most remote areas of each country. Bookings can be made through their websites or via the rural tourism association – **Estonian Rural Tourism** in Estonia, **Baltic Country Holidays** in Latvia and **Countryside Tourism Association** in Lithuania.

Rural tourism has become such a popular sector in the

Baltic States that many of these guesthouses are booked out all through the summer. It is advisable to make a reservation well in advance.

Hostels

The first accommodation choice for young travellers on a tight budget, hostels were once few and far between in the Baltic States. With the growth in tourism, even at the budget end, backpackers and other travellers looking for sociable and affordable accommodation are now well served throughout the three countries.

Most hostels are of a decent standard and have beds in communal dormitories for reasonable rates, as well as a small selection of private rooms, offered for considerably less than the average hotel rate. Hostels also offer a range of amenities, including at least Internet access, kitchen facilities and a common room, and extending to licensed bars, sightseeing tours and, in the case of the Red Emperor in Tallinn *(see p296)*, live music and a skateboard ramp.

Many hostels are privately run and you'll find some of these listed on pages 296–307. Others are affiliated with the worldwide network of youth hostel associations, **Hostelling International**. Membership is required to stay at one of these hostels, but joining is cheap and can be done while booking.

Understated suite in Rīga's stylish Neiburgs Hotel *(see p301)*

Swimming pool at Vanagupe hotel at the beach resort of Palanga, Lithuania *(see p307)*

Campsites

Camping is an extremely popular summer activity in Estonia, Latvia and Lithuania. As a result, there are a number of campsites scattered throughout each of the Baltic countries. These are usually very cheap and offer basic amenities such as communal showers and an on-site pub-style restaurant. However, not all camps are equipped with washing facilities and toilet blocks. National parks have official camping spots, which are free of charge. Many commercial campsites also offer basic cabin accommodation, sometimes with kitchen facilities.

In general, there is a very relaxed attitude towards camping in the Baltic States and people often camp alongside beaches and lakes and in forests at improvised campsites. Many guesthouses allow campers to pitch a tent in their grounds for a nominal fee. For camping on private property, however, it is imperative to obtain permission from the owner beforehand.

A full list of campsites can be found on national tourism websites *(see p365)* and rural tourism websites. In Estonia, **RMK** is an efficient organization that arranges camping.

Hidden Extras

Most decent hotels in cities throughout the three Baltic States operate in a transparent manner and will not add any hidden extras to the bill. However, it is worth checking the cost of drinks from the minibar and calls made from the hotel room telephone, before using either of these services – the price is often exorbitant. In smaller hotels, it is a good idea to find out if breakfast is included in the room rate.

Rural guesthouses tend to be peculiarly reticent about the cost of extra services. Therefore, it is advisable to check the exact prices of meals, drinks, saunas, guided tours, or any such additional services in advance, to avoid any awkwardness at the time of settling the bills.

Children

Children are amply catered for in nearly all hotels and guesthouses in all three countries. A number of hotels have rooms designed for families travelling with children. If not, then most hotels gladly provide extra beds for children. Many rural guesthouses offer special play areas and activities for children and most decent hotels can provide cots for very young children, while babysitting services are becoming increasingly common. Some larger hotels offer special family rates that include a number of family-oriented excursions.

Smoking

In keeping with the ban on smoking in public places in Estonia, Latvia and Lithuania, all hotels prohibit smoking in their public areas. Smoking is not allowed in lobbies and restaurants, although some larger hotels provide special smoking zones. These zones can be recognized by a green smoking-allowed symbol. Most

Well-appointed room at the Radisson Blu Astorija Hotel in Vilnius *(see p305)*

Dignified decor at the SamaraH Hotel Metropole, Rīga *(see p300)*

hotels still offer guests a choice between smoking and non-smoking rooms.

Disabled Travellers

Until recently, access and facilities for disabled travellers was limited to high-end establishments and large chain hotels. However, most major new hotels in the three capital cities have incorporated facilities for disabled guests into their design and the situation has greatly improved. In many upscale hotels, guest rooms are appointed with facilities for disabled people. It is important to remember, however, that very few rural guesthouses have facilities for disabled visitors.

Recommended Hotels

Estonia, Latvia and Lithuania have an excellent range of hotel accommodation, though the more luxurious options are mostly to be found in the historic Old Towns of the capitals. The listings on pages 296–307 cover a wide choice of accommodation types, from luxury and mid-range modern hotels to apartments, guest-houses, hostels and campsites.

Across the Baltic States there are wonderfully atmospheric historic hotels to be found. The Three Sisters Boutique Hotel in Tallinn is a magnificent conversion of three medieval houses *(see p297)*; Rīga's Hotel Justus occupies a 14th-century cathedral dormitory *(see p300)*; rooms in the 13th-century

Jaunpils Castle in Western Latvia have antique four-poster beds and fireplaces *(see p301)*; and Monte Pacis hotel in Kaunas, Lithuania, is housed in an elegantly furnished 17th-century monastery *(see p306)*.

There are also numerous rustic getaways, perfect for spa treatments or convening with nature. Akmenine Rezidencija in Lithuania *(see p306)* is a romantic bolthole on a lake, while Taevaskoja Salamaa in Estonia *(see p299)* is a simple rural retreat perfect for families.

Throughout the listings some venues are labelled DK Choice. These are outstanding in some way. They might have an atmospheric historic setting, magnificent views, particularly good amenities or an idyllic location. Whatever the reasons, a DK Choice will provide an especially memorable stay.

The pine-clad interior of Akmeninė Rezidencija, Trakai, Lithuania *(see p306)*

DIRECTORY

Apartments and Private Homes

Airbnb
w airbnb.com

Eldorado Apartments
Vilnius.
Tel +372 6991 7391.
w apartamentai.lt

Erel Apartments & Residences
Tartu mnt 14, Tallinn 10149, Estonia.
Tel +372 663 1640.
w erel.ee

Eugenijus Apartments
Vilniaus 25–1,
Vilnius.
Tel +372 6994 2456.
w vilniusapartments.lt

Goodson & Red Apartments
Jõe 5, Tallinn.
Tel +372 666 1650.
w goodsonandred.com

Lilija Plus Real Estate Agency
Rīdzenes iela 25, Rīga.
Tel +371 6721 6040.
w lilarealty.lv

Guesthouses

Baltic Country Holidays (Lauku ceļotājs)
Kalnciema 40, Rīga.
Tel +371 6761 7600.
w celotajs.lv

Estonian Rural Tourism
Vilmsi tänav 53 G,
Tallinn.
Tel +372 600 9999.
w maaturism.ee

Lithuanian Countryside Tourism Association
Donelaičio gatvė 2–201,
Kaunas.
Tel +370 37 400 354.
w atostogoskaime.lt

Hostels

Hostelling International
w hihostels.com

Campsites

RMK
Toompuiestee 24,
10149, Tallinn
Tel +372 676 7500.
w rmk.ee

Where to Stay in Estonia

Tallinn

Economy Hotel €
Modern   **Street Finder** B1
Kopli tee 2c, 10412
Tel 66/ 8300
[w] economyhotel.ee
The cosy Economy Hotel offers rooms with work desks and stripped wooden floors. It is conveniently close to the main train station.

Go Hotel Shnelli €
Modern   **Street Finder** B2
Toompuiestee 37, 10133
Tel 631 0100
[w] gohotels.ee
This stylish hotel offers spotless rooms, some with Old Town views. Generous breakfasts, a casino and spa facilities add to its appeal. Efficient, friendly staff and free parking.

Old Town Münkenhof €
Hostel   **Street Finder** D2
Munga 4, 10123
Tel 507 4766
[w] oldtownmunkenhof.ee
Choose between immaculate private rooms or 4- to 6-bed dorms at this hostel in an atmospheric Old Town house. There is a communal kitchen.

Red Emperor Hostel €
Hostel   **Street Finder** D2
Aia 10, 10111
Tel 608 7387
[w] redemperorhostel.com
A funky modern hostel with great facilities, private rooms and mixed dorms. Be warned that its lively bar attracts young locals who like to party until late.

Romeo Family Apartments €
Apartments   **Street Finder** C3
Suur-Karja 18, Apt 38, 10149
Tel 5690 4786
[w] romeofamily.ee
These family-run, great-value Old Town apartments come with microwaves and washing machines; some have full kitchens, too. Breakfast is included.

Vabriku €
Guesthouse   **Street Finder** B1
Vabriku 24, Põhja-Tallinn 15010
Tel 646 6287
[w] vabrikuhostel.eu
Simply furnished double and triple rooms are offered in this lovely house with a garden, a short walk from the Old Town. There are shared kitchen facilities, plus a barbecue area.

CRU Hotel €€
Historic   **Street Finder** D3
Viru 8, 10640
Tel 611 7600
[w] cruhotel.eu
A splendid hotel in a 15th-century building with exposed beams and period features. The restaurant is excellent.

Delta Apartments €€
Apartments   **Street Finder** C2
Raekoja plats 8, 10146
Tel 644 3534
These smart apartments in the Old Town are spacious, clean and have well-equipped kitchens. Some apartments have saunas.

Hotel Bern €€
Modern   **Street Finder** D2
Aia 10, 10111
Tel 680 6630
[w] bernhotelestonia.com
Rooms are on the small side, but service is great and the breakfast is plentiful at this pleasant hotel in a utilitarian brick building.

Hotel Palace €€
Modern   **Street Finder** C3
Vabaduse Väljak 3, 10141
Tel 680 6604
[w] tallinnhotels.ee
This chic hotel features an ultra-elegant interior. Rooms have Old Town views. Facilities include steam bath, sauna and small pool.

Kalev Spa Hotel & Waterpark €€
Spa hotel   **Street Finder** D2
Aia 18, 10111
Tel 649 3300
[w] kalevspa.ee
With an enormous waterpark that is free for guests and features three slides and a large pool, this central hotel is great for families. Spacious rooms are stylishly furnished.

A room with canopy bed in The Three Sisters Boutique Hotel, Tallinn

Tallinn Street Finder *see pp86–7;* **Road Map** *see back inside cover*

Price Guide
Prices are based on one night's stay in high season for a standard double room, inclusive of service charges and taxes.
€   up to €80
€€   €80 to €180
€€€   over €180

DK Choice

Merchant's House Hotel €€
Historic   **Street Finder** C2
Dunkri 4/6, 10123
Tel 697 7500
[w] merchantshousehotel.com
Set in a 16th-century building right at the heart of the Old Town, this boutique hotel offers wonderfully characterful rooms that make the most of the building's rustic medieval features. The vaulted basement houses a restaurant, where guests can enjoy a generous breakfast buffet.

My City Hotel €€
Modern   **Street Finder** C3
Vana-Posti 11/13, 10146
Tel 622 0900
[w] mycityhotel.ee
This delightful Old Town hotel, a few steps from the town square, has airy, elegantly furnished rooms and exceptionally high service standards.

Original Sokos Hotel Viru €€
Modern   **Street Finder** D3
Viru Väljak 4, 10111
Tel 680 9300
[w] sokoshotels.fi
A vast hotel complex, Original Sokos has two restaurants, a nightclub and a shopping centre. The wide range of well-appointed rooms are suitable for families as well as business travellers.

Videviku Villa Apartments €€
Apartments
Videviku 30, 10139
Tel 503 4107
Choose from several spacious apartments located in a peaceful neighbourhood. Facilities include fully equipped kitchens and antique-style furnishings.

Hotel Telegraaf €€€
Luxury   **Street Finder** C2
Vene 9, 10123
Tel 600 0600
[w] telegraafhotel.com
An old telegraph office has been transformed into one of Tallinn's top hotels. It offers sumptuously furnished rooms, faultless service and a great restaurant *(see p316)*.

Radisson Blu Sky Hotel €€€
Luxury   Street Finder E3
Rävala puiestee 3, 10143
Tel 682 3000
W radissonblu.com
An ultra-modern hotel in a glass building a short walk from the Old Town, Radisson Blu Sky has a rooftop bar with panoramic views of the sea and the city.

St Petersbourg Hotel €€€
Historic   Street Finder C2
Rataskaevu 7, 10123
Tel 628 6500
W hotelstpetersbourg.com
First opened in 1850, this is Tallinn's oldest hotel and one of its finest. The spacious rooms are extravagantly furnished with touches of Art Deco whimsy.

Schlössle Hotel €€€
Historic   Street Finder C2
Pühavaimu 13/15, 10123
Tel 699 7700
W schloesslehotel.com
This atmospheric five-star hotel occupies several 14th-century houses. Lavishly furnished rooms complement the medieval interior perfectly. Fine restaurant *(see p315)*.

Swissotel Tallinn €€€
Luxury   Street Finder E3
Tornimäe 3, 10145
Tel 624 0000
W swissotel.com
Occupying Tallinn's tallest building, this stunning hotel has a spa centre, a pool with sauna, and a top-floor bar and restaurant with spectacular city views.

The Three Sisters Boutique Hotel €€€
Historic   Street Finder D1
Pikk 71 / Tolli 2, 10133
Tel 630 6300
W threesistershotel.com
Three medieval houses have been magnificently converted into Tallinn's premiere luxury boutique hotel. Large, comfortable rooms feature both modern fittings and period detail.

Western Estonia

HAAPSALU: Lahe Guesthouse €
Guesthouse   Road Map C2
Lahe 7, 90503
Tel 516 3023
W lahemaja.com
In a century-old villa, this peaceful family-run guesthouse has large, classically furnished rooms. It is set in beautiful gardens a short walk from the sea and local sights.

Understated "Superior Double" room at the Schlössle Hotel, Tallinn

HAAPSALU: Fra Mare Thalasso Spa €€
Spa hotel   Road Map C2
Ranna tee 2, 90403
Tel 472 4600
W framare.ee
This modern seafront hotel offers a range of spa and beauty treatments. It has bright, airy rooms, an excellent pool complex and gym, and a large sauna.

HIIUMAA ISLAND: Kassari Puhkekeskus €€
Modern   Road Map C2
Kassari village, Käina parish, 92111
Tel 469 7169
W kassarikeskus.ee
Ideal for families, this superb hotel by the sea has a large garden, a children's play area and capacious rooms with kitchenettes.

KIHNU ISLAND: Tolli Tourism Farm €
Guesthouse   Road Map C2
Sääre village, Kihnu parish, 88005
Tel 527 7380
W kihnukallas.ee
An authentic farmstead in an idyllic rural setting. Guests can take trips out to sea with the island's fishermen. Sporting activites are also on offer.

MATSALU NATIONAL PARK: Altmõisa Guesthouse €
Guesthouse   Road Map C2
Tuuru village, Ridala parish, 90426
Tel 472 4680
W altmoisa.ee
An endearing guesthouse with sea views and great bird-watching and hiking opportunities.

MATSALU NATIONAL PARK: Algallika €€
Guesthouse   Road Map C2
Mäe farmstead, Ranna village, Hanila parish, 90115
Tel 5556 6088
W algallika.ee
This delightful rural guesthouse sits amidst acres of natural beauty. Rooms are large and cosy and there's space for backpackers in the hay loft.

MUHU ISLAND: Igaküla Matsi Puhkemaja €
Guesthouse   Road Map C2
Matsi farmstead, Igaküla village, 94722
Tel 5668 2681
W matsitalu.ee
This appealing 19th-century wooden farmhouse with a thatched roof is surrounded by immaculate gardens. The three spacious rooms are cosily furnished and accommodate up to five people. Three small log cabins are also available.

DK Choice

MUHU ISLAND: Pädaste Manor €€€
Luxury   Road Map C2
Pädaste, 94716
Tel 454 8800
W padaste.ee
A stunning, high-class hotel, Pädaste Manor is housed in a renovated 16th-century farmhouse ensconced in woods at the waterfront. Oozing period charm, it has antique furniture, open fires and exposed brickwork throughout. Its top-notch facilities include a helipad, spa centre, billiards room and a world-renowned restaurant *(see p317)*. The ideal place to get away from it all in style.

PALDISKI: Padise Manor €€
Historic   Road Map C1
Padise village, Padise parish, 76001
Tel 608 7877
W padisemois.ee
In an 18th-century manor house overlooking the ruins of a 13th-century monastery, this hugely atmospheric hotel has an elegant interior and flawless service.

For more information on types of hotels *see pp292–5*

PÄRNU: Rannahotell €€
Spa hotel   **Road Map** D2
Ranna puiestee 5, 80010
Tel *444 4444*
Ⓦ rannahotell.ee
Most of the rooms at this elegant
seafront hotel overlook the beach.
There is a spa centre, sauna,
tennis court and kids' play area.

PÄRNU: Villa Ammende €€€
Luxury   **Road Map** D2
Mere puiestee 7, 80010
Tel *447 3888*
Ⓦ ammende.ee
A glorious hotel in an Art Nouveau
mansion with a wonderful restaurant *(see p317)*. The service is faultless and the rooms are beautifully
furnished in authentic period style.
Close to the beach and Old Town.

PÄRNU: Frost Boutique
Hotel €€€
Luxury   **Road Map** D2
Kuninga 11a, 80011
Tel *5303 0424*
Ⓦ frosthotel.ee
A lovely Old Town hotel with
individually designed rooms
incorporating wood and
stone with modern accents.
Transparent bathroom doors are
one of the more unusual features.

SAAREMAA ISLAND:
Toomalõuka Tourist Farm €
Guesthouse   **Road Map** B2
*Kopli farmstead, Toomalõuka village,
Salme parish, 93261*
Tel *5646 6567*
Ⓦ toomaloukaturism.ee
This fantastic rustic farm complex
has a thatched guesthouse
boasting comfortable wood-
panelled rooms and a barn that
sleeps up to 20. The energetic
owners organize fishing, sea-
kayaking, cycling and diving tours.

SAAREMAA ISLAND:
Georg Ots Spa Hotel €€
Spa hotel   **Road Map** C2
Tori 2, Kuressaare, 93810
Tel *455 0000*
Ⓦ gospa.ee
Outstanding facilities and service
feature at this hotel that boasts
views of the sea or castle from
many rooms. Generous breakfast
and great restaurant *(see p318)*.

SAAREMAA ISLAND: Kuursaal
Guesthouse €€
Modern   **Road Map** C2
Lossipark 1, Kuressaare, 93815
Tel *453 9749*
Ⓦ kuressaarekuursaal.ee
A charming place next to the
castle, this guesthouse has airy
en-suite rooms with mosquito
nets and a restaurant serving
French and Estonian cuisine.

SAAREMAA ISLAND: Ekesparre
Boutique Hotel €€€
Luxury   **Road Map** C2
Lossi 27, Kuressaare, 93815
Tel *453 8778*
Ⓦ ekesparre.ee
Ekesparre is the island's oldest hotel
and one of its best. Outstanding
service and great location right
beside the Bishop's Castle *(see p98)*.

SOOMAA NATIONAL PARK:
Guesthouse Linnamehe €
Guesthouse   **Road Map** D2
Kuiaru village, Tori parish, 86806
Tel *517 8379*
Ⓦ linnamehe.ee
A pretty wooden cottage close to
Soomaa National Park offers
simple accommodation, verdant
gardens, a children's play area and
swimming pond. The hospitable
owners organize local tours.

VORMSI ISLAND: Elle-Malle €
Guesthouse   **Road Map** C1
Hullo village, 91301
Tel *473 2072*
This restful guesthouse has
several rustic rooms, a romantic
double in a converted windmill,
and a separate cottage. Bikes are
available to get around the island.

VORMSI ISLAND: Rumpo
Mäe Farm €
Guesthouse   **Road Map** C1
Rumpo village, 91309
Tel *472 9932*
Ⓦ rumpomae.ee
A charming converted farmstead
and campsite by the sea, Mäe
Farm offers simple, tidy rooms
and self-catering facilities.
Activities include sea-kayaking,
archery, fishing and cycling.

Eastern Estonia

KUREMÄE: Kuremäe Hostel €
Hostel   **Road Map** E1
Kuremäe village, Illuka parish, 41201
Tel *525 0896*
Basic but adequate twin rooms,
some with a shared bathroom,
are offered in this cosy house
close to Pühtitsa Convent. The
small café-bar serves light meals.

LAHEMAA NATIONAL PARK:
Sae Hostel €
Hostel   **Road Map** D1
Koljaku village, Vihula parish, 45419
Tel *5656 0901*
Ⓦ saehostel.weebly.com
In an idyllic cottage in the woods,
this hostel has simply furnished
rooms, a shared kitchen and living
area, and a sauna. The friendly
owners hire out bikes and can
advise on local trips.

The functionalist Rannahotell, Pärnu, built
in the 1930s

LAHEMAA NATIONAL PARK:
Merekalda Guesthouse €€
Guesthouse   **Road Map** D1
Neeme tee 2, Käsmu village, 45601
Tel *323 8451*
Ⓦ merekalda.ee
Snug apartments have a patio or
balcony and a kitchenette at this
seaside getaway in a stunning
spot ideal for hiking and cycling.

LAHEMAA NATIONAL PARK:
Sagadi Manor Hotel €€€
Luxury   **Road Map** D1
Sagadi village, Vihula parish, 45403
Tel *676 7888*
Ⓦ sagadi.ee
In the grounds of the beautiful
Sagadi Manor estate *(see p113)*,
this hotel has charming rooms in
the elegantly converted stables.

NARVA-JÕESUU: Pansionaat
Valentina €€
Guesthouse   **Road Map** E1
Aia 47, 29023
Tel *357 7468*
Ⓦ pansionaatvalentina.com
In a spectacular location amidst
dense woods beside the sea, this
guesthouse has a choice of two
simply furnished rooms and a
much smarter pair of apartments.

NARVA-JÕESUU: Meresuu Spa
& Hotel €€€
Spa hotel   **Road Map** E1
Aia 48a, 29023
Tel *357 9600*
Ⓦ meresuu.ee
A smart, modern hotel towering
over the tree tops, near the
beach. The spa facilities are first-
rate. Many rooms have sea views.

ONTIKA COAST: Toila Spa
Hotel €€
Spa hotel   **Road Map** E1
Ranna 12, Toila 41702
Tel *324 2900*
Ⓦ toilaspa.ee
The accommodation at this vast
seafront complex includes self-
catering apartments and a
campsite. Rather dated interior.

**OTEPÄÄ: Pühajärve Spa &
Holiday Resort**   €€
Spa hotel   **Road Map** E2
Pühajärve, 67414
Tel *766 5500*
w pyhajarve.com
In a beautiful location, this hotel
offers a range of wellness and
beauty treatments, as well as
billiards, a bowling alley, a gym
and a large pool.

**PÕLTSAMAA: Guesthouse Carl
Schmidt**   €
Guesthouse   **Road Map** D2
Kesk 4, 48105
Tel *5346 8303*
This well-run establishment in the
town centre has its own pub and
a delightfully rustic interior.
Rooms are on the small side, but
the friendly service compensates.

PÕLVA: Hotel Pesa   €
Modern   **Road Map** E2
Uus 5, 63308
Tel *799 8530*
w kagureis.ee
The congenial Hotel Pesa has
comfortable rooms and a large
pool with separate children's pool.
Local excursions can be arranged.

RAKVERE: Hotell Wesenbergh €
Modern   **Road Map** D1
Tallinna 25, 44311
Tel *322 3480*
w wesenbergh.ee
Named after the local castle, this
hotel is smartly furnished to a
high standard. Several rooms
come with a private sauna.

RÕUGE: Rõuge Suurjärve €
Guesthouse   **Road Map** E2
Metsa 5, 66201
Tel *785 9273*
w maremajutus.ee
A great base for exploring the
surrounding area, this wooden
guesthouse has simple, comfortable rooms and rustic-style breakfast. Lunch and dinner on request.

**SANGASTE MANOR: Sangaste
Castle Hotel**   €€
Historic   **Road Map** D2
Lossi village, Sangaste parish, 67005
Tel *529 5911*
w sangasteloss.com
This redbrick manor, built in
English Gothic Revival style,
offers wonderfully atmospheric
rooms with high ceilings and
old wooden beams.

SILLAMÄE: Hotel Krunk €€
Modern   **Road Map** E1
Kesk 23, 40231
Tel *392 9030*
w krunk.ee
Constructed in the 1950s
during the Soviet era, this is an
interesting example of Stalinist
Neo-Baroque architecture. The
rooms are spacious, but rather
dated and sparsely furnished.

**SUUR MUNAMÄGI: Haanjamehe
Talu**   €
Guesthouse   **Road Map** E2
Vakari village, Haanja parish, 65101
Tel *502 3103*
w haanjamehetalu.ee
This cosy log-built farmstead
offers accommodation in
converted granaries or in the
main house. Activities include
local excursions, kayaking and –
depending on the season –
sleigh or carriage rides.

DK Choice

**TAEVASKOJA: Taevaskoja
Salamaa**   €
Guesthouse   **Road Map** E2
*Taevaskoja tee 32, Põlva parish,
63229*
Tel *5345 6480*
w salamaa.eu
Tucked away in the woods,
this simple, peaceful
guesthouse makes for the
perfect rural retreat. Rooms are
individually furnished with folk-
tale themes and, with families
in mind, come with bunk beds.
Alternatively, visitors can pitch a
tent at the campsite. There's a
large shared kitchen and a great
outdoor play area complete
with trampoline and swings.
Kayaking, cycling and hiking are
among the activities on offer.

TARTU: Antonius Hotel €€
Luxury   **Road Map** E2
Ülikooli 15, 51003
Tel *737 0377*
w hotelantonius.ee
In a meticulously restored
16th-century house, this very
atmospheric Old Town hotel
features antique furniture and
exposed beams. Excellent service.

**VILJANDI: Just Rest
Automatic Hostel**   €
Hostel   **Road Map** D2
Ranna puiestee 6, 71003
Tel *520 6772*
w justrest.eu
A fantastic hostel with automated
check-in and space-age styling.
Rooms with one to four beds have
bathrooms and secure lockers.

**VILJANDI: Grand
Hotel Viljandi**   €€
Modern   **Road Map** D2
Tartu 11, 71004
Tel *435 5800*
w ghv.ee
An opulent hotel in an Art Deco
building with classically styled
rooms and good fitness facilities. A
morning sauna session is included.

VÕRU: Hämsaare Guesthouse €
Guesthouse   **Road Map** E2
Meegomäe village, 65603
Tel *5566 9472*
w hamsa.ee
This 19th-century log farmhouse
is now an idyllic lodging with
cosy rooms and a rustic tavern
serving traditional Estonian fare.

**VÕRU: Kubija Hotel and
Nature Spa**   €
Spa hotel   **Road Map** E2
Männiku 43a, 65603
Tel *504 5745*
w kubija.ee
This tranquil hotel in a forest has
five pools, four saunas and an
abundance of wellness treatments.
Remarkably good value.

**VÕRU: Piusa Ürgoru
Holiday Centre**   €
Guesthouse   **Road Map** E2
*Väiko-Härma village, Meremae
parish, 65554*
Tel *528 9134*
w puhkemaja.ee
A village-like complex with a main
house, converted granary, several
log cabins and a campsite. Trout
fishing and a traditional sauna.

Merekalda Guesthouse on the Gulf of Finland, within Lahemaa National Park

For more information on types of hotels *see pp292–5*

Where to Stay in Latvia

Rīga

Art Hotel Laine €
Guesthouse **Street Finder** E2
Skolas 11, LV-1010
Tel 6728 8818
🌐 laine.lv
Housed in an Art Nouveau building, this bright hotel has spotless en-suite doubles and cheaper rooms with shared facilities.

Elizabeth's Youth Hostel €
Hostel **Street Finder** E4
Elizabetes 103-2, LV-1050
Tel 6721 7890
🌐 youthhostel.lv
This large, clean hostel has mixed dorms and rooms with shared facilities. It is located close to the train station and the Old Town.

Guesthouse Jakob Lenz €
Guesthouse **Street Finder** D1
Lenču 2, LV-1010
Tel 6733 3343
🌐 guesthouselenz.lv
In the Art Nouveau district, this well-kept lodging has bright doubles with shared bathrooms and a few en-suite family rooms.

Hotel B&B Rīga €
Guesthouse **Street Finder** E3
Ģertrūdes 43, LV-1011
Tel 6727 8505
🌐 bb-riga.lv
A short walk from the Old Town, this family-run B&B overlooks a courtyard. Most of the spacious rooms have cooking facilities.

Hotel Edvards €
Modern **Street Finder** E2
Dzirnavu 45/47, LV-1010
Tel 6743 9960
🌐 hoteledvards.lv
An immaculate hotel with plain rooms in a 19th-century building. There's a good choice at breakfast and free tea and coffee all day.

Albert Hotel €€
Modern **Street Finder** D2
Dzirnavu 33, LV-1010
Tel 6733 1717
🌐 alberthotel.lv
This central hotel towers over its neighbours, offering superb city views from its rooftop bar and many of its rooms.

Apartments – Laipu €€
Apartments **Street Finder** C3
Laipu 1, LV-1050
Tel 6781 4680
Fully equipped apartments have elegant, high-ceilinged rooms. Great service; immaculate rooms.

Baltvilla €€
Spa hotel
Senču prospekts 45, Baltezers, LV-2164
Tel 6784 0640
🌐 baltvilla.lv
On the edge of Lake Baltezers, 15 km (9 miles) from the centre, Baltvilla specializes in spa and medical treatments. Good facilities for disabled guests.

Europa Royale Rīga €€
Historic **Street Finder** E3
K Barona 12, LV-1050
Tel 6707 9444
🌐 groupeuropa.com
Remarkably plush, this 19th-century building features high ceilings, huge doors, stained-glass windows and a casino.

Hotel Garden Palace €€
Historical **Street Finder** C4
Grēcinieku 28, LV-1079
Tel 6722 4650
🌐 hotelgardenpalace.lv
Indulge in old-fashioned elegance at this well-priced hotel. Rooms are opulently furnished and some have terraces.

DK Choice

Hotel Justus €€
Historic **Street Finder** C4
Jauniela 24, LV-1050
Tel 6721 2404
🌐 hoteljustus.lv
Occupying the 14th-century dormitories of the cathedral, this enormously atmospheric Old Town hotel has distressed period features and exposed brick walls, some with murals painted by the once-resident monks. Tastefully styled rooms have antique furniture along with air-conditioning and Wi-Fi.

The blue façade of Wellton Centrum Hotel & Spa, centrally located in Rīga's Old Town

Monika Centrum Hotels €€
Modern **Street Finder** C2
Elizabetes 21, LV-1010
Tel 6703 1900
🌐 monika.centrumhotels.com
Housed in an attractive Neo-Gothic building in the main Art Nouveau district, this spotless hotel offers spacious and cosy rooms.

SemaraH Hotel Metropole €€
Historic **Street Finder** D4
Aspazijas bulvāris 36/38, LV-1050
Tel 6601 0300
🌐 semarahhotels.com
Open since 1871, this is one of the city's oldest hotels. The renovated interior is thoroughly modern but there is no air-conditioning.

Wellton Centrum Hotel & Spa €€
Spa hotel **Street Finder** D4
Kalēju 33, LV-1050
Tel 6713 0670
🌐 wellton.com
This is an unusually central Old Town location for such a well-equipped spa hotel. Note that use of the spa is not included in the standard room-rate. The service is excellent though.

Astor Rīga Hotel €€€
Modern **Street Finder** D3
Z A Meierovica bulvāris 10, LV-1050
Tel 6721 7777
🌐 astorrigahotel.lv
Opened in 2012, this grand hotel in the Old Town acquired an excellent reputation in a very short period of time. Standard rooms are a little on the small side.

Dome Hotel & Spa €€€
Luxury **Street Finder** C3
Miesnieku 4, LV-1050
Tel 6750 9010
🌐 domehotel.lv
This five-star boutique hotel in a 17th-century Old Town mansion, which was renovated in 2009 by Latvian designers, is an absolute treat. Rates include use of the *hammam*, but the spa and wellness treatments are extra. The service is impeccable.

Gallery Park Hotel €€€
Luxury **Street Finder** D2
K Valdemāra 7, LV-1010
Tel 6733 8830
🌐 galleryparkhotel.com
In an imposing 19th-century building that is part of the Châteaux & Hôtels Collection, this opulent five-star hotel has an indoor pool, secure underground parking and a great restaurant.

Grand Palace Hotel €€€
Luxury **Street Finder** C3
Pils 12, LV-1050
Tel *6704 4000*
ⓦ grandpalaceriga.com
A first-rate hotel with an acclaimed restaurant and sophisticated bar. The rooms have heated floors and modern furnishings.

Hotel Bergs €€€
Luxury **Street Finder** C2
Elizabetes 83/85, LV-1050
Tel *6777 0900*
ⓦ hotelbergs.lv
This prestigious boutique hotel has large rooms and modern, understated decor. There is an excellent restaurant *(see p321)*.

DK Choice
Neiburgs Hotel €€€
Historic **Street Finder** C4
Jauniela 25/27, LV-1050
Tel *6711 5522*
ⓦ neiburgs.com
Occupying a splendid Art Nouveau mansion in the centre of the Old Town, this stylish hotel is among the best in the city. Large, smartly furnished rooms and apartments with full kitchen facilities are available, along with a sauna, a steam bath and an excellent restaurant.

Radisson Blu Hotel Latvija €€€
Modern **Street Finder** C2
Elizabetes 55, LV-1010
Tel *6777 2222*
ⓦ radissonblu.com
This monolithic 26-floor hotel looms over the city. Facilities are first-rate and the views from rooms and top floor bar are fabulous.

Western Latvia

BAUSKA: Hotel Bērzkalni €
Modern **Road Map** D4
Bērzkalni 11a, LV-3901
Tel *6392 6888*
ⓦ berzkalni.lv
This great-value hotel is 2 km (1 mile) from the centre and offers airy doubles and triples, some with shared bathroom, a small indoor pool and a restaurant.

DUNDAGA: Laumas €
Guesthouse **Road Map** C3
Laumas, LV-3261
Tel *2640 3240*
A wonderful retreat in the Laumas Nature Park with immaculate wood-panelled en-suite rooms and apartments, situated in idyllic woodlands. Activities include fishing, hiking and mini-golf.

Sleek room in the boutique Dome Hotel & Spa, set in a 400-year-old Riga building

DK Choice
JAUNPILS: Jaunpils Castle €€
Historic **Road Map** C4
Pils, Tukuma district, LV-3145
Tel *6310 7082*
ⓦ jaunpilspils.lv
Perfect for a romantic break, this 13th-century castle *(see p174)* is as atmospheric as they come. Most of the rooms are en-suite with four-poster beds, tiled or parquet floors and open fireplaces. Those on a lighter budget can opt for a bed in a mixed dorm within the castle.

JELGAVA: Hotel Jelgava €€
Modern **Road Map** C4
Lielā 6, LV-3001
Tel *6302 6193*
ⓦ hoteljelgava.lv
A short walk from Jelgava Palace, this smart hotel offers spacious, well-appointed rooms, a pleasant garden and a complimentary morning sauna for guests.

JŪRMALA: Dzintari Park Hostel €
Hostel **Road Map** C3
Piestātnes 6/14, LV-2010
Tel *2586 2000*
An impeccable hostel in a tastefully converted redbrick villa just 200 m (650 ft) from the sea. There's a choice of bright, spacious rooms and mixed or single-sex dorms.

JŪRMALA: Villa Joma €€
Historic **Road Map** C3
Jomas 90, LV-2015
Tel *6777 1999*
ⓦ villajoma.lv
This stately building first functioned as a hotel back in the late 19th century and has an enviable location right at the heart of the resort. It has a lovely elegant interior and fine restaurant *(see p322)*.

JŪRMALA: Light House €€€
Luxury **Road Map** C3
Gulbenes 1a, LV-1205,
Tel *6751 1445*
ⓦ lighthousejurmala.lv
This small luxury complex with a glass-fronted restaurant and terrace sits right on the beach. Each of the 11 individually themed rooms has full kitchen facilities.

KANDAVA: Hotel Kandava €
Modern **Road Map** C3
Sabiles 3, LV-3120
Tel *2640 6733*
ⓦ hotelkandava.lv
A good-value central option with clean and comfortable but unexceptional rooms. A simple café-restaurant offers a choice of local dishes. Helpful, efficient staff.

KOLKA: Guesthouse Vītoli €
Guesthouse **Road Map** C3
Vītoli, Kolka, LV-3275
Tel *2913 5764*
Close to the sea in the picturesque Slītere National Park, this modest guesthouse has a pretty garden and basic rooms with shared bathroom and kitchen facilities.

KULDĪGA: Metropole €
Modern **Road Map** B3
Baznīcas 11, LV-3301
Tel *6335 0588*
ⓦ hotel-metropole.lv
Although this hotel has kept its original façade dating from 1910, its interior was renovated in 2006 to a minimalist design. Sloping ceilings give it character. There is a fine restaurant *(see p322)*.

LAKE ENGURE: Guesthouse Mikas €
Guesthouse **Road Map** C3
Ābragciems, Engure district, LV-1048
Tel *2924 4653*
A short walk from the sea, this peaceful property has cosy rooms with shared bathroom and kitchen and a large garden.

LIEPĀJA: Pie Jāna €
Hostel   Road Map B4
Raiņa 43, LV-3401
Tel *2036 4552*
w hotelpiejana.lv
There is a choice of private rooms or beds in spacious dorms at this characterful, central hostel.

LIEPĀJA: Libava €€
Modern   Road Map B4
Vecā ostmala 29, LV-3401
Tel *6342 5318*
w libava.lv
This serene canal-side hotel in a converted 18th-century customs house has seven stylish rooms with contemporary decor, and a first-rate restaurant.

MEŽOTNE: Mežotnes Pils €€
Luxury   Road Map D4
Bauskas district, LV-3918
Tel *6396 0711*
w mezotnespils.lv
This exquisitely restored 19th-century manor house with a Neo-Classical interior is set in acres of grounds *(see p170)*. Stately rooms come with heavy antique furniture and woodland views.

NĪCA: Nīcava €
Guesthouse   Road Map B4
Nīcas parish, Nīcas district, LV-3473
Tel *6348 6379*
w nicava.lv
The large rooms are dated but comfortable at this lakeside villa set in charming gardens. It has a good restaurant with a tree-shaded terrace *(see p323)*.

PĀVILOSTA: Viga €
Guesthouse   Road Map B4
Viļņu 3, LV-3466
Tel *2642 4389*
In a quiet neighbourhood near the sea, this wonderful guesthouse has cosy rooms. Free tea and coffee throughout the day.

ROJA: Rēderi €
Modern   Road Map C3
Kaltene, Roja, LV-3264
Tel *6322 0558*
w hotelrederi.lv
A contemporary wood-clad hotel with bright, spacious rooms and sea views. Meals can be taken in the adjoining café-restaurant.

RUNDĀLE: Baltā Māja €
Historic   Road Map D4
Pils Rundāle, LV-3921
Tel *6396 2140*
w hotelbaltamaja.lv
Housed in the old servants' quarters of Rundāle Palace *(see pp172–3)*, rooms have shared bathrooms, original paved flooring and tiled stoves. Open out of season only by prior arrangement.

SABILE: Firks Pedvāle €
Historic   Road Map C4
Pedvāle, LV-3295
Tel *6325 2249*
This manor house in the grounds of Pedvāle Open-Air Museum *(see p182)* has basic, but atmospheric, rooms with shared bathrooms.

TALSI: Martinelli €€
Guesthouse   Road Map C3
Lielā 7, LV-3201
Tel *6329 1340*
w martinelli.lv
A tiny lodging with tastefully furnished rooms. The restaurant serves delicious Latvian cuisine as well as hearty breakfasts *(see p323)*.

TĒRVETE: Pūteļkrogs €
Guesthouse   Road Map C4
Zaļenieku parish, LV-3001
Tel *2925 5010*
w puteli.lv
A few minutes' drive from Tērvete Nature Park, this converted dairy offers snug rooms and a café-restaurant with a pretty garden.

TUKUMS: Hotel Tukums €
Modern   Road Map C3
Pils 9, LV-3101
Tel *6312 5747*
w hoteltukums.lv
On a quiet street a short walk from the centre, this pleasant hotel has en-suite rooms that are small but adequate.

TUKUMS: Jaunmoku Palace €€
Historic   Road Map C3
Tumes parish, Tukuma district
Tel *2618 7442*
w jaunmokupils.lv
This one-time aristocratic hunting lodge has five rooms, one of them reputedly haunted, and twenty more in the manor next door *(see p175)*. Popular for weddings.

VENTSPILS: Kupfernams €
Guesthouse   Road Map B3
Kārļa 5, LV-3601
Tel *6362 6999*
w hotelkupfernams.lv
A charming property with a traditional wooden façade and interior decor that blends modern style and period features.

Eastern Latvia

AGLONA: Aglonas Cakuli €
Guesthouse   Road Map E4
Ezera 4, LV-5304
Tel *2933 3422*
w aglonascakuli.lv
Friendly, family-run guesthouse with a rustic feel on Lake Cirīša. Breakfast includes home-made pancakes. Bikes and boats for hire.

Cosy wood-panelled room at Lacu Miga, "the Bear's Den", in Gauja National Park

DAUGAVPILS: Leo €
Modern   Road Map E4
Krāslavas 58, LV-5401
Tel *6542 6565*
w hotelleo.lv
A well-established motel-style hotel in the centre of town, Leo has reasonably sized rooms that are spotless and comfortable.

DAUGAVPILS: Villa Ksenija €€
Guesthouse   Road Map E4
Varšavas 17, LV-5400
Tel *6543 4317*
w villaks.lv
This beautifully restored 19th-century mansion, with an elegant interior, has smart, spacious rooms and a lovely shaded garden.

GAUJA NATIONAL PARK:
Eglaines €
Guesthouse   Road Map D3
Kārļi, Drabešu parish, LV-4139
Tel *2917 2332*
w hoteleglaines.lv
With just two rooms, this enchanting forest retreat is often booked up. An exceptionally charming place and great value.

GAUJA NATIONAL PARK:
Lacu Miga €
Guesthouse   Road Map D3
Gauja 22, Līgatne, LV-4110
Tel *6415 3481*
w lacumiga.lv
Lacu Miga is a snug log cabin with spacious rooms, deep inside the park. It is also home to an army of teddy bears.

GAUJA NATIONAL PARK:
Karlamuiza Country Hotel €€
Historic   Road Map D3
Kārļi, Drabešu parish, LV-4139
Tel *2616 5298*
w karlamuiza.lv
Large rooms have vintage furniture and basic kitchens at this manor on a forested estate.

GAUJA NATIONAL PARK: Spa Hotel Ezeri €€
Spa hotel **Road Map** D3
Siguldas parish, LV-2150
Tel *6797 3009*
w hotelezeri.lv
A well-run spa hotel set in several acres of gardens. Guests can enjoy a wide variety of wellness treatments as well as the chance to plunge into an icy pond following their sauna.

IKŠĶILE: Spadrops €
Modern **Road Map** D3
Rīgas 18 , LV-5052
Tel *2643 0430*
w meidrops.lv
A well-appointed hotel and recreation centre outside Rīga, with a good restaurant *(see p324)*, a pool, a sauna, cycling, hiking trails and croquet.

KOKNESE: Orinoko €
Guesthouse **Road Map** D4
Beģēni, Kokneses parish, LV-5113
Tel *2663 7918*
w orinoko.lv
This small guesthouse in a picturesque location has bright, airy rooms with river views. Activities include motorboat trips, badminton and volleyball.

KRĀSLAVE: Priedaine €
Guesthouse **Road Map** E4
Klusā 2, LV-5601
Tel *2643 0798*
A popular guesthouse on the banks of the Daugava river, just outside the town centre, Priedaine has spotless rooms with basic furnishings and river views.

DK Choice

LIMBAŽI: Bīriņu Pils €€
Luxury **Road Map** D3
Bīriņi, LV-4013
Tel *6402 4033*
w birinupils.lv
Surrounded by acres of parkland, Bīriņu manor house is a stately Neo-Gothic building dating from the mid-19th century. Book a comfortable en-suite room in the neighbouring Gardener's House or splash out on a regal room in the castle itself, though it's often booked up for weddings and other events. There is an excellent restaurant *(see p325)*.

LUDZA: Cirmas Ezerkrasts €
Guesthouse **Road Map** E3
Zvirgzdenes parish, Ezernieki, LV-4600
Tel *2833 2523*
w cirmasezerkrasts.lv
This is a secluded complex of smart log cabins of varying sizes,

some with self-catering facilities, on Lake Cirma. There is a common kitchen and living area with sauna.

LUDZA: Lucia €
Modern **Road Map** E3
Kr. Barona 20-1, LV-5701
Tel *2625 3535*
w lucia.lv
One of the few central options, this brightly decorated hotel has large, clean rooms, a café serving light meals, and helpful staff.

PREIĻI: Pie Pliča €
Historic **Road Map** E4
Raiņa bulvāris 9, LV-5301
Tel *2912 1689*
This peaceful establishment was the town's first hospital. Today it's a well-regarded guesthouse with characterful rooms and a sauna.

RĀZNA: Rāzna Hotel €
Modern **Road Map** E4
v. "Astici", Kaunata parish, LV-4622
Tel *2999 4444*
w razna.lv
On Lake Rāzna, this large recreation centre has smartly furnished rooms, self-catering villas and excellent facilities.

RĒZEKNE: Kolonna Hotel €
Modern **Road Map** E4
Brīvības 2, LV-4600
Tel *6460 7820*
w hotelkolonna.com
An unpretentious hotel with a good restaurant *(see p325)* and summer terrace overlooking the river, and attentive service. There is a generous breakfast buffet.

SALACGRĪVA: Kapteinu Osta €€
Guesthouse **Road Map** D3
Pērnavas 49a, LV-4033
Tel *6402 4930*
w kapteinuosta.lv
A seafront complex with spotless, nautically themed rooms, self-catering cabins, and a campsite. Guests can use the yacht club's living area and sauna.

SAULKRASTI: Medzābaki €
Guesthouse **Road Map** D3
Medzābaki-2, Lilaste, LV-2163
Tel *6714 7070*
w medzabaki.lv
A wonderful thatched-roof guesthouse on Lake Lilaste with bright, spacious rooms facing the water. Holiday cottages are available too.

SAULKRASTI: Pie Maijas €
Guesthouse **Road Map** D3
Murjāņu 3, LV-2160
Tel *2940 5480*
w hotelmaija.lv
An idyllic spot with self-catering cabins tucked away in the trees, just a short walk from the beach. Rooms are adequately furnished and there's a large garden with a children's play area.

STĀMERIENA: Vonadziņi €
Guesthouse **Road Map** E3
Skolas 1, LV-4406
Tel *2922 5805*
w vonadzini.lv
This thatched-roof hotel has pleasant rooms overlooking Lake Ludza. It offers a wide range of recreational activities.

VALMIERA: Wolmar €
Modern **Road Map** D3
Tērbatas 16a, LV-4201
Tel *6420 7301*
w hotelwolmar.lv
A large, central hotel that's a short walk from the main tourist sights, Wolmar offers spacious rooms with walk-in showers. Facilities include sauna and Jacuzzi.

VALMIERA: Dikli Palace Hotel €€
Luxury **Road Map** D3
Dikļi parish, Kocēnu district, LV-4223
Tel *6420 7480*
w diklipalacehotel.com
Housed in a beautifully restored 19th-century manor in wooded parkland, this hotel offers opulent rooms, a pool, relaxing spa treatments and a stunning restaurant *(see p325)*.

Façade of Kupfernams Guesthouse with traditional shuttered windows, Ventspils

For more information on types of hotels *see pp292–5*

Where to Stay in Lithuania

Vilnius

DK Choice

Comfort Hotel LT €
Modern **Street Finder** C5
Mindaugo gatvė 27, LT-03212
Tel *(5) 250 5111*
Ⓦ comforthotel.lt
Part of the Nordic Choice Hotel
chain, the hip Comfort Hotel LT
features large rooms with ultra-
stylish decor. There is free tea
and coffee for guests, as well as
use of the gym. The excellent
restaurant is run by a top
Lithuanian chef and the Old
Town is a 10-minute walk away.

Fabrika Hostel & Gallery €
Hostel **Street Finder** C2
A Vienuolio gatvė 4, LT-01104
Tel *(5) 203 1005*
Ⓦ fabrikahostel.com
This trendy hostel in an industrial
space hosts art exhibitions. It has
great facilities, but soundproofing
between rooms is minimal.

Litinterp Vilnius €
Guesthouse **Street Finder** E3
Bernardinu gatvė 7, LT-01124
Tel *(5) 212 3850*
Ⓦ litinterp.com
A simple B&B in an 18th-century
Old Town house, Litinterp has
bright, airy rooms with kitchen-
ettes and shared bathrooms.

Old Vilnius Apartments €
Apartments **Street Finder** E3
S Skapo gatvė 10, LT-01122
Tel *6114 3637*
Ⓦ oldvilniusapartments.lt
A 17th-century Old Town building
with five immaculate apartments,
a pleasant courtyard seating area
and free tea and coffee.

Park Villa €
Spa hotel
Vaidilutes gatvė 6a, LT-10100
Tel *(5) 211 3356*
Ⓦ parkvilla.lt
A perfect getaway from the
bustle of the city, this tranquil
hotel is set in wooded parkland a
10-minute drive from the centre.

Vilnius Home B&B €
Guesthouse **Street Finder** C3
Pylimo gatvė 14b, LT-01117
Tel *6560 5036*
Ⓦ vilniushome.eu
The rooms at this clean, central
B&B share bathrooms, a kitchen
and a living area. Breakfast is
pancakes and homemade jam.

Vivulskio Apartments €
Apartments **Street Finder** B4
Tel *6300 0162*
Ⓦ vivulskioapartamentai.lt
This complex of doubles and
apartments is a 10-minute walk
from the Old Town. There's a
sauna, hot tub and optional in-
room breakfast service.

Amberton €€
Modern **Street Finder** E4
L Stuokos-Gucevičiaus gatvė 1, 01122
Tel *(5) 210 7461*
Ⓦ ambertonhotels.com
Opposite Cathedral Square, this
chic hotel has a good choice of
large, smartly furnished rooms,
plus an excellent restaurant.

Artis €€
Spa hotel **Street Finder** D3
Totoriŭ gatvė 23, LT-01120
Tel *(5) 266 0366*
Ⓦ centrumhotels.com
Located in the Old Town, this
hotel offers free morning use of
the pool and sauna. Upper floor
rooms have lovely views.

Dvaras €€
Guesthouse **Street Finder** D3
Tilto gatvė 3, LT-01101
Tel *(5) 210 7370*
Ⓦ dvaras.lt
The creaky floorboards and fine
furnishings of this classy Old Town
guesthouse give it the feel of a
richly designed country cottage.

Hotel Domus Maria €€
Historic **Street Finder** D5
Aušros Vartŭ gatvė 12, LT-01129
Tel *(5) 264 4880*
Ⓦ domusmaria.com
This former 16th-century nunnery
has smart rooms with period
features and sloping ceilings.

Understated façade of Old Town guesthouse
Litinterp Vilnius

Hotel Rinno €€
Modern **Street Finder** C4
Vingriu gatvė 25, LT-01141
Tel *(5) 262 2828*
Ⓦ rinno.lt
This well-established Old Town
hotel has high standards of service
and rooms furnished in classical
style. Delicious pancake breakfast.

Mabre Residence €€
Historic **Street Finder** E4
Maironio gatvė 13, LT-01124
Tel *(5) 212 2087*
Ⓦ mabre.lt
This plush four-star hotel occupies
an imposing old monastery
with a courtyard garden. The
comfortable rooms lack historic
features but the restaurant
retains a vaulted ceiling.

Novotel Vilnius Centre €€
Modern **Street Finder** C3
Gedimino prospektas 16, LT-01103
Tel *(5) 266 6200*
Ⓦ novotel.com
Appealing to both tourists and
business travellers, this popular,
central hotel has excellent
facilities and consistently high
standards of service. Upper floor
rooms have great views.

**Secret Garden
Boutique B&B** €€
Guesthouse **Street Finder** E3
Bernardinu gatvė 4, LT-01124
Tel *6127 3210*
Ⓦ secretgarden.lt
This quaint cottage has a
courtyard garden and two comfy
en-suite rooms. High-speed Wi-Fi,
great breakfast and free parking.

**Gaono Residence
Apartments** €€€
Luxury **Street Finder** D4
Gaono gatvė 8, LT-01103
Tel *6878 4525*
Ⓦ g-rez.lt
Large, lavishly appointed apartments in a historic Old Town
mansion. Each apartment has its
own private entrance and
separate living area and
bedrooms, but no kitchen.

**Kempinski Hotel Cathedral
Square** €€€
Luxury **Street Finder** D3
Universiteto gatvė 14/2, LT-01122
Tel *(5) 220 1100*
Ⓦ kempinski.com
A flawless hotel overlooking the
cathedral and Gediminas Tower,
Kempinksi offers opulent rooms
and suites, excellent facilities
including a pool and spa and a
huge breakfast buffet.

The Narutis Hotel €€€
Historic **Street Finder** D3
Pilies gatvė 24, LT-01123
Tel *(5) 212 2894*
[w] narutis.com
Some of the luxurious rooms in
this 16th-century building have
original ceiling murals. There is a
spa centre and small pool.

Radisson Blu Astorija Hotel €€€
Luxury **Street Finder** D4
Didzioji gatvė 35/2, LT-01128
Tel *(5) 212 0110*
[w] radissonblu.com
In a century-old building, this is
one of the city's best hotels. It has
well-appointed rooms, superb
service and first-rate facilities.

DK Choice

Ramada Hotel & Suites €€€
Luxury **Street Finder** D4
Subačiaus gatvė 2, LT-01127
Tel *(5) 255 3355*
[w] ramadavilnius.lt
Rated among Lithuania's best
hotels, this regal place is housed
in a beautifully renovated 16th-
century building. The opulently
furnished rooms feature richly
patterned wallpaper, sumptuous
fabrics and marble bathrooms.

Relais & Châteaux Stikliai Hotel €€€
Luxury **Street Finder** D4
Gaono gatvė 7, LT-01131
Tel *(5) 264 9595*
[w] relaischateaux.com
Rooms boast beautiful upholstery
in rich fabrics and luxurious bathrooms in this lavish Old Town
hotel with Baroque and Gothic
features. Popular with celebrities.

Shakespeare Boutique Hotel €€€
Luxury **Street Finder** E3
Bernardinu gatvė 8/8, LT-01124
Tel *(5) 266 5885*
[w] shakespeare.lt
Converted from a 17th-century
mansion, this atmospheric Old
Town hotel has original oak beams
and an indulgent breakfast. Each
of its rooms is named after a writer.

Central Lithuania

ALYTUS: Motel Linas €
Guesthouse **Road Map** D6
Senoji gatvė 2, LT-62121
Tel *6826 5950*
[w] motelislinas.lt
This welcoming venue on a quiet
street near the town centre has
simply furnished en-suites, an outdoor pool and children's play area.

Traditional lobby of Hotel Rinno in Vilnius's Old Town

DK Choice

ANYKŠČIAI: SPA Vilnius Anykščiai €€
Spa hotel **Road Map** D5
Vilniaus gatvė 80, LT-29142
Tel *(313) 53 811*
[w] anyksciai.spa-vilnius.lt
This four-star spa complex
tucked away in the woods has a
striking modern design and large
rooms with balconies and floor-
to-ceiling windows. Its restaurant
caters for a wide range of dietary
needs. There are indoor and outdoor pools, a children's playroom
and a range of spa treatments.

AUKŠTAITIJA NATIONAL PARK: Šakarva €
Guesthouse **Road Map** E5
Šakarva, Ignalinos r. sav, LT-30204
Tel *6871 6136*
[w] sakarva.lt
A picturesque lakeside spot with
three wooden cottages, each of
which has a kitchen and will sleep
many. Kayaks and bicycles for hire.

AUKŠTAITIJA NATIONAL PARK: Žuvėdra €
Modern **Road Map** E5
*Mokyklos gatvė 11, Ignalina,
LT-30119*
Tel *6860 9069*
[w] zuvedra.com
Just outside the park, this lake-
side hotel has deluxe rooms with
lake views and a good restaurant
with a summer terrace *(see p328).*

AUKŠTAITIJA NATIONAL PARK: Miškiniškės €€
Guesthouse **Road Map** E5
Kazitiškio sen., Ignalina, LT-30252
Tel *6160 0692*
[w] miskiniskes.lt
Combining comfort with
isolation, this rustic farmstead has
log cabins and cottages with
stoves. Guests can try archery
and axe throwing.

BIRŠTONAS: Audenis €
Modern **Road Map** D6
Lelijų gatvė 3, LT-59207
Tel *(319) 61 300*
[w] audenis.lt
This smart hotel in the centre of
town has simply furnished rooms,
excellent service and a cosy café-
restaurant with a fireplace.

BIRŠTONAS: Nemuno Slėnis €€
Spa hotel **Road Map** D6
Kampiškių gatvė 8, LT-59107
Tel *6996 4028*
[w] nemunoslenis.lt
Hidden away in the woods, this
lakeside hotel has a flamboyant
interior and heavy, antique-style
furniture. Facilities include a spa
centre, pool and tennis courts.

DRUSKININKAI: ViLaima €
Guesthouse **Road Map** D6
Žalioji gatvė 28, LT-66116
Tel *6752 4494*
[w] vilaima.wordpress.com
Close to the river, this family-run
guesthouse has a pretty garden.
Guests have the use of a shared
kitchen and dining area.

DRUSKININKAI: Grand Spa Lietuva Hotel Druskininkai €€
Spa hotel **Road Map** D6
V Kudirkos gatvė 45, LT-66120
Tel *(313) 51 200*
[w] grandspa.lt
This well-equipped complex has
free access to the spa facilities and
two excellent restaurants *(see
p328).* It has a wave pool and
water slides for children.

DRUSKININKAI: Hotel Violeta €€
Spa hotel **Road Map** D6
Kurorto gatvė 4, LT-66126
Tel *(313) 60 600*
[w] violeta.lt
Surrounded by parkland, this
grand riverside hotel offers a
range of facilities including pools,
a spa centre and tennis courts.

For more information on types of hotels *see pp292–5*

KAUNAS: Kauno Arkivyskupijos Guesthouse €
Road Map D5
Rotušės aikštė 21, LT-44279
Tel *(37) 322 597*
W kaunas.lcn.lt
This Old Town guesthouse is run by the Kaunas Archdiocese. The clean, airy rooms have parquet floors and huge windows.

KAUNAS: The Monk's Bunk €
Hostel Road Map D5
Laisvės al. 48-2, LT-44238
Tel *6209 9695*
A popular hostel just outside the Old Town with clean, spacious dorms and a shared living area. Helpful staff ensure a pleasant stay.

KAUNAS: Best Western Santakos Hotel €€
Modern Road Map D5
J Gruodžio gatvė 21, LT-44293
Tel *(37) 302 702*
W santakahotel.eu
A reliable option on the edge of the Old Town with an appealing interior featuring exposed brickwork. Guests have free morning use of the pool and sauna.

DK Choice

KAUNAS: Monte Pacis €€
Historic Road Map D5
T Masiulio gatvė 31, LT-52436
Tel *(37) 458 282*
W montepacis.lt
Located in a still-functioning old monastery just outside Kaunas, Monte Pacis offers a hugely atmospheric stay. Baroque-style rooms feature four-poster beds, high ceilings and polished wood floors. It's a great spot to wind down in complete peace and quiet. Guests without transport will have to rely on taxis.

KĖDAINIAI: Grėjaus Namas €
Historic Road Map D5
Didžioji gatvė 36, LT-57257
Tel *(347) 51 500*
W grejausnamas.lt
One of Kėdainiai's best hotels, Grėjaus Namas has large, modern rooms and apartments in an 18th-century building. Excellent service and restaurant *(see p329)*, but only some rooms have air-conditioning.

MARIJAMPOLĖ: Mercure €
Modern Road Map C6
J Basanavičiaus a. 8, LT-68308
Tel *(343) 97 778*
W mercure.com
Overlooking the main square, this hotel with a restaurant is popular with both tourists and business travellers.

MOLĖTAI LAKELAND: Apple Island €
Campsite Road Map D5
Grabuostas lake, Žalvariai village
Tel *(383) 50 073*
W appleisland.lt
An idyllic island campsite with cosy wooden cottages. Numerous activities are available including canoeing, tennis and billiards.

MOLĖTAI LAKELAND: Spa Hotel Belvilis €€
Spa hotel Road Map D5
Kirneilės kaimas, LT-33166
Tel *(383) 51 098*
W belvilis.lt
This luxurious lakeside complex in picturesque woodlands offers beautifully designed rooms and cottages, and an exhaustive choice of spa treatments.

PANEVĖŽYS: Romantic Hotel €€
Historic Road Map D5
Kranto gatvė 24, LT-35173
Tel *(45) 584 860*
W romantic.lt
In an old flour mill, this hotel has well-designed rooms in earthy browns, a fitness centre, pool and upscale restaurant *(see p329)*.

TRAKAI: Villa Sofia €
Guesthouse Road Map D6
Zemaitės 13, LT-21142
Tel *6153 5113*
Wonderful cottage-style accommodation in a secluded villa with just three en-suite rooms. Guests have free use of the hotel's bikes.

TRAKAI: Akmeninė Rezidencija €€
Guesthouse Road Map D6
Bražuolė village, LT-21100
Tel *6983 0544*
W akmeninerezidencija.lt
This divine lakeside getaway has snug rooms and rustic villas with views of Trakai Castle, as well as a fine restaurant *(see p329)*. In winter the lake becomes a skating rink.

VARĖNA: Vila Ula €
Guesthouse Road Map D6
Burokaraistėlės km., Peroja, LT-65383
Tel *6799 3318*
W vilaula.lt
Each lakeside room, apartment and cabin here has a large balcony with a terrific view. Snorkelling, cycling and hiking are on offer.

VISAGINAS: Gabriella €
Modern Road Map E5
Jaunystės gatvė 21, LT- 31230
Tel *(386) 70 171*
W gabriella.lt
A functional hotel with clean, simple rooms. Guests have the use of a small fitness centre with sauna and steam bath.

Beautiful pine-clad double room at rustic getaway Akmeninė Rezidencija, Trakai

Western Lithuania

CURONIAN SPIT NATIONAL PARK: Nidos Kempingas €
Campsite Road Map B5
Taikos gatvė 45a, Nida, LT-93121
Tel *6824 1150*
W kempingas.lt
Offering a huge range of activities in a picturesque wood, this is a well organized and popular campsite. Rooms and self-catering apartments are also available. Book well ahead.

CURONIAN SPIT NATIONAL PARK: Mariu Krantas €€
Guesthouse Road Map B5
Purvynes gatvė 9-2, Nida, LT-93123
Tel *(469) 52 494*
W smilte.lt
In the woods just outside Nida, this peaceful guesthouse has large rooms with views of the lagoon through French windows. Attentive staff.

CURONIAN SPIT NATIONAL PARK: Nerija €€
Modern hotel Road Map B5
Pamario gatvė 13, Nida, LT-93124
Tel *6823 8948*
W neringahotels.lt
Located on a quiet road a short distance from the centre of Nida, Nerija has spacious rooms with large windows and balconies.

CURONIAN SPIT NATIONAL PARK: Nidos Seklyčia €€
Guesthouse Road Map B5
Lotmiškio gatvė 1, Nida, LT-93123
Tel *(469) 50 000*
W neringaonline.lt
This intimate four-room guesthouse has four-poster beds and antique-style furniture, plus good sauna and steam bath facilities. The restaurant has delicious home-cooked food *(see p330)*.

KLAIPĖDA: Klaipėda Hostel €
Hostel **Road Map** B5
Butku Juzes 7-4, LT-92228
Tel *(46) 211 879*
w klaipedahostel.com
Next to the bus and train
stations, this spotless hostel has
several large mixed dorms with
shared bathrooms.

KLAIPĖDA: Pirklių Namai €
Guesthouse **Road Map** B5
Naujoji Sodo gatvė 12, LT-91227
Tel *(46) 313 179*
w pirkliunamai.lt
Six elegantly furnished rooms
are offered at this intimate
guesthouse in a meticulously
restored 18th-century mansion.

KLAIPĖDA: Hotel Navalis €€
Modern **Road Map** B5
H Manto gatvė 23, LT-92234
Tel *(46) 404 200*
w navalis.lt
Housed in a 19th-century redbrick building, the contemporary
rooms here are elegant. There is
a good restaurant.

KLAIPĖDA: National Hotel €€
Historic **Road Map** B5
*Žvejų gatvė 21/Teatro gatvė 1,
LI-91247*
Tel *(46) 211 111*
w nationalhotel.lt
With an enviable location over-
looking the port and the Old Town,
this comfortable hotel makes a
good base. Excellent service.

**KLAIPĖDA: Radisson Blu Hotel
Klaipėda** €€€
Luxury **Road Map** B5
Sauliu gatvė 28, LT-92231
Tel *(46) 490 800*
w radissonblu.com
This four-star option with stylish,
well-appointed rooms and
consistently high standards is in a
central location. Facilities include
state-of-the-art conference rooms,
a fitness centre and a steam bath.

NEMUNAS DELTA: Ventainė €
Holiday complex **Map** B5
Marių gatvė 7, Ventė, LT-99361
Tel *(441) 68 525*
w ventaine.lt
On the shore of the Curonian
Lagoon, this guesthouse, campsite
and leisure centre complex is ideal
for boat trips, canoeing, tennis and
horse riding. There is also a sauna
and a restaurant *(see p331)*.

PALANGA: Villa Gamanta €
Guesthouse **Road Map** B5
Baltijos aikštė 12, LT-00131
Tel *(460) 48 885*
w gamanta.lt
Bright, modern self-catering rooms
are offered in this well-presented

guesthouse a short distance from
the centre. There's a pretty garden
with an outdoor seating area.

**PALANGA: Boutique Vila
Artemide** €€
Guesthouse **Road Map** B5
Ievu gatvė 8, LT-00155
Tel *6180 8158*
w vilaartemide.lt
In a quiet suburb, this lodging has
chunky wooden furniture and
antique design touches
throughout. Outdoor pool.

**PALANGA: Palanga Spa
Design Hotel** €€€
Luxury **Road Map** B5
Birutės al. 60, LT-00135
Tel *(460) 41 414*
w design.palangahotel.lt
This strikingly modern five-star
hotel has opulently furnished
rooms with comfortable seating
areas and private balconies.

PALANGA: Vanagupe €€€
Luxury **Road Map** B5
Vanagupes gatvė 31, LT-00169
Tel *(460) 41 199*
w vanagupe.lt
A plush five-star beach hotel, this
has a classy restaurant and a
well-equipped spa centre, plus
horse riding and tennis facilites.

> ### DK Choice
>
> **PALANGA: Villa Chateau
> Amber** €€€
> Luxury **Road Map** B5
> *Naglio aleja 17, LT-00136*
> **Tel** *6143 9919*
> w chateauamber.eu
> Right on the beach and edged
> by a pine forest, Villa Chateau
> Amber boasts one of the best
> locations in the region. Its
> windows overlook the sea and
> golden sand dunes, and the
> sunset views are unbeatable.
> The facilities and service are
> first-rate, too.

Cosy double room at Villa Sofia, Trakai

PLUNGĖ: Žemsodis €
Campsite **Road Map** C5
Mardosų kaimas , LT-90103
Tel *6202 6033*
w zemsodis.lt
Cosy log cabins at this riverside
campsite come with a fireplace
and a kitchenette. A popular spot
for fishing and canoeing.

**ŠIAULIAI: Saulininkas
Guesthouse** €
Guesthouse **Road Map** C4
Lukauskio gatvė 5, LT-76236
Tel *(41) 436 555*
w saulininkas.com
A functional option with bright,
simple rooms. A light breakfast
and simple meals are available in
the restaurant.

ŠIAULIAI: Turnė €
Modern **Road Map** C4
Rūdės str. 9, LT-77155
Tel *(41) 500 150*
w turne.lt
Simply furnished rooms, a decent
breakfast, and a warm welcome
are offered at this modest hotel
in a leafy neighbourhood. .

ŠIAULIAI: Girelė €€
Guesthouse **Road Map** C4
*Domantų kaim. 1a, Meškuičių
village, LT-81439*
Tel *(41) 211 043*
Conveniently located for a visit to
the Hill of Crosses, Girelė offers
spotless modern rooms in several
large timber cottages. There are
fishing opportunities nearby.

**ŽEMAITIJA NATIONAL PARK:
Linelis** €
Modern **Road Map** C4
Paplatelės village, LT-90423
Tel *6557 7666*
w linelis.lt
By far the best accommodation
in the park, this large leisure
complex has its own beach on
Lake Plateliai and organizes
canoeing, sailing and diving trips.
It has a good restaurant *(see p331)*.

For more information on types of hotels *see pp292–3*

WHERE TO EAT AND DRINK

Restaurant culture in Estonia, Latvia and Lithuania has changed dramatically in recent years. Although traditional food is still very popular, there has been a huge increase in all kinds of new restaurants specializing in everything from eclectic international cuisine to quality pizza. The considerable rise in the diversity and standards of restaurants has happened across all three Baltic States, although there is far more variety and choice of cuisine in the capital cities. A few other large cities and popular resort towns also have a fairly impressive choice of dining options.

Good food is an integral part of Baltic culture and the abundance of traditional-style restaurants in each country attests to the pride many people take in their national cuisine. Traditional Baltic food may not be particularly subtle, but it is tasty and makes for a hearty meal. It is often best enjoyed in the countryside where portions are generous and ingredients tend to be deliciously fresh.

Types of Restaurants

Restaurants and cafés in the Baltic States are locally referred to as *restoran* and *kohvik* in Estonia, *restorāns* and *kafejnīca* in Latvia, and *restoranas* and *kavinė* in Lithuania. Both types of establishment vary widely in the type of food they offer.

Restaurants can either be very luxurious and modern places or basic food-and-beer joints that do not differ significantly from pubs. Similarly, cafés can be pleasant and stylish. Most of them offer a decent but cheap meal of hearty proportions. Sometimes they act as a meeting place for local drinkers. All cafés have a good selection of alcohol on sale. Most modern bars often have a small but good-quality menu which is available until late. Locally run pubs are known as *kõrts* in Estonia, *krogs* in Latvia and *baras* in Lithuania. Although rare in Tallinn, Rīga and Vilnius, pubs

Rustic styling at Estonian restaurant Kuldse Notsu Körts in Tallinn *(see p315)*

are common in small towns and in the countryside. Sometimes, they are rustically furnished places that offer an excellent standard of traditional food and local beer. Fast food has not really taken off in the Baltic States and can only be found in central locations in the capitals.

Dining Hours

The rise in restaurant culture has seen a proliferation of restaurants which keep similar opening hours throughout the Baltic States. They open between 10 and 11am and close between 11pm and midnight. In small towns, restaurants are more likely to open later and close earlier, and in some very seasonal destinations a few restaurants are open only during summer months, closing entirely out of season.

Big breakfasts are rare in the Baltic States. Until quite recently, the only breakfast foods available were pastries or pancakes. These days, however, restaurants offer a range of breakfasts, including variations on the English fry-up. Lunch is still the main meal of the day for many people. Nonetheless, eating out has become such a recreational habit that restaurants often fill up in the evenings, although people tend to eat early, normally between 6pm and 9pm.

Café culture is big in the Baltic States. Most cafés open any time from 8am to 10am and close around 9pm or 10pm, although in small towns they often close earlier. In more remote places, many cafés remain closed on Sundays. Pubs and cafés always have an array of snacks available.

Bright contemporary dining room at one of Riga's best restaurants, Neiburgs *(see p321)*

Dining outside at Domini Canes, right at the heart of Rīga's Old Town *(see p321)*

Menus

English-language menus are commonplace in the capital cities and tourist resorts. In small towns and the countryside, however, such menus are much scarcer. Most people in the Baltic States speak some English, so it may be possible to ask for help in deciphering the menu. After Russian, German is the most common language in Latvia and Estonia. Consequently, menus often come with German or Russian translations.

Vegetarians

Meat is integral to Baltic cuisine. Although there is an increasing choice of vegetarian (*vegetaarlane* in Estonian, *veģetārie* in Latvian and *vegetaras* in Lithuanian) dishes on offer in most decent restaurants, these vegetarian menu options are limited to the capital cities.

Reservations

Reservations are usually made by phone, although in some cases they can be made via the Internet. It is unnecessary to make a booking for lunch, but it is sensible to reserve a table for dinner, in a good restaurant in one of the capital cities, particularly on a Friday or Saturday evening.

Paying

The price of eating out has increased considerably in the Baltic States, but it is still somewhat lower than in other European countries, as is the cost of alcoholic drinks. Prices are highest in the capital cities, particularly in tourist spots.

Tax is always included in the price. Cover charges are quite rare, and usually only apply to restaurants or bars which include special live music sets. Cafés are the most affordable eating option, but many only accept cash. However, credit and debit card payment is becoming common throughout the Baltic States.

Tipping

Tipping is a relatively new concept in the Baltic States. Service charges are usually included in the bill though some leading restaurants add a service charge to the total, which should be clearly indicated. Tipping is generally only expected in larger establishments with table service. The general rule is to leave 10 per cent or less of the total bill. Tipping in cafés and bars is rare.

Children

Although children are welcome in restaurants, only a few popular chains offer provisions such as half portions. In bigger towns and cities, however, menus for children are becoming more common. It is usually possible to arrange for something off the menu to be prepared to meet children's needs.

Disabled Visitors

Few restaurants, besides the new ones, offer easy access for disabled people in the Baltic States, but the situation is improving. Tallinn is slightly ahead of Vilnius and Rīga in this regard. Hotel restaurants are a good option for disabled visitors as they have more facilities.

Smoking

Smoking in enclosed public spaces, such as restaurants, bars, clubs, hotel lobbies, buses and trains, is banned in the Baltic States. The only option for smokers is to sit at an outdoor table in the summer, although some restaurants even prohibit outdoor smoking. However, a few cigar bars have been licensed to allow smoking.

Recommended Restaurants

There is a broad choice of restaurants in Estonia, Latvia and Lithuania, and the listings on pages 314–31 cover a wide range of eateries and cuisine types across all three Baltic States. They include characterful cafés, taverns and traditional restaurants serving hearty national or local fare, numerous ethnic eateries, some vegetarian venues and elegant fine-dining options offering international or marvellously inventive fusion menus.

Throughout the listings, those establishments that stand out from the crowd for their exceptional cuisine and service, ambience or historic or unique setting have been flagged as a DK Choice. Among these high-lighted restaurants are some of the Baltic States' finest and most innovative dining options. A few examples are Tchaikovsky in Tallinn *(see p316)*, serving superb Russian–French fusion cuisine, Dikļu Pils in Valmiera, Latvia *(see p325)*, offering modern takes of local specialities made with fresh ingredients and Lithuania's Uoksas restaurant in Kaunas *(see p329)*, serving highly creative international dishes prepared with the latest technologies.

The Flavours of Estonia, Latvia and Lithuania

Traditional Baltic cooking is hearty and filling, designed to satisfy after hard physical labour and during long, gloomy winters. In the past, staple dishes were mostly soups and porridges made with grains such as barley, although coastal communities also ate fresh and preserved fish. Meat was usually reserved for festivals. Today it is central to most dishes, typically accompanied by boiled potatoes and rye bread. Popular seasonings include garlic, onions, caraway seeds and dill. Baltic cuisines have been influenced by those of neighbouring countries, particularly Russia and Germany in Estonia and Latvia, and Poland in Lithuania.

Bunch of fresh dill

Basket of wild mushrooms gathered in the woods of Latvia

Meat, Poultry and Game

Pork is on almost every Baltic menu, whether breaded and fried like a schnitzel or in the form of bacon and sausages. Roast pork has long been a festive treat. Pork fat is also eaten, often accompanied by rye bread, and several dishes, such as Lithuanian *liežuvis* (cow's tongue), stem from a time when no part of the

animal could be wasted. Chicken and beef are also widely available, while game such as wild boar, hare and venison, may be found in both rural and urban restaurants.

Fish and Seafood

Fishing is a venerable history in the Baltic States, with the long coastlines of Estonia and Latvia

and an extensive network of rivers and lakes throughout the region. Many traditional recipes fell out of use during the Soviet era when most fish was exported. The Baltic sprat, in particular, was canned and eaten throughout the Soviet Union. Today, fish is usually prepared by frying or baking, but it is also smoked and salted. The prevalence of this in Estonia is said to show a link

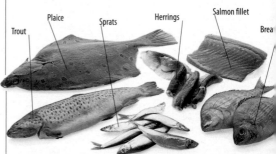

Some of the many varieties of fish caught in the clear Baltic waters

Trout · Plaice · Sprats · Herrings · Salmon fillet · Bream

Baltic Dishes and Specialities

The long list of Baltic soups and porridges includes Latvian *putra* (porridge with pork fat, often with meat or smoked fish added). Popular sausages include Lithuanian *vėdarai*, made from pig's intestines stuffed with potato. Estonia is noted for *verevoorst* (blood sausage) and *verileib* (blood bread). Latvia's signature dish is *pelēkie zirņi* (grey peas with bacon). Lithuania's *kugelis* (grated potato pudding often incorporating bacon, onion and eggs) is served with sour cream. A favourite Lithuanian snack is *kepta duona*, also known as *grauzdini* (fried rye bread with garlic) in Latvia and served with cheese. Throughout the region, you can sample Russian-style *pelmeni* (dumplings).

Red caviar on rye bread

Pīrāgi (Latvia) and *pirukas* (Estonia) are small leavened pasties, usually filled with bacon or cabbage.

Stalls in the bustling market square in Vilnius, Lithuania

with Scandinavian traditions. Popular freshwater fish include pike, eel and elvers. Caviar is also available, including the relatively affordable red variety.

Fruit and Vegetables

The Baltic climate limits the cultivation of fruit and vegetables, and they are not strongly represented in traditional recipes. By far the most common vegetable is the potato, introduced in the 18th century and now served at almost every meal. Other accompaniments include simple salads, often just cucumber and tomato. Mushrooms are popular and, every autumn, people roam the forests to gather mushrooms, either to eat or to sell (see p359). Cepe is preferred, although varieties such as chanterelle and rozites

caperata, meaning "gypsy mushrooms", are also picked.

Local apples, plums and pears appear in fruit pies and tarts, but the true fruit bounty of the region is its berries and currants. Picking berries is a popular summer pastime (see p359).

Freshly picked redcurrants at an Estonian farm

They are eaten raw, made into tarts, puddings or compotes, or preserved for the winter.

Dairy Produce

Dairy products feature strongly in Baltic cuisine. Local butter is held in high regard, while Estonian kefir (fermented cow's milk), Lithuanian varškė (cheese curd) and Latvian rūgušpiens (curdled milk) are also very popular. Caraway cheese is eaten by Latvians, especially in midsummer. The most ubiquitous dairy product is sour cream. A base for many Baltic sauces, it is also poured directly on to a wide range of dishes.

ON THE MENU

Kartupeļu pankūkas (Latvia) Potato pancakes.

Kibinai (Lithuania) Mutton and onion pies, a speciality of the Karaim community.

Šližikai (Lithuania) Biscuits served with poppy seed milk traditionally on Christmas Eve.

Rosolje (Estonia) Herring, meat, beetroot and apple salad, in a whipped cream and mustard dressing.

Seljanka (Estonia) and soļanka (Latvia) A soup made with meat, pickled vegetables or fish, which has Russian origins.

Zrazai (Lithuania) Thin slices of beef rolled with onion, bread and often mushrooms, then baked.

Šaltibarščiai (Lithuania) is a chilled soup made of beetroot, cucumber, chopped egg, kefir and dill.

Cepelinai (Lithuania), or "zeppelins", are meat-stuffed potato dumplings in a sour cream, onion and bacon sauce.

Pannkoogid (Estonia), huge, fluffy pancakes served with a berry compote, show the influence of Russian cuisine.

What to Drink

Beer is popular in the Baltic States and several of the region's breweries date back to the 19th century. Vodka is not as popular as it was during the Soviet era, although it is still widely drunk and both local and Russian brands are available. The region also has some unusual spirits and liqueurs made with herbs. Although wine-drinking does not have a distinguished history, imported wine is available in restaurants and many affordable local sparkling wines are available. The most prominent traditional soft drink, *kali* in Estonia, *kvass* in Latvia or *gira* in Lithuania, has been claimed as a forerunner of strong beer. Customarily made from rye bread and very mildly alcoholic, it is a refreshing alternative to aerated drinks such as cola.

Rīga Black Balsam, Latvia | Bobelinė, Lithuania

Wines

Although the Baltic States are not a major wine-producing region, both Latvia and Lithuania produce sparkling wines, such as Rīga Šampanietis and Alita Šampanas respectively. In Estonia, mulled red wine, known as *hõõgvein* or *glögg*, is popular in winter. Served warm, it has a spicy taste due to the cinnamon and cloves used to flavour it. Fruit wines, such as Põltsamaa Kuldne, which is made from apples, are also common.

Latvia appears in the *Guinness Book of World Records* for the northernmost open-air vineyard in the world. Sabile Wine Hill vineyard (Sabiles, Vīna Kalns) *(see p182)*, has a long history of viniculture, but production stopped during the Soviet occupation. It has been restarted but is very limited and often the only chance to try the wine is by attending the annual wine festival in summer.

Spirits and Liqueurs

The best-known Estonian liqueur is the sweet-tasting Vana Tallinn, which has ingredients such as citrus oils, cinnamon, vanilla and rum. It can be drunk neat but is worth trying in coffee or over ice cream. It is also used to make cocktails or mixed with white wine or champagne. Vodka is also popular in Estonia, and Viru Valge is the most common local brand. In addition to the original version, it is available in flavoured varieties such as vanilla, lemon and watermelon. For visitors to Latvia, Rīga Black Balsam is an unmissable drink and makes a popular souvenir, although perhaps as much for its ceramic bottle as for the liquid inside. Developed in 1752 as a medicinal tonic, it is composed of a top-secret list of ingredients and is an acquired taste. Occasionally drunk neat, it is often mixed with cola, hot

Vana Tallinn liqueur

blackcurrant juice or vodka. Specialist shops, and some bars, also sell Latvian liqueurs such as the caraway-flavoured Allažu Ķimelis.

Lithuania has a range of herbal liqueurs, including Trejos Devynerios. Concocted by a pharmacist in the late 19th century, Trejos Devynerios was listed as a legal patent medicine between the two world wars. Vodka drinkers may want to try Starka, which is distilled from rye grain, while other traditional drinks are honey-based mead and *bobelinė*, a liqueur made with cranberry juice. In rural areas throughout the region, local people brew their own, very potent, vodka. Visitors should be wary of this, as it is usually of low quality and there have been cases where batches have been contaminated with methanol. In Lithuania, a legitimate drink takes the name of this illegal vodka, Samanė, but is not as strong.

Beer

After independence in 1991, the region's state breweries were privatized and many of them were subsequently bought by large international corporations. Baltic Beverages Holdings, jointly owned by Carlsberg and Scottish & Newcastle, owns several of the region's biggest brands, such as Saku in Estonia, Aldaris in Latvia and Utenos in Lithuania. The Finnish company Olvi has bought Cēsis, which is Latvia's

Rīgas sparkling wine, Latvia | Põltsamaa Kuldne fruit wine, Estonia | Glögg mulled wine, Estonia

oldest brewery, A Le Coq in Estonia and Ragutis – now branded Volfas Engleman – in Lithuania. Also in Lithuania, Kalnapilis is owned by the Danish Brewery Group. These major brands predominate in both bars and shops, although some of the more popular international beers are also available in the three countries. The two main categories are light (*helein* in Estonian, *gaišais* in Latvian and *šviesus* in Lithuanian) and dark (*tume* in Estonian, *tumšais* in Latvian and *tamsus* in Lithuanian). However, the major breweries have diversified their ranges and produce everything from very light US-style ice beers to rich, dark porters. Lager drinkers will certainly find a light beer to suit their palate, although visitors often find the dark beers appealing.

The arguably more interesting products of small- and medium-sized breweries do make it into some bars, particularly in the area where they are produced and in the capital cities, and larger supermarkets also often have a decent range. Estonia's islands produce stronger drinks than most of the mainland breweries, and Saaremaa *õlu* is particularly well received. Interesting breweries in Latvia include Užavas, which produces unpasteurized beers that cannot be stored for long and are not exported. Other brands worth looking out for are Valmiermuižas, Tērvetes and Bauskas. The LIDO chain of restaurants brew their own brand of beer, with a

Saku Brewery, producer of some of the most popular beer in Estonia

microbrewery on the premises of the huge LIDO Recreation Centre, just outside Rīga. In Lithuania, the Biržai region is known for its longstanding brewing traditions and is home to several breweries, including the popular Rinkuškiai, which has both light and dark beer.

Soft Drinks

The most popular soft drink in the Baltic States is a drink traditionally made from fermented rye bread and sometimes flavoured with fruit or herbs, alternatively called *kali*, *kvass* and *gira*. Strictly speaking, it is not a soft drink and is beer-like, although it has a very low alcohol content, usually about 1 per cent. It vanished from the market at the time of the collapse of the Soviet Union because of concerns about the conditions of its production and storage, since it used to be dispensed from large outdoor tanks. Once reintroduced, it proved a threat to the market dominance of Coca-Cola, which responded by buying the drink manufacturers in the three countries, who now produce Linnuse Kali, Pilskalna Kvass and Bajorų Gira. Today, this

mass-produced drink is usually made from malt extract and flavourings. Another common lunchtime drink across the region is *kefir*, a very mildly alcoholic fermented milk, which is one of the key ingredients of *šaltibarščiai* (see p311).

Kefir, fermented milk, Lithuania | Kvass, malted drink, Latvia

A very popular soft drink in Estonia is Tartu Limonaad, while Latvia has the very rustic *bērzu sula*, made from birch sap. It is fermented in a barrel with barley seeds sprinkled on top and sometimes rye bread crusts are added. Traditional flavourings for the juice include peppermint and sprigs of blackcurrant, while more modern additions include lemon or orange zest, raisins and cinnamon. Something else to look out for in Latvia is *veselība*, which is a soft drink sold in vessels akin to beer bottles and advertised as being fortified with an abundance of vitamins.

Saku Originaal, Estonia | Aldaris Zelta, Latvia | Kalnapilis Grand, Lithuania | Švyturys Gintarinis, Lithuania

Where to Eat and Drink in Estonia

Tallinn

DK Choice

Ill Draakon   €
Estonian   **Street Finder** C2
Town Hall, Raekoja plats 1
Tel *627 9020*
Rough wooden tables, bare
stone walls and staff dressed in
traditional attire make for a
proper medieval experience at
this fantastic tavern in the city's
Town Hall. Elk soup is a popular
menu choice, as are the traditional pasties filled with meat,
vegetables or fruit, all washed
down with beer, wine or vodka.

Bogapott   €
Estonian   **Street Finder** C3
Pikk 9
Tel *631 3181*
Dishes are served on handmade
crockery at this café that doubles
as a ceramics studio. A great place
to sample some light Estonian
dishes such as *mulgipuder* (potato
and barley porridge).

Clayhills Gastropub   €
International   **Street Finder** C2
Pikk 13
Tel *641 9312*
Modelled on Britain's upmarket
gastropubs, Clayhills offers a
wide-ranging menu that
includes fish and chips, lamb
curry and New York steak. Lively
atmosphere and friendly staff.

Faeton   €
Azerbaijani   **Street Finder** F2
Köleri 2
Tel *687 2125*
In historic Kadriorg, this Azerbaijani
restaurant has an open fire and
bare stone walls. *Govurma*
(mutton stew) is typical of the
meat-heavy dishes, but there are
vegetarian options too.

Kompressor   €
Estonian   **Street Finder** C2
Rataskaevu 3
Tel *646 4210*
This self-styled "Legendary Pancake
House" lives up to its billing with
generous servings of sweet and
savoury pancakes. Soups and
salads are also available.

Lido   €
Latvian   **Street Finder** D3
Solaris Centre, Estonia puiestee 9
Tel *609 3364*
In a mall and part of a Latvian
chain, this bustling canteen has

faux rustic decor and Baltic
dishes at budget prices.

Pan y Vino   €
Mediterranean   **Street Finder** C1
Lai 35
Tel *521 4461*
At this tiny wine bar, the affable
owner cooks and serves light
meals accompanied by a good
choice of Italian, French and
South American wines.

Papa Joe   €
Middle Eastern   **Street Finder** E1
Sadama 25-4
Tel *5684 0103*   **Closed** *Mon*
This great little Lebanese take-
away, serving up the best falafel
sandwiches and hummus in
Tallinn, is perfect for vegetarians.
Baba ghanoush (stewed
aubergine) and *dolma* (vine
leaves stuffed with rice) are
also on the menu.

Pizza Americana   €
American   **Street Finder** C3
Müürivahe 2
Tel *644 8837*
One of the oldest pizzerias in town,
Pizza Americana serves large thin
and thick crust American-style
pizzas with a huge variety of
toppings. Great value.

Sushi Cat   €
Japanese   **Street Finder** C4
Roosikrantsi 16
Tel *503 0911*
This fun sushi restaurant extends
its *manga* and Japanese pop-
culture theme to life-size *anime*
portraits on the walls and staff
dressed-up as *anime* characters.
Top-notch sushi at bargain prices.

Intimate corner table in fine dining
restaurant M C Grill, Tallinn

Tallinn Street Finder *see pp86–7*

Vapiano   €
Italian   **Street Finder** E2
Hobujaama 10
Tel *682 9010*
This is part of a popular restaurant
chain where chefs cook pasta to
order in an open kitchen as diners
stand watching. It serves fresh,
tasty dishes at reasonable prices.

Vegan Restoran V   €
Vegan   **Street Finder** C2
Rataskaevu 12
Tel *626 9087*
Dishes from around the world,
such as yam and coconut curry,
spicy tofu and avocado coconut
pudding are served at this snug
restaurant with a fireplace.

African Kitchen   €€
African   **Street Finder** D2
Uus 32/34
Tel *644 2555*
This hip eatery with vibrant
African decor and cave-like rooms
has a broad menu. Among the
highlights are spicy fish curry and
obe agbon (beef in coconut sauce).

Alter Ego   €€
Mediterranean   **Street Finder** E2
Roseni 8
Tel *5456 0339*
Situated in the fashionable
Rotermanni Quarter, Alter Ego
serves exquisitely presented
Mediterranean-style dishes
prepared from local ingredients
such as wild venison. Home-made
bread and an exhaustive wine list.

Beer House   €€
German   **Street Finder** C2
Dunkri 5
Tel *5819 0670*
Resembling a German beer
hall, this pub serves a wide
range of brews including live,
unpasteurised beers and *medovar*
(honey beer). There's pizza, but
also plenty of sausage, plus crispy
pigs' ears and chicken gizzards.

Controvento   €€
Italian   **Street Finder** C2
Vene 12
Tel *644 0470*
A quintessential Italian restaurant
on a narrow cobbled street with
outdoor tables. Many ingredients
are imported from Italy.

Golden Dragon €€
Chinese **Street Finder** C2
Pikk 37
Tel 631 3506
Occupying a vaulted cellar, Golden Dragon is quite possibly the best Chinese restaurant in Tallinn. Portions are generous and the extensive menu has plenty of vegetarian options.

Grillhaus Daube €€
International **Street Finder** C3
Rüütli 11
Tel 645 5531
A great-value eatery with a blazing open fire and exposed brick walls. The meat-based menu features tender steaks along with grilled duck, chicken, pork and salmon.

Kuldse Notsu Kõrts €€
Estonian **Street Finder** C2
Dunkri 8
Tel 628 6567
This charming cellar restaurant serves a satisfying selection of typically meaty traditional dishes such as crispy pigs' ears and blood sausage, plus some vegetarian options.

Masha €€
Russian **Street Finder** F1
Lootsi 14-2
Tel 600 3633
This brightly lit restaurant, just outside the centre, serves excellent Russian staples such as *pelmeni* (stuffed dumplings) and *blini* (pancakes). There is live music and colourful folk dancing from 7pm, Wednesday to Saturday.

Mix €€
Fusion **Street Finder** C2
Pikk 33
Tel 621 7700 **Closed** *Sun*
Traditional European recipes are combined with those of Central Asia and the Far East at this smart Old Town restaurant. Creative dishes include tuna steak with rhubarb sauce and salmon stuffed with mussels.

Rataskaevu16 €€
Estonian **Street Finder** C2
Rataskaevu 16
Tel 642 4025
This great little restaurant with friendly staff and superb food is one of the city's best. Roast elk with blackcurrant sauce and warm chocolate cake are among the tempting options.

Restoran Spot €€
International **Street Finder** C2
Vene 4
Tel 600 4977
Run by an enthusiastic young team, this stylish restaurant

Restrained luxury at the elegant Bordoo in the Three Sisters Boutique Hotel, Tallinn

serves an excellent selection of reasonably priced international dishes. Grilled duck is a local favourite.

Von Krahli Aed €€
European **Street Finder** C2
Rataskaevu 8
Tel 626 9088
At this hip restaurant with comfy chairs and faded decor the emphasis is on healthy eating. There is a good selection for vegetarians; the menu indicates whether dishes contain lactose, egg or gluten.

Bocca €€€
International **Street Finder** C2
Olevimägi 9
Tel 611 7290
A sleek, minimalist restaurant with atmospheric lighting and a suitably contemporary menu. Among the enticing options are ravioli stuffed with rabbit, roast dove and grilled rack of lamb. First-rate service. Book ahead.

Bordoo €€€
International **Street Finder** D1
Pikk 71/ Tolli 2
Tel 630 6300
Luxurious Bordoo is nestled in the Three Sisters Boutique Hotel *(see p297)*. Intricate, artfully presented dishes are served by attentive staff. Tables are set well apart to ensure diners' privacy and there's also a pleasant courtyard.

Chedi €€€
Asian **Street Finder** C2
Sulevimägi 1
Tel 646 1676
This multiple award-winning restaurant has a stylish, modern interior with black slate cladding. Modern takes on traditional Asian recipes are stunningly presented. Advance booking recommended.

Dominic €€€
Estonian **Street Finder** C2
Vene 10
Tel 641 0400
This Old Town restaurant in a historic building has a classical interior, antique-style crockery and professional service. International dishes prepared with locally sourced ingredients include deer chops and mushroom risotto, all served with excellent wines.

Gloria €€€
French **Street Finder** D3
Müürivahe 2
Tel 640 6800 **Closed** *Sun*
This elegant restaurant and wine cellar dates from 1937 and specializes in old-fashioned haute cuisine. Favourites such as foie gras and duck confit can be accompanied by a splendid selection of wines. Heavy velvet curtains for privacy at some tables.

Korsaar €€€
Caribbean **Street Finder** C2
Dunkri 5
Tel 666 8064
A fun, nautically themed restaurant packed with aquariums swimming with live sharks, tropical fish and turtles. Superb exotic dishes include Patagonian toothfish steak with mango, grilled stingray fins with coconut-ginger tapioca, and Madagascar chocolate ganache.

M C Grill €€€
International **Street Finder** C2
Schlössle Hotel, Puhavaimu 13/15
Tel 699 7780
A welcoming cellar restaurant beneath the Schlössle Hotel *(see p297)*, with open fire, traditional decor and comfortable chairs. Finely cooked dishes such as grilled venison fillet and smoked duck are accompanied by an equally good wine list.

For more information on types of restaurants *see pp308–9*

DK Choice

Neh €€€
Estonian   **Street Finder** F2
Lootsi 4
Tel *602 2222*
This superb restaurant with an exposed redbrick interior sources its recipe ideas from the Nordic islands, so there's plenty of pickled, dried and salted ingredients on the menu. Dishes are imaginatively presented on wood, glass and slate, and the service is excellent. Advance booking is essential and can be done via the restaurant's website.

Restaurant Ö €€€
Estonian   **Street Finder** D2
Mere puiestee 6e
Tel *661 6150*   **Closed** *Sun*
At this smart, upmarket restaurant with a quirky modern interior and unerring service the award-winning chefs come up with short seasonal menus that use locally sourced ingredients wherever possible. Rabbit, quail and beef usually feature. There is an exemplary wine list. Advance booking is essential.

DK Choice

Tchaikovsky €€€
Russian–French   **Street**
fusion   **Finder** C2
Hotel Telegraaf, Vene 9
Tel *600 0610*
This atmospheric, glass-roofed restaurant in the luxury Hotel Telegraaf *(see p296)* consistently ranks among the top five in Flavour of Estonia's rigorous selection of the best restaurants in the country. Tchaikovsky's skilled chefs create an exquisite selection of dishes that fuse traditional Russian and French recipes. Fine wines and faultless service are provided by elegantly attired staff.

Western Estonia

HAAPSALU: Muuriaare Café €
International   **Road Map** C2
Karja 7
Tel *473 7527*
A cosy venue with comfy armchairs and a laid-back vibe, Muuriaare Café caters for all tastes with a good choice of dishes for vegetarians and vegans as well as meat-eaters. Gluten-free meals are indicated on the menu. The cakes are a highlight.

HAAPSALU: Hapsal Dietrich €€
International   **Road Map** C2
Karja 10
Tel *509 4549*   **Closed** *Sun, Mon*
This casual, café-restaurant with a 1930s feel serves fresh, locally caught fish, organic beef and crispy duck among other tempting options. There is separate children's menu and a choice of delicious cakes. There is outdoor patio seating in summer. Friendly service.

DK Choice

HAAPSALU: Kuursaal Summer Café €€
International   **Road Map** C2
Promenaadi 1
Tel *475 7500*   **Closed** *out of season*
One of the best restaurants in Haapsalu, Kuursaal occupies a delightful 19th-century building on the promenade. With its superb acoustics, the restaurant hall is the perfect spot to enjoy live classical music while tucking into the café's delicious selection of pasta and fish dishes. As its name implies, it is open only in summer.

HAAPSALU: Wiigi Kohvik €€
International   **Road Map** C2
Suur-Lossi 25
Tel *473 3112*
The west-facing summer terrace at this charming seafront restaurant is perfect for watching the sun go down. The wide-ranging menu of well-prepared dishes includes hummus, pasta, duck, beef and several fish options. Helpful service.

HIIUMAA ISLAND: Liilia €
Estonian   **Road Map** C2
Hiiu 22, Käina
Tel *463 6146*
This welcoming restaurant, part of the Lillia Hotel, has a friendly local vibe. The menu features plenty of tasty dishes that are made with local meat and fish, as well as some vegetarian options.

HIIUMAA ISLAND: Vetsi Tall €
Estonian   **Road Map** C2
Kassari village
Tel *462 2550*
Occupying the tastefully renovated stables of Kassari manor, Vetsi Tall is an old-style inn with a lovely central fireplace. It serves an enticing range of traditional Estonian dishes, including various types of smoked fish, as well as some international options.

Flower-filled roadside patio at Hapsal Dietrich, Haapsalu

KIHNU ISLAND: Kurase Café €
Estonian   **Road Map** C2
Sääre village
Tel *525 5172*   **Closed** *out of season*
Despite being a humble affair, Kihnu Island's only eatery serves surprisingly good food. The menu has a number of local specialities, including the island's renowned fish dishes. Open only in summer.

MATSALU NATIONAL PARK: Amanda Puhvet €
Estonian   **Road Map** C2
Üdrumal village, Kullamaa parish
Tel *5550 9223*
This is an appealing, out-of-the-way eatery just off the road to Saaremaa and Matsalu National Park – the large wooden watch-tower makes it hard to miss. It serves hearty soups, a range of mains and delicious pasties.

MATSALU NATIONAL PARK: Roosta Holiday Village Restaurant €
International   **Road Map** C2
Elbiku village , Noarootsi parish
Tel *525 6699*
Part of a lovely ensemble of holiday cottages, this smart restaurant offers a good mixture of well-prepared local and international dishes. The summer terrace has delightful sea views.

MUHU ISLAND: Muhu €
Estonian   **Road Map** C2
Liiva village
Tel *459 8160*   **Closed** *out of season*
This charming, friendly restaurant occupying a renovated dairy is decorated with traditional colourful blankets and local paraphernalia. The rather eclectic menu is prepared from local produce and includes ostrich meat from a nearby farm. Open only in summer.

DK Choice

MUHU ISLAND: Alexander Restaurant
Estonian   Road Map C2
Pädaste
Tel *454 8800*
Voted Estonia's best restaurant 4 years in a row, this exclusive venue within the luxurious Pädaste Manor hotel *(see p297)* offers an exceptional dining experience. Locally sourced ingredients, including herbs and vegetables from the manor's grounds, are used to prepare innovative dishes inspired by traditional Nordic cuisine. Superb service.

PALDISKI: Peetri Toll Tavern €
Russian/Estonian   Road Map C1
Mere 10
Tel *5647 7272*
Paldiski's oldest pub serves filling Russian, Estonian and international cuisine using local ingredients. Delicious desserts include *blini* (pancakes) and fruit pies.

PALDISKI: Wicca Restaurant at Laulasmaa Resort   €€
Estonian   Road Map C1
Puhkekodu 4, Laulasmaa
Tel *687 0870*
This relaxed, award-winning restaurant with splendid sea views from its summer terrace serves wonderful local dishes such as quail, marinated elk fillet and rhubarb sorbet.

PÄRNU: Ahoy Sushi Bar   €
Japanese   Road Map D2
Kuninga 34
Tel *443 8543*   **Closed** *Sun*
As the only sushi bar in Pärnu, Ahoy is a rather exotic spot and sports a white, minimalist interior. Polite, efficient service.

PÄRNU: Café XS   €
International   Road Map D2
Munga 2
Tel *443 1316*
With a stylish, modern interior and a summer terrace, Café XS offers a choice of meaty salads, sweet and savoury pancakes and pasta dishes along with a tempting selection of home-made cakes.

PÄRNU: Café Grand   €€
International   Road Map D2
Kuninga 25
Tel *444 3412*
Open since 1927, Café Grand offers a glimpse into Pärnu's high society of days past. Bow-tied waiting staff serve German and French-influenced specialities and there's afternoon tea from 5pm.

PÄRNU: Kohvik Supelsaksad €€
International   Road Map D2
Nikolai 32
Tel *442 2448*   **Closed** *Mon*
The award-winning design at this café-restaurant features vintage wallpaper and brightly upholstered furniture. It serves home-made cakes and first-rate Estonian and international dishes.

PÄRNU: Kuursaal   €€
International   Road Map D2
Mere puiestee 22
Tel *442 0368*
A popular, lively pub in a late 19th-century seafront building. The menu will please most, with satisfying main courses such as local herring with sour cream, T-bone steak and grilled sausages.

PÄRNU: Trahter Postipoiss €€
Russian   Road Map D2
Vee 12
Tel *446 4864*
This tavern-style restaurant with a rustic interior gets lively at weekends. Staff in folk costume serve *blini* (pancakes), Siberian *pelmeni* (dumplings), ox fillet and baked salmon, plus other Russian dishes.

PÄRNU: Villa Ammende   €€€
Mediterranean   Road Map D2
Mere puiestee 7
Tel *447 3888*
Exquisite Mediterranean and French food is served in three regal halls in this Art Nouveau manor house *(see p298)* with immaculate attention to detail. There is a lovely summer terrace.

SAAREMAA ISLAND: Kaali Tavern   €
Estonian   Road Map C2
Kaali village
Tel *459 1182*
Located close to the Kaali meteor impact site, this pub-restaurant in an old farm building is the perfect stop after a day's sightseeing.

SAAREMAA ISLAND: Pub Vaekoda   €
Estonian   Road Map C2
Tallinna 3, Kuressaare
Tel *453 3020*
Housed in a 17th-century weighing house in the centre of the Old Town, Pub Vaedoka is a lively tavern popular with both locals and tourists. Tasty Estonian cuisine is served in generous portions.

SAAREMAA ISLAND: Hotel Saaremaa Restaurant   €€
Estonian   Road Map C2
Mändjala village,
Kaarma parish
Tel *454 4100*
Occupying an idyllic wooded location overlooking Mändjala beach, this modern restaurant offers a seasonal choice ranging from gourmet-style Estonian cuisine to health food-style minimalism.

SAAREMAA ISLAND: La Perla €€
Italian   Road Map C2
Lossi 3, Kuressaare
Tel *453 6910*
At this acclaimed restaurant in the centre of Kuressaare the menu offers a broad choice of well-prepared pasta dishes that incorporate local ingredients such as bream, salmon and shrimp.

SAAREMAA ISLAND: Rose   €€
Estonian   Road Map C2
Grand Rose SPA Hotel, Tallinna 15,
Kuressaare
Tel *3726667000*
A cosy cellar restaurant, Rose is among the best eateries in town. The vaulted brick ceilings and partitioned rooms create an intimate setting perfect for sampling the beautifully presented local and international specialities such as boar sirloin and grilled ribs.

Bright blue furniture, part of the award-winning design at Kohvik Supelsaksad, Pärnu

For more information on types of restaurants *see pp308–9*

SAAREMAA ISLAND: Georg Ots Spa Hotel Restaurant €€€
Estonian   Road Map C2
Tori 2, Kuressaare
Tel *455 0000*
Set in the Georg Ots Spa Hotel *(see p298)*, this stylish restaurant creates wonderfully inventive cuisine that strikes a balance between healthy and indulgent ingredients. Mains include pork tenderloin, gently smoked trout and slow-cooked chicken breast.

VORMSI ISLAND: Krog €
Estonian   Road Map C1
Hullo village
Tel *5669 4268*
This is a friendly, family-run restaurant in a Swedish-style wooden cottage characteristic of Vormsi Island. Authentic home-cooked dishes include wild boar stew and freshly caught herring. Larger groups should book ahead.

Eastern Estonia

KUREMÄE: Wironia €€
Estonian   Road Map E1
Rakvere 7, Jõhvi, 41531
Tel *5303 6505*
This smart hotel restaurant serves well-presented, hearty local favourites such as sweet and savoury stuffed pancakes. The adjoining pub stays open until late.

LAHEMAA NATIONAL PARK: Kadaka-baar €
Estonian   Road Map D1
Viitna village, 45202
Tel *325 5550*
Tucked away in the dense woods, this welcoming log cabin pub is a cosy resting place for hikers and tourists. Expect large portions of meaty Estonian fare.

LAHEMAA NATIONAL PARK: Lahemaa Kohvikann €€
Estonian   Road Map D1
Palmse village, 45405
Tel *323 4148*   **Closed** *Mon, Tue*
Run by a hospitable couple, this simple, cheerful restaurant near the park serves hearty local food with German influences.

LAHEMAA NATIONAL PARK: Sagadi Manor €€
International   Road Map D1
Sagadi village, Vihula parish, 45403
Tel *676 7888*
On the Sagadi estate *(see p113)*, this classy restaurant offers an enjoyable dining experience with mutton, vegan lentil stew and Sagadi carrot cake on the menu.

Traditional table-settings at Italian trattoria, La Dolce Vita, Tartu

LAHEMAA NATIONAL PARK: Viitna Korts €€
Estonian   Road Map D1
Viitna village, Kadrina parish, 45202
Tel *520 9156*
Originally a staging post on the Tallinn-Narva highway, this atmospheric log cabin continues to be a popular resting place for travellers. There is plenty of fish and meat on the menu as well as *mulgipuder* (potato and barley porridge).

NARVA: 100% China €
Chinese   Road Map E1
Tallinna maantee 6b, 20304
Tel *552 4777*
This highly regarded restaurant with a colourful interior has managed to hire the only Chinese chef in the region, ensuring the food is close to authentic. The long menu includes many vegetarian options.

NARVA: Gulliver €
Estonian   Road Map E1
Lavretsovi 7
Tel *356 0777*
This rustic pub has a large summer terrace. The typically meat-based local food is prepared to a good standard and includes pork on a spit and schnitzel. It tends to get lively at weekends.

NARVA: German Pub €€
Estonian   Road Map E1
Pushkini 10, 20308
Tel *359 1548*
This popular pub in the centre of town offers hearty food in a relaxed interior adorned with antique paraphernalia and vintage boxing photographs. Pancakes, salted fish, caviar and herring are among the offerings along with some great German beers.

NARVA: Petchki-Lavotchki €€
Russian   Road Map E1
Tallinna maantee 19c, 20303
Tel *357 9333*
This pleasant restaurant attached to the Café Geneva nightclub serves traditional specialities such as *blini* (pancakes), *borsch* and *pelmeni* (dumplings) prepared by the resident Russian chef.

ONTIKA COAST: Mio Mare €€
Estonian   Road Map E1
Ranna 12, Toila, 41702
Tel *334 2915*
The low-key restaurant within the Toila Spa Hotel *(see p298)* offers an outstanding menu of exquisitely prepared meat and fish dishes including wild boar in red wine sauce and grilled lamb.

OTEPÄÄ: Hotel Karupesa €
International   Road Map E2
Tehvandi 1a
Tel *766 1500*
Located in the woods outside Otepää, this resaurant has romantic lighting and a cosy interior. The menu caters for both vegetarians and meat-eaters with a mixture of local and international dishes.

PAIDE: Paide €
Estonian   Road Map D1
Keskväljak 15, 72711
Tel *5698 8777*   **Closed** *Sun*
A somewhat simple, centrally located restaurant, Paide is geared towards large groups, but serves decent food. The traditional menu features pancakes, salads and grilled meat and fish.

PÕLTSAMAA: Rivaal Café €
Estonian   Road Map D2
Veski 1, 48106
Tel *776 2620*
This riverside café-restaurant offers a good choice of dishes. There is an open fire in winter and tree-shaded terrace in summer.

PÕLVA: Aal €
Estonian   Road Map E2
F Tuglase 2, 63308
Tel *517 1818*
About as good as it gets for eating out in Põlva, Aal is a lakeside café-restaurant with a menu of traditional staples. The summer terrace has picturesque lake views.

PÕLVA: Pizza Olive €
Italian   Road Map E2
Ihamaru village, Kõlleste parish, 63503
Tel *5663 0054*
At this secluded pizza restaurant well outside of Põlva hospitable staff serve fantastic traditional wood-fired pizzas and home-made desserts.

RAKVERE: Katariina Kelder €
Estonian   **Road Map** D1
Pikk 3, 44307
Tel *322 3943*
This simple restaurant in the cellar of a guesthouse is one of the best places in town for a satisfying meal. The menu features imaginatively presented local cuisine accompanied by a small selection of wines.

SILLAMÄE: Krunk €€
Estonian   **Road Map** E1
Kesk 23, 40231
Tel *392 9033*
Part of the town's refurbished Soviet-era hotel *(see p299)*, Krunk has an oddly appealing aura of faded elegance. The well-presented, meaty fare is the best food served in town. There is live music at weekends.

SUUR MUNAMÄGI: Café Suur Muna €
International   **Road Map** E2
Haanja village
Tel *786 6000*   **Closed** *Mon, Tue*
A peaceful rural café in an idyllic spot with a modern wood-panelled interior, Café Suur has a short menu of various egg-themed dishes in honour of Suur Munamägi (Big Egg Hill). There is a lovely summer terrace.

SUUR MUNAMÄGI: Suur Munamägi Tower Café €
International   **Road Map** E2
Haanja village
Tel *525 1364*
This little glass-fronted café at the top of the Suur Munamägi tower *(see p125)* sits at the highest point in the Baltic States, at 347 m (1,139 ft) above sea level. Enjoy fantastic views of the region along with a light refreshment.

TARTU: Vilde's Health Café €
International   **Road Map** E2
Vallikraavi 4
Tel *734 4191*   **Closed** *Sun*
Ultra-healthy dishes made from locally produced organic ingredients are served at this green café-restaurant with quirky decor. Meals that are gluten or lactose-free are marked as such on the menu and there's an abundance of vegetarian options.

TARTU: Yakuza Sushi Bar €
Japanese   **Road Map** E2
Tasku Shopping Centre 4th floor, Turu 2, 51014
Tel *741 2732*
Inside a central shopping mall, this restaurant serves a well-presented choice of sushi options along with soups and rice and noodle dishes.

Artfully mismatched tiles at Fellin, Viljandi

TARTU: Püssirohu Kelder €€
International   **Road Map** E2
Lossi 28, 51003
Tel *730 3555*
Built into a hillside, this popular pub-restaurant in an old gun-powder cellar has, at 11 m (36 ft), the world's highest pub ceiling. Great beers are served and the menu is packed with meaty dishes. It gets pretty lively late at night and at weekends.

TARTU: Chez André €€€
International   **Road Map** E2
Küütri 3, 51007
Tel *744 2085*
This acclaimed restaurant really pushes the boundaries with its innovative and artistic combinations of exquisite nouvelle cuisine. The intriguing menu includes strawberry and duck pasta, beef tenderloin steak with Alaska crab, and smoked ice cream.

DK Choice
TARTU: La Dolce Vita €€€
Italian   **Road Map** E2
Kompanii 10, 51007
Tel *740 7545*
Serving an enormous selection of authentic dishes, Old Town restaurant La Dolce Vita has won numerous awards. Pizzas are cooked in a traditional wood-fired oven, the pasta is home-made and many of the ingredients are imported from Italy. The delightful interior is reminiscent of an authentic trattoria and the service is excellent.

VÄRSKA: Hirvemä €
Estonian   **Road Map** E2
Silla 6
Tel *797 6105*
Part of a holiday complex close to Setu Village Museum, this

small café-restaurant serving typical Estonian food relies on the passing tourist trade. Sandwiches and snacks are also available.

VILJANDI: Fellin €€
International   **Road Map** D2
Kauba 11, 71011
Tel *435 9795*
The innovative menu at the wonderfully cosy Fellin has a great selection of health-conscious dishes made from locally sourced ingredients. Artfully presented options include smoked herring, and lamb and beetroot bouillon.

VILJANDI: Suur Vend €€
International   **Road Map** D2
Turu 4, 71003
Tel *433 3644*
Plenty of meat and fish dishes, as well as a few vegetarian options, are on the menu at this friendly pub. There is live music Wednesday to Saturday evenings.

VÕRU: Mõisa Ait €
International   **Road Map** E2
Jüri 20c, 65608
Tel *782 5587*
Meat-eaters are well catered for at this welcoming pub-restaurant in a lovely old building. There's a good choice of fish, beef, pork and chicken dishes, but far fewer options for vegetarians.

VÕRU: Café Spring €€
International   **Road Map** E2
Petseri 20
Tel *782 2777*   **Closed** *Sun*
In a stylishly renovated wooden house right beside Lake Tamula, Café Spring offers a good choice of artistically presented vegetarian and meat dishes. The pleasant interior has exposed brick, a wood-burning stove and a comfy upstairs lounge.

Where to Eat and Drink in Latvia

Rīga

Aragats
€
Armenian   **Street Finder** F1
Miera 15
Tel *6737 3445*   **Closed** *Mon*
The distinctly Soviet-era decor at this family-run restaurant in a converted apartment is offset by the delicious Caucasian cuisine on offer. The menu features much lamb, but there are also vegetarian options and fish is often available too.

Fazenda
€
International   **Street Finder** E2
Baznīcas 14
Tel *6724 0809*
Fazenda is a quaint little café and bakery which serves great fresh bread and pastries along with light Latvian and international dishes. Reminiscent of a country cottage, it has been deftly decorated with floral wallpaper, white-washed brick walls, carefully chosen antique furniture and old prints and tiles.

Himalajas
€
Nepalese   **Street Finder** F1
Brīvības 10
Tel *2037 2938*
Despite its rather unappealing decor, this family-run restaurant is one of the very best places in Rīga for authentic Nepalese and Indian cuisine. Dishes can be spiced according to each diner's request.

LIDO Alus Sēta
€
Latvian   **Street Finder** C3
Tirgoņu 6
Tel *6722 2431*
Serving authentic Latvian cuisine in a farmhouse-style setting, this is the most central of the popular LIDO chain of self-service restaurants. Queue up for chicken or pork *shashlik* (grilled meat on a skewer) and pile your plate high with chips.

Pelmeni XL
€
Russian   **Street Finder** D3
Kaļķu 7
Tel *6707 3956*
A cheerful buffet restaurant, Pelmeni XL is completely devoted to Russian dumplings (*pelmeni*). Diners can choose from chicken, beef, pork, vegetarian or seafood varieties. Portions are large, providing very good value for the low prices. A beer or a shot of vodka make for the perfect accompaniment.

Raw Garden
€
Vegetarian   **Street Finder** E2
Skolas 12
Tel *2778 0489*
Rīga's only raw food restaurant serves an imaginative selection of dishes packed with nutrients. It has great smoothies, juices and desserts as well as hot vegetarian meals.

DK Choice

Stock Pot
€
International   **Street Finder** E2
Gertrudes 6
Tel *2783 2165*   **Closed** *Sun, Mon*
This great little family-run restaurant with a short menu features original combinations of Mediterranean, Indian, Thai and Latvian dishes. Choices vary daily and might include Thai red curry with fish, Indian butter chicken or "chili con soya". There are plenty of meat-free options and vegan, vegetarian and lactose-free dishes are labelled as such. Excellent value.

Sweetday Café
€
International   **Street Finder** C4
Tirgonu 9
Tel *2653 7235*
A popular café in the city centre adorned with artworks and an eye-catching display of irresistible cakes and pastries. Sandwiches, snacks, salads and light meals are also served.

Terra
€
Vegetarian   **Street Finder** E3
Blaumaņa 9
Tel *6765 0001*
This stylish vegetarian eatery, with buffet-style self-service,

Patio seating outside self-service
LIDO Alus Sēta, Rīga

offers freshly baked bread along with dishes made from fresh, locally sourced fruit and vegetables. Eat in or take away in a funky box.

Victory Pub
Ġ
International   **Street Finder** C4
Tirgonu 10
Tel *2922 8310*
Popular with locals and tourists, this is an English-style pub in a historic Old Town building. The wide-ranging menu includes fish and chips, steak, bacon sandwiches, chicken curry and various omelettes.

Bellevue
€€
International   **Street Finder** A5
Slokas 1
Tel *6706 9040*
On the eleventh floor of the Maritim Park Hotel, this smart fusion-food restaurant has splendid views of the riverfront and Old Town. In a plush interior, it offers professional service and artistically presented versions of international and Latvian cuisine, often with a Chinese influence.

Benjamiņš
€€
International   **Street Finder** E3
Kr Barona 12
Tel *6707 9410*
Occupying five opulent rooms within a stately 19th-century building, Benjamiņš has retained many original features such as stained-glass windows and parquet floors. Expect superb service and fine international cuisine, such as monkfish fillet and roast duck.

Bon Vivant
€€
Belgian   **Street Finder** D4
Mārstaļu 8
Tel *6722 6585*
A café-restaurant with a dark wood interior, Flemish memorabilia and more than ten Belgian beers on tap. Bon Vivant serves meat-heavy dishes including sausages served in half-metre lengths, Flemish beef stew and several good mussel options.

Čemodāns
€€
Mediterranean   **Street Finder** F3
Ģertrūdes 39
Tel *6731 5050*
A popular restaurant, Čemodāns serves an attractive selection of wonderful dishes from France, Spain, Portugal and Italy, as well as Latvia. Classical interior styling and top-notch service add to its appeal.

Da Sergio €€
Italian **Street Finder** F2
Tērbatas 6
Tel *6731 2777*
This is one of Rīga's best Italian restaurants, with a well-established reputation for consistently high standards of service and cuisine. Pizzas are cooked in a traditional wood-fired oven and there's a great choice of pasta and seafood.

Demokrātisks Vīna Bārs Garage €€
Latvian **Street Finder** E3
Berga Bazārs, Elizabetes 83/85
Tel *2662 8833*
The menu changes daily, according to which seasonal ingredients are available, at this chic restaurant and wine bar in a starkly modern converted garage. Tapas complement the wide selection of wines.

Domini Canes €€
International **Street Finder** D4
Skārņu 18/20
Tel *2231 4122*
This intimate restaurant has just ten tables and is located right at the heart of the Old Town opposite St Peter's Church. Delicious international dishes with Latvian influences are prepared with locally sourced ingredients. Book ahead.

Honkonga €€
Chinese **Street Finder** D2
Dzirnavu 55
Tel *6781 2292*
An authentic Chinese restaurant with an extensive menu of delicious dishes served in atmospheric surroundings. Mouthwatering desserts include crispy fried bananas and apples. Book ahead at weekends.

International SV €€
International **Street Finder** F1
Hospitāļu 1
Tel *6749 1212*
At this top restaurant with a sleek, modern interior, diners can choose several mini-portions of exquisitely presented main dishes. Options include beef Wellington, ostrich fillet, potato *gnocchi* and cheese fondue. Outstanding service.

Ķiploku Krogs €€
International **Street Finder** C3
Jēkaba 3/5
Tel *6721 1451*
In keeping with its name, which means "garlic bar," this quirky little restaurant puts garlic in just about everything, including the ice cream.

Extra-long bar at modern and inventive restaurant Bibliotēka No 1, Rīga

Province €€
Latvian **Street Finder** C4
Kaļķu 2
Tel *6722 2566*
An Old Town restaurant with a rustic interior and some great local cuisine. The tasting menu is a good starting point; it includes beef fillet tart, black peas with bacon and herring tart.

Tēvocis Vaņa €€
Russian **Street Finder** C3
Smilšu 16
Tel *2788 6963*
"Uncle Vanya" is an upmarket Russian restaurant with an elegant interior featuring vintage wallpaper, ceramic knick-knacks, antique books and comfortable chairs. It serves a menu of Slavic classics including a highly-rated beef stroganoff.

Varzob €€
Uzbek **Street Finder** C4
Ratslaukuma iela 1
Tel *6722 4180* **Closed** *Sun*
A tiny, family-run café-restaurant serving Uzbek and Central Asian food in simple surroundings. Favourites include dumplings, roast lamb, *shashlik* (kebabs) and freshly baked bread. Hospitable staff provide excellent service.

DK Choice

3 Pavaru €€€
International **Street Finder** C3
Torņa 4/2b
Tel *2037 0537*
Run by three of Latvia's most promising chefs, 3 Pavaru is one of Rīga's most exciting dining experiences. Diners can watch the seasonal Latvian dishes being prepared with modern cooking techniques in the open kitchen, with chefs wielding blowtorches and pouring vapourizing liquid nitrogen.

Bergs €€€
International **Street Finder** E3
Berga Bazārs, Elizabetes 83/85
Tel *6777 0957* **Closed** *Sun*
Part of boutique Hotel Bergs *(see p301)*, this is one of Rīga's classiest restaurants. It offers an exciting fusion of Latvian and European cuisine created by top Latvian chef Kaspars Jansons.

Bibliotēka No 1 €€€
Latvian **Street Finder** D3
Tērbatas 2
Tel *2022 5000*
Boasting a summer terrace overlooking a leafy park, Bibliotēka No 1 serves a high standard of innovative cuisine. Smoked Latgale eel and chicken-liver ice cream are among the offerings.

Le Dome €€€
Latvian **Street Finder** C3
Miesnieku 4
Tel *6755 9884*
This award-winning fish restaurant on a quiet street is part of the Dome Hotel and Spa *(see p300)*. It specializes in freshly caught Baltic fish, but also serves beef, pork and chicken dishes.

Melnie Mūki €€€
International **Street Finder** D4
Jāņa Sēta 1
Tel *6721 5006*
The well-established Melnie Mūki, or Black Monks, occupies the cellar of an old monastery and serves an eclectic menu of Latvian and international cuisine.

Neiburgs €€€
Latvian **Street Finder** C4
Jauniela 25/27
Tel *6711 5544*
Part of the Neiburgs Hotel *(see p301)*, this charming restaurant is among the best in Rīga. It has a bright, classy, modern interior and beautifully presented Latvian and international dishes.

For more information on types of restaurants *see pp308–9*

Ostas Skati €€€
International Street Finder A1
Matrožu 15, Ķīpsala
Tel *2669 3693*
This sophisticated glass-fronted
riverside restaurant, serving a
variety of classy fish and meat
dishes, has lovely river views and
a great summer terrace. Best
reached by car or taxi.

Rozengrāls €€€
Latvian Street Finder C3
Rozena 1
Tel *6722 0356*
Occupying an enormously
atmospheric 13th-century cellar,
this medieval-themed restaurant
features waiting staff in full
costume and local dishes
prepared from historical recipes.
Smoked deer, rabbit stew and
oven-baked pumpkin are among
the offerings.

Vincents €€€
International Street Finder C2
Elizabetes 19
Tel *6733 2830* **Closed** *Sun*
Run by celebrity chef Mārtiņš
Rītiņš, Vincents is just as fresh
and innovative as it was when
it first opened in 1993. It serves
adventurous dishes with
spectacular presentation, often
aided by liquid nitrogen.
Impeccable service.

Western Latvia

DUNDAGA: Jūras Sapņi €
Latvian Road Map C3
Vīdales ielā 2, LV-3270
Tel *2946 2622* **Closed** *out of season*
Of the few dining options
available in Dundaga, Jūras Sapņi
is perhaps the best. Cheerful
nautical decor features palm
trees and boat-related paraphernalia. Standard fare such as pork,
chicken and potatoes is on offer.
Open only in summer.

DK Choice

JELGAVA: La Tour de Marie €€
French/Latvian Road Map C4
Akadēmijas 1, LV-3001
Tel *6308 1392* **Closed** *Mon*
Jelgava's finest restaurant is
located on the seventh floor of
the Holy Trinity Church Tower.
It's a remarkably atmospheric
location, with bare brick walls
and windows in the four clock
faces, plus views of the city that
are better than those from any
other restaurant in Latvia. It
serves superb French and
Latvian cuisine.

JŪRMALA: Café 53 €
Latvian Road Map C3
Jomas 53, LV-2015
Tel *6781 1771*
With a laid-back vibe, this great
centrally located restaurant
serves a reasonably priced choice
of specialities such as mutton
with beans, barley porridge and
jellied pike. There are delicious
pizzas and desserts too.

JŪRMALA: International €€
International Road Map C3
Vienības prospekts 6, LV-2010
Tel *6776 7735*
This chic centrally located
restaurant with a stylish modern
interior and an excellent
international menu offers a
broad range of fish and meat
dishes. Options include ostrich
fillet, beef Wellington, catfish
fillet and Burgundy snails.

JŪRMALA: Villa Joma €€
Mediterranean Road Map C3
Jomas 90, LV-2015
Tel *6777 1999*
The bright, airy restaurant in the
Villa Joma hotel *(see p301)* has a
cosy open fire in winter and a
pleasant summer terrace. It
serves well-prepared
Mediterranean cuisine with
some Latvian specialities.

JŪRMALA: MaMa €€€
Mediterranean Road Map C3
Tirgoņu 22, Majori, LV-2015
Tel *6776 1271*
Voted the best hotel restaurant
in Latvia for 4 years running,
this stunning venue with its
eclectic boutique interior
makes for a hugely enjoyable
dining experience. It has a
Mediterranean menu with
Latvian influences.

KOLKA: Zitari €
Latvian Road Map C3
Rutas iela, LV-3275
Tel *2001 9608* **Closed** *out of season*
One of the few eateries in tiny
Kolka, Zitari also functions as a
guesthouse. The hosts are
wonderfully hospitable and serve
large portions of hearty fare that
includes delicious locally smoked
fish. Open only during the
summer holiday season.

KULDĪGA: Stenders Pica €
Latvian Road Map B3
Suru 2, LV-3301
Tel *6332 3763*
As well as pizzas, this restaurant
in the centre of Kuldīga serves a
good selection of Latvian cuisine.
Various meaty mains and tasty
sweet and savoury pancakes are
among the possibilities.

Modern, somewhat quirky dining room at
MaMa, Jūrmala

KULDĪGA: Metropole €€
Latvian Road Map B3
Baznīcas 11, LV-3301
Tel *6335 0588*
Despite its faded elegance, this
hotel restaurant *(see p301)* is the
most upmarket dining option in
town. International and Latvian
dishes are prepared with fish and
game sourced from local farms.

LAKE ENGURE: Cope Café €
Latvian Road Map C3
*Rideļu Dzirnavas, Engure parish,
LV-3113*
Tel *2653 6532*
A cosy café serving wholesome
snacks and light meals prepared
with local ingredients. The home-
made bread and pancakes use
flour from the neighbouring
Rideji Watermill, while mushroom
and berry fillings are collected
from the surrounding forests.

LIEPĀJA: Boulangerie €
International Road Map B4
Kuršu 2, LV-3401
Tel *2713 4686*
Serving rustic home-made bread
and cakes, light snacks and
sandwiches, this enormously
popular café-bakery in the town
centre has downstairs seating as
well as a pleasant roof terrace
with great views. Excellent value.

LIEPĀJA: Bel Cibo €€
Italian Road Map B4
Graudu 21, LV-3401
Tel *2783 0274* **Closed** *Mon–Wed*
An enthusiastic team ensures
that customers have the best
possible dining experience at
this tiny, but highly regarded
Italian restaurant. Authentic
cuisine is prepared and
presented to an exceptionally
high standard.

LIEPĀJA: Olive €€
Fusion **Road Map** B4
Klaipēdas 104c, LV-3416
Tel *2666 0935*
On the second floor of the Baata shopping centre, Olive serves a range of pasta and Latvian–Asian fusion dishes such as Japanese dumplings and Tokyo salmon.

LIEPĀJA: Pastnieka Māja €€
Latvian **Road Map** B4
Fr Brīvzemnieka 53, LV-3401
Tel *2949 6233*
Occupying a former post office with a modernized interior, Pastnieka Māja is considered the town's best restaurant. Specialities include soft rabbit roll and stuffed bull's testicles.

MEŽOTNE: Mežotnes Pils €€
Latvian **Road Map** D4
Mežotnes pagasts, Bauskas novads, LV-3918
Tel *6396 0711*
The Mežotnes Pils hotel's *(see p302)* dining room has spectacular views of the palace grounds and serves traditional specialities. Impeccable service. Advance booking recommended.

NĪCA: Nīcava €
Latvian **Road Map** B4
Nīcas novads, Nīcas pagasts, LV-3473
Tel *6348 6379*
The elegant restaurant in the Nīcava hotel *(see p302)* has an attractive summer terrace. Smartly dressed waiting staff serve typically meaty cuisine.

PĀVILOSTA: Vēju Paradīze €
Latvian **Road Map** B4
Smilšu 14, LV-3466
Tel *2644 6644*
This bright café restaurant with floor-to-ceiling windows is in a hotel that's popular with windsurfers. It serves light meals and sandwiches.

ROJA: Dzintarkrasts €
Latvian **Road Map** C3
Žocene village, Rojas parish, LV-3264
Tel *2860 0600*
Part of a holiday complex, this sophisticated restaurant serves specialities from the local Kurzeme region such as sorrel and bacon soup.

ROJA: Otra Puse €
Latvian **Road Map** C3
Jūras iela 6, LV-3264
Tel *2947 7602*
Part of the Otra Puse recreation complex, this pretty stone building is a good spot to try some local cuisine, such as the fish that's smoked nearby. There is live music on Saturday evenings.

RUNDĀLE: Baltā Māja €
Latvian **Road Map** D4
Pils Rundāle, LV-3921
Tel *6396 2140*
In a 250-year-old house that also offers bed and breakfast *(see p302)*, this café-restaurant serves delicious home-cooked fare, served in an endearing, farmhouse-style dining room. The desserts and freshly baked black bread are particularly good. Open only by reservation out of season.

RUNDĀLE: Rundāles Pils €€
Latvian **Road Map** D4
Rundāle, LV-3921
Tel *6396 2274*
Conveniently located for visiting Rundāle Palace, this elegant restaurant occupies the Duke of Courland's former kitchens. It serves superb and exquisitely presented Latvian cuisine with plenty of choices for meat-eaters but few options for vegetarians.

SABILE: Dare €
Latvian **Road Map** C3
Pedvāle, LV-3294
Tel *6325 2273*
Right by the entrance to Pedvāle Open-Air Museum *(see p182)*, Dare serves a selection of traditional staples in a relaxed atmosphere. The outdoor terrace is a popular in summer.

SABILE: Zviedru Cepure €
Latvian **Road Map** C3
Pīltiņi Matkule parish, LV-3132
Tel *2640 5405*
Zviedru Cepure is a popular recreation centre 3.5 km (2 miles) from Sabile that offers children's activities, skiing, horse-riding and a lengthy toboggan run. Its rustic log cabin café-restaurant serves wholesome traditional dishes. The restaurant is open throughout summer, and in winter if there is snow.

TALSI: Martinelli €
Latvian **Road Map** C3
Lielā 7, LV-3200
Tel *6329 1340*
A cosy, farmhouse-style restaurant, the menu at Martinelli encompasses traditional fare and includes some family recipes. The dining room has a fireplace, hefty wooden beams and a summer terrace overlooking a peaceful garden. The owners also run a guesthouse here *(see p302)* and have a small winery next door.

TUKUMS: Karē €
Latvian **Road Map** C3
Pasta 25, LV-3101
Tel *6312 2555*
The menu at this restaurant in central Tukums features a well-prepared selection of typical chicken, pork, beef and fish dishes. The dining room is simple but comfortable. Friendly service.

TUKUMS: Liepaleja €€
Latvian **Road Map** C3
Tumes parish, Tukuma district, LV-3139
Tel *2618 7442* **Closed** *Sun*
Housed within the impressive Jaunmoku Pils *(see p175)*, a manor house set in acres of parkland, Liepaleja offers a relaxed dining experience in elegant surroundings. The menu has a good choice of salads, as well as meat and fish dishes.

VENTSPILS: Bugiņš €
Latvian **Road Map** B3
Lielā iela 1/3, LV-3601
Tel *2555 2958*
Featuring a log cabin-style interior adorned with sepia photographs, Bugiņš offers generous servings of traditional staples and good draught beers. It tends to get very busy at weekends.

Rustic outdoor seating at Pastnieka Māja, a former post office in Liepāja

For more information on types of restaurants *see pp308–9*

VENTSPILS: Melnais Sivēns
Pils Krogs €€
Latvian **Road Map** B3
Jana 17, LV-3601
Tel *6362 2396*
The "Black Piglet" is a wonderfully atmospheric pub-restaurant with candles and worn wooden tables, located in the cellar of the city's Livonian Order castle. Staff donning suitably traditional garb serve medieval-style dishes such as black pudding (blood sausage).

VENTSPILS: Skroderkrogs €€
Latvian **Road Map** B3
Skroderu 6, LV-3601
Tel *6362 7634*
Considered by many to be the best restaurant in Ventspils, this cosy spot with quirky tables made from antique sewing machines is a lovely venue in which to eat. It serves well-presented Latvian and international dishes.

Eastern Latvia

AGLONA: Upenīte €
Latvian **Road Map** E4
Tartakas 7, LV-5304
Tel *2631 2465*
As a member of the European Network of Culinary Heritage, the medieval-style dining room of the lakeside Upenīte Guesthouse is one of the more interesting dining options around Aglona. Curd pancakes made using a traditional Latgalian recipe are one of the specialities.

DAUGAVPILS: Gubernators €€
Latvian/Russian **Road Map** E4
Lāčplēša 10, LV-5401
Tel *6542 2455*
Decorated with an unusual assortment of Soviet-era paraphernalia, this quirky pub-restaurant with a lively atmosphere serves an extensive range of Russian-influenced Latvian cuisine. There is a good selection of draft beers, many of them local.

DAUGAVPILS: Plaza €€
Mediterranean **Road Map** E4
Gimnazijas 46, LV-5401
Tel *6540 4900*
Situated on the tenth floor of the Latgola Hotel in central Daugavpils, Plaza has a wall of floor-to-ceiling windows, which provides fantastic views of the city. It serves skilfully presented Mediterranean cuisine and some Latvian and regional specialities. Attentive service.

DAUGAVPILS: Villa Ksenija €€€
International **Road Map** E4
Varšavas 17, LV-5400
Tel *6543 4317*
This elegant, classically styled restaurant is in the imposing four-star Villa Ksenija guesthouse *(see p302)*. The menu has an emphasis on fish dishes, which are artfully presented. There is a lovely garden with shaded outdoor seating.

GAUJA NATIONAL PARK: Allas un Vinetas Kārumlāde €
International **Road Map** D3
Rīgas 12, Cēsis, LV-4101
Tel *2939 2810*
A bright and cheerful café where the friendly owners, Alla and Vineta, serve delicious home-made cakes and great coffee. They also prepare fresh and nicely presented salads, soups and sandwiches.

GAUJA NATIONAL PARK: Cili Pica €
Italian **Road Map** D3
Strēlnieku 2, Sigulda, LV-2150
Tel *6797 3955*
Part of a successful pizza chain with outlets all over the country, this centrally located pizzeria has a colourful modern interior. There is a reliable selection of pizzas, pasta dishes, salads and pancakes, and the service is fast and efficient.

GAUJA NATIONAL PARK: Mr. Biskvīts €
International **Road Map** D3
Ausekļa 9, Sigulda, LV-2150
Tel *6797 6611*
This great little self-service café, with a rugged interior hung with cow bells, is renowned for its superb cakes and has a good selection of light lunches and evening meals. It gets crowded at times, but there is extra space outdoors in the summer.

Wholesome food at Līgatne's busy pub, Vilhelmīnes Dzirnavas, Gauja National Park

GAUJA NATIONAL PARK: Vilhelmīnes Dzirnavas €
Latvian **Road Map** D3
Spriņģu 1, Līgatne, LV-4110
Tel *2755 1311*
This bustling pub in a tiny village serves wholesome cuisine in rustic surroundings. Dishes include home-made meatballs, grilled trout and grilled banana.

GAUJA NATIONAL PARK: Alexis €€
Latvian **Road Map** D3
Vienibas laukums 1, Cēsis LV-4101
Tel *6412 0122*
In the grand Kolonna Hotel, Alexis offers splendid views of the surrounding park. Traditional Latvian cuisine, as well as other European fare, is served by attentive staff.

GAUJA NATIONAL PARK: Aparjods €€
Latvian **Road Map** D3
Ventas 1a, Sigulda, LV-2150
Tel *6797 4414*
Part of a complex of thatched holiday cottages, Aparjods is decorated with antiques. It serves excellent Latvian and international cuisine.

GAUJA NATIONAL PARK: Kungu Rija €€
Latvian **Road Map** D3
Turaida, LV-2147
Tel *6797 1473*
Plenty of hearty Latvian dishes such as roast piglet, trout and leg of lamb are served at this log cabin restaurant with a large fireplace and a pleasant garden and pond.

GULBENE: Lācīte €
Latvian **Road Map** E3
Ranka parish, LV-4416
Tel *2659 9997*
Better than the average roadside eatery, this thatched log cabin has a very good selection of traditional cuisine.

IKŠĶILE: Meidrops €€
Latvian **Road Map** D3
Rīgas 18, LV-5052
Tel *6503 0466*
On the Daugava river, this tranquil thatched-roof restaurant is part of the Spadrops Hotel *(see p303)* and serves regional cuisine made with local ingredients.

JĒKABPILS: Uguntiņa €
Latvian **Road Map** D4
Pasta 23b
Tel *6523 1907*
Overlooking the Old Town square, this simple eatery is a local favourite. It offers a wide variety of local dishes as well as some more unusual options such as sushi.

JĒKABPILS: Luiize €€
International   Road Map D4
Brīvības 190
Tel *2770 5777*
A stylish restaurant in an old
building with a hotel and
nightclub attached, Luiize has
a menu that typically consists
of plenty of meat dishes. It
has expanded the choice even
further by adding more unusual
options such as crocodile,
kangaroo and quail.

KRĀSLAVA: Mārīte €
Latvian   Road Map E4
Tirgus 2, LV-5601
Tel *6562 4039*
This popular central café with
bright scarlet decor and cheerful
service is the best eatery in
Krāslava. It offers a straightforward menu of Latvian
standard dishes. There is live
music at weekends.

LIELVĀRDE: Baltu Ozols €€
International   Road Map D4
Lāčplēša 35, LV-5070
Tel *6505 5017*
Creatively presented dishes,
attentive service and a
reasonable wine list are the
recommendations at this
idyllically situated riverside
restaurant, located within
a small hotel.

LIMBAŽI: Bīriņu Pils €€
Latvian   Road Map D3
Bīriņi, LV-4013
Tel *6402 4033*
An excellent choice of
imaginative dishes based on
Latvian cuisine is served at this
atmospheric restaurant in the
brick-lined, vaulted cellar of
Bīriņu manor house *(see p303)*.
Options include beaver broth,
organic lamb with baked apple,
and pickled beaver.

PREIĻI: Levaž €
Latvian   Road Map E4
Kooperatīvā 1c, LV-5301
Tel *2643 2050*   **Closed** *Sun*
The menu has a simple choice of
local dishes at this small, modest
café in the centre of town. It is
known as "the greenhouse" for its
marvellous tropical-style interior,
glass walls and winter garden.

RĒZEKNE: Latgale €€
Latvian   Road Map E4
Atbrīvošanas aleja 98, LV-4601
Tel *2616 4444*
The Latgale Hotel's ground-floor
restaurant has a rather dated and
formal interior, but is a pleasant
place to eat nonetheless as the
traditional cuisine is well-
prepared and the service is good.

Bīriņu manor house with crenellated towers, containing a restaurant in its cellar, Limbaži

RĒZEKNE: Little Italy €€
Italian   Road Map E4
Atbrīvošanas aleja 100, LV-4601
Tel *6462 5771*
A first-floor restaurant with good
views of the city centre, Little
Italy is popular with locals for its
great selection of pasta dishes
and over 30 pizzas.

RĒZEKNE: Rozalija €€
International   Road Map E4
Brīvības 2, LV-4600
Tel *6460 7840*
A stylish dining option in the
Kolonna Hotel *(see p303)*, Rozalija
serves a good choice of meaty
regional dishes alongside
international favourites. It has a
terrace overlooking the river.

SALACGRĪVA: Rakari €
Latvian   Road Map D3
Rakari, Svētciems, LV-4033
Tel *2706 0869*
A smart pub-restaurant just off
the Via Baltica (Rīga–Tallinn)
motorway that's part of a well-
equipped recreation complex
with a children's play area. The
menu has the usual choice of
well-prepared traditional cuisine.

SALACGRĪVA: Zvejnieku Sēta €
Latvian   Road Map D3
Rīgas 1, LV-4033
Tel *2632 3846*
This well-established, central fish
restaurant, decked out with all
sorts of fishing paraphernalia,
serves a broad choice of cuisine
made with fresh fish and locally
sourced ingredients.

STĀMERIENA: Vonadziņi €€
International   Road Map E3
Skolas 1, LV-4406
Tel *2922 5805*
A lovely lakeside restaurant
within the Vonadziņi hotel
complex of thatched log
buildings *(see p303)*. A good
choice of dishes is served on the
summer terrace or, in the winter
months, by a blazing fire.

VALMIERA: Cili Pica €
Italian   Road Map D3
Georga Apiņa 10a, LV-4201
Tel *6422 8558*
Part of a national chain, this
brightly decorated pizzeria offers
quick service and delicious pizzas.
Pasta dishes, soups, salads and
desserts are also on the menu.

VALMIERA: Rātes Vārti €
International   Road Map D3
Lāčplēša 1, LV-4201
Tel *6428 1942*
A quaint little restaurant near
St Simon's church with stripped
wood floors, white tablecloths
and comfortable seating. The
wide selection of Latvian and
international dishes includes
several couscous options.

DK Choice

VALMIERA: Dikļu Pils €€
Latvian   Road Map D3
Dikļi parish, LV-4223
Tel *6420 7480*
Housed within the impeccably
restored Dikli Palace Hotel *(see
p303)*, this restaurant has a
formal yet relaxed dining
atmosphere. The menu features
exquisitely presented Latvian
specialities made with locally
sourced ingredients. Tempting
options include smoked pike
perch soup, roast rabbit with
apple sauce, and baked
pumpkin with marzipan for
dessert. Excellent service.

**VECPIEBALGA: Jumurdas
Muiža** €€
International   Road Map D3
Ērgļu district, LV-4844
Tel *6487 1791*
Part of a hotel complex of
converted manor buildings 19 km
(12 miles) south of Vecpiebalga,
this secluded lakeside restaurant
has a lovely summer terrace. A
sophisticated blend of Latvian
and European cuisine is served.

Where to Eat and Drink in Lithuania

Vilnius

Briusly €
Asian   **Street Finder** C3
Islandijos 4
Tel *0914 1203*
Named after legendary Kung Fu
fighter Bruce Lee, this informal and
reasonably priced restaurant serves
"food with attitude" – a tasty
selection of oriental dishes – and
attracts a young, trendy crowd.

Cozy €
International   **Street Finder** D4
Dominikonų 10
Tel *(5) 261 1137*
Contemporary jazz complements
the subtly lit interior and a DJ
plays most nights until late at this
hip café-restaurant in the Old
Town. The menu has a good
choice of pasta, soups, meaty
mains and desserts.

Forto Dvaras €
Lithuanian   **Street Finder** D3
Pilies gatvė 16
Tel *6561 3688*
Part of a popular chain of folksy
Lithuanian restaurants, Forto
Dvaras is a reliable option for
hearty local fare. Dishes include
potato pancakes with various
fillings and a choice of meat dishes.

Ltaste €
Lithuanian   **Street Finder** D3
Odminių 3
Tel *6982 6865*   **Closed** *Sun*
This welcoming café-restaurant-
shop opposite Cathedral Square
specializes in home-made bread,
cakes and a refreshingly modern
interpretation of Lithuanian
cuisine. The shelves of the
modern interior are stocked with
locally produced food.

Pilies Kepyklėlė €
International   **Street Finder** C3
Pilies gatvė 19
Tel *(5) 260 8992*
A popular meeting place, Pilies
Kepyklėlė offers a fantastic
selection of freshly made cakes
and pastries, as well as more
substantial savoury crêpes.

Pinavija €
International   **Street Finder** C3
Vilniaus 21
Tel *6764 4422*
Renowned for its cakes and
pastries and for its freshly baked
kibinai (see p311) in particular, this
laid-back, cosy café and bakery
serves great breakfasts. It has
some outdoor seating.

Prie Katedros €
International   **Street Finder** D3
Gedimino prospektas 5
Tel *6057 7555*
This well-established microbrewery is replete with gleaming
vats, piping and ducts. The tasty
honey beer is a local favourite, as
are the boar sausages and plums
wrapped in bacon.

RawRaw €
Vegetarian   **Street Finder** D3
Totorių gatvė 3
Tel *6995 2022*
As the name suggests, just
about every dish at this stylish
restaurant is served uncooked.
Vitamin-packed smoothies and
juices are on offer, and the
healthy, filling dishes include
turnip ravioli stuffed with nuts.
The open-plan kitchen lets diners
watch the action.

Užupio Klasika €
Lithuanian   **Street Finder** E4
Užupio 28
Tel *(5) 215 3677*
This tiny, romantic restaurant-
café is the perfect spot for an
intimate rendezvous. The food is
delicious, although service can
be slow. Expect to be serenaded
by a musician.

Vandens Malūnas €
Lithuanian
Verkių 100
Tel *(5) 271 1666*
Occupying a restored 19th-
century watermill in a lush valley
just below Verkiai Palace *(see
p249)*, this delightful restaurant
serves simple fare. The stone-
walled interior has a roaring fire
in winter and there is a shaded
terrace in summer.

Cellar dining area of popular traditional
restaurant Forto Dvaras in Vilnius

Vegafe €
Vegetarian   **Street Finder** D4
Augustijonų 2
Tel *6597 7072*   **Closed** *Sun*
A great place to cleanse your
system when you've had enough
of meat-heavy Lithuanian cuisine,
Vegafe is a wonderful vegetarian
and vegan restaurant with a yoga
centre upstairs. Diners can choose
to sit on chairs or floor cushions.

Burė No 1 €€
International   **Street Finder** D1
Lvovo 25
Tel *6717 8676*   **Closed** *Sat, Sun*
Ambitiously promising 365
different dishes a year upon
opening, the owners of Burė No 1
have done a great job of creating
an evolving menu of innovative
cuisine using locally sourced
organic ingredients.

Didžioji Kinija €€
Chinese   **Street Finder** C1
Konstitucijos 12
Tel *6864 0560*
Vilnius has a large number of
Chinese restaurants, but this
mainstay is one of the best. Browse
a catalogue-sized menu before
selecting such delicious dishes as
king prawns on a hot plate or the
fantastically presented carp in the
form of a chrysanthemum.

DK Choice

Druskos Namai €€
International   **Street Finder** D4
Savičiaus 6-19
Tel *(5) 215 3004*
Highly acclaimed by both locals
and visitors, Druskos Namai
places great emphasis on using
the freshest, highest-quality
ingredients. The brief menu
changes frequently depending
on what ingredients are available
locally. These are combined
with the best produce that the
owners can source from
around the world to produce
wonderful dishes such as horse
fillet and hanger steak.

Holy Miko's €€
International   **Street Finder** D3
Šv Mykolo 4
Tel *6882 2210*
A cosy, family-run restaurant with
friendly service and beautifully
presented food. Dishes are a
modern take on Lithuanian and
international cuisine and include
potato pancakes, dumplings with
cottage cheese, and strawberry
and rhubarb *gazpacho*.

Miyako €€
Japanese   **Street Finder** C1
Konstitucijos 7a
Tel *6185 2112*
This superb restaurant and sushi bar is located on the top floor of the Europa shopping centre. The high-quality sushi is prepared by expert chefs in full view of diners.

Rib Room €€
International   **Street Finder** D1
Šeimyniškių 1
Tel *(5) 210 3012*
The Holiday Inn's restaurant is the place to indulge in all things meaty, from thick rib soup to spicy spare ribs and grilled veal ribs. There's also a good choice of fish dishes.

Saint Germain €€
French   **Street Finder** D4
Literatų 9
Tel *(5) 262 1210*
Hugely popular with both ex-pats and locals, this shabby-chic French restaurant is among the best in the city. The food is impressive and reasonably priced, and there is an excellent choice of wines.

Senoji Trobelė €€
Lithuanian   **Street Finder** B4
Naugarduko 36
Tel *6099 9002*
The menu at this rustic-style restaurant offers an extensive choice of meaty national staples served on pretty traditional crockery. If you are taken by it, you can purchase the dining ware as a souvenir. There is a shaded outdoor terrace.

Sky Bar €€
International   **Street Finder** C1
Konstitucijos 20
Tel *(5) 231 4823*
The views from this 22nd-floor bar atop the Radisson Blu Hotel are the best in Vilnius. Guests can enjoy light meals accompanied by first-class cocktails.

Sofa de Pancho €€
Mexican   **Street Finder** D4
Visų Šventųjų 5
Tel *6738 9002*   **Closed** *Sun, Mon*
Enthusiastic staff prepare top-notch tacos, tortillas and *chili con carne*, as well as great cocktails, at this brilliant little restaurant with a smart yet eclectic interior.

Sue's Indian Raja €€
Indian   **Street Finder** D3
Odminių 3
Tel *(5) 266 1888*
Sue's is a reliable Old Town restaurant serving the city's most authentic Indian cuisine. Delectable dishes are labelled

Mexican restaurant Sofa de Pancho's homely interior, Vilnius

with heat warnings where necessary and the service from the energetic waiting staff is very professional.

Böff Steakhouse €€€
International   **Street Finder** D2
Olimpiečių 1
Tel *(5) 219 9498*   **Closed** *Sun*
Upon opening, this steakhouse quickly established itself as one of the city's best restaurants. The steaks, which are from all over the world, are cooked to perfection.

Brasserie de Verres en Vers €€€
French   **Street Finder** D4
Didžioji gatvė 35/2
Tel *(5) 236 0840*
This high-end restaurant in the Radisson Blu Astorija luxury Old Town hotel *(see p305)* has a small but carefully selected menu of dishes. House specialities include mussels steamed in white wine, roasted duck breast and seafood stew.

Da Antonio €€€
Italian   **Street Finder** C3
Vilnius 23
Tel *(5) 262 0109*
A grand entrance of columns and a portico welcomes diners to this well-established Italian restaurant. Pizzas are cooked in a wood-fired oven and the pasta is prepared fresh on site.

Imperial €€€
International   **Street Finder** D4
Subačiaus gatvė 2
Tel *(5) 238 8388*
Influenced by American gourmet cuisine, the menu at this restaurant in the Ramada Hotel *(see p305)* features fresh North Atlantic lobster, grilled veal and suckling pig. The opulent interior has gleaming chandeliers, a marble fireplace, and wood-panelled walls and ceilings.

Medininkai €€€
International   **Street Finder** D4
Aušros Vartų gatvė 8
Tel *6008 6491*
This well-respected Old Town establishment sports crisp white linens in the 16th-century courtyard dining areas. The service is impeccable, and the award-winning chef ensures that the standard of cuisine is consistently high.

Narutis €€€
International   **Street Finder** D3
Pilies gatvė 24
Tel *(5) 212 2894*
Serving an exceptionally high standard of both international cuisine and traditional Lithuanian dishes, Narutis offers quality dining in the elegant environment of the Narutis Hotel *(see p305)*, with thick carpets and plush furniture. The service is of course excellent.

La Pergola €€€
International   **Street Finder** D4
Ligoninės 7
Tel *(5) 266 0322*   **Closed** *Sun*
Part of the splendid Grotthuss Boutique hotel, La Pergola offers a high-end dining experience with first-class service and a menu of flawlessly prepared dishes. Enticing options include halibut fillet in crispy pastry, and roasted scallops with cream sauce.

La Provence €€€
Mediterranean   **Street Finder** D4
Vokiečių 22
Tel *(5) 262 0257*   **Closed** *Sun, Mon*
This exclusive restaurant attracts a constant flow of VIPs, diplomats and celebrities. The interior is theatrical and even a little bit quirky, while the menu is wide-ranging and expensive, featuring a skilful fusion of Mediterranean and Lithuanian cuisine.

Stikliai €€€
French **Street Finder** D4
Gaono gatvė 7
Tel *(5) 264 9580* **Closed** *Sun, Mon*
Part of the luxurious hotel of the same name, Stikliai offers a sophisticated French-influenced gourmet experience in an elegant glass-roofed dining room. Margaret Thatcher, Ronald Reagan and Mikhail Gorbachev have dined here in the past.

Telegrafas €€€
International **Street Finder** D3
Universiteto gatvė 14
Tel *(5) 220 1600*
With its high-class cuisine and splendid views over Cathedral Square from within the Kempinski Hotel *(see p305)*, Telegrafas is hard to beat. The international and Lithuanian menu includes a superb signature dish of *cepelinai* (potato dumplings).

Central Lithuania

ALYTUS: Dzūkų Svetainė €
Lithuanian **Road Map** D6
Rotušės aikštė 16
Tel *(315) 73 780*
In a town with few decent dining options, Dzūkų Svetainė stands out as a reliable venue for well-prepared Lithuanian food along with pizza and other international dishes.

ANYKŠČIAI: Nykščio Namai €
International **Road Map** D5
Liudiškių 18
Tel *6503 1881*
This smart restaurant is located in a recreation complex off the Molėtai road to the southeast of Anykščiai. It serves a good selection of well-presented international dishes, accompanied by local wines and brandies.

ANYKŠČIAI: Romuvos Parkas €
International **Road Map** D5
Žaliosios village, 20km (12 miles) east of Anykščiai
Tel *6867 7858*
The intimate restaurant in the Romuva Park Hotel and leisure complex has panoramic views of the surrounding pine forests. The menu offers a wide choice of local and international cuisine.

AUKŠTAITIJA NATIONAL PARK: Žuvėdra €
Lithuanian **Road Map** E5
Mokyklos gatvė 11, Ignalina
Tel *6860 9069*
Part of the Žuvėdra Hotel *(see p305)*, this pleasant restaurant is surrounded by pretty gardens

and has a lovely summer terrace with views of the nearby lake. It serves delicious national and regional dishes made with locally sourced ingredients.

BIRŠTONAS: Birštono Seklytėlė €
Lithuanian **Road Map** D6
Prienų 10
Tel *(319) 65 800*
Perched high above the Nemunas river, Birštono Seklytėlė's main attraction is the stunning views from its terrace. Tables along its rim are the most popular, but the window-side seats in the dining room also provide great views. Good national fare is served.

BIRŠTONAS: Sonata €
Lithuanian **Road Map** D6
Algirdo 34
Tel *(319) 65 825*
This secluded restaurant within the Sonata Hotel on the banks of the Nemunas river has lush forest views from its stylish redbrick interior. A broad selection of regional and international cuisine is on offer.

BIRŽAI: 19-tas Kilometras €
Lithuanian **Road Map** D4
Rauboniy village, Pasvalio region
Tel *(451) 39 676*
Located just off the Via Baltica motorway to Rīga, this canteen-style eatery serving cutlets, pancakes and salads is a good place to break the journey between capital cities. It also has its own zoo. A convenient pit stop rather than a dining destination in its own right.

BIRŽAI: Biržų Duona €
Lithuanian **Road Map** D4
Vytauto 26
Tel *65031993* **Closed** *Sat dinner, Sun*
This delightful café and bakery serves great coffee and a delicious range of traditional Lithuanian breads and pastries, along with sandwiches, pizza slices and other light snacks. It's a good spot to try *šakotis*, a distinctive local cake made by applying layers of dough onto a rotating spit over an open fire.

DRUSKININKAI: Kolonada €
Lithuanian **Road Map** D6
V Kudirkos gatvė 22
Tel *(313) 53 409*
Occupying an early 20th-century colonnaded building in a park, Kolonada is popular with the local arty crowd. A good selection of national dishes is served though service can be slow. There is live jazz, blues and classical music.

Minimalist, modern decor at Uoksas, one of Kaunas's top restaurants

DRUSKININKAI: Sicilia €
Italian **Road Map** D6
Taikos 9
Tel *(313) 51 865*
An enormously popular pizzeria in central Druskininkai, Sicilia boasts consistently high standards of service and cuisine. The wide-ranging menu includes pizza, sweet and savoury pancakes, potato pie, and various chicken, pork and beef dishes.

DRUSKININKAI: Keturi Vėjai €€
International **Road Map** D6
V Kudirkos gatvė 45
Tel *6180 0966*
The Grand Spa Lietuva Hotel *(see p305)* has two excellent restaurants – the elegant ground-floor Druskininkai and the smart eighth-floor Keturi Vėjai, which boasts panoramic views of the town and serves beautifully presented regional and international cuisine.

KAUNAS: Žalias Ratas €
Lithuanian **Road Map** D5
Laisvės 36b
Tel *6747 3815*
Providing great value and friendly service, this delightfully rustic restaurant, with a central open fireplace and shaded summer terrace, is a great place to sample reasonably priced, authentic local cuisine.

KAUNAS: Bernelių Užeiga €€
Lithuanian **Road Map** D5
M Valančiaus 9
Tel *6140 5236*
This tavern-style restaurant in an 18th-century building serves generous portions of traditional cuisine. Mouthwatering options include potato dumplings, mutton cooked in beer, rabbit stew and potato pancakes.

KAUNAS: Buon Giorno €€
Italian **Road Map** D5
Daukanto 14
Tel *6106 3777*
Revelling in Italian gastronomy, Buon Giorno serves great pizza, pasta and *bruschetta*. This branch is a *trattoria* with full meals. For drinks and lighter bites head to the *taverna* of the same name (and quality) found at Vilniaus 34.

KAUNAS: Moksha €€
Indian **Road Map** D5
Vasario 16-osios 6
Tel *6767 1649*
Highly regarded for its Indian and Thai food, Moksha is an intimate place in the Old Town with whitewashed walls and simple furniture. Dishes are spiced to European tastes, and the staff provide efficient service.

KAUNAS: Pompėja €€
Mediterranean **Road Map** D5
V Putvinskio 38
Tel *(37) 422 055*
Pompėja has a well-deserved reputation for fine Mediterranean food. Mock Classical frescoes and clay floor tiles conjure up the spirit of ancient Rome.

DK Choice

KAUNAS: Uoksas €€
International **Road Map** D5
Maironio 28
Tel *6863 8881* **Closed** *Sun*
One of Kaunas's best restaurants, Uoksas has an open kitchen where diners can watch the chefs prepare inventive dishes using liquid nitrogen and other cutting-edge cooking methods. Innovative food presentation features the use of slate, stone and wooden slabs in place of plates and rough woollen bread baskets instead of traditional wicker ones.

KĖDAINIAI: Grėjaus Namas €
Lithuanian **Road Map** D5
Didžioji gatvė 36
Tel *(347) 51 500*
Housed in the vaulted cellar of the Old Town hotel bearing the same name *(see p306)*, Grėjaus Namas is one of the loveliest restaurants in Central Lithuania and serves first-class cuisine in elegant surroundings.

KERNAVĖ: Pušynėlis €
Lithuanian **Road Map** D5
Verkšionys, near Dūkštai
Tel *6991 4103*
Situated above a thickly forested bend in the Neris river, Pušynėlis commands an almost primordial

view. The food cannot quite match the panorama, but the simple fare and a children's playground make it an attractive destination for families. On the Vilnius–Sudervė–Kernavė road, turn left towards Vievis, continue for a couple of kilometres and it's on the left.

MARIJAMPOLĖ: Sudavija €
Lithuanian **Road Map** C6
Sodo 1a
Tel *(343) 52 995*
Expect home-cooked food served by attentive waiting staff at this cosy dining room in the Sudavija Hotel. The relaxed interior features crisp white tablecloths, a fireplace and a piano.

PANEVĖŽYS: Hesburger
Panevėžys Babilonas II €
International **Road Map** D5
Klaipėdos 143
Tel *6730 2758*
Part of an ubiquitous Baltic chain of McDonald's-style fast-food restaurants, Hesburger has hamburgers, fries, wraps, cakes and salads. With efficient service, it is convenient for a quick meal.

PANEVĖŽYS: Déjà vu €€
International **Road Map** D5
Kranto gatvė 24
Tel *(45) 584 859*
Panevėžys' classiest restaurant is located within the Romantic Hotel *(see p306)* and features an elegant interior with paintings and soft furnishings. Imaginative dishes include caramelized duck breast, baby octopus risotto, and pear salad.

TRAKAI: Kybynlar €
Karaim **Road Map** D6
Karaimų 29
Tel *6980 6320*
This riverside restaurant with a pleasant summer terrace and traditionally decorated interior

serves an appetizing choice of Karaim cuisine, including fish baked in pastry and other similar pasty-style dishes.

TRAKAI: Senoji Kibininė €
Karaim **Road Map** D6
Karaimų 65
Tel *(528) 55 865*
Located in an atmospheric barn, Senoji Kibininė specializes in traditional *čenakai* (stewed cabbage) and *kibinai*, Karaim pasties stuffed with a choice of filling including mutton, beef and vegetables or, for dessert, chocolate and nuts.

TRAKAI: Bona €€
International **Road Map** D6
Karaimų 53a
Tel *(528) 55 595*
Bona is an upmarket pizzeria with an enviable lakeside spot providing wonderful views of the castle. Well-prepared international dishes are available in addition to pizza.

TRAKAI: Remus €€
International **Road Map** D6
Karaimų 93a
Tel *6981 3777*
Serving first-class European and Lithuanian cuisine, this luxurious venue modelled on an English rowing club features plenty of polished wood, antique boating paraphernalia and even a small museum dedicated to rowing.

TRAKAI: Akmeninė
Rezidencija €€€
Caucasian **Road Map** D6
Bražuolės village
Tel *6983 0544*
Nestled in a picturesque spot on the shore of Lake Akmena, the rustic yet elegant restaurant at this secluded hotel *(see p306)* serves dishes such as baked rabbit's liver, smoked eel, and meat and fish *shashlik* (kebab).

Alfresco eating at traditional Karaim restaurant, Kybynlar in Trakai

For more information on types of restaurants *see pp308–9*

TRAKAI: Apvalaus Stalo Klubas €€€
French/Lithuanian   Road Map D6
Karaimų 53a
Tel *(528) 55 595*
With floor-to-ceiling windows, this classy lakeside restaurant enjoys splendid views of the castle. It serves gourmet French food and exquisitely presented Lithuanian specialities.

VILNIUS-KLAIPĖDA MOTORWAY: Tvirtovė prie Didžiulio €
Lithuanian   Road Map D5
Dėdeliškių village, 20km (12 miles) west of Vilnius
Tel *(5) 243 2389*
In a modern three-storey brick castle by the A1 motorway, this restaurant with kitsch decor serves simple food and beer, and has fine views of the countryside.

VILNIUS-MOLĖTAI ROAD: Žaldokynė €
Lithuanian   Road Map D5
Molėtų plentas, 17km (11 miles) north of Vilnius
Tel *(5) 250 2289*
Just off the A14 to Molėtai, this thatched mansion has a warren of atmospheric dining rooms serving excellent dishes, including stewed dumplings and potato pasties.

VILNIUS-PANEVĖŽYS ROAD: Le Paysage €€€
French   Road Map D5
A2 motorway, 19km (12 miles) north of Vilnius
Tel *(5) 273 9700*
Part of the vast lakeside Le Meridien Villon Resort, Le Paysage is an upmarket restaurant with impeccable service and exquisite food. There are fabulous views from its summer terrace.

VISAGINAS: Prospektas €
Lithuanian   Road Map E5
Taikos 10
Tel *6206 0056*
Meaty mains, salads and desserts can be enjoyed at this smart restaurant, a popular choice for weddings and banquets.

Western Lithuania

CURONIAN SPIT NATIONAL PARK: Baras Po Vyšniom €
Lithuanian   Road Map B5
Nagliu 10, Nida
Tel *6125 2822*
Despite having a short menu, this café-restaurant in a pretty wooden house surrounded by idyllic gardens fills up quickly in season. Book in advance.

CURONIAN SPIT NATIONAL PARK: Ešerinė €
International   Road Map B5
Naglių 2, Nida
Tel *(469) 52 757*
A thatched-roof restaurant and bar with sweeping sea views in one of the loveliest parts of Nida. Popular with both drinkers and diners, it has a good choice of local and international cuisine.

CURONIAN SPIT NATIONAL PARK: Lyra €
Lithuanian   Road Map B5
Preilos 15, Preila
Tel *6124 6447*
Located in Preila, one of the Curonian Spit's smaller fishing villages, this unpretentious seasonal restaurant serves generous portions of Lithuanian food. The back garden's summer terrace has lovely views over the lagoon.

CURONIAN SPIT NATIONAL PARK: Tik Pas Joną €
Lithuanian   Road Map B5
Naglių 6-1, Nida
Tel *6208 2084*
A simple outdoor restaurant specializing in locally smoked fish. Smoked eel is a favourite, and all food is served on paper plates with plastic cutlery. Splendid sea views.

CURONIAN SPIT NATIONAL PARK: In Vino €€
International   Road Map B5
Taikos gatvė 32, Nida
Tel *6557 7997*
An excellent choice of well-prepared dishes is accompanied by an extensive wine list at this laid-back wine bar and restaurant. There are stunning views of the sea from both inside and on the rooftop terrace. Advance booking recommended.

Stairs leading down to Russian restaurant Stora Antis, Klaipėda

CURONIAN SPIT NATIONAL PARK: Nidos Seklyčia €€
International   Road Map B5
Lotmiškio gatvė 1, Nida
Tel *(469) 50 000*
One of Nida's classiest restaurants is located in the Nidos Seklyčia guesthouse *(see p306)*. The restaurant has an elegant interior and a tree-shaded summer terrace with gorgeous views out to sea. The menu features imaginative cuisine fusing Lithuanian and international recipes.

CURONIAN SPIT NATIONAL PARK: Vela Bianca €€
Italian   Road Map B5
L Rėzos 1a, Juodkrantė
Tel *6900 6544*
One of the Curonian Spit's finest restaurants, Vela Bianca occupies an enviable waterside spot with panoramic views of the lagoon and harbour. It specializes in fabulous seafood creations and great carrot cake.

KLAIPĖDA: Čili Pica €
Italian   Road Map B5
Liepų 2
Tel *(46) 210 201*
The most central of the national pizza chain's eateries in Klaipėda, this is a pleasant venue for tasty pizza, pasta and salad served by a busy team of enthusiastic young waiters.

KLAIPĖDA: Herkus Kantas €
International   Road Map B5
Kepėjų 17
Tel *6858 7338*   **Closed** *Sun, Mon*
This vibrant Old Town bar in the cramped cellar of a historic building specializes in beers from small Lithuanian breweries and serves a selection of international dishes. The waterfront terrace is open in summer.

KLAIPĖDA: Senoji Hansa €
Lithuanian   Road Map B5
Kurpių 1
Tel *(46) 400 056*
Popular during the day for coffee breaks and light meals, and in the evening for reasonably priced Lithuanian cuisine, this Old Town eatery has a great central location with outdoor seating.

KLAIPĖDA: Anikės Teatras €€
Lithuanian   Road Map B5
Sukilėlių 8
Tel *6135 3333*
With a grand modern dining room, this highly regarded Old Town restaurant has a superb choice of meat-based Lithuanian and international cuisine.

DK Choice

KLAIPĖDA: Ararat €€
Armenian **Road Map** B5
Liepų 48a
Tel (46) 410 001
For an exotic dining experience, head for this restaurant in the Ararat Hotel, where modern decor is combined with the bright colours of Armenian textiles. The meaty menu features beautifully presented dishes including sublime lamb options.

KLAIPĖDA: Momo Grill €€
International **Road Map** B5
Liepų 20
Tel 6931 2355 **Closed** Sun, Mon
Known as one of the best places in town for steak, this great little restaurant is often booked up well in advance thanks to its superb service and a weekly menu that changes according to what's in season.

KLAIPĖDA: Stora Antis €€
Russian **Road Map** B5
Tiltų gatvė 6
Tel (46) 493 910 **Closed** Sun, Mon
This candlelit restaurant occupies a vaulted brick cellar in the Old Town. Well-known favourites such as borsch (beetroot soup) and pelmeni (stuffed dumplings) are on the menu.

KLAIPĖDA: Viva la Vita €€€
International **Road Map** B5
Naujojo Sodo 1
Tel (46) 404 372
Though it serves exotic cocktails and exquisitely presented international cuisine, the main reason people come here is for the views from the 20th floor of the Amberton Hotel.

KRETINGA: Pas Grafą €
Lithuanian **Road Map** B5
Vilniaus 20
Tel (445) 51 366
This elegant café-restaurant in the glass-enclosed winter gardens of Count Tyskiewicz's 19th-century palace is perfect for coffee and a pastry. More substantial meals are available too.

NEMUNAS DELTA: Ventainė €
Lithuanian **Road Map** B5
Marių gatvė 7, Ventė village
Tel 6867 0490
Part of a secluded hotel, campsite and aquapark beside the Curonian Lagoon (see p307), this simple restaurant has great views from its summer terrace and serves freshly caught fish and regional dishes made with local ingredients.

Cellar dining room at Lithuanian restaurant Arkos in Šiauliai

PALANGA: 1925 €
International **Road Map** B5
J Basanavičiaus 4
Tel (460) 52 526
A pub-restaurant with a wood-panelled interior and open fireplace that has great food and first-class service. International dishes and Lithuanian staples such as smoked pigs' ears are on offer.

PALANGA: Vila Žvaigždė €
Ukrainian **Road Map** B5
S Daukanto 6
Tel 6565 9691
This well-established restaurant serves delicious food such as potato pancakes and home-made dumplings. Vintage wallpaper and black-and-white photographs add to the appeal.

PALANGA: De Cuba €€
International **Road Map** B5
J Basanavičiaus 28
Tel (460) 51 011
The huge menu at this lively bar-restaurant has potato pancakes, cepelinai (potato dumplings) and international choices. There is plenty of outdoor seating around an ornamental pond.

PALANGA: Žuvinė €€
International **Road Map** B5
J Basanavičiaus 37a
Tel (460) 48 070
This wonderful beachfront restaurant has an impressive choice of fish and seafood, from simple herrings to oysters and fine black caviar. Efficient service.

RASEINIAI: Karpynė €
Lithuanian **Road Map** C5
Karpynės 2, Gabšių village
Tel (428) 70 123
Try your luck catching carp, trout or pike in the lake or just stop by this thatched mini-village with rooms, a campsite, a brewery and saunas for a hearty fish or meat meal.

ŠIAULIAI: Juonė Pastuogė €
Lithuanian **Road Map** C4
Aušros al. 31a
Tel (41) 524 926
A broad choice of imaginative dishes is offered here. There is live pop and folk music most evenings and outdoor performances at weekends.

ŠIAULIAI: Arkos €€
Lithuanian **Road Map** C4
Vilniaus 213
Tel 6503 1330
Enjoy authentic cuisine at this cellar-based bar-restaurant with high wood-beamed ceilings. Fish predominates in summer while meats ranging from beef to ostrich are prevalent in winter. Excellent wine list.

ŠIAULIAI: My Thai €€
Thai **Road Map** C4
P Višinskio 41b, IIa
Tel 6000 3056
For those in search of something a little more exotic in Šiauliai, this peaceful restaurant run by Lithuanians with a passion for Thai cuisine is the perfect choice.

ŠILUTĖ: Rambynas €
International **Road Map** B5
Lietuvininkų gatvė 68a
Tel (441) 77 055
This central restaurant also serves as a bar, café and nightclub. The extensive menu includes Lithuanian staples as well as pizza, hamburgers and more.

ŽEMAITIJA NATIONAL PARK: Linelis €
International **Road Map** C4
Paplatelės village
Tel 6557 7666
This cosy lakeside restaurant is set amidst pretty gardens and is part of the Linelis hotel (see p307). The menu features local and international cuisine and a good selection of wines.

For more information on types of restaurants see pp308–9

SHOPPING IN ESTONIA

Traditional handicrafts and souvenirs can be found all over Estonia. The country's retail sector is, in general, quite uniform outside the major towns of Tallinn, Tartu and Pärnu. Shopping malls have had a considerable impact on smaller towns and the same stores and brand names fill out the bulk of these identikit malls. Despite this, towns and villages are good places to find local specialities, including handicrafts, locally woven textiles such as blankets and rugs, and high-quality organic honey from local farms. Most towns hold small markets where visitors can find food and household items. Antique stores also sell some interesting objects. Prices are usually lower outside Tallinn. Estonian chocolate, alcohol and cigars are readily available in most supermarkets.

Stockmann, one of the best department stores in Estonia

Opening Hours

Most shops are generally open from 10am to 6 or 7pm on weekdays, and from 10am to 5pm on Saturdays and Sundays. Shopping centres usually open from 10am to 8 or 9pm daily. In small towns and villages, opening hours are more erratic at weekends, with many shops only opening for half a day or staying closed. Grocery stores normally keep longer hours, and in Tallinn there are several 24-hour convenience stores.

How to Pay

All large stores and the majority of small shops throughout Estonia accept most major credit and debit cards. Retail outlets prominently display logos for accepted credit and debit cards. Visitors may be asked for proof of identity when paying with a credit card. However, most market stalls and out-of-the-way places accept only cash.

Rights and Refunds

In Estonia, all goods come with a two-year warranty under EU law. However, after a period of six months from the date of purchase, the customer might be asked to prove that the defect existed at the time of buying and was not introduced later. Warranties are only effective on production of a valid receipt.

Refunds remain discretionary on the part of the seller, although most major stores will provide a refund as long as there is no damage to the goods and the receipt is produced. Legal guidance can be sought from the Consumer Centre of Estonia (see p335), which protects consumer rights in the case of cross-border purchases.

VAT Exemption

Nearly all goods and services are subject to 20 per cent VAT, which is always included in the display prices. Non-EU citizens can claim a VAT refund on some goods over €127. Ask the shop for a VAT refund cheque, which then needs to be stamped by customs. You can get a refund at Tallinn Airport, or check www.globalrefund.com for locations.

Sales

Throughout Estonia, sales are usually held in the middle and at the end of a season, although the most significant reductions are reserved for the New Year sales. Watch out for a sign in shop windows, which may read as *allahindlus* (discount), *soodusmüük* (sale), *lõpumüük* (final sale), or *tühjendusmüük* (everything must go).

Markets

Just about every Estonian town has a market, known as a *turg*, although they often only sell fruit, vegetables, household goods and other everyday items. There is little in the way of souvenirs or curios to be found in these markets. Kuressaare market in Saaremaa is a rare exception. It also sells trinkets, such as dolomite-carved objects, in addition to local produce. For Estonian mementos the best bet is to attend one of the annual folk or town festivals held across the country. During these, temporary markets are set up, with stalls selling an array of local delicacies, quirky

Trendy clothes displayed in the window of a Kaubamaja store in Tartu

gifts and a fascinating range of handicrafts, including colourful ceramics, stained glass and woodcarvings.

Department Stores and Shopping Malls

The country's best department stores, such as Stockmann and Kaubamaja *(see p335)*, are in Tallinn, although Kaubamaja has opened a huge department store in Tartu. Shopping malls are far more prevalent and are springing up in town centres and suburbs all around the country at a phenomenal rate. Malls are good for essentials, but they offer little for the discerning shopper.

Supermarkets, such as Selver and Rimi, are extremely common throughout Estonia. These enormous hypermarkets sell just about everything one can think of, from everyday household items to an extensive range of alcoholic drinks, chocolates, cigarettes and music.

Regional Specialities

Visitors can buy a number of popular local products from all over Estonia. The country has a stunning selection of regional specialities that make ideal souvenirs. In Tallinn, traditional items, such as hand-knitted mittens and socks, lace, ceramics, amber, leather-bound books, silverware and objects carved out of limestone, are widely available. Kihnu Island *(see p105)* is famed for its colourful and elaborately patterned handmade rugs, as well as thick woollen fishermen's jumpers made by the island's inhabitants.

In southeastern Estonia, home to the Setu people *(see p124)*, one can purchase authentic examples of the embroidered shawls and ornate jewellery that are unique to their culture. The Setu were also the only people in Estonia to commonly use pottery, which is sold in several ceramics shops. Today, pottery fairs peddle their wares in the main Setu towns. The use of dolomite is unique to Saaremaa Island *(see pp96–9)*. Dolomite is used to make a wide range of souvenirs, such as carved ashtrays and pestles and mortars. Muhu Island is famous for its embroidered handmade slippers and bright orange knitwear. Pärnu *(see pp102–3)* is known for its linen and the most popular souvenirs in the coastal resort of Haapsalu *(see pp92–3)* are hand-woven and beautifully patterned white shawls.

Beautifully crafted cane baskets on sale in a local market

Shopping in Tallinn

Tallinn has witnessed a proliferation of sleek new shopping malls in recent years. Most international brand names can be found alongside a considerable range of popular Scandinavian brands. Tallinn's Old Town, which has some exclusive fashion boutiques and speciality art shops, is also one of the best places in the capital for gift shopping and souvenir hunting. Almost every street has something in the way of traditional handicrafts, such as ceramics, glassware, linen, wooden utensils and toys. There are plenty of stores and market stalls which specialize in art, antiques, jewellery, amber, knitted woollens, patchwork quilts and interesting knick-knacks. The Christmas Market in Town Hall Square is especially popular and brings together virtually every imaginable Estonian product.

Colourful ceramic collection at the stylish Bogapott studio

Russian dolls and amber jewellery for sale on one of Tallinn's souvenir stalls

Markets

Tallinn's main market, the open-air Central Market, offers a glimpse into the everyday life of the city's inhabitants. Stalls full of fresh produce may not offer much variety for the average souvenir-hunter, but the Central Market's bustling atmosphere is worth the experience. Those interested in shopping can try and haggle. The market selling knitwear at the corner of Viru and Müürivahe covers a sizeable stretch of the Old Town wall and is a great place to find a gift. Uus Käsitööturg, a popular stall in the market, has a good selection of traditional handicrafts and souvenirs. The Christmas Market in Town Hall Square (see pp62–3), which runs through December, features everything from knitwear and decorative items to marzipan.

Handicrafts

Much more than just souvenirs aimed at tourists, Estonian handicrafts are synonymous with a traditional way of life that persists even today. Tallinn abounds with a bewildering variety of handicrafts. Wooden toys and utensils are particularly common as are a wide range of ceramics, including candle-holders modelled after the Old Town buildings. Traditionally woven rugs are still made today, some of which are more like works of art with their beautiful and elaborate patterns.

Bogapott, an exclusive ceramics studio, and **Galerii Kaks**, with its wide range of textiles, are worthy of a visit. **Nukupood** stocks handmade toys as well as dolls dressed in traditional folk costumes of Estonia. In **Katariina Gild**, craftsmen can be seen creating handicrafts, jewellery and ceramics. **A-Galerii** has a dazzling selection of local handmade jewellery.

Art and Antiques

Tallinn's contemporary art scene offers plenty of galleries and small shops that stock all manner of attractive oil paintings, graphic art, textiles, sculpture and off-beat ceramics.

The city has several antique stores selling everything from Soviet-era paraphernalia to exorbitantly priced Russian icons. Emerging only in the 1990s, antique shops have quickly become a fascinating and flourishing retail niche.

Woven baskets, knitting wool and textiles at the Town Hall Square market

Special permission is needed to take some objects out of the country, so check with the shop manager before buying. With a stunning range of bronze items, silverware and crystals, **Reval Antiik** and **Shifara Art & Antiques** are among Tallinn's best antiques stores.

Books and Music

The best bookstore in Tallinn for English-language books is **Apollo**. This outlet has a range of gift books relating to Estonian culture and history, as well as a small selection of Estonian novels translated into English. Look out for the English translation of *The Czar's Madman* and *Treading Air* by Jaan Kross (1920–2007), the esteemed Estonian writer.

Estonia's wealth of choral and classical music also makes for a great gift. CDs of the works of renowned composers, such as Heino Eller (1887–1970), Eduard Tubin (1905–82) and Arvo Pärt *(see p27)*, are widely available, as are folk music and choral music compilations. **Lasering**, one of the leading music stores in Tallinn, has an impressive selection of various kinds of music and a separate section on classical music.

Apollo, Tallinn's primary bookstore, stocks a range of gift books

Food and Drink

Estonian food products are ubiquitous and can usually be found in any supermarket. Rye bread is a local staple, as are sprats, smoked fish and cheese,

Kaubamaja store, one of Tallinn's leading shopping venues

halvah and blood sausage, during the Christmas season. Try the gourmet section at **Kaubamaja** for a variety. For chocolate lovers, Kalev, Estonia's largest and oldest chocolate and confectionary producer, offers a wide range of luxury chocolates with picturesque prints of Tallinn on the box. These chocolates can be bought from local food stores. Real chocolate connoisseurs should try the handmade delicacies at **Anneli Viik**. There are also numerous bakeries selling delicious pastries and cakes. **Stockmann**, one of the largest department stores, also stocks cakes, bagels and savouries.

Vana Tallinn *(see p312)*, a very sweet brown liqueur, is considered to be the national drink of Estonia. Those without a sweet tooth may prefer it mixed with coffee, while some people even drink it with milk. In terms of sheer consumption, beer is by far the most popular drink in Estonia. Saku Originaal is the dominant brand, but Tartu Alexander and A Le Coq beers are popular brews as well. There is an abundance of locally made, as well as quality imported, vodka, which is considerably cheaper than in other European countries. Saare Džinn, a gin flavoured with berries from the Estonian islands, is good too. **Liviko**, one of Estonia's leading alcohol producers, has stores all over Tallinn.

Logo of
Kalev chocolate

DIRECTORY

Handicrafts

A-Galerii
Hobusepea 2. **Tel** 646 4101.

Bogapott
Pikk jalg 9. **Tel** 631 3181.
w bogapott.ee

Galerii Kaks
Lühike jalg 1. **Tel** 641 8308.

Katariina Gild
Vene 12. **Tel** 644 5365.

Nukupood
Raekoja plats 18. **Tel** 644 3058.

Art and Antiques

Reval Antiik
Harju 13. **Tel** 644 0747.
w reval-antique.ee

Shifara Art & Antiques
Vana-posti 7. **Tel** 644 3536.
w shifara-antique.ee

Books and Music

Apollo
Estonia pst 9. **Tel** 633 6000.
w apollo.ee
One of several branches.

Lasering
Pärnu mnt 38. **Tel** 627 9279.
w lasering.ee
One of several branches.

Food and Drink

Anneli Viik
Pikk 30. **Tel** 644 4530.
w anneliviik.ee

Kaubamaja
Gonsiori 2. **Tel** 667 3100.
w kaubamaja.ee

Liviko
Mere pst 6. **Tel** 683 7745.
w liviko.ee
One of several branches.

Stockmann
Liivalaia 53. **Tel** 633 9539.
w stockmann.ee

Rights and Refunds

Consumer Centre of Estonia
Rahukohtu 2. **Tel** 620 1708.
w consumer.ee

SHOPPING IN LATVIA

Numerous supermarkets and shopping centres have opened in major towns and cities throughout the country since 1991. However, Rīga undoubtedly has the country's largest range of shopping options. This is particularly true when it comes to items likely to be of interest to visitors, although outside the capital it is usually possible to find typical handicraft items such as amber jewellery and embroidered knitwear. Museum gift shops are normally good places to pick up interesting mementos when a town or village lacks a dedicated souvenir retailer. Several workshops across the country allow visitors to watch artisans at work and even make their own pottery, woodwork and other items to take home. Latvian markets cater mostly to local people, but can still be fascinating places to visit. Local honey, chocolate, beer or a bottle of Black Balsam can make excellent gifts.

Opening Hours

Most shops in Latvia open around 10am. Small shops close around 6 or 7pm, while bigger malls and shopping centres usually stay open until 10pm. Many small shops remain closed on Sundays.

How to Pay

In cities and large towns, it is possible to pay with debit cards and major credit cards such as MasterCard or VISA. Some places will also accept American Express and Diners Club. In smaller towns and villages cash payment in the local currency, the euro, may be the only option.

It is rare for traveller's cheques to be accepted as payment outside Rīga, the capital city, although those issued by major companies can usually be exchanged at most banks.

VAT Exemption

Visitors from non-EU countries are entitled to a VAT refund of up to 12 per cent, provided that the items were purchased in a shop displaying the "Tax Free" logo and the total price of purchases made from the shop was at least 50 euros. Identification must be shown at the point of purchase, and a Global Refund receipt completed. Purchased items cannot be used until the receipt is stamped by a customs official when leaving the country. The VAT can be reclaimed at the customs zone in the airport or the land borders with Russia, at Terehova and Grebņeva. For departures from other locations, the receipt should be stamped and sent to Global Blue Latvia (see p339), along with the visitor's bank details, within six months.

Sales

Although locally made items are fairly cheap compared to those in other EU countries, prices for imported goods tend to be high in Latvia, a situation which has not been helped by regular bouts of high inflation. One way of picking up a bargain is to visit the end-of-season sales, when shops reduce their prices.

Markets

Most Latvian towns have regular or even daily markets, although they are rarely aimed at tourists and are most useful for everyday food purchases. However, some markets are extremely atmospheric, such as Petertirgus in the covered market hall in Liepāja (see pp184–5), which is a real throwback to the Soviet era. In the summer months, some markets, like the ones in Jūrmala, sell souvenirs as well as fresh produce.

Department Stores and Shopping Malls

Most sizeable towns have at least one department store or supermarket. Several malls and shopping centres have been built in important cities such as Rīga, Ventspils, Liepāja and Daugavpils. Some of these malls are located in the outskirts of the cities, while others are more central and easy to access. The larger retailers include Rimi, Maxima and Mego.

Collection of fresh produce for sale at the Central Market, Rīga

Handcrafted items displayed at the Ludza Handicrafts Centre, Eastern Latvia

Handicrafts

Traditional Latvian handicrafts include handmade linen, amber jewellery, woodwork and knitwear embroidered with popular Latvian folk symbols. Motifs from the natural world, such as the sun, stars or trees, are commonly used as part of the repertoire of geometric designs found on many handcrafted goods. A particularly attractive example is the *Lielvārdes josta*, a long red-and-white woven belt which features symbolic patterns, and is a part of Latvian wedding costumes. These belts are available in souvenir shops in Rīga, and can be seen on display at the Pumpurs Museum in Lielvārde, or even made to order.

Visitors can watch artisans at work in several places, such as the House of Craftsmen in Liepāja. The Handicrafts Centre in Ludza has workshops where visitors can try their hand at crafting items themselves. Musical instruments can be purchased from the Musical Instruments Workshop in Gaigalava.

The Smithy of Ancient Jewellery in the New Castle in Cēsis calls itself a workshop of experimental archaeology, with master craftsman Daumants Kalniņš making replicas of ancient designs. Another place to find handicraft items is the branch of Tornis in the tower of Turaida Castle near Sigulda.

Food and Drink

Available in many varieties, Laima *(see p339)* chocolate has been made in Latvia for decades and is among the country's most popular buys.

A bar of Laima, Latvia's favourite chocolate

Another common gift is Rīga's Black Balsam, a herbal liqueur that is supposed to have medicinal properties, which comes in an attractive ceramic bottle. Visitors usually prefer it in cocktails or with blackcurrant juice rather than neat.

Beer also makes a good gift. Latvians are enthusiastic beer-drinkers so there are several brands to choose from. The most popular ones are internationally owned, but more unusual brews include the yeasty Užavas, which is made near Ventspils, and Valmiera's Valmiermuiža.

Art and Antiques

Genuinely valuable Latvian antiques are not easy to find, partly because the 20th century saw many of them destroyed or lost during war and occupation. In spite of this, antique shops are well worth exploring, especially because they often stock interesting items. The best place to buy art is in commercial art galleries. A licence, which is available at most shops, is usually required before genuine antiques can be exported. The shops are helpful with the paperwork.

Amber

Amber jewellery is a popular Latvian souvenir, despite the fact that resin is less commonly discovered in Latvia than Lithuania. It is readily available in tourist areas, such as Jūrmala, and in some museum shops.

Buyers should be aware that not all amber is genuine, as various plastics are used to emulate it. Visitors spending a large sum of money on amber objects should ask for a certificate of authenticity, and it is generally safer to buy from an established shop rather than a street-seller.

Roadside Stalls

In the countryside, especially in rural Latgale, it is common to see stalls at the side of the road selling fresh produce. Latvian honey is particularly delicious and also makes a good gift.

Shopping in Rīga

Once a member of the powerful Hanseatic League (see p36), the Latvian capital has had a distinguished mercantile history. Although its harbour is no longer one of the most important in the region, commerce has flourished since the restoration of independence, with boutiques and department stores springing up throughout the city. Specialist shops can be found all over the Old Town and in shopping malls, while major high-street brands are available in Centrs. Souvenir shops, mostly found in the Old Town, sell handicrafts of variable quality including linen, amber jewellery and knitwear. Handmade chocolates and Rīga Black Balsam, the city's signature drink, are popular gifts.

Department Stores and Shopping Malls

The years since independence have witnessed the development of many shopping centres and department stores as well as the renovation of stalwarts such as the 1920s **Galerija Centrs**.

Upmarket boutiques and galleries can be found at **Berga Bazārs**, a 19th-century enclave of shops, offices, restaurants and apartments. The **Galleria Rīga** shopping mall is the hub of designer fashion, while **mc²** has stores specializing in gourmet food and home accessories. For more basic shopping there is **Stockmann**, on the edge of the Old Town.

Markets

Housed in five huge zeppelin hangars, Rīga's Central Market has most of its indoor space dedicated to food, while the stalls and kiosks selling CDs, clothes and electrical goods are outside. Also of interest is the covered outdoor antiques and organic food market on the second and fourth Sunday of each month at Berga Bazārs. Latvians love to give flowers and the city's main Flower Market is open 24 hours a day, through the year.

Music

Folk music was a key part of the National Awakening Movement (1856), although in the years since independence it has become harder to find a sizeable clientele for folk recordings. Rīga's best music outlet is **Upe**, a chain owned by the former frontman of folk-rock band Jauns Mēness. Upe specializes in folk music from Latvia and beyond, and also has a wine bar. **Randoms** is perhaps the biggest music shop in the Baltic States. Cheap CDs can be bought at the Central Market, although bootleg versions are rife.

Clothing and Jewellery

Handwoven garments, lace items and knitwear are popular souvenirs. Designer clothes are available at upmarket stores, while smaller shops sell traditional woollen garments. **Tines** sells handmade wool and linen items in traditional designs, while modern styles from up-and-coming designers can be found at **Latvijas Modes Klase** in Berga Bazaars.

In addition to countless places selling amber necklaces and bracelets, there are several shops offering more unusual jewellery. The stylish **Putti** gallery stocks jewellery by Latvian designers and also holds exhibitions.

Handicrafts

There are numerous souvenir shops in the Old Town stocking items such as linen and wooden toys. In some cases, however, these are mass-produced rather than handmade. More unique and practical gifts can be found in **Riija**, which offers ecologically produced crafts and household items. **Pienene** boasts a wide range of souvenirs, while more can be found in the open-air **Egle** craft market. Some shops also sell Russian objects such as matryoshka, wooden dolls of various sizes that are placed one inside the other.

Decorative wall lamp

Art and Antiques

There are many commercial art galleries in Rīga and the tourist information office can provide an up-to-date list. **Māksla XO** is one of the city's most highly regarded galleries. **Art Nouveau Rīga**, a

A shopper browsing for souvenirs at Art Nouveau Rīga

Amber jewellery displayed in a shop window

Food and Drink

Laima has been one of Latvia's leading chocolate makers since 1870 and it has many shops throughout Rīga. In recent years, however, its position has been challenged by the more upmarket **Emils Gustavs Chocolate**, which also has stores all over Rīga, including one in the Valters un Rapa bookshop.

For something more traditional, many varieties of honey are available for tasting at the **Jāṇa Bišu** Honey Room, along with other bee-related products. **Desa & Co** (Sausage & Company) is one of the few places in the city where visitors can taste and buy deer, wild pig and bison, all raised on their farm in the Latvian countryside, along with other locally produced ecological items. The famous Rīga Black Balsam also makes a popular gift, which probably has as much to do with the ceramic bottles it comes in as with the drink itself. It is widely available throughout the city.

Rīga Black Balsam

leading souvenir shop, offers attractive reproductions, along with scarves, mugs and other objects inspired by early 20th-century designs. The shop is conveniently located at the end of Alberta iela, a street with the city's most impressive Art Nouveau buildings.

Rīga also has a fine selection of antique shops, mostly clustered around Brīvības iela. Upmarket emporiums include **Doma Antikvariāts**, while **Art Embassy** specializes in diverse artworks created in Latvia during the 20th century. Religious icons and musical instruments are available at **Volmar**.

Amber

Rīga has dozens of shops selling amber jewellery. Hard to miss is **Amber Line**, which has numerous branches all over the city. **IG Romuls**, under the Town Hall, sells amber jewellery in traditional and more modern styles, designed by two generations of the Romuls family. Amber can also be bought from street stalls and even in the Central Market, but be aware that such items might not be the genuine article.

DIRECTORY

Department Stores and Shopping Malls

Berga Bazārs
Dzirnavu iela 84.
🌐 bergabazars.lv

Galerija Centrs
Audēju iela16.
Tel 6701 8018.
🌐 galerijacentrs.lv

Galleria Rīga
Dzirnavu iela 67. **Tel** 6750 8000. 🌐 galleriariga.lv

mc²
Krasta iela 68a.
Tel 6700 6868. 🌐 mc2.lv

Stockmann
13 Janvāra iela 8.
🌐 stockmann.lv

Music

Randoms
Kaļķu iela 4. **Tel** 6722 5212. 🌐 randoms.lv

Upe
Vaļņu iela 26. **Tel** 6720 5509. 🌐 upeveikals.lv

Clothing and Jewellery

Latvijas Modes Klase
Elizabetes iela 85a.
Tel 2779 1635.
🌐 modesklase.eu

Putti
Mārstaļu iela 16.
Tel 6721 4229.
🌐 putti.lv

Tines
Vāgnera iela 5.
Tel 2542 4477. 🌐 tines.lv

Handicrafts

Egle
Kalķu iela 1a. **Tel** 2550 5268. 🌐 spogulegle.lv

Pienene
Kungu iela 7/9.
Tel 6721 0400.

Riija
Tērbatas iela 6/8.
Tel 6728 4828. 🌐 riija.lv

Art and Antiques

Art Embassy
Ausekla iela 6A.
Tel 2918 5957.

Art Nouveau Rīga
Strēlnieku 9.
Tel 6733 3030.

Doma Antikvariāts
Smilšu iela 8.
Tel 2916 6504.

Māksla XO
Elizabetes iela 14.
Tel 2948 2098.

Volmar
Krāmu iela 4.
Tel 6721 4278.

Amber

Amber Line
Torņa iela 4. **Tel** 6732 5058. 🌐 amberline.lv

IG Romuls
Ratslaukums 1. **Tel** 2655 5363. 🌐 romuls.lv

Food and Drink

Desa & Co
Maskavas iela 4.
Tel 6721 6186.
🌐 zemitani.lv

Emils Gustavs Chocolate
Aspazijas bulvāris 24.
Tel 6722 8333.
🌐 emilsgustavs.com

Jāņa Bišu
Pēterbaznīcas iela 17.
Tel 6722 4355.
🌐 daugmalesmedus.lv

Laima
Audēja iela 16. **Tel** 6710 4431. 🌐 laima.lv

VAT Exemption

Global Blue Latvia
🌐 global-blue.com

SHOPPING IN LITHUANIA

The souvenirs and gifts available in Lithuania usually consist of traditional arts and handicrafts made from local materials such as amber, ceramics and wood. Beautiful handmade flax or linen tablecloths and throw blankets, garments and soft toys are often available at reasonable prices. The shops and stalls of the Old Towns in the larger cities, as well as the various resorts, are flooded with most of these objects. Handicrafts of a superior quality and in greater variety can be found at specialist shops, which are commonly located close to the major tourist sights. Food and drink in Lithuania are distinctive in taste. The local cheeses and smoked meats on offer are varied and delicious. The wide choice of Lithuanian alcohol – such as *trauktinės*, often described as a bitter brandy – as well as vodka and beer, are great souvenirs to carry back home.

Opening Hours

Shops in Lithuania are usually open from 9 or 10am until 6pm on weekdays. Some gift and souvenir shops open at 10am. Food shops and supermarkets belonging to larger chains often open at 8am and close late in the evening.

The Soviet-era practice of closing for an hour for lunch is slowly fading and a handful of supermarkets are open 24 hours a day. Many shops open on Saturdays until 4pm, and some in tourist areas and in large city and town centres are open on Sundays as well. In smaller towns and villages, local stores close early so visitors should avoid leaving shopping until the evening.

How to Pay

As in the other countries of the Baltic region, almost all shops in Lithuania accept major international credit and debit cards. Some smaller retail outlets may accept only cash. Bargaining is rarely practised except at some market and souvenir stalls, but visitors are welcome to try.

VAT and Tax-Free Shopping

In Lithuania sales tax, known locally as *pridėtinės vertės mokestis* (PVM), is levied on most goods at a flat rate of 21 per cent. By law, visitors from non-EU nations can claim a refund of sales tax from customs when they leave the country, provided they have completed a tax-free shopping cheque, available at stores where the "Tax-Free Shopping" sign is displayed. Shoppers should have their passport with them at the time of purchase. VAT can be paid back only if the outward journey is made by air, road or sea; rail is exempt. Visitors need to spend a minimum of 50 euros, including VAT, in a shop in one day to claim the refund of sales tax.

Department Stores and Shopping Malls

To meet the growing demands of local consumers, sprawling modern shopping complexes are being constructed in Vilnius as well as in most of Lithuania's large towns and cities. The malls are replacing the old department stores dating from the Soviet era, whose interiors were usually adapted in the 1990s to fit the needs of small traders.

Shopping malls have a main anchor tenant, which tends to be one of the leading nation-wide supermarket chains. As a result, the range of goods available is practically the same as that found in the rest of Europe. For more authentic shops, visit the Old Towns in the major cities.

Amber

Lithuanian artisans have applied great imagination to the crafting of amber, an indis-putable part of the country's cultural heritage. They fashion it into jewellery, lampshades, writing materials and a great range of other objects.

Amber comes in browns, greens and other colours, besides the more familiar yellow. It is also available as original polished stones, of which the most valuable and exquisite are those that

Europa *(see p342)*, a stylish shopping mall in Vilnius

Souvenir stall on Theatre Square, Old Town, Klaipėda

have insects, plants, leaves and feathers preserved in the fossilized resin.

Handicrafts and Regional Specialities

Lithuanian craftsmen make all manner of objects out of wood, such as handcarved spatulas and spoons, and grotesque masks of devils and witches, whose distorted, freakish faces are traditionally displayed every Shrovetide. A far more acceptable wooden memento is the *rūpintojėlis*, a constantly worrying Christ-like figure who sits with his chin on one hand. Another religiously themed souvenir commonly made out of wood is the crucifix

For the musically inclined, handcarved musical instruments, such as the alluring Lithuanian *kanklės*, or zither, make an ideal gift. Russian *matryoshka* dolls can be easily bought from local markets.

Some of the most original items of clothing that can be bought in Lithuania are made of flax. Shirts and blouses, dresses and hand-crocheted hats are all widely available, particularly in the capital's gift and souvenir shops. A hand-woven *juosta*, which is a sash or waistband often used as wedding attire besides being used as a traditional form of fortune-telling, is also widely available and makes a good souvenir to take home.

The agricultural nature of Lithuania has helped in preserving many local customs and traditions. Black ceramics, in the form of pots, jugs, cups and figures, are among the specialities of the southern region of Dzūkija. Further north, Aukštaitija is known for its rich tradition of music and instruments, especially its horns and pipes. In the west, the people of Žemaitija value their religious images, miniatures and shrines, which often incorporate traditional pagan symbols.

Cognac bottles on display

Food and Drink

Traditional foods of all kinds are sold in Lithuanian shops, including *blynai* (a thin potato pancake similar to a crêpe with both sweet and savoury fillings), *spurgos* (doughnuts), smoked and steamed cheeses and a range of products made from curd and sour milk.

Smoked meats are usually sold as long, thick sausages or, even more authentically, bound in balls. The best local fish to buy is herring, normally marinated and sold in sealed packets. Some supermarkets also have cafés where a traditional Lithuanian meal of *cepelinai* (potato dumplings), as well as *kugelis* (baked potato pudding) and *vėdarai* (potato sausage) can be sampled. Lithuanian rye bread, such as the widely used black bread or the greyer *palangos*, can be bought from local stores. Traditional *šakotis* (tree cake) and *tinginys* (handmade cakes) are commonly available. Mushrooms and forest berries can also make unusual gifts, but visitors need a customs clearance to carry them back. Local favourites, such as *starka* (aged, caramel-coloured vodka), or *trejos devynerios* (herbal panacea), should not be missed. The best of the many varieties of *degtinė* (Lithuanian vodka) include the excellent gold-topped Lithuanian vodkas, while the company Alita makes a popular eponymous brand of brandy. Švyturys Premium Pils and the Švyturys Ekstra Draught are both very fine bottled beers. For more information on food and drinks see pages 310–13.

Matryoshka dolls for sale at one of the many souvenir stalls in Lithuania

Shopping in Vilnius

The main streets of the Old Town are lined with countless souvenir shops, stalls and galleries that specialize in the national favourites of amber, linen, wood and ceramics. Many of the better quality craft shops and art galleries are also hidden in the Old Town's labyrinth of narrow lanes and courtyards, so it is worth exploring off the beaten track. Away from the Old Town, Gedimino prospektas (avenue) has a number of clothing stores, bookshops and several shopping centres, while bigger malls with huge spaces for fashionable shopping can be found further afield. With so many choices, Vilnius has evolved into a shopper's paradise.

mini-malls dotting the avenue, boasts the Baltic region's first Marks & Spencer and Lindex stores. However, most of the outlets for more expensive brands tend to be found in the Old Town along Vokiečių and Didžioji gatvė (street). Vilnius also has its own treasured and highly sought-after designers with their individual boutiques, such as **Ramunė Piekautaitė**. Perhaps Lithuania's most visually impressive shopping mall is **Europa**, which brands itself as a fashion and style centre.

Markets

The most extraordinary market in Lithuania is **Gariūnai**, located next to Vilnius's towering water-heating facility, about 5 km (3 miles) southwest of the city centre. The market sells everything from cheap clothes, shoes, toys, toiletries and cosmetics to food, gadgets and even cars. Traders come from far and wide to sell their wares and, unlike at other markets in the country, bargaining is widely practised in Gariūnai. It is open from sunrise to lunch-time every day of the week except Mondays. The best time to visit the market is during the weekend.

At the southern edge of the Old Town, near the bus and train stations, is **Halės Market**,

One of the paintings for sale on Pilies gatvė

which mostly stocks a variety of fresh fruit and vegetables, cheese, meat and cakes.

Fashion and Clothing

The spruced-up Gedimino prospektas is the best place to shop for clothes and footwear. **Gedimino 9**, one of the new

Traditional Arts and Crafts

Shops and stalls selling traditional Lithuanian arts and crafts are most easily found along Pilies, Didžioji and Aušros vartų streets. Prices vary, so it is best to scan the market stalls before buying anything. Quaint outlets selling handmade artifacts at cheaper rates are tucked away in the narrow lanes leading off the Old Town artery.

Linen & Amber Studio, a chain of gift shops, is among the best places to find handicrafts made of amber and flax. These shops stretch up the entire length of Pilies gatvė and beyond; the one on Stiklių gatvė is among the largest.

Market stall displaying traditional amber jewellery in Vilnius's Old Town

For those interested in gifts and accessories made by local textile artists, a good destination is **Aukso Avis**. Funky felt hats, bags and jewellery, screen-printed shirts, garments and silk-printed wall pieces can be purchased here. Visitors can also craft their own souvenirs on the spot. **Sauluva** is one of the best and most reliable options as it stocks an assortment of Lithuanian handicraft items made of wood, ceramics, glass, dried flowers and amber.

Inside the elaborately frescoed Littera bookshop, Vilnius University

Art Galleries

Vilnius has an astonishing range of imaginative gift ideas, displayed in a number of small art galleries such as **Galerija R&A**. Quirky paintings, colourful plates designed with old photographs, vases and curios for shelves and mantelpieces cover the gallery space. At **e.k.art** in the Old Town, original artwork and antiques from the last few centuries, from Lithuania and abroad, are eclectically displayed in one place. Many upscale galleries in Vilnius mount shows of the work of Lithuania's foremost painters and sculptors. These works are regularly offered for sale.

The bohemian district of Užupis is lined with a surfeit of galleries and gift shops. Among them, **Užupio Galerija**, a working gallery selling metal and enamel pieces, is the most interesting.

Colourful painting at an art gallery

Books and Music

Vilnius has a large number of small, yet very intriguing, book-stores. Most of them sell locally published English-language reference and coffee-table books, original as well as translated local and international fiction, along with maps and postcards. **Vaga** has a whole upper floor which has a good collection of books in English. **Littera** *(see p226)*, the bookshop within the Vilnius University complex, is attractive and has a lively atmosphere. It is worth visiting as much for the stunning frescoed walls and ceiling as it is for its books.

There is a lack of a single, all-encompassing record store in Vilnius. However, Muzikos Bomba in the Europa mall has a fair collection of Lithuanian and international music. It also sells music under its own record label. Fans of jazz, blues and rock should not forget to visit **Thelonious**, a quirky basement store in the Old Town stacked with records, CDs and old-fashioned hi-fi equipment. The **Humanitas** bookstore has a fine selection of art books in English, as well as a small collection of local music CDs.

DIRECTORY

Markets

Gariūnai Market
Vilnius–Kaunas highway.

Halės Market
Pylimo & Bazilijonų street corner.

Fashion and Clothing

Europa
Konstitucijos 7a. **Tel** 204 7109. W **pceuropa.lt**

Gedimino 9
Gedimino 9. **Tel** 262 9812. W **gedimino9.lt**

Ramunė Piekautaitė
Didžioji 20.
Tel 231 2270.

Traditional Arts and Crafts

Aukso Avis
Pilies 38.
Tel 261 0421.

Linen & Amber Studio
Didžioji 5.
Tel 262 4986.
W **lgstudija.lt**
One of several branches.

Sauluva
Literatų 3 & Pilies 21.
Tel 212 1227.
W **sauluva.lt**

Art Galleries

e.k.art
Didžioji 27. **Tel** 6052 2222.
W **ek-art.lt**

Galerija R&A
Pranciškonų 8. **Tel** 6858 0080. W **galerijara.lt**

Užupio Galerija
Užupio 3–I. **Tel** 231 2318.
W **uzupiogalerija.lt**

Books and Music

Humanitas
Dominikonų 5.
Tel 249 8392.
W **humanitas.lt**

Littera
Vilnius University,
Universiteto 5.
Tel 212 7786.

Thelonious
Stiklių 12.
Tel 212 1076.

Vaga
Gedimino 50. **Tel** 249 8392. W **vaga.lt**

ENTERTAINMENT IN ESTONIA

Estonia has a strikingly dynamic and eclectic entertainment scene. The larger towns and cities, especially Tartu and Pärnu, have a crowded cultural calendar as well as a good nightlife scene. Classical music lovers are spoiled for choice all through the year as a range of nationwide and local concerts takes place, given by a fine selection of national and international performers. Saaremaa Island hosts many classical music festivals throughout the summer. Estonians are fond of wining and dining, which plays an integral part in their social lives. A vast array of rustic-style pubs can be found in major towns and cities, offering a hearty meal, a friendly environment and sometimes vibrant, toe-tapping folk music. Smaller towns, such as Haapsalu, Narva and Kuressaare, have numerous bustling nightclubs and bars. A major part of Estonia's cultural life revolves around folk festivals, with almost every town hosting some kind of celebration throughout the year. For entertainment in Tallinn, refer to pages 346–7.

A jam session in progress at the Viljandi Early Music Festival

Information

A good starting point for news about local concerts and events is the nearest tourist information office. *The Baltic Times* also offers information on arts and entertainment. All Estonian towns have their own websites, which usually carry listings of what is happening when. The publication *In Your Pocket* covers Tallinn, Tartu, Pärnu and other major Estonian cities.

Booking and Prices

Bookings for cultural events can be made at the venue or through ticket agencies. **Piletilevi**, the biggest ticketing agency, offers both online booking and ticket purchase. A number of retail outlets throughout Estonia also offer the same service, particularly at the Selver supermarket chain and Statoil petrol stations.

Classical Music and Ballet

Estonia has an outstanding tradition of classical music and recitals are regularly hosted all over the country. Tartu's main concert venue, the **Vanemuine**, stages theatre, classical music performances, ballet, comedy, musicals and special shows for children. Pärnu Concert Hall *(see p102)* hosts a wide range of concerts and music events.

Music Festivals

A number of festivals are organized to promote modern and traditional music. Vilandi's annual Suure-Jaani Music Festival is held to commemorate popular composers Mart Saar and Villem Kapp, while Muhu Island's Juu Jääb

Logo of Illusioon nightclub, Tartu

Music Festival, held in June, was established to explore the connections between traditional and world music. Other events that draw large numbers of local and international musicians are the Viljandi Early Music Festival and the Saaremaa Opera Days. For indie music fans, the highlight is the annual Plink Plonk festival in Tartu. **Eesti Muusika-festivalid**, available online, has the details of all nationwide festivals.

Nightlife

Tartu has an impressive range of pubs, clubs and bars to choose from. One of the best-known nightclubs is **Atlantis**, while the most exclusive is **Illusioon**. Another favourite is the **Eduard Vilde Lokaal**, which has consistently attracted a huge clientele. For

Brightly illuminated exterior of Tartu's favourite nightclub, Atlantis

Performers at one of the many folk festivals held in Estonia

something more laid-back, head to **Möku**, which has a casual, bohemian feel.

Pärnu also has a lively nightlife. **Lime Lounge** is a stylish place for a drink, while **Postipoiss** is a restaurant-cum-pub with frequent live music. The slickest nightclub in town is **Bravo**, while **Mirage**, another club, is often packed.

In Narva, head for the **German Pub** for a drink in enjoyable surroundings. **Africa** is the biggest and most popular pub in Haapsalu and doubles up as a disco at weekends. Kuressaare has a good choice of quality restaurants, pubs and bars. With an attractive outdoor deck, the **John Bull Pub** is cheerful.

Folk Festivals

Some of the most important festivals take place in July. Of these, the Viljandi Folk Festival is the biggest, attracting vast numbers of dancers, musicians and singers each year. Another is the Hiiu Folk Festival in Hiiumaa (see pp94–5), which has a particularly authentic ambience created by its rustic setting.

August is also a busy month. The splendid Narva Historic Festival stages an enactment of the Great Northern War (see p37) in Narva. Obinitsa hosts several festivals celebrating Setu culture (see p124). The White Lady Days, held on the August full moon, is a festival filled with merry-making in the grounds of the castle in Haapsalu (see p92).

Cinema

Films are shown in their original language with Russian subtitles, though the choice of films outside Tallinn is decidedly poor. Most reasonably large towns have a small cinema which shows the latest blockbusters a few weeks after they are shown in the capital. Hollywood films are regularly shown at Pärnu's small **Apollo Kino**. Tartu's trendy **Kino Ekraan**, located in a shopping mall, is part of the same chain as **Forum Cinemas Astri**.

The Black Nights Film Festival (see p53), celebrated in November and December, travels to Tartu, Viljandi, Narva, Jõhvi and Kärdla, while Pärnu has a small film festival of its own in July.

Poster for an Estonian-language film, *Sigade Revolutsioon*

Entertainment in Tallinn

Entertainment in Tallinn is astonishingly vibrant. Its classical music and opera performances are world renowned and a major tourist draw. In recent years, the city has also started to attract some big international pop artists, although its local live-music scene is far more enjoyable. A plethora of venues in Tallinn regularly host rock, jazz, blues and alternative music performances by local bands. The city's pulsating nightclub scene covers diverse genres, from mainstream pop to underground club music. There is a large choice of places to enjoy a drink. These usually stay open late into the night and range from ultra-chic lounge bars to good old-fashioned, pint-in-hand pubs. Theatre in Tallinn is generally of a very high quality, but is mostly performed in Estonian, except during international festivals.

A scene from *Carlo Gozzi II Corvo* at the Tallinn Linnateater

Information

Visitors can check *Tallinn In Your Pocket*, *The Baltic Times* and booking website Piletilevi *(see p345)* for upcoming events in the city.

Theatre

Tallinn has a proud tradition of theatre and the flagship Estonian Drama Theatre *(see p76)* does a fine job of preserving the national repertoire. The **Tallinn Linnateater** specializes in contemporary work. The best place for serious theatre lovers is the **Von Krahl Theatre**, the leading avant-garde theatre, though English translations are rare. It often stages various intensely visual multimedia productions. Russian-speakers can visit the **Russian Drama Theatre**, which puts on a range of classic and contemporary Russian theatre.

Classical Music, Opera and Dance

Concerts by the Estonian National Symphony Orchestra, which are often held in the Estonian Concert Hall *(see pp76–7)* and the Estonian National Opera, regularly sell out thanks to their consistently high-quality performances and productions. However, there are also wonderful chamber and choral concerts held in churches and other more intimate Old Town locations every week, such as Niguliste Church *(see pp68–9)*, the House of Blackheads *(see p70)* and the **Estonian Music Academy**. The best of both contemporary Estonian as well as international dance performances are usually hosted at **Kanuti Gildi Saal**.

Logo of Hell Hunt pub

Rock, Pop, Jazz and Blues

Live music lovers are spoiled for choice in Tallinn. **Café Amigo** attracts the biggest local rock, pop and blues bands and holds nightly performances. **Von Krahl Baar** is one of the best places in the city to experience the local alternative music scene, while the industrial setting of the **Rock Café** has a diverse range of live music, ranging from blues to funk. Most of the popular international acts that come to Tallinn play at the outdoor Song Festival Grounds *(see p82)*. **No99** hosts cosy jazz concerts on Fridays and Saturdays, as well as some jazz acts during the Jazzkaar festival *(see p52)*.

Pubs and Bars

Tallinn's Old Town is packed with bars and pubs of every imaginable size and description. There are several well-acclaimed Irish and English-style pubs, such as **Mad Murphy's** and **Scotland Yard**, which are as much favoured by expats as by foreign visitors. Stylish and classy lounge bars are also extremely popular among the city's well-heeled. Some of the best venues include the chic **Déjà Vu** and the extravagant **Lounge 24**, which affords spectacular views from the 24th floor of the Radisson Blu Sky Hotel *(see p297)*. There are also several smaller, cosier pubs

Atmospheric interior of the stylish Déjà Vu lounge bar

Parlament, one of Tallinn's most popular nightspots

scattered around the Old Town, which are far less frequented by boisterous visitors. Intimate places, such as **Hell Hunt**, Tallinn's first real tavern, and the **Drink Bar**, which occasionally features live bands, offer an amiable atmosphere for a chat over a relaxing drink.

Nightclubs

The amazing choice and variety of nightclubs draws people from far and wide to Tallinn. Most of the city's best clubs are situated in the Old Town, or within walking distance of it. Many, such as Café Amigo, Déjà

Vu and **Parlament**, are just good, simple, fun places and are equally popular with locals and foreign visitors. For the most exclusive hangouts head to **Club Privé** or **BonBon** and marvel at the preening clientele. For showy bartending, clubbers could try out **Venus Club**.

Not all nightclubs in Tallinn will suit all tastes, and some are downright dubious and as a result are best avoided. Rather than wandering into the first nightclub they come across, visitors are advised to do some research and choose their places of evening entertainment carefully.

Cinema

In Tallinn, films are screened in their original language with subtitles. The diversity of choice has dwindled due to the arrival of the multi-screen **Coca-Cola Plaza** and **Solaris**, which show the latest Hollywood blockbusters and Estonian films. Arthouse and independent films are screened at the impressive **Sõprus** and **Kino Artis**. The Black Nights Film Festival *(see p53)* is a cinema lover's treat, when the best in world cinema gets a rare screening in smaller cinemas.

Movie posters displayed at the Coca-Cola Plaza

DIRECTORY

Theatre

Russian Drama Theatre
Vabaduse väljak 5.
Tel 641 8246.
W veneteater.ee

Tallinn Linnateater
Lai 23.
Tel 665 0800.
W linnateater.ee

Von Krahl Theatre
Rataskaevu 10.
Tel 626 9090.
W vonkrahl.ee

Classical Music, Dance and Opera

Estonian Music Academy
Rävala 16.
Tel 667 5700.
W ema.edu.ee

Kanuti Gildi Saal
Pikk 20.
Tel 646 4704. W saal.ee

Rock, Pop, Jazz and Blues

Café Amigo
Hotel Viru, Viru väljak 4.
Tel 680 9380.
W amigo.ee

No99
Sakala 3. Tel 668 8798.

Rock Café
Tartu mnt 80d. Tel 681 0878. W rockcafe.ee

Von Krahl Baar
Rataskaevu 10/12.
Tel 626 9090.
W vonkrahl.ee

Pubs and Bars

Déjà Vu
Vana Viru 8.
Tel 5688 4455.
W dejavu.ee

Drink Bar
Väike-Karja 8.
Tel 644 9433.

Hell Hunt
Pikk 39. Tel 681 8333.
W hellhunt.ee

Lounge 24
Radisson Blu Sky Hotel, Rävala pst 3.
Tel 682 3424.

Mad Murphy's
Mündi 2.
Tel 601 1070.
W madmurphys.ee

Scotland Yard
Mere pst 6e.
Tel 653 5190.
W scotlandyard.ee

Nightclubs

BonBon
Mere pst 6e.
Tel 5400 5411.
W bonbon.ee

Club Privé
Harju 6.
Tel 631 0580.
W clubprive.ee

Parlament
Ahtri 10.
Tel 611 6145.
W clubparlament.com

Venus Club
Vana-Viru 14.
Tel 551 9999.

Cinema

Coca-Cola Plaza
Hobujaama 5.
Tel 680 0684.
W superkinod.ee

Solaris, Kino Artis
Estonia Pst 9.
Tel 630 4111.

Sõprus
Vana-Posti 8.
Tel 644 1919.
W kinosoprus.ee

ENTERTAINMENT IN LATVIA

Latvia's major cultural events are concentrated in Rīga, although the dynamic festival calendar includes plenty of reasons to explore the country beyond the capital. A few concerts and events are scheduled through the year, but visitors need to consult a website or the tourist board as they are not regular. The major exception is Liepāja, which has a vibrant cultural life and its own symphony orchestra. The city is also considered the home of Latvian rock bands, and DJs perform in clubs every evening. There are also some good rock clubs, in addition to numerous bars that host live music. The seaside resort of Jūrmala is another hotspot during summer. Here, many bars and clubs open only for the tourist season and the Dzintari Concert Hall hosts concerts ranging from classical to pop. Valmiera, considered to be the cultural capital of the Vidzeme region, is another lively city. For entertainment options in Rīga, see pages 350–51.

One of Rīga's tourist offices, which has details of events in the capital

Information

Tourist information offices in Rīga provide details of entertainment in the capital and the rest of the country, while regional tourist offices focus on local areas. Online resources include the **Latvian Culture Portal**, which has a searchable nationwide calendar, and **Latvijas Koncerti** for classical music events.

Booking and Prices

Tickets for cultural events are generally very affordable in Latvia, and bookings can be made at the venue or through a ticket agency. **Biļešu Paradīze** has offices in several of Rīga's shopping centres and major venues as well as concert halls and cultural centres around Latvia. Tickets can be delivered internationally for an extra fee. **Ticket Service** has an even larger network of outlets, including at many post offices, Narvesen stores and Statoil petrol stations. Tickets can be booked online and collected from a sales office, or delivered to an address within Latvia. Both agencies' websites have instructions in English, although most event descriptions are only in Latvian.

Theatre

Most theatrical performances are in Latvian or Russian. **Liepāja Theatre** produces a mix of intimate drama and expansive theatrical works. The building's restored Art Nouveau and Neo-Classical interior is well worth a look. There are also occasional travelling performances at **Saulkrasti Open-Air Stage** and at the open-air stage in Reņķa Gardens, Ventspils.

Classical Music and Opera

The **Latvian Music Information Centre** is a good resource for details of musical performances across the country. Some of the best classical music concerts take place at annual events, such as the International Early Music Festival, which includes outdoor concerts in Rundāle Palace (see pp172–3) and Bauska Castle (see pp170–71).

In Jūrmala, the Dzintari Concert Hall (see p175) stages very high-quality events from June to August, on Saturdays. Liepāja's Holy Trinity Church (see p184) hosts organ recitals. The **Liepāja Symphony Orchestra** specializes in romantic music and hosts concerts throughout Latvia in major cities such as Rīga, Valmiera and Cēsis.

With the exception of special events, such as the annual Sigulda Opera Festival, there

Scene from *Uncle Vanya*, by Anton Chekhov, performed at Liepāja Theatre

The open-air theatre near Rundāle Palace

are few chances to see opera outside Rīga. The Latvian National Opera does leave the capital to perform elsewhere in Latvia, but venues for these shows include cultural centres in several towns and **Krustpils Open-Air Stage** near Jēkabpils.

Rock, Pop and Alternative

The liveliest music scene outside the capital is in Liepāja, which boasts a few decent places to see a band. **Fire Bar** features mostly jazz bands, but does host rock acts too. It's a small place and can get rather smoky. Another option is **Fontaine Palace**, which features a mixture of bands and DJs. It has a more relaxed bar downstairs, and a fast-food outlet next door. The summer sees performances on Liepāja's open-air stage, **Pūt Vējiņi**, as well as the Summer Sound festival (see p136) in July.

Jūrmala hosts plenty of live music in summer. The programme at the Dzintari Concert Hall features popular Latvian and Russian musicians. The major Russian-language pop competition, New Wave, held every July, attracts huge crowds, while the biggest music festival, **Positivus**, takes place near Salacgrīva and features bands from all over the globe (see p137). The schedule at the open-air stage in Ogre, on the way to Daugavpils, includes rock and pop acts, while the nightlife in Jelgava is enlivened

by **Jelgavas Baltie Krekli**. Like its sister club, Četri Balti Krekli in Rīga, it has a strictly-Latvian music policy.

Jazz

Regular jazz nights are scarce outside Rīga, but local tourist offices may provide information. **Saulkrasti Jazz Festival** is an important event in the calendar, as is the **Sigulda Jazz Festival** in Liepāja.

Bars and Clubs

Most places in Latvia have at least a couple of bars, some of which turn into discos on weekend nights. Some of the better ones include the Fire Bar and Fontaine Palace, both in Liepāja.

Cēsis Historical Film Festival, held every August in Cēsis Castle

Cinema

State funding for Latvian films has almost dried up and many cinemas have closed since independence. Most cinemas tend to screen Hollywood movies with Latvian and Russian subtitles. Cēsis Castle hosts the annual **Cēsis Historical Film Festival** in August.

DIRECTORY

Information

Latvian Culture Portal
W culture.lv

Latvijas Koncerti
W latvijaskoncerti.lv

Booking and Prices

Biļešu Paradīze
W ticketparadise.lv

Ticket Service
W ticketservice.lv

Theatre

Liepāja Theatre
Teātra iela 4. **Tel** 6340 7811.
W liepajasteatris.lv

Saulkrasti Open-Air Stage
Ainažu iela 42a.

Classical Music and Opera

Krustpils Open-Air Stage
Tel 6522 1051.

Latvian Music Information Centre
Tel 6722 6797. W lmic.lv

Liepāja Symphony Orchestra
Tel 6348 9272. W lso.lv

Rock, Pop and Alternative

Fire Bar
Stūrmaņu 1, Liepāja. **Tel** 6348 9777. W firebar.lv

Fontaine Palace
Dzirnavu iela 4, Liepāja. **Tel** 6348 8510. W fontainepalace.lv

Jelgavas Baltie Krekli
Lielajā ielā 19a. **Tel** 6302 2259.
W tamitami.lv

Positivus
W positivus.lv

Pūt Vējiņi
Peldu iela 57, Liepāja.

Jazz

Saulkrasti Jazz Festival
W saulkrastijazz.lv

Sigulda Jazz Festival
W jazzfest.lv

Cinema

Cēsis Historical Film Festival
W filmuskate.cesis.lv

Entertainment in Rīga

Since independence Rīga has been working hard to recapture its reputation as the cultural capital of the Baltic region. Apart from world-class performances of opera, ballet and classical music, the city also has a thriving live-music scene. Local bands play diverse genres from jazz to rock, often alongside international performers. The summer months see a few festivals offering music and more, but in winter there is usually some form of cultural event or other taking place regularly. The city is also renowned for its energetic nightlife. On Friday and Saturday nights, many Old Town bars buzz with foreign visitors, though it is not difficult to find a peaceful place for a drink among local people. Clubs, which range from small and hip to huge and mainstream, stay open throughout the night.

Information

Most hotels in Rīga stock an assortment of free pocket-sized magazines containing listings and other information, of which the best is *RigaNOW!* The affordably priced and comprehensive bi-monthly *Rīga In Your Pocket* is available to browse or download as a PDF from the company's website. The Latvian Culture Portal *(see p349)* website is also helpful.

Theatre

Theatre performances are mainly in Latvian or Russian, making them of limited interest to most visitors. The **Latvian National Theatre**, housed in a Neo-Classical building, has a significant place in Latvian history, as independence was declared here on 18 November 1918. The **Dailes Theatre**, directed by Eduards Smiļģis (1886–1966) for 40 years, puts on a range of productions, from traditional to experimental. Other options include the **New Rīga Theatre** and the **Russian Drama Theatre**. Rīga's most important theatre festival is Homo Novus, held in September, usually every alternate year. It concentrates on cutting-edge experimental theatre and dance.

Opera and Ballet

Since the 18th century, Rīga has maintained a strong tradition of opera and ballet. The **Latvian National Opera** has an imposing Neo-Classical building with a Baroque interior. It is the venue for world-class performances that are usually in their original language with subtitles in Latvian and English. The building that houses the Latvian National Opera is also home to the Rīga Ballet. The strong ballet tradition established during the Soviet period continues today.

Although the National Opera closes in the summer, there are special performances in August. Tours of the building are also available for a minimum of 10 people.

Classical Music

There are a number of concert venues in Rīga, including the Dome Cathedral *(see p146)*, which hosts regular recitals. **Ave Sol** hosts chamber and choral music performances. The Latvian Philharmonic Orchestra performs at the Great Guild *(see p149)*, while chamber music is played at the Small Guild across the road. **Spīķeri Concert Hall**, located in the warehouses next to Rīga's Central Market, is a contemporary venue for classical music and is the home of the Sinfonietta Rīga chamber orchestra.

Rock, Pop and Alternative

Major international artists perform at the **Arēna Rīga**, while local bands play at a host of smaller venues. **Kaļķu Vārti** is noted for booking some of the country's top artists. **Depo** features alternative music from ska to metal and **Sapņu Fabrika** offers a range of diverse genres from world music to rock. **Četri Balti Krekli** offers Latvian music.

Jazz and Blues

The best blues venue in the city is **Bites Blūza Klubs**, which has live music on weekend evenings. It also serves surprisingly good food, while the photographs on the walls are testament to the number of international performers who have visited over the years. The smaller-scale **Hamlets** club hosts jazz performances. **Rīgas Ritmi** (Rīga's Rhythms) organizes concerts featuring local and international jazz, blues and world musicians at various venues throughout the year.

A lavishly decorated hall in the Latvian National Theatre

Bars and Clubs

With a wide range of bars and clubs, Rīga has a swinging nightlife. **Balzambārs** is a popular place to try various cocktails. **Skyline Bar** in the Radisson Blu Hotel Latvija *(see p301)* is one of the favourite bars in town. **I Love You** attracts a youthful local crowd, while **Paddy Whelan's** Irish pub is a favourite among expats. The best-known nightclubs,

Pulkvedim Neviens Neraksta and **Studio 69**, feature DJs on the weekend, while **Folkklubs Ala** offers a mix of folk bands and more traditional music, plus tasty traditional food too.

Rīga's gay scene remains low-profile. **XXL**, the only well-advertised gay club, has live shows on Friday and Saturday nights. **Golden**, a gay-friendly bar, plays house music in a warm ambience.

Casinos

Although there are numerous establishments that describe themselves as casinos, most provide only slot machines. Establishments with gaming tables include the **Olympic Voodoo Casino** in the Radisson Blu Hotel Latvija *(see p301)* and the **Royal Casino**. It is compulsory to register at casinos, so you must be sure to carry valid photo ID.

Cinema

There are several multi-screen cinemas in Rīga, mostly offering Hollywood films. The largest is the **Coca-Cola Forum**, which has 14 halls and several cafés. **Splendid Palace**, the city's first cinema house, has been renovated and also shows non-Hollywood films. **K Suns** is the best place for art-house cinema.

Sweeping view of Rīga from the Skyline Bar, Radisson Blu Hotel Latvija

DIRECTORY

Theatre

Dailes Theatre
Brīvības iela 75.
Tel 6727 0463.
W dailesteatris.lv

Latvian National Theatre
Kronvalda bulvāris 2.
Tel 6700 6337.
W teatris.lv

New Rīga Theatre
Lāčplēša iela 25.
Tel 6728 0765. W jrt.lv

Russian Drama Theatre
Kaļķu iela 16.
Tel 6722 4660.
W trd.lv

Opera and Ballet

Latvian National Opera
Aspāzijas bulvāris 3.
Tel 6707 3777.
W opera.lv

Classical Music

Ave Sol
Citadeles iela 7.
Tel 6718 1637.
W avesol.riga.lv

Spīķeri Concert Hall
Maskavas iela 4/1.
Tel 6721 5018.
W sinfoniettariga.lv

Rock, Pop and Alternative

Arēna Rīga
Skanstes iela 21. **Tel** 6738 8200. W arenariga.com

Četri Balti Krekli
Vecpilsētas iela 12. **Tel** 6721 3885. W krekli.lv

Depo
Vaļņu iela 32.
Tel 6721 1374.
W klubsdepo.lv

Kaļķu Vārti
Kaļķu iela 11a.
Tel 6722 4576.
W kalkuvarti.lv

Sapņu Fabrika
Lāčplēša 101.
Tel 2201 1811.
W sapnufabrika.lv

Jazz & Blues

Bites Blūza Klubs
Dzirnavu iela 34a.
Tel 6733 3123.
W bluesclub.lv

Hamlets
Jāņa sēta 5. **Tel** 6722 9938. W hamlets.lv

Rīgas Ritmi
W rigasritmi.lv

Bars and Clubs

Balzambārs
Torņa iela 4.
Tel 6721 4494.

Folkklubs Ala
Peldu iela 19. **Tel** 2779 6914. W folkklubs.lv

Golden
Ģertrūdes iela 33–35.
Tel 2550 5050.
W mygoldenclub.com

I Love You
Aldaru iela 9. **Tel** 6722 5304. W iloveyou.lv

Paddy Whelan's
Grēcinieku iela 4.
Tel 6721 0150.

Pulkvedim Neviens Neraksta
Peldu iela 26–28. **Tel** 6721 3886. W pulkvedis.lv

Skyline Bar
Radisson Blu Hotel Latvija, Elizabetes iela 55.
Tel 6777 2222.

Studio 69
Terbatas 73.
Tel 6750 6030.
W info.studio69.lv

XXL
Kalniņa iela 4.
Tel 6728 2276.
W xxl.lv

Casinos

Olympic Voodoo Casino
Radisson Blu Hotel Latvija, Elizabetes iela 55.
Tel 6782 8777.

Royal Casino
Tērbatas iela 73.
Tel 6709 2299.

Cinema

Coca-Cola Forum
Janvara iela 8.
W forumcinemas.lv

K Suns
Elizabetes iela 83–85.
W kinogalerija.lv

Splendid Palace
Elizabetes iela 61.
W splendidpalace.lv

ENTERTAINMENT IN LITHUANIA

Lithuania offers its visitors a wide variety of entertainment, with something for everybody. Most cities have a strong cultural tradition Panevėžys has a popular drama theatre, while the residents of Klaipėda are more inspired by music, embracing both improvised and traditional jazz, blues and operetta. Trakai and Kernavė provide scenic backdrops to summer events, including medieval festivals of archery and swordfighting and mystical celebrations of the summer solstice. Lively pop festivals sometimes brighten up summer resorts such as Palanga and Juodkrantė. Outside Vilnius the entertainment options tend to be limited, although Klaipėda provides some atmospheric venues for live music. Baroque and chamber music concerts are regularly performed throughout the year in many of Lithuania's churches. For entertainment options in Vilnius see pages 354–5.

Information

The English-language *In Your Pocket* guides, found in hotels, at newsstands and online, cover restaurants, hotels, shopping and nightlife in most of Lithuania's livelier towns. The official websites of **Lithuanian Tourism** and **Tourism Vilnius** are also useful resources.

Lithuania has a large number of visitor information centres with English-speaking staff and English-language leaflets, booklets and up-to-date local information. All of Lithuania's towns and cities have their own dedicated websites, which usually contain schedules and information on culture and events.

Booking and Prices

The booking service **Bilietai** has kiosks in most concert venues and shopping centres in major cities, where tickets can be bought with credit cards or cash. Tickets can also be booked by telephone or through a website and can be collected from a sales office, or delivered to any address in Lithuania. Prices usually vary anywhere between 10 and 50 euros per person.

Theatre

Lithuanian theatre developed during the period of independence between the world wars, producing young and talented playwrights such as Balys Sruoga and Kazys Binkis. Vilnius has a particularly strong

Imposing exterior of the Klaipėda State Drama Theatre in Klaipėda

theatre culture, although an equal passion for theatre exists outside the city.

The **Klaipėda State Drama Theatre**, which dates from 1819, is one of the oldest functioning theatres in Lithuania and the most famous outside Vilnius. In Panevėžys, the **Juozo Miltinio Drama Theatre** is named after legendary stage actor and director Juozas Miltinis (1907–94), who taught actors to reject conservatism and to draw on their own life experiences while acting.

Classical Music

Kaunas has several concert halls that feature music regularly. The **Kaunas State Musical Theatre** and the **Great Hall** of Vytauto Didžiojo University are among the preferred venues, but the Kaunas City Symphony Orchestra and Kaunas State Choir also perform at less formal venues including the Mykolas Žilinskas Art Gallery *(see p264)*. Some churches host classical music recitals that often have no entry charges. Zapyškis Church *(see p265)*, outside Kaunas, is a particularly atmospheric venue in the countryside.

On the coast, the **Klaipėda State Music Theatre** holds a wide array of classical music concerts, opera and other performances. Panevėžys Civic Art Gallery *(see p268)* and Kėdainiai's Multicultural Centre *(see p265)* also hold regular concerts.

Beautiful exterior of the Kaunas State Musical Theatre

Music Festivals

Several music festivals have grown in popularity over the years. The magnificent Baroque Pažaislis Monastery complex (see p265), near Kaunas, forms the backdrop to the annual **Pažaislis Music Festival**. The **Edvard Grieg and M K Čiurlionis Festival**, hosted in Kaunas each spring, features classical music concerts. The **Muzikinis Pajūris** (Musical Seaside) festival of opera and symphony takes place every summer in Klaipėda.

Nightlife

Club life is not limited to the capital city. Klaipėda has an increasingly lively and varied nightlife. A popular place is **Pabo Latino**, a branch of the successful club of the same name in Vilnius. Newer venues are gradually taking the place of the duller bars and discos in and around the Old Town. They offer casinos, concerts and restaurants, besides dance floors. Klaipėda's Kanto Street also has some spirited bars full of fun and revelry.

Kaunas has a mix of low-key bars such as **BO** in the Old Town and the swinging **Nautilus Centre**, a club frequented by the young. The other party-town in Lithuania is the coastal resort of Palanga, where in summer the entire area around Basanavičiaus gatvė (street) turns into a pulsating open-air disco from dusk virtually until dawn.

Colourfully lit interior of a nightclub on Basanavičiaus Street in Palanga

Jazz, Blues and Folk Music

Jazz features prominently in the country's cultural scene. Among the best jazz festivals is Kaunas Jazz (see p212). **Kurpiai** in Klaipėda also hosts jazz and blues performances. Folk music features at the Days of Live Archaeology amid the ancient hills forts of Kernavė (see p258), in July.

Cinema

Movies screened in Lithuania are shown in their original language, which means that they can be enjoyed by locals and visitors. Only one modern multiplex, the **Forum Cinemas**, exists in both Vilnius and Kaunas. However, other cities have decent cinemas, such as **Cinamon** in Klaipėda.

Entertainment in Vilnius

The range of entertainment on offer in Vilnius has changed rapidly in recent years. Trendy clubs and lounge bars have sprung up, but, at the same time, there has been a resurgence of traditional folk singing and dancing. *Sutartinės*, music with rural roots, helped sustain national identity through the periods of occupation and today it has made a comeback in folk-themed restaurants. Classical music was promoted during the Soviet period, but it was also significant in the 20th-century national revivals. Classical music, opera and ballet performances in Vilnius are excellent. Live music is played in several key venues frequented by a small but enthusiastic and faithful crowd. Tourist information points provide news on most cultural events.

A scene from the play *Three Sisters* at the State Small Theatre of Vilnius

Information

Vilnius In Your Pocket, which covers the whole spectrum of restaurants, entertainment and shopping, as well as upcoming events, is available at numerous shops and kiosks and most of the city's hotels. Brochures and leaflets about cultural events can be found at the capital's tourist information centres. Posters are another source of information.

Tickets for concerts, opera, ballet and plays can be purchased at the appropriate venue or booking kiosks. Tickets for all major events in Lithuania can be bought online from **Bilietai LT**.

Theatre

The residents of Vilnius have a passion for theatre. Productions by two of the country's most outstanding directors, Oskaras Koršunovas and Eimuntas Nekrošius, are highly recommended. The **Lithuanian National Drama Theatre** and the more avant-garde **State Small Theatre of Vilnius** provide pre-recorded English translations for some performances, which can be heard using headphones.

Classical Music, Opera and Ballet

Vilnius has a good classical music scene. Both the opulent **National Philharmonic** and the contemporary **Congress Palace** hold superb concerts. Chamber music concerts are often held at the atmospheric Church of St Catherine *(see p241)* and, occasionally, at the Church of St Casimir *(see p236)*. On weekdays during term time, students and professors at the Lithuanian Academy of Music often give free-of-charge recitals at different venues in the city.

The standard of opera and ballet is generally high in Vilnius, although the repertoire is fairly conservative. In addition to classical performances, the innovative choreography of the **Anželika Cholina Dance Theatre** attracts big audiences and is very popular among locals and visitors. The famous **National Opera & Ballet Theatre** is funded by Lithuania's Ministry of Culture. Tickets for its performances often sell out quickly and it is advisable to visit the ticket office to check on availability.

Folk Music

Lithuania's folk music can be heard in folk-themed restaurants, which are as popular with locals as they are with visitors. For an authentic experience, enjoy the music with a traditional meal of meat-and-potatoes and Lithuanian beer at venues such as the rustic **Fort Dvaras** *(see p326)* or the atmospheric **Marceliukės Klėtis**. Folk festivals are often played out in the courtyards and halls of Vilnius University *(see pp224–5)*, or in more low-key spots such as the **Teachers' House**.

Rock, Blues and Pop

Several outstanding Lithuanian rock and pop performers play regularly at atmospheric venues such as **Tamsta Club**, **Brodvėjus** and the **Forum Palace**. Names

A classical music concert in progress at the Congress Palace

Live band playing at the Tamsta Club in the Old Town

Nightlife

Though a little quieter than many other European capitals, Vilnius has an abundance of bars and clubs featuring a variety of music genres and both local and international DJs. The uproarious **Bix** is for heavy metal fans, while **Mojo Lounge**, hosting parties of all kinds in the Old Town, attracts the best DJs. A little more central are **Paparazzi**, popular for its friendly atmosphere and wide range of cocktails, and **Pabo Latino**, a nightclub specializing in Latin rhythms. Bands often play live at **Ala**.

to look out for include the punky Biplan, the singer and songwriter Andrius Mamontovas and the more soulful Jurga. International artistes on tour tend to play at the modern **Siemens Arena** or the less pretentious **Utenos Entertainment Centre**, which doubles as an ice rink.

Jazz

With a small but fanatical following, jazz forms an inextricable part of the Lithuanian lifestyle. During the Soviet era,

jazz was associated with freedom. The birth of Lithuania's modern jazz scene came in 1961, at a recital by 17-year-old pianist Vyacheslav Ganelin at the Academy of Music, during which the audience was mesmerized. Ganelin still makes rare appearances in Vilnius, often with saxophonist Petras Vyšniauskas. Another big name to look out for is singer-flautist Neda Malūnavičiūtė.

The best jazz in town is showcased at the **Vilnius Jazz** festival, which is held in October *(see p213)*.

Cinema

Vilnius has two modern multiplex cinemas, both operated by Forum Cinemas *(see p353)*. One of them is housed in the Coca-Cola Plaza, while the other is in the Akropolis shopping centre. Films from other countries are usually screened in their original language with Lithuanian subtitles. Lithuanian films do not usually have English subtitles. Art-house cinemas have all but disappeared. A rare survivor, however, is **Skalvija**.

DIRECTORY

Information

Bilietai LT
w bilietai.lt

Theatre

Lithuanian National Drama Theatre
Gedimino 4.
Tel 262 1593.
w teatras.lt

State Small Theatre of Vilnius
Gedimino 22.
Tel 249 9869.
w vmt.lt

Classical Music, Opera and Ballet

Anželika Cholina Dance Theatre
Šimulionio 4–103.
Tel 6883 4181.
w ach.lt

Congress Palace
Vilniaus 6–14.
Tel 261 8828,
w lvso.lt

National Opera & Ballet Theatre
Vienuolio 1.
Tel 262 0727.
w opera.lt

National Philharmonic
Aušros vartų 5.
Tel 266 5216.
w filharmonija.lt

Folk Music

Marceliukės Klėtis
Tuskulėnų gatvė 35.
Tel 5272 5087.

Teachers' House
Vilniaus 39.
Tel 262 3514.
w kultura.lt

Rock, Blues and Pop

Brodvėjus
Vokiečių 4.
Tel 210 7208.
w brodvejus.lt

Forum Palace
Konstitucijos 26.
Tel 263 6666.
w forumpalace.lt

Siemens Arena
Ozo 14.
Tel 247 7576.
w siemens-arena.lt

Tamsta Club
A Strazdelio 1.
Tel 212 4498.
w tamstaclub.lt

Utenos Entertainment Centre
Ąžuolyno 9.
Tel 242 4444.

Jazz

Vilnius Jazz
w vilniusjazz.lt

Nightlife

Ala
Pilies 11. Tel 268 7173.

Bix
Etmonų 6. Tel 262 7791.

Mojo Lounge
Vokiečių 2.
Tel 6576 6500.

Pablo Latino
Trakų 3. Tel 6576 6500.

Paparazzi
Totorių 3. Tel 212 0135.

Cinema

Skalvija
A Goštauto 2–15.
w skalvija.lt

OUTDOOR ACTIVITIES AND SPECIALIST HOLIDAYS

Bereft of dramatic peaks and raging rivers, the Baltic States nevertheless abound with subtle charms and this has helped develop rural tourism in the three countries. Exploring the lakes and rivers allows the scenery to unfold at a leisurely pace, while back on land, the forests are perfect for rambling. Fishing, berry- and mushroom-picking and bird-watching are among the most popular activities and can easily be arranged by reputable tour operators. The opportunities for those who wish to discover the region on horseback are endless, with excursions for both novices and experienced riders. Winter changes the landscape, and skiing, ice-skating, snowboarding and snowmobiling take over. For visitors who simply want to relax, the region has a series of stylish spa resorts which draw on decades of tradition. Brewery tours tempt those impressed by local beer. However, the infrastructure varies from region to region and it is best to contact a reputable tour operator.

Information

In the Baltic States, most tourist information centres have lists of both state-run and private tour operators, who organize a variety of outdoor activities depending on the time of year. Most companies have their own dedicated websites (see p361).

Rural Tourism

The development of rural tourism as an organized activity began in the mid-1990s with support from the Ministry of Agriculture, along with other organizations. It has now become one of the biggest tourist attractions in the Baltic region, and it is often advisable to arrange for accommodation well in advance. Bookings can be made through the various rural tourism associations (see p295), such as Estonian Rural Tourism, Latvia's Country Holidays (Lauku ceļotājs) and the Lithuanian Countryside Tourism Association.

Bird-Watching

Located on major migration routes, with a high proportion of fish-rich wetlands and little intensive farming, the Baltic States are an ideal destination for bird-watchers. Ducks, geese, swans, corncrakes, bitterns, common coots and white storks are easily spotted.

It has been estimated that around 50 million waterfowl, including most of the world's tundra swans and barnacle geese, visit Estonia's coastal wetlands every spring. The peak time for bird-watching is the beginning of May at sites such as Matsalu National Park (see p93). The autumn migration is at its

Bird-watching tower near Lake Lubans, Latvia

best in October at Põõsaspea Cape, close to Haapsalu. Several tour operators, including **Estonian Nature Tours**, arrange bird-watching trips. For further information contact **Estonian Ornithological Society**.

Good bird-watching spots in Latvia include Gauja National Park (see pp190–93) and Lake Lubans (see p202). The **Engure Ornithological Centre**, situated in Lake Engure (see p176), has been monitoring and protecting duck populations since 1958. The **Latvian Birding** website keeps up-to-date lists of sightings in the country.

Over 330 species of birds can be spotted in Lithuania, including great snipes, white-tailed eagles, ferruginous ducks, corncrakes and aquatic warblers, among which are endangered species that breed in the country. The main migration route follows the

Latvia's Ķemeri National Park, home to a large number of birds

Cyclists on a winding path in Gauja National Park, Latvia

coast and crosses the Curonian Spit, and a particularly good spot is the Vente Horn on the tip of the Nemunas Delta National Park (see p287). The biggest draws are the migrations in spring and autumn, mainly between September and early October. Early spring is a good time to observe seabirds, owls, woodpeckers and grouse, while the largest number of species can be spotted during the breeding season between late May and early June. The **Lithuanian Society of Ornithologists** also arranges bird-watching tours.

Hiking and Trekking

Despite their lack of hilly terrain, the Baltic States attract walkers with their extensive forests, attractive rivers, lakes and rural calm. The relatively high chance of spotting wildlife such as roe deer, wild boar, moose and wolves also draws a number of walkers here. Each country has a good selection of well-marked trails with campsites and guesthouses along the way, and local tourist offices can suggest routes or arrange guides for visitors.

In Estonia, Lahemaa National Park (see pp110–111) has trails of varying lengths covering a diverse terrain. There are also pleasant routes surrounding Tartu (see pp118–19) and on the islands of Saaremaa (see pp96–7) and Hiiumaa (see pp94–5). A more unusual activity is bog-walking in Soomaa National Park (see pp104–5).

Latvia's Gauja National Park is good for walking, particularly along the well-marked Līgatne Nature Trail (see p193). There are also numerous short trails in the Tērvete Nature Park (see p171) and visitors looking for hills might head for the Latgale Uplands (see p202). Tour companies, such as **Eži**, organize walking trips in Valmiera (see p194).

Lithuania has almost 300 hiking trails, of which around 170 are in regional or national parks. Dzūkija National Park (see p260) is a favourite and some of its paths and facilities have been especially adapted for disabled visitors. Short, well-signposted walks include the 5-km (3-mile) long Šeirė Nature Trail and the route through the Čepkelių bog from the park's headquarters.

A cycle sign at Vaide, Latvia

The rolling hills of Dzukija National Park, Lithuania

Among the Lithuanian companies offering walking trips, the **Nemunas Tour** is one of the most popular.

Cycling

The relatively flat terrain and breathtaking scenery of the Baltic States makes cycling a pleasant way to get around. However, mountain bikers will find little to challenge their skills. It is not all smooth riding, though, as some roads are in poor condition. A popular international route is the EuroVelo route 10, which runs along the north of Estonia through Tallinn, across to the islands of Hiiumaa and Saaremaa via ferry, on to Rīga and then further south to Klaipėda.

Bicycle rental is easy in Estonia and Latvia, while in Lithuania there are hire outlets in the larger towns and cities. A good point of contact for all three countries is **BaltiCCycle**, a non-profit organization which provides details of organized tours, bicycle rental and self-guided cycling. It is also possible to hire a bike in one Baltic country and return it in another.

In Estonia, popular areas for cycling include Lahemaa National Park and the islands of Muhu (see p95), Saaremaa and Hiiumaa. **City Bike** is a notable organization that provides cycling tours and rental services in Estonia.

Easy rides in Latvia include the route from Rīga to Jūrmala (see pp174–5), while the best opportunity for mountain biking is in the Gauja Valley near Sigulda (see p192). There are marked biking routes around Kuldīga (see p183) and from Cēsis (see p192–3) to Valmiera; Eži arranges trips in the latter area.

The Lithuanian section of the Baltic Coast route includes an attractive stretch between Palanga (see p286) and Klaipėda (see pp284–5). There is also a marked route along the coast of the Curonian Lagoon to Nemunas Delta National Park.

Riders practising their equestrian skills, Pärnu, Estonia

Horse-Riding

Horses are a common sight in the rural areas of the Baltic States, especially in Latvia's Latgale region, where traditional ploughing methods still persist alongside mechanized farming. Horses can be hired at most horse-breeding farms; some farms also offer instruction. It may be possible to hire carriages, traps and even horse-drawn sleighs during winter.

The sandy tracks of Lahemaa National Park are popular for horse-riding in Estonia. One unusual option is the **Tihuse Riding Farm** on the island of Muhu, where guests can also participate in ploughing fields with the help of horses. Visitors to the Tori Stud Farm (see p105), in Estonia, can enjoy a tour of the farm in a horse-drawn carriage.

In Latvia, tourist attractions offering horse-riding include the Līgatne Nature Trail. Disabled visitors may be interested in riding therapy at **Kavalkāde** in Jūrmala. One of Lithuania's most renowned horse-breeding farms, **Žagarė Stud Farm**, about 34 km (21 miles) north of Šiauliai, has stalls built and decorated with materials brought from England at the end of the 19th century.

Fishing

Fishing is a very popular year-round activity in the Baltic States. In winter, hardy local people trek out onto frozen lakes and cut holes in the ice. Common fish include perch, brown trout, pike, carp, bream, tench and grayling. Fishing

permits are required throughout the region, and additional licences are required for some areas. Major tour operators can provide or assist visitors in obtaining the required permits.

Estonia's long coastline offers numerous angling opportunities. Inland, several companies organize fishing trips to Lake Peipsi (see p127) and Lahemaa National Park. A good starting point is the **Tallinn Fishing Club**, which issues permits that can otherwise be difficult to arrange. The club's staff provide assistance, although most of them speak only Estonian.

In Latvia, Lake Engure and Lake Kaņieris in Ķemeri National Park (see p174) are particularly good for pike. There are also many other suitable lakes in the Latgale and Vidzeme regions, and fish farms around the country. The **Latvian Fishing Association** can provide information on fishing sites, and permits are usually easy to obtain.

The key spots in Lithuania are in the east of the country, particularly near Ignalina in the Aukštaitija National Park (see pp270–71) and Molėtai Lakelands (see p269), and in the south. The Nemunas river is also popular, particularly around the town of Rusnė, as is the Curonian Spit (see pp288–9). Most fishing tackle shops and park offices sell licences; otherwise they are available from the **Department of Water Resources**.

Fishermen angling from the banks of the Lielupe river in Jelgava, Latvia

Mushroom- and Berry-Picking

Picking berries in spring and mushrooms during autumn are popular activities in the Baltic States. In fact, mushrooms are often a source of income in rural areas.

Often, the best way to arrange mushroom- and berry-picking is to ask your hotel or guesthouse to organize it. It is advisable to take a local along for guidance on both where to look and which varieties of mushroom are edible and tasty. The Estonian Rural Tourism website has details of farms which can offer mushroom- and berry-picking. The Džukija and Aukštaitija national parks offer some of the best opportunities. Visitors must bear in mind that it is usually illegal to pick the cranberries which grow on peat bogs. Berry-picking with **Vaskna Turismitalu** near Võru also teaches visitors how to make traditional alcoholic Christmas drinks. The website of Countryside Tourism of Lithuania has useful information on mushroom- and berry-picking. The **Žervynos Hostel** can also help with arrangements for the same.

Winter Sports

With long winters usually providing several months of snow coverage, it is not surprising that cross-country skiing is popular. What may be more unexpected is the number of downhill ski runs in a region where the highest point is just about 318 m (1,043 ft) above sea level. Although the Baltic States do not attract hardcore skiers and snowboarders, there are adequate opportunities for those who enjoy the sport.

In Estonia, some of the best skiing, snowboarding, snowmobiling, snowtubing and ski-jumping are found around Otepää (see p122), such as at **Kuutsemäe Resort**. Cross-country skiing is also possible at the Soomaa National Park. Details for winter activities are listed on the Estonian Rural Tourism website (see p295). A premier spot for downhill

Canoeing in Soomaa National Park, Estonia

skiing in Latvia is **Žagarkalns**, located close to Cēsis, but there are numerous other options listed in the Country Holidays website (see p295). Visitors seeking adventure should try the bobsleigh run in Sigulda operated by **Taxi Bob**. In Lithuania, Ignalina is a favoured destination for skiers. The **Lithuanian Winter Sports Centre** is one of several options in the area, with four downhill pistes, cross-country skiing and a skating rink. For ice-skating on frozen lakes, including Trakai, visitors may contact **Kempingas Slėnyje**. **Camping Villa Ventainė** regularly organizes snowmobiling and ice-fishing on the Curonian Lagoon.

Enthusiasts enjoying skiing in Kuutsemäe, Otepää, Estonia

Water Activities

With hundreds of rivers and lakes, and an extensive coastline, the Baltic States offer ample opportunities for canoeing, kayaking, windsurfing and rafting. The lack of any serious rapids may deter keen white-water enthusiasts, but it is perfect for leisurely river excursions.

Canoeing is one of the best ways to explore the wilderness of Soomaa National Park in Estonia, where visitors can also try to build haabjas (longboats). A number of water activities are provided by **Vesipapp**, **Surf Paradise** and **Reimann Retked**. Of the Baltic countries, Latvia has the most developed water tourism and the Gauja river is a popular spot. Specialist operator **Campo** offers a range of river trips and **Pāvilosta Marina** arranges catamaran sailing lessons. In Lithuania, the Aukštaitija region, with almost 300 lakes linked by waterways, allows tour companies to create multi-day sailing trips. Elsewhere, the **Trakai National Sports and Health Centre** offers kayaking, canoeing, yachting and diving. Similarly, the **Zarasai Water Sports Centre** offers water-skiing and windsurfing. Klaipėda's **Oktopusas** diving centre arranges dives in lakes and the Baltic Sea.

Latvian ice-hockey player in action in an IIHF World Championship match

Spectator Sports

The Baltic States are among the few parts of Europe where football is not the dominant spectator sport. The region's most enthusiastic football fans are the Estonians, and their national team has improved in recent years. However, in Estonia, the biggest of the stadium sports is basketball and major fixtures can be seen at the **Kalev Stadium**.

In Latvia, the most popular sport is ice hockey, particularly since the national team beat Russia in the 2000 Ice Hockey Championships. Many of the best players are members of overseas teams, making domestic games a little lacklustre, but support is enthusiastic for international games at the **Arena Rīga**. Visitors to Daugavpils will find the city in the thrall of speedway racing. Enthusiasts should not miss a visit to the **Lokomotive Stadium**.

The most popular spectator sport in Lithuania is basketball. The national team has won a bronze medal at the Olympic Games three times and was the European champion in 2003. Žalgiris Kaunas and Lietuvos Rytas Vilnius are the leading domestic teams. To watch players practising, visit the **Siemens Arena**.

Golf

Soviet Russians were not keen on golf, so the sport is relatively new to the region and there are few good courses. In Estonia, a number of golf clubs are members of the **Estonian Golf Association**. The **Estonian Golf & Country Club** is seeking to be a part of the PGA Tour. There are 18-hole courses in Otepää, Saaremaa and Tallinn, the last of which is well maintained.

The premier course in Latvia is at the **Ozo Golf Club** on Rīga's outskirts, while the country's other 18-hole course is **Saliena**, located between Rīga and Jūrmala. Golf clubs in Lithuania with 18-hole courses include **Sostinių** and **Europos Centro**. There are also plans to open a golf complex near Klaipėda, featuring an additional spa hotel.

Spa Breaks

There have been health resorts in the Baltic States since the 19th century, although there is evidence of mud and spring water being used in folk medicine much earlier. The resorts were hugely popular during the Soviet era, drawing visitors from across the former Soviet Union for relaxation or medical treatment. There was a decline in the spa industry after independence. However, since then new spa hotels have opened and older ones have been renovated. Treatments are cheaper than in Western Europe, and there are special deals in winter.

There are several spa hotels on the Estonian islands and also establishments within, and close to, the capital, such as the **Kalev Spa**, a huge facility on the edge of the Old Town, and **Meriton Spa**. The **Estonian Spa Association** represents several of the country's spas.

The main spot for a spa break in Latvia is Jūrmala, a string of seaside towns providing everything from lively bars to secluded beaches. Another good choice is the Spa Hotel Ezeri *(see p303)*.

In Lithuania, the best spas can be found in Druskininkai *(see p259)*, one of which is **Spa Vilnius**. Palanga is also a popular spa destination.

Brewery Tours

Beer brewing has a celebrated history in the Baltic States, and there are several brewery tours available in the region. Try **A Le Coq Brewery** in Estonia or the **Užavas** or **Valmiermuižas** facilities in Latvia. Lithuania has the best choice of breweries open to the public, including **Utenos**, **Švyturys**, **Volfas Engelman**, **Kalnapilis** and **Rinkuškiai**.

Entrance to the Spa Vilnius, one of the best spas in Druskininkai, Lithuania

DIRECTORY

Bird-Watching

Engure Ornithological Centre
Tel 742 2195.
W eedp.lv

Estonian Nature Tours
Linnuse tee 1, Läänemaa.
Tel 477 8214.
W naturetours.ee

Estonian Ornithological Society
Veski 4, Tartu.
Tel 742 2195.
W eoy.ee

Latvian Birding
W putni.lv

Lithuanian Society of Ornithologists
Naugarduko 47–33, Vilnius. Tel 8521 30498.
W birdlife.lt

Hiking and Trekking

Eži
Beātes iela 30a, Valmiera, Latvia. Tel 6420 7263.
W ezi.lv

Nemunas Tour
Gėlių 50, Ringaudai, Lithuania. Tel 3756 3766.
W nemunastour.com

Cycling

BaltiCCycle
Tel 6995 6009.
W bicycle.lt

City Bike
Uus 33, Estonia.
Tel 683 6383.
W citybike.ee

Horse-Riding

Kavalkāde
Skautu iela 2, Jūrmala, Latvia. Tel 2940 6955.

Tihuse Riding Farm
Hellamaa, Muhu, Estonia.
Tel 514 8667.
W tihuse.ee

Žagarė Stud Farm
Žagariškų k, Žagarė, Lithuania.
Tel 4266 0860.

Fishing

Department of Water Resources
Juozapavičiaus 9, Vilnius.
Tel 5272 3786.

Latvian Fishing Association
Stabu iela, Rīga.
Tel 6731 6943.

Tallinn Fishing Club
Pärnu mnt 42.
Tel 525 4488.

Mushroom- and Berry-Picking

Vaskna Turismitalu
Haanja vald, Võrumaa, Estonia. Tel 782 9173.

Žervynos Hostel
Tel 3103 9583.

Winter Sports

Camping Villa Ventainė
Ventės k, Lithuania. Tel 4416 8525. W ventaine.lt

Kempingas Slėnyje
Slėnio 1, Trakai, Lithuania.
Tel 5285 3880.
W camptrakai.lt

Kuutsemäe Resort
Tel 766 9007.
W kuutsemae.ee

Lithuanian Winter Sports Centre
Sporto 3. Tel 3865 4193.
W lzsc.lt

Taxi Bob
Peldu iela 2, Sigulda, Latvia. Tel 2924 4948.
W taxibob.lv

Žagarkalns
Tel 2626 6266.
W zagarkalns.lv

Water Activities

Campo
Kronu 23d, Rīga. Tel 2922 2339. W campo.laivas.lv

Oktopusas
Šilutės 79, Klaipėda, Lithuania. Tel 4638 1850.
W godive.lt

Pāvilosta Marina
Ostmalas 4, Pāvilosta, Latvia. Tel 6349 8581.
W pavilostamarina.lv

Reimann Retked
Tel 511 4099.
W retked.ee

Surf Paradise
Ristna, Hiiumaa, Estonia.
W paap.ee

Trakai National Sports and Health Centre
Karaimų 73, Lithuania.
Tel 5285 5501.

Vesipapp
Tel 511 9117.
W vesipapp.ee

Zarasai Water Sports Centre
Laukesos village, Zarasai, Lithuania. Tel 3855 3426.
W poilsiobaze.lt

Spectator Sports

Arena Rīga
Skanstes iela 21.
Tel 6738 8200.
W arenariga.lv

Kalev Stadium
Juhkentali tänav 12, Tallinn. Tel 644 5171.

Lokomotive Stadium
Jelgavas iela 54, Daugavpils, Lithuania.
W lokomotive.lv

Siemens Arena
Ozo 14a, Lithuania.
Tel 5247 7576.
W siemensarena.lt

Golf

Estonian Golf Association
Tel 504 1792.
W golf.ee

Estonian Golf & Country Club
Manniva küla, Jõelähtme, Harjumaa. Tel 602 5290.
W egcc.ee

Europos Centro
Girijos village, Lithuania.
Tel 6162 6366.
W golflub.lt

Ozo Golf Club
Milgravja 16, Rīga.
Tel 739 4399.
W ozogolf.lv

Saliena
Egluciems, Babītes Pagasts, Latvia. Tel 716 0300. W salienagolf.lv

Sostinių
Pipiriškių k, Pastrėvio sen, Lithuania. Tel 6199 9999.

Spa Breaks

Estonian Spa Association
Sadama 9–11, Haapsalu.
W estonianspas.eu

Kalev Spa
Aia 18, Tallinn. Tel 649 3300. W kalevspa.ee

Meriton Spa
Toompuiestee 27, Estonia.
Tel 667 7111.
W meritonhotels.com

Spa Vilnius
Dineikos k 1, Druskininkai.
Tel 3135 3811.
W spa-vilnius.lt

Brewery Tours

A Le Coq Brewery
Tähtvere 56–62, Tartu, Estonia. Tel 744 9711.
W alecoq.ee

Kalnapilis
Taikos avenue 1, Panevėžys, Lithuania.
Tel 4550 5219.
W kalnapilis.lt

Rinkuškiai
Alyvų 8, Birži, Lithuania.
Tel 4503 5293.
W rinkuskiai.lt

Švyturys
Kulių vartų 7, Klaipėda, Lithuania.
Tel 4648 4000.
W svyturys.lt

Utenos
Pramonės 12, Utena, Lithuania.
W utenosalus.lt

Užavas
Užavas pagasts, Ventspils, Latvia.
Tel 2921 9145.
W uzavas-alus.lv

Valmiermuižas
Dzirnavu iela 2, Valmiera, Latvia.
Tel 2026 4269.
W valmiermuiza.lv

Volfas Engelman
Kaunakiemio 2, Kaunas, Lithuania.
Tel 8007 2427.
W volfasengelman.lt

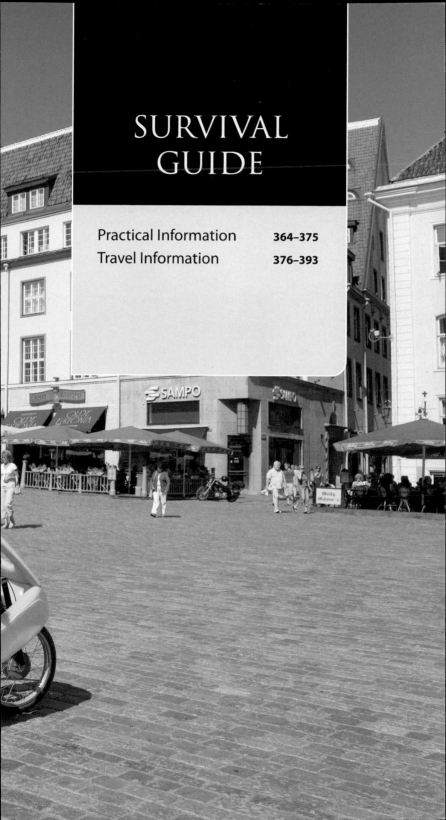

SURVIVAL GUIDE

PRACTICAL INFORMATION

After so many years of being excluded from the map of Europe, the Baltic States of Estonia, Latvia and Lithuania are now drawing a great number of eager visitors to discover the region's hidden treasures. These countries are extremely visitor-friendly destinations that offer a wealth of historic sights and cultural activities as well as great natural beauty, good food and fascinating insights into the region's complex past. Each country has a well-developed network of tourist information centres that often extends into small towns and offers an abundance of useful literature to help visitors get the best out of their trip. Moreover, with the region's capitals only a relatively short drive away from each other, it is easy to explore the Baltic States either individually or as a whole. Tour operators are growing in number and offer a good variety of packages. The practical information below and on pages 366–7 covers each of the three Baltic States.

When to Visit

The best time to visit the Baltic States is from May to October, when the weather is generally mild and rarely very cold. It is an ideal time to explore the region's natural wonders by visiting one of the many national parks or taking long treks in the countryside, camping or going swimming in the sea or one of the numerous lakes. Nearly all the best festivals take place in summer, while some small museums and historic sights are only open between May and September.

The Old Towns of Tallinn and Rīga are especially crowded at the peak of summer due to their compact size. Vilnius's larger Old Town, however, is less cramped. Autumn is often splendid in the Baltic States, but the weather can abruptly turn chilly as early as October.

Impressive building of the French Embassy in Rīga, Latvia

The capitals are also very atmospheric in winter, when they are blanketed in snow, although temperatures can plunge significantly at any time. The least pleasant time to visit is January, the coldest month, and the rainy month of April, when the snow melts into a mass of sludge.

Visas and Passports

Citizens of EU member states, the USA, Canada, Australia and New Zealand only need a valid passport for entry into Estonia, Latvia and Lithuania for a period of up to 90 days in a half-year period. Those wishing to stay beyond the permitted 90 days will need to apply for a national long-term visa or a residence permit. Visitors from other countries should enquire at the relevant embassy or consulate for visa requirements before travelling. The official websites of the Ministry of Foreign Affairs for each of the three countries offers information on visa regulations.

Customs Regulations

EU citizens are not subject to customs regulations, provided they adhere to EU guidelines. All visitors should check for any customs duty or special permission required to export a cultural object, before buying it. For detailed information on all these guidelines, entrance regulations and visa cost, it is advisable to visit the official website of the European Commission.

Street café close to Vilnius Cathedral, Vilnius, Lithuania

◀ Velo-taxi on Tallinn's Town Hall Square

Visitors at the tourist information office in Tallinn, Estonia

Tourist Information

Estonia, Latvia and Lithuania have a remarkably well-developed network of tourist information centres supported by an equally advanced structure of tourism websites. All cities and most major towns have a tourist information office, which is usually located in or close to the town square. In the case of very small towns, the office is often situated in a museum or within some other historic building. Tourist offices in cities and larger towns are open from 9am to 6pm on weekdays. The offices are open for shorter hours on Saturdays and are usually open on Sundays. In remote places, opening hours are more erratic and it is advisable to check in advance.

Tourist offices are staffed by friendly, English-speaking local people, who are always eager to promote their area and can offer information on accommodation, museums, historic sights, nature trails, entertainment and restaurants. Free brochures covering local and national sights and events are available at these offices, which also sell more detailed maps and guidebooks at nominal rates. For a full list of all tourist information offices across each country, visit their websites. Latvia and Lithuania also have tourist information centres in the UK, Finland, Germany, Sweden and Russia.

Logo,
Lithuanian Tourism

Business Hours

Throughout Estonia, Latvia and Lithuania, banks and state institutions are generally open from 9am to 5 or 6pm. Private businesses are increasingly working longer hours and are open from 9am to anywhere between 6 and 8pm. For opening hours of shops, see pages 332, 336 and 340.

Imposing exterior of the Hipoteku Bank in Limbaži, Latvia

DIRECTORY

Visas and Passports

Estonia
W vm.ee

Latvia
W am.gov.lv

Lithuania
W urm.lt

Customs Regulations

W ec.europa.eu

Tourist Information

W visitestonia.com
W latvia.travel
W lithuania.travel

Embassies and Consulates in Tallinn

Canada
Toomkooli 13. **Tel** 627 3311.
W canada.ee

United Kingdom
Wismari 6. **Tel** 667 4700.
W ukinestonia.fco.gov.uk

United States
Kentmanni 20. **Tel** 668 8100.
W estonia.usembassy.gov

Embassies and Consulates in Rīga

Australia
Vilandes iela 7. **Tel** 6732 0509.

Canada
Baznīcas iela 20/22.
Tel 6781 3945.

France
Raina bulvāris 9. **Tel** 6703 6600.

United Kingdom
J Alunana iela 5. **Tel** 6777 4700.
W ukinlatvia.fco.gov.uk

United States
S Velsa 1. **Tel** 6710 7000.

Embassies and Consulates in Vilnius

Australia
Vilniaus 23. **Tel** 212 3369.

Canada
Jogailos 4. **Tel** 249 0950.
W canada.lt

United Kingdom
Antakalnio 2. **Tel** 246 2900.
W ukinlithuania.fco.gov.uk

United States
Akmenų 6. **Tel** 266 5500.
W usembassy.lt

Exhibition on the Lithuanian partisans, in the KGB Museum *(see p242)* in Vilnius, Lithuania

Museums, Churches and Historic Sights

Museums in the Baltic States keep rather erratic hours, so it is advisable to check opening times before visiting. Usually, they open from 10am to 5 or 6pm during summer, although in some cases they open at 11am or even midday. Monday is the official closing day for most museums, though some are also closed on Tuesdays. Nearly all museums open on Saturdays and many on Sundays. However, tour operators often arrange for museums to open for a group.

Other sights, such as castles and churches, tend to have fairly regular opening hours in summer, between 9 or 10am and 4 or 5pm, Tuesday to Saturday. In winter, however,

St Nicholas's Orthodox Cathedral *(see p185)* in Liepāja, Latvia

many museums open for shorter hours or just remain closed. Some historic sights can only be visited as part of a guided tour. Organizers often try to accommodate single visitors into a group.

Discount Card Schemes

A cost-effective way of exploring Tallinn, Vilnius and Rīga is to purchase a city card. The Tallinn Card costs €31 for 24 hours, €19 for 48 hours and €49 for 72 hours. It entitles holders to free entrance to 40 major museums and tourist sights, free sightseeing tours, use of public transport and admission to a range of entertainment venues, including a bowling centre, a water park and a major nightclub. It can also get visitors a discount in many restaurants and shops. The card is on sale at tourist information centres, hotels, travel agents, Tallinn Airport, Tallinn Port and online. The Rīga Card costs €16 for 24 hours, €20 for 48 hours and €26 for 72 hours. It entitles holders to free admission to many museums, a walking tour of the Old Town and a discount at a range of hotels. There are two types of Vilnius City Card, 24 hours and 72 hours. The card entitles holders to free public transport

KONTROLES TALONS

Ticket to
St Peter's, Rīga

(both buses and trolleybuses), free entry to museums and discounts on tours, accommodation and restaurants.

Admission Charges

In all three Baltic States, admission charges vary considerably depending on the type of museum and where it is located. Most museums away from the capitals are quite reasonably priced. Ticket prices in Tallinn, Rīga and Vilnius are more expensive, but still reasonable. Students and senior citizens can obtain discounts. State museums in Estonia offer free entrance on the last Saturday of each month. In Latvia, state museums give free admission on the last Wednesday of each month, and in Lithuania many museums do not charge an entrance fee on Wednesdays.

What to Wear

The chilly winters in the Baltic countries make thick layers of clothing necessary, as well as gloves, hats and thick-soled waterproof shoes. In summer, lightweight garments are usually adequate, but it is best to carry a jacket for the evenings. In spring, carry an umbrella. Comfortable footwear is recommended for walking on the cobbled streets of Rīga and Tallinn.

Travelling with Children

The Baltic States are extremely child-friendly. Most parks have play areas and some even have a range of distractions, such as bouncy toy castles and trampolines. Many traditional-style taverns and ethnographic museums also provide some wonderfully old-fashioned play apparatus for children. Some hotels offer childcare facilities. For information on eating out with children, see pages 308–9.

Disabled Travellers

Although there has been a significant improvement in recent years, Estonia, Latvia and Lithuania do not provide many facilities for disabled people. Most of the new upmarket hotels and restaurants have taken disabled travellers' needs into consideration, but such places are few and far between. Owing to their historic structure, the Old Towns of the three capital cities are extremely difficult for disabled people to negotiate. In Tallinn, there are several steep, winding cobblestoned streets, and Rīga's Old Town is also predominantly cobbled. Although very little of Vilnius's Old Town is cobbled, it is still difficult to get around in many

Children playing at the Seaside Open-Air Museum *(see p181)*, Ventspils, Latvia

places due to the extremely narrow streets and pavements.

Public transport is another major obstacle as trams, trolleybuses and trains do not provide wheelchair access in Tallinn and Rīga, and only a very limited number of buses do. The situation is better in Vilnius, where a large number of buses and trolleybuses have access for disabled people. For information on access for disabled travellers in hotels, see page 295.

Signpost at Limbaži, Latvia

Language

Both Latvian and Lithuanian belong to the Baltic family of languages. Estonians speak a Finno-Ugric dialect, which is

closer to Finnish. German is quite commonly spoken as a second language in all three Baltic States, while virtually everybody is fluent in Russian. However, communicating in English in the capital cities is seldom a problem – most people speak it to some extent. Knowledge of English is less wide-spread in rural areas. For common words and phrases used in the three languages, refer to the Phrase Book on pages 411–16.

Measures and Electrical Appliances

The Baltic States all use the metric system. The mains voltage is 230 volts in Estonia and Lithuania and 220 volts in Latvia. Standard Continental European two-pin plugs are used. Although UK plug adapters are available, they are not easy to find, so it is advisable to bring any necessary adapters with you.

Local Time

The clocks of the Baltic States are set to Eastern European Standard Time and are two hours ahead of Greenwich Mean Time (GMT+2) and seven hours ahead of Eastern Standard Time (EST+7). Clocks go forward one hour on the last Sunday in March and go back one hour on the last Sunday in October.

The cobbled Viru Street in Tallinn's Old Town

Personal Security and Health

Estonia, Latvia and Lithuania are generally safe countries, with relatively rare instances of theft and mugging. However, visitors should remain vigilant in the capitals, particularly in and around the Old Towns. Generally, Tallinn, Rīga and Vilnius are far safer than many other Western capitals, although the same precautions should be exercised as in any other major city in the world. The quality of medical care is improving and is mostly level with that of Western European countries. Pharmacies in bigger cities are open all day and all three countries provide free emergency care.

Busy western end of Basanavičiaus Street in Palanga, Lithuania

Police

The Estonian *politsei (police)* usually wear a dark blue jacket and trousers, black boots and a baseball-like cap. They drive white cars with a blue stripe and the word *politsei* written on the side doors and bonnet. In Tallinn, the police have a significant street presence, especially in the Old Town, during summer. The municipal police force wear dark green uniforms and have limited powers. Therefore, the state police should be contacted to report a crime.

In Latvia, the *policija (police)* wear dark blue uniforms consisting of a suit-like jacket with epaulets and a maroon tie, although when on patrol they mostly wear dark blue overalls with a luminous yellow vest and a broad cap. The Latvian police drive white cars with a grey stripe along the side. The Rīga municipal police usually wear all-black uniforms and patrol the Old Town, although they have

limited powers of arrest. In an emergency, it is best to call the state police.

In Lithuania, the *policija* (police) uniform consists of a dark green jacket and trousers, black boots and a cap. They drive white cars with a green stripe along the side and "police" written in large letters across the car's bonnet.

General Precautions

Although the vast majority of visitors to the Baltic States do not have any problems with theft, it always helps to take some basic precautions to safeguard valuables. Car theft remains a persistent problem in all three Baltic States, so park in central and well-lit areas, and keep expensive objects hidden from view. Using a guarded parking lot is safer still. Pickpocketing is a minor problem, but visitors should take care of wallets and handbags.

In Rīga, avoid using the tunnels around Central Station at night; use the traffic light crossings instead. It is also a good idea to avoid using ATMs in quiet spots at night. Also, never carry large amounts of cash around with you while visiting popular tourist destinations.

Personal Safety

As you would do anywhere, using common sense is the best way to ensure your personal safety. Never accept drinks from strangers, no matter how affable they might seem, and never accept invitations from people to go with them to another bar or nightclub. Be vigilant and avoid disreputable-looking clubs, as a number of scams can happen in such places. It is advisable to carry a mobile phone, with a record of all emergency numbers.

Avoid drinking excessively. There are a handful of thugs in each of the Baltic capitals who make a point of preying on inebriated foreigners as they stumble out of bars in the early hours and head back to their hotels, although they normally target solitary people. Also, refrain from ostentatious behaviour, such as carrying luxury items.

Estonian police car

Latvian police car

Health Care

Standards of health care in the Baltics are now at least equal to those in other European countries. EU citizens will be treated free of charge provided they bring their Health Insurance card (EHIC) with them, together with another form of photographic identification.

Minor medical complaints can be dealt with at a pharmacy. Most pharmacies stock a wide range of international drugs. For serious health concerns visit the nearest hospital.

Private clinics exist in all major cities and are an option if you require non-emergency treatment. Tallinn, Vilnius and

Interior of the Town Hall Pharmacy *(see p64)*, in Tallinn's Old Town

Exterior of the Medical Diagnostic Centre, Vilnius

Rīga all have a choice of standard Western European clinics that are significantly cheaper than private clinics in the West. Check to see if your existing insurance policy covers all emergencies. If not, it is advisable to take out comprehensive travel insurance.

As there are virtually no significant health risks in the Baltic States, precautionary immunization is not mandatory. However, there is the risk of acquiring tick-borne encephalitis in woodland areas, so if you are planning to spend any length of time in a forest in summer, you should get vaccinated against it. In Tallinn, Rīga and Vilnius, tap water is

safe to drink, but is best avoided as it does not taste very good. Bottled mineral water is better.

Pharmacies

Minor ailments and accidents can often be treated by staff at a local pharmacy (*apteek* in Estonian, *aptieka* in Latvian and *vaistinė* in Lithuanian), which will usually stock a large selection of international drugs as well as many herbal medicines that are produced locally. Pharmacies generally open from 8am to 7 or 8pm on weekdays and until 3 or 4pm on Saturdays. There are a few 24-hour pharmacies in Tallinn, Rīga and Vilnius.

DIRECTORY

Emergency in Estonia

Ambulance
Tel 112.

Fire
Tel 112.

Police
Tel 112.

Roadside Assistance
Tel 1888.

Medical Help in Tallinn

24-Hour Pharmacy
Tõnismägi 5.
Tel 644 2282.

Qvalitas Swedish-Estonian Medical Centre
Parnu mnt 102c.
Tel 605 1500.
W qvalitas.ee

Tallinn Central Hospital
Ravi 18.
Tel 622 7070.
W itk.ee

Tallinn Mustamäe Hospital
J Sütiste 19.
Tel 617 1300.
W regionaalhaigla.ee

Emergency in Latvia

Ambulance
Tel 03, 112.

Fire
Tel 01, 112.

Police
Tel 02, 112.

Roadside Assistance
Tel 1888.

Medical Help in Rīga

24-Hour Pharmacy
Audēju 20.
Tel 6721 3340.

ARS
Skolas 5. **Tel** 6720 1007.
W ars-med.lv

Paul Stradiņš Clinical University Hospital
Pilsoņu 13.
Tel 6706 9600.
W stradini.lv

Rīga Hospital Number One
Bruņinieku 5. **Tel** 6727 0491. W 1slimnica.lv

Emergency in Lithuania

Ambulance
Tel 03, 112.

Fire
Tel 01, 112.

Police
Tel 02, 112.

Roadside Assistance
Tel 1888.

Medical Help in Vilnius

24-Hour Pharmacy
Gedimino pr 27.
Tel 261 0135.

Medical Diagnostic and Treatment Centre
V. Grybo 32A.
Tel 233 3000 or 698 00000.
W medcentras.lt

Vilnius University Emergency Hospital
Šiltnamių 29.
Tel 216 9140.

Banking and Currency in Estonia, Latvia and Lithuania

The Baltic States have a thriving banking sector and all three countries have now joined the Eurozone, using the common currency, the euro. The best and most convenient way to obtain euros while travelling in the Baltic States is by withdrawing them from debit accounts using the ATMs of major banks. Bureaux de change and banks offer money-changing services, as do hotels but the exchange rates are unfavourable. Check rates of commission before changing currency, and shop around as exchange rates may vary considerably.

Banking Hours

In Estonia and Latvia, banks are usually open from Monday to Friday between 9am and 6pm. Major banks in big cities stay open on Saturdays, from 9am to 2pm in Estonia and from 10am to 3pm in Latvia. In Lithuania, opening hours vary, with bank branches operating from 8am to 5pm on weekdays. Banks in big cities open on Saturdays from 8am to 3pm or 10am to 5pm, and, in rare cases, for a few hours on Sundays.

ATMs

There is an extremely wide network of ATMs in the Baltic States, spread across most major town centres and the capital cities. Some petrol stations have few ATMs and most small towns have at least two or three. Most ATMs have English-language options and accept all major international credit and debit cards, such as **MasterCard**, **Visa Electron**, VisaPlus and Cirrus/Maestro, and you can withdraw cash with no additional charges. However, most ATMs issue high-denomination banknotes.

Distinctively signposted bureau de change in Latvia

Banks and Bureaux de Change

Estonia, Latvia and Lithuania have a staggering number of banks. The biggest is the Swedish-owned, pan-Baltic **Swedbank**. It has branches in just about every town as well as many branches and ATMs in the cities. Sampo Bank and **SEB** are major banks in Estonia. In Latvia, **Latvijas Banka**, SEB, Citadele and Nordea are well established. In Lithuania, Vilniaus Bankas (SEB) and **Lietuvos Bankas** have the

largest networks. Banks usually charge between 2 and 3 per cent commission for changing money.

Bureaux de change are extremely widespread in the three capitals and are open for long hours, 7 days a week. They offer rates competitive to the banks, except in Estonia, where commission can be as high as 25 per cent. Changing money in hotels in all three countries should also be avoided, as they often offer unfavourable exchange rates.

Credit Cards and Traveller's Cheques

Traveller's cheques are best avoided as very few banks now change them and they are unheard of in shops. As there is a wide network of ATMs across all three countries, either cash or a credit card is a preferable option.

All the major credit cards are widely accepted, except in the smallest shops and cafés. Some museums outside the capitals also require cash payment. Bus and train fares must usually be paid in cash, both at the stations and on board.

One of the many 24-hour ATMs of Snoras, a bank in Lithuania

The Euro

The euro (€) is the common currency of the European Union. It went into general circulation on 1 January 2002, initially for 12 participating countries. Estonia joined in January 2011, with the kroon phased out later that year; Latvia's lat was replaced in January 2014; and Lithuania's lita in January 2015.

EU members using the euro as their sole official currency are known as the Eurozone. Euro notes are identical throughout the Eurozone countries, each one featuring designs of fictional architectural structures. The coins, however, have one side identical (the value side), and one side with an image unique to each country. Both notes and coins are exchangeable in each of the participating Eurozone countries.

Banknotes

Euro banknotes have seven denominations. The €5 note (grey in colour) is the smallest, followed by the €10 note (pink), €20 note (blue), €50 note (orange), €100 note (green), €200 note (yellow) and €500 note (purple). All notes show the stars of the European Union.

5 euros

10 euros

20 euros

50 euros

100 euros

200 euros

500 euros

2 euros | 1 euro | 50 cents | 20 cents | 10 cents

Coins

The euro has eight coin denominations: €1 and €2; 50 cents, 20 cents, 10 cents, 5 cents, 2 cents and 1 cent. The 2- and 1-euro coins are both silver and gold in colour. The 50-, 20- and 10-cent coins are gold. The 5-, 2- and 1-cent coins are bronze.

5 cents | 2 cents | 1 cent

Communications and Media

The three Baltic States have a highly developed communications network that is on a par with those of Western Europe. Mobile phone usage Is extremely high and access to Wi-Fi is widespread. It's advisable to travel with a mobile phone as public telephones no longer exist in Latvia or Estonia, and there are very few public phones left in Lithuania. The flat terrain in the Baltic countries has always ensured good mobile phone coverage, although you may discover the occasional blind spot in the remoter areas. For long-distance calls, international calling cards are readily available. The national postal services are generally dependable and major international couriers operate in all three countries.

Mobile Phones

GSM mobile phone networks have complete coverage in the Baltic States. The main mobile networks have partnerships with Western European service providers such as Orange and Vodafone, so travelling with your own phone is generally straightforward. Another option is to buy a prepaid SIM card from a local provider and insert it into your own handset for relatively cheap calls and SMS rates.

However, roaming rules introduced in the European Union mean that the cost of making and receiving calls when abroad in the EU is now substantially cheaper than it used to be. The EU has imposed maximum tariffs on all member states for calls, texts and downloading. For travellers from outside the EU, high roaming charges will likely still apply. Contact your service provider to determine the rates.

As of 2014, European operators are not allowed to exceed the following rates for mobile use: €0.19 per minute for outgoing voice calls; €0.05 per minute for incoming voice calls; €0.06 per SMS messsage for outgoing texts; and €0.20 per megabyte for online data downloads.

The Internet

Nearly all hotels have Internet connections and many cafés and restaurants have Wi-Fi access, most of which is free. Internet cafés are not as widespread as they used to be. In smaller towns, those that still exist are signposted with an "@" sign. Some hotels have business centres or PCs for public use, but most presume that guests arrive with their own devices.

Postal Services

Mail services in the Baltic States are efficient and very dependable. Post offices provide a range of services at competitive postal rates. Mail can be sent *poste restante* to any post office in the Baltic region, but a passport is usually needed to collect it. Post offices sell cheaper postcards than many shops.

Newspapers and Magazines

The Baltic Times is the only pan-Baltic, English-language newspaper. It comes out once a month and covers news, business, arts and entertainment across Estonia, Latvia and Lithuania. It includes weekly entertainment listings and information on concerts, exhibitions and films. *In Your Pocket* (around €1) provides comprehensive and well researched write-ups on everything from restaurants and bars to nightclubs and shopping, as well as up-to-date information on musem opening times. Both publications are widely available at kiosks and some retail outlets. Free listings magazines come and go in all three capitals and are available at hotel reception desks.

International editions of British and American newspapers and magazines, such as *The New York Times*, *International Herald Tribune* and *The Economist*, can be found in some news outlets in central Tallinn, Rīga and Vilnius.

Radio and Televison

BBC Radio is easily found in all three Baltic countries. Most other international radio stations can be easily accessed via the web. Hotels of all kinds continue to provide televisions in all rooms with access to the major international television stations, such as the BBC, CNN and Euronews, as well as sports and music channels. A few five-star hotels are starting to introduce smart TVs that integrate entertainment and wirelessly stream data from smartphones.

Customers at a newspaper kiosk in Ventspils, Latvia

Communications in Estonia

Estonia's communications infrastructure is very efficient. All phone lines are digital, ensuring high-quality connections and easy-to-make international calls. Internet and mobile phone usage is particularly high. A wide range of services can be paid for through mobile phones, including parking charges. Wi-Fi coverage in Estonia is almost total, and mostly free, including on the main islands and even on some beaches. The post offices offer a range of express delivery options, including a special pan-Baltic option.

Accessing the free Wi-Fi available just about everywhere across Estonia

Making a Phone Call

Estonia has an extremely simple and efficient digital telephone network. In 2004, the country did away with all city codes, as a result of which all landline numbers are now seven digits. Calls to landlines are usually less expensive than those to mobile phones. The public phone system has been decommissioned, and there are now no public telephones to be found anywhere in the country.

Mobile Phones

Estonian mobile numbers start with 5 or 8 and usually have seven or eight digits. The main mobile phone operators are **EMT**, **Elisa** and the pan-Baltic **Tele2**. EMT Simpel and Tele2 both offer pre-paid SIM cards, which are useful for visitors planning to stay in Estonia for a significant length of time.

The Internet

Virtually everywhere you go in Tallinn and the rest of Estonia, Wi-Fi internet access is available in public places. Almost every café, restaurant, hotel and public building offers Wi-Fi openly and free of charge, making Internet cafés all but redundant, though one or two are still around.

Postal Services

The state-owned Estonian *postkontor (post office)*, called **Omniva**, is an efficiently run enterprise. It has 500 outlets around the country opening from 9am to 6 or 7pm on weekdays, and between 9am and 3pm on Saturdays. **Tallinn Central Post Office** is open from 8am to 8pm on weekdays, and from 10am to 4pm on Saturdays and Sundays.

The cost of sending a letter of up to 50 g (about four pages) in Europe is €1.20. To send it registered costs around €3. It is possible to package, label and pay for sending letters and parcels via Omniva's online e-service.

Major international couriers such as **DHL** and **DPD** operate

Estonian postbox outside the Central Post Office, Tallinn

in Estonia, while **Cargobus** is a reliable Estonian parcel delivery company. The cheapest way of sending a parcel home is probably with the state post office company Omniva. They can send parcels to a specific address, from post office to post office, or via courier.

Dialling Codes

- All mobile numbers begin with 5 or 8; almost all other lines start with other numbers.
- Toll-free numbers start with 80; premium rate numbers start with 70.
- To make an international call from Estonia, first press "+", then the destination's country code and number.
- To call Estonia from abroad dial the international access code (00 from the UK, 011 from the US and Canada), followed by 372, Estonia's country code.

Communications in Latvia

The telephone and mail networks in Latvia are both efficient and reliable, although some post office branches need modernization. Nevertheless, post offices are present in most towns and villages of significant size. With the rise of mobile phone use, under used public phones have been removed across the country. Internet access is excellent in Rīga and other major cities, with Wi-Fi hotspots in many cafés and hotels, and continues to improve throughout Latvia.

A Plus Punkts kiosk selling SIM-card packages and top-up credit, Rīga

Making a Phone Call

All valid telephone numbers in Latvia have eight digits, except those for contacting some special public services. All mobile numbers start with 2; landlines start with 6, and occasionally 5.

Now that public telephones have been withdrawn, the easiest way to make international calls is simply with your own mobile phone after registering with one of the three mobile phone operators active in the country, LMT, Tele2 or Bite. EU regulations ensure that roaming charges are not extortionate for those using a European phone. If roaming charges are a concern, you could purchase a prepaid calling card for international calls, which allows connection through a toll-free number and gives automated instructions in numerous languages.

Mobile Phones

Latvia's three mobile phone operators **LMT**, **Tele2** and **Bite** provide prepaid SIM cards (your own phone will need to be unlocked). Visitors staying in Latvia for longer periods have the option of buying a cheap second phone, which can be found at shops and stalls in shopping malls, and signing up to a pay-as-you-go plan.

The Internet

Speedy, free-of-charge Wi-Fi is widely available at restaurants, hotels and cafés in Rīga and much of the rest of Latvia. The rapid growth of its availability means that Internet cafés are not as popular as they once were. One of the survivors, **Planēta**, is open 24 hours a day.

Postal Services

Branches of Latvia's state-owned post office, **Latvijas Pasts**, are found all over the country. In Rīga the biggest is located at Brivibas iela 32 (entrance on Merkela iela), but there are smaller post offices in the city centre. Sending a letter of up to 50 g within Europe costs €0.90; to send it registered costs €1.70.

The busy Brivibas post office branch is open from 7:30am to 7pm on weekdays and from 9am to 3pm on Saturdays, but is closed on Sundays. A branch at the central train station is open longer, from 7am to 9pm, on weekdays, from 9am to 8pm on Saturdays and from10am to 8pm on Sundays.

Major international couriers such as **DHL** and **DPD** operate in Latvia, but the cheapest way of sending a parcel home is probably with Latvijas Pasts. They can send parcels to a specific address, from post office to post office, or via courier.

DIRECTORY

Useful Numbers

Directory Enquiries
Tel 1188.

Mobile Phones

Bite
w bite.lv

LMT
w lmt.lv

Tele2
w tele2.lv

The Internet

Planēta
Valnu iela 41, Rīga.

Postal Services

DHL
w dhl.lv

DPD
w dpd.lv

Latvijas Pasts
Brīvības bulvāris 32, Rīga.
Tel 6750 2815.
w pasts.lv

Dialling Codes

- Mobile numbers start with 2; landline numbers tend to start with 6.
- Toll-free numbers begin with 80; premium-rate numbers start with 8 or 9.
- To make an international call from Latvia, first press "+", then the destination's country code and number.
- To call Latvia from abroad dial the international access code (00 from the UK, 011 from US and Canada), followed by 371, Latvia's country code.

Communications in Lithuania

The widespread network of telephone and mail services in Lithuania is very efficient. The huge popularity of mobile phones has ensured that the few public phones that exist are rarely used. Post offices can be found in all towns and larger villages. Internet usage is virtually universal and finding an access point is seldom a problem.

Phone card, available with the service provider, Teo LT

Making a Phone Call

Public telephones are steadily disappearing from Lithuania, but a few can still be found. All valid telephone numbers in Lithuania have eight digits (including the area code), with the exception of special public services such as four-digit numbers for taxi companies. All mobile numbers currently start with 6.

Area codes are one to three digits and need to be left off when dialling locally from a land line. In Vilnius for example the area code is 5. When in Vilnius you dial seven digits, leaving off the 5. When dialling from another area code, dial 8 first, then the full eight digit number including the area code. When calling any number from a mobile phone, dial the complete eight-digit number, including the area code.

Now that public telephones have been withdrawn, the easiest way to make international calls is simply with your own mobile phone after registering with one of the three mobile phone operators active in the country, Omnitel, Tele2 and Bitė. EU regulations ensure that roaming charges are not extortionate. If roaming charges are a concern, you could purchase a prepaid calling card for international calls, which allows connection through a toll-free number and gives automated instructions in many languages.

Mobile Phones

There are three mobile phone operators in Lithuania, namely **Omnitel**, **Tele2** and **Bitė**. They provide prepaid SIM cards which might be helpful to those from outside the EU who are concerned about roaming charges. Keep in mind that your phone would need to be unlocked. Visitors staying for longer periods have the option of buying a cheap phone on a pay-as-you-go basis to take advantage of low local rates. Phones can be purchased in shops and stalls in indoor shopping centres.

The Internet

Fast, free-of-charge Wi-Fi can be found at restaurants, hotels and cafés in Vilnius and much of the rest of Lithuania, and old-fashioned internet cafés are becoming difficult to find. If you find that Wi-Fi is not immediately available wherever you happen to be, a local will undoubtedly be able to tell you where you might find it.

Postal Services

Branches of **Lietuvos Paštas**, Lithuania's state-owned post office company, are found all over the country. In large towns and cities they are increasingly located in indoor shopping centres where opening hours are long and include Sundays. In Vilnius, the main post office is on the main street, at Gedimino 7, and is open from 8:30am to 7pm on weekdays and from 9am to 2pm on Saturdays, but is closed on Sundays. A branch at the central train station is open longer: from 7am to 9pm on weekdays, from 9am to 8pm

on Saturdays and from 10am to 8pm on Sundays.

Sending a letter of up to 20 g in Europe costs €0.75; to send it by registered mail costs €2.84.

Major international couriers such as **DHL** and **DPD** operate in Lithuania, but the cheapest way of sending a parcel home is probably with Lietuvos Paštas, either to a specific address, from post office to post office, or shipped via courier.

DIRECTORY

Useful Numbers

Directory Enquiries
Tel 118.

Mobile Phones

Bitė
w bite.lt

Omnitel
w omnitel.lt

Tele2
w tele2.lt

Postal Services

DHL
w dhl.lv

DPD
w dpd.lv

Lietuvos Paštas
Gedimino 7, Vilnius. Tel 261 6759.
w post.lt

Dialling Codes

- Mobile numbers start with 6.
- Lithuania's city codes include 5 for Vilnius, 37 for Kaunas, 46 for Klaipėda, 313 for Druskininkai, 460 for Palanga and 469 for Nida.
- Toll-free numbers start with 8; premium-rate numbers start with 9.
- To make an international call from Lithuania, first press "+", then the destination's country code and number.
- To call Lithuania from abroad dial the international access code (00 from the UK, 011 from US and Canada), followed by 370, Lithuania's country code.

TRAVELLING TO ESTONIA

It is easy to reach Estonia by air, as several major international carriers from many European cities provide links to Tallinn, the capital of Estonia. The country is also well served by ferries, with regular services to Tallinn and the island of Saaremaa. In Tallinn, the ferry port and main railway station are conveniently located close to the Old Town and city centre, while the airport and coach station are only a short taxi or bus ride away. Tallinn has good coach connections with the rest of Europe, although travelling by coach can be slow. Reaching Estonia from Western Europe by train is almost impossible, as the only international service is from Russia. A pan-Baltic train, Rail Baltica, is in the works, but is a complex and expensive undertaking, with completion set for 2024.

Gleaming interior of Lennart Meri Tallinn Airport

Arriving by Air

The sleek-looking **Lennart Meri Tallinn Airport** is the only Estonian airport with regular scheduled flights. In recent years, the airport has become a regional hub with approximately 12 airlines using the airport, including major carriers such as **Finnair** and **Lufthansa**. The Latvian airline **airBaltic** makes regular flights to Tallinn with a quick stop in Rīga.

Founded in 1991, **Estonian Air** is the country's national carrier. Based in Tallinn, it offers a good standard of service in both business and tourist class. The airline has direct links with several major European destinations as well as some Estonian cities and islands. Visitors from outside Europe need to catch a connecting flight from cities such as London, Helsinki, Copenhagen or Stockholm.

A couple of low-cost carriers provide daily flights to Tallinn from the UK: **Ryanair** flies from London Stansted and Manchester; **easyjet** flies from London Gatwick.

From Tallinn Airport to the City Centre

Lennart Meri Tallinn Airport is about 3 km (2 miles) from the city centre. Taxis wait outside and the ride to the city centre costs around €10. Bus number 2 takes up to 15 minutes to reach the centre and costs around €1.50. It leaves every 20 minutes from Monday to Saturday, and every 30 minutes on Sunday.

Taxi stand near Lennart Meri Tallinn Airport

Other Estonian Airports

Estonia's other airports are situated in Pärnu, Kuressaare and Kärdla. These are serviced by small regional airlines with connections to Tallinn. There are special summer flight services from Sweden to Saaremaa Island and from Finland to Tartu's recently upgraded airport.

Arriving by Sea

Estonia is very well served by ferry, with Tallinn's **Passenger Port** (*reisisadam*) handling about 7 million passengers a year. The main line, **Tallink**, has routes to Helsinki (Finland), Rostock (Germany) and Stockholm (Sweden), while other carriers, such as **Viking Line** and Eckerö Line, are accessible from Helsinki and Stockholm. Linda Line runs a hydrofoil service to Helsinki.

Travellers from Helsinki are spoiled for choice, with a range of catamarans and ferries making the crossing. The Passenger Port is within walking distance of Tallin's Old Town and a taxi ride should cost between €3 and €5, although it is close enough to walk. The local bus no. 2 connects the port with the city centre, bus station and airport.

Tallinn is also included in a choice of Baltic Sea cruises. Pärnu and Saaremaa Island are also included in some cruise ship itineraries.

Tallink shuttle on its way to Rīga from Helsinki

Arriving by Coach

International coach routes to Estonia are provided by **Lux Express** and **Ecolines**, which operate connections between Tallinn and Berlin, Munich, Kaliningrad, Warsaw and St Petersburg, among others. International coaches arrive at **Tallinn Bus Station** (*bussijaam*), which is a short taxi ride from the city centre. Alternatively, catch the numbers 2 or 4 trams, or numbers 17, 17a or 23 buses from the main bus station into the city centre. Passengers travelling to Tallinn by bus from Rīga or Vilnius can get off at the more central Viru väljak bus stop. There are also limited international coach connections with Pärnu, Narva and Tartu. The coach network is efficiently run and cheap. Services are clearly posted in coach and bus stations.

Lux Express coach, connecting Tallinn to Germany, Poland and Russia

Arriving by Train

Tallinn's main railway station, Balti Jaam, is a short walk away from the Old Town. There is a nightly train to Moscow. Tickets should be pre-booked, since Russian visa specifications insist on dates of entry and exit. In 2010, the Tartu–Volga line reopened, making it possible to travel from Tallinn to Rīga. There are plans to build the Rail Baltica route to Warsaw.

Arriving by Car

Since 2007, when the Baltic States agreed to the Schengen Agreement (under which systematic border controls were abolished), there are no border restrictions for Schengen visa holders. Crossing the border from Latvia is easy, especially for EU passport holders. The border crossing with Russia is slower and border guards are likely to scrutinize your documents. To bring your own car into Estonia, the Vehicle Registration document, an international driving permit and a valid Green Card insurance policy are mandatory.

Arriving by Helicopter

Copterline's 12-seater helicopter service between Helsinki and Tallinn takes 18 minutes. There are about 13 hourly services between 7am and 8pm, from Monday to Saturday. Tallinn's heliport is a 5-minute drive from the city centre. A minibus service is available.

Getting Around Estonia

The best way of getting around Estonia is by car, as all the main sights are, at most, a few hours' drive away from each other. The country's rail network is cheap but with a limited reach and often frustratingly slow. A far better public transport option is the country's well-developed bus system, which links all the major towns and cities as well as more remote areas. However, rural bus services are sparse, and the buses tend to crawl along at no more than about 30 kmph (19 mph). Alternatively, there is a good range of ferries serving the islands but many of these do not run in winter, when the sea freezes over. Some regular domestic flights connect Estonia's mainland cities, and there are regular air connections to several islands.

Local train waiting at Tallinn railway station

Travelling by Train

Estonia's rail network is the least efficient way to see the country. Services have been so drastically reduced that the choice of destinations is limited. There are rail routes between Tallinn and Narva, Tartu, Pärnu and Viljandi, and an electric train runs between Tallinn and Paldiski 10 times a day. It is usually advisable to catch a *kiirrong* (fast train), although these are still relatively slow compared to those in Western Europe. However, there are now express trains, with first-class carriages, between Tallinn and Tartu. **Edelaraudtee** runs inter-city passenger services and **Elektriraudtee**, belonging to the same company, runs local electric trains.

It is best to buy *pilet* (tickets) on board, although some can be bought online or at the ticket offices in Tallinn. There are no passes for rail travel. Timetables are rarely printed or updated and services are usually posted on large display boards at the stations.

Travelling by Bus

The bus network in Estonia is efficiently run and is good value for money. Inter-city buses run regularly and are generally comfortable. Some companies run express routes, which avoid endless stops in small towns and villages. Route operators include **SEBE** and **Taisto**. The Tartu–Tallinn route is the busiest and most convenient, with coaches departing every hour until late at night. Tickets can be bought from the bus station or the driver on boarding. On busier routes, it is best to buy tickets in advance. Although ticket prices vary, they are generally very reasonable, but slightly higher than those for rail travel. The fares of buses bound for the islands are usually higher as they always include the price of the ferry crossing. To check bus schedules visit **Bussireisid**'s website.

Luggage is usually carried onto the bus and passengers may have to pay a small additional fee to stow any large items in the compartment underneath the bus.

Travelling by Ferry

The Estonian islands are well served by a number of car and passenger ferry connections. There are also regular services between Rohuküla harbour (near Haapsalu), Heltermaa (on Hiiumaa Island) and Vormsi. Virtsu harbour (north of Pärnu) has hourly connections with Muhu Island, which is linked with nearby Saaremaa Island by road. Saaremaa itself is connected with Hiiumaa from Triigi harbour in the northeast. Saaremaa has a special summertime ferry service to Ventspils in Latvia. Check **Saaremaa Shipping Company Limited**'s official website for

Bussireisid's air-conditioned inter-city express bus en route from Tartu

Ferry from Virtsu on its way to Saaremaa Island

route details. **Veeteed** runs a ferry service between Pärnu and the islands of Kihnu and Vormsi, although the service is less regular. In summer, ferries tend to quickly fill up and passengers can be left waiting in long queues if they don't reserve their tickets well in advance. Passengers travelling by car should arrive at the harbour about 20 minutes before the scheduled departure time.

In winter, ferry services are often cancelled when the sea freezes over, although officially designated ice roads are established if the ice is thick enough.

Travelling by Air

Estonian Air, the country's national carrier (see p376), operates domestic flights that connect the major cities. **Avies** also runs a few daily flights between Tallinn, Kuressaare and Kärdla. It is best to book well in advance because their planes are very small and can only seat up to seven passengers. There are also some flights from Pärnu Airport to Kuressaare and Kihnu which are reasonably priced, and a good option in winter when the sea is frozen. Tartu Airport has connections to Rīga and Stockholm. Kärdla acts mainly as a stopover point for chartered flights in Europe. The daily domestic service to Tallinn is the only regular service coming from the airport at Kärdla.

Travelling by Car

Driving is by far the best way to get around Estonia. Conditions are generally good on main roads and distances are relatively short. However, country roads are severely potholed and dirt roads are also common in many rural parts of the country.

There are no motorways and overtaking is the norm. It is mandatory by law to drive with the headlights on at all times of the day. Wearing a seatbelt is compulsory for drivers as well as passengers. The speed limit is 50 kmph (31 mph) in built-up areas and 90 kmph (56 mph) on the main roads. In Estonia, drinking alcohol and driving is illegal. By law, winter tyres must be fitted between December and March.

Petrol stations are quite rare in remote places so it is advisable to fill up on petrol when leaving a city or town.

Car Hire

There are numerous car rental firms, including **Avis**, **Budget**, **Europcar**, **Hertz** and **National**. A local company, **Easy Car Rent**, also offers good deals. All require a major credit card and a valid international driver's licence. Rental rates are comparable to those in Western Europe. Outside Tallinn, there are few rental options except in major towns. However, some of the Tallinn-based chains can organize car hire in other parts of the country.

DIRECTORY

Travelling by Train

Edelaraudtee
w edel.ee

Elektriraudtee
w elektriraudtee.ee

Travelling by Bus

Bussireisid
w bussireisid.ee

SEBE
w sebe.ee

Taisto
w taisto.ee

Travelling by Ferry

Saaremaa Shipping Company Limited
w tuulelaevad.ee

Veeteed
w veeteed.com

Travelling by Air

Avies
w avies.ee

Car Hire

Avis
w avis.com

Budget
w budget.com

Easy Car Rent
w easycarrent.eu

Europcar
w europcar.com

Hertz
w hertz.com

National
w nationalcar.com

Autorent Terminal of Avis, a global car rental chain

Getting Around Tallinn

Most of the main sights in Tallinn are within comfortable walking distance of each other. The Old Town is so compact that it can easily be covered on foot. Public transport in Tallinn is cheap and efficient. It is made up of an integrated network of trolleybuses, buses and trams serving sites away from the city centre. Cycling is another good way of getting around the city. In general, Tallinn's transport options are very good, and there is no need for a car unless you plan to take a day trip or explore the outer parts of the city.

Buses, Trolleybuses and Trams

Tallinn's public transport system operates daily between 6am and midnight. Buses are the best way to reach the airport and other outlying areas. The terminal for many routes is in Viru Keskus, the central shopping mall. The nine trolleybus lines mainly connect to residential areas near the centre. The main stops are on Vabaduse väljak and Balti Jaam. Trams follow the main arteries in and out of the city centre. The four tram lines running across the city converge at the Hobujaama stop on Narva maanti (road).

The same tickets can be used on all three systems and schedules in English can be found at the **Tallinn Bus Company**'s website. As drivers only sell single tickets at a premium, it is best to buy tickets, either individual or as booklets, at kiosks. Tallinn Card *(see p366)* holders are entitled to unlimited travel on all public transport.

Bus sign, Tallinn

Minibuses

Minibuses, or route-taxis as they are often called, are a faster option for travellers. They connect the city centre to outlying residential areas. These white vans, operated by many small private companies, follow set routes, picking up and dropping off passengers at any spot they request along the route. Most minibuses leave from a stop at Estonia puiestee (boulevard) just opposite the Estonian Drama Theatre. Destinations are usually displayed in the window. Tickets cost between €1 and €2 depending on how far the destination is. Tickets can only be purchased from the drivers on boarding.

Driving

Driving around Tallinn may be a little disorienting for visitors. There are several confusing one-way systems and traffic jams are common during rush hour. Also, tram tracks are often in the middle of the road. Drivers have to stop and wait for a tram when it pulls in at a station so that passengers can safely alight. Driving conditions are especially difficult at night because of the dangerous habit of overtaking on narrow roads and speeding. The speed limit in Tallinn is 50 kmph (31 mph), except on some larger roads where the limit is 70 kmph (43 mph).

Parking

There are plenty of parking options in Tallinn, though it can be hard to find a good spot in the heart of the city during weekdays. In the city centre, paid parking is in force between 7am and 7pm on weekdays and 8am and 3pm on Saturdays, although the first 15 minutes are free. Tickets can be bought from street-side machines or kiosks or, in some areas, by

Tallinn tram, a convenient mode of transport for short hops around the city

A taxi waiting in a cobblestoned street in the Old Town, Tallinn

using a mobile phone, following instructions posted on signs. Rates range from around €1 per 15 minutes to €4.60 per hour. The Old Town has a seven-day, 24-hour paid parking in effect, which starts at €0.75 per 15 minutes. A relatively convenient option might be to leave your car at one of several centrally located guarded parking lots. These range in price from about €0.75 to €1.90 per hour. In the summer months, paid parking is also in effect in the Pirita istrict.

Taxis

There is an abundance of taxis in Tallinn, although it is best to take one from a taxi stand or to book one in advance from reputable companies such as **Tulika Takso**, **Tallink Takso** or **Reval Takso**. Taxi stands can be found near large hotels, major intersections and also next to the Estonian Drama Theatre. Hailing a taxi on the street is risky, as there are many dishonest taxi drivers who overcharge foreign visitors. However, legislation has been introduced to help improve the situation. All taxi drivers are obliged to display their prices in English, on the vehicle's rear right-hand window, and to provide a receipt on request. If the driver fails to give a receipt, the passenger is legally entitled not to pay the fare.

Starting fares normally range from €2.25 to €4.50, with a rate of about €0.50 per kilometre, although prices can vary considerably from operator to operator. It is advisable to ask the driver for an approximate price before starting your

journey and ensure that the meter is running.

Cycling

Getting around Tallinn by bicycle is a good option, although it is not so practical in the cobbled streets of the Old Town. There are plenty of bicycle rental firms in the city, such as **CityBike**, that offer a wide range of organized tours accompanied by a guide. It is also possible to rent a bicycle and take off by yourself. As there are hardly any bicycle lanes in Tallinn, special care should be taken when cycling along congested streets.

Walking

Walking is the ideal way to experience the busy streets of Tallinn's Old Town and the city centre. In general, Tallinn is a pedestrian-friendly environment, although a good road map is useful to avoid getting lost in its labyrinthine streets. A huge number of walking tours are available

DIRECTORY

Buses, Trolley Buses and Trams

Tallinn Bus Company
w tak.ee

Taxis

Reval Takso
Tel 601 4600.
w reval-takso.ee

Tallink Takso
Tel 640 8921.
w tallinktakso.ee

Tulika Takso
Tel 612 0001.
w tulika.ee

Cycling

CityBike
Tel 5111 819.
w citybike.ee

Velotaxi

Tel 5811 6051.
w velotakso.ee

from most hotels and tourist information centres.

Velotaxi

Velotaxis, or bicycle-taxis, are a novel way of seeing the city. They operate from March to October and cost around €2.25 for an adult and €0.95 for a child, and can be ordered on the **Velotaxi** website.

The fascinatingly novel velotaxi, available for hire in Tallinn

TRAVELLING TO LATVIA

Most visitors arrive in Latvia by air, at Rīga International Airport. Since independence there has been a rapid growth in the number of European cities directly linked to Rīga, mainly because of the arrival of low-cost carriers that raised the capital's profile as a destination for weekend breaks. In contrast, the country's regional airports are little used for international passenger flights. For those who wish to avoid air travel and who have more time, there are sea routes from Germany and Scandinavia, as well as comfortable trains and coaches from other parts of the Continent. Arriving by car is also perfectly feasible, provided the driver has the correct documents and is willing to tackle a variable road network.

Arriving by Air

The majority of visitors to Latvia arrive at **Rīga International Airport**, the largest airport in the Baltic region by passenger numbers. The airport is connected to most Western European cities as well as to Prague, Moscow, Kiev, Tallinn, Vilnius and Warsaw. Services at the airport include a currency exchange and ATMs, which remain open until the last flight arrives.

The country's national carrier, **airBaltic**, was established in 1995 and offers some very affordable flights. Rīga is also served by other major airlines including **LOT**, **SAS**, **Lufthansa** and **Finnair**. Several low-cost carriers, such as **Wizz Air** and **Ryanair**, also fly to Rīga from various European cities.

There are very few direct flights to Latvia from the USA, New Zealand, Canada or Australia. Visitors often transfer at another European airport such as Copenhagen or Helsinki. It may be more economical to arrange a long-haul flight to a transport hub such as London, along with a separate onward flight.

Riga International Airport

From Rīga Airport to the City Centre

Rīga Airport is located about 8 km (5 miles) from the city centre. The cheapest way to reach the city is by taking a bus from outside the airport terminal. Bus 22 runs approximately every 10 to 20 minutes, from 5:45am to midnight, and takes 30 minutes to reach Abrenes iela (street); stops along the way include 11 Novembra krastmala and the Central Railway Station. airBaltic operates the Airport Express every 30 minutes, from 5:30am to 12:30pm; it costs €5. Taxis reach the city centre in 15 minutes.

Other Latvian Airports

The other international airports are in **Ventspils** and **Liepāja**. Neither is much used by scheduled passenger services.

Arriving by Sea

Passenger ferries take longer than air travel, though crossing the Baltic Sea has its own appeal. Ferries operated by **Tallink** connect Rīga to Stockholm (Sweden). **Stena Line** connects Liepāja to Lübeck (Germany), and Ventspils to Nynashamn (Sweden) and Lübeck. Rīga's main **Ferry Terminal** can be reached by trams 5, 7 or 9 from the bus station or outside the National Opera. There are marinas at Rīga, Jūrmala, Liepāja, Pāvilosta, Salacgrīva and Ventspils for those with their own boats. The Latvian Coast website offers information.

Arriving by Coach

This is the best way to travel between the three Baltic capitals. International carriers,

Express bus waiting outside Rīga International Airport

such as **Ecolines**, **Lux Express** and **Nordeka**, run services between Rīga and several other European and Russian cities. Rīga's main bus terminal, Autoosta (see p385), is five minutes south of the Old Town.

Travelling by coach costs less than travelling by air, although the difference is negligible, except during peak season. International coaches are equipped with air conditioning and reclining seats, and some, such as those in Lux Express's lounge class, have well-spaced single seats, extra legroom and in-seat touch-screen consoles.

Passengers queuing up outside the ticket office at a bus station

Arriving by Train

The main railway station in Rīga, Central Railway Station (see p385), is located south of the Old Town. Although there are no trains from Vilnius to Rīga, it is possible to ride the rails between Talinn and Rīga, although passengers need to change trains at the border. There are rail routes heading east towards Moscow, Vitebsk, Odessa and St Petersburg. The most comfortable way to travel on most routes is a kupeja (four-bunk compartment). However, there

are more luxurious two-bunk compartments on the trains from Moscow.

Arriving by Car

Since the Schengen Agreement (see p377), there are no border controls between Estonia, Latvia and Lithuania. Entering from Russia or Belarus may take several hours.

It is essential to bring along the vehicle's registration document, a valid third-party insurance policy and either a European driving licence or an International Driving Permit. Vehicles must be in roadworthy condition and it is compulsory to carry a first-aid kit, fire extinguisher and hazard-warning triangle in your vehicle at all times. From December to March, winter tyres must be used, and between September and April, drivers should fit spiked tyres.

Arriving by Bicycle

Since Latvia acceded to the Schengen Agreement, cycling into Latvia from Estonia or Lithuania has been simple. The flat landscape makes it an attractive option during summer. Carry appropriate spares and a waterproof jacket.

There are two EuroVelo cycle routes passing through Latvia, though they are not always well marked, and much of the riding is on country roads. EV10 follows the Baltic coastline, while EV11 crosses the Estonian border at Valka and traverses Eastern Latvia to Daugavpils.

DIRECTORY

Airports

Liepāja Airport
W liepaja-airport.lv

Rīga International Airport
10/1 Mārupes civil parish.
Tel 1187.
W riga-airport.com

Ventspils Airport
W airport.ventspils.lv

Airlines

airBaltic
W airbaltic.com

Finnair
W finnair.com

LOT
W lot.com

Lufthansa
W lufthansa.com

Ryanair
W ryanair.com

SAS
W flysas.com

Wizz Air
W wizzair.com

Ferry Companies

Stena Line
W stenaline.com

Tallink
W tallink.lv

Ferry Port

Ferry Terminal
Eksporta iela 3A, Rīga.
Tel 6732 6200. W rigapt.lv

Ventspils Port
Tel 636 22586.
W portofventspils.lv

Coach Companies

Ecolines
W ecolines.ee

Lux Express
W luxexpress.eu

Nordeka
W nordeka.lv

Passenger train passing through the lush pine forests of the Latvian countryside

Getting Around Latvia

The public transport network in Latvia is extensive and affordable. Travelling by coach tends to be quicker than by train, although the buses are often old and can be uncomfortable. Major urban areas and places of interest to visitors usually benefit from frequent coach services. However, in the countryside, there may be only one bus or train per day in each direction. This means that visitors who wish to get off the beaten path will find it difficult to rely on public transport. Car hire is a popular choice, despite the variable state of the roads in the country. The combination of a flat landscape and relatively short distances makes cycling pleasant, especially in good weather.

Commuters entering the Central Railway Station, Rīga

Travelling by Train

The state-owned **Latvian Railways** runs all trains in the country. Trains tend to take a little longer than buses to reach their destinations, but the journey is slightly more comfortable, especially if travellers bring along cushions for the hard benches. However, the windows rarely open, making the carriages stuffy in summer. The heating can be erratic.

The most useful routes are from Rīga to Jūrmala Beach, Jelgava and destinations in Gauja National Park. There are also train services to places further afield such as Valmiera, Daugavpils and Rēzekne. Rail enthusiasts should take the narrow-gauge line between Alūksne and Gulbene.

Travelling by Coach

Regular coach services run between most large towns and cities. Other places are less frequently served, therefore careful planning is important to visit several towns in a single day. Although more expensive than travelling by train, bus travel is still good value. For overnight journeys, it is advisable to carry a blanket or sleeping bag.

Autoosta (Rīga's central bus station) runs services to Bauska, Cēsis, Sigulda, Daugavpils, Liepāja, Valmiera and Ventspils.

If the journey starts at a major station, it is best to buy a ticket before boarding. Otherwise tickets can be purchased from the driver. If your luggage is very large, you may have to pay to stow it in the luggage compartment, but otherwise it is normal to take it on board.

Understanding Timetables

Outside of Rīga, it can be difficult to find station staff who speak English. Timetables are written on boards at the railway station and are also available by telephone and on the Internet. Details of several common routes are also available in the publication *Rīga in Your Pocket (see p387)*. For further enquiries visit the Latvian Railways website.

Timetables at train or bus stations rarely include timings of return journeys from various destinations. Express buses are generally indicated by the letter "E", while the equivalent for trains is indicated by three-digit route numbers. *Pietur* indicates that a train or bus stops at a particular destination, while *nepietur* means that it does not. Buses and trains listed as *darbdienās* run on weekdays, and the days of the week are often listed by their initial. Latvian stations number their *perons* (platform) and *ceļš* (track) separately.

One of the many extra-long public buses typical of Daugavpils

Autonomas Car Rentals

Typical car rental sign at the Domestic Airport, Rīga

Travelling by Car and Motorcycle

Bringing or renting a vehicle is an excellent way to see Latvia for those who come for short trips, or wish to visit out-of-the-way corners of the country. However, neither car rental nor petrol is cheap, and road conditions vary dramatically. Most major routes are in an acceptable state, but minor roads can be in poor condition. Many are surfaced with gravel or dirt. In winter, gritting is not widespread, and some minor roads become impassable without a sturdy four-wheel-drive vehicle.

Latvians tend to drive aggressively and overtaking on blind corners is common. Congestion is rare outside the capital. The legal blood alcohol limit is 0.05 per cent, with a 10-day prison sentence for exceeding it. Seat belt use is mandatory in the front seats, as well as in the rear if fitted, and crash helmets must be used on motorcycles. It is compulsory to drive with the headlights switched on at all times. The speed limit is 50 kmph (31 mph) in built-up areas and 90 kmph (56 mph) elsewhere. Traffic police cannot always be spotted outside towns and cities, but they are strict about speeding and collect fines on the spot. Remember to ask for a receipt if you are fined.

In the countryside, changes in speed limit are not always sign-posted and it is up to the driver to notice signs indicating built-up areas. These are white rectangles usually bearing the name of the town or village.

Signposting is poor across the country, making it essential to buy a good roadmap. For vehicle breakdown and towing, it is advisable to contact

SOS Motor Club. On major roads, *degvielas stacija* (service stations) are often open 24 hours, but in rural areas it can be hard to find a place to refuel.

Parking is usually easy outside Rīga, although some cities, notably Daugavpils and Liepāja, have parking meters in certain areas. There is also a fee of €2 to enter Jūrmala, collected at a roadside booth.

Car Hire

Vehicle hire is most easily arranged in Rīga, although other towns and cities have hire offices. Most international car rental companies are represented in the capital, and many of them have offices at the airport. There are many smaller companies as well.

3.1 km

Bumpy road sign at Krāslava

Check the condition of the vehicle and the insurance cover provided. Car hire services are operated by companies such as **Budget Rent A Car**. Most companies stipulate a minimum age for the person hiring the car. Requirements state that the driver should have held a licence for at least a year. The driver may also need to leave his credit card details or a large deposit.

Travelling by Bicycle

Cycling is a good way to get around the relatively flat terrain of Latvia. Bicycles can be hired in many towns and cities. The tourist information board can provide details of cycle routes, such as the popular and easy trail from Rīga to Jūrmala and routes in Gauja National Park and its surrounding valley. There are also two European Cycle Routes in Latvia, one of which, part of the EuroVelo 10, runs along the entire coast.

Bicycles are permitted on trains, although you need to buy a ticket for them. There are designated areas at the end of each carriage, marked with a bicycle symbol.

Cyclists riding through a field of dandelions in Gauja National Park

Getting Around Rīga

Rīga's compact Old Town is a pleasure to wander around and is best explored on foot. The cobbled streets, however, can prove difficult for those with mobility problems. Several hotels are located within the Old Town, while many others are within easy walking distance. It is also a short walk to the unmissable Art Nouveau district from the city centre. Attractions further afield, such as the Latvian Ethnographic Open-Air Museum, can be reached via the city's extensive network of buses, minibuses, trolleybuses and trams. Tickets are available on board, while passes valid for various lengths of time can be purchased from newspaper kiosks. Taxis are readily available outside the Old Town.

Passengers boarding a bus at Rīga Bus Station

Buses, Trolleybuses and Trams

With several bus, trolleybus and tram routes, Rīga's public transport system is a cheap and efficient way of getting around outside the Old Town. It brings many museums, hostels and hotels within easy reach of the town centre and also offers access to the zoo, the Song Festival grounds and to several large parks.

There are timetables at the various bus stops, but usually no route maps are shown; therefore it is advisable to carry one when travelling. Public transport on most routes runs between 5:30am and 11:30pm, with some services operating hourly throughout the night. Autoosta (see p385) is close to both the Central Railway Station and Central Market. Other transport hubs include the stretch in front of the Orthodox Cathedral.

Various organizations merged in 2005 to form a single body responsible for public transport, **SIA Rīgas Satiksme**. Until 2009 different payment systems operated for buses, trams and trolleybuses but now they have finally been integrated. There is a single fare of €1.20 paid to the driver on boarding. There is no extra charge for luggage. However, it is better to purchase your ticket first from a kiosk for €0.60. The etalon smart card covers five, ten or twenty journeys at a discount. Public transport is free to holders of a **Rīga Card** (see p366).

Minibuses

Rīga's mikroautobuss (minibus) network runs along the major boulevards and out into the suburbs, and usually offers great comfort and speed. The main stops are outside the Central Railway Station and the Orthodox Cathedral. Tickets cost marginally more than those for other public transport.

Driving

Driving in Rīga is seldom a pleasant experience, marred by heavy traffic during peak hours and aggressive drivers. Petrol stations are readily found, and roads tend to be in good condition, with just a few potholes.

It is worth noting that you must not pass a tram that has its doors open, since this might endanger passengers, and you must be careful not to block the tram lines.

Parking

Parking can be difficult to find in the city centre. It is also expensive. Rates are €2 for the first hour and €3 per hour on the streets of the Old Town. For those who really need a car, it is best to choose a hotel with parking space.

Taxis

Taxis are abundant in Rīga and are a comfortable, though relatively expensive, way of getting around. They do not come in a standard colour, although all official cabs have yellow licence plates. Fares vary from €0.35 to €0.70 per kilometre depending on the

Taxis for hire outside Rīga International Airport

taxi company. Fares tend to increase by about 50 per cent after midnight. It is usually better to book a taxi in advance, rather than flag one down in the street, and you might obtain a better price by calling a reputable company such as **Rīga Taxi** or **Rīgas Taxometru Parks**. Taxis waiting outside the upmarket hotels tend to be more expensive.

Passengers must note that drivers often refuse to accept a fare of less than €5, and try to charge at least that much to take passengers from the bus or railway station to a nearby hotel. Visitors must ensure that the meter is used, or at least negotiate a fare in advance, before entering the taxi. It is rarely difficult to find a taxi during the day, while at night taxis congregate at each end of Kaļķu iela.

Pedestrians at a zebra crossing, Aspazijas bulvāris

Cycling in Rīga, a quick and easy way of getting around the city

Cycling

Getting around Rīga by bicycle is a good option, despite the Old Town's cobbled streets and the heavy traffic in other parts of the city. One of the more pleasant places for a ride is the pristine suburb of Mežaparks (see p160). **Eat Rīga** can offer help with bicycle rental in the city.

Walking

The Old Town is relatively small, with plenty of recognizable landmarks, making the walk manageable as well as enjoyable, in spite of the cobblestoned streets. It is particularly pleasant to wander around in summer, when many streets and squares are lined with terrace seating outside bars and cafés, and the weather is more suitable for walking. The area immediately north of the Old Town is home to some impressive Art Nouveau buildings and several smart shops and restaurants. The main street in Rīga's Art Nouveau district is Elizabetes iela, which intersects with Brīvības bulvāris (avenue). In addition, Alberta and Strēlnieku iela also feature examples of this style.

The Rīga Card (see p366) offers free entry to many museums, a free walking tour of the Old Town, and free public transport within Rīga and Jūrmala. Since public transport is already so cheap in the country, investing in the card is worthwhile only if visitors are interested in the walking tour or in visiting several museums in a single day. The card is available in hotels, at Rīga Airport and in the tourist information offices.

Maps

The most widely available map of the city is published by Jāņa Sēta, at a scale of 1:20,000 with the centre shown at a detailed 1:7000. A much smaller version of the map is included in the popular Rīga In Your Pocket guide, but it is only detailed enough if you do not plan to stray far from the centre. The guide also indicates public transport routes.

DIRECTORY

Buses, Trolleybuses and Trams

SIA Rīgas Satiksme
Tel 8000 1919.
W rigassatiksme.lv

Taxis

Rīga Taxi
Tel 8000 1010. W taxi.lv

Rīgas Taksometru Parks
Tel 8383. W rtp.lv

Cycling

Eat Rīga
Tel 2246 9888.
W eatriga.lv

City Card

Rīga Card
Tel 6721 7217. W rigacard.lv

Maps

Rīga in Your Pocket
Laipu iela 8–9a. **Tel** 6722 0580.
W inyourpocket.com

TRAVELLING TO LITHUANIA

The quickest and easiest way to reach Lithuania is by air. Most airlines fly to Vilnius, which has direct connections with many European cities. Some international flights arrive at Kaunas and Palanga airports. Lithuania has only one sea port, at Klaipėda, which offers a limited number of passenger ferry services across the Baltic Sea to Germany and Scandinavia. By land, it is best to travel to Lithuania by coach. There are regular departures from London, Paris and other European capitals. However, getting to Lithuania by car is long and hazardous, given the bad roads in Poland. A daily train service links Warsaw with Kaunas and Vilnius, with a change at Sestokai, on the Polish-Lithuanian frontier. Lithuania is not covered by Eurail or InterRail, making travelling by train from Western Europe expensive.

Arriving by Air

Lithuania is well connected with Europe and, via major European transport hubs such as London, Copenhagen and Amsterdam, to the rest of the world. Connectivity has improved, with flights to and from Vilnius timing in well with intercontinental flights. Since March 2008, the control of internal borders among the Schengen states, which also include Estonia, Latvia and Lithuania, was abolished.

Opened in 1944, **Vilnius Airport** is the arrival point for most flights. It is the only airport among the Baltic capitals to have maintained its original appearance of a formulaic, erstwhile Soviet-era terminal. Services at the airport include car rental offices, currency exchange and cafés, as well as newspaper kiosks which also sell bus tickets.

airBaltic offers increased services between Rīga and Vilnius, and direct services from Vilnius to several European cities, including Amsterdam, Copenhagen, Dublin and London. British Airways pulled out of serving Vilnius due to low-cost airline competition. As a result, major international flights and low-cost carriers from around 40 cities arrive in Lithuanian airports. These include almost all the capitals of Western Europe, as well as Prague, Moscow, Minsk, Gomel, Kiev, St Petersburg, Tbilisi, Kaliningrad, Baku, Tel Aviv and other cities further east. Other European carriers that serve Vilnius include **Austrian**

International check-in hall at Vilnius Airport

Airlines, Norwegian, Estonian Air, Finnair, Lufthansa, Ryanair and **SAS**.

From the United States, the most common routes to Lithuania are via Warsaw, then on to Vilnius with **LOT**; Stockholm or Copenhagen, then on to Vilnius with SAS; or Helsinki, then on to Vilnius with Finnair. Norwegian airlines fly via Oslo.

Canadian visitors tend to fly via Frankfurt and Brussels with Lufthansa.

Travelling from Australia or New Zealand also requires multiple carriers, and it is worth shopping around for the best prices.

airBaltic has implemented a one-way ticket system, which ensures the prices of tickets depend directly on demand. The traditional "Sunday rule", with prices being higher on weekdays than on the weekends, does not hold true, as the majority of tickets are purchased on the Internet. In accordance with international agreements, most airline services operate a system of reduced rates for children, students and pensioners, as well as pre-arranged groups.

From Vilnius Airport to the City Centre

Vilnius Airport is located 5 km (3 miles) south of the city centre. There is a train from the airport to Vilnius Main Station, which takes about 7 minutes, although buses also operate. Tickets are cheaper if bought at airport kiosks.

The bus stop and taxi rank are both outside the arrivals area. The official rate for taxis into town is about €8, but tourists will find it difficult to pay less than €15. Taxis take about 20 minutes to reach the city centre.

Other Lithuanian Airports

The airports at Kaunas and Palanga have scheduled international flights, although they are fairly limited compared to those at Vilnius Airport. New terminals are being built at both the airports in an effort to make them better equipped. From **Kaunas Airport**, shuttle bus number 120 goes to Savanorių prospektas (avenue) and the Old Town, while bus number 29 goes to the bus station. A minibus shuttle travels twice daily between Kaunas Airport and Vilnius, connecting all Ryanair flights, as that is the only carrier operating in Kaunas at the moment. For information on airport bus services, log on to **Ollex**. There are hourly buses from **Palanga Airport** to Palanga and many buses operate between Palanga and Klaipėda. airBaltic offers its passengers free minibus services from Palanga Airport to Klaipėda. Buses head north from the airport to Liepāja in Latvia.

Arriving by Car

As Lithuania is part of the Schengen zone, there are no restrictions on entering it from Schengen countries. Drivers entering the country by car do not need an international driver's licence, but it is essential that they carry the vehicle's registration documents, insurance papers, a passport and a licence from their country. All cars must carry a first-aid kit and fire extinguisher.

International cargo and passenger carrier sailing out of Klaipėda

Arriving by Sea

Lithuania's only commercial maritime harbour, **Klaipėda State Sea Port**, is linked by ferry to ports in Germany, Sweden and Denmark. There are connections between Klaipėda and Kiel and Mukran in Germany, Copenhagen-Fredericia, Aabenraa-Aarhus in Denmark and Karlshamn in Sweden.

Arriving by Coach

Lithuania has an extensive network of roads connecting the country to neighbouring states. It is fairly simple to reach Lithuania by bus or coach from Estonia or Latvia as there are numerous crossing points. There are express passenger coaches from Vilnius to Rīga and Tallinn, as well as other cities including Warsaw, Berlin, Prague, Vienna, Kaliningrad and Moscow. On the other hand, the journey from countries such as Germany or the UK is very long and the inconvenience is best avoided.

Airport terminal building, Palanga Airport in Western Lithuania

Getting Around Lithuania

Lithuania's excellent road network makes it very easy to get around. Buses are the fastest and most convenient mode of public transport in the country. Express buses link virtually every town in Lithuania and are also a great way to see the countryside. Trains are cheaper, but also less frequent and with far fewer routes. The roads in Lithuania are some of the best-maintained in Central and Eastern Europe, which often makes hiring a car the most comfortable way to travel. The country's relatively flat landscape, punctuated by low hills, makes it ideal for cycling as well.

International luxury coach at the bus station in Panevėžys

Travelling by Bus

Buses form the main mode of Lithuania's public transport network. The privately owned bus company **Toks** operates comfortable buses on more than 50 routes countrywide as well as 11 international routes for **Eurolines**. Although travelling by bus is usually a little more expensive than by train, buses are quicker and connect more places.

Schedules are written on signs at the head of each stand, as well as inside the bus station building. Express buses, marked by an "E" in the schedules, sometimes operate on intercity routes, bypassing smaller towns and villages along the way. Many of the bus services to the coast, for instance to Palanga or Nida, are seasonal and operate in summer only. For more information on frequency of services check the official website for Toks.

Vilnius Bus Station is the country's biggest bus transport hub, although **Kaunas Bus Station** also has links with various European cities.

Tickets can be bought at ticket desks in bus stations in larger towns, although you can also buy them from the driver on boarding, especially on minor routes. In summer, or during weekends when services are more regularly used, it is worth buying tickets in advance. Tickets have to be paid for in cash and there are no facilities for reserving them by telephone or on the Internet. Disabled passengers, senior citizens over the age of 70 and children below the age of ten, are entitled to a 50 per cent discount. Pre-school children travel free. Groups of ten passengers or more get price reductions if travel is arranged in advance.

Travelling by Train

The national rail network is run by **Lietuvos Geležinkeliai** (Lithuanian Railways). The main routes are from Vilnius to Šiauliai and Klaipėda, Vilnius to Visaginas, which passes by Ignalina and Aukštaitija National Park, Šiauliai to Panevėžys and Rokiškis, and the comparatively speedy and regular Vilnius to Kaunas route. The Vilnius to Varėna line continues to Dzūkija National Park before heading into Belarus. One of the most enjoyable and scenic train journeys in Lithuania is on the Narrow-Gauge Railway, which runs from Panevėžys to Lake Rubikiai.

All train tickets must be purchased at the ticket desks at railway stations. Reductions are available for young children, pensioners and also disabled passengers.

Lithuania's *autobusų stotis* (bus stations) and *traukinių stotis* (railway stations) are generally located close to one another and are within easy walking distance of the town centre. Theft is rare, although it is best to keep an eye on your belongings. Risk to personal safety is seldom an issue when travelling in Lithuania, but security guards are often deployed at Vilnius Bus Station.

However, bus and train stations place little emphasis on cleanliness and hygiene, although the stations at Vilnius and Kaunas have now been modernized. At the larger railway stations it is also possible to leave your baggage at the

The Narrow-Gauge Railway, one of the most scenic and enjoyable train journeys

Well-maintained ticket office in the railway station, Vilnius

left luggage room for a small fee, or deposit it in a self-service locker.

Travelling by Car

Roads in Lithuania are excellent by post-Soviet standards, and present no special problems to drivers. There are different categories of road, with different speed restrictions. The highest category is the motorway, but there are only two of these, Kaunas to Klaipėda (A1), and Vilnius to Panevėžys (A2). Although the Vilnius–Kaunas and Kaunas–Klaipėda roads look the same, the former stretch is not the "motorway" class because of its hilly terrain. There are no toll roads in Lithuania, except through the Curonian Spit National Park.

Lithuanian regulations state that every car must carry a small fire extinguisher, a first-aid kit, a reflective warning triangle and reflective safety vest. It is mandatory for the driver and passengers to wear seat belts. Motorists must use headlights at all times, both during the day and night. The traffic police may not be able to speak fluent English but are stringent about rules and can collect fines on the spot.

The maximum permissible speed limit on motorways is 130 kmph (81 mph) from May to October and 110 kmph (68 mph) for the rest of the year, the exception being the Vilnius–Kaunas motorway where the speed limit remains 110 kmph (68 mph). The speed limit in built-up areas is 50 kmph (31 mph), but drivers are rarely stopped for speeding unless they exceed a speed of 60 kmph (37 mph).

Drink driving is a punishable offence and local authorities sometimes use roadblocks and breathalyzer tests as enforcement tools.

Car Hire

A large number of local and well-known international car hire companies offer a wide range of vehicles for rental in Lithuania. Some have desks at Vilnius Airport and upmarket hotels. Many others can be found in Vilnius city centre. Local firms, such as **Aunela**, have a range of newer and older Western makes of car. The minimum rental period is usually 24 hours. Payments for car hire can be made with cash or through any major credit card.

Road Signs

Signposting on motorways, country roads and minor roads is comprehensible. When entering a town or village, the settlement's name appears on a sign with black lettering on a white background. This indicates that drivers must slow down to the speed limit for built-up areas. Small blue signs near road junctions in Vilnius city centre point the way to streets, sights and landmarks. Key road signs to look out for are those regulating speed, controlling roadside parking and preventing right or left turns. These are often monitored by traffic police.

Part of Klaipėda's recently modernized road network

Getting Around Vilnius

The best way to explore Vilnius is on foot as most sights such as churches, museums, restaurants and cafés are within easy walking distance of each other. It is only a short walk to the main sights from the city's main thoroughfare, Gedimino Avenue. Vilnius's Old Town is among the biggest in Europe and much of the city's inner traffic is kept to roads that circle its boundary. To reach the sights and restaurants that lie outside the city centre, visitors can use the reliable network of trolleybuses and buses. Taxi services are usually trustworthy but getting around by road is best avoided at rush hour.

Modern trolleybus, part of Vilnius's public transport network

Buses and Trolleybuses

Vilnius has a very dependable network of trolleybuses and buses with frequent services that span the city. Some of the older vehicles are now being replaced with modern ones. However, public transport is best avoided during rush hour, when trolleybuses and buses are crowded.

A detailed map of the city's bus routes is available on the **Vilnius Transport** website. The timetables for every *stotelė* (stop) can be viewed by clicking "*autobusų*" for buses and "*troleibusų*" for trolleybuses. Few services run between 11pm and 5am.

A standard *bilietas* (ticket) is valid on both buses and trolleybuses. This must be bought in advance at a kiosk or from the driver on boarding, and then validated by punching it in one of the machines on board. Passes for one, three and ten days are available. Penalties for travelling without a valid ticket are high.

Driving in Vilnius

Traffic density has increased rapidly in Vilnius in recent years, resulting in congestion during peak hours, especially early mornings and late evenings. The problem is further compounded by the erstwhile Soviet city planning. The lack of roads is a serious issue that Vilnius's city council is struggling to solve with the help of EU funds. However, road construction causes further blockades, adding to drivers' woes in the short term. With the rise in the number of vehicles, tailgating and overtaking have become standard practice. Central Vilnius has an extensive one-way system, which can be quite tricky to negotiate without a road map.

Parking

Multi-storey car parks in Vilnius are few. Most often drivers use roadside parking. In the city centre, drivers can use controlled parking between 8am and 6pm, using a pay-and-display machine. Parking is more expensive in the Old Town. Failing to pay results in a wheel-clamp, a lengthy wait and then a very heavy fine.

In parked cars, all objects, including bags and clothing should be locked out of sight.

Taxis

Taxis are easily available in Vilnius, although during rush hour and late on weekend evenings it may be necessary to call several companies before finding a free cab. Ordering a taxi by telephone is cheaper than hailing one on the street. The average charge is €0.50 per kilometre, though prices are higher at night. Companies such as **Romerta**

A busy road in Vilnius during peak traffic hour

Martono Taksi, an expensive but reliable option

and **Ekipažas** are generally reliable. All taxis must have a working meter, so check the initial reading as you get in.

Cycling

Conditions for cyclists vary considerably around the city. Bicycle routes are clearly marked on many of the pavements in the Old Town, along roads such as Gedimino and Konstitucijos avenues and into districts such as Žvėrynas and Vingis Park. EuroVelo route 11 is an Eastern European cycle route that runs through the eastern Baltic region, taking in Vilnius and Tartu. It has now been extended to Vilnius from the southwest to the northeast, towards Verkiai. However, cycling along roads that do not have bicycle lanes is not recommended. Bicycles can be rented at **Baltic Cycle**.

Walking

Each sight is just a few steps from the next one, allowing visitors to experience the Old Town's magnificent architecture from close quarters. There are many pedestrianized streets and, despite the occasional reckless driver, traffic is rarely a hindrance.

Crossing roads in Vilnius can sometimes be hazardous. At many crossings a "red man" and "green man" guide pedestrians on when to cross. However, at road junctions, there are traffic lights just for cars. When at a pedestrian crossing without lights, cars must give way to pedestrians, but they do not always do so. Gedimino Avenue is the city's main street for

shopping, festivals and parades, besides being an attraction in itself. Stretching from Cathedral Square in the east to Žvėrynas in the west, it becomes pedestrianized in the evenings. The lush districts of Žvėrynas and Užupis are on either sides of the Old Town. The former leads to the splendid views of the Neris river and Vingis Park, reachable by a pedestrian bridge. A walk to Užupis may culminate in a peaceful wander around Bernardinų Cemetery, or you could continue on as far as Belmontas and the Church of Sts Peter and Paul.

Visitors walking down Pilies Street towards Upper Castle, Old Town

Sightseeing Tours

Tour guides in Vilnius are professional and speak fluent English. A typical sightseeing tour arranged by **Senamiesčio Gidas** includes a trip to the Old Town, Užupis and the Church of Sts Peter and Paul. Customized tours can also be arranged. Travel agencies such as **Visit Lithuania** also arrange guided tours as well as accommodation

and transport. **West Express** organizes specialized tours, such as Jewish Vilnius. Balloon flights with **Ballooning Centre** are especially memorable.

Car Hire

A convenient alternative for getting around the city and taking day-trips to nearby attractions such as Trakai is to hire a car. International car rental companies, such as **Europcar**, **Avis** and **Hertz**, and local companies such as Aunela, offer insured vehicles.

DIRECTORY

Buses and Trolleybuses

Vilnius Transport
Sodų 22. **Tel** 216 0054.
W vilniustransport.lt

Taxis

Ekipažas
Šv Stepono 33a. **Tel** 233 7958.
W ekipazastaksi.lt

Romerta
Garsioji 9. **Tel** 275 6969.
W romerta.lt

Cycling

Baltic Cycle
Vytenio 6–110. **Tel** 6995 6009.
W bicycle.lt

Sightseeing Tours

Ballooning Centre
Upės 5. **Tel** 6520 0510.
W ballooning.lt

Senamiesčio Gidas
Aušros vartų 7. **Tel** 6995 4064.
W vilniuscitytour.com

Visit Lithuania
L Stuokos-Gucevičiaus 1.
Tel 262 5241.
W visitlithuania.net

West Express
A Stulginskio 5. **Tel** 255 3255.
W westexpress.lt

Car Hire

Avis
W avis.com

Europcar
W europcar.com

Hertz
W hertz.com

General Index

Page numbers in **bold** type refer to main entries

GENERAL INDEX | 399

Käsmu Boulder Walk 13, 112, **114**
Erratic boulders 22, 114
Käsmu Peninsula 114
Käsmu village 114
Saartneem 114
Käsmu Peninsula 22, **114**
Kassari 12, **95**
Hiiumaa Museum 95
Kastaldi, Philippo 198
Katariina Guild (Tallinn) 335
Kaubamaja (Tallinn) 335
Kaudzīte, Matīss and Reinis 203
Kaunas 16–17, 253, **262–5**
Cathedral of Sts Peter and Paul **263**
Church of the Holy Trinity **262**
Church of the Resurrection **264**
Church of St George **262**
climate 32
Devil's Museum **264**
festivals 212
Folk Music Museum **263**
history 42, 218, 221
hotels 306
Kaunas Castle **262**
Laisvės Avenue **264**
M K Čiurlionis Art Museum **264**
Mykolas Zilinskas Art Gallery **264**
Ninth Fort **264**
Old Town Hall 21, **262**
Pažaislis Monastery 20, **265**
Perkūnas House 21, **263**
Pharmacy Museum **262–3**
Raudondvaris **265**
restaurants 328–9
Rumšiškės Open-Air Museum **265**
Vytautas Church **263**
Vytautas the Great War Museum **264**
Zapyškis Church **265**
Kaunas Bus Station 390, 391
Kaušėnai 281
Kavinė 308
Kazaks, Jēkabs 155
Kėdainiai **265**
hotels 306
Multicultural Centre 265
restaurants 329
Kefir 311, 313
Ķemeri **174**
Ķemeri National Park 174
Ķemeri Park 174
Kenesa synagogue (Trakai) 41, **257**
Kepta duona 310
Kernavė 35, 204–5, 207, 253, **258**
restaurants 329
Kettler, Duke Gotthard 167, 183
Kettler, Duke Jakob 37, 139, 167, 184, 198
KGB Cells Museum (Tartu) **119**
KGB Museum (Vilnius) **242**, 366
Kibinai 311
Kiek-in-de-Kök (Tallinn) 65, 72–3, **75**
Kihnu Island **105**
hotels 297
Linaküla 105
restaurants 316
Kiidjärve Watermill 13, **126**
Akste Anthills 126
Kiipsaare Lighthouse (Saaremaa) 100–101
Kissing Students Fountain (Tartu) 118
Kistler-Ritso 75
Kits, Elmar 119
Klaipėda 17, 35, 42, 272, 273, **284–5**
Ännchen of Tharau **284**
Blacksmiths' Museum **284**
Castle Museum **284**
climate 32
Clock Museum **284–5**
festivals 213
history 218, 219
hotels 307
Lithuanian Minor History Museum **284**

Klaipėda (cont.)
Picture Gallery and Sculpture Park **285**
restaurants 330–31
Theatre Square 284
Klaipėda State Sea Port 389
Kmieliauskas, Antanas 221, 226, 240
Knackfus, Marcin 249
Knights' House (Tallinn) 73, *75*
Koguva (Muhu Island) 95
Kohtla Underground Mining Museum 10, 13, **115**
Kohtla-Järve 107, 115
Kohvik 308
Koidula, Lydia 39, **103**
My Country is My Love 103
Kokle 29
Koknese **197**
hotels 303
Kolbe, H 102
Kolkja 127
Kolvja 127
Kononenko, Sergejs 154
Konventa Sēta 150–51
Kõpu Lighthouse (Hiiumaa Island) 10, **95**
Kõrts 308
Košrags 177
Kraków 215
Krāslava **198–9**
hotels 303
Krāslava Castle 198
Krāslava Museum 198–9
restaurants 325
Kretinga 273, **286**
Church of the Annunciation 286
Kretinga Museum 286
restaurants 331
Winter Garden 286
Kreutzwald, Friedrich 26, 78, **125**
Kalevipoeg 78, 85, 125
Kriaunos 268
Krimulda 191, **192**
Krogs 308
Kross, Jaan 26
Krustpils Castle (Jēkabpils) 198
Kugelis 310
Kuldīga 138, 167, **183**
Holy Trinity 183
hotels 301
restaurants 322
Rižupe Sand Caves 183
St Catherine's Church 183
Venta Waterfall 183
Kuldīga District Museum 183
Kulnev, Jaan 203
Kuremäe **116**
Dormition Cathedral 116
hotels 298
Pühtitsa Convent 116
restaurants 318
Kuressaare 12, 36, 96, **98**
St Nicholas' Church 98
Vaekoja 98
Weigh House 98
Kuressaare Castle 20
Kurzeme 135, 154, 163, 167, 177, 182–3, 185
Kurzeme Peasants' Homestead (Latvian Ethnographic Open-Air Museum) 163
Kuuraniidu Study Trail (Soomaa National Park) 105
Kuutsemäe Ski Resort 123
Kvass 313

L

Laar, Mart 57
Labanoras Regional Park 269
Lāčplēsis 154, **197**
Ladakalnis Hill 17, **270**
Lahemaa National Park 13, 47, 107, 109, **110–14**
Altja 111, **113**

Lahemaa National Park (cont.)
fauna and flora 110
hotels 298
Käsmu **112**
Käsmu Boulder Walk **114**
Käsmu Peninsula 110
Oandu Beaver Trail 113
Oandu Forest Trail 111, 113
Palmse Manor House 111, **112**
restaurants 318
Sagadi Manor 111, **113**
Viinistu 110, **113**
Võsu 111, **112**
Laima (Rīga) 339
Lais, B 66
Laisvės Avenue (Kaunas) **264**
Lake Asveja 269
Lake Baltieji 269
Lake Baluošas 271
Lake Dringis 271
Lake Dviragis 268
Lake Engure **176**
hotels 301
Ornithological Centre 176
restaurants 322
Lake Ežezers 15, **202**
Lake Galvė 257
Lake Jugla 163
Lake Juodieji Lakajai 269
Lake Linkmenas 270
Lake Lubāns 15, **202**
Lake Lūkstas 280
Lake Mastis 280
Lake Orija 261
Lake Pape Nature Reserve **185**
Vītolnieki 185
Lake Peipsi 13, 23, 25, 47, 107, **127**
Kasepää 127
Kolkja 127
Mustvee 127
Piirissaar 127
Raja 127
Värska 127
Lake Plateliai 273, 274, 281, **282–3**
Folk Legends **283**
Lake Põlva 126
Lake Pühajärv 122
Lake Rāzna 202
Lake Rõuge 124
Lake Rubikiai 269
Lake Širvėna 268
Lake Talšos 277
Lake Tamula 125
Lake Taurāgnas 270
Lake Võrtsjärv 10, 13, **122**
Jõgeveste 122
Lake Želva 269
Land of Blue Lakes *see* Latgale Lakes
Landscape and wildlife **22–3**
Arctic lichen 23
barn swallows **23**
bees 22, 271
black storks 22
brown bears 23
elks 23
mushrooms 23
orchids 23
ringed seals 23
white storks 22
wolves 22
Language **367**
Estonian 411–12
Latvian 413–14
Lithuanian 415–16
Lasering (Tallinn) 335
Lasnamäe (Tallinn) **85**
The Last Supper (Kihelkonna Church, Saaremaa) 99
Latgale 154, 163, 187, 198–9, 202
Latgale Art and Craft Centre (Līvāni) 198
Latgale Lakes 11, 15, 128–9, 131, **202**
Gaiglava 202

Acknowledgments

Dorling Kindersley would like to thank the many people whose help and assistance contributed to the preparation of this book.

Contributors

Howard Jarvis has been editor of numerous publications including *RigaNOW!*, *The Baltic Times*, *TTG Nordic* and *Minsk In Your Pocket*. He has been a regular contributor for the Jane's Information Group since 2000.

John Oates, winner of the Guardian newspaper's Young Travel Writer of the Year award, has contributed to numerous newspapers, magazines and guidebooks.

Tim Ochser has been living in Rīga and Vilnius since 2001 where he has been working as a teacher and freelance journalist. He has written several novels and plays.

Neil Taylor is a writer, a tour operator and a consultant. He writes for British newspapers on the Baltics and has published several guidebooks on the region.

Fact Checkers
Eat Latvia, Nicholas Archdeacon, Joel Dullroy, Irja Luks, Brigita Pantelejeva, Nat Singer

Proofreaders
Deepthi Talwar, Debra Wolter

Indexers
Ajay Lal Das, Helen Peters

Design and Editorial
Managing Editor Douglas Amrine
Managing Art Editor Jane Ewart
Senior Editor Michelle Crane
Production Controller Lousie Daly
Picture Research Ellen Root
DTP Designer Natasha Lu

Additional Photography
Peter Dennis, Rose Horridge, Rajnish Kashyap, Ian O'Leary.

Additional Illustrations
Chapel Design & Marketing Ltd

Cartography
Casper Morris, Stuart James

Cartographic Research
Netmaps

Special Assistance
Dorling Kindersley would like to thank the following for their assistance:
Sonata Šiaučiulytė at Vilnius Tourist Information Centre

Revisions Team
Emma Anacootee, Claire Baranowski, Marta Bescos, Imogen Corke, Joel Dullroy, Anna Freiberger, Howard Jarvis, Kathryn Lane, Maite Lanturon, Carly Madden, Alison McGill, George Nimmo, Vikki Nousiainen, Susie Peachey, Rada Radojicic, Lucy Richards, Ellen Root, Sands Publishing Solutions, Susana Smith, Neil Taylor, Richa Verma, Matt Willis

Photography Permissions
Dorling Kindersley would like to thank the following for their assistance and kind permission to photograph at their establishments:

Ainaži Naval College Museum, Andrejs Pumpurs Museum, Anton Hansen Tammsaare Museum, Aqua Park, Arsenal Museum of Art, Art Nouveau in Riga, Aviation Museum, Beekeeping Museum, Bicycle Museum, Calvary Church of the Holy Cross, Cathedral of Christ the King, Cathedral of St Anthony of Padua, Cathedral of St Mary the Virgin (Toomkirik), Cathedral of Sts Boris and Glebe, Cat's House, Church of St Casimir's, Church of St Theresa, Church of Sts Peter and Paul, Coca Cola Plaza, Tallinn, Contemporary Art Centre, Dauderi, Déjà Vu Lounge Bar, Tallinn, Dome Cathedral, Dominican Church, Dominican Monastery, Old town, Dundaga, Europa Mall, Vilnius, Folk House of the Livs, Franciscan Church, Friary of the Virgin Mary, Tytuvenai, House of Blackheads, KGB Cells Museum, KGB Museum, Vilnius, Kohtla Underground Mining Museum, Kiek in de Kök, Tallinn, Kumu Art Museum, Latgale Culture and History Museum, The Latvian Ethnographic Open-Air Museum, Latvian Museum of Photography, Rēzekne, Liepāja Museum, Lithuanian National Museum, Littera Bookshop, Vilnius University, Mentzendorff House, The Mihkli Farm Museum, Mikalojus Konstantinas Čiurlionis National Museum of Art, Motor Museum, Museum of the Barricades of 1991, Museum of Decorative Arts and Design, Museum of History and Applied Arts, Preiļi, Museum of Horns, Museum of Rīga's History and Navigation, Niguliste Church, Tallinn, Palmse Manor House, Pedvāle Open-Air Museum, Peter The Great House Museum, The Palanga Amber Museum, Photo Museum, Tallinn, Porcelain Museum, Powder Tower/ Latvian War Museum, Railway Station, Vilnius, Rundāle Palace, Latvia, Sea Museum-Aquarium and Dolphinarium in Smiltynė, Setu Village Museum (Lake Peipsi), Shakespeare Boutique Hotel, Skaistkalne Roman Catholic Church, Skyline Bar (Reval Hotel, Latvija), St Anne's Basilica, St John's Church, Tallinn International Airport, Tamsta Club, Tērvete Nature Park, Theatre, Music and Film Museum, Town Hall Pharmacy in Tallinn, Trakai Island Castle, Tukums, Vilnius Cathedral, Vilnius Picture Gallery, Vilnius University, Vincents Restaurant, Rīga, Vytautas The Great War Museum, Žemaitija National Park

Picture Credits

The publisher would like to thank the following for their kind permission to reproduce their photographs:

Key: a-above; b-below/bottom; c-centre; f-far; l-left; r-right; t-top.

4Corners: Cozzi Guido 253b; Giovanni Simeone/SIME 178-179.

akg-images: 36cl, 38br, 40tr, 40-41c, 54crb, 55tl, 139bc, 140tc, 219tl; Erich Lessing 34, 216-217c; RIA Nowosti 43t, 43c, 216cl.

Akmenine Rezidencija: 295bc, 306tr.

Alamy Images: A.P. 167b, 185br; Urmas Ääro 49b, Stuart Abraham 46br, Ace Stock Limited 21br, 97crb; age fotostock 332cla; AllOver photography 210b; Arco Images 237cb; Arco Images GmbH 10cla; Andrew Barnes 30bc; Caro 206bl, 210tr; China Span/Keren Su 187b; Content Mine International 133b, 135tr, Gary Cook 191tl; Danita Delimont 28br, 135br, 357tl, 385br; Ilja Dubovskis 288cl, Cody Duncan 23cr; epa european pressphoto agency b.v. 123crb; Sindre Ellingsen 257tl; Maciej Figiel 31tl, 31cla; Johan Furusjö 137bl; Goddard New Era 325tr; Christopher Griffin 73cr; Andrew Harrington 89b; Simon Hathaway 310cl; Pete Hill 374cla; Ula Holigrad 22cr; Imagebroker 23cl, 84tr, 97tl; INSADCO Photography 373bc; Jevgenija 191br; Stanislovas Kairys 243bl; Christian Klein 349tl; Stan Kujawa 311c; Yadid Levy 41cr, 247tl; Robin Mckelvie 114crb, 176bl; Natural Visions 30br; The Natural History Museum 31tc; Kari Niemeläinen 381br; Jaak Nilson 13tr; Indrek Parli 52bl, PCL 137tl, Pictorial Press Ltd 26cl; Les polders 62br; Recognition 346c; Robert Harding World Imagery 17tl,134t; Joeri de Rocker 348cla; Jonathan Smith 28cla; Kitt Cooper-Smith 31ca; David Soulsby 378cl; Sylvia Cordaiy Photo Library Ltd 362tc; Vario images GmbH & Co.KG/Stefan Kiefer 379br, / Jesper Dijohn 57c; Tiit Veermae 21tr, 22tr, 51t, 110clb, 114cra, 121br; Martyn Vickery 24br, 72clb, 247cr, 342b; Visual&Written SL 74tl; World Pictures 51br; Sven Zacek 96cla, 107b; Imagebroker/Michael Zegers 382cra.

Apollo Raamatud: 335bl.

Archive of the Latvian Tourism Development Agency: 145tr, 202cl, 202bc.

Arkos: 331tr.

Aukstaitijos siaurasis gelezinkelis: 390br.

AWL Images: Walter Bibikow 48, 88, 166; Danita Delimont Stock 186; Ian Trower 2-3, 220.

Bank of Lithuania: 43bl.

Bibliotēka No.1: 321tr.

Bogapott: 334tr.

Bridgeman Images: *A View of Tallinn with Hattorpe Tower,* Schlater, Alexander Georg (1834-1879) © Art Museum of Estonia, Tallinn, Estonia/Bridgeman Images 8-9; *King Charles XII (1682-1718) of Sweden, on horseback,* 1702 37br; *Catherine the Great,* 1793 38bl; *Arms of the Hanseatic League Stone* 138bc; *Shipping off a Baltic Port* 139crb.

Bussi Reisid: 378br.

Cēsis Historical Film Festival: 349cb.

Club Illusion: 344c.

Corbis: Niall Benvie 356bl; Christophe Boisvieux 61br; Franz-Marc Frei 206cl; Jon Hicks 236t; Robert Harding World Imagery/Yadid Levy 25tr; Hans Georg Roth 350bl; Sygma/Gérard Rancinan 26bl; Peter Turnley 219crb; Zefa/ Goebel 20cl, 207br.

Corbis. epa/Kay Nietfeld 123bc; epa/Toms Kalnins 211br; Sven Zacek/Nature Picture Library 123cra.

Courtesy of Tallin City Museum: 77c.

Danita Delimont Stock Photography: Keren Su 221b.

La Dolce Vita: 318tc.

Vydas Dolinskas: 217tl, 217tc.

Dome Hotel & Spa: 300bc.

Domni Canes: 309tl.

Dorling Kindersley: Ian O'Leary 310-311.

Dreamstime.com: Aistija 204-205; Alisbalb 16bl; Valery Bareta 58; Milda Basinskiene 288clb; Coplandj 272; Dennis Dolkens 16tr; Gadagj 12br; Gorshkov13 132, 290-291; Kaspars Grinvalds 11tr; Helen Kattai 100-101; Konstik 12tc; Kristina Kuodiene 208; Alexey Kuznetsov 15tr; Lindawelsa 128-129; Aliaksandr Mazurkevich 17bc; Antony Mcaulay 142; Rihards Plivch 15bl; Dmitry Rukhlenko 14tr; Tatiana Savvateeva 61cra; Scanrail 44-45; Alexander Tolstykh 14bl; Vikau 11br.

Ethnographic Open-Air Museum of Latvia: 163cra; Uldis Veisbuks 163cla, 163clb.

Fellin: Renee Altrov 319tr.

Focus: Kaido Haagen 28clb; Tiit I Iunt 94tl, Jarek Jõepera 23cra, 50tl, 127tr; Didzis Kadaks 30crb, 175br, 190bc; Mati Kose 53cr; Arnold Kristjuhan 23ca; Heinrich Lukk 33br; Kalju Suur 27tc, 27cra, 29tl, 57tl; Tiina Tammet 79tl; Andres Teiss 345tl, 34/tl, 359tr; Ioomas Tuul 50br, 52cra, 78cl, 93b, 96bl, 97bl, 98cl, 105br, 109cr, 110cla, 111cra, 117br, 313tr, 344br, 358tl, 359bc, 379tl.

Forto Dvaras: 326bc.

Getty Images: AFP/Ilmars Znotins 134br; AFP/Petras Malukas/Stringer 211tl; AFP/Stringer 41br; AFP/Tim Sloan 141bc; Jeff Gross 360tl; Arnd Hemmersbach/NordicFocus 123br; Hulton Archive/Austrian Archives/Imagno 216br; Hulton Archive/Stringer 40br, 140clb, 218c; Janek Skarzynski/Staff 123cl; Stu Forster 27bl; Time & Life Pictures/Ben Martin 200bl; Time & Life Pictures/David Rubinger 141tl.

The Granger Collection, New York: Ullstein Bild 141crb.

Hapsal Dietrich: 316tr.

Ilgi: Ilgi 29tr.

Howard Jarvis: 224cl.

Jon Smith: 311tl.

Jonathan Smith Photography: 28-29c, 212bc, 213tl, 273b, 352cra.

Didzis Kadaks: 157bl.

Kalev Chocolates: 335c.

Rajnish Kashyap: 20br, 21cla, 35bc, 60tr, 69cb, 69br, 224bl, 224br, 225crb, 228br, 235br, 256tr, 257cr, 262bl, 263crb, 333tl.

Kaubamaja Store: 335tc.

KGB Cells Museum: 119cb.

Klaipeda Clock Museum: 284crb.

Kohvik Supelsaksad: 317br.

Kolonna Hotel: 292br.

Kupfernams: 303br.

Kybynlar: 329br.
Lacu Miga: 302tr.
LIDO Altus Sēta: 320bc.
Liepaja Theatre: 348br.
Lithuanian Tourism: 365c.
Liitintero Vilnius: 304bc.
Lonely Planet Images: Jonathan Smith 212tl.
Boutique Hotel & Restaurant MaMa: 322tr.
Mary Evans Picture Library: 38tl, 56c, 138bl.
Merekalda Guesthouse: 299br.
Mikalojus Konstantinas Čiurlionis: Mikalojus Konstantinas
Čiurlionis Museum 26cra.
Molly Malone's: 360c.
National Geographic Stock: Klaus Nigge 22bl.
naturepl.com: Niall Benvie 23crb; William Osborn 23clb;
Igor Shpilenok 23bc; Artur Tabor 22br.
Neiburgs Hotel: 293br, 308bl.
NHPA/Photoshot: Lee Dalton 22cb.
Land Nomad: 20ca.
North Wind Picture Archives: 30cl.
Pädaste Manor: 293tl.
Palangos TIC: Tomas Smilingis 31br.
Joan Parenti: 279br.
Pastnieka Māja: 323br.
Patricia Tourist Office Riga - www.RigaLatvia.net: 386br.
Photolibrary: JTB Photo 333b; Roland Marske/Voller Ernst
209b.
Private Collection: 26tr, 28tr, 37tl, 37crb, 38cb, 39ca, 39bc,
40cl, 40bl, 42tl, 54ca, 55cr, 56tl, 81tr, 83cl, 83cr, 83bl, 103cr,
139tc, 202cra, 214c, 214crb, 214bc, 215tc, 215crb, 216bl,
217tr, 217bl, 217br, 218br, 243cl, 243cr.
Radisso Blue Royal Astorija Hotel: 294br.
Rannahotell, Parnu: 298tr.
Elmar Reich: Flickr 377bl.
Riga Opera Festival: 136bl.
Hotel Rinno: 305tr.
Robert Harding Picture Library: Piotr Ciesla 357bc; Peter
Erik Forsberg 13clb; Jaak Nilson 362-363.
Aivar Ruukel: 104cla, 104cl, 104br, 105cl.
Salacgrvas Novada TIC: 194cr.
Scanpix Baltics: 137cr, F64 27crb, 136cr; LT 29cr; Postimees/
Henn Soodla 23cla; Postimees/Lauri Kulpsoo 23tc.

Schlössle Hotel: 297tr, 314bc.
SemaraH Hotel Metropole: 295tl.
Sigade Revolutsioon LLC: 345bc.
Sofa de Pancho: 327tr.
Villa Sofia: 307br.
Hotel St. Petersbourg: 308cra.
Starover.ee: Pilrissaale 126bc.
State Small Theatre: Dmitrij Matvejev 354cla.
Stora Antis: 330bc.
Superstock: age fotostock 152tl, 252; fge fotostock/Wojtek
Buss 261cl; MIVA Stock 266-267; Yoshio Tomii 53bl.
Tallinn City Theatre: Siim Vahur 346cl.
Three Sisters Boutique Hotel: 296bc; Bordoo Restaurant
315tr.
Toomalõuna Tourist Farm: 292cla.
TopFoto.co.uk: The British Library/HIP 218tl.
Travel-Images.com: 247crb; A. Dnieprowsky 47br, 169tr,
188bl.
Uoksas: 328tr.
Vanagupė Hotel: 294tl.
Vilhelmines Dzirnavas: 324bc.
Vilnius Congress Concert Hall: 354br.
Vilnius Jazz Festival: Vytautas Suslavicius 213bl.
Visit Estonia: Marin Sild 373cla.
Wandering Spirit Travel Images: Louise Batalla Duran/
Photographersdirect.com 59b.
Jonathan Wasserstein: 76crb.
Wellton Centrum Hotel & Spa: 301tr.
Wikipedia: 24cl, 26crb, 27cl, 30bl, 35br, 39cb, 41tl, 42bc,
55crb, 55bc, 56br, 57bl, 215bc, 378tc; National Archives &
Records Administration, nara.gov 42cb; U.S. Department of
Defense 57bc.

Jacket front and spine: AWL Images: Peter Adams.

Front Endpapers: AWL Images: Walter Bibikow Ltl, Rcr;
Danita Delimont Stock Rbr; Ian Trower Rbc; Dreamstime.
com: Valery Bareta Lcl; Coplandj Lbl; Antony Mcaulay Rtr;
Vapsik662 Ltc; SuperStock: age fotostock Lbc.

All other images © Dorling Kindersley
For further information see: www.dkimages.com

Special Editions of DK Travel Guides

DK Travel Guides can be purchased in bulk quantities at discounted prices for use in promotions or as premiums. We are also able to offer special editions and personalized jackets, corporate imprints, and excerpts from all of our books, tailored specifically to meet your own needs.

To find out more, please contact:
in the United States **SpecialSales@dk.com**
in the UK **travelspecialsales@uk.dk.com**
in Canada DK Special Sales at **general@ tourmaline.ca**
in Australia **business.development@pearson. com.au**

Phrase Book: Estonian

In Emergency

Help!	**Appi!**	*Awpy!*
Stop!	**Peatuge!**	*Beh-atu-gay!*
Call a doctor!	**Kutsuge arst!**	*Coot-soo-gay arst!*
Call an ambulance!	**Kutsuge kiirabi!**	*Coot-soo-gay keer-awbi!*
Call the police!	**Kutsuge politsei!**	*Coot-soo-gay po-leet-say!*
Call the fire department!	**Kutsuge tuletõrje!**	*Coot-soo-gay too-lei-tur-ye!*
Where is the nearest telephone?	**Kus on lähim telefon?**	*Coos onn la-him telefon?*
Where is the nearest hospital?	**Kus on lähim haigla?**	*Coos onn la-him high-glaa?*

Communication Essentials

Yes	**Jah**	*Yah*
No	**Ei**	*Ey*
Please	**Palun**	*Pa-loon*
Thank you	**Aitäh**	*Ai-tah*
Excuse me	**Vabandage**	*Va-ban-da-gay*
Hello	**Tere**	*Te-re*
Goodbye	**Head aega**	*Heyad ayga*
Good night	**Head õhtut**	*Heyad ewh-toot*
morning	**hommik**	*hom-mik*
afternoon	**pärastlõuna**	*pa-rawst-lew-na*
evening	**õhtu**	*ewh-tu*
yesterday	**eile**	*eilay*
today	**täna**	*ta-naw*
tomorrow	**homme**	*hom-may*
What?	**Mida?**	*Meeda?*
When?	**Millal?**	*Meelal?*
Why?	**Miks?**	*Meeks?*
Where?	**Kus?**	*Coos?*

Guidelines for Pronunciation

The Estonian alphabet consists of the following letters: a, b, d, e, f, g, h, i, j, k, l, m, n, o, p, r, s, š, z, ž, t, u, v, o, ä, ö, ü. The letters c, q, x, y, z are used only in proper names (of places and people) and in words borrowed from foreign languages. Unlike English, all letters in Estonian are pronounced (for example: the silent k in "knee").

Some letter sounds:
a   as in the "u" in cut
b   similar to "p" in English
g   similar to "k" in English
j   as in the "y" in yes
r   like in English, but rolled
š   "sh"
ž   as in the "s" in pleasure
õ   like the "o" in own
ä   as in the "a" in bat
ö   similar to the "u" in fur
ü   as in the "u" in cube
Some letter combination sounds:
ai as in the "ai" in aisle
ei as in the "ei" in vein
oo   as in the "a" in water
uu   as in the "oo" in boot
öö   as in the "u" in fur
Some points to remember:
• Usually the first syllable of a word is stressed. However, quite a few words with foreign origins and some native Estonian words, such as aitäh, don't follow this pattern.
• Vowels and consonants can be short (written with one letter), long or extra long (written with two letters).

Useful Phrases

How are you?	**Kuidas läheb?**	*Cooi-das la-heb?*
Very well, thank you.	**Aitäh, väga hästi.**	*Ai-tah, va-ga has-ti.*
Pleased to meet you.	**Meeldiv tuttavaks saada.**	*Mayl-div too-taw vawks saa daw.*
See you soon!	**Varsti näeme!**	*Vaarsti nay-me!*
Is there … here?	**Kas siin on …?**	*Cos scene onn …?*
Where can I get …?	**Kust ma saaksin …?**	*Coost ma sawk-sin …?*
How do you get to?	**Kuidas minna …?**	*Cooi-dass min-na …?*
How far is …?	**Kui kaugel on …?**	*Cooi cow-kel onn …?*
Do you speak English?	**Kas te räägite inglise keelt?**	*Cos tay ra-gi-tay ing-li-say keylt?*
I can't speak Estonian.	**Ma ei oska eesti keelt.**	*Maw ey oska eysti kaylt.*
I don't understand.	**Ma ei saa aru.**	*Maw ey saw aru.*
Can you help me?	**Kas saate mind aidata?**	*Cos saw-tay meend eye-data?*
Please speak slowly.	**Palun rääkige aeglaselt.**	*Pa-loon ra-ki-gay ayg-la-selt.*
Sorry!	**Vabandust!**	*Va-ban-doost!*

Useful Words

big	**suur**	*suur*
small	**väike**	*vayke*
hot	**kuum**	*coom*
cold	**külm**	*kewlm*
good	**hea**	*he-ya*
bad	**halb**	*halb*
enough	**küllalt**	*cool-alt*
well	**hästi**	*hasti*
open	**avatud**	*aw-va-tud*
closed	**suletud**	*soo-laytud*
left	**vasak**	*vaw-sawk*
right	**parem**	*paw-rem*
straight	**otse**	*ot-say*
near	**lähedal**	*la-hay-dawl*
far	**kaugel**	*kaw-ghell*
up	**ülal**	*oolal*
down	**all**	*all*
early	**vara**	*va-raw*
late	**hilja**	*hill-yaw*
entrance	**sissepääs**	*see-say-pa-es*
exit	**väljapääs**	*val-yaw-pa-es*
toilet	**tualett**	*too-a-lett*
free/unoccupied	**vaba**	*vaw-baw*
free/no charge	**tasuta**	*taw-soo-taw*

Making a Telephone Call

Can I call abroad from here?	**Kas ma saan siit välismaale helistada?**	*Cos maw sawn seet va-lees-maw-lay hay-lees-taw-da?*
I would like to call collect.	**Tahaksin helistada vastaja kulul.**	*Taw-haw-ksin hay-lees-taw-da vaws-taya koo-lool.*
local call	**kohalik kõne**	*kohaw-lik kew-ne*
I'll ring back later.	**Helistan hiljem tagasi.**	*Hay-lees-tawn heel-yem taw-gaw-si.*
Could I leave a message?	**Kas ma saaksin teate jätta?**	*Cos maw sawk-seen tyate ya-taw?*
Could you speak up a little, please?	**Kas saate natuke valjemini rääkida?**	*Cos saw-tay naw-too-kay vawl-ye-meenee ra-ki-daw?*

Shopping

How much is this?	**Kui palju see maksab?**	*Cooi pawl-yu say mawk-sab?*
I would like …	**Tahaksin …**	*Taw-hawk-sin …*
Do you have …?	**Kas teil on …?**	*Cos tayl onn …?*
I'm just looking.	**Vaatan lihtsalt.**	*Vaw-tan liht-sawlt.*
Do you take credit cards?	**Kas krediitkaardiga saab maksta?**	*Cos kre-diit-kawrd-eega sawb mawk-sta?*
What time do you open?	**Mis kell teil avatakse?**	*Mees kell tayl a-vaw-tawk-say?*
What time do you close?	**Mis kell teil suletakse?**	*Mees kell tayl su-lay-tawk-say?*
this one	**see**	*cee*
that one	**too**	*toe*
expensive	**kallis**	*kaw-lees*
cheap	**odav**	*oh-dav*
size	**suurus**	*soo-rus*

antique dealer	**antiigipood**	an-**tiiki**-pode
souvenir shop	**suveniiripood**	sou-ve-**niiri**-pode
bookshop	**raamatupood**	**raw**-maw-too-pode
café	**kohvik**	koh-fik
chemist	**apteek**	ap-tayk
newspaper kiosk	**ajalehekiosk**	a-ya-le-he-**kii**-osk
department store	**kaubamaja**	cow-ba-mawya
market	**turg**	toorg

Staying in a Hotel

Have you any	**Kas teil on vaba**	Los tayl onn
vacancies?	**tuba?**	vawba too ba?
double room	**kahene tuba**	ka-hay-ne tooba
with double bed	**laia voodiga**	la-ya **vo**-diga
twin room	**kahe voodiga tuba**	ka-hay **vo**-diga too
single room	**ühene tuba**	ew-hene tooba
non-smoking	**mittesuitsetajatele**	meetay-sooitse-ta-ya-lay
room with a	**tuba**	too-ba
bath/shower	**vanniga/dušiga**	vaw-niga/doosh-iga
porter	**portjee**	port-ye
key	**võti**	vew-ti
I have a	**Mul on**	Mool onn re-se-**veri**-tood.
reservation.	**reserveeritud.**	

Sightseeing

bus	**buss**	boos
tram	**tramm**	trawm
trolley bus	**troll**	trol
train	**rong**	row-ng
bus stop	**bussipeatus**	boo-si-peya-toos
tram stop	**trammipeatus**	tra-mi-peya-toos
art gallery	**kunstigalerii**	koonsti-gale-**ree**
palace	**palee**	pa-**lay**
castle	**loss**	lowss
cathedral	**katedraal**	caw-tay-dral
church	**kirik**	kee-reek
garden	**aed**	eye-ed
library	**raamatukogu**	raw-maw-too-kogu
museum	**muuseum**	mu-seum
tourist information	**turismiinfo**	too-ris-me-info
closed for public	**külastajatele suletud**	koo-las-taya-tayle soo-le-tood
holiday	**puhkepäev**	pooh-ke-payev
travel agent	**reisibüroo**	ray-see-bu-roh

Eating Out

A table for …	**Palun üks laud …**	Pa-loon ooks
please	**inimesele**	la-ood …eenee-me-selay
I want to reserve	**Tahaksin reserveerida**	Taw-hawk-sin re-ser-**veri**-da la-ooda.
a table.	**lauda.**	
The bill, please	**Palun arve**	Pa-loon arvay
I am a vegetarian.	**Olen taimetoitlane.**	Olayn tai-may-toyt-lanay.
I'd like …	**Tahaksin …**	Ta-hawk-sin…
waiter/waitress	**kelner/ettekandja**	kel-ner/etay-kandya
menu	**menüü**	men-oo
wine list	**veinimenüü**	veini-men-**oo**
chef's special	**firmaroog**	feer-ma-rogue
tip	**jootraha**	**yot**-rawha
glass	**klaas**	klas
bottle	**pudel**	poo-del
knife	**nuga**	noo-ga
fork	**kahvel**	kawf-fel
spoon	**lusikas**	loo-si-kaws
breakfast	**hommikusöök**	hom-miku-sook
lunch	**lõuna**	lewna
dinner	**õhtusöök**	euh-tu-sook
main courses	**praed**	prayed
starters	**eelroad**	el-rowad
vegetables	**köögiviljad**	koo-gi-vilyad
desserts	**magustoidud**	maw-gus-toy-dud
rare	**pooltoores**	pole-**toe**-res
well done	**küps**	cewps

Menu Decoder

äädikas	a-di-kaws	vinegar
aurutatud	ow-ru-tawtud	steamed
friikartul	free-kartool	chips
grillitud	grilly-tud	grilled
jäätis	ya-tis	ice cream
juust	youst	cheese
kala	kaw-la	fish
kana	kawna	chicken
kartul	kar-tool	potatoes
kaste	kaws-tey	sauce
keedetud	kay-day-tud	boiled
klimbid	klim-bid	dumplings

kohv	k-oh-v	coffee
kook, saiad	coke, sigh-ad	cake, pastry
koor	core	cream
küüslauk	koos-lauk	garlic
lambaliha	lawm-ba-leeha	lamb
leib/sai	layb/sei	bread
liha	lee-ha	meat
loomaliha	**lo**-ma-leeha	beef
mereannid	mayrey-awnid	seafood
mineraalvesi	min-e-**rawl**-vaysi	mineral water
muna	moona	egg
õli	ewli	oil
õlu	ewlu	beer
pannkook	pawn-coke	pancake
peekon	paykon	bacon
piim	peem	milk
pipar	peepar	pepper
pirukas	piru-kaws	pie
praeliha	praey-leeha	steak
praetud	praeytud	fried
punane vein	poo-naw-nay vein	red wine
puuvili	**puu**-veelee	fruit
puuviljamahl	**puu**-vil-ya-mawhl	fruit juice
riis	rees	rice
rull	rule	roll
salat	sawlat	salad
sealiha	seya-leeha	pork
seened	say-ned	mushrooms
sink	sink	ham
šokolaad	shok-o-lawd	chocolate
sool	sole	salt
suhkur	suhkoor	sugar
suitsukala	suit-soo-kawla	smoked fish
supp	soup	soup
tee	te	tea
täidetud	tayde-tood	stuffed
valge vein	val-gay vein	white wine
vorst	vorst	sausage
võileib	voi-layb	sandwich

Numbers

0	**null**	nul
1	**üks**	ewks
2	**kaks**	kawks
3	**kolm**	colm
4	**neli**	ne-li
5	**viis**	viis
6	**kuus**	kuus
7	**seitse**	say-tsey
8	**kaheksa**	kaw-hex-a
9	**üheksa**	ew-hex-a
10	**kümme**	kewmme
11	**üksteist**	ewx-taste
12	**kaksteist**	kawks-taste
13	**kolmteist**	colm-taste
14	**neliteist**	nayli-taste
15	**viisteist**	viis-taste
16	**kuusteist**	kuus-taste
17	**seitseteist**	saytse-taste
18	**kaheksateist**	kawheksaw-taste
19	**üheksateist**	ewheksaw-taste
20	**kakskümmend**	kawks-kew-mend
30	**kolmkümmend**	colm-kew-mend
40	**nelikümmend**	nayli-kew-mend
50	**viiskümmend**	viis-kew-mend
60	**kuuskümmend**	kuus-kew-mend
70	**seitsekümmend**	say-tse-kew-mend
80	**kaheksakümmend**	kaw-heksa-kew-mend
90	**üheksakümmend**	ew-heksa-kew-mend
100	**sada**	sa-da
1000	**tuhat**	too-hawt

Time

one minute	**üks minut**	ewks minut
hour	**tund**	toond
half an hour	**pool tundi**	pole toondi
Sunday	**pühapäev**	pew-ha-payev
Monday	**esmaspäev**	esmas-payev
Tuesday	**teisipäev**	taysi-payev
Wednesday	**kolmapäev**	kolma-payev
Thursday	**neljapäev**	nelya-payev
Friday	**reede**	re-de
Saturday	**laupäev**	lauw-payev

Phrase Book: Latvian

In Emergency

Help!	Palīgā!	Pu-lee-gaa!
Stop!	Apstāties!	Up-staat-eas!
Call a doctor!	Izsauciet ārstu	Iz-sowts-eat ahr-stoo!
Call an ambulance!	Izsauciet ātro palīdzību!	Iz-sowts-eat aa-troa pu-leedz-ee-boo!
Call the police!	Izsauclet policiju!	Iz-sowts-eat po-lits-ee-yoo!
Call the fire department!	Izsauciet ugunsdzēsējus!	Iz-sowts-eat oo-goons-dseh-say-oos!
Where is the nearest telephone?	Kur ir tuvākais telefons?	Koor ir too-vaak-ais tel-e-fons?
Where is the nearest hospital?	Kur ir tuvākā slimnīca?	Koor ir too-vaak-aa slim-neets-u?

Communication Essentials

Yes	Jā	Yaa
No	Nē	Neh
Please	Lūdzu	Loodz-oo
Thank you	Paldies	Pul-deas
Excuse me	Atvainojiet	Ut-vy-noa-yeat
Hello	Sveiki / Labdien	Svay-key / lub-dean
Goodbye	Uz redzēšanos	Ooz redz-ee-shun-oas
Good night	Ar labu nakti	Ur lub-oo nukt-i
morning	rīts	reets
afternoon	pēcpusdiena	pehts-poos-dea-nu
evening	vakars	vu-kars
yesterday	vakar	vu-kar
today	šodien	shoa-dean
tomorrow	rīt	reet
What?	Ko?	Kuah?
When?	Kad?	Kud?

Guidelines for Prouunciation

Latvian is, for the most part, a phonetic language and the stress is almost always on the first syllable. Each letter and vowel combination (dipthong) has a particular sound, as indicated below:

Vowels
Either short or long (with a macron):
a like "u" in "under"
ā like "a" in "star"
e like "e" in "bed", or "a" in "cat"
ē like "ai" in "hair", or "a" in "glad"
i like "i" in "sit"
ī like "ee" in "feet"
o like "o" in "corn", or "oa" in "oar"
u like "oo" in "book"
ū like "oo" in "school"

Dipthongs
ai like "i" in "line"
au like "ow" in "cow"
ei like "ay" in "clay"
ie like "ea" in "clear"
oi like "oy" in "boy"
ui like "ui" in "ruin"

Consonants
Same as English, except for:
c like "ts" in "hats"
č like "ch" in "church"
dz like "ds" in "hands"
dž like "j" in "joke"
ģ like "d" in "duty"
j like "y" in "yellow"
ķ like "c" in "cute"
ļ like "li" in "million"
ņ like "n" in "new"
r like "r" in "run"
š like "sh" in "shut"
ž like "s" in "treasure"

Why?	Kāpēc?	Kaa-pehts?
Where?	Kur?	Koor?

Useful Phrases

How are you?	Kā jums klājas?	Kaa yooms klaa-yus?
Very well	Ļoti labi	Lyot-ee lu bi
Pleased to meet you.	Prieks iepazīties.	Preaks ea-pu-zeet-eas.
See you soon!	Uz drīz redzēšanos!	Ooz dreez redz-e-shun-oas!
Is there ... here?	Vai šeit ir ....?	Vi shayt eer ...?
Where can I get ...?	Kur es varu dabūt ...?	Koor es vu-roo du-boot ...?
How do you get to?	Kā es varu tikt līdz?	Kaa es vu-roo tikt leedz?
How far is ...?	Cik tālu atrodas ...?	Tsik taa-loo ut-roa-dus ...?
Do you speak English?	Vai jūs runājat angliski?	Vy yoos roon-aa-yut ung-lees-kee?
I can't speak Latvian.	Es nerunāju latviski.	Es ne-roon-aa-yoo lut-vees-kee.
I don't understand.	Es nesaprotu.	es ne-sup-rat-oo.
Can you help me?	Vai varat man palīdzēt?	Vy vu-rut mun pu-leedz-eht?
Please speak slowly.	Lūdzu, runājiet lēnām.	Loodz-oo roon-aa-yeat lehn aam.
Sorry!	Atvainojiet!	ut-vy-noa-yeat!

Useful Words

big	liels	leals
small	mazs	muzs
hot	karsts	kahrsts
cold	auksts	owksts
good	labs	lubs
bad	slikts	slikts
enough	pietiekami	pea-teak-um-ee
well	vesels	vas-als
open	atvērts	ut-vehrts
closed	slēgts	slehgts
left	kreisi	pu krays-i
right	labi	pu lu-bi
straight	taisni	tai-sni
near	tuvu	toov-u
far	tālu	taal-oo
up	augšā	owg-shaa
down	lejā	lay-aa
here	šeit	shayt
there	tur	toor
early	agri	ug-ri
late	vēlu	vehl-oo
entrance	ieeja	ea-ey-u
exit	izeja	iz-ey-u
toilet	tualete	toou-le-te
free/unoccupied	brīvs	breevs
free/no charge	bezmaksas	bez-muk-sus

Making a Telephone Call

Can I call abroad from here?	Vai no šejienes var zvanīt uz ārzemēm?	Vy noa shay-ean-ess vur zvun-eet ooz aar-zem-ehm?
I would like to call collect.	Es gribu, lai maksā zvana saņēmējs.	Es grib-oo, lai muks-aa zvu-nu suny-eh-mehs.
local call	vietējā saruna	veat-ay-aa su-roo-nu
I'll ring back later.	Es atzvanīšu vēlāk.	Es ut-zvun-ee-shoo vehl-aak.
Could I leave a message?	Vai es varu atstāt ziņu?	Vy es vuroo ut-staat ziny-oo?
Could you speak up a little, please?	Lūdzu, runājiet mazliet skaļāk?	Loodz-oo, roon-aa yeat muz-leat skuly-aak?

Shopping

How much is this?	Cik tas maksā?	Tsik tus muk-saa?
I would like ...	Es vēlētos ...	Es veh-leh-toas ...
Do you have ...?	Vai Jums ir ...?	Vy yooms ir ..?
I'm just looking.	Es tikai skatos.	Es tik-ai skut-oas.
Do you take credit cards?	Vai es varu maksāt ar kredītkarti?	Vy es vu-roo muk-saat ur kred-eet-kurti?
What time do you open?	Cikos tiek atvērts veikals?	Tsik-oas teak ut-vehrts vay-kuls?
What time do you close?	Cikos tiek slēgts veikals?	Tsik-oas teak slehgts vay-kuls?
this one	šo	shoa

that one	**to**	*toa*
expensive	**dārgs**	*daargs*
cheap	**lēts**	*lehts*
size	**izmērs**	*iz-mehrs*
antique dealer	**antikvariāts**	*un-teek-vur-i-aats*
souvenir shop	**suvenīru veikals**	*soo-ve-near-oo vay-kuls*
bookshop	**grāmatu veikals**	*graa-mut-oo vay-kuls*
café	**kafējnīca**	*ku-fay-neets-u*
chemist	**aptīciku**	*up-tsee-ku*
newspaper kiosk	**avīžu kiosks**	*u-veezh-oo kee-osks*
department store	**universālveikals**	*oo-ni-ver-saal-vay-kuls*
market	**tirgus**	*tir-gus*

Staying in a Hotel

Have you any vacancies?	**Vai jums ir brīvas istabas?**	*Vy yooms ir breev-us is-tu?*
double room with double bed	**istaba ar divvietīgu gultu**	*is-tu-bu ur div-veat-ee-goo gool-too*
twin room	**divvietīga istaba**	*div-veat-ee-gu is-tu-bu*
single room	**vienvietīga istaba**	*vean-veat-ee gu is-tu-bu*
non-smoking	**nesmēķētāju**	*ne-smee-kyeh-taay-oo*
room with a ...	**istaba ar vannu/dušu ...**	*is-tu-bu ur vun-oo/doosh-oo ...*
porter	**portjē**	*port-yay*
key	**atslēga**	*ut-sleh-gu*
I have a reservation	**Man ir pasūtīts**	*mun ir pus-oo-teets*

Sightseeing

bus	**autobuss**	*ow-to-boos*
tram	**tramvajs**	*trum-vuys*
trolley bus	**trolejbuss**	*trol-ay-boos*
train	**vilciens**	*vilts-eans*
bus stop	**autobusa pietura**	*ow-to-boos-u pea-too-ru*
tram stop	**tramvaja pietura**	*trum-vuy-u pea-too-ru*
art gallery	**mākslas galerija**	*maak-slus gul-e-ree-yu*
palace/castle	**pils**	*pils*
cathedral	**katedrāle**	*kut-e-draa-le*
church	**baznica**	*buz-neets-u*
garden	**dārzs**	*daarz*
library	**biblioteka**	*bib-li-oa-te-ku*
museum	**muzejs**	*mooz-ays*
tourist information	**tūristu informācija**	*toor-is-too in-for-maats-i-ya*
closed	**slēgts**	*slehgts*
holiday	**brīvdiena**	*breev-dea-nu*
travel agent	**ceļojumu aģentūra**	*tsely-oy-oo-moo udy-en-toor-u*

Eating Out

A table for ... please.	**Galdiņu .... personām, lūdzu.**	*Guld iny oo...pehr soa naam, loodz oo.*
The bill ...	**Rēķinu ...**	*Rehky-i-noo ...*
I am a vegetarian.	**Es esmu veģetārietis.**	*Es as-moo vedy-e-taar-ea-tis.*
I'd like ...	**Es vēlos ...**	*Es veh-loas ...*
waiter/waitress	**oficiants / oficiante**	*of-its-i-unts/of-its-i-unte*
menu	**ēdienkarte**	*eh-dean-kurt-e*
wine list	**vīnu karte**	*veen-oo kurt-e*
chef's special	**īpašais šefpavāra ieteikums**	*ee-push-ais shef-pu-vaa-ru eat-ay-kums*
tip	**dzeramnauda**	*dzer-um-now-du*
bottle	**pudele**	*poo-de-le*
knife	**nazis**	*nu-zis*
fork	**dakša**	*duk-shu*
spoon	**karote**	*kur-oa-te*
breakfast	**brokastis**	*broa-kus-tis*
lunch	**pusdienas**	*poos-dea-nus*
dinner	**vakariņas**	*vuk-ur-iny-us*
main courses	**galvenie ēdieni**	*gul-ven-ea eh-dea-ni*
starters	**uzkodas**	*ooz-koa-dus*
vegetables	**dārzeņi**	*daarz-eny-i*
desserts	**saldie ēdieni/deserti**	*sul-dea ee-dea-ni/dess-er-ti*
rare	**asiņains**	*us-iny-ains*
well done	**labi sacepts**	*lu-bi suts-apts*

Menu Decoder

alus	*ul-oos*	beer
augļu sula	*ow-gly-oo soo-la*	fruit juice
baltvīns	*bult-veens*	white wine
bekons	*bek-ons*	bacon
cepts	*tsepts*	fried
cūkgaļa	*tsook-guly-u*	pork
cukurs	*tsoo-koors*	sugar
desa	*des-u*	sausage
etiķis	*et-iky-is*	vinegar
frī kartupeļi	*free kur-too-pely-i*	chips
grilēts	*gril-ehts*	grilled
jēra gaļa	*yehr-u guly-u*	lamb
jūras veltes	*yoor-us vel-tes*	seafood
kafija	*kuf-i-yu*	coffee
kartupeļi	*kur-too-pely-i*	potatoes
kūpinātas zivis	*koop-in-aat-us ziv-is*	smoked fish
krējums	*kray-ooms*	cream
liellopa gaļa	*leal-loap-u guly-u*	beef
maize	*maiz-e*	bread
mērce	*mehr-tse*	sauce
minerālūdens	*min-er-aal-oo-dens*	mineral water
ola	*oal-u*	egg
pankūka	*pun-koo-ku*	pancake
piens	*peans*	milk
pildīts	*pild-eets*	stuffed
pipars	*pi-purs*	pepper
rīsi	*rees-i*	rice
saldējums	*sul-day-ums*	ice cream
sāls	*saals*	salt
salāti	*sul-aa-ti*	salad
sarkanvīns	*sur-kun-veens*	red wine
siers	*sears*	cheese
šķiņkis	*shkyinky-is*	ham
smalkmaizīte	*smulk-maiz-ee-te*	pastry
šokolāde	*shok-o-laa-de*	chocolate
steiks	*stayks*	steak
tēja	*they-u*	tea
tvaicēts	*tvai-tsehts*	steamed
vārīts	*vaar-eets*	boiled
vista	*vis-tu*	chicken
zivis	*ziv-is*	fish
zupa	*zoop-u*	soup

Numbers

0	**nulle**	*nooll-e*
1	**viens**	*veans*
2	**divi**	*di-vi*
3	**trīs**	*trees*
4	**četri**	*chet-ri*
5	**pieci**	*peat-si*
6	**seši**	*se-shi*
7	**septiņi**	*sept-iny-i*
8	**astoņi**	*us-toany-i*
9	**deviņi**	*dev-iny-i*
10	**desmit**	*des-mit*
11	**vienpadsmit**	*vean-puds-mit*
12	**divpadsmit**	*div-puds-mit*
13	**trīspadsmit**	*trees-puds-mit*
14	**četrpadsmit**	*chet-r-puds-mit*
15	**piecpadsmit**	*peats-puds-mit*
16	**sešpadsmit**	*sesh-puds-mit*
17	**septiņpadsmit**	*sept-iny-puds-mit*
18	**astoņpadsmit**	*us-toany-puds-mit*
19	**deviņpadsmit**	*dev-iny-puds-mit*
20	**divdesmit**	*div-des-mit*
30	**trīsdesmit**	*trees-des-mit*
40	**četrdesmit**	*chet-r-des-mit*
50	**piecdesmit**	*peats-des-mit*
60	**sešdesmit**	*sesh-des-mit*
70	**septiņdesmit**	*sept-iny-des-mit*
80	**astoņdesmit**	*us-toany-des-mit*
90	**deviņdesmit**	*de-viny-des-mit*
100	**simts**	*simts*
1000	**tūkstotis**	*took-stoa-tis*

Time

one minute	**viena minūte**	*vean-u min-oo-te*
hour	**stunda**	*stoon-du*
half an hour	**pus stunda**	*poos stoon-du*
Sunday	**svētdiena**	*sveet-dea-nu*
Monday	**pirmdiena**	*pirm-dea-nu*
Tuesday	**otrdiena**	*oa-tr-dea-nu*
Wednesday	**trešdiena**	*tresh-dea-nu*
Thursday	**ceturtdiena**	*tset-oort-dea-nu*
Friday	**piektdiena**	*peakt-dea-nu*
Saturday	**sestdiena**	*sest-dea-nu*

Phrase Book: Lithuanian

In Emergency

Help!	Gelbėkit!	Galbekit!
Stop!	Sustokit!	Soostokit!
Look out!	Atsargiai!	Aatsaargyai!
Call a doctor!	Kvieskit gydytoją!	Kvieskit geedeetoyaa!
Call an ambulance!	Kvieskit greitąją!	Kvieskit greitaayaa!
Call the police!	Kvieskit policiją!	Kvieskit politsiyaa!
Call the fire department!	Kvieskit gaisrinę!	Kvieskit gisrine!
Where is the nearest telephone?	Kur yra artimiausias telefonas?	Koor eeraa artimyowsyaas telefonaas?
Where is the nearest hospital?	Kur yra artimiausia ligoninė?	Koor eeraa artimyaausyaa ligonine?

Communication Essentials

Yes	Taip	Taip
No	Ne	Ne
Please	Prašom	Praashom
Thank you	Ačiū	Aachyoo
Excuse me	Atsiprašau	Aatsipraashoa
Hello	Sveiki	Sveiki
Goodbye	Viso gero	Viso gero
Good night	Labanakt	Laabaanaakt
morning	rytas	reetaas
afternoon	popietė	popiete
evening	vakaras	vaakaraas
yesterday	vakar	vaakar
today	šiandien	shyaandien
tomorrow	rytoj	reetoy
What?	Kas?	Kaas?

Guidelines for Prounciation

Lithuanian has a complicated wandering accent that can change whenever a word changes its ending, as is seen with "mato matoe" (he/she/it/ they see) and "matau matoe" (I see).

Diphthongs hold the sound longer than that of a simple vowel:
ai like "a" in "made" or "i" in "child"
au like "ow" in "cow" or "o" in "note"
ei like "a" in "made"
ie like "ie" in "sienna"
ui like "ooey" in "gooey"
uo like the word "woe"

Vowels have only one sound:
a like "a" in "father"
e like "e" in "bet"
ę like "a" in "man"
ė like "a" in "made"
i like "i" in "bit" but before an "a", "o", or "u", it is sounds like the "y" in "canyon"
y like į
o like "o" in "boat"
u like "oo" in "wood"
ą, į, ų, and ū just hold the sound of a, i, and u longer

Any consonant before an "e", "i", or "y" is palatalized or softened like "n" in "bunion". Consonants that do not sound like their English counterparts include:
c like "ts" in "Betsy"
č like "ch" in "chunk"
j like "y" in "yellow"
š like "sh" in "shot"
ž like "s" in "measure"
g is always hard like in "go"
r is trilled on the tip of the tongue.

When?	Kada?	Kaadaa?
Why?	Kodėl?	Kodel?
Where?	Kur?	Koor?

Useful Phrases

How are you?	Kaip sekasi?	Kaip sakaasi?
Very well, thank you.	Ačiū, labai gerai.	Aachyoo, laabai gerai.
Pleased to meet you.	Malonu susipažinti.	Maalonoo soosipaazhinti.
See you soon!	Iki greito pasimatymo!	Iki greito paasimaateemo!
Is there … here?	Ar čia yra …?	Ar che eeraa …?
Where can I get …?	Kur galiu gauti …?	Koor gaalyoo gowti …?
How do you get to …?	Kaip nuvykti iki …?	Kaip nooveekti iki …?
How far is …?	Koks atstumas iki …?	Koks aatstoomaas iki …?
Do you speak English?	Ar kalbate angliškai?	Ar kaalbaate aanglishkai?
I can't speak Lithuanian.	Aš nekalbu lietuviškai.	Aash nekaalboo lietoovishkai.
I don't understand.	Aš nesuprantu.	Aash nesoopraantoo.
Can you help me?	Ar galite man padėti?	Ar gaalite maan paadeti?
Please speak slowly.	Prašau kalbėti lėčiau.	Praashoa kaalbeti lechyoa.
Sorry!	Apgailestauju!	Aapgilestowyoo!

Useful Words

big	didelis	didelis
small	mažas	maazhaas
hot	karštas	karshtaas
cold	šaltas	shaaltaas
good	geras	geraas
bad	blogas	blogaas
enough	gana	gaanaa
well	gerai	gerai
open	atidarytas	aatidareetaas
closed	uždarytas	oozhdareetaas
left	kairė	kire
right	dešinė	dashine
straight	tiesiai	tiesyai
near	šalia	shaalyaa
far	toli	toli
up	aukštyn	owkshteen
down	žemyn	zhemeen
early	anksti	aanksti
late	vėlai	velai
entrance	įėjimas	eeyeyimaas
exit	išėjimas	isheyimaas
toilet	tualetas	tualetaas
free/unoccupied	laisva/neužimta	lisvaa/neoozhimtaa
free/no charge	nemokamai	nemokaamai

Making a Telephone Call

Can I call abroad from here?	Ar galiu iš čia paskambinti į užsienį?	Ar gaalyoo ish che paaskaambinti ee oozhsienee?
I would like to call collect.	Aš norėčiau paskambinti abonentui jo sąskaita.	Aash norechyoa paaskaambinti aabonentui yo saaskitaa.
local call	vietinis pokalbis	vietinis pokaalbis
I'll ring back later.	Aš pats vėliau paskambinsiu.	Aash paats velyoa paaskaambinsyoo.
Could I leave a message?	Ar galiu palikti žinutę?	Ar gaalyoo paalikti zhinoote?
Could you speak up a little, please?	Ar galite kalbėti šiek tiek garsiau?	Ar gaalite kaalbeti shiek tiek garsyoa?

Shopping

How much is this?	Kiek tai kainuoja?	Kiek tai kinuoyaa?
I would like …	Aš norėčiau …	Aash norechyoa …
Do you have …?	Ar turite …?	Ar toorite …?
I'm just looking	Aš tik žiūriu	Aash tik zhyooryoo
Do you take credit cards?	Ar priimate kreditines korteles?	Ar priimaate kreditines korteles?
What time do you open?	Kada pradedate darbą?	Kaadaa praadedaate darbaa?
What time do you close?	Kada baigiate darbą?	Kaadaa baigyaate darbaa?

this one	**šitas**	*shitaas*
that one	**anas**	*aanaas*
antique dealer	**antikvariatas**	*aantikvaryaataas*
bookshop	**knygynas**	*kneegeenaas*
department store	**universalinė parduotuvė**	*ooniversaaline parduotoove*
market	**turgus**	*toorgoos*
newspaper kiosk	**spaudos kioskas**	*spqados kyoskaas*
souvenir shop	**suvenyrų parduotuvė**	*sooveneeroo parduotoove*

Staying in a Hotel

Have you any vacancies?	**Ar turite laisvų kambarių?**	*Ar toorite lisvoo kaambaryoo?*
double room	**dvivietis**	*dvivietis*
with double bed	**kambarys**	*kaambarees*
twin room	**kambarys su dviem lovom**	*kaambarees soo dviem lovom*
single room	**vienvietis kambarys**	*vienvietis kaambarees*
non-smoking	**nerūkantiems**	*nerookaantiems*
room with a bath/shower	**kambarys su vonia/dušu**	*kaambarees soo vonyaa/dooshoo*
porter	**nešikas**	*neshikaas*
key	**raktas**	*raaktaas*
I have a reservation.	**Mano vardu rezervuotas.**	*Maano vardoo rezervuotaas.*

Sightseeing

bus	**autobusas**	*owtoboosaas*
tram	**tramvajus**	*traamvaayoos*
trolley bus	**troleibusas**	*troleiboosaas*
train	**traukinys**	*troakinees*
bus stop	**autobusų stotelė**	*owtoboosoo stotale*
tram stop	**tramvajaus stotelė**	*traamvaayoas stotale*
art gallery	**meno galerija**	*mano gaaleriyaa*
palace	**rūmai**	*roomai*
castle	**pilis**	*pilis*
cathedral	**katedra**	*kaatedraa*
church	**bažnyčia**	*baazhneechyaa*
garden	**sodas**	*sodaas*
library	**biblioteka**	*biblyotekaa*
museum	**muziejus**	*moozieyoos*
tourist information	**turizmo informacija**	*toorizmo informaatsiyaa*
closed for public holiday	**nedirbama – valstybinės šventės**	*nedirbama – vaalsteebines shventes*

Eating Out

A table for … please	**Ar yra staliukas …**	*Ar eeraa staalyookaas …*
I want to reserve a table.	**Norėčiau rezervuoti staliuką.**	*Norechyoa rezervuoti staalyookaa.*
The bill, please!	**Prašom sąskaitą!**	*Praashom saaskitaa!*
I am a vegetarian.	**Aš vegetaras.**	*Aash vegetaraas.*
I'd like …	**Norėčiau …**	*Norechyoa …*
waiter/waitress	**padavėjas/padavėja**	*paadaaveyaas/ paadaaveyaa*
menu	**meniu**	*menyoo*
wine list	**vynų sąrašas**	*veenoo saaraashaas*
chef's special	**rekomenduojama paragauti**	*rekomenduojaamaa paraagowti*
tip	**arbatpinigiai**	*arbaatpinigyai*
glass	**stiklinė**	*stikline*
bottle	**butelis**	*bootelis*
knife	**peilis**	*peilis*
fork	**šakutė**	*shaakoote*
spoon	**šaukštas**	*showkshtaas*
breakfast	**pusryčiai**	*poosreechyai*
lunch	**pietūs**	*pietoos*
dinner	**vakarienė**	*vaakariene*
main courses	**pagrindiniai patiekalai**	*paagrindinyai paatiekaalai*
starters	**pirmieji patiekalai**	*pirmieyi paatiekaalai*
desserts	**desertai**	*desertai*
rare	**pušlais**	*pooszhaalis*
well done	**gerai išvirtas**	*gerai ishvirtaas*

Menu Decoder

actas	*aatstaas*	vinegar
alus	*aaloos*	beer
arbata	*arbaataa*	tea
baltas vynas	*baaltaas veenaas*	white wine
bekonas	*bekonaas*	bacon
bifšteksas	*bifshteksaas*	steak
blynas	*bleenaas*	pancake
cukrus	*tsookroos*	sugar

dešra	*dashraa*	sausage
duona	*duonaa*	bread
druska	*drooskaa*	salt
ėriena	*erienaa*	lamb
grietinėlė	*grietinele*	cream
įdarytas	*eedareetaas*	stuffed
jautiena	*yowtienaa*	beef
jūros gėrybės	*jyooros gereebes*	seafood
kava	*kaavaa*	coffee
kepenėlės	*kepeneles*	liver
keptas ant grotelių	*kaptaas gant grotalyoo*	grilled
keptas	*kaptaas*	fried/roasted
keptuvėje/ orkaitėje	*keptooveye/ orkaiteye*	
kiauliena	*kyoalienaa*	pork
kiaušinis	*kyoashinis*	egg
košė	*koshe*	porridge
kumpis	*koompis*	ham
ledai	*ledai*	ice cream
mėsa	*mesaa*	meat
mineralinis vanduo	*mineraalinis vaanduo*	mineral water
padažas	*paadaazhaas*	sauce
pienas	*pienaas*	milk
pipirai	*pipirai*	pepper
pyragas	*peeraagaas*	pie/cake
raudonas vynas	*roadonaas veenaas*	red wine
rūkyta žuvis	*rookeetaa zhoovis*	smoked fish
ryžiai	*reezhyai*	rice
salotos	*saalotos*	salad
šokoladas	*shokolaadas*	chocolate
sumuštinis	*soomooshtinis*	sandwich
sūris	*sooris*	cheese
sriuba	*sryoobaa*	soup
vaisių sultys	*visyoo sooltees*	fruit juice
virtas	*virtaas*	boiled
virtas garuose	*virtaas garuose*	steamed
virtiniai	*virtinyai*	dumplings
vištiena	*vishtienaa*	chicken
žuvis	*zhoovis*	fish

Numbers

0	**nulis**	*noolis*
1	**vienas**	*vienaas*
2	**du**	*doo*
3	**trys**	*trees*
4	**keturi**	*ketoori*
5	**penki**	*penki*
6	**šeši**	*sheshi*
7	**septyni**	*septeeni*
8	**aštuoni**	*aashtuoni*
9	**devyni**	*deveeni*
10	**dešimt**	*dashimt*
11	**vienuolika**	*vienuolikaa*
12	**dvylika**	*dveelikaa*
13	**trylika**	*treelikaa*
14	**keturiolika**	*ketooryolikaa*
15	**penkiolika**	*penkyolikaa*
16	**šešiolika**	*sheshyolikaa*
17	**septyniolika**	*septeenyolikaa*
18	**aštuoniolika**	*aashtuonyolikaa*
19	**devyniolika**	*deveenyolikaa*
20	**dvidešimt**	*dvideshimt*
30	**trisdešimt**	*trisdeshimt*
40	**keturiasdešimt**	*ketooryaasdashimt*
50	**penkiasdešimt**	*penkyaasdashimt*
60	**šešiasdešimt**	*shashyaasdashimt*
70	**septyniasdešimt**	*septeenyaasdashimt*
80	**aštuoniasdešimt**	*aashtuonyaas-dashimt*
90	**devyniasdešimt**	*deveenyaasdashimt*
100	**šimtas**	*shimtaas*
1000	**tūkstantis**	*tookstaantis*

Time

one minute	**minutė**	*minoote*
hour	**valanda**	*vaalaandaa*
half an hour	**pusvalandis**	*poosvaalaandis*
Sunday	**sekmadienis**	*sekmaadienis*
Monday	**pirmadienis**	*pirmaadienis*
Tuesday	**antradienis**	*aantraadienis*
Wednesday	**trečiadienis**	*trechyaadienis*
Thursday	**ketvirtadienis**	*ketvirtaadienis*
Friday	**penktadienis**	*penktaadienis*
Saturday	**šeštadienis**	*sheshtaadienis*